TAJIK

practical dictionary

TAJIK
practical dictionary

Jon Jilani

Tajik-English
English-Tajik

Hippocrene Books, Inc.
New York

For information, address:
Hippocrene Books, Inc.
171 Madison Avenue
New York, NY 10016
www.hippocrenebooks.com

Library of Congress Cataloging-in-Publication Data

Jilani, Jon.
Tajik-English/English-Tajik practical dictionary / Jon Jilani.
p. cm.
ISBN-13: 978-0-7818-1233-7 (alk. paper)
1. Tajik language—Dictionaries—English. 2. English language—Dictionaries—Tajik. I. Title.

PK6976.J55 2008
491'.57—dc22 2007034003

Contents

Introduction

Tajik is a member of the Iranian language family, and is the official language of Tajikistan, where it is the mother tongue of more than 66% of the population. Beyond Tajikistan, Tajiks make up the second-largest ethnic group in Afghanistan, and are also found in Uzbekistan. Tajik is a form of Persian, which differs from the dialects of Iran and Afghanistan in that it is written in the Cyrillic alphabet. Additionally, it retains archaic vocabulary and grammatical features that are not found elsewhere.

The fall of the Soviet Union has led to a revival in the use of Tajik, which has now supplanted Russian as the language of business and government in Tajikistan. Since independence, numerous Russian loanwords have fallen out of use, to be replaced by existing Tajik words or by neologisms. Contact with the Persian-language media in Iran and Afghanistan has also begun to influence the development of the language.

As Tajikistan becomes a more active player in the world community, increased contact between speakers of English and Tajik is bound to occur. This book attempts to fill a void in reference material for speakers of both languages in order to facilitate contact between the two.

Guide to Pronunciation

Letter	Transcription	Equivalent Sound
А, а	a	r**u**n, t**o**n, b**u**zz
Б, б	b	**b**ook
В, в	v	**v**endor
Г, г	g	**g**ood, **g**ift
Ғ, ғ	gh	uvular trill – like Parisian "r"
Д, д	d	**d**oor
Е, е	e	m**e**rry, l**e**ft (if first letter in word, then "**ye**")
Ё, ё	yo	**yaw**n
Ж, ж	zh	occa**s**ion, tria**ge**
З, з	z	**z**ebra
И, и	i	f**ee**t, l**ea**n *or* h**i**t
ӣ	i	f**ee**t, l**ea**n
Й, й	y	**y**es
К, к	k	**k**angaroo
Қ, қ	q	voiceless uvular plosive – like "q" in "**Q**atar"
Л, л	l	**l**ift
М, м	m	**m**eat
Н, н	n	**n**ever
О, о	o	l**aw**n
П, п	p	**p**ut
Р, р	r	rolled r, as in Spanish
С, с	s	mu**s**t, **s**end
Т, т	t	**t**ook
У, у	u	r**oo**m, y**ou**
Ӯ, ӯ	ü	h**er**
ф	f	**f**riend
Х, х	x	like "ch" in Scottish "lo**ch**"
Ҳ, ҳ	h	**h**elp, **h**and

Ч, ч	ch	**ch**isel
Ҷ, ҷ	j	**j**unk
Ш, ш	sh	**sh**ort
ъ	'	no English equivalent – denotes a slight pause
Э, э	e	**e**very
Ю, ю	yu	**you**
Я, я	ya	**yu**mmy, **you**ng

Note 1: **ай** [ay] is pronounced like the "y" in "m**y**" or the "i" in "m**i**nd"

Note 2: On the rare occasions where **з** and **ҳ** occur next to each other in a word, this has been denoted as [z-h] to avoid confusion with **ж** [zh]. Similarly, on the rare occasions when **с** and **ҳ** occur next to each other in a word, this has been denoted as [s-h] to avoid confusion with **ш** [sh].

List of Abbreviations

Abbreviation	English	Tajik
abbrev.	abbreviation	ихтисор
adj.	adjective	сифат
adv.	adverb	зарф
anat.	anatomical	анатомӣ
art.	article	артикл
aux.	auxiliary verb	феъли ёридиҳанда
conj.	conjunction	пайвандак
geo.	geographical	ҷуғрофӣ
gram.	grammatical	грамматикӣ
med.	medical	тиббӣ
mil.	military	ҳарбӣ
mus.	musical	мусиқӣ
n.	noun	исм
n.pl.	plural noun	исми ҷамъ
opp.	opposite	акс
pref.	prefix	префикс
prep.	preposition	пешоянд
sb	somebody	касе
sth	something	чизе
v.i.	intransitive verb	феъли монда
v.t.	transitive verb	феъли гузаранда

Tajik-English Dictionary

А

абзатс [abzats] *n.* paragraph
абзор [abzor] *n.* apparatus, appliance, device, implement, tool, utensil
аблаҳ [ablah] *n.* fool, idiot / *adj.* silly
аблаҳона [ablahona] *adj.* foolish, silly
абр [abr] *n.* cloud
абрешим [abreshim] *n.* silk
абрешимӣ [abreshimi] *adj.* silk
абрнок [abrnok] *adj.* cloudy
абрӯ [abrü] *n.* eyebrow
аввал [avval] *adj.* first
аввалан [avvalan] *adv.* at first, first of all
август [avgust] *n.* August
авлод [avlod] *n.* posterity
авранг [avrang] *n.* throne
Аврупо [Avrupo] *n.* Europe
аврупоӣ [avrupoi] *n./adj.* European; **Иттиҳоди Аврупо** [Ittihodi Avrupo] European Union
австралиягӣ [avstraliyagi] *n./adj.* Australian
автобус [avtobus] *n.* bus
автоматонӣ [avtomatoni] *n.* automation
автомобил [avtomobil] *n.* automobile
авусун [avusun] *n.pl.* wives of two brothers
авҷ [avj] *n.* climax, peak, zenith
агар [agar] *conj.* if
агарчи [agarchi] *conj.* although, though
агба [aghba] *n.* mountain pass
адабиёт [adabiyot] *n.* literature
адабӣ [adabi] *adj.* literary
адад [adad, raqam] *n.* number, figure
адаптер [adapter] *n.* adapter
адвия [adviya] *n.* spice
адвокат [advokat] *n.* lawyer
адлия [adliya] *n.* justice
адмирал [admiral] *n.* admiral
аждар [azhdar] *n.* dragon; monster
аждаҳо [azhdaho] *n.* dragon
аз [az] *prep.* from, of; off, though / *conj.* than
аз даст додан [az dast dodan] *v.t.* lose *(metaphorically)*
аз ёд баромадан [az yod baromadan] *v.i.* forget
аз миёни [az miyoni] *prep.* through
аз нав кардан [az nav kardan] *v.t.* renovate
аз навбатдорӣ озод [az navbatdori ozod] *adj.* Off-duty
аз паҳлӯ [az pahlü] *adv.* sideways
аз худ кардан [az xud kardan] *v.t.* assimilate *(physiologically)*
азамат [azamat] *n.* majesty
аздастдиҳӣ [azdastdihi] *n.* loss *(metaphorical)*
аздаҳонмонда [azdahonmonda] *adj.* old-fashioned
азиз [aziz] *adj.* esteemed, dear
азим [azim] *adj.* giant
азнавбавуҷудоварӣ [aznavbavujudovari] *n.* reproduction
азнавсозӣ [aznavsozi] *n.* renewal
азоб [azob] *n.* anguish, misery, torment
азоб дидан [azob didan] *v.i.* suffer

азоб додан [azob dodan] *v.t.* torment
азодорӣ [azodori] *n.* mourning
азодорӣ кардан [azodori kardan] *v.t.* mourn
азот [azot] *n.* nitrogen
айб [ayb] *n.* fault
айбдор [aybdor] *n.* defendant / *adj.* guilty
айбдорӣ [aybdori] *n.* guilt
айвон [ayvon] *n.* porch, terrace
айнак [aynak] *n.pl.* glasses
айнак офтобпанаҳ [aynaki oftobpanah] *n.pl.* sunglasses
ака [aka] *n.* older brother
академия [akademiya] *n.* academy
академӣ [akademi] *adj.* academic
акварел [akvarel] *n.* watercolor
аккос [akkos] *n.* bark *(of a dog)*
аккос задан [akkos zadan] *v.i.* bark
акнун [aknun] *adv.* now
акр [akr] *n.* acre
аксарият [aksariyat] *n.* majority
акс [aks] *n.* opposite; photograph
акс гирифтан [aks giriftan] *v.t.* photograph, take a picture
аксгир [akkos, aksgir] *n.* photographer
аксгирак [aksgirak] *n.* camera
аксгирӣ [aksgiri] *n.* photography
акси садо [aksi sado] *n.* echo
аксуламал [aksulamal] *n.* reaction
акула [akula] *n.* shark
акушер [akusher] *n.* obstetrician
ақаллият [aqalliyat] *n.* minority
ақиб [aqib] *n.* rear
ақида [aqida] *n.* attitude, belief, concept, idea, notion
ақл [aql] *n.* intelligence, reason, wisdom
ақрабак [aqrabak] *n.* hand *(of a timepiece)*
ақрабаки дақиқашумор [aqrabaki daqiqashumor] *n.* minute hand *(of a timepiece)*
ақрабаки соатнамо [aqrabaki soatnamo] *n.* hour hand *(of a timepiece)*
аланга [alanga] *n.* blaze, flame
албатта [albatta] *adv.* of course
алвонҷ додан [alvonj dodan] *v.t.* rock, swing
алвонҷ хӯрдан [alvonj xürdan] *v.i.* rock, swing
алифбо [alifbo] *n.* alphabet
алиш [alish] *n.* exchange
алиш кардан [alish kardan] *v.t.* replace, exchange, trade
аллакай [allakay] *adv.* already
аллергия [allergiya] *n.* allergy; **аллергия доштан** [allergiya doshtan] be allergic
аллергӣ [allergi] *adj.* allergic
алмос [almos] *n.* diamond; **алмоси сеқирота** [almosi seqirota] a three-carat diamond; **ангуштарини алмосдор** [angushtarini almosdor] diamond ring
алмосшакл [almosshakl] *adj.* diamond-shaped
ало [alo] *n.* hello *(telephone greeting)*
алов [alov] *n.* fire, flame

алоқа [aloqa] *n.* association, relationship, contact

алоқа кардан [aloqa kardan] *v.t.* contact

алоқаи электронӣ [aloqai elektroni] *n.* e-mail

алоқаманд кардан [tamos kardan] *v.t.* connect *(via phone or other communications circuit)*

аломат [alomat] *n.* notation, note, sign, notice, symptom

аломати қайд [alomati qayd] *n.* check mark

аломати нидо [alomati nido] *n.* exclamation mark

аломати тақсим [alomati taqsim] *n.* colon *(gram.)*

аломати ҷамъ [alomati jam'] *n.* plus, plus sign

аломатҳои китобатӣ [alomathoi kitobati] *n.* punctuation

аломоҳӣ [alomohi] *n.* perch *(fish)*

алюминий [alyuminiy] *n.* aluminum

амад [amad] *n.* raft

амадронӣ [amadroni] *n.* rafting

амак [amak] *n.* paternal uncle

амакбача [amakbacha] *n.* cousin *(paternal uncle's son)*

амал [amal] *n.* action, operation, practice

амалан [amalan] *adv.* virtually

амалӣ [amali] *adj.* practical, virtual

амма [amma] *n.* paternal aunt

аммабача [ammabacha] *n.* cousin *(paternal aunt's son)*

аммиак [ammiak] *n.* ammonia

аммо [ammo] *conj.* but, however

амният [amniyat] *n.* security, safety

амри воқеъ [amri voqe'] *n.* fact

амри хаттӣ [amri xatti] *n.* warrant

Америкои Лотинӣ [Amrikoi Lotini] *n./adj.* Latin American

америкоӣ [amrikoi] *n./adj.* American

амсиласозӣ [amsilasozi] *n.* simulation

амудӣ [amudi] *adj.* perpendicular, vertical

ананас [ananas] *n.* pineapple

анатомия [anatomiya] *n.* anatomy

анбор [anbor] *n.* pantry, shed, storeroom, storage room, warehouse

анбоштан [anboshtan] *v.t.* fill

анбӯр [anbür] *n.pl.* pincers, pliers, tongs

анбӯҳ [anbüh] *n.* crowd, mass *(of people, animals, etc.)*

ангабин [angabin] *n.* honey

ангар [angar] *n.* hangar

ангеза [angeza] *n.* incentive, urge, impulse

ангишт [angisht] *n.* coal

англис [anglis] *n.* English

англисӣ [anglisi] *n.* English *(language)* / *adj.* English

ангора [angora] *n.* rough draft, outline, sketch, study *(painting)*

ангур [angur] *n.* grape

ангушт [angusht] *n.* finger

ангушти пой [angushti poy] *n.* toe

ангуштарин [angushtarin] *n.* ring; **ангуштарини номзадӣ** [angushtarini nomzadi] engagement ring

ангуштпона [angushtpona] *n.* thimble
андармонӣ [andarmoni] *n.* delay
андармон кардан [andarmon kardan] *v.t.* occupy, keep amused, delay, detain
андармон шудан [andarmon shudan] *v.i.* skid
андарун [andarun] *n.* interior
андеша [andesha] *n.* idea, thought
андешаманд [andeshamand] *adj.* thoughtful
андешида ёфтан [andeshida yoftan] *v.t.* devise
андешидан [andeshidan] *v.i.* think, reason
андова кардан [andova kardan] *v.t.* plaster
андовидан [andovidan] *v.t.* plaster
андоз [andoz] *n.* tax
андоза [andoza] *n.* dimension, size, gauge, quantity
андоза будан [andoza budan] *v.i.* fit
андохтан [andoxtan] *v.t.* cast
андӯхтан [andüxtan] *v.t.* accumulate
андӯҳ [andüh] *n.* grief, sorrow, sadness
андӯҳгин [andühgin] *adj.* sad
андӯҳгин кардан [andühgin kardan] *v.t.* sadden
андӯҳгин шудан [andühgin shudan] *v.i.* sadden
анестизия [anesteziya] *n.* anesthesia
аниқ [aniq] *adj.* definite, certain, precise, exact
ансур [ansur] *n.* element *(physical/chemical)*
антенна [antenna] *n.* antenna, aerial
антибиотик [antibiotik] *n.* antibiotic
антибиотикӣ [antibiotiki] *adj.* antibiotic
антисептикӣ [antiseptiki] *adj.* antiseptic
анча [ancha] *adv.* pretty
анҷир [anjir] *n.* fig
анҷом [anjom] *n.* accomplishment, achievement, conclusion, ending, finish
анҷом додан [anjom dodan] *v.t.* accomplish, achieve
анҷом ёфтан [anjom yoftan] *v.i.* finish
анҷуман [anjuman] *n.* association, club
анъана [an'ana] *n.* tradition
анъанавӣ [an'anavi] *adj.* traditional
апа [apa] *n.* older sister
апортумон [aportumon] *n.* apartment
аппендикс [appendiks] *n.* appendix *(anat.)*
аппендисит [appendisit] *n.* appendicitis
апрел [aprel] *n.* April
араб [arab] *n.* Arab
арабӣ [arabi] *n.* Arabic / *adj.* Arab
арақ [araq] *n.* liquor, perspiration, sweat
арақ кардан [araq kardan] *v.i.* perspire, sweat
аралаш [aralash] *n.* mixture
аралаш кардан [aralash kardan] *v.t.* mix
аралашкарда шудан [aralashkarda shudan] *v.i.* mingle, mix

арафа [arafa] *n.* eve; **арафаи Соли нав** [arafai Soli nav] New Year's Eve
арғамчин [arghamchin] *n.* rope
арғувонӣ [arghuvoni] *adj.* purple
арғунун [arghunun] *n.* organ *(mus.)*
арз [arz] *n.* latitude
арзамӯрак [arzamürak] *n.* termite
арзанда [arzanda] *adj.* worthy, having worth
арзёбӣ [arzyobi] *n.* evaluation
арзидан [arzanda budan] *v.i.* be worth
арзиз [arziz] *n.* tin
арзиш [arzish] *n.* value, worth
арзишдор [arzishdor] *adj.* valuable, worthwhile
арзон [arzon] *adj.* cheap
ариза [ariza] *n.* petition
арифметика [arifmetika] *n.* arithmetic
арман [arman] *n.* Armenian *(person)*
арманӣ [armani] *n.* Armenian *(language)* / *adj.* Armenian
армуғон [armughon] *n.* souvenir
ароба [aroba] *n.* cart, wagon
арра [arra] *n.* saw
арра кардан [arra kardan] *v.t.* saw
аррамайда [arramayda] *n.* sawdust
аррапушт [arrapusht] *n.* backbone, spine
артикл [artikl] *gram.* article
артиш [artish] *n.* military
арӯс [arüs] *n.* bride, daughter-in-law
арӯсӣ [arüsi] *n.* wedding
асаб [asab] *n.* nerve
асабдард [asabdard] *n.* neuralgia
асабӣ [asabi] *adj.* nervous, neural
асабонӣ [asaboni] *adj.* nervous
асал [asal] *n.* honey
асар [asar, ta'sir] *n.* effect
асбоб [asbob] *n.* appliance, device, implement, tool, instrument
асбобу анҷом [asbobu anjom] *n.* equipment
асилзода [asilzoda] *n.* noble
аскар [askar] *n.* soldier
аскиягӯй [askiyagüy] *adj.* witty
асл [asl] *n.* essence, origin
аслан [aslan] *adv.* originally
аслиҳа [asliha, yaroq] *n.* weapon
аслӣ [asli] *adj.* authentic, original, substantial
асо [aso] *n.* walking stick, cane, staff
асобағал [asobaghal] *n.* crutch
ассортимент [assortiment] *n.* assortment, mixture
асос [asos] *n.* basis, base, principle
асосӣ [asosi] *adj.* basic, fundamental, major, principal, substantial
асоснок [asosnok] *adj.* sound, solid
асп [asp] *n.* horse
аспаки баҳрӣ [aspaki bahri] *n.* seahorse
аспдавонӣ [aspdavoni] *n.* horse race
аспи обӣ [aspi obi] *n.* hippopotamus
аспирин [aspirin] *n.* aspirin

аспсавор [aspsavor] *adj.* on horseback
аспхона [aspxona] *n.* stable
аср [asr] *n.* era, age
астар [astar] *n.* lining
асфалт [asfalt] *n.* asphalt
атиқа [atiqa] *n.* antique
атиқафурӯшӣ [atiqafurüshi] *n.* antique shop
атом [atom] *n.* atom
атр [atr] *n.* perfume
атроф [atrof] *n.* environs
атрофи шаҳр [atrofi shahr] *n.* suburbs
атса [atsa] *n.* sneeze
атса задан [atsa zadan] *v.i.* sneeze
афғон [afghon] *n./adj.* Afghan
афзоёндан [afzoyondan] *v.t.* increase, multiply
афзоиш [afzoish] *n.* addition, something added, increase, rise
афзоли асп [afzoli asp] *n.* harness
афзудан [afzudan] *v.t.* increase, rise, add, augment
афлесун [aflesun] *n.* orange
африқоӣ [afriqoi] *n./adj.* African
афрӯзиш [afrüzish] *n.* ignition
афрӯхтан [afrüxtan] *v.t.* kindle, ignite, light, spark
афсар [afsar] *n.* officer
афсона [afsona] *n.* fairy tale, fiction, legend, myth
афсонашиносӣ [afsonashinosi] *n.* study of myths, mythology
афсун [afsun] *n.* incantation, charm
афсун кардан [afsun kardan] *v.t.* cast a spell, charm
афсурда [afsurda] *adj.* depressed
афсурда кардан [afsurda kardan] *v.t.* depress
афсурдагӣ [afsurdagi] *n.* depression
афсӯс [afsüs] *n.* regret
афсӯс хӯрдан [afsüs xürdan] *v.t.* regret
афтидан [aftidan] *v.i.* fall
афтиш [aftish] *n.* fall
афтодан [aftodan] *v.i.* fall
афтондан [aftondan] *v.t.* drop
афшондан [afshondan] *v.i.* flap
ахлоқ [axloq] *n.* moral, morals
ахлот [axlot] *n.* garbage, refuse, waste
ахлотқуттӣ [axlotqutti] *n.* wastebasket, wastepaper basket
ахта кардан [axta kardan] *v.t.* castrate, sterilize *(a male)*
аҳамият [ahamiyat] *n.* importance
аҳамиятнок [ahamiyatnok] *adj.* important
аҳднома [ahdnoma] *n.* contract, treaty
аҳмақ [ahmaq] *n.* idiot / *adj.* stupid
аҳолӣ [aholi] *n.* population
аҳром [ahrom] *n.* pyramid
аҷиб [ajib] *adj.* eccentric, strange, odd, weird
аҷоиб [ajoib] *adj.* marvelous
ашк [ashk] *n.* tear
ашроф [ashrof] *n.* noble
аъзо [a'zo] *n.* limb

Б

ба [ba] *prep.* against *(touching)*, at, on, to
ба боло [ba bolo] *prep.* up / *adv.* upstairs

ба василаи [ba vasilai] *prep.* by way of
ба вижа [ba vizha] *adv.* especially
ба воситаи [ba vositai] *prep.* via
ба вуҷуд овардан [ba vujud ovardan] *v.t.* generate
ба даст овардан [ba dast ovardan] *v.t.* acquire, gain possession, get
ба зудӣ [ba zudi] *adv.* shortly, soon
ба изтироб овардан [ba iztirob ovardan] *v.t.* upset, agitate, alarm, harrass
ба кор бурдан [ba kor burdan] *v.t.* use, apply, utilize
ба наздикӣ [ba nazdiki] *adv.* soon
ба осонӣ [ba ozoni] *adv.* easily
ба пеш [ba pesh] *adv.* ahead, forward
ба ростӣ [ba rosti] *adv.* truly
ба тартиб овардан [ba tartib ovardan] *v.t.* arrange
ба худ кашидан [ba xud kashidan] *v.t.* attract
ба ҷуз [ba juz] *prep.* except
ба эътибор гирифтан [ba e'tibor giriftan] *v.i.* acknowledge someone
ба эътибор нагирифтан [ba e'tibor nagiriftan] *v.t.* ignore
бабр [babr] *n.* tiger
бавосир [bavosir] *n.pl.* hemorrhoids, piles
бағоҷ [baghoj] *n.* baggage, luggage
бағоҷи дастӣ [baghoji dasti] *n.* carry-on luggage
бад [bad] *adj.* bad, evil, wicked / *adv.* badly
бадан [badan] *n.* body
бадарға кардан [badargha kardan] *v.t.* exile
бадарғагӣ [badargha] *n.* exile
бадарғакунӣ [badarghakuni] *n.* ostracism
бадарғашуда [badarghashuda] *n.* outcast, exile / *adj.* exiled
бадастдарорӣ [badastdarori] *adj.* obtainable
бадахлоқ [badaxloq] *adj.* immoral
бадбахт [badbaxt] *adj.* unfortunate, unlucky
бадбахтӣ [badbaxti] *n.* affliction, bad luck, misfortune, misadventure
бадбин [badbin] *n.* pessimist / *adj.* cynical, pessimistic
бадгумон [badgumon] *adj.* suspicious
бадгумон шудан [badgumon shudan] *v.i.* suspect
бадгумонӣ [badgumoni] *n.* prejudice
бадзот [badzot] *n.* jerk *(person)*
бадӣ [badi] *n.* evil, vice
бадкирдорӣ [badkirdori] *n.* misdeed
бадқасд [badqasd] *adj.* malignant, ill-intentioned
бадният [badniyat] *adj.* malignant, ill-intentioned
бадрашк [badrashk] *adj.* jealous
бадрашкӣ [badrashki] *n.* jealousy
бадтар [badtar] *adj./adv.* worse
бадтар кардан [badtar kardan] *v.t.* aggravate, make worse

бадтарин [badtarin] *adj.* worst
бадхоҳона [badxohona] *adj.* unfriendly
баён [bayon] *n.* statement
баён кардан [bayon kardan] *v.t.* state
базеб [bazeb] *adj.* elegant *(object)*
базм [bazm] *n.* feast, party
байзавӣ [bayzashakl *adj.* oval
байналмилалӣ [baynalmilali] *adj.* international
байналхалқӣ [baynalxalqi] *adj.* international
байни [bayni] *prep.* between
байрақ [bayraq] *n.* banner, flag
байтал [baytal] *n.* mare
байтор [baytor] *n.* veterinarian
байторӣ [baytori] *adj.* veterinary
бактерия [bakteriya] *n.* bacteria
бактериядор [bakteriyador] *adj.* bacterial
бақияи пул [baqiyai pul] *n.* change *(balance of money)*
баққол [baqqol] *n.* grocer
баққолӣ [baqqoli] *n.* grocery
баланд [baland] *adj.* high, loud
баланд кардан [baland kardan] *v.t.* hoist, lift, raise, mount, put up
баланд шудан [baland shudan] *v.i.* rise
баландӣ [balandi] *n.* altitude
баландтар кардан [balandtar kardan] *v.t.* amplify
балғам [balgham] *n.* phlegm
бале [bale] *n.* hello *(telephone greeting)* / *adv.* yes
балкон [balkon] *n.* balcony
балоғат [baloghat] *n.* maturity, adulthood
банан [banan] *n.* banana
банд [band] *n.* article *(legal)*; joint, link
банд кардан [band kardan] *v.t.* obstruct
банда [banda] *n.* slave
бандагӣ [bandagi] *n.* slavery
банди ангушт [bandi angusht] *n.* knuckle
банди об [bandi ob] *n.* dam
бандак [bandak] *n.* clip, suffix
бандaнда [bandanda] *adj.* astringent
бандар [bandar] *n.* harbor, port
бандаргоҳи баҳрӣ [bandargohi bahri] *n.* seaport
банди даст [bandi dast] *n.* wrist
бандина [bandina] *n.* bandage
бандиш [bandish] *n.* bandage
бандча [bandcha] *n.* package
банка [banka] *n.* can, jar
бар [bar] *n.* bar, pub; width / *prep.* upon
бар зидди [bar ziddi] *prep.* against *(in opposition to)*
баракат [barakat] *n.* boon, blessing
баракгирак [barakgirak] *n.* strainer
барангезиш [barangezish] *n.* excitement
барангехтан [barangextan] *v.t.* excite, stimulate
баранда [baranda] *n.* winner
бараҳна [barahna] *adj.* naked, bare, nude
бараҳнагӣ [barahnagi] *n.* nudity
барбод кардан [barbod kardan] *v.t.* frustrate *(about a plan)*

барбодравӣ [barbodravi] *n.* frustration *(about a plan)*
барвақт [barvaqt] *adj./adv.* early; **пагоҳи барвақт** [pagohi barvaqt] early morning
барг [barg] *n.* leaf
баргардондан [bargardondan] *v.t.* restore, give back, return
баргардондани пул [bargardondani pul] *n.* refund
баргашт [bargasht] *n.* return
баргаштан [bargashtan] *v.i.* return
баргаштнопазир [bargashtnopazir] *adj.* irreversible
баргузидан [barguzidan] *v.t./v.i.* choose
бардошт [bardosht] *n.* tolerance
бардошт кардан [bardosht kardan] *v.t.* tolerate, withstand
бардоштан [bardoshtan] *v.t.* hoist, lift, remove, withstand, tolerate
бардурӯғ [bardurügh] *adj.* false
бардурӯғӣ [bardurüghi] *n.* sham
барзагов [barzagov] *n.* ox
барзиёд [barziyod] *adj.* surplus, excessive
баркас [barkas] *n.* launch *(type of boat)*
баркашидан [barkashidan] *v.t.* weigh, determine weight
барқ [barq] *n.* electricity, lightning
барқарор кардан [barqaror kardan] *v.t.* determine, install, institute
барқарорӣ [barqarori] *n.* installation
барқасд [barqasd, maqsadnok] *adj.* deliberate, intentional
барқӣ [barqi] *adj.* electric
барнома [barnoma] *n.* program *(radio, television, concert, etc.)*
баробар [barobar] *adj.* equal, equivalent, level
баробар будан [barobar budan] *v.t.* equal
баробарӣ [barobari] *n.* equality
баровард [barovard] *n.* estimate
баровард кардан [barovard kardan] *v.t.* estimate
баровярда партофтан [barovarda partoftan] *v.t.* throw out, throw away
баровардан [barovardan] *v.t.* emit, extract, issue
бародар [barodar] *n.* brother
бародарандар [barodarandar] *n.* stepbrother
бародарзода [barodarzoda] *n.* nephew *(brother's son)*
барои [baroi] *prep.* for
баромад [baromad] *n.* number in a play or show, act
баромадан [baromadan] *v.i.* exit
баромадгоҳ [baromadgoh] *n.* exit
барориш [barorish] *n.* issue *(stamps, coins, etc.)*
бароҳат [barohat] *adj.* handy
барпо кардан [barpo kardan] *v.t.* establish, found, institute
барра [barra] *n.* lamb
бартараф кардан [bartaraf kardan] *v.t.* eliminate
бартар [bartar] *adj.* superior

бартарин [bartarin] *adj.* excellent, superior
бартарӣ [bartari] *n.* superiority, merit, preference
барф [barf] *n.* snow
барф боридан [barf boridan] *v.i.* snow
барх [barx] *n.* portion, part
бархато [barxato] *adj.* mistaken
бархостан [barxostan] *v.i.* rise up
бархӯрд [barxürd] *n.* collision
бархӯрдан [barxürdan] *v.i.* collide
барҷаста [barjasta] *adj.* outstanding
баромадгоҳи эҳтиётӣ [baromadgohi ehtiyoti] *n.* emergency exit
баръакс [bar'aks] *adj.* reverse
бас шудан [bas shudan] *v.i.* cease
басанда [basanda] *adj.* adequate, sufficient, enough
басанда будан [basanda budan] *v.i.* suffice
басарӣ [basari] *adj.* visual
басират [basirat] *n.* insight, vision
баскетбол [basketbol] *n.* basketball
баста [basta] *adj.* closed
бастак [bastak] *n.* clutch *(mechanical)*
бастан [bastan] *v.t.* bind, close, shut, fasten, harness, tie
батарея [batareya] *n.* battery
бахмал [baxmal] *n.* velvet
бахмалин [baxmalin] *adj.* velvet
бахт [baxt] *n.* luck, fate, fortune
бахш кардан [baxsh kardan] *v.t.* deal
бахшидан [baxshidan] *v.t.* bestow, grant, dedicate, donate; excuse, forgive, pardon
бахшиш [baxshish] *n.* grant, pardon
ба худ печидан [ba xud pechidan] *v.i.* curl up *(one's body)*
баҳмут [bahmut] *n.* hippopotamus
баҳо [baho] *n.* cost, price
баҳодор [bahodor] *adj.* valuable
баҳона [bahona] *n.* excuse
баҳор [bahor] *n.* spring *(season)*
баҳористон [bahoriston] *n.* tropics
баҳр [bahr] *n.* sea
баҳрӣ [bahri] *adj.* marine, naval
баҳрнаворд [bahrnavard] *n.* sailor
баҳс [bahs] *n.* argument
баҳс кардан [bahs kardan] *v.i.* argue
бача [bacha] *n.* child, boy, son
бачабардор [bachabardor] *n.* nanny
бачагӣ [bachagi, kudaki] *n.* childhood
бачагона [bachagona] *adj.* childish
бачадон [bachadon] *n.* uterus, womb
бачапартоёнӣ [bachapartoyoni] *n.* abortion
бачапартоӣ [bachapartoi] *n.* abortion
башарият [bashariyat] *n.* humanity, mankind
башарӣ [bashari] *adj.* human
баъд [ba'd] *adv.* after, next
баъд аз [ba'd az] *prep.* after

бе [be] *prep.* without
беадаб [beadab] *adj.* impolite
беадолат [beadolat] *adj.* unjust, unfair
беандеша [beandesha] *adj.* rash
беарзиш [bearzish] *adj.* worthless, without value
беаҳамият [beahamiyat] *adj.* unimportant
бебарг [bebarg] *adj.* without leaves, bare
бебаҳо [bebaho] *adj.* priceless
бебор [bebor] *adj.* barren *(land)*
бебӯй [bebüy] *adj.* odorless
бева [beva] *n.* widow, widower
бевазан [bevazan] *n.* widow
беваколат [bevakolat] *adj.* without authority, unauthorized
бевақт [bevaqt] *adv.* late
бевамард [bevamard] *n.* widower
бевосита [bevosita] *adj.* direct
бегона [begona] *n.* stranger / *adj.* foreign, alien, unfamiliar, strange / **аз ситораи бегона** [az sitorai begona] *n./adj.* extra-terrestrial
бегоҳ [begoh] *n.* evening
бегоҳӣ [begohi] *adj.* p.m.
бегуноҳ [begunoh] *adj.* innocent
бегӯшт [begüsht] *adj.* meatless, vegetarian
беғараз [begharaz] *adj.* objective
беғубор [beghubor] *adj.* pure
бед [bed] *n.* willow
беда [beda] *n.* hay
бедалел [bedalel] *adj.* arbitrary
бедам [bedam] *adj.* lifeless
бедард [bedard] *adj.* painless
бедиққат [bediqqat] *adj.* careless
бедин [bedin] *n.* atheist
бединӣ [bedini] *n.* atheism
бедона [bedona] *n.* quail
бедор [bedor] *adj.* awake
бедор кардан [bedor kardan] *v.t.* wake, wake up
бедор шудан [bedor shudan] *v.i.* awaken, wake up
бедору дарахт [bedoru daraxt] *adj.* bare *(landscape)*
бедорхобӣ [bedorxobi] *n.* insomnia
безарар [bezarar] *adj.* harmless
безеб [bezeb] *adj.* ugly
безиён [beziyon] *adj.* harmless, benign, undamaged
безор кардан [bezor kardan] *v.t.* annoy, pester, tease
безорӣ [bezori] *n.* annoyance
беинсоф [beinsof] *adj.* dishonest, unfair
беинсофӣ [beinsofi] *n.* dishonesty
беист [beist] *adj.* constant, ceaseless
беихтиёрона [beixtiyorona] *adj.* spontaneous / *adv.* spontaneously
беихтисос [beixtisos] *adj.* unskilled
беиҷозат [beijozat] *adj.* without permission, unauthorized
бейсбол [beysbol] *n.* baseball
бекор [bekor] *adj.* idle, null, off, unemployed
бекор кардан [bekor kardan] *v.t.* annul, nullify, cancel, revoke
бекорӣ [bekori] *n.* unemployment

беқарор [beqaror] *adj.* restless
беқасд [beqasd] *adj.* unintentional
беқобилият [beqobiliyat] *adj.* unable
бел [bel] *n.* oar, shovel, spade
бел задан [bel zadan] *v.t.* row
бел кашидан [bel kashidan] *v.t.* row
белкашӣ [belkashi] *n.* boating
белча [belcha] *n.* trowel
бемадор [bemor] *adj.* unwell
бемадор шудан [bemor shudan] *v.i.* sicken, decline in health
бемасъулият [bemas'uliyat] *adj.* unaccountable, without responsibility
бемаънӣ [bema'ni] *adj.* absurd, mindless
бемор [bemor] *n.* sick person, patient / *adj.* ill, sick, unhealthy, unwell
беморӣ [bemori] *n.* disease, illness, sickness
бемории қанд [bemorii qand] *n.* diabetes
беморхона [bemorxona] *n.* hospital
бемуваффақият [bemuvaffaqiyat] *adj.* unsuccessful
бенавоӣ [benavoi] *n.* misery
бензин [benzin] *n.* gasoline
бензинкаш [benzinkash] *n.* gasoline tanker
бенигоҳубин мондан [benigohubin mondan] *v.t.* neglect
бенозунузона [benozunuzona] *adj.* simple, unadorned
бенӯхта [benüxta] *adj.* frantic
беоб [beob] *adj.* dehydrated
беобрӯӣ [beobrüi] *n.* disgrace
беовоз [beovoz] *adj.* quiet
беовозӣ [beovozi] *n.* quiet
беодоб [beodob] *adj.* obscene
бепаноҳ [besarpanoh] *adj.* without shelter; bleak
бепарво [beparvo] *adj.* indifferent
бепоён [bepoyon] *adj.* endless, unending
бераҳм [berahm] *adj.* brutal, merciless
берун [berun] *n./adv.* outside
берун кардан [berun kardan] *v.t.* expel
берунӣ [beruni] *adj.* external, outer, outside
бесабр [besabr] *adj.* impatient
бесавод [besavod] *adj.* illiterate, uneducated
бесарӣ [besari] *n.* anarchy
бетараф [betaraf] *adj.* neutral, objective
бетарафӣ [betarafi] *n.* neutrality
бетартиб [betartib] *adj.* chaotic, messy, sloppy
бетартибӣ [betartibi] *n.* chaos, mess
бетаъсир [beta'sir] *adj.* impotent
бетон [beton] *n.* concrete
бефаъолият [befa'oliyat] *adj.* inactive
бефоида [befoida] *adj.* useless
бех [bex] *n.* flower bulb
бехабар [bexabar] *adj.* unaware
бехатар [bexatar] *adj.* without danger, safe
бехатарӣ [bexatari] *n.* lack of danger, safety
бехобӣ [bexobi] *n.* insomnia
бехтан [bextan] *v.t.* sift
беҳавсала [kamhavsala] *adj.* apathetic

беҳамто [behamto] *adj.* unique
беҳаракат [beharakat] *adj.* passive, still
беҳдошт [behdosht] *n.* hygiene
беҳдоштӣ [behdoshti] *adj.* sanitary
беҳис [behis] *adj.* numb
беҳокимиятӣ [behokimiyati] *n.* anarchy
беҳосил [behosil] *adj.* barren *(land)*
беҳтар [behtar] *adj./adv.* better
беҳтар донистан [behtar donistan] *v.t.* prefer
беҳтар кардан [behtar kardan] *v.t.* improve
беҳтар шудан [behtar shudan] *v.i.* improve
беҳтарин [behtarin] *adj./adv.* best
беҳуда [behuda] *adj.* needless, vain, without result
беҳунар [behunar] *adj.* incompetent
беҳурматӣ [behurmati] *n.* slight
беҳуш [behush] *adj.* unconscious
беҳуш шудан [behush shudan] *v.i.* faint
беҳшавӣ [behshavi] *n.* improvement
бечора [bechora] *adj.* unfortunate
бечорагӣ [bechoragi] *n.* hardship, misery
беҷинс [bejins] *adj.* neuter, unisex
беҷо [bejo] *adj.* improper
беҷон [bejon] *adj.* lifeless
беш [besh] *adj./adv.* more
бешак [beshak] *adj.* without doubt, definite
бешарм [besharm] *adj.* shameless, obscene
бештар [beshtar] *adj./adv.* more
бештарин [beshtarin] *adj./ adv.* most /*adj.* maximum, utmost
беэҳтиёт [beehtiyot] *adj.* careless
беэътино [bee'tino] *adj.* casual
беэътиноӣ [bee'tinoi] *n.* disregard
беэътиноӣ кардан [bee'tinoi kardan] *v.t.* disregard
беяроқ [beyaroq] *adj.* unarmed
бибикалон [bibikalon] *n.* great-grandmother
бибӣ [bibi] *n.* grandmother
биёбон [biyobon] *n.* desert
билет [bilet] *n.* ticket
билярд [bilyard] *n.* billiards
бим [bim] *n.* dread, fright
бим доштан [bim doshtan] *v.t.* dread
бима [bima] *n.* insurance
бимнок [bimnok] *adj.* frightening
бинанда [binanda] *n.* spectator
биниш [binish] *n.* faculty of sight, vision
бинӣ [bini] *n.* nose
бино [bino] *n.* building, structure
бинобар ин [binobar in] *adv.* therefore
бинои фаръӣ [binoi far'i] *n.* annex
биноӣ [binoi] *n.* faculty of sight, vision
биология [biologiya] *n.* biology

биологӣ [biologi] *adj.* biological
бирён [biryon] *adj.* fried
бирён кардан [biryon kardan] *v.t.* fry
бирёндан [biryondan] *v.t.* fry
биринҷ [birinj] *n.* bronze; rice
биринҷӣ [birinji] *adj.* bronze
бисёр [bisyor] *n.* a lot / *adj./ adv.* very, many, much / *adj.* numerous
бист [bist] *num.* twenty
бистар [bistar] *n.* mattress
бистум [bistum] *adj.* twentieth
бифштекс [bifshteks] *n.* steak
биҳишт [bihisht] *n.* heaven, paradise
блузка [bluzka] *n.* blouse
бо [bo] *prep.* with
боадаб [boadab] *adj.* polite
боазамат [boazamat] *adj.* grand, majestic
боақл [boaql] *adj.* intelligent
боандеша [boandesha] *adj.* thoughtful, reasonable
боб [bob] *n.* chapter
бобо [bobo] *n.* grandfather
бобокалон [bobokalon] *n.* great-grandfather
бовар [bovari] *n.* trust
бовар доштан [bovar doshtan] *v.i.* trust
бовар кардан [bovar kardan] *v.i.* believe
бовар кунондан [bovar kunondan] *v.t.* assure, persuade
бовар накардан [bovar nakardan] *v.t.* distrust, mistrust
боваркунонӣ [bovarkunoni] *n.* assurance
бовиҷдон [bovijdon] *adj.* conscientious, scrupulous
боғ [bogh] *n.* garden, park
боғи ҳайвонот [boghi hayvonot] *n.* zoo
боғбон [boghbon] *n.* gardener
боғайрат [boghayrat] *adj.* diligent
боғча [boghcha] *n.* kindergarten
бод [bod] *n.* wind
бодбарак [bodbarak] *n.* kite
бодбезак [bodbezak] *n.* fan
бодбон [bodbon] *n.* sail
бодиққат [bodiqqat] *adj.* attentive, careful, mindful
бодинҷон [bodinjon] *n.* eggplant
бодом [bodom] *n.* almond
бодпо [bodpo] *adj.* fleet, swift
боз [boz] *adj.* open / *adv.* again, else, more
боз кардан [boz kardan] *v.t.* open
бозгашт [bozgasht] *n.* return
бозгаштан [bozgashtan] *v.i.* return
боздид [bozdid] *n.* visit
боздид кардан [bozdid kardan] *v.t.* visit
боздоштан [bozdoshtan] *v.t.* curb, restrain, hinder, stop, detain
бозёфт [bozyoft] *n.* find
бозидан [bozidan] *v.i.* act, perform, play
бозии рӯимизӣ [bozii rüimizi] *n.* board game
бозингар [bozingar] *n.* player
бозича [bozicha] *n.* toy
бозӣ [bozi] *n.* game, sports match
бозӣ кардан [bozi kardan] *v.t./v.i.* act, perform, play
бозмонда [bozmonda] *n.* survivor / *adj.* remaining, surviving

бозор [bozor] *n.* market, bazaar
бозори саҳом [bozori sahom] *n.* stock market
бозоргир [bozorgir] *adj.* salable
бозорёбӣ [bozoryobi] *n.* marketing
бозу [bozu] *n.* arm
боигарӣ [boigari] *n.* wealth, riches
боинсоф [boinsof] *adj.* just, fair
боистан [boistan] *v.i.* should
боистеъдод [boiste'dod] *adj.* talented
боихтисос [boixtisos] *adj.* qualified
бой [boy] *adj.* rich, wealthy
бой додан [boy dodan] *v.i.* lose
бойгонӣ [boygoni] *n.* archive
бойгонӣ кардан [boygoni kardan] *v.t.* file away, keep on file
бокарруфар [bokarrufar] *adj.* luxurious
бокира [bokira] *n.* virgin
бокс [boks] *n.* boxing
боқимонда [boqimonda] *adj.* remaining
бол [bol] *n.* wing
болға [bolgha] *n.* hammer
болға задан [bolgha zadan] *v.t.* hammer
болиғ [boligh] *n./adj.* adult, grown-up, mature
болишт [bolisht] *n.* cushion, pillow
боло [bolo] *adv./prep.* above, aloft, up / *adj.* up, upper, upstairs
боло баромадан [bolo baromadan] *v.t.* climb
боло рафтан [bolo raftan] *v.i.* climb, mount
болобарой [bolobaroi] *n.* climb
болои [boloi] *adv.* over
болой [boloi] *adj.* upper
болор [bolor] *n.* beam
болотар аз ҳама [bolotar az hama] *adv.* above all
бом [bom] *n.* roof
бомаза [bomaza] *adj.* savory, tasty
бомантиқ [bomantiq] *adj.* logical
бомба [bomba] *n.* bomb
бомба андохтан [bomba andoxtan] *v.t.* throw a bomb, bomb
бомбаборон кардан [bombaboron kardan] *v.t.* bombard, bomb heavily
бомдод [bomdod] *n.* morning, first Islamic prayer of the day
бонг [bong] *n.* call
бонги хатар [bongi xatar] *n.* alarm, alert
бонги хатар задан [bongi xatar zadan] *v.t.* sound the alarm, sound the alert
бонк [bonk] *n.* bank
бонкир [bonkir] *n.* banker
боодоб [boodob] *adj.* polite, tactful
боодобӣ [boodobi] *n.* politeness, tact
бор [bor] *n.* freight, load; occasion, time
бор кардан [bor kardan] *v.t.* load
борбандӣ [borbandi] *n.* packing
бордор [bordor] *adj.* pregnant
борик [borik] *adj.* slender, slim, fine, tenuous

борикбин [borikbin] *adj.* shrewd
боркаш [borkash] *n.* porter
боркашонӣ [borkashoni] *n.* transmission
борон [boron] *n.* rain
борон боридан [boron boridan] *v.i.* rain
боронӣ [boroni] *n.* raincoat
бору банд [boru band] *n.pl.* belongings
борхалта [borxalta] *n.* knapsack, rucksack
босабр [bosabr] *adj.* patient
босалиқа [bosaliqa] *adj.* elegant *(person)*
бостон [boston] *adj.* ancient
бостоншинос [bostonshinos] *n.* archeologist
бостоншиносӣ [bostonshinosi] *n.* archeology
босуръат рафтан [bosur'at raftan] *v.i.* speed
ботартиб [botartib] *adj.* regular, tidy
ботил [botil] *adj.* null, void
ботлоқ [botloq] *n.* marsh, swamp
бофанда [bofanda] *n.* weaver
бофта [bofta] *n.* tissue *(anat.)*, web / *adj.* woven, knitted, wicker
бофтан [boftan] *v.t./v.i.* knit, weave
бохтан [boxtan] *v.i.* lose
бохтар [boxtar] *n.* west / *adj.* western
бохтарӣ [boxtari] *adj.* western
боҳуш [bohush] *adj.* conscious, mentally perceptive
боҷ [boj] *n.* toll, tribute
боҷа [boja] *n.pl.* husbands of two sisters
бошараф [bosharaf] *adj.* noble
бошиддат [boshiddat] *adj.* intense
бошишгоҳ [boshishgoh] *n.* dwelling
бошукӯҳ [boshuküh] *adj.* luxurious, magnificent
боэътимод [boe'timod] *adj.* reliable
бояд [boyad] *aux.* must, got to, have to
бразилиягӣ [braziliyagi] *n./adj.* Brazilian
бригада [brigada] *n.* crew
британиягӣ [britaniyagi] *n./adj.* British
брокколи [brokkoli] *n.* broccoli
брон [bron] *n.* booking, reservation
брон кардан [bron kardan] *v.t.* make a reservation, book
бронхит [bronxit] *n.* bronchitis
Бубахшед! [bubaxshed!] Excuse me!
буғ [bugh] *n.* horn *(mus. or of car)*; steam, vapor
буғ додан [bugh dodan] *v.t.* steam, expose to steam
буғӣ кардан [bughi kardan] *v.t.* strangle
буғранҷ [bughranj] *adj.* complicated
буғранҷ кардан [bughranj kardan] *v.t.* complicate
буғум [bughum] *n.* joint
будан [budan] *v.i.* be
буз [buz] *n.* goat
буздил [buzdil] *n.* coward
бузича [buzicha] *n.* kid *(young goat)*
бузург [buzurg] *adj.* enormous, huge, immense, massive, great

бузургии пойдор [buzurgii poydor] *n.* constant
бузургӣ [buzurgi] *n.* greatness
булғорӣ [bulghori] *n.* green pepper
булка [bulka] *n.* bread roll
булут [bulut] *n.* oak
булӯр [bulür] *n.* crystal
булӯрин [bulürin] *adj.* crystal
бум [bum] *n.* owl
бумазӣ [bumazi] *n.* flannel
бумӣ [bumi] *adj.* native
бунафш [bunafsh] *adj.* violet
бунафша [bunafsha] *n.* violet
бунгоҳ [bungoh] *n.* institute
бунёд [bunyod] *n.* foundation, groundwork
бунёдӣ [bunyodi] *adj.* fundamental
бунёдгаро [bunyodgaro] *n.* fundamentalist
бунёдкор [bunyodkor] *adj.* founder
бурд [burd] *n.* win
бурда расондан [burda rasondan] *v.t.* deliver
бурдан [burdan] *v.t.* bear, carry, convey; win
бурдарасонӣ [burdarasoni] *n.* delivery
бурида партофтан [burida partoftan] *v.t.* amputate
буридан [buridan] *v.t.* cut, slice
буридапартоӣ [buridapartoi] *n.* amputation
буриш [burish] *n.* cut, section cut away
бурро [burro] *adj.* sharp
бурут [burut] *n.* mustache, whisker
бурҷ [burj] *n.* constellation; tower
бутпараст [butparast] *n.* pagan, idol-worshipper
буттамева [buttameva] *n.* berry
буханка [buxanka] *n.* loaf
буҷа [buja] *n.* budget
буҷулак [bujulak] *n.* ankle
бӯғча [büghcha] *n.* bundle
бӯзина [büzina] *n.* monkey
бӯидан [büidan] *v.t.* smell
бӯй [büy] *n.* odor, smell
бӯй кардан [büy kardan] *v.t.* smell
бӯйоӣ [büyoi] *n.* sense of smell
бӯр [bür] *n.* chalk
бӯрё [büryo] *n.* mat
бӯрон [büron] *n.* snowstorm
бӯса [büsa] *n.* kiss
бӯсидан [büsidan] *v.t.* kiss
бӯҳрон [bühron] *n.* crisis
бӯҳтон [bühton] *n.* libel
бӯҳтон кардан [bühton kardan] *v.t.* libel
бюро [byuro] *n.* bureau *(government)*

В

ва [va] *conj.* and
ва ғайра [va ghayra] etc., and so forth, and so on
вазидан [vazidan] *v.i.* blow
вазир [vazir] *n.* minister
вазифа [vazifa] *n.* position, post, appointment *(ministerial)*, duty, function, job, task, obligation
вазифаи хонагӣ [vazifai xonagi] *n.* homework
вазиш [vazish] *n.* puff of air
вазн [vazn] *n.* rhythm, weight
вазн [vazna] *n.* weight *(for exercise)*
вазнин [vaznin] *adj.* heavy
вазорат [vazorat] *n.* ministry
вазъ [vaz'] *n.* sermon

вазъият [vaz'iyat] *n.* situation, status
вазъияти таъҷилӣ [vaz'iyati ta'jili] *n.* emergency
вай [vay] *pron.* he, him, she, her, it
вайрон кардан [vayroni] *v.t.* destroy, ruin, spoil, violate
вайрон шудан [vayron shudan] *v.i.* become ruined, become destroyed
вайрона [vayrona] *n.pl.* ruins
вайронӣ [vayron kardan] *n.* destruction
вайроншавӣ [vayronshavi] *n.* violation, decay
вакил [vakil] *n.* attorney
ваксина [vaksina] *n.* vaccine
ваксина гузарондан [vaksina guzarondan] *v.t.* vaccinate
ваксинагузаронӣ [vaksinaguzaroni] *n.* vaccination
вақт [vaqt] *n.* time
вақтгузаронӣ [vaqtguzaroni] *n.* pastime
вақте ки [vaqte ki] *conj.* when, while
вақтхушӣ [vaqtxushi] *n.* recreation
вақтчоқ кардан [vaqtchoq kardan] *v.t.* cause to laugh, amuse
валӣ [vali] *n.* saint
ванил [vanil] *n.* vanilla
ванна [vanna] *n.* bathtub
варақа [varaqa] *n.* sheet *(of paper)*
варақаи қарз [varaqai qarz] *n.* credit card
варақасанг [varaqasang] *n.* slate
варам [varam] *n.* inflammation, swelling, tumor
варам кардан [varam kardan] *v.i.* swell
варамкарда [varamkarda] *adj.* inflamed
варзиш [varzish] *n.* athletics, sport
варзишгар [varzishgar] *n.* athlete, sportsman
варзишгоҳ [varzishgoh] *n.* gymnasium
вартиш [vartish] *n.* quail
варшикаст [varshikast] *adj.* bankrupt
васат [vasat] *n./adj.* middle
васваса [vasvasa] *n.* temptation
васваса кардан [vasvasa kardan] *v.t.* tempt
васеъ [vase'] *adj.* wide
васила [vasila] *n.* means
васият [vasiyat] *n.* will *(legal)*
ватан [vatan] *n.* homeland
ватандӯст [vatandüst] *n.* patriot / *adj.* patriotic
ватт [vatt] *n.* watt
вафодор [vafodor] *adj.* loyal, faithful
вафодорӣ [vafodori] *n.* loyalty, devotion
ваҳй [vahy] *n.* revelation
ваҳшиёна [vahshiyona] *adj.* savage / *adv.* savagely
ваҳшӣ [vahshi] *n.* savage, wild
ваҷд [vajd] *n.* ecstacy, trance
ваъда [va'da] *n.* promise
ваъда додан [va'da dodan] *v.t.* promise
вергул [vergul] *n.* comma
вермут [vermut] *n.* vermouth
вертолёт [vertolyot] *n.* helicopter
видео [video] *n.* video
видеокассета [videokasseta] *n.* videotape
видеомагнитофон [videomagnitofon] *n.* VCR

вижа [vizha] *adj.* special, characteristic
вилла [villa] *n.* villa
вилоят [viloyat] *n.* province
виолинчел [violinchel] *n.* cello, violoncello
вирус [virus] *n.* virus
вирусӣ [virusi] *adj.* viral
виски [viski] *n.* whiskey
витамин [vitamin] *n.* vitamin
вобаста [vobasta] *adj.* dependent
вобаста будан [vobasta budan] *v.i.* depend, hinge
вобаста кардан [vobasta kardan] *v.t.* associate
вогузорӣ [voguzori] *n.* transfer
вогузоштан [voguzoshtan] *v.t.* transfer, give over
водӣ [vodi] *n.* valley
водопроводчӣ [vodoprovodchi] *n.* plumber
водор кардан [vodor kardan] *v.t.* force, oblige
водоштан [vodoshtan] *v.t.* force, oblige
вожа [vozha] *n.* word
вокуниш [vokunish] *n.* reaction
вокуниш доштан [vokunish doshtan] *v.t.* react
воқеа [voqea] *n.* event, instance, occurrence
воқеият [voqeiyat] *n.* reality
воқеӣ [voqei] *adj.* actual, real
воқеъ шудан [voqe' shudan] *v.i.* occur
волидайн [volidayn] *n.pl.* parents
волт [volt] *n.* volt
волтаж [voltazh] *n.* voltage
вом [vom] *n.* credit, debt, loan
вом додан [vom dodan] *v.t.* credit, lend, loan
вомдиҳанда [vomdihanda] *n.* creditor
вонамуд кардан [vonamud kardan] *v.t.* simulate
вонамуд [vonamud] *n.* simulation
вора [vora] *n.* gum *(anat.)*
ворид кардан [vorid kardan] *v.t.* import
воридот [voridot] *n.* import, imports
восита [vosita] *n.* means, medium
вохӯрдан [voxürdan] *v.t.* meet
вохӯрӣ [voxüri] *n.* get-together, date, meeting
вохӯрӣ кардан [voxüri kardan] *v.t.* shake hands, meet
воҳид [vohid] *n.* unit
воҳима [vohima] *n.* panic
воя [voya] *n.* dose, ration
воясозӣ кардан [voyasozi kardan] *v.* ration
вуруд [vurud] *n.* arrival

Г

гавазн [gavazn] *n.* deer
гавҳарак [gavharak] *n.* pupil *(anat.)*
гадо [gado] *n.* beggar
гадоӣ кардан [gadoi kardan] *v.i.* beg
газ [gaz] *n.* gas
газак [gazak] *n.* appetizer, hors d'oeuvre, snack; inflammation
газакгирифта [gazakgirifta] *adj.* inflamed
газанд [gazand] *n.* harm
газвор [gazvor] *n.* cloth, fabric, material, textile
газгун [gazgun] *adj.* gassy
газидан [gazidan] *v.t.* bite, sting

газоф [gazof] *adj.* extravagant
гала [gala] *n.* flock
галаситора [galasitora] *n.* constellation
галлон [gallon] *n.* gallon
галстук [galstuk] *n.* necktie
гамбуск [gambusk] *n.* beetle
ганг [gang] *n.* bedbug
ганда [ganda] *adj.* bad, nasty / *adv.* badly
гандидан [gandidan] *v.i.* spoil, go bad
гандум [gandum] *n.* wheat
ганҷ [ganj] *n.* treasure
ганҷдор [ganjdor] *n.* treasurer
ганҷина [ganjina] *n.* treasury
ганҷур [ganjur] *n.* treasurer
гап задан [gap zadan] *v.i.* speak, talk
гарав [garav] *n.* bet, mortgage
гарав бастан [garav bastan] *v.t.* bet
гарав гузоштан [garav guzoshtan] *v.t.* pawn
гаравгон [garavgon] *n.* hostage
гараж [garazh] *n.* garage
гард [gard] *n.* dust, powder
гардан [gardan] *n.* neck
гардан тофтан [gardan toftan] *v.t.* renounce
гарданбанд [gardanband] *n.* necklace
гарданпеч [gardanpech] *n.* scarf
гардероб [garderob] *n.* wardrobe
гардгир [gardgir] *n.* whisk
гардидан [gardidan] *v.i.* revolve
гардиш [gardish] *n.* circulation, cycle, revolution; walk
гардолуд [gardolud] *adj.* dusty
гардон [gardon] *n.* chorus *(refrain)*
гардондан [gardondan] *v.t.* revolve, spin, walk
гарева [gareva] *adj.* hilly
гарм [garm] *adj.* hot, warm
гармича [garmicha] *n.* acne, pimple
гармӣ [garmi] *n.* heat, warmth
гармкунак [garmkunak] *n.* heater, radiator
гармкунӣ [garmkuni] *n.* heating
гармоба [garmoba] *n.* bathroom *(for bathing)*
гарон [garon] *adj.* expensive; heavy
гаронбаҳо [garonbaho] *adj.* precious, valuable
гаҳвора [gahvora] *n.* cradle
гач [gach] *n.* plaster
гаштан [gashtan] *v.i.* walk
гаштугузор [gashtuguzor] *n.* hike
гаштугузор кардан [gashtuguzor kardan] *v.i.* hike, wander
гелос [gelos] *n.* cherry
гемофилия [gemofiliya] *n.* hemophilia
генерал [general] *n.* general
генетикӣ [genetiki] *adj.* genetic
гетӣ [geti] *n.* world
гил [gil] *n.* clay, soil, dirt, mud
гила [gila] *n.* complaint, grievance
гила кардан [gila kardan] *v.i.* complain
гилем [gilem] *n.* rug
гиро [giro] *n.* grip
гира [gira] *n.* vise
гирд [gird] *adj.* round
гирд гаштан [gird gashtan] *v.i.* circulate, move through a circuit

гирди [girdi] *prep.* around
гирдоб [girdob] *n.* whirlpool
гирдогирд [girdogird] *adv.* around / *adj.* indirect
гирду атроф [girdu atrof] *n.* vicinity
гиребон [girebon] *n.* collar
гиреҳ [gireh] *n.* knot, loop
гиреҳ бастан [gireh bastan] *v.t.* tie a knot
гиристан [giristan] *v.t./v.i.* weep, cry
гирифтан [giriftan] *v.t.* derive, dial, get, take; **рақами телефонро гирифтан** [raqami telefonro giriftan] dial a telephone number
гирифтор кардан [giriftor kardan] *v.t.* expose
гирифтор шудан [giriftor shudan] *v.i.* undergo
гиромӣ [giromi] *adj.* esteemed, dear
гиря кардан [girya kardan] *v.t./v.i.* weep, cry
гитара [gitara] *n.* guitar
гиҷ [gij] *adj.* dizzy
гиҷ кардан [gij kardan] *v.t.* stun
гобелен [gobelen] *n.* tapestry
гов [gov] *n.* cow
гол задан [gol zadan] *v.t.* score a goal
голф [golf] *n.* golf
гом [gom] *n.* step, pace
гоҳ-гоҳ [goh-goh] *adj.* occasional
гоҳ-гоҳӣ [goh-gohi] *adv.* occasionally
граф [graf] *n.* count *(nobleman)*
график [grafik] *n.* graph
графикӣ [grafiki] *adj.* graphic
грамм [gramm] *n.* gram
грамматика [grammatika] *n.* grammar
грипп [gripp] *n.* flu, influenza
гуворидан [guvoridan] *v.t.* digest
гувориш [guvorish] *n.* digestion
гуворо [guvoro] *adj.* wholesome
гувоҳ [guvoh] *n.* witness
гувоҳинома [guvohinoma] *n.* certificate, record
гувоҳӣ [guvohi] *n.* testimony
гувоҳӣ додан [guvohi dodan] *n.* testify
гудохтан [gudoxtan] *v.t.* melt
гузаранда [guzaranda] *adj.* infectious, transferable / *gram.* transitive
гузаргоҳ [guzargoh] *n.* passage
гузарондан [guzarondan] *v.t.* transfer, pass from one side to the other, transmit
гузашт [guzasht] *n.* concession
гузашт кардан [guzasht kardan] *v.t.* concede
гузашта [guzashta] *n./adj.* past
гузашта [guzashta] *aux.* could *(past of* can*)*
гузаштан [guzashtan] *v.t.* cross, pass
гузориш [guzorish] *n.* installation; report
гузориш додан [guzorish dodan] *v.t.* report
гузоштан [guzoshtan] *v.t.* leave, place, put, install, lay, let
гул [gul] *n.* flower, rose
гул-гул шукуфтан [gul-gul shukuftan] *v.i.* prosper, thrive

гулбарг [gulbarg] *n.* petal
гулбутта [gulbutta] *n.* rosebush
гулгун [gulgun] *adj.* scarlet
гулдон [guldon] *n.* vase
гулдӯзӣ [guldüzi] *n.* embroidery
гулдӯзӣ кардан [guldüzi kardan] *v.t.* embroider
гулдӯзӣ [guldüzi] *adj.* embroidered
гулдуррос [guldurros] *n.* crash, rumble
гулдуррос зада афтондан [guldurros zada aftondan] *v.t.* crash
гулдуррос задан [guldurros zadan] *v.i.* rumble
гулкарам [gulkaram] *n.* cauliflower
гулмоҳӣ [gulmohi] *n.* trout
гулобӣ [gulobi] *adj.* pink, rose
гулӯ [gulü] *n.* throat
гулӯгир кардан [gulügir kardan] *v.t.* choke
гулӯгоҳ [gulügoh] *n.* strait
гулфурӯш [gulfurüsh] *n.* florist
гулхона [gulxona] *n.* greenhouse
гум кардан [gum kardan] *v.t.* lose
гумshuda [gumshuda] *adj.* lost
гумон [gumon] *n.* opinion
гумон доштан [gumon doshtan] *v.i.* suppose
гумонбар [gumonbar] *n.* suspect
гумони бад [gumoni bad] *n.* suspicion
гумошта [gumoshta] *n.* agent *(one empowered to act)*
гумоштан [gumoshtan] *v.t.* appoint
гумроҳ [gumroh] *adj./adv.* astray
гумрук [gumruk] *n.* customs
гумрукчӣ [gumrukchi] *n.* customs official
гумшуда [gumshuda] *adj.* lost
гуна [guna] *n.* kind, sort
гунбад [gunbad] *n.* dome
гунбаз [gunbaz] *n.* dome
гунг [gung] *adj.* mute, dumb
гуногун [gunogun] *adj.* diverse, manifold, various
гуноҳ [gunoh] *n.* sin; fault
гуноҳ кардан [gunoh kardan] *v.i.* sin
гуноҳгор [gunohgor] *adj.* guilty
гуноҳгорӣ [gunohgori] *n.* guilt
гунҷишк [gunjishk] *n.* sparrow
гунҷоиш [gunjoish] *n.* capacity, volume
гунҷондан [gunjondan] *v.t.* accommodate
гуппос [guppos] *n.* engine fumes, exhaust
гурба [gurba] *n.* cat
гурбача [gurbacha] *n.* kitten
гург [gurg] *n.* wolf
гурда [gurda] *n.* kidney
гурез [gurez] *n.* escape
гуреза [gureza] *n./adj.* fugitive, refugee
гурезпо [gurezpo] *n.* fugitive
гурехтан [gurextan] *v.t.* escape, flee
гурусна [gurusna] *adj.* hungry
гуруснагӣ [gurusnagi] *n.* hunger
гуруснамонӣ [gurusnamoni] *n.* starvation
гурӯҳ [gurüh] *n.* group
гурҷӣ [gurji] *n./adj.* Georgian
гуфтан [guftan] *v.t.* say, speak, tell / *v.i.* say, utter

гуфтугӯ [guftugü] *n.* chat, conversation, talk, dialogue
гуфтугӯ кардан [guftugü kardan] *v.i.* chat
гуфтушунид [guftushunid] *n.* negotiation
гуфтушунид кардан [guftushunid kardan] *v.i.* negotiate
гушн [gushn] *n.* heat *(female animal mating period)*
гӯгирд [gügird] *n.* match, matches
гӯр [gür] *n.* grave, tomb
гӯристон [güriston] *n.* cemetery
гӯрхар [gürxar] *n.* zebra
гӯсола [güsola] *n.* calf *(young cow)*
гӯсфанд [güsfand] *n.* sheep
гӯш [güsh] *n.* ear
гӯш кардан [güsh kardan] *v.t.* listen
гӯш накардан [güsh nakardan] *v.t.* disobey
гӯша [güsha] *n.* corner
гӯшанишинӣ [güshanishini] *n.* seclusion
гӯшак [güshak] *n.* receiver *(telephone)*
гӯшвора [güshvora] *n.* earring
гӯшмонак [güshmonak] *n.* earphone
гӯшпӯшакҳо [güshpüshakho] *n.pl.* earmuffs
гӯшт [güsht] *n.* flesh, meat
гӯшт гирифтан [güsht giriftan] *v.t.* gain weight
гӯштингир [güshtingir] *n.* wrestler
гӯштӣ [güshti] *n.* wrestling
гӯштӣ гирифтан [güshti giriftan] *v.t.* wrestle
гӯштнахӯранда [güshtnaxüranda] *n.* vegetarian

Ғ

ғаввос [ghavvos] *n.* diver
ғаввосӣ [ghavvosi] *n.* diving
ғаввосӣ кардан [ghavvosi kardan] *v.i.* dive
ғавғо [ghavgho] *n.* noise, uproar
ғадуд [ghadud] *n.* gland
ғадуди бодомшакл [ghadudi bodomshakl] *n.pl.* tonsils
ғайбат [ghaybat] *n.* absence
ғайр аз [ghayr az] *adv.* aside from
ғайрат [ghayrat] *n.* zeal
ғайридинӣ [ghayridini] *adj.* secular
ғайриқаноатбахш [ghayriqanoatbaxsh] *adj.* unsatisfactory
ғайриқонунӣ [ghayriqonuni] *adj.* illegal
ғайримарказӣ [ghayrimarkazi] *adj.* peripheral
ғайриоддӣ [ghayrioddi] *adj.* abnormal
ғайрирасмӣ [ghayrirasmi] *adj.* unofficial
ғайрисайёр [ghayrisayyor] *adj.* stationary
ғайриҳатмӣ [ghayrihatmi] *adj.* optional
ғалақа [ghalaqa] *n.* bolt, locking device
ғалақаи дар [ghalaqai dar] *n.* latch
ғалат [ghalat] *adj.* mistaken, wrong
ғалатфаҳмӣ [ghalatfahmi] *n.* misunderstanding

ғалбер [ghalber] *n.* large-holed sieve
ғалевоҷ [ghalevoj *n.* hawk
ғалла [ghalla] *n.* cereal, grain
ғалсама [ghalsama] *n.* gill
ғалтак [ghaltak] *n.* reel
ғалтидан [ghaltidan] *v.i.* fall, tip over
ғалтиш [ghaltish] *n.* fall
ғалтондан [ghaltondan] *v.t.* cause to fall, tip over
ғам [gham] *n.* affliction, sadness, sorrow
ғамгин [ghamgin] *adj.* sad
ғамгин кардан [ghamgin kardan] *v.t.* afflict, sadden
ғамгин шудан [ghamgin shudan] *v.i.* sadden
ғанаб [ghanab] *n.* nap
ғанаб кардан [ghanab kardan] *v.i.* nap, take a nap
ғарб [gharb] *n.* west / *adj.* western
ғарбӣ [gharbi] *adj.* western
ғарғара [gharghara] *n.* pulley
ғарғара кардан [gharghara kardan] *v.t.* gargle
ғариб [gharib] *adj.* strange, odd
ғариза [ghariza] *n.* instinct
ғарқ кардан [gharq kardan] *v.t.* drown
ғарқ шудан [gharq shudan] *v.i.* drown
ғарчос кардан [gharchos kardan] *v.t.* crunch
ғасб кардан [ghasb kardan] *v.t.* annex
ғафлат [ghaflat] *n.* omission
ғафлат кардан [ghaflat kardan] *v.t.* omit
ғафс [ghafs] *adj.* plump, thick
ғафс кардан [ghafs kardan] *v.t.* thicken
ғафс шудан [ghafs shudan] *v.i.* thicken
ғафсӣ [ghafsi] *n.* thickness
ғафсрӯда [ghafsrüda] *n.* colon *(anat.)*
ғаюр [ghayur] *adj.* zealous
ғел задан [ghel zadan] *v.i.* roll
ғелида рафтан [ghelida raftan] *v.i.* roll
ғелондан [ghelondan] *v.t.* roll
ғеҷондан [ghejondan] *v.t.* drag from side to side, slide *(for instance, heavy objects)*
ғилофак [ghilofak] *n.* capsule, pod
ғирғирак [ghirghirak] *n.* top *(toy)*
ғиҷҷак [ghijjak] *n.* fiddle, violin
ғоиб [ghoib] *adj.* absent
ғор [ghor] *n.* cave
ғорат [ghorat] *n.* robbery
ғорат кардан [ghorat kardan] *v.t.* ransack, rob
ғоратгар [ghoratgar] *n.* robber
ғубор [ghubor] *n.* dust
ғук [ghuk] *n.* toad
ғулом [ghulom] *n.* slave
ғун кардан [ghun kardan] *v.t.* collect, gather, bring together
ғун шудан [ghun shudan] *v.i.* gather
ғундоштан [ghundoshtan] *v.t.* accumulate, collect, gather
ғурридан [ghurridan] *v.i.* roar
ғурриш [ghurrish] *n.* roar
ғуррос [ghurros] *n.* growl, roar
ғуррос задан [ghurros zadan] *v.i.* growl, roar
ғуруб кардан [ghurub kardan] *v.i.* set
ғуруби офтоб [ghurubi oftob] *n.* sunset
ғурур [ghurur] *n.* arrogance

ғусса хӯрдан [ghussa xürdan] *v.i.* grieve
ғӯзаи чашм [ghüzai chashm] *n.* eyeball
ғӯлачӯб [ghülachüb] *n.* log
ғӯта задан [ghüta zadan] *v.i.* dive, plunge
ғӯтазан [ghütazan] *n.* diver
ғӯтазанӣ [ghütazani] *n.* diving
ғӯтондан [ghütondan] *v.t.* dip

Д

дабба [dabba] *n.* hernia
даббоғӣ кардан [dabboghi kardan] *v.t.* tan
дав [dav] *n.* run
давак [davak] *n.* runner *(device on which things are moved)*
даванда [davanda] *n.* one who runs, runner
давидан [davidan] *v.i.* run
давиш [davish] *n.* run, dash
давлат [davlat] *n.* government, regime
давлатманд [davlatmand] *adj.* prosperous, rich
давлатмандӣ [davlatmandi] *n.* prosperity
даво кардан [davo kardan] *v.t.* heal, cure
даводавӣ [davodavi] *n.* running
давом [davom] *n.* sequel
давом додан [davom dodan] *v.i.* continue, proceed
давомдор [davomdor] *adj.* continuous
давомнок [davomnok] *adj.* chronic
давр [davr] *n.* tour
давр задан [davr zadan] *v.t.* tour
давра [davra] *n.* circuit *(circular course)*, circumference; era, period of time
даврӣ [davri] *adj.* of a period
дағал [daghal] *adj.* rude, vulgar
дада [dada] *n.* dad, daddy
дайр [dayr] *n.* convent, monastery
дакка хӯрдан [dakka xürdan] *v.i.* stumble
дақиқ [daqiq] *adj.* precise, exact, thorough
дақиқа [daqiqa] *n.* minute
далел [dalel] *n.* proof, reason, argument
далел овардан [dalel ovardan] *v.t.* to give reason for
далер [daler] *adj.* brave, courageous, valiant
далерӣ [daleri] *n.* courage
дам [dam] *n.* instant, moment
дам баровардан [dam barovardan] *v.i.* exhale
дам гирифтан [dam giriftan] *v.i.* rest, relax
дамгирӣ [damgiri] *n.* rest, relaxation
даммал [dammal] *n.* boil *(med.)*
дампухт [dampuxt] *adj.* steamed
данд [dand] *adj.* tart
данда [danda] *n.* gear
дандон [dandon] *n.* tooth
дандон нишон додан [dandon nishon dodan] *v.i.* snarl
дандонак [dandonak] *n.* trigger
дандонпизишк [dandonpizishk] *n.* dentist
дар [dar] *n.* door / *prep.* in, into, within / *adv.* within

дар бораи [dar borai] *prep.* about, concerning, regarding
дар зери [dar zeri] *prep.* below, underneath
дар киштӣ [dar kishti] *adv.* aboard a ship
дар куҷое [dar kujoe] *adv.* somewhere
дар пеш [dar pesh] *adj.* ahead
дар пеш шудан [dar pesh shudan] *v.* get ahead
дар саф овардан [dar saf ovardan] *v.t.* align
дар ҳавопаймо [dar havopaymo] *adv.* aboard a plane
дар ҷое [dar joe] *adv.* somewhere
дара [dara] *n.* valley
даравидан [daravidan] *v.t.* reap
даранг [darang] *n.* pause
дарахт [daraxt] *n.* tree
дарахти ҷалғӯза [daraxti jalghüza] *n.* cedar
дараҷа [daraja] *n.* degree, level
дараҷа бастан [daraja bastan] *v.t.* graduate
дарбеҳ [darbeh] *n.* patch
дарбеҳ кардан [darbeh kardan] *v.t.* fix, patch
дарбон [darbon] *n.* doorman
дарбор [darbor] *n.* royal court
дарвоза [darvoza] *n.* gate; goal *(sports)*
дарвозаи обпарто [darvozai obparto] *n.* sluice
дарвозабон [darvozabon] *n.* goalkeeper
даргирондан [dargirondan] *v.t.* kindle, light, switch on
дард [dard] *n.* ache, pain, anguish
дард кардан [dard kardan] *v.i.* ache, hurt
дарднок [dardnok] *adj.* painful, sore
дарё [daryo] *n.* river; sea
дарёӣ [daryoi] *adj.* marine, naval
дарёнаворд [daryonavard] *n.* sailor
дарёфт [daryoft] *n.* perception
дарёфтан [daryoftan] *v.t.* perceive
дарз [darz] *n.* seam
дарзӣ [darzi] *n.* tailor
дарзигӣ кардан [darzigi kardan] *v.t.* tailor
дарзмол [darzmol] *n.* iron *(for clothing, etc.)*
дарзмол кардан [darzmol kardan] *v.t.* iron
дарди сари дил [dardi sari dil] *n.* chest pains
дарида [darida] *adj.* ragged, torn
даридагӣ [daridagi] *n.* rip, tear
даридан [daridan] *v.i.* rip, tear
дарк [dark] *n.* perception
дарк кардан [dark kardan] *v.* perceive
даркор [darkor] *adj.* vital, necessary
даркорӣ [darkori] *adj.* due, necessary
дармон [darmon] *n.* cure
дармонгоҳ [darmongoh] *n.* clinic
даровардан [darovardan] *v.t.* include, bring in, insert
дароз [daroz] *adj.* long
дароз кашидан [daroz kashidan] *v.i.* lie down
дарозӣ [darozi] *n.* length
дарозрӯя [darozrüya] *adj.* oblong

дарозтар кардан [daroztar kardan] *v.t.* lengthen
даромад [daromad] *n.* income, revenue; entry
даромадан [daromadan] *n.* admission / *v.i.* enter; **даромадани бепул** [daromadani bepul] free admission
даромадгоҳ [daromadgoh] *n.* entrance
дарранда [darranda] *adj.* fierce
даррондан [darrondan] *v.t.* rip, tear
дарс [dars] *n.* lesson
дарс хондан [dars xondan] *v.i.* study
дарсад [darsad] *n.* percent, percentage
sinfхона [darsxona] *n.* classroom
дарун [darun] *n./adj.* inside, interior
даруни [daruni] *prep.* into, within
дарунӣ [daruni] *adj.* indoor, inner, interior, internal
дарунравӣ [darunravi] *n.* diarrhea
дархост [darxost] *n.* request, solicitation, application
дархост кардан [darxost kardan] *v.t./v.i.* request, solicit, apply
дарҷ кардан [darj kardan] *v.t.* insert
дасиса [dasisa] *n.* plot, intrigue
даст [dast] *n.* hand
даст кашидан [dast kashidan] *v.t.* refuse
даст расондан [dast rasondan] *v.t.* touch
даста [dasta] *n.* group, party, team, band *(of people)*; batch, cluster; pack, set; shaft
даста шудан [dasta shudan] *v.i.* cluster
дастабандӣ кардан [dastabandi kardan] *v.t.* classify
дастак [dastak] *n.* handle
дастархон [dastarxon] *n.* tablecloth
дастгирӣ [dastgiri] *n.* arrest
дастгир кардан [dastgir kardan] *v.t.* arrest
дастгоҳ [dastgoh] *n.* apparatus
дастгоҳи бофандагӣ [dastgohi bofandagi] *n.* loom
дастгоҳи дуредгарӣ [dastgohi duredgari] *n.* lathe
дастгоҳи кабобкунӣ [dastgohi kabobkuni] *n.* grill
дастгоҳи нусхабардорӣ [dastgohi nusxabardori] *n.* copier
дастёр [dastyor] *n.* assistant, helper, attendant
дастёрӣ кардан [dastyori kardan] *v.i.* wait upon, attend
дастӣ [dasti] *adj.* handmade
дастрushak [dastkash] *n.* glove
дастнавис [dastnavis] *n.* manuscript
дастнорас [dastnoras] *adj.* inaccessible
дастомӯз [dastomüz] *adj.* tame
дастомӯз кардан [dastomüz kardan] *v.t.* tame
дастпӯшак [dastpüshak] *n.* glove
дастрас [dastras] *n.* reach / *adj.* accessible, available
дастрасӣ [dastrasi] *n.* access, accessibility, availability

даструмолча [dastrümolcha] *n.* handkerchief
дастур [dastur] *n.* instructions, regulation, rule
дастшӯяк [dastshüyak] *n.* sink
дафн кардан [dafn kardan] *v.t.* bury
дафтар [daftar] *n.* notebook
дафтари хотира [daftari xotira] *n.* diary, journal
дахма [daxma] *n.* funeral vault
дахолат кардан [daxolat kardan] *v.t.* interfere, tamper
даҳ [dah] *num.* ten
даҳан [dahan] *n.* mouth
даҳана [dahana] *n.* funnel
даҳанакӣ [dahanaki] *adj.* oral
даҳантиққӣ [dahantiqqi] *n.* cork
даҳӣ [dahi] *adj.* decimal; **нуқтаи даҳӣ** [nuqtai dahi] decimal point
даҳлез [dahlez] *n.* lobby
даҳо [daho] *n.* genius *(quality)*
даҳон [dahon] *n.* mouth
даҳонбанд [dahonband] *n.* gag
даҳригӣ [dahrigi] *n.* atheism
даҳрӣ [dahri] *n.* atheist
даҳум [dahum] *adj.* tenth
даҳшат [dahshat] *n.* horror, terror
даҳшатангез [dahshatangez] *adj.* terrifying
даҳшатнок [dahshatnok] *adj.* awful, horrible, terrible
дашном [dashnom] *n.* verbal abuse, insult
дашном додан [dashnom dodan] *v.t.* abuse verbally, insult, swear
дашномдиҳанда [dashnomdihanda] *adj.* verbally abusive, insulting
дашт [dasht] *n.* plain, steppe
даъват [da'vat] *n.* challenge; draft *(mil.)*; invitation
даъват кардан [da'vat kardan] *v.t.* challenge; invite
даъватнома [da'vatnoma] *n.* invitation card
даъво [da'vo] *n.* claim, lawsuit
даъво кардан [da'vo kardan] *v.t.* claim
дев [dev] *n.* monster, demon
девона [devona] *n.* lunatic / *adj.* crazy, insane
девор [devor] *n.* wall
девора [devora] *n.* barrier
деворча [devorcha] *n.* fence
дег [deg] *n.* pot
дегдон [degdon] *n.* hearth
дегхона [degxona] *n.* boiler room
дегча [degcha] *n.* saucepan
декабр [dekabr] *n.* December
делфин [delfin] *n.* dolphin
демократия [demokratiya] *n.* democracy
демократӣ [demokrati] *adj.* democratic
дер [der] *adj./adv.* late
дерина [derina] *adj.* quaint
десерт [desert] *n.* dessert
деҳа [deha] *n.* village, settlement
деҳқон [dehqon] *n.* farmer, peasant
диван [divan] *n.* couch, sofa
диванкат [divankat] *n.* sofa bed
дигар [digar] *adj.* another, else, following, next / *n.* late afternoon; Islamic prayer performed in late afternoon
дигаргун кардан [digargun kardan] *v.t.* alter, change, modify, vary

дигаргун шудан [digargun shudan] *v.i.* change, vary
дигаргунӣ [digarguni] *n.* alteration, change, shift, variation
дигаргуншавӣ [digargunshavi] *n.* modification
дигарсон [digarson] *adj.* different
дигархел [digarxel] *adj.* different
дида баромадан [dida baromadan] *v.t.* think carefully, consider / *v.i.* watch
дида мондан [dida mondan] *v.t.* note, notice
дидан [didan] *v.t.* witness / *v.i.* behold, see
диданашаванда [didanashavanda] *adj.* invisible
дидашаванда [didashavanda] *adj.* apparent, visible
дидбонӣ [didboni] *n.* observation
дидор [didor] *n.* get-together, date
диж [dizh] *n.* fortress
дизел [dizel] *n.* diesel; **сӯзишвории дизелӣ** [süzishvorii dizeli] diesel fuel
дикта [dikta] *n.* dictation
дикта кардан [dikta kardan] *v.t.* dictate
диққат [diqqat] *n.* attention, caution, care
диққат кардан [diqqat kardan] *v.i.* pay attention
дил [dil] *n.* heart
дил рабудан [dil rabudan] *v.t.* fascinate
дила [dila] *n.* core
дилбардорӣ [dilbardori] *n.* consolation, comfort
дилбардорӣ кардан [dilbardori kardan] *v.t.* comfort, console
дилбеҳузурӣ [dilbehuzuri] *n.* qualm
дилбеҷо [dilbejo] *adj.* nauseated
дилбеҷокунанда [dilbejokunanda] *adj.* nauseating, nauseous
дилбеҷошавӣ [dilbejoshavi] *n.* nausea; qualm
дилгиркунанда [dilgirkunanda] *adj.* dreary, tiresome
дилдорӣ [dildori] *n.* comfort, solace
дилдорӣ кардан [dildori kardan] *v.t.* comfort, console
дилкаш [dilkash] *adj.* attractive, pretty, cute
дилнокаш [dilnokash] *adj.* unattractive, unpleasant
диловар [dilovar] *adj.* brave, courageous, daring, valiant
диловарӣ [dilovari] *n.* courage, valor
диловез [dilovez] *adj.* lovely
дилписанд [dilpisand] *adj.* desirable, agreeable
дилпур [dilpur] *adj.* confidence, assured, sure
дилпур будан [dilpur budan] *v.t.* to be sure
дилпурӣ [dilpuri] *n.* confidence, trust
дилпуркунӣ [dilpurkuni] *n.* assurance
дилрабо [dilrabo] *adj.* charming, fascinating
дилрабоӣ [dilraboi] *n.* charm *(pleasing characteristic)*, fascination

дилсӯз будан [dilsüz budan] *v.i.* pity
дилсӯзӣ [dilsüzi] *n.* pity
дилхоҳ [dilxoh] *adj.* desirable
дилхунукӣ [dilxunuki] *n.* disappointment
дилхунук кардан [dilxunuk kardan] *v.t.* disappoint
дилхушӣ [dilxushi] *n.* fun
дилчасп [dilchasp] *adj.* interesting
дилчаспӣ [dilchaspi] *n.* interest
димоғ [dimogh] *n.* nose; mood
димоға [dimogha] *n.* cape *(geo.)*
дин [din] *n.* religion
дина [dina] *n./adv.* yesterday
диндор [dindor] *adj.* devout, pious
динӣ [dini] *adj.* pertaining to religion
дипломат [diplomat] *n.* diplomat
дипломатӣ [diplomati] *adj.* diplomatic
дирӯз [dirüz] *n./adv.* yesterday
диск [disk] *n.* computer disk
дискотека [diskoteka] *n.* nightclub
дифоъ [difo'] *n.* defense
дифоъ кардан [difo' kardan] *v.t.* defend
довар [dovar] *n.* judge
довталаб [dovtalab] *n.* volunteer
доғ [dogh] *n.* scar, stain
доғдор кардан [doghdor kardan] *v.t.* stain
доғдор шудан [doghdor shudan] *v.i.* stain
доғдорнашуда [doghdornashuda] *adj.* stainless
дод [dod] *n.* justice; yell
дод задан [dod zadan] *v.i.* scream, yell
додан [dodan] *v.t.* give
додгоҳ [dodgoh] *n.* court of law
додо [dodo] *n.* dad, daddy
додрасӣ [dodrasi] *n.* court hearing
додситон [dodsiton] *n.* Attorney General, public prosecutor
додугирифт [dodugirift] *n.* transaction
доимӣ [doimi] *adj.* stationary
доира [doira] *n.* topic, subject, circle, cycle, scope
Доираи Қутби Шимол [Doirai Qutbi Shimol] *n.* Arctic Circle
доиратулмаориф [doiratulmaorif] *n.* encyclopedia
доллар [dollar] *n.* dollar
дом [dom] *n.* trap
доман [doman] *n.* lap; skirt
домод [domod] *n.* bridegroom, groom; son-in-law
дона [dona] *n.* kernel
донаи дом [donai dom] *n.* bait
донаӣ [donai] *adv.* each
донистан [donistan] *v.t./v.i.* know; deem
дониш [donish] *n.* knowledge
донишгоҳ [donishgoh] *n.* university
донишкада [donishkada] *n.* college, university department
донишманд [donishmand] *n.* scholar, learned; scientist
донишмандӣ [donishmandi] *n.* scholarship
донишҷӯ [donishjü] *n.* student

доранда [doranda] *n.* proprietor
доро [doro] *adj.* rich, wealthy
дорой [doroi] *n.* belongings; wealth, riches
дору [doru] *n.* medicine, medication
дору фармудан [doru farmudan] *v.t.* prescribe
дору фиристодан [doru firistodan] *v.t.* inject
дорувор [doruvor] *n.* spice
дорусоз [dorusoz] *n.* pharmacist
дорухона [doruxona] *n.* pharmacy
дорушиносӣ [dorushinosi] *n.* pharmacology
дорчин [dorchin] *n.* cinnamon
дорчинӣ [dorchini] *adj.* maroon
доси дастадароз [dosi dastadaroz] *n.* scythe
дохилӣ [doxili] *adj.* internal, domestic
дохилшавӣ [doxilshavi] *n.* admission
доҳӣ [dohi] *n.* leader, chief; genius *(person)*
дош [dosh] *n.* furnace
дошта [doshta] *n.* possession *(something owned)*
дошта истодан [doshta istodan] *v.t.* hold up, support
доштан [doshtan] *v.t.* have, hold
доя [doya] *n.* midwife, nanny
драма [drama] *n.* drama
дроссел [drossel] *n.* throttle
ду [du] *num.* two
ду бор [du bor] *adv.* twice
дубора гуфтан [dubora guftan] *v.t.* repeat *(a word or sentence)*
дубора кардан [dubora kardan] *v.t.* repeat *(an action or occurrence)*
дувоздаҳ [duvozdah] *num.* twelve
дувоздаҳ дона [duvozdah dona] *n.* dozen
дувоздаҳум [duvozdahum] *adj.* twelfth
дугона [dugona] *n.* girl or woman's female friend
дугоник [dugonik] *n.* twin
дуд [dud] *n.* smoke
дудила [dudila] *adj.* hesitant, uncertain, undecided
дудила шудан [dudila shudan] *v.i.* hesitate, waver
дудилагӣ [dudilagi] *n.* hesitation, scruple
дудкаш [dudkash] *n.* chimney
дуднок [dudnok] *adj.* smoky
дузабона [duzabona] *adj.* bilingual
дузд [duzd] *n.* robber, thief
дуздидан [duzdidan] *v.t.* rob, steal
дуздӣ [duzdi] *n.* robbery
дузону шудан [duzonu shudan] *v.i.* kneel
дуқат кардан [duqat kardan] *v.t.* fold
дум [dum] *n.* tail
дунболагирӣ [dunbolagiri] *n.* chase, pursuit
дунболагирӣ кардан [dunbolagiri kardan] *v.t.* chase, pursue
дунё [dunyo] *n.* world
дуо [duo] *n.* prayer
дуо кардан [duo kardan] *v.i.* pray
дуои хайр [duoi xayr] *n.* blessing

дуои хайр гуфтан [duoi xayr guftan] *v.t.* bless
дур [dur] *adj./adv.* far, distant
дур кардан [dur kardan] *v.t.* get rid of, dispose of
дуранг [durang] *n.* tie *(in a sports match, game)* / *adj.* tied
дурандеш [durandesh] *adj.* having foresight, farsighted
дурахш [duraxsh] *n.* flash
дурахшидан [duraxshidan] *v.i.* shine
дурахшон [duraxshon] *adj.* brilliant, vivid
дурбин [durbin] *adj.* hyperopic, farsighted
дурдаст [durdast] *adj.* remote, faraway
дуредгар [duredgar] *n.* carpenter
дурӣ [duri] *n.* distance
дурӣ ҷустан [duri justan] *v.i.* avoid
дуртар [durtar] *adj.* further
дурӯғ [durugh] *n.* lie
дурӯғ гуфтан [durugh guftan] *v.t.* tell a lie
дурӯғгӯй [durughgüy] *n.* liar
дуруд [durud] *n.* greeting
дуруд гуфтан [durud guftan] *v.t.* greet
дуруст [durust] *adj.* correct, right, accurate, decent
дуруст кардан [durust kardan] *v.t.* correct, fix, mend
дурусткор [durustkor] *adj.* honest
дурусткорӣ [durustkori] *n.* honesty
дурушт [durusht] *adj.* coarse, rough, tough, vulgar
дуруштӣ [durushti] *n.* toughness, roughness
дутарафа [dutarafa] *adj.* mutual
духтар [duxtar] *n.* girl, daughter
духтарандар [duxtarandar] *n.* stepdaughter
духтари амак [duxtari amak] *n.* cousin *(paternal uncle's daughter)*
духтари амма [duxtari amma] *n.* cousin *(paternal aunt's daughter)*
духтари бародар [duxtari barodar] *n.* niece *(brother's daughter)*
духтари тағо [duxtari tagho] *n.* cousin *(maternal uncle's daughter)*
духтари хола [duxtari xola] *n.* cousin *(maternal aunt's daughter)*
духтари хоҳар [duxtari xohar] *n.* niece *(sister's daughter)*
духтур [duxtur] *n.* doctor, physician
духтури дандон [duxturi dandon] *n.* dentist
духтури занҳо [duxturi zanho] *n.* gynecologist, obstetrician
духтури ҷонварҳо [duxturi jonvarho] *n.* veterinarian
духӯра [duxüra] *adj.* ambiguous
дуҳул [duhul] *n.* drum
дучанд [duchand] *adj.* double
дучарха [ducharxa] *n.* bicycle
дучор [duchor] *n.* encounter
дучор кардан [duchor kardan] *v.t.* expose
дучор шудан [duchor shudan] *v.t.* encounter / *v.i.* undergo
дучоршавӣ [duchorshavi] *n.* encounter
душ [dush] *n.* shower

душ кардан [dush kardan] *v.i.* shower
душанбе [dushanbe] *n.* Monday
душвор [dushvor] *adj.* difficult, tough
душвор кардан [dushvor kardan] *v.t.* make difficult, obstruct
душворӣ [dushvori] *n.* difficulty, obstacle
душман [dushman] *n.* enemy
душманона [dushmanona] *adj.* hostile, unfriendly
дуюм [duyum] *adj.* second
дӯғ [dügh] *n.* menace, threat
дӯзанда [düzanda] *n.* seamstress
дӯзах [düzax] *n.* hell
дӯкон [dükon] *n.* shop, store
дӯкондор [dükondor] *n.* shopkeeper
дӯконча [dükoncha] *n.* kiosk, newsstand, stand
дӯст [düst] *n.* friend
дӯст доштан [düst doshtan] *v.t./v.i.* love, like
дӯст надоштан [düst nadoshtan] *v.t.* dislike
дӯстдошта [düstdoshta] *adj.* favorite
дӯстдухтар [düstduxtar] *n.* girlfriend
дӯстӣ [düsti] *n.* friendship
дӯстона [düstona] *adj.* friendly
дӯстписар [düstpisar] *n.* boyfriend
дӯхт [düxt] *n.* sewing
дӯхтан [düxtan] *v.t.* sew
дӯш [düsh] *n.* shoulder
дӯшиза [düshiza] *n.* virgin, maiden
дюйм [dyuym] *n.* inch

Е

-е [-e] *art.* a, an: писар**е** [pisare] a boy; китоб**е** [kitobe] a book
елим [yelim] *n.* glue

Ё

ё [yo] *conj.* or
ёбоӣ [yoboi] *adj.* wild
ёва [yova] *n.* nonsense
ёвар [yovar] *n.* assistant, helper
ёд [yod] *n.* memory
ёд гирифтан [yod giriftan] *v.t.* learn, acquire *(knowledge)*, study
ёд додан [yod dodan] *v.t.* teach
ёд кардан [yod kardan] *v.t.* remember
ёдгорӣ [yodgori] *n.* memory, memento
ёддошт [yoddosht] *n.* reminiscence, memory; record
ёддошт кардан [yoddosht kardan] *v.t.* record
ёдоварӣ [yodovari] *n.* reminder
ёзанда [yozanda] *adj.* elastic
ёздаҳ [yozdah] *num.* eleven
ёздаҳум [yozdahum] *adj.* eleventh
ёзондан [yozondan] *v.t.* extend
ёзониш [yozonish] *n.* extension
ёқа [yoqa] *n.* collar
ёқути кабуд [yoquti kabud] *n.* sapphire
ёқути сурх [yoquti surx] *n.* ruby
ёрӣ [yori] *n.* assistance, aid, help, support

ёрӣ додан [yori dodan] *v.t.* aid, assist, help, support
ёрии таъҷилӣ [yorii ta'jili] *n.* emergency assistance
ёрлиқ [yorliq] *n.* label, tag
ёрлиқ часпондан [yorliq chaspondan] *v.t.* label
ёрмандӣ [yormandi] *n.* contribution
ёрмандӣ расондан [yormandi rasondan] *v.t.* assist, contribute
ёфтан [yoftan] *v.t.* find

Ж

жарф [zharf] *adj.* deep
жарфо [zharfo] *n.* depth
желе [zhele] *n.* jelly
жола [zhola] *n.* hail
жонглёрӣ кардан [zhonglyori kardan] *v.t.* juggle
журнал [zhurnal] *n.* journal *(publication)*, magazine
журналист [zhurnalist] *n.* journalist
жюри [zhyuri] *n.* jury

З

забон [zabon] *n.* language, tongue
забон гирифтагӣ [zabon giriftagi] *n.* stammer
забонак [zabonak] *n.* trigger
забонхат [zabonxat] *n.* receipt, voucher
завод [zavod] *n.* factory
завраки комагӣ [zavraqi komagi] *n.* canoe
заған [zaghan] *n.* kite *(type of bird)*
зада [zada] *n.* stress *(gram.)*
зада буридан [zada buridan] *v.t.* slash
зада гардондан [zada gardondan] *v.t.* repel militarily, repel with force
задан [zadan] *v.t.* beat, hit, strike / *v.i.* throb
задухӯрд [zaduxürd] *n.* conflict *(physical)*
заиф [zaif] *adj.* weak
заиф кардан [zaif kardan] *v.t.* weaken
заифӣ [zaifi] *n.* weakness
зайтун [zaytun] *n.* olive
зайтунранг [zaytunrang] *adj.* olive-green
замима [zamima] *n.* addendum, appendix, enclosure
замин [zamin] *n.* earth, soil, Earth, ground, land
замина [zamina] *n.* groundwork
заминдор [zamindor] *n.* landlord
заминӣ [zamini] *n.* relating to the earth, terrestrial
заминҷунбӣ [zaminjunbi] *n.* earthquake
заминшиносӣ [zaminshinosi] *n.* geology
замон [zamon] *n.* grammatical tense
замонат [zamonat] *n.* bail, guarantee, safeguard, surety
замонат кардан [zamonat kardan] *v.t.* guarantee
зан [zan] *n.* female, woman, wife
занах [zanax] *n.* chin
занбар [zanbar] *n.* stretcher; wheelbarrow
занбӯр [zanbüri] *n.* wasp
занбӯри асал [zanbüri asal] *n.* bee
занбӯруғ [zanbürugh] *n.* mushroom

занг [zang] *n.* bell; rust
занг задан [zang zadan] *v.t.* telephone, call *(on the phone)*, ring / *v.i.* ring; rust
занг занондан [zang zanondan] *v.t.* rust
зангзада [zangzada] *adj.* rusty
зангногир [zangnogir] *adj.* stainless *(as in "stainless steel")*
зандор [zandor] *adj.* married *(man)*
занона [zanona] *adj.* feminine, female
занҷир [zanjir] *n.* chain
занҷирак [zanjirak] *n.* zipper
занҷирча [zanjircha] *n.* wreath
запас [zapas] *n.* military reserve
зар [zar] *n.* gold
заандуд кардан [zarandud kardan] *v.t.* gild
зарандуд [zarandud] *adj.* gilt, gilded
зарар [zarar] *n.* harm, injury
зарар кардан [zarar kardan] *v.t.* harm, injure
зарарнок [zararnok] *adj.* harmful, noxious
зарб [zarb] *n.* beat
зарб kardan [zarb zadan] *v.t.* multiply *(mathematics)*
зарба [zarba] *n.* blow, stroke
зарб [zarbzani] *n.* multiplication
зарбулмасал [zarbulmasal] *n.* proverb
заргӯш [zargüsh] *n.* hare
зард [zard] *adj.* yellow
зарда [zarda] *n.* bile, gall
зардаҷӯш [zardajüsh] *n.* heartburn
зардии тухм [zardii tuxm] *n.* egg yolk
зардолу [zardolu] *n.* apricot
зардпарвин [zardparvin] *n.* hepatitis
зардуштӣ [zardushti] *n./adj.* Zoroastrian
зарин [zarin] *adj.* golden, gold
зарофат [zarofat] *n.* humor
зарра [zarra] *n.* particle
заррабин [zarrabin] *n.* microscope
зарраи барф [zarrai barf] *n.* snowflake
зарранг [zarrang] *adj.* gold-colored
зарур [zarur] *adj.* vital, necessary
зарурат [zarurat] *n.* necessity, urgency
зарурӣ [zaruri] *adj.* essential, necessary
зарф [zarf] *n.* container, dish, vessel / *(gram.)* adverb
зархез [zarxez] *adj.* fertile
зарҳал [zarhal] *n.* gilt
зафар [zafar] *n.* victory
захира [zaxira] *n.* reserve, stock
захира кардан [zaxira kardan] *v.t.* reserve, stock
захм [zaxm] *n.* wound, ulcer
захмдор [zaxmdor] *n.* casualty
захмдор кардан [zaxmdor kardan] *v.t.* wound
заҳ [zah] *adj.* damp
заҳбур кандан [zahbur kandan] *v.t.* drain
заҳмат [zahmat] *n.* nuisance
заҳр [zahr] *n.* poison, venom
заҳра [zahra] *n.* bile, gall
заҳрадон [zahradon] *n.* gall bladder
заҳрдор [zahrdor] *adj.* poisonous
зеб [zeb] *n.* decoration
зеб додан [zeb dodan] *v.t.* decorate

зебидан [zebidan] *v.i.* look attractive, suit
зебо [zebo] *adj.* beautiful, pretty
зебоӣ [zeboi] *n.* beauty
зевар [zevar] *n.* jewelry
зер [zer] *adv.* under
зери [zeri] *prep.* beneath, under
зери бағал [zeri baghal] *n.* armpit
зеризаминӣ [zerizamini] *n.* basement; bank vault
зер кардан [zer kardan] *v.t.* dent
зердаст кардан [zerdast kardan] *v.t.* subdue
зеризаминӣ [zerizamini] *adj.* underground, below ground
зериобӣ [zeriobi] *adj.* submarine, underwater
зеро [zero] *conj.* because
зертахтаи тиреза [zertaxtai tireza] *n.* windowsill
зеҳкалон [zehkalon] *n.* lapel
зеҳн [zehn] *n.* mind
зид [zid] *adj.* contrary, opposite
зидди [ziddi] *pref.* anti-
зидди уфунӣ [ziddi ufuni] *adj.* antiseptic
зиддият [ziddiyat] *n.* contrast
зиёд [ziyod] *adj.* excessive / *adv.* too
зиёд баромадан [ziyod baromadan] *v.t.* exceed
зиёд кардан [ziyod kardan] *v.t.* augment, increase, multiply
зиёд шудан [ziyod shudan] *v.t.* exceed
зиёдӣ [ziyodi] *n.* excess
зиён [ziyon] *n.* damage, harm, hurt, business loss
зиён расондан [ziyon rasondan] *v.t.* damage, harm, hurt
зиёнрасон [ziyonrason] *adj.* harmful, malignant *(med.)*
зиёрат [ziyorat] *n.* pilgrimage
зиёраткунанда [ziyoratkunanda] *n.* pilgrim
зиёфат [ziyofat] *n.* banquet, feast
зикр [zikr] *n.* mention
зикр кардан [zikr kardan] *v.t.* mention
зиқ будан [ziq budan] *v.i.* be stressed
зиққи нафас [ziqqi nafas] *n.* asthma / *adj.* asthmatic
зиқшуда [ziqshuda] *adj.* stressed out
зимистон [zimiston] *n.* winter
зимнан фаҳмондан [zimnan fahmondan] *v.t.* imply
зимни [zimni] *prep.* during
зимом [zimom] *n.* helm
зин [zin] *n.* saddle
зин кардан [zin kardan] *v.t.* saddle
зина [zina] *n.* stair, staircase
зинаи равон [zinai ravon] *n.* escalator
зинапоя [zinapoya] *n.* stair, staircase
зинда [zinda] *adj.* alive, live, living
зинда кардан [zinda kardan] *v.t.* revive
зинда мондан [zinda mondan] *v.i.* survive
зинда шудан [zinda shudan] *v.i.* revive
зиндагинома [zindaginoma] *n.* biography
зиндагӣ [zindagi] *n.* life
зиндагӣ кардан [zindagi kardan] *v.i.* dwell, live, reside
зиндагонӣ [zindagoni] *n.* life

зиндадил [zindadil] *adj.* lively
зиндон [zindon] *n.* jail, prison
зиндонӣ [zindoni] *n.* prisoner
зиндонӣ кардан [zindoni kardan] *v.t.* imprison
зирак [zirak] *adj.* astute, clever, smart, intelligent, shrewd
зиреҳ [zireh] *n.* shell *(of animals)*
зироат [ziroat] *n.* agriculture
зироатӣ [ziroati] *adj.* agricultural
зистан [zistan] *v.i.* live
зистшинос [zistshinos] *n.* biologist
зистшиносӣ [zistshinosi] *n.* biology
зич [zich] *adj.* compact, dense
зичӣ [zichi] *n.* density
зоғ [zogh] *n.* crow
зоғнӯл [zoghnül] *n.* pick, plectrum
зода [zoda] *adj.* born
зодгоҳ [zodgoh] *n.* birthplace
зодрӯз [zodrüz] *n.* birthday
зоида [zoida] *adj.* born
зоиш [zoish] *n.* birth; **гувоҳиномаи зоиш** [guvohinomai zoish] birth certificate
золим [zolim] *adj.* brutal, cruel
зомин [zomin] *n.* sponsor
зомин будан [zomin budan] *v.t.* sponsor
зону [zonu] *n.* knee
зонуқат нишастан [zonuqat nishastan] *v.i.* crouch
зор шудан [zor shudan] *v.i.* long
зор-зор гиристан [zor-zor giristan] *v.i.* sob, weep
зот [zot] *n.* ace *(cards)*; **зоти таппон** [zoti tappon] ace of hearts
зотулкабид [zotulkabid] *n.* hepatitis
зоҳир кардан [zohir kardan] *v.t.* develop *(film)*
зоча [zocha] *n.* puppet
зуд [zud] *adj.* agile, fast, quick
зуд-зуд [zud-zud] *adj.* frequent / *adv.* frequently, often
зудбовар [zudbovar] *adj.* trusting
зудранҷ [zudranj] *adj.* touchy
зудшикан [zudshikan] *adj.* fragile
зулф [zulf] *n.* curl
зумуррад [zumurrad] *n.* emerald
зуррият [zurriyat] *n.* posterity
зӯр [zür] *n.* force, strength, vigor

И

ибодатгоҳ [ibodatgoh] *n.* holy place, sanctuary
иборат будан [iborat budan] *v.i.* consist
ибтидоӣ [ibtidoi] *adj.* elementary, primary
иваз [ivaz] *n.* exchange
иваз кардан [ivaz kardan] *v.t.* change, exchange, replace, switch, shift
ивазкунӣ [ivazkuni] *n.* shift
иғво [ighvo] *n.* provocation, temptation
иғво кардан [ighvo kardan] *v.t.* provocate, tempt
ид [id] *n.* carnival, festival, holiday
идиома [idioma] *n.* idiom
идора [idora] *n.* administration, management, office

идора кардан [idora kardan] *v.t.* administer, conduct, direct, manage, operate, steer, wield
идорӣ [idori] *adj.* administrative
иёлат [iyolat] *n.* state
из [iz] *n.* scar, track, trace
издивоҷ [izdivoj] *n.* marriage
издивоҷ кардан [izdivoj kardan] *v.t.* marry
иззат [izzat] *n.* dignity, honor
иззат кардан [izzat kardan] *v.t.* honor
изофагӣ [izofagi] *adj.* extra
изтирор [iztiror] *n.* trance
изҳор [iz-hor] *n.* declaration, statement
изҳор кардан [iz-hor kardan] *v.t.* declare, express, state
иқлим [iqlim] *n.* climate
иқрор кардан [iqror kardan] *v.i.* admit, acknowledge, confess
иқрор [iqror] *n.* acknowledgement
иқтибос [iqtibos] *n.* quotation, quote
иқтибос овардан [iqtibos ovardan] *v.t.* cite, quote
иқтисод [iqtisod] *n.* economy
иқтисодиёт [iqtisodiyot] *n.* economics
иқтисодӣ [iqtisodi] *adj.* economical
иқтисодчӣ [iqtisodchi] *n.* economist
илқо [ilqo] *n.* suggestion
илқо кардан [ilqo kardan] *v.t.* suggest
илм [ilm] *n.* science
илми ҳисоб [ilmi hisob] *n.* arithmetic
илмӣ [ilmi] *adj.* scientific
илова [ilova] *n.* addition, something added, increase, supplement
илова бар ин [ilova bar in] *adv.* further
илова кардан [ilova kardan] *v.t.* increase, add
иловагӣ [ilovagi] *adj.* accessory, additional, extra
илоҳиёт [ilohiyot] *n.* theology
илтимос [iltimos] *adv.* please
илтимоснома [iltimosnoma] *n.* petition
илтифотнок [iltifotnok] *adj.* polite
илҳом [ilhom] *n.* inspiration, revelation
илҳом бахшидан [ilhom baxshidan] *v.t.* inspire
имконият додан [imkoniyat dodan] *v.t.* enable
имзо [imzo] *n.* signature
имзо кардан [imzo kardan] *v.t.* sign
имову ишорат [imovu ishorat] *n.* gesture
имову ишорат кардан [imovu ishorat kardan] *v.i.* gesture
имон [imon] *n.* faith
импаротӯр [imparotür] *n.* emperor
импаротӯрӣ [imparotüri] *n.* empire
имрӯз [imrüz] *adv.* today
имтиёз [imtiyoz] *n.* concession *(business)*; privilege
имтиҳон [imtihon] *n.* examination, test
имтиҳон кардан [imtihon kardan] *v.t.* test
ин [in] *conj./adj.* this
ин қадар [in qadar] *adv.* to such an extent, so

ин хел [in xel] *adv.* in the manner shown, thus
ин ҷо [in jo] *adv.* here
инвентар [inventar] *n.* inventory
индекс [indeks] *n.* index
индонезиягӣ [indoneziyagi] *n.* Indonesian
индонезӣ [indonezi] *adj.* Indonesian
инкор кардан [inkor kardan] *v.t.* deny, renounce
инқилоб [inqilob] *n.* political revolution
инсон [inson] *n.* human
инсонӣ [insoni] *adj.* human
инсоф [insof] *n.* equity
институт [institut] *n.* institute
интернет [internet] *n.* Internet
интизом [intizom] *n.* state of order, discipline
интизордошта [intizordoshta] *adj.* prospective
интизорӣ [intizori] *n.* wait
интиқом [intiqom] *n.* revenge, vengeance
интихоб [intixob] *n.* choice, option, selection
интихоб кардан [intixob kardan] *v.t.* choose, pick, select, elect
интихобот [intixobot] *n.* election
инҳисор [inhisor] *n.* monopoly
инҳо [inho] *pron.* these
Инҷил [Injil] *n.* Bible
иншо [insho] *n.* essay
инъикос [in'ikos] *n.* reflection
инъом [in'om] *n.* reward
инъом додан [in'om dodan] *v.t.* reward
ирландӣ [irlandi] *n./adj.* Irish
ирода [iroda] *n.* will
ирода кардан [iroda kardan] *v.i.* will
ирсол [irsol] *n.* transmission
исбот [isbot] *n.* affirmation, assertion; evidence, proof
исбот кардан [isbot kardan] *v.t.* affirm, assert, state positively, prove
исён [isyon] *n.* mutiny, riot
исъён кардан [is'yon kardan] *v.i.* riot
искана [iskana] *n.* chisel
исканҷа кардан [iskanja kardan] *v.t.* clip
ислом [islom] *n.* Islam
исломӣ [islomi] *adj.* Islamic
ислоҳ [isloh] *n.* amendment, correction
ислоҳ кардан [isloh kardan] *v.t.* correct, mend, revise
ислоҳот даровардан [islohot darovardan] *v.i.* reform
исм [ism] *gram.* noun
исмоилӣ [ismoili] *n./adj.* Ismaili *(sect of Islam)*
испанӣ [ispani] *n./adj.* Spanish
испаноқ [ispanoq] *n.* spinach
исроилӣ [isroili] *n./adj.* Israeli
исрор [isror] *n.* insistence
исрор кардан [isror kardan] *v.i.* insist
исроф [isrof] *n.* waste
исроф кардан [isrof kardan] *v.t.* waste
ист [ist] *n.* halt, stop
истгоҳ [istgoh] *n.* train/bus station; train/bus stop
истеҳзо [istehzo] *n.* irony
истеҳзоомез [istehzoomez] *adj.* ironic
истеҳсол кардан [istehsol kardan] *v.t.* produce
истеъдод [iste'dod] *n.* talent

истеъмол [iste'mol] *n.* consumption, usage, use
истеъмол кардан [iste'mol kardan] *v.t.* consume
истеъмолкунанда [iste'molkunanda] *n.* consumer, user
истеъфо [iste'fo] *n.* resignation
истеъфо додан [iste'fo dodan] *v.i.* resign
истиқлол [istiqlol] *n.* independence
истиқомат кардан [istiqomat kardan] *v.i.* lodge, reside
истиқоматгоҳ [istiqomatgoh] *n.* lodging, residence
истило [istilo] *n.* conquest
истило кардан [istilo kardan] *v.t.* conquer
истисно [istisno] *n.* exception
истифода кардан [istifoda kardan] *v.t.* use, utilize
истода [istoda] *adj.* standing, upright
истодагарӣ кардан [istodagari kardan] *v.i.* persist
истодан [istodan] *v.t.* cost / *v.i.* stand; stop
исфаноҷ [isfanoj] *n.* spinach
исфанҷ [isfanj] *n.* sponge
исҳоловар [is-holovar] *n./adj.* laxative
итоат кардан [itoat kardan] *v.i.* comply
итолиёӣ [itoliyoi] *n./adj.* Italian
иттифоқ [ittifoq] *n.* unity, agreement *(contract)*, alliance, union
иттифоқчӣ [ittifoqchi] *n.* ally
иттиҳод [ittihod] *n.* union
ифлос [iflos] *adj.* dirty
ифода [ifoda] *n.* phrase, expression
ифода кардан [ifoda kardan] *v.t.* express, voice, phrase
ифротӣ [ifroti] *adj.* extreme, radical
ифроткор [ifrotkor] *adj.* extravagant
ифтихор [iftixor] *n.* pride
ифтихорманд [iftixormand] *adj.* proud
ихлос [ixlos] *n.* sincerity, devotion
ихтиёрӣ [ixtiyori] *adj.* arbitrary, voluntary / *adv.* willingly
ихтилоф [ixtilof] *n.* conflict *(ideological)*
ихтилоҷ [ixtiloj] *n.* cramp
ихтироъ [ixtiro'] *n.* invention
ихтироъ кардан [ixtiro' kardan] *v.t.* devise, invent
ихтисор [ixtisor] *n.* abbreviation
ихчам [ixcham] *adj.* compact
ихчамсохт [ixchamsoxt] *adj.* portable
иҳота кардан [ihota kardan] *v.t./v.i.* surround
иҳотакунанда [ihotakunanda] *adj.* surrounding
иҷозат [ijozat] *n.* authorization, license, permit
иҷозат додан [ijozat dodan] *v.t.* authorize, permit
иҷозатнома [ijozatnoma] *n.* license
иҷора [ijora] *n.* lease
иҷора кардан [ijora kardan] *v.t.* lease / *v.i.* lodge
иҷорагир [ijoragir] *n.* tenant
иҷро [ijro] *n.* performance
иҷро кардан [ijro kardan] *v.t.* carry out, execute *(a plan, etc.)*, implement, perform

ичрогар [ijrogar] *n.* executive
ичтимоӣ [ijtimoi] *adj.* social
ишғол кардан [ishghol kardan] *v.t.* occupy militarily
ишкамба [ishkamba] *n.* paunch
ишқ [ishq] *n.* love, affection
ишқороб [ishqorob] *n.* lye
ишора [ishora] *n.* sign, signal
ишора кардан [ishora kardan] *v.t.* indicate / *v.i.* sign, signal
иштибоҳ [ishtiboh] *n.* error, mistake
иштибоҳ кардан [ishtiboh kardan] *v.t.* make a mistake, mistake
иштирок [ishtirok] *n.* participation,
иштирок кардан [ishtirok kardan] *v.i.* participate, share / *v.t.* contribute *(to a newspaper, etc.)*
иштиҳо [ishtiho] *n.* appetite
июл [iyul] *n.* July
июн [iyun] *n.* June

Й

йилт-йилт кардан [yilt-yilt kardan] *v.i.* twinkle
йога [yoga] *n.* yoga

К

кабел [kabel] *n.* cable
кабоб [kabob] *n.* kebab, roast/grilled/broiled meat / *adj.* roast, roasted
кабоб кардан [kabob kardan] *v.t.* grill, roast
кабуд [kabud] *adj.* blue
кабӯтар [kabütar] *n.* dove, pigeon
кадбону [kadbonu] *n.* housekeeper, mistress, female head of household
кадом [kadom] *adj.* which
каду [kadu] *n.* pumpkin, squash
каждум [kazhdum] *n.* scorpion
кай [kay] *adv.* when
кайк [kayk] *n.* flea
кайф [kayf] *n.* amusement, enjoyment, fun
кайф кардан [kayf kardan] *v.t.* enjoy
кайҳо [kayho] *adv.* long ago
кайҳон [kayhon] *n.* universe
какав [kakav] *n.* cocoa
кал [kal] *adj.* bald
каланд [kaland] *n.* hoe
калид [kalid] *n.* key, clue; wrench
калидак [kalidak] *n.* electric switch
калима [kalima] *n.* word
калисо [kaliso] *n.* church
калисои ҷомеъ [kalisoi jome'] *n.* cathedral
калкулятор [kalkulyator] *n.* calculator
калоғ [kalogh] *n.* crow
калламуш [kallamush] *n.* rat
калон [kalon] *n.* senior / *adj.* big, large; senior
калон кардан [kalon kardan] *v.t.* magnify; raise, rear *(children)*
калон шудан [kalon shudan] *v.i.* get bigger, grow
калонтар кардан [kalontar kardan] *v.t.* enlarge, expand
калонтарин [kalontarin] *adj.* largest, maximum
калоншавӣ [kalonshavi] *n.* growth
калпеса [kalpesa] *n.* lizard

калтак [kaltak] *n.* cudgel, club, stick
калтакалос [kaltakalos] *n.* lizard
калтсий [kaltsiy] *n.* calcium
кам [kam] *n./adj.* few, little / *adj.* meager, scarce / *adv.* seldom
камбуд доштан [kam doshtan] *v.t.* lack
камакак [kamakak] *n.* small amount, dash
камар [kamar] *n.* belt, waist
камарбанд [kamarband] *n.* belt
камарзиш [kamarzish] *adj.* inexpensive
камбағал [kambaghal] *adj.* poor
камбала [kambala] *n.* sole *(fish)*
каме [kame] *adv.* little, a little, somewhat
камёб [kamyob] *adj.* rare
камзӯлча [kamzülcha] *n.* vest
камӣ [kami] *n.* flaw, lack, shortage
камонаки милтиқ [kamonaki miltiq] *n.* trigger *(of a gun)*
камонча [kamoncha] *n.* fiddle
кампал [kampal] *n.* blanket
камтар [kamtar] *adj./adv.* less
камтар кардан [kamtar kardan] *v.t.* decrease, reduce, diminish
камтар шудан [kamtar shudan] *v.i.* decrease
камтарин [kamtarin] *adj.* least
камхунӣ [kamxuni] *n.* anemia
кана [kana] *n.* tick
канадагӣ [kanadagi] *n./adj.* Canadian
канал [kanal] *n.* channel
канализатсия [kanalizatsiya] *n.* sewer
канда гирифтан [kanda giriftan] *v.t.* yank
канда шудан [kanda shudan] *v.i.* interrupt
кандакорӣ [kandakori] *n.* carving, engraving
кандакорӣ кардан [kandakori kardan] *v.t.* carve, engrave
кандан [kandan] *v.t.* chisel, dig; interrupt, yank
кандашавӣ [kandashavi] *n.* interruption
канду [kandu] *n.* hive
каниса [kanisa] *n.* synagogue
канондан [kanondan] *v.t.* inoculate
канор [kanor] *n.* edge, rim, verge, margin, outskirts, shore
канорачӯӣ кардан [kanorajui kardan] *v.i.* avoid
канори дарё [kanori daryo] *n.* coast, bank, beach
кар [kar] *adj.* deaf
карам [karam] *n.* cabbage
карантин [karantin] *n.* quarantine
карасин [karasin] *n.* kerosene
карахт [karaxt] *adj.* numb
карахш [karaxsh] *n.* scab
карашма кардан [karashma kardan] *v.i.* flirt
карбогидрат [karbogidrat] *n.* carbohydrate
карбос [karbos] *n.* canvas
карда [karda] *n.* deed, act
кардан [kardan] *v.t.* do
карикатура [karikatura] *n.* cartoon
карнай [karnay] *n.* horn *(mus.)*; pipe *(mus.)*; loudspeaker

карнайи радио [karnayi radio] *n.* loudspeaker
карнайчӣ [karnaychi] *n.* piper
картошка [kartoshka] *n.* potato
кас [kas] *n.* person
касал [kasal] *n.* sick person, patient / *adj.* ill, sick
касалии баҳрӣ [kasali bahri] *adj.* seasick
касалии баҳрӣ [kasalii bahri] *n.* seasickness
касалӣ [kasali] *n.* disease, illness, sickness
касалхона [kasalxona] *n.* hospital
касб [kasb] *n.* profession, occupation, trade
касбӣ [kasbi] *adj.* professional
касе [kase] *pron.* anybody, anyone, somebody
каснорас [kasnoras] *adj.* inaccessible
каср [kasr] *n.* fraction
кассир [kassir] *n.* cashier
кат [kat] *n.* bed
каталог [katalog] *n.* catalog
католик [katolik] *n.* Catholic
католикӣ [katoliki] *adj.* Catholic
католитсизм [katolitsizm] *n.* Catholicism
катон [katon] *n.* linen
каучук [kauchuk] *n.* rubber
каф задан [kaf zadan] *v.t.* clap, applaud
кафкӯбӣ [kafkübi] *n.* clapping, applause
кафи даст [kafi dast] *n.* palm *(anat.)*
кафи пой [kafi poy] *n.* sole *(anat.)*
кафидан [kafidan] *v.i.* crack, split
кафк [kafk] *n.* foam, scum
кафолатнома [kafolatnoma] *n.* voucher, guaranty, warranty
кафондан [kafondan] *v.t.* chop, split, break up, slash
кафтар [kaftar] *n.* dove, pigeon
кафш [kafsh] *n.* shoe
кафшер [kafsher] *n.* welding
кафшер кардан [kafsher kardan] *v.t.* weld
кач [kaj] *adj.* bent, crooked
кач кардан [kaj kardan] *v.t.* bend
кач нигаристан [kaj nigaristan] *v.i.* squint
кач шудан [kaj shudan] *v.i.* bend, slant
качак [kajak] *n.* curl
качу килеб гаштан [kaju kileb gashtan] *v.i.* zigzag
качфаҳмӣ [kajfahmi] *n.* misunderstanding
кашида бурдан [kashida burdan] *v.t.* tow
кашида гирифтан [kashida giriftan] *v.t.* snatch
кашида дароз кардан [kashida daroz kardan] *v.t.* extend
кашидан [kashidan] *v.t.* haul, tug, pull, remove
кашиш [kashish] *n.* priest; traction
кашол ёфтан [kashol yoftan] *v.i.* last
кашола кардан [kashola kardan] *v.t.* drag, haul, tug
кашонда шудан [kashonda shudan] *v.i.* trail
кашондан [kashondan] *v.t.* convey, transport, trail
кашф [kashf] *n.* detection, discovery
кашф кардан [kashf kardan] *v.t.* discover

квадрат [kvadrat] *n.* square
квадратӣ [kvadrati] *adj.* square
кварта [kvarta] *n.* quart
кварталӣ [kvartali] *adj.* quarterly
квартс [kvarts] *n.* quartz
келин [kelin] *n.* bride; daughter-in-law
кенгуру [kenguru] *n.* kangaroo
ки [ki] *adv.* as / *pron.* which
кило(грамм) [kilo(gramm)] *n.* kilo(gram)
километр [kilometr] *n.* kilometer
ким-кӣ [kim-ki] *pron.* someone
ким-куҷо [kim-kujo] *adv.* someplace
ким-чӣ [kim-chi] *pron.* something
ким-чӣ хел [kim-chi xel] *adv.* somehow
кимиё [kimiyo] *n.* chemistry
кина [kina] *n.* spite, grudge
киноя [kinoya] *n.* hint
кирдор [kirdor] *n.* deed, act, action
кирм [kirm] *n.* worm
киро [kiro] *n.* lease / *pron.* whom
киро кардан [kiro kardan] *v.t.* charter, hire, lease
киропулӣ [kiropuli] *n.* fare
киса [kisa] *n.* pocket
кисабур [kisabur] *n.* pickpocket
кит [kit] *n.* whale
китоб [kitob] *n.* book
китобдор [kitobdor] *n.* librarian
китоби дарсӣ [kitobi darsi] *n.* textbook
китобфурӯшӣ [kitobfurüshi] *n.* bookstore
китобхона [kitobxona] *n.* library
китобча [kitobcha] *n.* pamphlet
китф [kitf] *n.* shoulder
кифоя [kifoya] *adj.* sufficient, enough
кифоя будан [kifoya budan] *v.i.* suffice
кифтпӯшак [kiftpüshak] *n.* cape *(item of clothing)*
кишвар [kishvar] *n.* country
кишоварз [kishovarz] *n.* farmer
кишоварзӣ [kishovarzi] *n.* agriculture
кишт [kisht] *n.* cultivation
киштзор [kishtzor] *n.* farm
киштии буғ [kishtii bugh] *n.* steamship
киштии гузора [kishtii guzora] *n.* ferryboat
киштии зериобӣ [kishtii zeriobi] *n.* submarine
киштии нафткашон [kishtii naftkashon] *n.* oil tanker
киштиронӣ [kishtironi] *n.* navigate
киштиронӣ кардан [kishtironi kardan] *v.t.* navigate
киштӣ [kishti] *n.* ship
кӣ [ki] *pron.* who
классикӣ [klassiki] *adj.* classical
клем [klem] *n.* clam
клиника [klinika] *n.* clinic
клуб [klub] *n.* club
ковиш [kovish] *n.* excavation
ковок [kovok] *adj.* hollow
коғаз [koghaz] *n.* paper
коғази папирос [koghazi papiros] *n.* tissue paper

коғазбоз [koghazboz] *n.* bureaucrat
коғаздору [koghazdoru] *n.* prescription
коғазин [koghazin] *adj.* paper
коғазпеч [koghazpech] *n.* packet
козургарии кимиёӣ [kozurgarii kimiyoi] *n.* dry cleaner
коктейл [kokteyl] *n.* cocktail
кокул [kokul] *n.* crest *(of a bird)*
колбадшиносӣ [kolbadshinosi] *n.* anatomy
колбаса [kolbasa] *n.* sausage
колготки [kolgotki] *n.pl.* tights
команда [komanda] *n.* team
комедия [komediya] *n.* comedy
комедиявӣ [komediyavi] *adj.* comic
комёб шудан [komyob shudan] *v.i.* succeed
комёбӣ [komyobi] *n.* success
комил [komil] *adj.* perfect
комилан [komilan] *adv.* completely, quite
комиссия [komissiya] *n.* commission *(group of people)*
кумита [kumita] *n.* committee
коммунизм [kommunizm] *n.* communism
коммунист [kommunist] *n.* communist
коммунистӣ [kommunisti] *adj.* communist
комод [komod] *n.* bureau *(piece of furniture)*
компютер [kompyuter] *n.* computer
кон [kon] *n.* mine
конгресс [kongress] *n.* congress
кондуктор [konduktor] *n.* conductor *(on a train)*
конканӣ [konkani] *n.* mining
консерт [konsert] *n.* concert
константа [konstanta] *n.* constant
консул [konsul] *n.* consul
консулхона [konsulxona] *n.* consulate
контур [kontur] *n.* circuit *(electronic)*
конфет [konfet] *n.* candy
кор [kor] *n.* deed, act, action, affair, work, business, employment, function, job, task
кор кардан [kor kardan] *v.i.* take action, function, work / *v.t.* manipulate
корбурд [korburd] *n.* usage, use, application
коргар [korgar] *n.* worker
коргоҳ [korgoh] *n.* workshop
корд [kord] *n.* knife
кордон [kordon] *adj.* competent / *n.* expert
кордонӣ [kordoni] *n.* competence
кордча [kordcha] *n.* penknife
корез [korez] *n.* canal *(subterranean)*
кореягӣ [koreyagi] *n./adj.* Korean
корзор [korzor] *n.* battle
коридан [koridan] *v.t.* sow, cultivate
коркӯфта [korküfta] *adj.* physically exhausted
корманд [kormand] *n.* employee
корозмуда [korozmuda] *adj.* experienced, qualified
короям будан [koroyam budan] *v.i.* fit
короянда [koroyanda] *adj.* fit

корпартой [korpartoi] *n.* strike
корпартой кардан [korpartoi kardan] *v.i.* strike, go on strike
корт [kort] *n.* sports court
корфармо [korfarmo] *n.* employer
корхона [korxona] *n.* factory, office, workshop
корчаллон [korchallon] *n.* businessman
косаи сар [kosai sar] *n.* skull
косаи чашм [kosai chashm] *n.* eye socket
косача [kosacha] *n.* cup
косметика [kosmetika] *n.* make-up
костан [kostan] *v.i.* shrink
котиб [kotib] *n.* clerk, secretary
кофеин [kofein] *n.* caffeine
кофӣ [kofi] *adj.* adequate, enough
кофтан [koftan] *v.t.* dig, search
кофтуков [koftukov] *n.* search
кофтуков кардан [koftukov kardan] *v.t.* search thoroughly
кох [kox] *n.* mansion, palace
коҳ [koh] *n.* straw
коҳида [kohida] *adj.* weary
коҳилак [kohilak] *n.* sloth *(animal)*
коҳилӣ [kohili] *n.* laziness, sloth
коҳиш [kohish] *n.* decrease
коҳондан [kohondan] *v.t.* shrink
коҳу [kohu] *n.* lettuce
кошер [kosher] *adj.* kosher
кошин [koshin] *n.* tile
коштан [koshtan] *v.t.* cultivate, grow, sow
крани борбардор [krani borbardor] *n.* crane *(mechanical)*
креветка [krevetka] *n.* prawn, shrimp
крем [krem] *n.* cream *(topical application)*
крикет [kriket] *n.* cricket *(sport)*
кроссворд [krossvord] *n.* crossword
круиз [kruiz] *n.* cruise; **круиз рафтан** [kruiz raftan] go on a cruise
ксилофон [ksilofon] *n.* xylophone
кузур [kuzur] *n.* trump
куланг [kulang] *n.* crane *(bird)*, heron
кулаҳхӯд [kulahxüd] *n.* helmet
кулба [kulba] *n.* cottage, cabin, hut
кулолӣ [kuloli] *n.* pottery
кулоҳ [kuloh] *n.* hat, cap
кулӯла [kulüla] *n.* wad
кулӯх [kulüx] *n.* wad
кулӯхпора [kulüxpora] *n.* lump
кулча [kulcha] *n.* biscuit
кулчаи қандин [kulchai qandin] *n.* cookie
кулчаи хушк [kulchai xushk] *n.* cracker
кунд [kund] *adj.* blunt
кунда [kunda] *n.* log, block
куништ [kunisht] *n.* synagogue
кунҷ [kunj] *n.* angle; corner; **кунҷи рост** [kunji rost] right angle
кунҷков [kunjkov] *adj.* curious
кура [kura] *n.* globe, sphere
курсив [kursiv] *n.* italics

курсии паҳлӯдор [kursii pahlüdor] *n.* armchair
курс [kurs] *n.* course *(academic)*
курсӣ [kursi] *n.* chair
курта [kurta] *n.* shirt, dress
куртаи занона [kurtai zanona] *n.* dress
куртаи таг [kurtai tag] *n.* undershirt
куртка [kurtka] *n.* jacket
куҷо [kujo] *adv.* where
куҷое ки [kujoe ki] *adv./conj.* wherever
куҷое [kujoe] *pron.* anywhere
кушанда [kushanda] *adj.* killer
кушод [kushod] *adj.* loose
кушода [kushoda] *adj.* open
кушода шудан [kushoda shudan] *v.i.* open
кушодадаст [kushodadast] *adj.* lavish, generous
кушодан [kushodan] *v.t.* open, undo, unpack, unwrap
кушоиш [kushoish] *n.* opening
куштан [kushtan] *v.t.* kill, murder, extinguish, switch off
куштор [kushtor] *n.* murder, killing
куя [kuya] *n.* clothes moth
кӯдак [küdak] *n.* baby, infant, child, kid
кӯдакӣ [küdaki] *n.* childhood
кӯдакона [küdakona] *adj.* childish
кӯж [küzh] *n.* hump
кӯз [küz] *n.* hump
кӯза [küza] *n.* jug, pitcher
кӯк [kük] *n.* stitch
кӯкнор [küknor] *n.* poppy
кӯл [kül] *n.* lake
кӯмак [kümak] *n.* aid, assistance, help
кӯмак кардан [kümak kardan] *v.t.* aid, assist, help
кӯпала [küpala] *n.* clutch *(mechanical)*
кӯр [kür] *adj.* blind
кӯра [küra] *n.* furnace
кӯрӣ [küri] *n.* blindness
кӯрпа [kürpa] *n.* quilt
кӯршабпарак [kürshabparak] *n.* bat *(animal)*
кӯсамоҳӣ [küsamohi] *n.* shark
кӯтал [kütal] *n.* mountain pass
кӯтара [kütara] *adj.* wholesale
кӯтоҳ [kütoh] *adj.* brief, short
кӯтоҳ кардан [kütoh kardan] *v.t.* shorten
кӯфта [küfta] *adj.* ground
кӯфтан [küftan] *v.t.* batter, grind, pound
кӯҳ [küh] *n.* mountain
кӯҳна [kühna] *adj.* old, antique, quaint; stale
кӯҳнавард [kühnavard] *n.* mountain climber
кӯҳнавардӣ [kühnavardi] *n.* mountain climbing
кӯҳнакола [kühnakola] *n.* junk, trash
кӯҳнапараст [kühnaparast] *adj.* conservative
кӯҳон [kühon] *n.* hump *(of an animal)*
кӯча [kücha] *n.* street
кӯчидан [küchidan] *v.i.* migrate, move *(to a new house, state, city, etc.)*
кӯчондан [küchondan] *v.t.* move *(to a new house, state, city, etc.),* transfer, transport
кӯшидан [küshidan] *v.i.* try, attempt
кӯшиш [küshish] *n.* effort, attempt

кӯшиш кардан [küshish kardan] *v.i.* try, attempt
кӯшк [küshk] *n.* castle, villa

Қ

қабат [qabat] *n.* crust, layer
қабзият [qabziyat] *n.* constipation
қабила [qabila] *n.* tribe
қабл аз милод [qabl az milod] B.C. *(Before Christ)*
қабр [qabr] *n.* grave, tomb
қабул [qabul] *n.* acceptance
қабул кардан [qabul kardan] *v.t.* accept, adopt *(a custom, etc.)*
қабул накардан [qabul nakardan] *v.t.* reject, decline *(a request, an invitation, etc.)*
қабулгоҳ [qabulgoh] *n.* waiting room
қабурға [qaburgha] *n.* rib
қавӣ [qavi] *adj.* powerful, strong
қад [qad] *n.* height, size
қадаған [qadaghan] *n.* embargo, prohibition / *adj.* forbidden
қадаған кардан [qadaghan kardan] *v.t.* forbid
қадам [qadam] *n.* step, pace
қадам задан [qadam zadan] *v.i.* step
қадбаланд [qadbaland] *adj.* tall
қадим [qadim] *adj.* ancient
қадима [qadima] *adj.* old-fashioned
қадкашак [qadkashak] *n.* groin
қадпаст [qadpast] *adj.* short in stature
қадр кардан [qadr kardan] *v.t.* appreciate
қадрас [qadras] *adj.* grown-up
қадрдонӣ [qadrdoni] *n.* appreciation
қазоқ [qazoq] *n./adj.* Kazakh
қазоқӣ [qazoqi] *n.* Kazakh *(language)*
қаиқ [qaiq] *n.* boat, rowboat
қаиқронӣ [qaiqroni] *n.* boating
қай кардан [qay kardan] *v.t.* vomit, throw up
қайд [qayd] *n.* remark
қайд кардан [qayd kardan] *v.t.* register
қайла [qayla] *n.* sauce
қаймоқ [qaymoq] *n.* cream *(dairy product)*
қаймоқ гирифтан [qaymoq giriftan] *v.t.* skim
қаймоқак [qaymoqak] *n.* thin layer, film
қайовар [qayovar] *adj.* nauseating, nauseous
қайчӣ [qaychi] *n.* scissors, shears
қайчӣ кардан [qaychi kardan] *v.t.* shear
қалам [qalam] *n.* pencil
қаламрав [qalamrav] *n.* domain, territory of control
қаламфур [qalamfur] *n.* chili pepper
қалбакӣ [qalbaki] *adj.* counterfeit
қалбакӣ кардан [qalbaki kardan] *v.t.* falsify
қалъа [qal'a] *n.* castle, fortress
қалъагӣ [qal'agi] *n.* tin
қалъача [qal'acha] *n.* fort
қамарӣ [qamari] *adj.* lunar
қамиш [qamish] *n.* rush, reed
қамчин [qamchin] *n.* whip
қанд [qand] *n.* candy, lump sugar

қанддон [qanddon] *n.* sugar bowl
қандшиканак [qandshikanak] *n.* tongs
қаноат [qanoat] *n.* satisfaction
қаноатбахш [qanoatbaxsh] *adj.* satisfactory
қаноатманд [qanoatmand] *adj.* satisfied
қапидан [qapidan] *v.t.* seize, catch, grasp
қапқоқ [qapqoq] *n.* valve *(anat.)*
қапқон [qapqon] *n.* trap
қапчуқ [qapchuq] *n.* purse, wallet
қаравулхона [qaravulxona] *n.* lodge
қарамашшоқ [qaramashshoq] *n.* spades *(cards)*
қарз [qarz] *n.* credit, debt, loan; **бақарз** [baqarz] on credit
қарз додан [qarz dodan] *v.t.* credit, lend, loan
қарздиҳанда [qarzdihanda] *n.* creditor
қарздор [qarzdor] *n.* debtor / *adj.* in debt
қарздор будан [qarzdor budan] *v.t.* owe
қарн [qarn] *n.* century
қаровул [qarovul] *n.* guard
қаровулӣ кардан [qarovuli kardan] *v.t.* guard, watch
қарор [qaror] *n.* decision
қарор додан [qaror dodan] *v.t.* decide
қарор доштан [qaror doshtan] *v.i.* decide
қарс-қурс кардан [qars-qurs kardan] *v.i.* emit a snapping or crackling sound
қарсак задан [qarsak zadan] *v.t.* clap, applaud
қарсакзанӣ [qarsakzani] *n.* clapping, applause
қарта [qarta] *n.* card
қарта кашидан [qarta kashidan] *v.t.* deal cards
қасам [qasam] *n.* oath, vow
қасам хӯрдан [qasam xürdan] *v.t.* take an oath, swear, vow
қасд [qasd] *n.* intention, purpose
қасд кардан [qasd kardan] *v.t.* intend
қаср [qasr] *n.* palace
қат [qat] *n.* fold
қат кардан [qat kardan] *v.t.* fold
қатл [qatl] *n.* murder
қатл кардан [qatl kardan] *v.t.* murder
қатор [qator] *n.* row; train
қаторкӯҳ [qatorküh] *n.* mountain range
қаторовоз [qatorovoz] *n.* musical scale
қатра [qatra] *n.* drop
қатрон [qatron] *n.* resin, tar
қатъ кардан [qat' kardan] *v.t.* interrupt
қатъ шудан [qat' shudan] *v.i.* interrupt
қатъӣ [qat'i] *adj.* decisive, definitive; dire
қатъшавӣ [qat'shavi] *n.* interruption
қафас [qafas] *n.* cage
қафо [qafo] *n.* rear
қаҳва [qahva] *n.* coffee
қаҳвагӣ [qahvagi] *adj.* tan
қаҳвахона [qahvaxona] *n.* café, coffee shop
қаҳвачӯшонак [qahvajüshonak] *n.* coffee pot

қаҳрамон [qahramon] *n.* champion, hero
қаҳрамонӣ [qahramoni] *adj.* heroic
қаҳрамонона [qahramonona] *adj.* heroic / *adv.* heroically
қаҳтӣ [qahti] *n.* famine, starvation
қиём [qiyom] *n.* rebellion, uprising
қиём кардан [qiyom kardan] *v.i.* rebel
қиёс [qiyos] *n.* analogy, logical deduction
қиқир-қиқир [qiqir-qiqir] *n.* giggle
қиқир-қиқир хандидан [qiqir-qiqir xandidan] *v.i.* giggle
қиқиррос [qiqirros] *n.* giggle
қиқиррос задан [qiqirros zadan] *v.i.* giggle
қимат [qimat] *adj.* expensive
қиматбаҳо [qimatbaho] *adj.* precious
қир [qir] *n.* asphalt
қирғиз [qirghiz] *n./adj.* Kirghiz
қирғизӣ [qirghizi] *n.* Kirghiz *(language)*
қисм [qism] *n.* part, portion, section
қисмат [qismat] *n.* segment
қисматбандӣ кардан [qismatbandi kardan] *v.t.* link
қисса [qissa] *n.* story
қисса гуфтан [qissa guftan] *v.i.* tell a story
қитиқ кардан [qitiq kardan] *v.t.* tickle
қитъа [qit'a] *n.* continent
қиф [qif] *n.* funnel
қишлоқ [qishloq] *n.* village
қобил [qobil] *adj.* able, capable
қобил кардан [qobil kardan] *v.t.* enable
қобилият [qobiliyat] *n.* ability
қоз [qoz] *n.* goose
қоида [qoida] *n.* rule, regulation
қоқ [qoq] *adj.* stale
қолиб [qolib] *n.* mold
қолин [qolin] *n.* rug
қонеъ [qone'] *adj.* content, satisfied
қонеъ гардондан [qone' gardondan] *v.t.* satisfy
қонун [qonun] *n.* law, rule
қонунбарорӣ [qonunbarori] *n.* legislation
қонунгузорӣ [qonunguzori] *n.* legislation
қонунӣ [qonuni] *adj.* lawful, legal, legitimate, statutory
қорч [qorch] *n.* mushroom
қосид [qosid] *n.* messenger
қотил [qotil] *n.* murderer
қофия [qofiya] *n.* rhyme
қочоқ бурдан [qochoq burdan] *v.t.* smuggle
қочоқчигӣ [qochoqchigi] *n.* smuggling
қочоқчӣ [qochoqchi] *n.* smuggler
қош [qosh] *n.* eyebrow
қошуқ [qoshuq] *n.* spoon
қошуқча [qoshuqcha] *n.* teaspoon
қошуқи хӯокхӯрӣ [qoshuqi xürokxüri] *n.* tablespoon
қу [qu] *n.* swan
қубод [qubod] *n.* hepatitis
қубур [qubur] *n.* pipe, tube
қувва [quvva] *n.* energy, force, power
қувваи асп [quvvai asp] *n.* horsepower
қувватфизо [quvvatfizo] *n.* amplifier

қувваҳои ҳарбии ҳавой [quvvahoi harbii havoi] *n.* air force
қудрат [qudrat] *n.* strength
қулай [qulay] *adj.* comfortable, convenient
қулай будан [qulay budan] *v.i.* be convenient
қулла [qulla] *n.* peak, summit
қулт [qult] *n.* sip, swallow
қулфинай [qulfinay] *n.* strawberry
қумқума [qumquma] *n.* flask
қунғуз [qunghuz] *n.* beetle
қундуз [qunduz] *n.* beaver
қурб [qurb] *n.* stock market quote
қурбоққа [qurboqqa] *n.* frog
қурбон [qurbon] *n.* sacrifice
қурбон кардан [qurbon kardan] *v.t.* sacrifice
қурбон шудан [qurbon shudan] *v.i.* sacrifice
қурбонгоҳ [qurbongoh] *n.* sacrificial altar
қурбонӣ [qurboni] *n.* victim
қуръа партофтан [qur'a partoftan] *v.t.* draw lots
Қуръон [Qur'on] *n.* Koran
қутб [qutb] *n.* pole *(geo.)*
Қутби Шимолӣ [Qutbi Shimoli] *adj.* Arctic
қутбнамо [qutbnamo] *n.* compass
қутр [qutr] *n.* diameter
қуттӣ [qutti] *n.* box, can, case
қуттии муқовагӣ [quttii muqovagi] *n.* carton
қуттии упо [quttii upo] *n.* compact
қуттича [quttícha] *n.* can, tin can
қуфл [qufl] *n.* lock
қуфл кардан [qufl kardan] *v.t.* lock
қӯрс [qürs] *adj.* rude
қӯшун [qüshun] *n.* army, military

Л

лаб [lab] *n.* lip, edge, rim, verge
лаббай [labbay] *n.* hello *(telephone greeting)*
лабгир [labgir] *n.* mouthpiece *(of a musical instrument)*
лаби [labi] *prep.* at the edge of, by
лаблабу [lablabu] *n.* beet
лабханд [labxand] *n.* smile
лабханд кардан [labxand kardan] *v.i.* smile
лавозимот [lavozimot] *n.pl.* accessories, amenities
лабиринт [labirint] *n.* labyrinth
лаборатория [laboratorya] *n.* laboratory
лавҳаи соат [lavhai soat] *n.* dial
лагад [lagad] *n.* kick
лагад задан [lagad zadan] *v.t.* kick
лаган [lagan] *n.* basin
лагер [lager] *n.* camp
лагер сохтан [lager soxtan] *v.i.* camp
лағв [laghv] *n.* cancellation, revocation / *adj.* null
лағв кардан [laghv kardan] *v.t.* annul, nullify, cancel, revoke
лағжидан [laghzhidan] *v.i.* slip
лағжиш [laghzhish] *n.* slip
лағжонак [laghzhonak] *adj.* slippery
лазер [lazer] *n.* laser
лаззат [lazzat] *n.* amusement, treat

лакка [lakka] *n.* stain, mark
лаккадор кардан [lakkador kardan] *v.t.* stain
лаккадор шудан [lakkador shudan] *v.i.* stain
лаккадорнашуда [lakkadornashuda] *adj.* stainless
лаклак [laklak] *n.* stork
лакнати забон [laknati zabon] *n.* stammer
лақаб [laqab] *n.* nickname, title
лаққидан [laqqidan] *v.i.* chatter
лаққӣ [laqqi] *adj.* talkative
лампочка [lampochka] *n.* lightbulb
ламс [lams] *n.* touch
ланг [lang] *adj.* crippled, lame
лангар [langar] *n.* anchor
лангар андохтан [langar andoxtan] *v.i.* anchor, weigh anchor
лангаргоҳ [langargoh] *n.* harbor
лангидан [langidan] *v.i.* limp
лангӣ [langi] *n.* limp
лангон-лангон гаштан [langon-langon gashtan] *v.i.* limp
лаппас [lappas] *n.* splash
лаппас задан [lappas zadan] *v.i.* splash
ларзидан [larzidan] *v.i.* shake, shiver, tremble, vibrate, oscillate
ларзиш [larzish] *n.* vibration
ларингит [laringit] *n.* laryngitis
лас [las] *n.* elastic
латифа [latifa] *n.* anecdote
латта [latta] *n.* rag; tampon
латта-путта [latta-putta] *n.* junk
лаҳза [lahza] *n.* instant, moment
лаҳистонӣ [lahistoni] *n.* Pole, Polish *(language)* / *adj.* Polish
лаҳҷа [lahja] *n.* accent, dialect
лаҷом [lajom] *n.* rein
лашкар [lashkar] *n.* army, military
лаъл [la'l] *n.* ruby
лаълича [la'licha] *n.* disk
лаълӣ [la'li] *n.* tray
лаънат кардан [la'nat kardan] *v.t.* damn
лейтенант [leytenant] *n.* lieutenant
лекин [lekin] *conj.* but
лексия [leksiya] *n.* lecture
лента [lenta] *n.* ribbon
лесидан [lesidan] *v.t.* lick
либералӣ [liberali] *adj.* liberal *(political)*
либос [libos] *n.* clothing
либосовезак [libosovezak] *n.* hanger
лижа [lizha] *n.* ski
лижаронӣ кардан [lizharoni kardan] *v.i.* ski
ликёр [likyor] *n.* liqueur
лиққонак [liqqonak] *adj.* rickety
лимӯ [limü] *n.* lemon, lime
линг [ling] *n.* leg
линза [linza] *n.* lens
лифофа [lifofa] *n.* envelope
лифт [lift] *n.* elevator
лоғар [loghar] *adj.* lean, skinny
лоғар шудан [loghar shudan] *v.t.* lose weight
лозим [lozim] *adj.* necessary
лоиҳа [loiha] *n.* project
лоиҳаи қонун [loihai qonun] *n.* legislative bill
лой [loy] *n.* clay, dirt, mire, mud

лок [lok] *n.* varnish
лок задан [lok zadan] *v.t.* varnish
локомотив [lokomotiv] *n.* locomotive
лол [lol] *adj.* mute, dumb
лола [lola] *n.* tulip
лона [lona] *n.* den, nest
лона сохтан [lona soxtan] *v.i.* nest
лотерея [lotereya] *n.* raffle, lottery
лотинӣ [lotini] *n./adj.* Latin
лоша [losha] *n.* corpse
луғат [lughat] *n.* dictionary, vocabulary
луч [luch] *adj.* naked, bare, nude
луч кардан [luch kardan] *v.t.* strip, uncover
луч шудан [luch shudan] *v.i.* strip
лӯбиё [lübiyo] *n.* bean
лӯлӣ [lüli] *n.* Gypsy
лӯнда [lünda] *n.* small piece / *adj.* round
лӯхтак [lüxtak] *n.* doll, puppet
люкс [lyuks] *n.* luxury

М

маблағ [mablagh] *n.* finances, sum, amount
маблағ додан [mablagh dodan] *v.t.* finance
мавзӯъ [mavzü'] *n.* topic, matter, subject, theme
мавиз [maviz] *n.* raisin
мавқеъ [mavqe'] *n.* occasion, position
мавлуди Исо [mavludi Iso] *n.* Christmas
маврид [mavrid] *n.* circumstance, occasion
мавҷ [mavj] *n.* wave
мавҷуд будан [mavjud budan] *v.i.* be present, attend
мавҷуда [mavjuda] *adj.* present, available
мавҷудият [mavjudiyat] *n.* presence, attendance
мавҷудӣ [mavjudi] *n.* presence, availability
мавҷудот [mavjudot] *n.* wildlife
магас [magas] *n.* fly
магнит [magnit] *n.* magnet
магнитнок [magnitnok] *adj.* magnetic
магнитофон [magnitofon] *n.* tape player
мағал [maghal] *n.* turmoil
мағз [maghz] *n.* brain; marrow; nut
мағзи устухон [maghzi ustuxon] *n.* bone marrow
мағоза [maghoza] *n.* store, shop
мағок [maghok] *n.* pit, deep hole
мағор [maghor] *n.* fungus
мағрур [maghrur] *adj.* arrogant
мад [mad] *n.* high tide
мадду ҷазр [maddu jazr] *n.* tide
мадор [mador] *n.* tropic
мадҳия [madhiya] *n.* hymn
маза [maza] *n.* flavor, taste
маза додан [maza dodan] *v.i.* taste
мазаммат кардан [mazammat kardan] *v.t.* disapprove, condemn
мазор [mazor] *n.* shrine
май [may] *n.* May; wine
майда [mayda] *adj.* little, small, minute, petty, insignificant

майда кардан [mayda kardan] *v.t.* grind
майда шудан [mayda shudan] *v.i.* crumble
майдагап [maydagap] *adj.* petty *(person)*
майдаяк [maydayak] *adj.* tiny
майдон [maydon] *n.* field, flat expanse, village/town/city square
майзада [mayzada] *n.* alcoholic *(person)*
майкада [maykada] *n.* tavern, pub
майл [mayl] *n.* inclination, preference, tendency
майлаш [maylash] *adv.* OK
майлон [maylon] *n.* incline, trend
маймун [maymun] *n.* monkey
майна [mayna] *n.* brain
майонез [mayonez] *n.* mayonnaise
майор [mayor] *n.* major
майхона [mayxona] *n.* tavern, bar, pub
майҳан [mayhan] *n.* homeland
макидан [makidan] *v.t./v.i.* suck
маккондан [makkondan] *v.t.* nurse *(a baby)*
маконӣ [makoni] *adj.* spatial
мактаб [maktab] *n.* school
мактаб-интернат [maktab-internat] *n.* boarding school
мактаббача [maktabbacha] *n.* schoolchild
мактабгурез [maktabgurez] *adj.* truant
мактабхон [maktabxon] *n.* schoolchild
мақол [maqol] *n.* saying
мақола [maqola] *n.* article *(written piece)*
мақсад [maqsad] *n.* intention
малах [malax] *n.* grasshopper, locust
малика [malika] *n.* queen
малла [malla] *adj.* blond; **малламӯй** [mallamüy] blond-haired
малофа [malofa] *n.* sheet *(bedding)*
мамлакат [mamlakat] *n.* country
мамониат кардан [mamoniat kardan] *v.t.* hinder
ман [man] *pron.* I, me
манаҳ [manah] *n.* chin
манекен [maneken] *n.* mannequin
манёвр кардан [manyovr kardan] *v.i.* maneuver
манзара [manzara] *n.* landscape, scene, scenery, sight, view
манзил [manzil] *n.* accommodation
манманӣ [manmani] *n.* conceit
манора [manora] *n.* tower
мансаб [mansab] *n.* position, rank
мансабдор [mansabdor] *n.* official
мансабпараст [mansabparast] *adj.* ambitious
мансабпарастӣ [mansabparasti] *n.* ambition
мантиқ [mantiq] *n.* logic
мантиқӣ [mantiqi] *adj.* logical
манфиат [manfiat] *n.* benefit
манфиат гирифтан [manfiat giriftan] *v.i.* benefit
манфиатбахш [manfiatbaxsh] *adj.* beneficial
манфӣ [manfi] *adj.* negative

манъ [man'] *n.* prohibition
манъ кардан [man' kardan] *v.t.* forbid, prohibit
манъшуда [man'shuda] *adj.* forbidden
мараз [maraz] *n.* infection
марафон [marafon] *n.* marathon
марбут будан [marbut budan] *v.t.* concern(s) with, related to
марворид [marvorid] *n.* pearl
марг [marg] *n.* death
маргарин [margarin] *n.* margarine
марговар [margovar] *adj.* fatal
марғзор [marghzor] *n.* meadow
мард [mard] *n.* man, guy, male *(human)*
мардона [mardona] *adj.* masculine
мардонагӣ [mardonagi] *n.* manhood, masculinity
мардум [mardum] *n.* people
мардумак [mardumak] *n.* pupil *(anat.)*
мардумшинос [mardumshinos] *n.* ethnographist
мардумшиносӣ [mardumshinosi] *n.* ethnography
марз [marz] *n.* border
марзангӯш [marzangüsh] *n.* forget-me-not
марказ [markaz] *n.* center, focus
марказӣ [markazi] *adj.* central
маркаи почта [markai pochta] *n.* postage stamp
мармалод [marmalod] *n.* marmalade
мармар [marmar] *n.* marble
марминҷон [marminjon] *n.* blackberry
маро [maro] *pron.* me
маросим [marosim] *n.* ceremony
март [mart] *n.* March
марҳала [marhala] *n.* phase, stage
марҳам [marham] *n.* ointment
марҷон [marjon] *n.* coral
маршал [marshal] *n.* marshal
масал [masal] *n.* saying
маска [maska] *n.* butter
маскан [maskan] *n.* dwelling
маслиҳат [maslihat] *n.* advice
маслиҳат додан [maslihat dodan] *v.t.* advise
масома [masoma] *n.* pore
масона [masona] *n.* bladder
масоҳат [masohat] *n.* area *(mathematical)*
маст [mast] *adj.* drunk
масхарабоз [masxaraboz] *n.* clown
масхараомез [masxaraomez] *adj.* ridiculous
масҳ [mas-h] *n.* massage
масҷид [masjid] *n.* mosque
масъул [mas'ul] *adj.* liable, responsible
масъулият [mas'uliyat] *n.* liability, responsibility
матарс [matars] *n.* scarecrow
матбуот [matbuot] *n.* press
математика [matematika] *n.* mathematics
материк [materik] *n.* mainland
матлуб [matlub] *adj.* desirable
матн [matn] *n.* text
матоъ [mato'] *n.* cloth, material
мафтун кардан [maftun kardan] *v.t.* fascinate

махрут [maxrut] *n.* cone
махсус [maxsus] *adj.* distinct, particular, special
махсусан [maxsusan] *adv.* namely
маҳал [mahal] *n.* site, location
маҳалла [mahalla] *n.* neighborhood
маҳаллӣ [mahalli] *adj.* native, traditional, regional
маҳдуд кардан [mahdud kardan] *v.t.* restrict
маҳдудият [mahdudiyat] *n.* restriction
маҳин [mahin] *adj.* slender, fine, tenuous
маҳкам кардан [mahkam kardan] *v.t.* fasten, reinforce, close
маҳкум кардан [mahkum kardan] *v.t.* pass judgment against, condemn
маҳмез [mahmez] *n.* spur
маҳмез задан [mahmez zadan] *v.t.* spur
маҳорат [mahorat] *n.* mastery, expertise
маҳрам [mahram] *adj.* intimate
маҳрум кардан [mahrum kardan] *v.t.* deprive
маҳсул [mahsul] *n.* product
маҳсулот [mahsulot] *n.pl.* ingredients
маҷалла [majalla] *n.* journal *(publication)*, magazine
маҷбур кардан [majbur kardan] *v.t.* oblige
маҷлис [majlis] *n.* assembly, convention, session
маҷмӯа [majmüa] *n.* collection, set
маҷнунбед [majnunbed] *n.* weeping willow
машварат кардан [mashvarat kardan] *v.i.* consult
машғул [mashghul] *adj.* engaged, busy, occupied
машғул кардан [mashghul kardan] *v.t.* engage in, involve in, occupy
машқ [mashq] *n.* rehearsal, practice
машқ кардан [mashq kardan] *v.t./v.i.* practice, rehearse
машҳур [mashhur] *adj.* famous
машъал [mash'al] *n.* torch
маъдан [ma'dan] *n.* ore
маъзур доштан [ma'zur doshtan] *v.t.* excuse
маъқул донистан [ma'qul donistan] *v.t.* approve, endorse
маълумот [ma'lumot] *n. pl.* data / *n.* information
маълумотнома [ma'lumotnoma] *n.* handbook, reference book
маъмулан [ma'mulan] *adv.* normally
маънавӣ [ma'navi] *adj.* spiritual
маънӣ [ma'ni] *n.* meaning
маъно [ma'no] *n.* meaning
маъно доштан [ma'no doshtan] *v.t.* mean, signify
маъюс кардан [ma'yus kardan] *v.t.* disappoint
маъюсӣ [ma'yusi] *n.* disappointment
мебел [mebel] *n.* furniture
мебелдор кардан [mebeldor kardan] *v.t.* provide with furniture, furnish
мева [meva] *n.* fruit
медал [medal] *n.* medal

медуза [meduza] *n.* jellyfish
мексикой [meksikoi] *n./adj.* Mexican
мембрана [membrana] *n.* membrane
меню [menyu] *n.* menu
мерос [meros] *n.* inheritance
мерос гирифтан [meros giriftan] *v.t.* inherit
меросхӯр [merosxür] *n.* heir
металл [metall] *n.* metal
метр [metr] *n.* meter
метро [metro] *n.* metro, subway
мех [mex] *n.* nail *(hardware)*
мех задан [mex zadan] *v.t.* nail
механизм [mexanizm] *n.* gear
механик [mexanik] *n.* mechanic
мехи печдор [mexi pechdor] *n.* bolt *(mechanical)*, screw
меҳвар [mehvar] *n.* axis
меҳмон [mehmon] *n.* guest, visitor
меҳмон кардан [mehmon kardan] *v.t.* receive guests, entertain, host, treat *(to a meal, etc.)*
меҳмондӯст [mehmondüst] *adj.* hospitable
меҳмоннавоз [mehmonnavoz] *adj.* hospitable
меҳмонхона [mehmonxona] *n.* guesthouse, hotel, inn, living room
меҳнатдӯст [mehnatdüst] *adj.* industrious
меҳнат [mehnat] *n.* labor, toil
меҳнат кашидан [mehnat kashidan] *v.i.* toil
меҳнаткаш [mehnatkash] *n.* laborer
меҳр [mehr] *n.* affection
меҳроб [mehrob] *n.* altar *(of a church)*
меҳрубон [mehrubon] *adj.* affectionate, tender, kind, gracious, merciful
меҳрубонӣ [mehruboni] *n.* kindness, mercy
меъда [me'da] *n.* stomach
меъдача [me'dacha] *n.* ventricle
меъёр [me'yor] *n.* standard, criterion
меъмор [me'mor] *n.* architect
меъморӣ [me'mori] *n.* architecture / *adj.* architectural
мидия [midiya] *n.* mussel
миён [miyon] *n.* waist / *adj.* medium
миёна [miyona] *n./adj.* average, mean, medium, mid-, middle, temperate; **ба ҳисоби миёна** [ba hisobi miyona] on average
миёнагир кардан [miyonagir kardan] *v.t./v.i.* surround
миёни [miyoni] *prep.* amid, among, between
миёнсол [miyonsol] *adj.* middle-aged
миёнҷой [miyonjoy] *n./adj.* middle
мижа [mizha] *n.* eyelash
мижа задан [mizha zadan] *v.i.* blink
миз [miz] *n.* table
мизбон [mizbon] *n.* host
мизбонзан [mizbonzan] *n.* hostess
мизи хатнависӣ [mizi xatnavisi] *n.* desk
микроб [mikrob] *n.* germ
микроскоп [mikroskop] *n.* microscope

микрофон [mikrofon] *n.* microphone
микдор [miqdor] *n.* quantity
микёс [miqyos] *n.* scale *(system of measurement)*
мил [mil] *n.* mile
мила [mila] *n.* rod
милиса [milisa] *n.* police, cop
милки дандон [milki dandon] *n.* gum *(anat.)*
миллат [millat] *n.* nation, nationality
миллиметр [millimetr] *n.* millimeter
миллион [million] *n.* million
миллият [milliyat] *n.* nationality
миллӣ [milli] *adj.* national
милодӣ [milodi] A.D. *(Anno Domini)*
милтиқ [miltiq] *n.* gun, rifle
мино [mino] *n.* enamel
минои баҳрӣ [minoi bahri] *n.* lighthouse
минтақа [mintaqa] *n.* region, zone
минус [minus] *prep.* minus
мир [mir] *n.* mayor
мирук [miruk] *n.* termite
мис [mis] *n.* copper
мисли [misli] *adv.* like, as
мисол [misol] *n.* example, instance; **масалан** [masalan] for example
мисрӣ [misri] *n./adj.* Egyptian
мобайн [mobayn] *adj.* medium
мо [mo] *pron.* we, us
мод [mod] *n.* fashion, style
мода [moda] *adj.* female *(non-human)*
модар [modar] *n.* mother
модарандар [modarandar] *n.* stepmother
модаркалон [modarkalon] *n.* grandmother
модахук [modaxuk] *n.* sow
модда [modda] *n.* article *(legal)*, good, item, substance, matter
модем [modem] *n.* modem
модиён [modiyon] *n.* mare
модул [modul] *n.* module
модулӣ [moduli] *adj.* modular
модшуда [modshuda] *adj.* fashionable, stylish
моеъ [moe'] *n.* fluid, liquid
моил будан [moil budan] *v.i.* tend, inclined to
мокиён [mokiyon] *n.* hen
мол [mol] *n.* goods, ware, merchandise, property
моли чорпой [moli chorpoy] *n.* cattle
молидан [molidan] *v.t.* rub
молия [moliya] *n.* finances
молиявӣ [moliyavi] *adj.* financial
моллюскҳо [mollyuskho] *n.* shellfish
момодоя [momodoya] *n.* midwife
монанд [monand] *adj.* similar, alike, like
монанд будан [monand budan] *v.t.* resemble
монанд кардан [monand kardan] *v.t.* mistake for something else, confuse
монандӣ [monandi] *n.* similarity, likeness, resemblance
монанднабуда [monandnabuda] *adj.* unlike
монда [monda] *adj.* tired / *gram.* intransitive
монда кардан [monda kardan] *v.t.* tire

монда шудан [monda shudan] *v.i.* tire
мондагӣ [mondagi] *n.* tiredness / *adj.* remaining
мондан [mondan] *v.t.* allow, let, leave, place, put / *v.i.* remain, stay
монданашаванда [mondanashavanda] *adj.* tireless
монеа [monea] *n.* handicap, obstacle
монондан [manondan] *v.t.* defer
монополия [monopoliya] *n.* monopoly
мор [mor] *n.* snake
мори айнакӣ [mori aynaki] *n.* cobra
мормоҳӣ [mormohi] *n.* eel
морпеч [morpech] *adj.* spiral
мортира [mortira] *n.* mortar *(mil.)*
мост [most] *n.* yogurt
мот кардан [mot kardan] *v.t.* checkmate
мотосикл [motosikl] *n.* motorcycle
мотор [motor] *n.* engine, motor
моҳ [moh] *n.* moon; month
моҳвора [mohvora] *n.* satellite
моҳи асал [mohi asal] *n.* honeymoon
моҳигир [mohigir] *n.* fisherman
моҳигирӣ [mohigiri] *n.* fishing
моҳигирӣ кардан [mohigiri kardan] *v.t.* fish
моҳихӯрак [mohixürak] *n.* seagull
моҳӣ [mohi] *n.* fish
моҳӣ гирифтан [mohi giriftan] *v.t.* fish
моҳона [mohona] *n.* salary, wages
моҳтоб [mohtob] *n.* moon; moonlight
мошин [moshin] *n.* car, machine
мошин мондан [moshin mondan] *v.t.* park a car
мошини боркаш [moshini borkash] *n.* truck
мошини ёрии таъҷилӣ [moshini yorii ta'jili] *n.* ambulance
мошини хатнависӣ [moshini xatnavisi] *n.* typewriter
мошини ҷомашӯӣ [moshini jomashüi] *n.* washing machine
мошинка [moshinka] *n.* typewriter
муайян [muayyan] *adj.* definite *(gram.)*
муайян кардан [muayyan kardan] *v.t.* schedule
муайянкунанда [muayyankunanda] *adj.* definitive *(gram.)*
муаллим [muallim] *n.* schoolteacher, teacher
муаллиф [muallif] *n.* author
мубодила [mubodila] *n.* exchange
мубодила кардан [mubodila kardan] *v.t.* exchange
муболиға [mubaligha] *n.* exaggeration
муболиға кардан [mubaligha kardan] *v.t.* exaggerate
муборак [muborak] *n.* congratulations
муборакбод гуфтан [muborakbod guftan] *v.t.* congratulate

мубориза бурдан [muboriza burdan] *v.t.* fight
мубоҳиса [mubohisa] *n.* debate, discussion
мубоҳиса кардан [mubohisa kardan] *v.t.* contest, debate, discuss
мубтало кардан [mubtalo kardan] *v.t.* infect
мубҳам [mubham] *adj.* obscure
мубҳам кардан [mubham kardan] *v.t.* obscure
муваққатӣ [muvaqqati] *adj.* temporary
мувозина [muvozina] *n.* equilibrium, *(sense of)* balance
мувозӣ [muvozi] *adj.* parallel
мувофиқ будан [muvofiq budan] *v.i.* agree, be in accord
мувофиқ набудан [muvofiq nabudan] *v.i.* disagree
мувофиқат [muvofiqat] *n.* accord, agreement
мувофиқи [muvofiqi] *prep.* according to
муддат [muddat] *n.* period of time, while, phase
мудир [mudir] *n.* director, manager
мудофиа [mudofia] *n.* plea; protection
мудофиа кардан [mudofia kardan] *v.t.* defend, protect / *v.i.* plead
мудохила кардан [mudoxila kardan] *v.i.* intervene
мужда [muzhda] *n.* good news
музд [muzd] *n.* salary, wages
музей [muzey] *n.* museum
музикирот [muzokirot] *n.* negotiation
музикирот кардан [muzokirot kardan] *v.i.* negotiate
музофоти шаҳр [muzofoti shahr] *n.* suburbs
музояда [muzoyada] *n.* auction
мукааб [mukaab] *n.* cube
мукаммал [mukammal] *adj.* complete, comprehensive
мукаммал кардан [mukammal kardan] *v.t.* complete, supplement
муколима [mukolima] *n.* dialogue
мукотиба доштан [mukotiba doshtan] *v.i.* correspond
мукотибот [mukotibot] *n.* correspondence
мукофот [mukofot] *n.* award, prize
мукофот додан [mukofot dodan] *v.t.* award
муқаддас [muqaddas] *adj.* holy, sacred
муқаррар кардан [muqarrar kardan] *v.t.* appoint, set in place, fix
муқобил [muqobil] *adj.* opposite
муқова [muqova] *n.* cardboard
муқовимат [muqovimat] *n.* resistance
муқовимат кардан [muqovimat kardan] *v.t.* resist
муқовиматкунанда [muqovimatkunanda] *adj.* resistant
муқоиса [muqoisa] *n.* comparison
муқоиса кардан [muqoisa kardan] *v.t.* compare
мулк [mulk] *n.* estate

мулоим [muloim] *adj.* soft, tender
мулоқот [muloqot] *n.* meeting, appointment
мулоқот кардан [muloqot kardan] *v.t.* meet
мулоҳиза [mulohiza] *n.* consideration
мулоҳиза кардан [mulohiza kardan] *v.t.* think carefully, consider
мум [mum] *n.* wax
мум задан [mum zadan] *v.t.* wax
мумкин [mumkin] *adj.* likely, possible
мунисипалитет [munisipalitet] *n.* municipality
мунозира [munozira] *n.* debate
мунозира кардан [munozira kardan] *v.t.* debate
мунокиша [munoqisha] *n.* dispute
мунокиша кардан [munoqisha kardan] *v.t.* dispute
муносиб [munosib] *adj.* appropriate, proper, suitable, apt, fit, decent; due
муносиб будан [munosib budan] *v.i.* be appropriate
муносиб кардан [munosib kardan] *v.t.* fit
муносибат [munosibat] *n.* suitability; relationship
мунтазам [muntazam] *adj.* methodical, neat, regular
мунтазир шудан [muntazir shudan] *v.i.* wait
мунтазира [muntazira] *adj.* prospective
мунъакис кардан [mun'akis kardan] *v.t.* reflect
мунъакис шудан [mun'akis shudan] *v.i.* reflect
муовин [muovin] *n.* deputy
муоина [muoina] *n.* medical examination
муоина кардан [muoina kardan] *v.t.* examine
муоличa [muolija] *n.* medical procedure, medical treatment
муоличa кардан [muolija kardan] *v.t.* treat medically
муомила [muomila] *n.* bargain, deal, transaction; behavior, conduct
муомила кардан [muomila kardan] *v.i.* deal
муомила доштан [muomila doshtan] *v.i.* treat
мураббаъ [murabba'] *n./adj.* square
мураббо [murabbo] *n.* jam, preserves
мураккаб [murakkab] *adj.* compound
мураттаб [murattab] *adj.* methodical, systematic
мурваттобак [murvattobak] *n.* screwdriver
мурғ [murgh] *n.* chicken, fowl
мурғи марҷон [murghi marjon] *n.* turkey
мурғобӣ [murghobi] *n.* duck
мурда [murda] *adj.* dead
мурдадил [murdadil] *adj.* apathetic
мурдан [murdan] *v.i.* die
мурданӣ [murdani] *adj.* dying
мурдоб [murdob] *n.* swamp
мурдор [murdor] *adj.* filthy
муродиф [murodif] *n.* synonym / *adj.* synonymous
мурофиа [murofia] *n.* lawsuit
мурочиат кардан [murojiat kardan] *v.i.* seek redress, appeal

мурӯд [murüd] *n.* pear
мурч [murch] *n.* black pepper
мусалмон [musalmon] *n.* Muslim
мусалмонӣ [musalmoni] *adj.* Muslim
мусбӣ [musbi] *adj.* positive
мусиқӣ [musiqi] *n.* music
мусобиқа [musobiqa] *n.* competition, contest, tournament
мусодира [musodira] *n.* confiscation, seizure
мусофир [musofir] *n.* passenger, traveler
мусоҳиба [musohiba] *n.* interview
мусоҳиба кардан [musohiba kardan] *v.t.* interview
мустақил [mustaqil] *adj.* independent
мустақим [mustaqim] *adj.* direct
мустақиман [mustaqiman] *adv.* direct, directly
мустамлика [mustamlika] *n.* colony
мустаҳкам [mustahkam] *adj.* tenacious
мутаассир кардан [mutaassir kardan] *v.t.* tamper
мутаассиф [mutaassif] *adj.* sorry
мутаассифона [mutaassifona] *adv.* unfortunately
мутараққӣ [mutaraqqi] *adj.* progressive
мутахассис [mutaxassis] *n.* specialist
мутеъ кардан [mute' kardan] *v.t.* subdue
мутлақ [mutlaq] *adj.* absolute
мутмаин [mutmain] *adj.* sure
муттаҳам кардан [muttaham kardan] *v.t.* accuse
муттаҳид кардан [muttahid kardan] *v.t.* unite
муттаҳид гардидан [muttahid gardidan] *v.i.* unite with, join
муфаттиши махфӣ [mufattishi maxfi] *n.* detective
мухолиф [muxolif] *n.* opponent
мухолифат [muxolifat] *n.* disagreement, opposition
мухолифат кардан [muxolifat kardan] *v.t.* oppose
мухолифин [muxolifin] *n.* political opposition
мухталиф [muxtalif] *adj.* contrary, different
мухтасар [muxtasar] *adj.* concise
мухтасар кардан [muxtasar kardan] *v.t.* abbreviate
мухтор [muxtor] *adj.* autonomous
муҳаббат [muhabbat] *n.* love
муҳандис [muhandis] *n.* engineer
муҳаррик [muharrik] *n.* engine, motor
муҳим [muhim] *adj.* major, important
муҳит [muhit] *n.* environment, surroundings
муҳокима [muhokima] *n.* trial *(legal)*
муҳокима кардан [muhokima kardan] *v.t.* try in court
муҳофизат [muhofizat] *n.* conservation
муҳофизат кардан [muhofizat kardan] *v.t.* conserve, preserve

мухоҷир [muhojir] *n.* emigrant
мухоҷират [muhojirat] *n.* emigration
мухоҷират кардан [muhojirat kardan] *v.i.* emigrate
муҷаррад [mujarrad] *adj.* abstract
муҷассама [mujassama] *n.* statue
муш [mush] *n.* mouse
мушак [mushak] *n.* muscle; missile
мушкил [mushkil] *adj.* difficult
мушкилӣ [mushkili] *n.* difficulty
мушовир [mushovir] *n.* adviser, consultant
мушт [musht] *n.* fist, punch
мушт задан [musht zadan] *v.t.* punch
муштарак [mushtarak] *adj.* shared
муштарӣ [mushtari] *n.* client, customer
муштзанӣ [mushtzani] *n.* boxing
муътадил [mu'tadil] *adj.* mild
мӯза [müza] *n.* boot
мӯина [müina] *n.* fur
мӯй [müy] *n.* hair
мӯйдор [müydor] *adj.* hairy
мӯйи сохта [müyi soxta] *n.* wig
мӯйлаб [müylab] *n.* mustache, whisker
мӯйчинак [müychinak] *n.pl.* tweezers
мӯрча [mürcha] *n.* ant
мӯҳр [mühr] *n.* seal
мӯҳр задан [mühr zadan] *v.t.* impress with a seal, seal
мӯҳра [mühra] *n.* dice; vertebra
муътадил [mu'tadil] *adj.* temperate, moderate
мӯҳтарам [mühtaram] *adj.* dignified
мӯъҷиза [mü'jiza] *n.* miracle
мӯъҷизакорона [mü'jizakorona] *adj.* miraculous

Н

на [na] *conj.* nor
набера [nabera] *n.* grandchild
набз [nabz] *n.* pulse
набот [nabot] *n.* rock candy
нав [nav] *adj.* new, novel, recent / *adv.* just
навад [navad] *num.* ninety
навакак [navakak] *adv.* just
навбаромад [navbaromad] *adj.* novel
навбатӣ [navbati] *adj.* following, recurring
навбатдор [navbatdor] *adj.* on duty
навбора [navbora] *n.* teenager
навда [navda] *n.* sprout
навда баровардан [navda barovardan] *v.i.* sprout
навдин [navdin] *n.* convert
навзод [navzod] *n./adj.* newborn
навигарӣ [navigari] *n.* news
нависанда [navisanda] *n.* writer
навишта гирифтан [navishta giriftan] *v.t.* record
навишта шудан [navishta shudan] *v.i.* spell
навиштан [navishtan] *v.t./v.i.* write
навӣ [navi] *n.* novelty, newness
навкеш [navkesh] *n.* convert

навкор [navkor] *n.* beginner, pioneer
наво [navo] *n.* tune
навозанда [navozanda] *n.* musician
навозиш кардан [navozish kardan] *v.t.* cherish, pet
навозишкор [navozishkor] *adj.* soft-hearted, gentle, tender
навомӯз [navomüz] *n.* beginner
навор [navor] *n.* strip, band, ribbon; camera film, tape *(audio/video)*
навохтан [navoxtan] *v.t.* play an instrument
наврас [navras] *n.* teenager
навсозӣ [navsozi] *n.* renovation
Навӯз [Navrüz] *n.* Tajik New Year
нағз [naghz] *adj.* good, well, fine, nice / *adv.* well
нағз дидан [naghz didan] *v.t.* like
нажод [nazhod] *n.* race, descent, ethnicity
нажодӣ [nazhodi] *adj.* ethnic, racial
назар [nazar] *n.* attitude
назария [nazariya] *n.* theory
назариявӣ [nazariyavi] *adj.* theoretical
назди [nazdi] *prep.* close to, by
наздик [nazdik] *adv.* about, close, near / *adj.* adjacent, close, near, nearby, handy, intimate
наздик шудан [nazdik shudan] *v.i.* approach
наздикбин [nazdikbin] *adj.* nearsighted
наздики [nazdiki] *adv.* nearly
наздикшавӣ [nazdikshavi] *n.* approach
назира [nazira] *n.* example, instance
назм [nazm] *n.* verse
назокат [nazokat] *n.* delicacy
назорат [nazorat] *n.* verification, check, control; supervision, observation
назорат кардан [nazorat kardan] *v.t.* verify, check, control
назоратчӣ [nazoratchi] *n.* inspector, supervisor
най [nay] *n.* reed, cane
найранг [nayrang] *n.* plot, intrigue
найрангбозӣ [nayrangbozi] *n.* trick *(cards, magic, etc.)*
найча [naycha] *n.* spool, tube
накҳат [nakhat] *n.* aroma, scent
наққош [naqqosh] *n.* painter
наққошӣ [naqqoshi] *n.* painting *(artform)*
нақл кардан [naql kardan] *v.t.* narrate, recite, tell
нақрасанг [naqrasang] *n.* gem
нақш [naqsh] *n.* role
нақш бандондан [naqsh bandondan] *v.t.* imprint
нақша [naqsha] *n.* chart, plan, project
нақша кашидан [naqsha kashidan] *v.t.* chart, draw an architectural plan, plot, trace
нақши ангушт [naqshi angusht] *n.* fingerprint
налдавон [naldavon] *n.* plumber
нам [nam] *adj.* moist
нам кардан [nam kardan] *v.t.* dampen, moisten
намад [namad] *n.* felt
намак [namak] *n.* salt

намак андохтан [namak andoxtan] *v.t.* salt
намак задан [namak zadan] *v.t.* preserve with salt
намакин [namakin] *adj.* salty
намакоб [namakob] *n.* pickle
намиранда [namiranda] *adj.* immortal
намӣ [nami] *n.* moisture
намнок [namnok] *adj.* damp, humid
намнокӣ [namnoki] *n.* humidity
намо [namo] *n.* façade
намоён [namoyon] *adj.* evident, noticeable
намоён кардан [namoyon kardan] *v.t.* represent, reveal
намоён шудан [namoyon shudan] *v.i.* appear
намоёнӣ [namoyoni] *n.* visibility
намоз хондан [namoz xondan] *v.i.* pray
намоиш [namoish] *n.* demonstration, display, exhibit, scene *(theatrical)*, show
намоиш дода шудан [namoish doda shudan] *v.i.* demonstrate
намоиш додан [namoish dodan] *v.t.* demonstrate, display, exhibit
намоянда [namoyanda] *n.* deputy, representative
намудан [namudan] *v.i.* seem
намуна [namuna] *n.* model, sample, specimen, pattern
намунавӣ [namunavi] *adj.* typical
нана [nana] *n.* mom, mommy
нар [nar] *n./adj.* male *(animal)*
нарангушт [narangusht] *n.* thumb
нардбон [nardbon] *n.* ladder
нарм [narm] *adj.* soft, gentle, tender
нармдил [narmdil] *adj.* soft-hearted
нарх [narx] *n.* cost, price, rate
нарх доштан [narx doshtan] *v.t.* cost
нарх мондан [narx mondan] *v.t.* price, value
насаб [nasab] *n.* surname, last name
насим [nasim] *n.* breeze
наск [nask] *n.* lentil
насл [nasl] *n.* generation
насос [nasos] *n.* pump
наср [nasr] *n.* prose
насронӣ [nasroni] *n./adj.* Christian
натиҷа [natija] *n.* consequence, outcome, result
натрий [natriy] *n.* sodium
нафақа [nafaqa] *n.* pension
нафақахӯр [nafaqaxür] *n.* pensioner
нафас баровардан [nafas barovardan] *v.i.* exhale
нафас даровардан [nafas darovardan] *v.i.* inhale
нафас кашидан [nafas kashidan] *v.i.* breathe
нафоридан [naforidan] *v.t.* displease
нафрат [nafrat] *n.* disgust, hate
нафрат кардан [nafrat kardan] *v.t.* hate
нафратангез [nafratangez] *adj.* disgusting
нафрин [nafrin] *n.* curse
нафрин кардан [nafrin kardan] *v.t.* curse
нафт [naft] *n.* crude oil, petroleum
нах [nax] *n.* fiber, thread

нахл [naxl] *n.* palm tree
нахуст [naxust] *adj.* first
нахустин [naxustin] *adj.* first, initial, primary
нахӯд [naxüd] *n.* pea
наҳв [nahv] *n.* syntax
наҷот [najot] *n.* rescue, salvation
наҷот додан [najot dodan] *v.t.* rescue, save
наҷотдиҳанда [najotdihanda] *n.* savior
нашр [nashr] *n.* edition, issue, publication
нашр кардан [nashr kardan] *v.t.* publish
нашркунанда [nashrkunanda] *n.* publisher
нашъа [nash'a] *n.* narcotic, drug
нашъадор [nash'ador] *adj.* narcotic
наъл [na'l] *n.* horseshoe
не [ne] *adv.* no, not
невралгия [nevralgiya] *n.* neuralgia
неврозӣ [nevrozi] *adj.* neurotic
невропатолог [nevropatolog] *n.* neurologist
негатив [negativ] *n.* photographic negative
некахтар [nekaxtar] *adj.* fortunate, blessed
некбахт [nekbaxt] *adj.* fortunate, blessed
некбин [nekbin] *n.* optimist / *adj.* optimistic
неккирдорӣ [nekkirdori] *n.* virtue
некӯаҳволӣ [neküahvoli] *n.* welfare
некӯӣ [neküi] *n.* virtue
неккоҳӣ [nekxohi] *n.* favor, courtesy
неккоҳӣ кардан [nekxohi kardan] *v.t.* do a favor
немис [nemis] *n.* German
немисӣ [nemisi] *n.* German *(language)* / *adj.* German
нерӯ [nerü] *n.* energy, power
нерӯманд [nerümand] *adj.* powerful, strong
нест кардан [nest kardan] *v.t.* eliminate
нестшавӣ [nestshavi] *n.* extinction
неш [nesh] *n.* sting
неш задан [nesh zadan] *v.t.* sting / *v.i.* sprout
нигаристан [nigaristan] *v.t.* view / *v.i.* look
нигарон [nigaron] *adj.* anxious
нигаронӣ [nigaroni] *n.* anxiety, suspense
нигористон [nigoriston] *n.* art gallery
нигоҳ [nigoh] *n.* look
нигоҳ доштан [nigoh doshtan] *v.t.* conserve, preserve, retain, keep, maintain, reserve, set aside, withhold
нигоҳ кардан [nigoh kardan] *v.t.* view / *v.i.* look, watch
нигоҳдоранда [nigohdoranda] *n.* keeper
нигоҳдорӣ [nigohdori] *n.* conservation, storage
нигоҳдошта [nigohdoshta] *adj.* kept aside, maintained, kept, preserved
нигоҳубин кардан [nigohubin kardan] *v.t.* look after, tend
нидо [nido] *n.* exclamation
нидо кардан [nido kardan] *v.t.* exclaim
ниё [niyo] *n.* ancestor

ниёз [niyoz] *n.* need, requirement
ниёз доштан [niyoz doshtan] *v.t.* need
ниёзманд будан [niyozmand budan] *v.t.* require, need
низ [niz] *adv.* too, also
низом [nizom] *n.* routine
низомнома [nizomnoma] *n.* charter
низоъ [nizo'] *n.* legal dispute, quarrel
низоъ андохтан [nizo' andoxtan] *v.i.* quarrel
никел [nikel] *n.* nickel *(type of metal)*
никоҳ [nikoh] *n.* marriage
ниқоб [niqob] *n.* disguise, mask
нил [nil] *n.* indigo
ним [nim] *n.* half
нимдошт [nimdosht] *adj.* used
нимишаб [nimishab] *n.* midnight
нимкола [nimkola] *adj.* sloppy, poorly done
нимранг [nimrang] *adj.* pale
нимрух [nimrux] *n.* profile
нимрӯз [nimrüz] *n.* midday, noon
нимторикӣ [nimtoriki] *n.* dusk, twilight
нимҷон [nimjon] *adj.* weak, queasy
нисбат [nisbat] *n.* relationship
нисбат додан [nisbat dodan] *v.t.* attribute, refer
нисбӣ [nisbi] *adj.* relative
нисф [nisf] *n.* half
нисфирӯз [nisfirüz] *n.* midday, noon
нисфишаб [nisfishab] *n.* midnight
нитроген [nitrogen] *n.* nitrogen
ниҳодан [nihodan] *v.t.* lay, place
ниҳолхона [niholxona] *n.* agricultural/horticultural nursery
ниҳонӣ [nihoni] *adj.* hidden, secret
ниҳоят [nihoyat] *adv.* extra, extremely, terribly
ниҳоят монда [nihoyat monda] *adj.* physically exhausted
нишастан [nishastan] *v.i.* sit
нишастгоҳ [nishastgoh] *n.* place to sit, seat
нишеб [nisheb] *n.* incline, slope, ramp, slant
нишебӣ [nishebi] *n.* slope
нишон [nishon] *n.* target, objective, goal; badge, coat-of-arms, crest
нишон гирифтан [nishon giriftan] *v.t.* take aim, target
нишон додан [nishon dodan] *v.t.* exhibit, indicate, show
нишона [nishona] *n.* mark, notation, note, symbol, token
нишона кардан [nishona kardan] *v.t.* mark
нишонӣ [nishoni] *n.* address
нишоста [nishosta] *n.* starch
ният [niyat] *n.* intent, aim, intention
ният доштан [niyat doshtan] *v.t.* intend, aim
нобаробар [nobarobar] *adj.* unequal
нобиға [nobigha] *n.* genius *(person)*
нобино [nobino] *adj.* blind
нобиноӣ [nobinoi] *n.* blindness

нобоварӣ [nobovari] *n.* distrust

нобудшавӣ [nobudshavi] *n.* ruin, perdition

нова [nova] *n.* gutter

новадон [novadon] *n.* drain, gutter

новгон [novgon] *n.* fleet

ногаҳон [nogahon] *adv.* suddenly

ногаҳонӣ [nogahoni] *adj.* sudden

ногузир [noguzir] *adj.* fatal, unavoidable

нодаркор [nodarkor] *adj.* needless, unnecessary

нодон [nodon] *n.* fool / *adj.* foolish, stupid, ignorant

нодонӣ [nodoni] *n.* foolishness, ignorance

нодуруст [nodurust] *adj.* incorrect, untrue, wrong

ноз кардан [noz kardan] *v.i.* flirt

нозо [nozo] *adj.* barren *(unable to conceive)*

нозо кардан [nozo kardan] *v.t.* render barren, sterilize *(a woman)*

нозпарвард [nozparvard] *n.* snob / *adj.* snobbish

нозпарвардона [nozparvardona] *adj.* snobbish / *adv.* snobbishly

нозук [nozuk] *adj.* delicate, subtle

нои нафас [noi nafas] *n.* trachea, windpipe

ноиб-президент [noib prezident] *n.* vice-president

ноил шудан [noil shudan] *v.i.* achieve

ноилшавӣ [noilshavi] *n.* achievement

ноиттифоқӣ [noittifoqi] *n.* disagreement

нок [nok] *n.* pear

нокифоя [nokifoya] *adj.* insufficient, meager

ноком [nokom] *adj.* unsuccessful

ноком шудан [nokom shudan] *v.i.* fail

нокомӣ [nokomi] *n.* failure

ноқил [noqil] *n.* conductor *(of electricity, etc.)*; narrator

ноқис [noqis] *adj.* handicapped

ноқулай [noqulay] *adj.* awkward, uncomfortable

нол [nol] *num.* zero

нола [nola] *n.* groan, moan

нолидан [nolidan] *v.i.* groan

ном [nom] *n.* name; reputation

ном бурдан [nom burdan] *v.t.* mention

нома [noma] *n.* letter

номавҷуда [nomavjuda] *adj.* away

номақбул [nomaqbul] *adj.* unacceptable

номаъқул шумурдан [noma'qul shumurdan] *v.t.* disapprove, condemn

номаълум [noma'lum] *adj.* anonymous, unknown

номбар [nombar] *n.* mention

номдор [nomdor] *adj.* famous

номдорӣ [nomdori] *n.* fame

номзад [nomzad] *n.* candidate, fiancé

номзадӣ [nomzadi] *n.* engagement

номи шаб [nomi shab] *n.* password

номидан [nomidan] *v.t.* name, christen

номуайян [nomuayyan] *adj.* vague
номукаммал [nomukammal] *adj.* incomplete, imperfect
номумкин [nomumkin] *adj.* impossible
номуносиб [nomunosib] *adj.* improper
нон [non] *n.* bread
нонамоён [nonamoyon] *adj.* invisible
нонамоён шудан [nonamoyon shudan] *v.i.* vanish
нонвой [nonvoy] *n.* baker
ноништа [nonishta] *n.* breakfast
ноништаи дуюм [nonishtai duyum] *n.* lunch
ноништаи дуюм кардан [nonishtai duyum kardan] *v.i.* lunch, have lunch
нонпаз [nonpaz] *n.* baker
нонхӯр [nonxür] *n.* dependent
ноором [noorom] *adj.* anxious, uneasy, restless
ноороми [nooromi] *n.* anxiety, uneasiness, worry, concern; suspense
ноошно [nooshno] *adj.* unfamiliar
нопадид шудан [nopadid shudan] *v.i.* disappear, vanish
нописанди [nopisandi] *n.* disregard
нопурра [nopurra] *adj.* crude, incomplete, imperfect
норавшан [noravshan] *adj.* dim, unclear, vague
норанг [norang] *n.* tangerine
норасои [norasoi] *n.* flaw; shortage
норинҷи [norinji] *adj.* orange
нороста [norosta] *adj.* indirect
нору [noru] *n.* robin
носоз будан [nosoz budan] *v.i.* disagree
носози [nosozi] *n.* disagreement
нота [nota] *n.* musical note
нотавон [notavon] *adj.* impotent, unable
нотавони [notavoni] *n.* inability
нотарс [notars] *adj.* bold, daring
нотиқ [notiq] *n.* speaker
ноумед [noumed] *adj.* hopeless, bleak
ноумеди [noumedi] *n.* despair
ноумед шудан [noumed shudan] *v.i.* despair
ноустувор [noustuvor] *adj.* changeable, precarious, unstable
ноӯҳдабаро [noühdabaro] *adj.* incompetent, inefficient
ноф [nof] *n.* navel
нофорам [noforam] *adj.* unpleasant
нохоно [noxono] *adj.* illegible
нохун [noxun] *n.* nail *(anat.)*
нохуш [noxush] *adj.* unhappy; unhealthy
ноҳамгун [nohamgun] *adj.* unlike, different
ноҳия [nohiya] *n.* region, district
ночиз [nochiz] *n.* trifle, minor matter / *adj.* minor, trivial, worthless
ношинос [noshinos] *adj.* unfamiliar, unknown
ноябр [noyabr] *n.* November
нубуғ [nubugh] *n.* genius *(quality)*
нуқра [nuqra] *n.* silver
нуқсон [nuqson] *n.* defect
нуқсондор [nuqsondor] *adj.* defective, faulty

нуқта [nuqta] *n.* dot, point, period; full stop
нуқтавергул [nuqtavergul] *n.* semicolon
нур [nur] *n.* light
нурафкан [nurafkan] *n.* projector
нусха [nusxa] *n.* copy, mold
нусха бардоштан [nusxa bardoshtan] *v.t.* make a copy
нутқ [nutq] *n.* faculty of speech
нуфуз кардан [nufuz kardan] *v.t.* penetrate
нуҷум [nujum] *n.* astrology
нӯг [nüg] *n.* tip, point
нӯги по [nügi po] *v.* tiptoe
нӯгостин [nügostin] *n.* cuff
нӯздаҳ [nüzdah] *num.* nineteen
нӯздаҳум [nüzdahum] *adj.* nineteenth
нӯк [nük] *n.* spire
нӯкар [nükar] *n.* servant
нӯҳ [nüh] *num.* nine
нӯҳум [nühum] *adj.* ninth
нӯл [nül] *n.* beak, bill
нӯшидан [nüshidan] *v.t.* drink
нӯшиданӣ [nüshidani] *n.* drink
нӯшоба [nüshoba] *n.* beverage, soft drink
нӯшокӣ [nüshoki] *n.* beverage

О

об [ob] *n.* water
об додан [ob dodan] *v.t.* water
об кардан [ob kardan] *v.t.* melt, liquefy, thaw
об шудан [ob shudan] *v.i.* melt, liquefy, thaw
обакӣ [obaki] *adj.* fluid, liquid, watery
обанбор [obanbor] *n.* reservoir
оббоз [obboz] *n.* bather, swimmer
оббозӣ [obbozi] *n.* bathing, swimming
оббозӣ кардан [obbozi kardan] *v.i.* bathe, swim
оббозӣ кунондан [obbozi kunondan] *v.t.* bathe
обгардон [obgardon] *n.* ladle
обгармкунак [obgarmkunak] *n.* boiler
обдон [obdon] *n.* flask
обёрӣ [obyori] *n.* irrigation
обёрӣ кардан [obyori kardan] *v.t.* irrigate
оби баҳрӣ [obi bahri] *n.* seawater
оби даҳан [obi dahan] *n.* saliva
оби ҷав [obi jav] *n.* beer
обистан [obistan] *adj.* pregnant
обӣ [obi] *adj.* aquatic
обкунанда [obkunanda] *n.* solvent
обкунӣ [obkuni] *n.* solution *(mixture of substances)*
обногузар [obnoguzar] *adj.* waterproof
обрӯ [obrü] *n.* prestige, reputation
обу ҳаво [obu havo] *n.* climate
обуна [obuna] *n.* subscription
обуна кардан [obuna kardan] *v.i.* subscribe
обхокӣ [obxoki] *adj.* amphibian
обшор [obshor] *n.* waterfall
овардан [ovardan] *v.t.* bring, cause
овезон кардан [ovezon kardan] *v.t.* hang
овезон карда шудан [ovezon karda shudan] *v.i.* hang
овехтан [ovextan] *v.t.* hang

овехта шудан [ovexta shudan] *v.i.* hang
овоз [ovoz] *n.* sound, voice, volume, vote
овоз додан [ovoz dodan] *v.i.* vote
овоза [ovoza] *n.* rumor
овоздиҳанда [ovozdihanda] *n.* voter
овоздиҳӣ [ovozdihi] *n.* poll, vote, ballot
овозӣ [ovozi] *adj.* vocal
огоҳ [ogoh] *adj.* aware
огоҳ будан [ogoh budan] *v.i.* know
огоҳинома [ogohinoma] *n.* notification
огоҳӣ [ogohi] *n.* reminder, warning
огоҳонидан [ogohonidan] *v.t.* notify
оғил [oghil] *n.* stable
оғоз [oghoz] *n.* start, beginning
оғоз кардан [oghoz kardan] *v.t.* begin
оғоз шудан [oghoz shudan] *v.i.* begin, commence
оғӯш [oghüsh] *n.* embrace, hug
оғӯш кардан [oghüsh kardan] *v.t.* embrace, hug
одам [odam] *n.* person, human, man
одам чида гирифтан [odam chida giriftan] *v.t.* recruit
одамак [odamak] *n.* mannequin
одамдӯст [odamdüst] *adj.* humane
одамӣ [odami] *adj.* human
одамкуш [odamkush] *n.* murderer
одат [odat] *n.* habit
одат кардан [odat kardan] *v.i.* accustom, become accustomed
одатан [odatan] *adv.* generally, normally, usually
одатӣ [odati] *adj.* usual
оддӣ [oddi] *adj.* ordinary, common, normal, routine
одил [odil] *adj.* just, fair
одина [odina] *n.* Friday
ожанг [ozhang] *n.* wrinkle
озарбойҷонӣ [ozarboyjoni] *n./adj.* Azerbaijani
озах [ozax] *n.* wart
озмоишгоҳ [ozmoishgoh] *n.* laboratory
озмоишӣ [ozmoishi] *adj.* tentative, experimental
озмудан [ozmudan] *v.t.* test, sample
озмун [ozmun] *n.* examination, test
озод [ozod] *adj.* free
озод кардан [ozod kardan] *v.t.* free, release
озодӣ [ozodi] *n.* freedom, liberty
озодмоҳӣ [ozodmohi] *n.* salmon
озодона [ozodona] *adj.* fluently, freely
озон [ozon] *n.* ozone
озор [ozor] *n.* abuse, anguish
озор додан [ozor dodan] *v.t.* cause anguish, abuse, annoy, gall, tease
озуқа [ozuqa] *n.* ration
озурдагӣ [ozurdagi] *n.* annoyance
озурдан [ozurdan] *v.i.* cause anguish, abuse; annoy, gall, tease
оила [oila] *n.* family, swarm
оин [oin] *n.* custom
оина [oina] *n.* mirror
оинаи шамолгардон [oinai shamolgardon] *n.* windshield
оксиген [oksigen] *n.* oxygen

октябр [oktyabr] *n.* October
оқибат [oqibat] *n.* consequence, solution, settlement
оқил [oqil] *adj.* rational, thinking, sane, wise
оқо [oqo] *n.* Mister *(abbrev.* Mr.*)*
олам [olam] *n.* world
олат [olat] *n.* organ *(anat.)*
олим [olim] *n.* scholar, scientist
олимпӣ [olimpi] *adj.* Olympic
олиҳа [oliha] *n.* goddess
олӣ [oli] *adj.* excellent
олмонӣ [olmoni] *n./adj.* German
олу [olu] *n.* plum
олуда [oluda] *adj.* polluted, contaminated
олуда кардан [oluda kardan] *v.t.* infect
олудагӣ [oludagi] *n.* pollution, contamination
олудан [oludan] *v.t.* contaminate, pollute
олуқоқ [oluqoq] *n.* prune
омадан [omadan] *v.i.* come; **пас омадан** [pas omadan] be back
омезиш [omezish] *n.* mix
омехта шудан [omexta shudan] *v.i.* mingle, mix
омехтан [omextan] *v.t.* mix
омиёна [omiyona] *adj.* ordinary, common
омил [omil] *n.* agent *(chemical substance, etc.)*
омлет [omlet] *n.* omelette
омманофаҳм [ommanofahm] *adj.* unpopular
омода [omoda] *adj.* ready
омода кардан [omoda kardan] *v.t.* prepare
омода шудан [omoda shudan] *v.i.* prepare, provide
омор [omor] *n.* statistics
оморӣ [omori] *adj.* statistical
омос [omos] *n.* swelling, tumor
омоси кӯррӯда [omosi kürrüda] *n.* appendicitis
омосидан [omosidan] *v.i.* swell
омӯзанда [omüzanda] *n.* learner
омӯзгор [omüzgor] *n.* instructor, schoolteacher, teacher
омӯзиш [omüzish] *n.* education, instruction; study
омӯзондан [omüzondan] *v.t.* instruct
омӯхта шудан [omüxta shudan] *v.i.* accustom, become accustomed; **ба … омӯхта будан** [ba … omüxta budan] be accustomed to …
омӯхтан [omüxtan] *v.t.* educate, teach / *v.i.* learn, study
он [on] *pron./adj.* that
он ҷо [on jo] *adv.* there, yonder
она [ona] *n.* mom, mommy
онсӯйи [onsüyi] *prep.* beyond
онҳо [onho] *pron.* they, them, those
опера [opera] *n.* opera
оператор [operator] *n.* operator
оптик [optik] *n.* optician
оптикӣ [optiki] *adj.* optical
орд [ord] *n.* flour
орд кардан [ord kardan] *v.t.* grind
орзу [orzu] *n.* desire, wish
орзу кардан [orzu kardan] *v.t.* wish, desire / *v.i.* yearn
оринҷ [orinj] *n.* elbow
оркестр [orkestr] *n.* orchestra
ороиш [oroish] *n.* decoration, ornament

ором [orom] *adj.* calm, sedate, quiet, still
ором кардан [orom kardan] *v.t.* calm, sedate
ором шудан [orom shudan] *v.i.* calm
оромиш [oromish] *n.* tranquility, calm
оромӣ [oromi] *n.* calm, comfort
оростан [orostan] *v.t.* decorate
ору [oru] *n.* wasp
оруи асал [orui asal] *n.* bee
осеб [oseb] *n.* damage, hurt
осеб овардан [oseb ovardan] *v.t.* damage, harm, hurt, injure
осебнок [osebnok] *adj.* harmful, noxious
Осиё [Osiyo] *n.* Asia
осиё [osiyo] *n.* mill
осиёб [osiyob] *n.* mill
осиёби бодӣ [osiyobi bodi] *n.* windmill
осиёбон [osiyobon] *n.* miller
осиёӣ [osiyoi] *n./adj.* Asian
осмон [osmon] *n.* sky
осоиш [osoish] *n.* tranquility, peace
осоишгоҳ [osoishgoh] *n.* health resort, place of respite
осоишта [osoishta] *adj.* tranquil, calm
осон [oson] *adj.* easy
осон кардан [oson kardan] *v.t.* facilitate
осонӣ [osoni] *n.* ease
осонтар кардан [osontar kardan] *v.t.* simplify
осорхона [osorxona] *n.* museum
остар [ostar] *n.* lining
остин [ostin] *n.* sleeve
остона [ostona] *n.* threshold
оташ [otash] *n.* fire, blaze
оташгирак [otashgirak] *n.pl.* tongs, fire-tongs
оташдон [otashdon] *n.* hearth, oven
оташин [otashin] *adj.* furious
оташфишон [otashfishon] *n.* volcano
офарида [ofarida] *n.* being, creature
офаридан [ofaridan] *v.t.* create
офарин [ofarin] *n.* acclamation, praise / *interj.* Bravo!, Well done!
офаринанда [ofarinanda] *n.* creator, maker
офариниш [ofarinish] *n.* creation
офат [ofat] *n.* disaster, plague; **офати табиӣ** [ofati tabii] natural disaster
офият [ofiyat] *n.* medical rehabilitation
офтоб [oftob] *n.* sun
офтобзанӣ [oftobzani] *n.* heatstroke
офтобӣ [oftobi] *adj.* solar, sunny
офтобпанаҳ [oftobpanah] *n.* sun visor, visor
офтобпараст [oftobparast] *n.* sunflower
охир [oxir] *adv.* finally, after all
охирин [oxirin] *adj.* final, last
охур [oxur] *n.* stall
оҳ [oh] *n.* sigh
оҳ кашидан [oh kashidan] *v.i.* sigh
оҳак [ohak] *n.* lime *(calcium oxide)*; mortar
оҳан [ohan] *n.* iron *(metal)*
оҳанг [ohang] *n.* nuance, tone, tune
оҳангар [ohangar] *n.* smith

оҳанин [ohanin] *adj.* iron
оҳанрабо [ohanrabo] *n.* magnet
оҳиста [ohista] *adj.* soft, gentle, slow
оҳиста-оҳиста [ohista-ohista] *adj.* gradual
оҳор [ohor] *n.* starch
оҳор додан [ohor dodan] *v.t.* starch
оча [ocha] *n.* mom, mommy
оҷ [oj] *n.* ivory
ош додан [osh dodan] *v.t.* tan
ошёна [oshyona] *n.* floor, level *(of a building)*, story *(of a building)*; nest
ошёна сохтан [oshyona soxtan] *v.i.* nest
ошиқ [oshiq] *n.* lover
ошиқ-маъшуқ [oshiq-ma'shuq] *n.* hinge
ошиқӣ [oshiqi] *n.* romance
ошиқона [oshiqona] *adj.* romantic
ошиқпечон [oshiqpechon] *n.* ivy
ошкор [oshkor] *adj.* evident, noticeable, obvious
ошкор кардан [oshkor kardan] *v.t.* detect
ошно [oshno] *n.* acquaintance *(a person)* / *adj.* familiar
ошно кардан [oshno kardan] *v.t.* acquaint
ошноӣ [oshnoi] *n.* acquaintance *(of someone)*
ошпазӣ [oshpazi] *n.* cooking; **китоби ошпазӣ** [kitobi oshpazi] cookbook
ошпазхона [oshpazxona] *n.* kitchen
оштинопазир [oshtinopazir] *adj.* irreconcilable
оштӣ [oshti] *n.* peace, reconciliation
оштӣ додан [oshti dodan] *v.t.* reconcile
ошуфтан [oshuftan] *v.t.* disturb
ошӯб [oshüb] *n.* unrest
ошхона [oshxona] *n.* cafeteria
ошхонача [oshxonacha] *n.* snack bar
ошхӯрак [oshxürak] *n.* bib
оянда [oyanda] *n./adj.* future / *adj.* next

П

пагоҳ [pagoh] *adv.* tomorrow
пагоҳӣ [pagohi] *n.* morning / *adj.* a.m.
падар [padar] *n.* father
падарандар [padarandar] *n.* stepfather
падаркалон [padarkalon] *n.* grandfather
падеж [padezh] *n.* grammatical case
падид омадан [padid omadan] *v.i.* emerge, form
падида [padida] *n.* phenomenon
падидор [padidor] *adj.* apparent
падидор кардан [padidor kardan] *v.t.* reveal
падруд [padrud] *n.* goodbye
падруд гуфтан [padrud guftan] *v.t.* abandon, bid goodbye
паём [payom] *n.* message
пажвок [pazhvok] *n.* echo
пажмурда шудан [pazhmurda] *adj.* faded, withered
пажмурда шудан [pazhmurda shudan] *v.i.* fade, wither

пажмурдан [pazhmurdan] *v.i.* fade
пажӯҳиш [pazhühish] *n.* research
пажӯҳиш кардан [pazhühish kardan] *v.t.* research
пазириш [pazirish] *n.* acceptance
пазирой [paziroi] *n.* reception, welcome
пазирой кардан [paziroi kardan] *v.t.* receive someone
пазируфтан [paziruftan] *v.t.* accept, adopt *(a custom, etc.)*
пазмон шудан [pazmon shudan] *v.i.* miss, long for
пай [pay] *n.* sinew, tendon; track, trace
пай бурдан [pay burden] *v.t.* realize
пайванд кардан [payvand kardan] *v.t.* connect; graft; inoculate
пайвандак [payvandak] *gram.* conjunction
пайванднавда [payvandnavda] *n.* graft
пайваста [payvasta] *adj.* fixed, standing, permanent
пайваста будан [payvasta budan] *v.i.* adjoin
пайвастан [payvastan] *v.t.* associate, attach, connect, join, link
пайвастшавӣ [payvastshavi] *n.* composition *(gram.)*
пайғамбар [payghambar] *n.* prophet
пайғом [payghom] *n.* message
пайғу [payghu] *n.* hawk
пайдо кардан [paydo kardan] *v.t.* find, obtain
пайдо шудан [paydo shudan] *v.i.* appear, come into being, arise
пайдоиш [paydoish] *n.* appearance
пайдокунӣ [paydokuni] *adj.* obtainable
пайк [payk] *n.* messenger
пайкара [paykara] *n.* statue
пайкон [paykon] *n.* tip *(of a spear, arrow, etc.)*, point
пайкора [paykora] *n.* mop
паймон [paymon] *n.* treaty
пайрав [payrav] *n.* follower
пайравӣ кардан [payravi kardan] *v.t.* be a follower, follow
пайроҳа [payroha] *n.* path, trail
пакет [paket] *n.* packet
пал [pal] *n.* vegetable patch
паланг [palang] *n.* leopard
палкона [palkona] *n.* trapdoor
палто [palto] *n.* coat
панаҳ кардан [panah kardan] *v.t.* screen, cover, shield
панд [pand] *n.* advice
панд додан [pand dodan] *v.t.* advise
панир [panir] *n.* cheese
паноҳ [panoh] *n.* asylum, refuge, shelter
паноҳ додан [panoh dodan] *v.t.* shelter
паноҳанда [panohanda] *n.* refugee
паноҳгоҳ [panohgoh] *n.* refuge, sanctuary
панҷ [panj] *num.* five
панҷа [panja] *n.* finger, fork, paw
панҷара [panjara] *n.* banister, handrail, railing
панҷоҳ [panjoh] *num.* fifty
панҷоҳум [panjohum] *adj.* fiftieth
панҷум [panjum] *adj.* fifth

панҷшанбе [panjshanbe] *n.* Thursday
папа [papa] *n.* pope
папка [papka] *n.* dossier, file, folder
папоротник [paporotnik] *n.* fern
пар [par] *n.* feather, plume
парад [parad] *n.* parade
паразит [parazit] *n.* parasite
паразитӣ [paraziti] *adj.* parasitic
парастанда [parastanda] *n.* worshipper
парастидан [parastidan] *v.t.* worship, venerate
парастиш [parastish] *n.* worship
парастор [parastor] *n.* nanny
парасторӣ кардан [parastori kardan] *v.t.* nurse, tend
парасту [parastu] *n.* swallow *(bird)*
парашют [parashyut] *n.* parachute
парванда [parvanda] *n.* legal case, dossier, file
парвардан [parvardan] *v.t.* nurture, take care of, cherish, foster, raise, rear *(children)*
парвардахона [parvardaxona] *n.* agricultural/horticultural nursery
парвариш [parvarish] *n.* nurture, care
парво [parvo] *n.* concern, care
парвоз [parvoz] *n.* flight
парвоз кардан [parvoz kardan] *v.i.* fly
парвона [parvona] *n.* moth
парда [parda] *n.* curtain, screen, partition; act *(in a play, etc.)*; musical tone
пардапӯш кардан [pardapüsh kardan] *v.t.* dissemble
пардача [pardacha] *n.* thin layer, film
пардоз [pardoz] *n.* polish
пардоз додан [pardoz dodan] *v.t.* polish
пардохт [pardoxt] *n.* fee, payment
пардохтан [pardoxtan] *v.t.* pay
парешонӣ [pareshoni] *n.* distress
паридан [paridan] *v.i.* fly
парӣ [pari] *n.* fairy
парма [parma] *n.* drill
парма кардан [parma kardan] *v.t.* drill
пароканда кардан [parokanda kardan] *v.t.* scatter
пароканда шудан [parokanda shudan] *v.i.* scatter
парпеч [parpech] *n.* diaper
парра [parra] *n.* propeller
парраи чарх [parrai charx] *n.* spoke
парранда [parranda] *n.* bird
паррондан [parrondan] *v.t.* fire, shoot, launch
партизан [partizan] *n.* guerilla
партизанӣ [partizani] *adj.* guerilla
партия [partiya] *n.* party
партовтозакунӣ [partovtozakuni] *n.* recycling
партоиш [partoish] *n.* throw
партофтан [partoftan] *v.t.* throw, cast, toss; shed *(skin)* / vomit, throw up
парҳез [parhez] *n.* diet

пархез кардан [parhez kardan] *v.i.* diet
парчам [parcham] *n.* flag, standard
пас [pas] *adv.* after, then, therefore
пас аз [pas az] *prep.* after, next
пас додан [pas dodan] *v.t.* restore, give back, return
пасандоз кардан [pasandoz kardan] *v.t.* save *(money, etc.)*
паси [pasi] *prep.* behind
паскӯча [paskücha] *n.* alley
пасманзар [pasmanzar] *n.* background
пасмонда [pasmonda] *n.* residue / *adj.* leftover
паспорт [pasport] *n.* passport
паст [past] *adj.* low, inferior, mean
паст кардан [past kardan] *v.t.* diminish
паст шудан [past shudan] *v.i.* decline
пастеризатсия кардашуда [pasterizatsiya kardashuda] *adj.* pasteurized
пастоб [pastob] *n.* shallow body of water
пастсифат [pastsifat] *adj.* inferior
пасттар кардан [pasttar kardan] *v.t.* reduce
пастхамӣ [pastxami] *n.* depression *(geo.)*; ramp
пастшавӣ [pastshavi] *n.* decline
пат [pat] *n.* fluff
патент [patent] *n.* patent
патинка [patinka] *n.* boot
патрон [patron] *n.* cartridge
пахмоқ [paxmoq] *adj.* shaggy
пахта [paxta] *n.* cotton
пахтагин [paxtagin] *adj.* cotton
пахтагӣ [paxtagi] *adj.* cotton
пахш кардан [paxsh kardan] *v.t.* muffle
паҳлӯ [pahlü] *n.* side *(of a person, animal, object)*
паҳлӯйи [pahlüyi] *prep.* beside, by, next to
паҳн кардашуда [pahn kardashuda] *adj.* widespread
паҳн кардан [pahn kardan] *v.t.* spread
паҳн шудан [pahn shudan] *v.i.* disseminate, circulate, spread
паҳншавӣ [pahnshavi] *n.* epidemic
паҳншуда [pahnshuda] *adj.* widespread
пачақ кардан [pachaq kardan] *v.t.* squash
пашм [pashm] *n.* wool
пашмин [pashmin] *adj.* woolen
пашша [pashsha] *n.* fly
педал [pedal] *n.* pedal
пенитсиллин [penitsillin] *n.* penicillin
пергамент [pergament] *n.* parchment
пероҳан [perohan] *n.* shirt, dress
перспектива [perspektiva] *n.* perspective
песа [pesa] *n.* play, theater piece
печ [pech] *n.* coil, screw
печида [pechida] *adj.* complicated
печида кардан [pechida kardan] *v.t.* complicate
печонда бастан [pechonda bastan] *v.t.* pack
печондан [pechondan] *v.t.* envelop, wrap

печтобак [pechtobak] *n.* screwdriver
пеш [pesh] *n./adj.* front / *adv.* ago
пеш аз [pesh az] *prep.* before, ahead of
пеш гирифтан [pesh giriftan] *v.t.* cover, shield
пеш гузаштан [pesh guzashtan] *v.t.* precede, surpass
пеш кашидан [pesh kashidan] *v.t.* advance, bring forward
пеш рафтан [pesh raftan] *v.i.* advance, progress, develop; **ба пеш рафтан** [ba pesh raftan] go ahead
пеша [pesha] *n.* craft, profession, trade
пешавар [peshavar] *n.* artisan, craftsman
пешайвон [peshayvon] *n.* terrace
пешакӣ [peshaki] *adv.* in advance
пешбинӣ [peshbini] *n.* foresight
пешбинӣ кардан [peshbini kardan] *v.t.* realize beforehand, anticipate
пешгирӣ [peshgiri] *n.* prevention
пешгирӣ кардан [peshgiri kardan] *v.t.* prevent
пешгиркунанда [peshgirkunanda] *adj.* preventive
пешгиркунандаи обистанӣ [peshgirkunandai obistani] *adj.* contraceptive
пешгуфтор [peshguftor] *n.* foreward, prologue
пешгӯӣ [peshgüi] *n.* forecast, prophecy
пешгӯӣ кардан [peshgüi kardan] *v.t.* predict
пешдастӣ кардан [peshdasti kardan] *v.t.* surpass
пешдоман [peshdoman] *n.* apron
пешин [peshin] *n.* afternoon, noon; Islamic prayer performed at noon / *adj.* former
пешина [peshina] *adj.* previous, former
пешкаш [peshkash] *n.* grant
пешкаш кардан [peshkash kardan] *v.t.* present
пешниҳод [peshnihod] *n.* offer, proposal, suggestion
пешниҳод кардан [peshnihod kardan] *v.t.* offer, submit, propose, suggest
пешоб [peshob] *n.* urine
пешоб кардан [peshob kardan] *v.i.* urinate
пешобдон [peshobdon] *n.* bladder
пешобӣ [peshobi] *adj.* urinary
пешона [peshona] *n.* forehead
пешонӣ [peshoni] *n.* forehead
пешопеш [peshopesh] *adv.* ahead
пешопеш рафтан [peshopesh raftan] *v.t.* precede
пешоянд [peshoyand] *gram.* preposition
пешпардохт [peshpardoxt] *n.* pre-payment, deposit
пешпо хӯрдан [peshpo xürdan] *v.i.* stub
пешравона [peshravona] *adj.* progressive
пешранда [peshranda] *n.* chip
пешрафт [peshraft] *n.* progress, advancement, development

пешрафт додан [peshraft dodan] *v.t.* develop *(a country)*
пешрафт кардан [peshraft kardan] *v.i.* progress
пештар [peshtar] *adv.* before
пештара [peshtara] *adj.* former
пештахта [peshtaxta] *n.* counter
пешхизмат [peshxizmat] *n.* waiter, waitress
пиво [pivo] *n.* beer
пиёба [piyoba] *n.* broth
пиёда [piyoda] *n.* pawn *(chess piece)* / *adj.* on foot
пиёдагард [piyodagard] *n.* pavement, sidewalk; pedestrian
пиёз [piyoz] *n.* onion
пиёла [piyola] *n.* cup, teacup
пизишк [pizishk] *n.* doctor, physician
пизишкӣ [pizishki] *n.* medicine *(science)*
пилки чашм [pilki chashm] *n.* eyelid
пиллагон [pillagon] *n.* staircase
пилта [pilta] *n.* wick
пина [pina] *n.* patch
пина кардан [pina kardan] *v.t.* patch
пинак [pinak] *n.* nap
пинак кардан [pinak kardan] *v.i.* nap, take a nap
пиндор [pindor] *n.* imagination
пиндоштан [pindoshtan] *v.t./v.i.* suppose, imagine
пинта [pinta] *n.* pint
пинҳон кардан [pinhon kardan] *v.t.* conceal, hide
пинҳон шудан [pinhon shudan] *v.i.* hide
пинҳонӣ [pinhoni] *adj.* hidden, secret, occult
пионер [pioner] *n.* pioneer
пир [pir] *adj.* elderly, old *(person)*
пирог [pirog] *n.* pastry, pie
пирожнӣ [pirozhni] *n.* pastry
пирӯз шудан [pirüz shudan] *v.i.* triumph, win
пирӯзӣ [pirüzi] *n.* triumph, victory
писанд [pisand] *n.* preference, choice
писанд накардан [pisand nakardan] *v.t.* ignore, disregard
писандидан [pisandidan] *v.t.* admire; approve, endorse / *v.i.* choose
писар [pisar] *n.* boy, son
писарандар [pisarandar] *n.* stepson
пичиррос [pichirros] *n.* whisper
пичиррос задан [pichirros zadan] *v.i.* whisper
пиҷак [pijak] *n.* jacket
пишак [pishak] *n.* cat
пишакбача [pishakbacha] *n.* kitten
плазма [plazma] *n.* plasma
план [plan] *n.* plan
план гузоштан [plan guzoshtan] *v.t.* plan
пластик [plastic] *n.* plastic
пластикӣ [plastiki] *adj.* plastic
пластмасӣ [plastmasi] *adj.* plastic
платина [platina] *n.* platinum
платформа [platforma] *n.* platform
по [po] *n.* foot, leg
пода [poda] *n.* herd

подош [podosh] *n.* award, prize, reward, recompense
подош додан [podosh dodan] *v.t.* award, reward, recompense
подшоҳ [podshoh] *n.* king, monarch
подшоҳӣ [podshohi] *n.* kingdom / *adj.* royal
поезд [poezd] *n.* train
поён [poyon] *n.* end, ending, finish
поин [poin] *adv.* down
пой [poy] *n.* foot, leg
пойафзол [poyafzol] *n.* shoe
пойга [poyga] *n.* race
пойгоҳ [poygoh] *n.* base *(mil.)*
пойдор [poydor] *adj.* fixed, permanent
пойдорӣ [poydori] *n.* permanence
пойдос [poydos] *n.* scythe
пойобнамо [poyobnamo] *n.* buoy
пойтахт [poytaxt] *n.* capital city
пойҷома [poyjoma] *n.pl.* pajamas
пок [pok] *adj.* clean
пок кардан [pok kardan] *v.t.* clean, delete, erase, wipe
покиза [pokiza] *adj.* neat, pure
покистонӣ [pokistoni] *n./adj.* Pakistani
поку [poku] *n.* razor blade
полковник [polkovnik] *n.* colonel
полкона [polkona] *n.* balcony
полоиш [poloish] *n.* purification, refining
полоишгоҳ [poloishgoh] *n.* refinery
полондан [polondan] *v.t.* strain, filter
полуда [poluda] *n.* jelly
полудан [poludan] *v.t./v.i.* purify, refine
полшагӣ [polshagi] *n.* Pole, Polish / *adj.* Polish
помидор [pomidor] *n.* tomato
понздаҳ [ponzdah] *num.* fifteen
понздаҳум [ponzdahum] *adj.* fifteenth
поп [pop] *n.* pope
пора [pora] *n.* crumb, splinter
пора кардан [pora kardan] *v.t.* rip, tear
пора шудан [pora shudan] *v.i.* rip, tear
пора-пора шудан [pora-pora shudan] *v.i.* crumble
порагӣ [poragi] *n.* rip, tear
порашуда [porashuda] *adj.* ragged, torn
порлумон [porlumon] *n.* parliament
порлумонӣ [porlumoni] *adj.* parliamentary
порсӣ [porsi] *n./adj.* Persian
порсо [porso] *adj.* devout, pious
португалӣ [portugali] *n./adj.* Portuguese
пору [poru] *n.* dung, manure
порча [porcha] *n.* small piece, scrap, cloth
поршен [porshen] *n.* piston
посбон [posbon] *n.* guard, watchman, keeper
посбонӣ кардан [posboni kardan] *v.t.* guard / *v.i.* patrol
посух [posux] *n.* answer, reply, response
посух додан [posux dodan] *v.t./v.i.* answer, reply, respond
почта [pochta] *n.* mail
почтаи ҳавоӣ [pochtai havoi] *n.* airmail

пошида шудан [poshida shudan] *v.i.* scatter
пошидан [poshidan] *v.t.* scatter, splash, spray, sprinkle
пошна [poshna] *n.* heel
поя [poya] *n.* basis, base; rack; stalk
презерватив [preservativ] *n.* condom
президент [prezident] *n.* president
префикс [prefiks] *gram.* prefix
приоритет [prioritet] *n.* priority
проблема [problema] *n.* problem
программа [programma] *n.* program
программа сохтан [programma soxtan] *v.t.* program
программасоз [programmasoz] *n.* programmer
простата [prostata] *n.* prostate
протестант [protestant] *n.* Protestant
протестантизм [protestantizm] *n.* Protestantism
протестантӣ [protestanti] *adj.* Protestant
профессор [professor] *n.* professor
пудина [pudina] *n.* mint
пул [pul] *n.* money, currency; **табдили пул** [tabdili pul] currency exchange
пул баргардондан [pul bargardondan] *v.t.* refund
пул додан [pul dodan] *v.t.* pay
пулакча [pulakcha] *n.* fish scale
пули майда [puli mayda] *n.* small change *(coins)*
пули нақд [puli naqd] *n.* cash
пулӣ [puli] *adj.* financial
пулфиристонӣ [pulfiristoni] *n.* remittance
пунба [punba] *n.* cotton
пур [pur] *adj.* full
пур кардан [pur kardan] *v.t.* fill, stuff
пургӯ [purgü] *adj.* talkative
пурдуд [purdud] *adj.* smoky
пурзаҳмат [purzahmat] *adj.* troublesome
пурзӯр [purzür] *adj.* strong
пуркибр [purkibr] *adj.* arrogant
пуркунанда [purkunanda] *n.* object *(gram.)*
пурмавҷ [purmavj] *adj.* stormy *(water)*, full of waves
пурмеҳр [purmehr] *adj.* affectionate
пуропур [puropur] *adj.* crowded
пурра [purra] *adj.* complete, whole, comprehensive, entire, utter
пурра кардан [purra kardan] *v.t.* complete, supplement
пурсидан [pursidan] *v.t./v.i.* ask
пурсиш [pursish] *n.* inquiry, question
пуртаҷриба [purtajriba] *adj.* experienced, veteran
пуртаъсир [purta'sir] *adj.* touching, affecting
пуртӯфон [purtüfon] *adj.* stormy
пурчанг [purchang] *adj.* dusty
пурҷӯшухурӯш [purjüshuxurüsh] *adj.* lively, passionate
пуршаҳват [purshahvat] *adj.* romantically passionate

пуф кардан [puf kardan] *v.t.* blow

пуфак [pufak] *n.* balloon; bubble

пухта [puxta] *adj.* ripe

пухта шудан [puxta shudan] *v.i.* cook, bake

пухтакор [puxtakor] *adj.* thorough

пухтан [puxtan] *v.t.* cook, bake

пушаймон [pushaymon] *adj.* regretful

пушаймон шудан [pushaymon shudan] *v.t.* regret

пушаймонӣ [pushaymoni] *n.* regret, remorse

пушт [pusht] *n.* back, rear, reverse; **дарди пушт** [dardi pusht] back pain

пуштакӯҳ [pushtaküh] *n.* plateau

пушти [pushti] *prep.* behind

пуштнокӣ [pushtnoki] *adv.* backward, in reverse; **пуштнокӣ рафтан** [pushtnoki raftan] back up *(an automobile, etc.)*

пӯз [püz] *n.* snout, animal's nose

пӯзбанд [püzband] *n.* muzzle

пӯзиш [püzish] *n.* apology

пӯзиш хостан [püzish xostan] *v.i.* apologize

пӯка [püka] *n.* cork, plug

пӯлод [pülod] *n.* steel

пӯлодин [pülodin] *adj.* steel

пӯпанак [püpanak] *n.* fungus, mold

пӯписа [püpisa] *n.* menace, threat

пӯртахол [pürtaxol] *n.* orange

пӯсида [püsida] *adj.* rotten, septic

пӯсидан [püsidan] *v.i.* decay, rot

пӯсиш [püsish] *n.* decay

пӯст [püst] *n.* skin, peel, rind

пӯст кандан [püst kandan] *v.t.* peel

пӯчоқ [püchoq] *n.* rind, shell *(of nuts, seeds, etc.)*

пӯшидан [püshidan] *v.t.* wear / *v.i.* dress

пӯшок [püshok] *n.* clothing, apparel, garment, costume

пӯшоки расмӣ [püshoki rasmi] *n.* official clothing, uniform

пӯшоки таг [püshoki tag] *n.* underwear

пӯшоковезак [püshokovezak] *n.* hanger

пӯшонидан [püshonidan] *v.t.* close, shut; clothe, dress, cover

Р

рабудан [rabudan] *v.t.* kidnap, seize

равған [ravghan] *n.* grease, oil

равған kardan [ravghan kardan] *v.t.* grease

равған молидан [ravghan molidan] *v.t.* grease, oil

равғанin [ravghanin] *adj.* oily

равғани офтобпанаҳ [ravghani oftobpanah] *n.* sunscreen, suntan lotion

равғанин [ravghanin] *adj.* fatty

равғанӣ [ravghani] *adj.* oily

равғанмоҳӣ [ravghanmohi] *n.* cod

равия [raviya] *n.* trend

равиш [ravish] *n.* method, process

равнақ [ravnaq] *n.* prosperity
равнақ ёфтан [ravnaq yoftan] *v.i.* prosper, thrive
раводид [ravodid] *n.* visa
равоқ [ravoq] *n.* alcove
равон [ravon] *n.* spirit / *adj.* fluent / *adv.* fluently
равон шудан [ravon shudan] *v.i.* flow
равона кардан [ravona kardan] *v.t.* send
равона шудан [ravona shudan] *v.i.* depart
равонашавӣ [ravonashavi] *n.* departure
равонӣ [ravoni] *adj.* psychological
равоншинос [ravonshinos] *n.* psychologist
равоншиносӣ [ravonshinosi] *n.* psychology
равшан [ravshan] *adj.* bright; fair *(of hair or skin)*, light
равшан кардан [ravshan kardan] *v.t.* lighten in color, brighten
равшанӣ [ravshani] *n.* light
раг [rag] *n.* blood vessel
раг кандан [rag kandan] *v.t.* sprain
раги варид [ragi varid] *n.* vein
рагканӣ [ragkani] *n.* sprain
рад [rad] *n.* rejection
рад кардан [rad kardan] *v.t.* reject, decline, rebuff, refuse
раддия [raddiya] *n.* refusal
радикал [radikal] *n.* radical
радио [radio] *n.* radio
радиоактив [radioaktiv] *adj.* radioactive
радиошунавонӣ [radioshunavoni] *n.* radio transmission
ракета [raketa] *n.* missile, rocket; racket
рақам [raqam] *n.* number, figure
рақамномаи телефон [raqamnomai telefon] *n.* telephone directory
рақиб [raqib] *n./adj.* rival
рақобат [raqobat] *n.* rivalry, competition
рақобат кардан [raqobat kardan] *v.i.* contend
рақс [raqs] *n.* dance
рақсидан [raqsidan] *v.i.* dance
рама [rama] *n.* flock
рамз [ramz] *n.* code, symbol
рамзӣ [ramzi] *adj.* symbolic
ранг [rang] *n.* color, dye, paint
ранг кардан [rang kardan] *v.t.* dye, paint, tint
ранги обӣ [rangi obi] *n.* watercolor
рангинкамон [ranginkamon] *n.* rainbow
рангоранг [rangorang] *adj.* diverse
рангорангӣ [rangorangi] *n.* variety
рангпарида [rangparida] *adj.* pale
ранда кардан [randa kardan] *v.t.* chip
ранҷидан [ranjidan] *v.t.* resent
ранҷиш [ranjish] *n.* indignation
ранҷондан [ranjondan] *v.t.* afflict
расан [rasan] *n.* rope
расадхона [rasadxona] *n.* observatory
расвоӣ [rasvoi] *n.* scandal
расида [rasida] *adj.* ripe
расидагӣ [rasidagi] *n.* investigation
расидагӣ кардан [rasidagi kardan] *v.t.* investigate
расидан [rasidan] *v.t.* reach / *v.i.* arrive

расиш [rasish] *n.* growth, progress
расм [rasm] *n.* custom; drawing, illustration, painting
расм кашидан [rasm kashidan] *v.t.* draw, paint a picture
расмиятпараст [rasmiyatparast] *n.* bureaucrat
расмиятпарастӣ [rasmiyatparasti] *n.* bureaucracy
расмӣ [rasmi] *adj.* formal, official
расондан [rasondan] *v.t.* transmit, cause to go from one place to another
рассом [rassom] *n.* painter
рассомӣ [rassomi] *n.* painting *(artform)*
рассомӣ кардан [rassomi kardan] *v.i.* paint
растагорӣ [rastagori] *n.* salvation
растании баҳрӣ [rastanii bahri] *n.* seaweed
растанӣ [rastani] *n.* plant
раф [raf] *n.* shelf
рафак [rafak] *n.* console
рафиқ [rafiq] *n.* comrade, friend
рафт [raft] *n.* flow, process
рафтан [raftan] *v.i.* go
рафтор [raftor] *n.* bearing, behavior, conduct
рафтор кардан [raftor kardan] *v.i.* behave
рафтуомад [raftuomad] *n.* traffic
рах [rax] *n.* line, streak, stripe
рах-рах [rax-rax] *adj.* striped
рахдор [raxdor] *adj.* striped
рахна [raxna] *n.* breach
рахна кардан [raxna kardan] *v.t.* breach
раҳм [rahm] *n.* mercy
раҳмат гуфтан [rahmat guftan] *v.t.* thank
раҳмдил [rahmdil] *adj.* merciful
раҳмдилӣ [rahmdili] *n.* mercy
раҳо кардан [raho kardan] *v.t.* rescue, save
раҳоӣ [rahoi] *n.* release, deliverance, rescue
раҳокунанда [rahokunanda] *n.* savior
раҳонидан [rahonidan] *v.t.* release, rescue, save
раҳсипор шудан [rahsipor shudan] *v.i.* depart
раҳсипорӣ [rahsipori] *n.* departure
раъд [ra'd] *n.* thunder
рег [reg] *n.* sand
реза [reza] *n.* splinter / *adj.* minute
реза кардан [reza kardan] *v.t.* chop
резгӣ [rezgi] *n.* crumb
резина [rezina] *n.* rubber
резиш [rezish] *n.* spill
резондан [rezondan] *v.t.* spill
реклама [reklama] *v.* reclaim
рекорд [rekord] *n.* record *(sports, world, etc.)*
рентген [rentgen] *n.* X-ray
ресидан [residan] *v.t.* spin *(thread, etc.)*
ресмон [resmon] *n.* thread
респиратор [respirator] *n.* respirator
ресторан [restoran] *n.* restaurant
ретсепт [retsept] *n.* recipe
рехта шудан [rexta shudan] *v.i.* spill
рехтан [rextan] *v.t.* leak, pour, shed *(blood, tears, etc.)*, spill / *v.i.* pour, spill

реш [resh] *n.* injury, sore
реша [resha] *n.* root
ривоҷ додан [rivoj dodan] *v.t.* develop *(industry, resources, etc.)*
рикоб [rikob] *n.* stirrup
риққатовар [riqqatovar] *adj.* pathetic, touching
рим [rim] *n.* pus
рисола [risola] *n.* thesis
риоя кардан [rioya kardan] *v.i.* comply with, adhere to *(rules, etc.)*
рихинак [rixinak] *n.* acne, pimple
риш [rish] *n.* beard
ришва [rishva] *n.* bribe
ришва додан [rishva dodan] *v.t.* bribe
ришватхӯр [rishvatxür] *adj.* corrupt
ришгирак [rishgirak] *n.* razor
ришта [rishta] *n.* tie, bond
риштан [rishtan] *v.t.* spin *(thread, etc.)*
риштарошак [rishtaroshak] *n.* razor
робита [robita] *n.* association, relationship
робот [robot] *n.* robot
роғи садопардаҳо [roghi sadopardaho] *n.* glottis
роз [roz] *n.* mystery, secret
розӣ [rozi] *adj.* content, willing
розигӣ [rozigi] *n.* consent
розигӣ додан [rozigi dodan] *v.t.* consent
рол [rol] *n.* role *(theatrical)*
ром [rom] *n.* rum / *adj.* tame
ром кардан [rom kardan] *v.t.* tame
роман [roman] *n.* novel
рон [ron] *n.* thigh
ронанда [ronanda] *n.* driver; **гувоҳномаи ронандагӣ** [guvohnomai ronandagi] driver's license
ронда шудан [ronda shudan] *v.i.* steer
рондан [rondan] *v.t.* drive, propel, steer
рост [rost] *adj.* candid, true, direct; right *(opp. of left)*; straight / *adv.* direct
рост мондан [rost mondan] *v.t.* stand
рост омадан [rost omadan] *v.i.* coincide
ростадаст [rostadast] *adj.* right-handed
ростгӯй [rostgüy] *adj.* candid, truthful
ростӣ [rosti] *n.* truth
росткарда [rostkarda] *adj.* erect
росткунҷа [rostkunja] *n.* rectangle / *adj.* rectangular
ростфуромада [rostfuromada] *adj.* steep
роҳ [roh] *n.* road, way; canal *(anat.)*
роҳ надодан [roh nadodan] *v.t.* exclude
роҳ намудан [roh namudan] *v.t.* guide
роҳ рафтан [roh raftan] *v.i.* walk
роҳат [rohat] *adj.* casual / *n.* comfort, convenience
роҳбар [rohbar] *n.* leader, sports team captain
роҳбарӣ [rohbari] *n.* leadership
роҳбарӣ кардан [rohbari kardan] *v.t.* direct, lead, provide leadership
роҳгузар [rohguzar] *n.* passerby

роҳзан [rohzan] *n.* highway robber
роҳзанӣ кардан [rohzani kardan] *v.t.* commit highway robbery
роҳи асосӣ [rohi asosi] *n.* artery *(roadway)*
роҳи оҳан [rohi ohan] *n.* railroad, railway
роҳи ҳавоӣ [rohi havoi] *n.* airline
роҳиб [rohib] *n.* monk
роҳиба [rohiba] *n.* nun
роҳнамо [rohnamo] *n.* guide, guidebook
роҳнамоӣ кардан [rohnamoi kardan] *v.t.* guide, lead
роҳпаймоӣ [rohpaymoi] *n.* parade
роҳрав [rohrav] *n.* aisle, corridor, hallway
роҳхат [rohxat] *n.* permit, pass
рус [rus] *n.* Russian
русӣ [rusi] *n.* Russian *(language)* / *adj.* Russian
рустоӣ [rustoi] *adj.* rustic
рутба [rutba] *n.* position, rank
рухсат додан [ruxsat dodan] *v.t.* dismiss
рухсатӣ [ruxsati] *n.* vacation, holiday
рухсор [ruxsor] *n.* cheek
руҳ [ruh] *n.* zinc
ручка [ruchka] *n.* pen
рӯбоҳ [rüboh] *n.* fox
рӯд [rüd] *n.* river
рӯда [rüda] *n.* intestine; hose
рӯёндан [rüyondan] *v.t.* cultivate, grow
рӯз [rüz] *n.* day
рӯзи кор [rüzi kor] *n.* weekday, workday
рӯзмарра [rüzmarra] *adj.* ordinary
рӯзнома [rüznoma] *n.* newspaper
рӯзномаи маҷлис [rüznomai majlis] *n.* agenda
рӯзноманигор [rüznomanigor] *n.* journalist, reporter
рӯзноманигорӣ кардан [rüznomanigori kardan] *v.i.* report
рӯзона [rüzona] *adj.* daily
рӯзҳои дамгирӣ [rüzhoi damgiri] *n.* weekend
рӯидан [rüidan] *v.i.* grow *(plants)*
рӯй [rüy] *n.* face
рӯй додан [rüy dodan] *v.i.* happen, occur
рӯй турш кардан [rüy tursh kardan] *v.i.* frown
рӯйдод [rüydod] *n.* event, occurrence
рӯйи [rüyi] *prep.* on, upon
рӯйхат [rüyxat] *n.* directory, list, registry
рӯйхат кардан [rüyxat kardan] *v.t.* register
рӯнавискунанда [rünaviskunanda] *n.* typist
рӯфтан [rüftan] *v.t.* sweep
рӯҳ [rüh] *n.* soul, spirit
рӯҳӣ [rühi] *adj.* psychological
рӯҳонӣ [rühoni] *adj.* spiritual
рӯҳшинос [rühshinos] *n.* psychologist
рӯҳшиносӣ [rühshinosi] *n.* psychology
рӯъё [rü'yo] *n.* manifestation, vision
рӯякӣ [rüyaki] *adj.* shallow, superficial

С

сабаб [sabab] *n.* cause, motivation, reason
сабаб шудан [sabab shudan] *v.t.* cause

сабад [sabad] *n.* basket
сабз [sabz] *adj.* green
сабза [sabza] *n.* grass
сабзавот [sabzavot] *n.* vegetable
сабзидан [sabzidan] *v.i.* grow *(plants)*, sprout
сабзиш [sabzish] *n.* growth *(of plants)*
сабк [sabk] *n.* style
сабр [sabr] *n.* patience
сабт кардан [sabt kardan] *v.t.* tape, record on tape
сабук [sabuk] *n.* light *(not heavy)*
сабук кардан [sabuk kardan] *v.t.* relieve
сабукӣ [sabuki] *n.* relief
сабуктар кардан [sabuktar kardan] *v.t.* make less heavy, lighten
савганд [savgand] *n.* oath, vow
савганд хӯрдан [savgand xürdan] *v.t.* take an oath, swear, vow
савғотӣ [savghoti] *n.* souvenir
савдо [savdo] *n.* commerce, trade
савдо кардан [savdo kardan] *v.i.* trade, traffic
савдогар [savdogar] *n.* merchant, trader
савқи табиӣ [savqi tabii] *n.* instinct
савол [savol] *n.* question
савор [savor] *n.* rider
савор кардан [savor kardan] *v.t.* mount, get on, ride
савор шудан [savor shudan] *v.i.* mount, get on, ride
саворӣ [savori] *n.* ride, riding
савсан [savsan] *n.* iris *(flower)*
саг [sag] *n.* dog
сагбача [sagbacha] *n.* puppy
сагхона [sagxona] *n.* kennel
сағир [saghir] *n.* orphan
сағона [saghona] *n.* shrine
сад [sad] *num.* hundred / *n.* obstacle
садақа [sadaqa] *n.* donation
садақа додан [sadaqa dodan] *v.t.* donate
садама [sadama] *n.* collision; shock, trauma
садафак [sadafak] *n.* oyster
садбарг [sadbarg] *n.* rose
садд [sadd] *n.* barrier; **аз садди садо гузаштан** [az saddi sado guzashtan] break the sound barrier
садо [sado] *n.* sound, voice
садо додан [sado dodan] *v.i.* sound
садонишонак [sadonishonak] *n.* muffler *(car/mechanical part)*
садонок [sadonok] *n.* vowel
садсола [sadsola] *n.* century
садум [sadum] *adj.* hundredth
саёҳат [sayohat] *n.* tourism
сазо [sazo] *n.* penalty, punishment
сазо додан [sazo dodan] *v.t.* punish
сазовор будан [sazovor budan] *v.t.* deserve
сайёра [sayyora] *n.* planet
сайёҳ [sayyoh] *n.* tourist
сайри чорбоғ [sayri chorbogh] *n.* picnic
сакта [sakta] *n.* stroke *(med.)*
сақич [saqich] *n.* chewing gum
сал [sal] *n.* raft
салат [salat] *n.* salad
салиб [salib] *n.* cross
салиқа [saliqa] *n.* sense of style, taste
салқин [salqin] *adj.* cool
салом [salom] *n.* greeting, hello

салом додан [salom dodan] *v.t.* greet
салронӣ [salroni] *n.* rafting
салют [salyut] *n.* salute
салют додан [salyut dodan] *v.t.* salute
самимият [samimiyat] *n.* sincerity
самимӣ [samimi] *adj.* sincere
самимона [samimona] *adv.* cordially
санавбар [sanavbar] *n.* pine
санад [sanad] *n.* document, deed
санбӯса [sanbüsa] *n.* meat pie
санг [sang] *n.* stone
сангдил [sangdil] *adj.* merciless
санги заҳрадон [sangi zahradon] *n.* gallstone
сангин [sangin] *adj.* heavy; stone
сангӣ [sangi] *adj.* stone
сангпушт [sangpusht] *n.* turtle
сангреза [sangreza] *n.* gravel
сангшуда [sangshuda] *adj.* fossilized
сандуқ [sanduq] *n.* trunk, large box, chest, crate
сандуқдор [sanduqdor] *n.* cashier
санитарӣ [sanitari] *adj.* sanitary
саноат [sanoat] *n.* industry
саноатӣ [sanoati] *adj.* industrial
сантиметр [santimetr] *n.* centimeter
санҷидан [sanjidan] *v.t.* gauge, sample, test, evaluate; weigh
санҷиш [sanjish] *n.* test
санҷоб [sanjob] *n.* squirrel
санъат [san'at] *n.* art
санъатӣ [san'ati] *adj.* artistic
санъаткор [san'atkor] *n.* artist
сапедадам [sapedadam] *n.* dawn
сар [sar] *n.* head
сар додан [sar dodan] *v.t.* launch
сар кардан [sar kardan] *v.t.* begin, start, embark
сар то сари [sar to sari] *prep.* across, throughout
сар шудан [sar shudan] *v.i.* begin, commence, start
сарангушт [sarangusht] *n.* thumb
саратон [saraton] *n.* cancer
сарбаланд [sarbaland] *adj.* proud
сарбоз [sarboz] *n.* soldier
сарбозгирӣ кардан [sarbozgiri kardan] *v.t.* recruit *(mil.)*
сарбозхона [sarbozxona] *n.* barrack
сарв [sarv] *n.* cypress
саргардон будан [sargardon budan] *v.i.* wander aimlessly
саргарм кардан [sargarm kardan] *v.t.* entertain
саргармӣ [sargarmi] *n.* pastime
саргармкунанда [sargarmkunanda] *adj.* entertaining
саргармкунӣ [sargarmkuni] *n.* entertainment
саргин [sargin] *n.* dung
саргузашт [sarguzasht] *n.* adventure
сард [sard] *adj.* cold, chilly
сардӣ [sardi] *n.* cold
сард кардан [sard kardan] *v.t.* cool
сардаста [sardasta] *n.* sports team captain

сардина [sardina] *n.* sardine
сардор [sardor] *n.* chief
сардори киштӣ [sardori kishti] *n.* ship captain
сардорӣ кардан [sardori kardan] *v.t.* head
сарзамин [sarzamin] *n.* territory, land
сарзаниш [sarzanish] *n.* reprimand
сарзаниш кардан [sarzanish kardan] *v.t.* reprimand, scold
сари [sari] *prep.* on
саркашӣ кардан [sarkashi kardan] *v.t.* disobey
саркор [sarkor] *n.* boss
сарқонун [sarqonun] *n.* constitution
сарлавҳа [sarlavha] *n.* heading, headline, title
сарлавҳаи зер [sarlavhai zer] *n.* subtitle
сармо [sarmo] *n.* chill, frost
сармоя [sarmoya] *n.* financial capital, funds
сармоя гузоштан [sarmoya guzoshtan] *v.t.* fund, invest
сармоягузорӣ [sarmoyaguzori] *n.* investment
сарнавишт [sarnavisht] *n.* destiny
сароб [sarob] *n.* mirage
саросар [sarosar] *adv.* throughout
саросема кардан [sarosema kardan] *v.t.* confuse, throw off
саросемагӣ [sarosemagi] *n.* confusion
саростин [sarostin] *n.* cuff
сароянда [saroyanda] *n.* singer
сарпанох [sarpanoh] *n.* shelter
сарпӯш [sarpüsh] *n.* lid, top
сарпӯшак [sarpüshak] *n.* valve *(mechanical)*
сарсупурдагӣ [sarsupurdagi] *n.* devotion, dedication
сарсухан [sarsuxan] *n.* introduction
сартарош [sartarosh] *n.* barber, hairdresser
сартарошхона [sartaroshxona] *n.* barbershop
сарф [sarf] *n.* consumption, expense
сарф кардан [sarf kardan] *v.t.* consume, spend
сарфаҷӯӣ [sarfajüi] *n.* thrift
сарфаҷӯй [sarfajüy] *adj.* thrifty
сарфкунанда [sarfkunanda] *n.* consumer
сарҳад [sarhad] *n.* border, frontier
сарҳанг [sarhang] *n.* colonel
сарҳарф [sarharf] *n.* capital letter
сарчархзанӣ [sarcharxzani] *n.* dizziness
сарчашма [sarchashma] *n.* source
сарҷӯш [sarjüsh] *n.* sauce
саршир [sarshir] *n.* cream *(dairy product)*
саръ [sar'] *n.* epilepsy
сатил [satil] *n.* bucket, pail
сатҳ [sath] *n.* level, surface
саф [saf] *n.* line, column
саф кашондан [saf kashondan] *v.t.* line up
сафар [safar] *n.* journey, travel, tour
сафар кардан [safar kardan] *v.t.* tour / *v.i.* journey, travel
сафед [safed] *adj.* white
сафед кардан [safed kardan] *v.t.* justify; whiten

сафеда [safeda] *n.* protein
сафедкунӣ [safedkuni] *n.* justification
сафир [safir] *n.* ambassador
сафол [safol] *n.* tile
сафолӣ [safoli] *n./adj.* ceramic
сафорат [saforat] *n.* diplomatic mission
сафоратхона [saforatxona] *n.* embassy
сафсата [safsata] *n.* chatter
сафҳаи калид [safhai kalid] *n.* keyboard
сафҳаи намоиш [safhai namoish] *n.* computer monitor, computer screen
сахарин [saxarin] *n.* saccharine
сахӣ [saxi] *adj.* generous, lavish
сахт [saxt] *adj.* firm, hard, solid, rigid, stiff; harsh, tough, severe; violent
сахт кардан [saxt kardan] *v.t.* toughen
сахт шудан [saxt shudan] *v.i.* harden
сахтгир [saxtgir] *adj.* stern
сахтӣ [saxti] *n.* hardship, toughness; violence
саҳар [sahar] *n.* dawn
саҳеҳ [saheh] *adj.* authentic
саҳифа [sahifa] *n.* page
саҳм [sahm] *n.* stock market share, stock, quota
саҳмдор [sahmdor] *n.* shareholder, stockholder
саҳна [sahna] *n.* stage
сачоқ [sachoq] *n.* napkin
саъба [ca'ba] *n.* robin
свитер [sviter] *n.* sweater
се [se] *num.* three
себ [seb] *n.* apple
сездаҳ [sezdah] *n.* thirteen
сездаҳум [sezdahum] *adj.* thirteenth
сейф [seyf] *n.* safe
секунҷа [sekunja] *n.* triangle / *adj.* triangular
сел [sel] *n.* flood
селоб [selob] *n.* flood
селоба [seloba] *n.* torrent
семестр [semestr] *n.* semester, term
сенат [senat] *n.* senate
сенатор [senator] *n.* senator
септикӣ [septiki] *adj.* septic
серамал [seramal] *adj.* dynamic
серборон [serboron] *adj.* rainy
сергап [sergap] *adj.* talkative
серғавғо [serghavgho] *adj.* noisy
сержант [serzhant] *n.* sergeant
серкор [serkor] *adj.* busy
серкӯшиш [serküshish] *adj.* diligent
сермушак [sermushak] *adj.* muscular
сермӯй [sermüy] *adj.* hairy, shaggy
серпашм [serpashm] *adj.* shaggy
серравған [serravghan] *adj.* fatty
серсоя [sersoya] *adj.* shady
сертеппа [serteppa] *adj.* hilly
серун кардан [serun kardan] *v.t.* renew
серхарсанг [serxarsang] *adj.* rocky
серҳаракат [serharakat] *adj.* energetic
сершавшув [sershavshuv] *adj.* noisy
сершамол [sershamol] *adj.* windy
сершумор [sershumor] *adj.* numerous

сершух [sershux] *adj.* rocky
сесанбар [sesanbar] *n.* thyme
сечарха [secharxa] *n.* tricycle
сешанбе [seshanbe] *n.* Tuesday
сеюм [seyum] *adj.* third
сигара [sigara] *n.* cigar
сигарет [sigaret] *n.* cigarette
сигор [sigor] *n.* cigarette
сигор кашидан [sigor kashidan] *v.t.* smoke
сиёсат [siyosat] *n.* politics
сиёсатмадор [siyosatmador] *n.* politician
сиёсӣ [siyosi] *adj.* political
сиёҳ [siyoh] *adj.* black
сиёҳӣ [siyohi] *n.* ink; nightmare
сиёҳраг [siyohrag] *n.* vein
сикка [sikka] *n.* coin
сикка задан [sikka zadan] *v.t.* impress *(a design on metal, coins, etc.)*
сила кардан [sila kardan] *v.t.* caress, stroke
силиқ [siliq] *adj.* sleek
силсила [silsila] *n.pl.* series
сим [sim] *n.* silver; wire
симон [simon] *n.* cement
сим-сим боридан [sim-sim boridan] *v.i.* drizzle
симчӯб [simchüb] *n.* telephone/telegraph pole
син [sin] *n.* age *(stage in life)*
сина [sina] *n.* chest *(anat.)*
синамо [sinamo] *n.* cinema, movie
синтетикӣ [sintetiki] *adj.* synthetic
синф [sinf] *n.* class, classroom
синҷи киштӣ [sinji kishti] *n.* keel
сипар [sipar] *n.* shield
сипас [sipas] *adv.* next, after, afterward
сипор [sipor] *n.* plow
сипос [sipos] *n.pl.* thanks
сипосгузор [siposguzor] *adj.* grateful, thankful
сипосгузорӣ [siposguzori] *n.* gratitude, thankfulness / *n.pl.* thanks
сипосгузорӣ кардан [siposguzori kardan] *v.t.* thank
сир [sir] *n.* enamel *(anat.)*; garlic; mystery, secret; **сири дандон** [siri dandon] tooth enamel
сириштан [sirishtan] *v.t.* knead
сирк [sirk] *n.* circus
сирко [sirko] *n.* vinegar
сирояткунанда [siroyatkunanda] *adj.* contagious, infectious
система [sistema] *n.* system
ситам [sitam] *n.* oppression
ситам кардан [sitam kardan] *v.t.* oppress
ситамкунанда [sitamkunanda] *adj.* oppressive
ситеғ [sitegh] *n.* summit, peak
ситоиш [sitoish] *n.* praise
ситоиш кардан [sitoish kardan] *v.t.* praise
ситора [sitora] *n.* star
ситораи баҳрӣ [sitorai bahri] *n.* starfish
ситорашинос [sitorashinos] *n.* astronomer
ситорашиносӣ [sitorashinosi] *n.* astronomy
сифат [sifat] *n.* merit, qualification; *gram.* adjective
сифр [sifr] *num.* zero
сиҳат [sihat] *adj.* healthy
сиҳат шудан [sihat shudan] *v.i.* heal, recuperate

сиҳатӣ [sihati] *n.* health
сӣ [si] *num.* thirty
скандинав [skandinav] *n.* Scandinavian
скандинавӣ [skandinavi] *adj.* Scandinavian
сквош [skvosh] *n.* squash *(sport)*
скрипка [skripka] *n.* violin
смог [smog] *n.* smog
соат [soat] *n.* clock, watch, hour
соати [soati] *adv.* o'clock
соати дастӣ [soati dasti] *n.* wristwatch
соати зангдор [soati zangdor] *n.* alarm clock
собун [sobun] *n.* soap; **кулчаи собун** [kulchai sobun] bar of soap
собун задан [sobun zadan] *v.t.* soap
сода [soda] *n.* soda
содда [sodda] *adj.* naïve, plain, simple
соддадил [soddadil] *adj.* naïve
содирот [sodirot] *n.* export
содирот кардан [sodirot kardan] *v.t.* export
соз кардан [soz kardan] *v.t.* fit, tune
созгор кардан [sozgor kardan] *v.t.* adapt
созгор шудан [sozgor shudan] *v.i.* adapt
созиш [sozish] *n.* agreement *(contract)*, compromise
Созмони милали муттаҳид [Sozmoni milali muttahid] *n.* United Nations
соид [soid] *n.* forearm
соидан [soidan] *v.t.* wear away
сой [soy] *n.* ravine
сок [sok] *n.* juice
сокин [sokin] *n.* inhabitant, resident
сокин будан [sokin budan] *v.i.* dwell, inhabit
соқ [soq] *n.* calf *(anat.)*
сол [sol] *n.* year; age *(stage in life)*
солгард [solgard] *n.* anniversary
соли кабиса [soli kabisa] *n.* leap year
солнома [solnoma] *n.* calendar
солона [solona] *adj.* annual, yearly
солхӯрда [solxürda] *adj.* elderly
сомонаи интернетӣ [somonai interneti] *n.* website
сон [son] *n.* hip
сония [soniya] *n.* second
сотсиализм [sotsializm] *n.* socialism
сотсиалист [sotsialist] *n.* socialist
сотсиалистӣ [sotsialisti] *adj.* socialist
соф [sof] *adj.* clear
соф кардан [sof kardan] *v.t.* clear
софдил [sofdil] *adj.* honest
софӣ кардан [sofi kardan] *v.t.* strain, filter
сохт [soxt] *n.* manufacture, structure
сохта [soxta] *adj.* artificial, counterfeit, false
сохтагӣ [soxtagi] *adj.* artificial, counterfeit, false
сохтакорӣ кардан [soxtakori kardan] *v.t.* falsify, simulate
сохтан [soxtan] *v.t.* erect, form, make, manufacture

сохтмон [soxtmon] *n.* structure, building
соҳа [soha] *n.* topic, subject, domain
соҳиб [sohib] *n.* owner, master, proprietor
соҳиб будан [sohib budan] *v.t.* own, possess
соҳибистиқлол [sohibistiqlol] *adj.* sovereign
соҳибӣ [sohibi] *adj.* possessive
соҳибкор [sohibkor] *n.* principal
соҳибхоназан [sohibxonazan] *n.* housewife
соҳил [sohil] *n.* coast, shore
соҳира [sohira] *n.* witch
соя [soya] *n.* shadow, shade, soy
соябон [soyabon] *n.* parasol
соягоҳ [soyagoh] *n.* shade, place of shadow
сосядор [soyador] *adj.* shady
СПИД [SPID] *n.* AIDS
спирт [spirt] *n.* alcohol, spirits
спиртдор [spirtdor] *adj.* alcoholic *(containing alcohol)*; **нӯшокии спиртдор** [nüshokii spirtdor] alcoholic drink
спорт [sport] *n.* sport
стадион [stadion] *n.* stadium
стандарт [standart] *n.* standard
стандартӣ [standarti] *adj.* standard
статистика [statistika] *n.* statistics
статистикӣ [statistiki] *adj.* statistical
стетоскоп [stetoskop] *n.* stethoscope
стипендия [stipendiya] *n.* scholarship, stipend
стюард [styuard] *n.* steward
стюардесса [styuardessa] *n.* stewardess
суботкор [subotkor] *adj.* tenacious
субҳ [subh] *n.* morning
суғурта [sughurta] *n.* insurance
суғурта кардан [sughurta kardan] *v.t.* insure
суд [sud] *n.* court of law, trial in court; gain, profit
суд бурдан [sud burdan] *v.i.* gain, profit
суд кардан [sud kardan] *v.t.* judge, try in court
судманд [sudmand] *adj.* profitable, helpful
сужет [suzhet] *n.* storyline, plot
суиқасд [suiqasd] *n.* attempt *(on someone, i.e. assassination, etc.)*; plot *(political, etc.)*
суккон [sukkon] *n.* rudder
сулҳ [sulh] *n.* peace
сулҳдӯст [sulhdüst] *adj.* peace-loving
сум [sum] *n.* hoof
сумка [sumka] *n.* handbag
сунъати дастӣ [sun'ati dasti] *n.* handicraft
сунъӣ [sun'i] *adj.* artificial
суп-сурх [sup-surx] *adj.* bright red
супермаркет [supermarket] *n.* supermarket
супориш [suporish] *n.* mission
супурдан [supurdan] *v.t.* allot, assign *(a job, homework, etc.)*; entrust; surrender, yield
сурат [surat] *n.* illustration, picture, photograph, portrait

сурат гирифтан [surat giriftan] *v.t.* photograph, take a picture
суратгир [suratgir] *n.* photographer
суратгирак [suratgirak] *n.* camera
суратгирӣ [suratgiri] *n.* photography
суратдор кардан [suratdor kardan] *v.t.* illustrate *(a book, etc.)*
сурб [surb] *n.* lead
сурин [surin] *n.pl.* buttocks
сурма [surma] *n.* eyeliner
суроға [surogha] *n.* address
суруд [surud] *n.* song
сурудан [surudan] *v.t./v.i.* sing
сурудхонӣ [surudxoni] *n.* singing
сурфа [surfa] *n.* cough
сурфидан [surfidan] *v.i.* cough
сурх [surx] *adj.* red
сурх шудан [surx shudan] *v.i.* blush
сурхак [surxak] *adj.* reddish
сурхӣ [surxi] *n.* redness, rouge
сурхраг [surxrag] *n.* artery *(anat.)*
сурхтоб [surxtob] *adj.* reddish
суръат [sur'at] *n.* frequency, speed
суръат додан [sur'at dodan] *v.t.* accelerate
суръатсанҷ [sur'atsanj] *n.* speedometer
суръатфизо [sur'atfizo] *n.* accelerator
суст [sust] *adj.* weak, passive, sluggish, slack
суст кардан [sust kardan] *v.t.* loosen, relax, slacken, slow, weaken
суст шудан [sust shudan] *v.i.* untense, relax, slow
сустӣ [susti] *n.* weakness
сусттар кардан [susttar kardan] *v.t.* loosen
сутун [sutun] *n.* pillar, column
сутуни киштӣ [sutuni kishti] *n.* mast
сутунмӯҳра [sutunmühra] *n.* spine, backbone
суфрамоҳӣ [suframohi] *n.* skate, ray *(type of fish)*
суфта [sufta] *adj.* smooth
сухан [suxan] *n.* faculty of speech, word
суханвар [suxanvar] *n.* speaker
сухангарӣ кардан [suxangari kardan] *v.t.* recite
суханронӣ [suxanroni] *n.* speech, oration
суханчин [suxanchin] *n.* gossip *(person)*
суханчинӣ [suxanchini] *n.* gossip
суханчинӣ кардан [suxanchini kardan] *v.i.* gossip
суҳбат [suhbat] *n.* talk
сӯ [sü] *n.* direction, side
сӯгворӣ [sügvori] *n.* mourning
сӯгворӣ кардан [sügvori kardan] *v.t./v.i.* mourn
сӯзан [süzan] *n.* needle
сӯзанак [süzanak] *n.* pin
сӯзишворӣ [süzishvori] *n.* fuel
сӯи [süi] *prep.* toward, towards
сӯй [süy] *n.* direction, side
сӯлуқ [süluq] *n.* bit *(of a bridle)*
сӯрох [sürox] *n.* hole, leak, puncture, slot
сӯрох кардан [sürox kardan] *v.t.* pierce
сӯрохи бинӣ [süroxi bini] *n.* nostril

сӯрохи қуфл [süroxi qufl] *n.* keyhole
сӯҳон [sühon] *n.* file *(steel tool)*
сӯҳон кардан [sühon kardan] *v.t.* file

Т

тааҷҷуб [taajjub] *n.* astonishment, amazement, surprise, wonder
тааҷҷуб кардан [taajjub kardan] *v.i.* wonder
тааҷҷубовар [taajjubovar] *adj.* marvelous, wonderful
таб [tab] *n.* fever
табақ [tabaq] *n.* serving plate
табақча [tabaqcha] *n.* small plate
табар [tabar] *n.* ax
табассум [tabassum] *n.* smile
табассум кардан [tabassum kardan] *v.i.* smile
табиат [tabiat] *n.* temperament, temper
табиатан [tabiatan] *adv.* naturally
табиӣ [tabii] *adj.* natural, organic
таблак [tablak] *n.* drum
таблиғот [tablighot] *n.* propaganda
табрик [tabrik] *n.* congratulations
табрик кардан [tabrik kardan] *v.t.* congratulate
табъид [tab'id] *n.* ostracism
табъиз кардан [tab'iz kardan] *v.i.* discriminate
таваққуф [tavaqquf] *n.* halt, pause
таваққуф кардан [tavaqquf kardan] *v.t.* halt, stop, pause
таваққуф шудан [tavaqquf shudan] *v.i.* pause
таваллуд [tavallud] *n.* birth
таваррум [tavarrum] *n.* inflation
таваҷҷӯҳ [tavajjüh] *n.* attention
тавба кардан [tavba kardan] *v.i.* repent
тавлид кардан [tavlid kardan] *v.t.* generate, produce
тавонистан [tavonistan] *v.i.* be able; *aux.* can
тавоно [tavono] *adj.* able, capable, powerful
тавоноӣ [tavonoi] *n.* ability, power
тавора [tavora] *n.* fence
тавсиф [tavsif] *n.* description
тавсиф кардан [tavsif kardan] *v.t.* describe
тавсия [tavsiya] *n.* recommendation
тавсия кардан [tavsiya kardan] *v.t.* recommend
тавсиянома [tavsiyanoma] *n.* letter of reference
таг [tag] *n.* bottom, sole of a shoe / *adv.* under
тагарг [tagarg] *n.* hail
таги [tagi] *prep.* beneath, under
тагу рӯ кардан [tagu rü kardan] *v.t.* shuffle, stir
тағйир [taghyir] *n.* change, variation
тағйир додан [taghyir dodan] *v.t.* modify, vary
тағйирёбанда [taghyiryobanda] *adj.* variable
тағйирёбӣ [taghyiryobi] *n.* modification
тағйир ёфтан [taghyir yoftan] *v.i.* vary
тағо [tagho] *n.* maternal uncle

тағобача [taghobacha] *n.* cousin *(maternal uncle's son)*
тағора [taghora] *n.* basin
тағояк [taghoyak] *n.* cartilage
тадқиқ кардан [tadqiq kardan] *v.t.* explore
тадриҷӣ [tadriji] *adj.* gradual
таёқ [tayoq] *n.* cudgel, club
тазарв [tazarv] *n.* pheasant
тазоҳур [tazohur] *n.* demonstration, public rally
тазриқ [tazriq] *n.* injection
тазриқ кардан [tazriq kardan] *v.t.* inject
тайёр [tayyor] *adj.* ready
тайёр кардан [tayyor kardan] *v.t.* make, prepare
тайёр шудан [tayyor shudan] *v.i.* prepare
тайёрӣ [tayyori] *n.* preparation
такаббур [takabbur] *n.* arrogance
таклиф [taklif] *n.* invitation, offer
таклиф кардан [taklif kardan] *v.t.* invite, offer
таклифнома [taklifnoma] *n.* invitation card
такмил [takmil] *n.* supplement
такон [takon] *n.* jerk, jolt, shock
такондан [takondan] *v.t.* jerk, shake, shock
такрор [takror] *n.* recurrence, relapse, repetition, repeat
такроршавӣ [takrorshavi] *n.* relapse, repeat *(of an action or occurrence)*
таксӣ [taksi] *n.* taxi
тактик [taktik] *n.* tactic
такя [takya] *n.* support, prop
такя кардан [takya kardan] *v.i.* lean
такя кунондан [takya kunondan] *v.t.* lean
тақ-тақ [taq-taq] *n.* knock
тақ-тақ кардан [taq-taq kardan] *v.t./v.i.* knock
тақвим [taqvim] *n.* calendar
тақвият [taqviyat] *n.* corroboration, support
тақвият додан [taqviyat dodan] *v.t.* strengthen, support, corroborate
тақдим кардан [taqdim kardan] *v.t.* present
тақлид [taqlid] *n.* imitation
тақлид кардан [taqlid kardan] *v.t.* imitate, copy
таққӣ задан [taqqi zadan] *v.t.* crash
тақозо [taqozo] *n.* demand
тақозо кардан [taqozo kardan] *v.t.* demand
тақрибан [taqriban] *adv.* about, almost, practically, approximately / *prep.* about,
тақрибӣ [taqribi] *adj.* approximate
тақсим кардан [taqsim kardan] *v.t.* distribute, share, divide
тақсимича [taqsimicha] *n.* saucer
тақсимкунӣ [taqsimkuni] *n.* partition
тақсимот [taqsimot] *n.* distribution
тақсимшавӣ [taqsimshavi] *n.* division
тақсир [taqsir] *n.* fault
тақтир кардан [taqtir kardan] *v.t.* distill
талаба [talaba] *n.* pupil, student
талаф кардан [talaf kardan] *v.t.* waste
талафкор [talafkor] *adj.* wasteful
талаффуз [talaffuz] *n.* pronunciation

талаффуз кардан [talaffuz kardan] *v.t.* pronounce
талқ [talq] *n.* talc, talcum powder
талқин кардан [talqin kardan] *v.t.* instill, inculcate
талоқ [taloq] *n.* divorce
талоқ гирифтан [taloq giriftan] *v.i.* divorce; **Талоқ гирифтанд.** [Taloq giriftand.] They got a divorce.
талоқ додан [taloq dodan] *v.t.* divorce
талофӣ [talofi] *n.* recompense, reimbursement
талофӣ додан [talofi dodan] *v.t.* recompense, reimburse
талош [talosh] *n.* struggle
талош кардан [talosh kardan] *v.i.* struggle
талх [talx] *adj.* bitter
талхшуда [talxshuda] *adj.* rancid
тамаддун [tamaddun] *n.* civilization
тамашк [tamashk] *n.* raspberry
тамбр [tambr] *n.* postage stamp
тамға [tamgha] *n.* emblem, mark, seal
тамғакоғаз [tamghakoghaz] *n.* tag
тамоку [tamoku] *n.* tobacco
тамом [tamom] *adj.* utter, total, whole
тамом кардан [tamom kardan] *v.t.* finish, use up / *v.i.* graduate
тамоман [tamoman] *adv.* completely, totally
тамомшуда [tamomshuda] *adj.* exhausted *(finished, completed in terms of money, resources, etc.)*
тамос [tamos] *n.* contact
тамос гирифтан [tamos giriftan] *v.t.* contact
тамошо [tamosho] *n.* show
тамошо кардан [tamosho kardan] *v.t.* observe, watch
тамошобин [tamoshobin] *n.* spectator
тамсила [tamsila] *n.* model
тамъиз кардан [tam'iz kardan] *v.t.* disinfect, sterilize
тамъизшуда [tam'izshuda] *adj.* disinfected, sterilized
тан [tan] *n.* body
тан додан [tan dodan] *v.i.* submit, surrender
тана [tana] *n.* stem
таназзул [tanazzul] *n.* decline, depression *(economic)*
таназзул кардан [tanazzul kardan] *v.i.* decline
танаи ҳавопаймо [tanai havopaimo] *n.* fuselage
танаффус [tanaffus] *n.* break; **танаффуси қаҳванӯшӣ** [tanaffusi qahvanüshi] coffee break
танбал [tanbal] *adj.* lazy
танбалӣ [tanbali] *n.* laziness, sloth
танг [tang] *adj.* narrow, tight
танг кардан [tang kardan] *v.t.* tighten
танг шудан [tang shudan] *v.i.* tighten
танга [tanga] *n.* coin
тангкӯча [tangkücha] *n.* alley, lane
тангназар [tangnazar] *adj.* narrow-minded
тандуруст [tandurust] *adj.* healthy, well
тандурустӣ [tandurusti] *n.* physical fitness, health
танзим [tanzim] *n.* regulation

танк [tank] *n.* tank
танқид [tanqid] *n.* criticism
танқид кардан [tanqid kardan] *v.t.* criticize
тановул [tanovul] *n.* meal
таносуб [tanosub] *n.* symmetry
таносулӣ [tanosuli] *adj.* genital
тануманд [tanumand] *adj.* stout
танӯр [tanür] *n.* oven
танӯра [tanüra] *n.* crater
танфурӯш [tanfurüsh] *n.* prostitute
танҳо [tanho] *adj.* alone, lone, lonely / *adv.* only, merely, simply
танҳоӣ [tanhoi] *n.* privacy
тапидан [tapidan] *v.i.* throb
тапиш [tapish] *n.* palpitation
таппон [tappon] *n.* hearts *(cards)*
таппонча [tapponcha] *n.* pistol
тар [tar] *adj.* moist, wet
тар кардан [tar kardan] *v.t.* moisten, soak, wet
тар шудан [tar shudan] *v.i.* soak, become wet
тараққӣ [taraqqi] *n.* progress
тараққӣ кардан [taraqqi kardan] *v.i.* progress
таранг [tarang] *adj.* tense, taut
таранг кардан [tarang kardan] *v.t.* stretch, strain
тарангшавӣ [tarangshavi] *n.* tension, tautness
тараф [taraf] *n.* direction
тарафдор [tarafdor] *n.* supporter, partisan
тарафдорӣ [tarafdori] *n.* support, taking a side
тарашшӯҳ кардан [tarashshüh kardan] *v.t.* exude
тарбия [tarbiya] *n.* training
тарбия кардан [tarbiya kardan] *v.t.* train
тарбуз [tarbuz] *n.* watermelon
тарз [tarz] *n.* manner, method, mode
тариқа [tariqa] *n.* mode
тариф [tarif] *n.* tariff
тарӣ [tari] *n.* moisture
тарк кардан [tark kardan] *v.t.* abandon / *v.i.* quit
таркиб [tarkib] *n.* make-up, composition; chemical compound
таркиб ёфтан [tarkib yoftan] *v.i.* consist
таркиб кардан [tarkib kardan] *v.t.* comprise
таркибӣ [tarkibi] *adj.* compound
тарқ [tarq] *n.* crack
тарқидан [tarqidan] *v.i.* crack, explode
тарқиш [tarqish] *n.* explosion
тарқондан [tarqondan] *v.t.* crack, explode
тармим [tarmim] *n.* repair
тармим кардан [tarmim kardan] *v.t.* repair
тармимӣ [tarmimi] *n.* maintenance
тарнов [tarnov] *n.* drain
тароват бахшидан [tarovat baxshidan] *v.t.* refresh
таровида гузаштан [tarovida guzashtan] *v.i.* leak
таровидан [tarovidan] *v.i.* leak, trickle
тарозу [tarozu] *n.* scale *(for weighing)*; balance
тароша [tarosha] *n.* chip
тарошидан [taroshidan] *v.t.* chip, scrape, shave
тарс [tars] *n.* fear, fright

тарсангез [tarsangez] *adj.* frightening, sinister
тарсидан [tarsidan] *v.i.* fear, be afraid; **тарсидан аз** [tarsidan az] be afraid of
тарснок [tarsnok] *adj.* frightening
тарсон [tarson] *adj.* afraid
тарсондан [tarsondan] *v.t.* frighten, scare
тарсончак [tarsonchak] *n.* coward
тартиб [tartib] *n.* arrangement, system, routine
тартибот [tartibot] *n.* regimen, regime
тартиб додан [tartib dodan] *v.t.* plan
тару тоза [taru toza] *adj.* fresh
тарҳ [tarh] *n.* subtraction, deduction from a total; design; outline / *prep.* minus
тарҳ кардан [tarh kardan] *v.t.* subtract
тарҳ кашидан [tarh kashidan] *v.t.* design, outline
тарҳкаш [tarhkash] *n.* designer
тарҷума [tarjuma] *n.* translation
тарҷума кардан [tarjuma kardan] *v.t.* translate
тарҷумаи ҳол [tarjumai hol] *n.* biography
тарҷумон [tarjumon] *n.* interpreter
таршавӣ [tarshavi] *n.* soaking
тасаввур [tasavvur] *n.* imagination
тасаввур кардан [tasavvur kardan] *v.t.* imagine
тасалло [tasallo] *n.* consolation
тасарруф [tasarruf] *n.* possession *(of something)*
тасбеҳ [tasbeh] *n.* rosary
тасвир [tasvir] *n.* image, picture
тасвир кардан [tasvir kardan] *v.t.* depict
тасдиқ [tasdiq] *n.* confirmation, verification, ratification
тасдиқ кардан [tasdiq kardan] *v.t.* certify, verify, confirm, notarize, ratify
таскин [taskin] *n.* relief
таскин додан [taskin dodan] *v.t.* relieve
таслим кардан [taslim kardan] *v.t.* surrender
таслим шудан [taslim shudan] *v.i.* submit, surrender
тасма [tasma] *n.* strap
тасниф [tasnif] *n.* composition *(writing, music, etc.)*
тасниф кардан [tasnif kardan] *v.t.* classify, specify
тасодуф [tasoduf] *n.* chance, coincidence
тасодуфан [tasodufan] *adv.* accidentally
тасодуфӣ [tasodufi] *adj.* accidental, coincidental, random
тасфияи ҳаво [tasfiyai havo] *n.* air conditioning
тасҳеҳ кардан [tas-heh kardan] *v.t.* revise
тафовут [tafovut] *n.* difference
тафоҳум [tafohum] *n.* mutual understanding
тафсир [tafsir] *n.* comment, commentary
тафсир кардан [tafsir kardan] *v.i.* comment
тафсон [tafson] *adj.* hot
тафт [taft] *n.* heat

тафтиш [taftish] *n.* verification, check, inspection
тафтиш кардан [taftish kardan] *v.t.* verify, check, inspect
тахлия [taxliya] *n.* evacuation
тахлия кардан [taxliya kardan] *v.t.* evacuate
тахмин [taxmin] *n.* estimate, guess
тахмин кардан [taxmin kardan] *v.t.* approximate, estimate / *v.i.* guess
тахмин карда ёфтан [taxmin karda yoftan] *v.t.* guess
тахминан [taxminan] *adv.* approximately
тахминӣ [taxmini] *adj.* approximate
тахт [taxt] *n.* throne
тахти равон [taxti ravon] *n.* litter, palanquin
тахта [taxta] *n.* board, plank
тахтаи синф [taxtai sinf] *n.* blackboard
тахтакана [taxtakana] *n.* bedbug
тахтача [taxtacha] *n.* splint
тахтачабанд [taxtachaband] *n.* splint
тахтачаи шикастабандӣ [taxtachai shikastabandi] *n.* cast *(med.)*
тахтмон [taxtmon] *n.* alcove
тахфиф [taxfif] *n.* discount, rebate
таҳ [tah] *n.* bottom
таҳаввул [tahavvul] *n.* evolution
таҳаммул [tahammul] *n.* tolerance
таҳаммулнопазир [tahammulnopazir] *adj.* unbearable
таҳдид [tahdid] *n.* menace, threat
таҳдид кардан [tahdid kardan] *v.t.* threaten
таҳия кардан [tahiya kardan] *v.t.* develop *(a plan)*
таҳқиқ [tahqiq] *n.* investigation, research
таҳқиқ кардан [tahqiq kardan] *v.t.* investigate, research
таҳқир [tahqir] *n.* scorn
таҳқир кардан [tahqir kardan] *v.t.* cause insult, scorn
таҳлил [tahlil] *n.* analysis
таҳлил кардан [tahlil kardan] *v.t.* analyze
таҳрир кардан [tahrir kardan] *v.t.* edit
таҳриф кардан [tahrif kardan] *v.t.* distort
таҳсин [tahsin] *n.* approval
таҳхона [tahxona] *n.* basement, cellar
таҷдид [tajdid] *n.* rehabilitation
таҷовуз кардан [tajovuz kardan] *v.t.* infringe
таҷовузкор [tajovuzkor] *n.* aggressive
таҷриба [tajriba] *n.* experience, practice
таҷриба кардан [tajriba kardan] *v.t.* experience
таҷҳиз кардан [tajhiz kardan] *v.t.* equip
таҷҳизот [tajhizot] *n.* equipment, amenities
ташаббус [tashabbus] *n.* enterprise, initiative
ташаккур гуфтан [tashakkur kardan] *v.t.* thank
ташвиш [tashvish] *n.* trouble

ташвиш додан [tashvish dodan] *v.t.* disturb, trouble
ташкил додан [tashkil dodan] *v.t.* constitute, form
ташкил кардан [tashkil kardan] *v.t.* organize
ташкила [tashkila] *n.* formation
ташкилот [tashkilot] *n.* organization
ташна [tashna] *adj.* thirsty
ташнагӣ [tashnagi] *n.* thirst
ташноб [tashnob] *n.* bathroom, restroom
ташхис [tashxis] *n.* diagnosis, identification
ташхис кардан [tashxis kardan] *v.t.* identify
таъбир рехта [ta'biri rexta] *n.* idiom
таъдил кардан [ta'dil kardan] *v.t.* adjust
таъзия [ta'ziya] *n.* condolence
таъин кардан [ta'in kardan] *v.t.* appoint, designate, set, nominate
таъкид [ta'kid] *n.* confirmation; emphasis, stress
таъкид кардан [ta'kid kardan] *v.t.* confirm, emphasize, stress
таъқиб кардан [ta'qib kardan] *v.t.* pursue
таълим додан [ta'lim dodan] *v.t.* educate
таълимӣ [ta'limi] *adj.* educational
таълиму тарбия [ta'limu tarbiya] *n.* education
таълиф [ta'lif] *n.* composition *(writing, music, etc.)*
таълиф кардан [ta'lif kardan] *v.t.* compose
таъмид [ta'mid] *n.* baptism
таъмид кардан [ta'mid kardan] *v.t.* baptize
таъмин кардан [ta'min kardan] *v.t.* ensure, secure; supply, furnish
таъминот [ta'minot] *n.* supply
таъмир [ta'mir] *n.* repair
таъмир кардан [ta'mir kardan] *v.t.* refit, repair
таъриф [ta'rif] *n.* compliment; definition
таъриф кардан [ta'rif kardan] *v.t.* compliment; define
таърих [ta'rix] *n.* date *(in time)*; history
таърих мондан [ta'rix mondan] *v.t.* date *(a document, etc.)*
таърихӣ [ta'rixi] *adj.* historical
таърихшинос [ta'rixshinos] *n.* historian
таъсир [ta'sir] *n.* effect, influence
таъсир гузоштан [ta'sir guzoshtan] *v.t.* influence
таъсир кардан [ta'sir kardan] *v.t.* affect, impress
таъсирбахш [ta'sirbaxsh] *adj.* effective, impressive
таътил [ta'til] *n.* school vacation, break
таъхир [ta'xir] *n.* delay
таъхир кардан [ta'xir kardan] *v.t.* delay
театр [teatr] *n.* theater
теғ [tegh] *n.* blade, razor blade
теға [tegha] *n.* ridge, crest *(of a wave)*
тез [tez] *adj.* acute, astute, keen, sharp; fast, rapid, quick
тез-тез [tez-tez] *adv.* often

тез кардан [tez kardan] *v.t.* sharpen
тезвайроншаванда [tezvayronshavanda] *adj.* perishable
тезгард [tezgard] *adj.* fleet, swift
тезй [tezi] *n.* speed
тезондан [tezondan] *v.t.* accelerate
тезтар шудан [teztar shudan] *v.i.* accelerate
тела [tela] *n.* push, shove
тела додан [tela dodan] *v.t.* push, shove
телевизион [televizion] *n.* television
телевизор [televizor] *n.* television
телеграмма [telegramma] *n.* telegram
телескоп [teleskop] *n.* telescope
телефон [telefon] *n.* telephone
телефон кардан [telefon kardan] *v.t.* telephone, call on the telephone
телефони дастй [telefoni dasti] *n.* cellular phone, mobile phone
теннис [tennis] *n.* tennis
тенор [tenor] *n./adj.* tenor
теппа [teppa] *n.* hill
терапия [terapiya] *n.* therapy
термос [termos] *n.* thermos
термостат [termostat] *n.* thermostat
терроризм [terrorizm] *n.* terrorism
террорист [terrorist] *n.* terrorist
тиб [tib] *n.* science of medicine
тиббй [tibbi] *adj.* medical
тикка [tikka] *n.* piece, small piece
тиққондан [tiqqondan] *v.t.* plug
тиққонҷ [tiqqonj] *n.* gag, plug
тилисм [tilism] *n.* amulet, talisman
тилло [tillo] *n.* gold
тиллой [tilloi] *adj.* golden, gold
тиллоранг [tillorang] *adj.* gold-colored
тимоб [timob] *n.* flu, influenza
тимор [timor] *n.* nurture, care
тимор кардан [timor kardan] *v.t.* nurture, take care of
тиморхона [timorxona] *n.* insane asylum
тимсол [timsol] *n.* image
тир [tir] *n.* arrow; fourth month of the Persian calendar; axle; bullet
тир андохтан [tir andoxtan] *v.t.* fire, shoot
тира [tira] *adj.* gloomy, somber, obscure
тирак [tirak] *n.* rolling pin
тира кардан [tira kardan] *v.t.* obscure
тирагй [tiragi] *n.* gloom
тирамоҳ [tiramoh] *n.* autumn, fall
тиргак [tirgak] *n.* rack
тире [tire] *n.* hyphen, dash
тиреза [tireza] *n.* window
тирукамон [tirukamon] *n.* rainbow
тифл [tifl] *n.* baby
тиҳй [tihi] *adj.* empty, vacant
тиҳй кардан [tihi kardan] *v.t.* empty
тиҷорат [tijorat] *n.* commerce
тиҷоратй [tijorati] *adj.* commercial
то [to] *prep.* until
тоб [tob] *n.* endurance, strength; twist

тоб овардан [tob ovardan] *v.t.* endure
тоба [toba] *n.* frying pan, pan
тобеъ [tobe'] *n.* subject / *adj.* dependent
тобеъ будан [tobe' budan] *v.i.* depend
тобидан [tobidan] *v.i.* glow, shine
тобистон [tobiston] *n.* summer
тобистона [tobistona] *adj.* summer
тобиш [tobish] *n.* glow; shade *(color, meaning, etc.)*; tint, tone
тобоварӣ [tobovari] *n.* endurance
тобут [tobut] *n.* coffin
товон додан [tovon dodan] *v.t.* recompense, reimburse
товус [tovus] *n.* peacock
тоза [toza] *adj.* clean, fresh
тоза кардан [toza kardan] *v.t.* clean; refine; renovate
тозиёна [toziyona] *n.* whip
тозиёна задан [toziyona zadan] *v.t.* whip
той [toy] *n.* package
ток [tok] *n.* vine
токзор [tokzor] *n.* vineyard
тоқ [toq] *n.* arch
тоқа [toqa] *adj.* alone, lone / lonely
тоқат кардан [toqat kardan] *v.t.* tolerate, endure
тоқатфарсо [toqatfarso] *adj.* unbearable
тоқча [toqcha] *n.* niche
толоб [tolob] *n.* pond
толор [tolor] *n.* hall
тонна [tonna] *n.* ton
тоннаж [tonnazh] *n.* tonnage
тор [tor] *n.* fiber; string
тори тортанак [tori tortanak] *n.* cobweb
торик [torik] *adj.* dark
торик кардан [torik kardan] *v.t.* darken
торикӣ [toriki] *n.* darkness
тормоз [tormoz] *n.* brake
тормоз додан [tormoz dodan] *v.t.* brake
торт [tort] *n.* cake
тортанак [tortanak] *n.* spider
тортанакхона [tortanakxona] *n.* cobweb, spiderweb
тосида [tosida] *adj.* rotten
тосидан [tosidan] *v.i.* rot
тоталитарӣ [totalitari] *adj.* totalitarian
тоту [totu] *n.* pony
тофтан [toftan] *v.t./v.i.* twist, wind
тохт [toxt] *n.* run
тохтан [toxtan] *v.i.* run
тохтутоз [toxtutoz] *n.* invasion
тоҷ [toj] *n.* crown
тоҷик [tojik] *n./adj.* Tajik
тоҷикӣ [tojiki] *n.* Tajik *(language)*
тоҷир [tojir] *n.* merchant
трактор [traktor] *n.* tractor
транзит [tranzit] *n.* transit
триместр [trimestr] *n.* trimester *(academic)*
тропикӣ [tropiki] *adj.* tropical
ту [tu] *pron.* you *(singular/ informal)*
тугма [tugma] *n.* button
тугмахона [tugmaxona] *n.* keyboard
тулӯи офтоб [tulüi oftob] *n.* sunset
туман [tuman] *n.* fog, mist
тумангирифта [tumangirifta] *adj.* foggy, hazy

тумандор [tumandor] *adj.* foggy, hazy
тунд [tund] *adj.* spicy
тундар [tundar] *n.* thunder
тундбод [tundbod] *n.* gust, blast of wind
тундмаза [tundmaza] *adj.* spicy
туннел [tunnel] *n.* tunnel
тунук [tunuk] *adj.* thin, slight of build
турбина [turbina] *n.* turbine
турк [turk] *n.* Turk
туркӣ [turki] *n.* Turkish *(language)* / *adj.* Turkish
туркман [turkman] *n./adj.* Turkmen
туркманӣ [turkmani] *n.* Turkmen *(language)*
турна [turna] *n.* swan
турш [tursh] *adj.* acid, sour, tart
турш кардан [tursh kardan] *v.t.* ferment
туршӣ [turshi] *n.* acid *(sour substance)*, acidity
туршрӯй [turshrüy] *adj.* sullen, surly
тутқулоқ [tutquloq] *n.* epilepsy
туф кардан [tuf kardan] *v.t.* spit
туфанг [tufang] *n.* gun, rifle
тухм [tuxm] *n.* egg, seed
тӯб [tüb] *n.* ball
тӯда [tüda] *n.* crowd, swarm, mass *(of people, animals, etc.)*; heap, pile
тӯй [tüy] *n.* wedding
тӯқумшуллуқ [tüqumshulluq] *n.* snail
тӯл [tül] *n.* longitude
тӯмор [tümor] *n.* amulet, talisman
тӯп [tüp] *n.* cannon
тӯпаланг [tüpalang] *n.* turmoil
тӯр [tür] *n.* mesh, net
тӯтӣ [tüti] *n.* parrot
тӯфон [tüfon] *n.* storm
тӯҳмат [tühmat] *n.* accusation, libel
тӯҳмат кардан [tühmat kardan] *v.t.* libel
тӯҳфа [tühfa] *n.* gift, present
тюлен [tyulen] *n.* seal *(animal)*

У

-у [u] *conj.* and
убур кардан [ubur kardan] *v.t.* cross
угро [ugro] *n.* noodle
уд [ud] *n.* harp
узангу [uzangu] *n.* stirrup
узбак [uzbak] *n./adj.* Uzbek
узбакӣ [uzbaki] *n.* Uzbek *(language)*
узв [uzv] *n.* limb; organ *(anat.)*; member
узвҳои таносул [uzvhoi tanosul] *n.pl.* genitals
узр [uzr] *n.* apology
узр хостан [uzr xostan] *v.i.* apologize
уқёнус [uqyonus] *n.* ocean
уқоб [uqob] *n.* eagle
уллос [ullos] *n.* howl
уллос кашидан [ullos kashidan] *v.i.* howl
ултрабунафш [ultrabunafsh] *adj.* ultraviolet
умда [umda] *adj.* prime, top-quality
умед [umed] *n.* hope
умед доштан [umed doshtan] *v.t.* hope
умедвор [umedvor] *adj.* hopeful

умедвор будан [umedvor budan] *v.t.* hope, be hopeful
умр [umr] *n.* lifetime
умуман [umuman] *adv.* in general, generally
умумӣ [umumi] *adj.* general, universal, public
унвон [unvon] *n.* degree *(academic)*; heading, headline; title
ура [ura] *interj.* hurray
урдугоҳ [urdugoh] *n.* camp, campsite
уреб [ureb] *adj.* diagonal
услуб [uslub] *n.* style
усто [usto] *n.* master, expert
устогӣ [ustogi] *n.* mastery, expertise
устод [ustod] *n.* master, expert
устокор [ustokor] *adj.* ingenious
устувона [ustuvona] *n.* cylinder
устувор [ustuvor] *adj.* determined; solid, stable, steady
устуворӣ [ustuvori] *n.* determination
устухон [ustuxon] *n.* bone
устухонбандӣ [ustuxonbandi] *n.* skeleton
усул [usul] *n.* principle
утоқ [utoq] *n.* room, chamber
уттӣ [utti] *n.* iron *(for clothes, etc.)*
уттӣ кардан [utti kardan] *v.t.* iron
уфуқ [ufuq] *n.* horizon
уфуқӣ [ufuqi] *adj.* horizontal
уштур [ushtur] *n.* camel

Ӯ

ӯ [ü] *pron.* he, him, she, her, it
ӯгурхоҳӣ [ügurxohi] *n.* heat *(of female animals)*
ӯзак [üzak] *n.* core
ӯҳда [ühda] *n.* responsibility, duty
ӯҳдабаро [ühdabaro] *adj.* competent
ӯҳдабароӣ [ühdabaroi] *n.* competence
ӯчоқ [üjoq] *n.* stove

Ф

фабрика [fabrika] *n.* factory
фаввора [favvora] *n.* fountain
фавқулодда [favqulodda] *adj.* extraordinary
фавра [favra] *n.* jet *(of water)*, spout
фаврак [favrak] *n.* trickle
фавран [favran] *adv.* instantly
фаврӣ [favri] *adj.* instant
фазо [fazo] *n.* cosmic space
фазоӣ [fazoi] *adj.* spatial
файл [fayl] *n.* computer file
факс [faks] *n.* fax
факс фиристодан [faks firistodan] *v.t.* fax
фактура [faktura] *n.* invoice
факулта [fakulta] *n.* university department
фақат [faqat] *adv.* only, merely, simply
фалахмон [falaxmon] *n.* sling *(weapon)*
фалсафа [falsafa] *n.* philosophy
фан [fan] *n.* branch of knowledge, discipline; subject; science
фанар [fanar] *n.* spring *(mechanical)*
фарбеҳ [farbeh] *adj.* fat
фарбеҳ шудан [farbeh shudan] *v.i.* gain weight
фардо [fardo] *adv.* tomorrow
фарёд [faryod] *n.* call, cry, yell

фарёд задан [faryod zadan] *v.i.* yell, cry out
фарз кардан [farz kardan] *v.t.* assume / *v.i.* suppose
фарзанд хондан [farzand xondan] *v.t.* adopt *(a child)*
фарзандхонд [farzandxond] *n.* adoption
фарзона [farzona] *adj.* prudent
фариштa [farishta] *n.* angel
фарқ [farq] *n.* difference, distinction
фарқ доштан [farq doshtan] *v.i.* differ
фарқ кардан [farq kardan] *v.t.* distinguish
фармакология [farmakologiya] *n.* pharmacology
фармоиш [farmoish] *n.* order *(in a restaurant, etc.)*
фармоиш додан [farmoish dodan] *v.t.* place an order
фармон [farmon] *n.* command, order, warrant
фармон додан [farmon dodan] *v.t.* command, order
фармонбардор [farmonbardor] *adj.* obedient
фармонбардорӣ [farmonbardori] *n.* obedience
фармонбардорӣ кардан [farmonbardori kardan] *v.t.* obey
фармонбардорӣ накардан [farmonbardori nakardan] *v.t.* defy
фармоянда [farmoyanda] *n.* customer
фарн [farn] *n.* fern
фаровон [farovon] *adj.* abundant
фаровонӣ [farovoni] *n.* abundance, plenty
фарогиранда [farogiranda] *adj.* surrounding
фароғат [faroghat] *n.* leisure
фаромадан [faromadan] *v.i.* get down, get off
фаромӯш кардан [faromüsh kardan] *v.t.* forget
фаромӯшшуда [faromüshshuda] *adj.* forgotten
фаронсавӣ [faronsavi] *n./adj.* French
фарох [farox] *adj.* wide
фарохӣ [faroxi] *n.* width
фарохкунӣ [faroxkuni] *n.* expansion
фарохтар кардан [faroxtar kardan] *v.t.* expand, widen
фароштурук [faroshturuk] *n.* swallow *(bird)*
фаррош [farrosh] *n.* cleaning person
фарсангсор [farsangsor] *n.* landmark
фарсуда [farsuda] *adj.* shabby, worn out
фарсудашуда [farsudashuda] *adj.* shabby, worn out
фархунда [farxunda] *adj.* merry, happy
фарҳанг [farhang] *n.* culture; dictionary
фарҳангӣ [farhangi] *adj.* cultural
фарш [farsh] *n.* floor
фарш кардан [farsh kardan] *v.t.* pave
фаръӣ [far'i] *adj.* accessory
фасл [fasl] *n.* season
фаслӣ [fasli] *adj.* seasonal
фасод [fasod] *n.* corruption
фатила [fatila] *n.* wick
фатҳ [fath] *n.* conquest
фатҳ кардан [fath kardan] *v.t.* conquer

фахфур [faxfur] *n.* china, porcelain
фахфурӣ [faxfuri] *adj.* china, porcelain
фаҳмидан [fahmidan] *v.t./v.i.* understand, realize
фаҳмиш [fahmish] *n.* comprehension, understanding
фаҳул [fahul] *adj.* loose
фашанг [fashang] *n.* lever
фашшос задан [fashshos zadan] *v.i.* hiss
фаъол [fa'ol] *adj.* active
фаъолият [fa'oliyat] *n.* activity
феврал [fevral] *n.* February
ферма [ferma] *n.* farm
феҳрист [fehrist] *n.* index, inventory, list
феъл [fe'l] *gram.* verb
феълӣ [fe'li] *adj.* verbal
фиғон [fighon] *n.* moan
фидия [fidiya] *n.* ransom
физик [fizik] *n.* physicist
физика [fizika] *n.* physics
фикр [fikr] *n.* mind, thought, worry
фикр кардан [fikr kardan] *v.i.* think
фикрӣ [fikri] *adj.* mental
фил [fil] *n.* elephant
филм [film] *n.* movie, film
филм гирифтан [film giriftan] *v.t.* film
финдиқи заминӣ [findiqi zamini] *n.* peanut
фиреб [fireb] *n.* deceit, deception, fraud, trick, seduction
фиребгар [firebgar] *n.* swindler
фиребгарӣ кардан [firebgari kardan] *v.t.* tamper, falsify
фирефтан [fireftan] *v.t.* deceive, trick, seduce
фиринӣ [firini] *n.* pudding
фиристанда [firistanda] *n.* sender
фиристодан [firistodan] *v.t.* send
фирқ-фирқ [firq-firq] *n.* snort
фирқ-фирқ кардан [firq-firq kardan] *v.i.* snort
фишор [fishor] *n.* pressure
фишор додан [fishor dodan] *v.t.* pressure
фишор овардан [fishor ovardan] *v.i.* push
флот [flot] *n.* fleet
флоти ҳарбӣ [floti harbi] *n.* navy
фоида [foida] *n.* benefit, gain, utility
фоида бахшидан [foida baxshidan] *v.t.* benefit
фоида бурдан [foida burden] *v.i.* gain
фоиданок [foidanok] *adj.* beneficial, helpful, useful, worthwhile
фойтун [foytun] *n.* coach, carriage
фона [fona] *n.* wedge
фона задан [fona zadan] *v.t.* drive a wedge
фонетика [fonetika] *n.* phonetics
фонетикӣ [fonetiki] *adj.* phonetic
фонуси [fonus] *n.* lantern
фонуси кӯчагӣ [fonusi küchagi] *n.* lamppost
форам [foram] *adj.* agreeable, pleasant
форидан [foridan] *v.t.* please
форма [forma] *n.* uniform
формула [formula] *n.* formula
форсӣ [forsi] *n./adj.* Persian

фортепяно [fortepyano] *n.* piano
фосила [fosila] *n.* gap, interval
фотонусха [fotonusxa] *n.* photocopy
фотонусха гирифтан [fotonusxa giriftan] *v.t.* photocopy
фоҷиа [fojia] *n.* tragedy
фоҷианок [fojianok] *adj.* tragic, terrible
фош кардан [fosh kardan] *v.t.* divulge, uncover
фук [fuk] *n.* snout
фулуз [fuluz] *n.* metal
фунт [funt] *n.* pound
фуровардан [furovardan] *v.t.* bring down, unload / *v.i.* descend
фуромадан [furomadan] *v.i.* get down, get off
фурориш [furorish] *n.* descent
фурсат [fursat] *n.* opportunity
фурудгоҳ [furudgoh] *n.* airport
фурӯ бурдан [furü burdan] *v.t.* swallow
фурӯ нишондан [furü nishondan] *v.t.* repress, suppress, restrain
фурӯ рафтан [furü raftan] *v.i.* set
фурӯнишонӣ [furünishoni] *n.* repression
фурӯтан [furütan] *adj.* humble
фурӯхтан [furüxtan] *v.t./v.i.* sell
фурӯш [furüsh] *n.* sale
фурӯшанда [furüshanda] *n.* dealer, seller, salesman/woman
фурӯшгор [furüshgor] *n.* seller, salesman/woman
фурӯшгоҳ [furüshgoh] *n.* department store
фурӯшӣ [furüshi] *adj.* for sale
фут [fut] *n.* foot *(unit of measurement)*
футбол [futbol] *n.* soccer
фуфайка [fufayka] *n.* jersey
фушурдан [fushurdan] *v.t.* crush, press

X

хабар [xabar] *n.* information, news
хабар додан [xabar dodan] *v.t.* communicate, notify
хабар кардан [xabar kardan] *v.t.* inform
хабар шудан [xabar shudan] *v.i.* learn
хабардиҳӣ [xabardihi] *n.* communication
хабардор шудан [xabardor shudan] *v.i.* learn
хабарнигор [xabarnigor] *n.* correspondent, journalist, reporter
хабарнигорӣ кардан [xabarnigori kardan] *v.i.* report
хабарнома [xabarnoma] *n.* notification
хабаррасон [xabarrason] *n.* messenger
хабаррасонӣ [xabarrasoni] *n.* communication
хавотир кардан [xavotir kardan] *v.t.* harass
хавотир шудан [xavotir shudan] *v.i.* worry
хаданг [xadang] *n.* arrow
хаёл [xayol] *n.* phantom
хаёлӣ [xayoli] *adj.* imaginary
хазанда [xazanda] *n.* reptile

хазидан [xazidan] *v.i.* crawl, creep
хазон [xazon] *n.* autumn, fall
хайрот [xayrot] *n.* charity
хайрхоҳӣ [xayrxohi] *n.* favor
хайрхоҳӣ кардан [xayrxohi kardan] *v.t.* do a favor
халабон [xalabon] *n.* pilot
халал додан [xalal dodan] *v.t.* infringe
халат [xalat] *n.* robe
халиҷ [xalij] *n.* bay, gulf
халқ [xalq] *n.* people
халондан [xalondan] *v.t.* pierce
хало [xalo] *n.* toilet
халоҷо [xalojo] *n.* latrine
халта [xalta] *n.* bag, sack
халтача [xaltacha] *n.* pouch
хам [xam] *n.* curve
хам шудан [xam shudan] *v.i.* curve, tilt
хамёза [xamyoza] *n.* yawn
хамёза кашидан [xamyoza kashidan] *v.i.* yawn
хамида [xamida] *adj.* bent
хамидан [xamidan] *v.i.* bend
хамир [xamir] *n.* dough, thick mixture, paste
хамира [xamira] *n.* sealant
хамира молидан [xamira molidan] *v.t.* seal up
хамиртуруш [xamirturush] *n.* yeast
хамкунӣ [xamkuni] *n.* deviation
хамондан [xamondan] *v.t.* bend
хамма [xamma] *n.* bin
хамнашаванда [xamnashavanda] *adj.* stiff
ханда [xanda] *n.* laugh
ханда кардан [xanda kardan] *v.i.* laugh
хандақ [xandaq] *n.* ditch, trench
хандаовар [xandaovar] *adj.* funny
хандидан [xandidan] *v.i.* laugh
хандондан [xandondan] *v.t.* cause to laugh
ханҷол кардан [xanjol kardan] *v.t.* scratch
хар [xar] *n.* donkey
харак [xarak] *n.* bench
харбуза [xarbuza] *n.* melon
харгӯш [xargüsh] *n.* rabbit
хардал [xardal] *n.* mustard
харид [xarid] *n.* purchase, shopping
харид кардан [xarid kardan] *v.i.* shop
харидан [xaridan] *v.t.* buy, purchase
харидор [xaridor] *n.* buyer
харидуфурӯш [xaridufurüsh] *n.* bargain, deal
харидуфурӯш кардан [xaridufurüsh kardan] *v.i.* deal
харита [xarita] *n.* chart, map
харита кашидан [xarita kashidan] *v.t.* chart
хароб кардан [xarob kardan] *v.t.* destroy, ruin, smash
хароб шудан [xarob shudan] *v.t.* lose weight
хароба [xaroba] *n.* ruins
харобӣ [xarobi] *n.* destruction
харошидан [xaroshidan] *v.t.* scrape, scribble
харсанг [xarsang] *n.* rock
хартум [xartum] *n.* trunk
харчанг [xarchang] *n.* crab; lobster
харҷ [xarj] *n.* expense
харҷумарҷ [xarjumarj] *adj.* chaotic

хасбеда [xasbeda] *n.* hay
хасис [xasis] *n.* miser
хаскашак [xaskashak] *n.* rake
хаста [xasta] *adj.* tired, weary
хаста кардан [xasta kardan] *v.t.* tire
хаста шудан [xasta shudan] *v.i.* tire
хастагӣ [xastagi] *n.* tiredness
хастакунанда [xastakunanda] *adj.* tiresome, tiring, causing fatigue
хастанашаванда [xastanashavanda] *adj.* tireless
хат [xat] *n.* letter, writing; line, streak
хат кашидан [xat kashidan] *v.t.* line, draw a line
хатар [xatar] *n.* danger, hazard, peril, risk
хатарнок [xatarnok] *adj.* dangerous, unsafe
хати истиво [xati istivo] *n.* equator
хатибӣ кардан [xatibi kardan] *v.t.* preach
хаткашак [xatkashak] *n.* ruler; straight-edge
хаткӯркунак [xatkürkunak] *n.* eraser
хатм кардан [xatm kardan] *v.t.* terminate
хатна [xatna] *n.* circumcision
хатнасурӣ [xatnasuri] *n.* circumcision ceremony
хатнатӯй [xatnatüy] *n.* circumcision ceremony
хато [xato] *n.* error, mistake, miss
хато кардан [xato kardan] *v.t.* miss, make a mistake, mistake
хаттӣ [xatti] *adj.* in writing
хатча [xatcha] *n.* note, short letter
хатчӯб [xatchüb] *n.* bookmark
хафа кардан [xafa kardan] *v.t.* choke, throttle; offend, upset
хафагиангез [xafagiangez] *adj.* offensive
хафагӣ [xafagi] *n.* offense
хафасозанда [xafasozanda] *adj.* upsetting, offensive
хашм [xashm] *n.* anger, wrath, rage, fury
хашмгин [xashmgin] *adj.* angry, furious
хашмгин кардан [xashmgin kardan] *v.t.* anger
хашмгин шудан [xashmgin shudan] *v.i.* anger
хашхош [xashxosh] *n.* poppy
хез задан [xez zadan] *v.i.* spring, jump
хекиртак [xekirtak] *n.* Adam's apple
хел [xel] *n.* sort, kind, type
хел-хел кардан [xel-xel kardan] *v.t.* sort
хеле [xele] *adj./adv.* much, very
хестан [xestan] *v.i.* get up, arise
хеш [xesh] *n.* relative
хешӣ [xeshi] *n.* familial relationship
хиёбон [xiyobon] *n.* avenue
хиёнат [xiyonat] *n.* treason
хиёнат кардан [xiyonat kardan] *v.t.* betray
хиёнаткор [xiyonatkor] *n.* traitor
хизмат [xizmat] *n.* service
хизмат кардан [xizmat kardan] *v.i.* wait upon, attend, serve
хизматгор [xizmatgor] *n.* attendant, valet, servant
хизматгорзан [xizmatgorzan] *n.* maid

химия [ximiya] *n.* chemistry
химиявӣ [ximiyavi] *adj.* chemical
хира [xira] *adj.* dim, faint
хира кардан [xira kardan] *v.t.* dim
хирад [xirad] *n.* intelligence, mind, reason, wisdom, wit
хирадманд [xiradmand] *adj.* intelligent, wise; reasonable
хиргоҳ [xirgoh] *n.* halo; tent
хиромон [xiromon] *adv.* gracefully
хиррӣ [xirri] *adj.* hoarse
хиррос [xirros] *n.* wheeze
хиррос задан [xirros zadan] *v.i.* wheeze
хирс [xirs] *n.* bear
хислати вежа [xislati vezha] *n.* characteristic
хитой [xitoi] *n./adj.* Chinese
хиҷолат [xijolat] *n.* shame
хишова кардан [xishova kardan] *v.t.* weed
хишт [xisht] *n.* brick; diamonds *(card suit)*
хиштин [xishtin] *adj.* brick
хоб [xob] *n.* dream
хобгоҳ [xobgoh] *n.* bedchamber
хобида [xobida] *adj./adv.* asleep
хобидан [xobidan] *v.i.* sleep
хоболуд [xobolud] *adj.* sleepy
ховар [xovar] *n.* east; **Ховари Миёна** [Xovari Miyona] Middle East
ховарӣ [xovari] *adj.* eastern, east
хода [xoda] *n.* pole, shaft
хоин [xoin] *n.* traitor
хойидан [xoyidan] *v.t.* chew
хок [xok] *n.* soil, territory
хока [xoka] *n.* powder
хокиранг [xokirang] *adj.* khaki
хокистар [xokistar] *n.* ash, cinders
хокистардон [xokistardon] *n.* ashtray
хокистарӣ [xokistari] *adj.* gray
хокӣ [xoki] *adj.* khaki
хоккей [xokkey] *n.* hockey
хоксор [xoksor] *adj.* humble
хол [xol] *n.* spot, beauty spot, mole
хола [xola] *n.* maternal aunt
холабача [xolabacha] *n.* cousin *(maternal aunt's son)*
холестрин [xolestrin] *n.* cholesterol
холис [xolis] *adj.* net; pure
холӣ [xoli] *adj.* empty, vacant
холӣ кардан [xoli kardan] *v.t.* empty
хом [xom] *adj.* crude, raw
хомӯш [xomüsh] *adj.* silent, off
хомӯш кардан [xomüsh kardan] *v.t.* silence, extinguish, muffle, suppress, switch off
хомӯшак [xomüshak] *n.* mosquito
хомӯшӣ [xomüshi] *n.* silence
хона [xona] *n.* house, home
хонавода [xonavoda] *n.* household
хонагӣ [xonagi] *adj.* domestic, household, indoor
хонадор [xonador] *adj.* married
хонадон [xonadon] *n.* household
хонаи даромад [xonai daromad] *n.* lobby
хонаи дастшӯй [xonai dastshüi] *n.* restroom
хонаи кӯдакон [xonai küdakon] *n.* nursery

хонаи нигоҳдорӣ [xonai nigohdori] *n.* storeroom, storage room
хонаи пӯшоккашӣ [xonai püshokkashi] *n.* changing room
хонаи хоб [xonai xob] *n.* bedroom
хонаи хӯрокхӯрӣ [xonai xürokxüri] *n.* dining room
хонанда [xonanda] *n.* reader
хонанишин [xonanishin] *adj.* retired
хонанишин шудан [xonanishin shudan] *v.i.* retire
хонача [xonacha] *n.* compartment
хондан [xondan] *v.t./v.i.* read
хониш [xonish] *n.* reading
хоно [xono] *adj.* legible
хонум [xonum] *n.* lady, madam, Mrs., wife
хонумдухтар [xonumduxtar] *n.* miss
хор [xor] *n.* choir, chorus; thorn
хоридан [xoridan] *v.i.* itch, tickle
хориҷ кардан [xorij kardan] *v.t.* exclude
хориҷа [xorija] *adv./adj.* abroad
хориҷӣ [xoriji] *n.* foreigner / *adj.* from a foreign land, foreign
хоришак [xorishak] *n.* itch
хоро [xoro] *n.* granite
хорпушт [xorpusht] *n.* hedgehog
хос [xos] *adj.* characteristic, special
хоста гирифтан [xosta giriftan] *v.t.* pick, choose
хостагирӣ [xostagiri] *n.* option
хостан [xostan] *v.t.* want, wish / *v.i.* will
хостгор [xostgor] *n.* suitor
хотир [xotir] *n.* behalf; **ба хотири** [ba xotiri] on behalf of
хоҳар [xohar] *n.* sister
хоҳарандар [xoharandar] *n.* stepsister
хоҳарарӯс [xohararüs] *n.* sister-in-law *(wife's sister)*
хоҳарзода [xoharzoda] *n.* nephew *(sister's son)*
хоҳаршӯй [xoharshüy] *n.* sister-in-law *(husband's sister)*
хоҳиш [xohish] *n.* desire, want, wish, request
хоҳиш кардан [xohish kardan] *v.i.* request, desire
хоҷ [xoj] *n.* cross
хоҷа [xoja] *n.* lord
хуб [xub] *adj.* good, well, fine / *adv.* well; pretty
худ [xud] *n./pron.* self / *adj.* own
худ ба худ [xud ba xud] *adj.* automatic
худам [xudam] *pron.* myself
худат [xudat] *pron.* yourself *(informal)*
худатон [xudaton] *pron.* yourself *(polite)*, yourselves
худаш [xudash] *pron.* himself, herself, itself
худашон [xudashon] *pron.* themselves
худбин [xudbin] *adj.* vain, egotistical
худдорӣ [xuddori] *n.* self-restraint, willpower
худдорӣ кардан [xuddori kardan] *v.t.* restrain oneself
худкушӣ [xudkushi] *n.* suicide

худкушӣ кардан [xudkushi kardan] *v.i.* commit suicide
худо [xudo] *n.* god
худписандӣ [xudpisandi] *n.* conceit
худсар [xudsar] *adj.* wayward, headstrong
хук [xuk] *n.* pig
хулоса [xulosa] *n.* résumé; summary
хумор [xumor] *n.* hangover
хун [xun] *n.* blood
хун рафтан [xun raftan] *v.i.* bleed
хуноба [xunoba] *n.* serum
хунук [xunuk] *adj.* cold, chilly
хунук занондагӣ [xunuk zanondagi] *n.* frostbite
хунук кардан [xunuk kardan] *v.t.* chill, cool
хунукӣ [xunuki] *n.* cold, chill, frost
хунхор [xunxor] *adj.* fierce
хурд [xurd] *adj.* small, minor
хурд кардан [xurd kardan] *v.t.* shrink
хурд шудан [xurd shudan] *v.i.* shrink
хурдсол [xurdsol] *n.* minor / *adj.* junior, juvenile, youthful
хурмо [xurmo] *n.* date *(fruit)*
хурофотпараст [xurofotparast] *adj.* superstitious
хуррок кашидан [xurrok kashidan] *v.i.* snore
хурсандӣ [xursandi] *n.* delight, pleasure
хурсандӣ кардан [xursandi kardan] *v.i.* exult
хурӯс [xurüs] *n.* rooster, cock
хурӯҷ [xurüj] *n.* fit
хуршед [xurshed] *n.* sun
хусур [xusur] *n.* father-in-law
хусусият [xususiyat] *n.* attribute, trait
хусусӣ [xususi] *adj.* private
хутба [xutba] *n.* sermon
хуҷаста [xujasta] *adj.* blessed, auspicious
хуш [xush] *adj.* happy, gay
хуш наомадан [xush naomadan] *v.t.* displease
хуш омадед гуфтан [xush omaded guftan] *v.t.* welcome
хушандом [xushandom] *adj.* graceful
хушандомӣ [xushandomi] *n.* grace
хушбахт [xushbaxt] *adj.* fortunate, lucky
хушбахтӣ [xushbaxti] *n.* good luck
хушбахтона [xushbaxtona] *adv.* fortunately, luckily
хушбӯӣ [xushbüi] *n.* aroma, scent
хушдоман [xushdoman] *n.* mother-in-law
хушӣ [xushi] *n.* happiness
хушк [xushk] *adj.* dry
хушкигард [xushkigard] *adj.* non-aquatic, terrestrial
хушкӣ [xushki] *n.* land, dry land
хушккунак [xushkkunak] *n.* dryer
хушмаза кардан [xushmaza kardan] *v.t.* flavor
хушманзара [xushmanzara] *adj.* picturesque
хушмуомилагӣ [xushmuomilagi] *n.* courteous behavior, courtesy
хушнуд [xushnud] *adj.* happy
хушнуд кардан [xushnud kardan] *v.t.* please
хушомадгӯӣ кардан [xushomadgüi kardan] *v.t.* flatter
хушрӯ [xushrü] *adj.* handsome, pretty

хушсарулибос [xushsarulibos] *adj.* well-dressed, smart
хӯд [xüd] *n.* helmet
хӯй [xüy] *n.* temperament, temper; habit
хӯр-хӯрак [xür-xürak] *n.* bait
хӯрдан [xürdan] *v.t./v.i.* eat, dine
хӯрданӣ [xürdani] *adj.* edible
хӯриш [xürish] *n.* appetizer, hors d'oeuvre, snack
хӯрок [xürok] *n.* food, meal, nourishment
хӯрок додан [xürok dodan] *v.t.* feed
хӯрокдиҳанда [xürokdihanda] *adj.* nourishing, nutritious
хӯрокдиҳӣ [xürokdihi] *n.* nourishment, nutrition
хӯроки пешин [xüroki peshin] *n.* lunch
хӯроки пешин кардан [xüroki peshin kardan] *v.i.* lunch, have lunch
хӯроки шом [xüroki shom] *n.* dinner, supper
хӯрондан [xürondan] *v.t.* feed
хӯса [xüsa] *n.* scarecrow
хӯҷаин [xüjain] *n.* master, principal
хӯша [xüsha] *n.* cluster

Ҳ

ҳаб [hab] *n.* pill
ҳабдаҳ [habdah] *num.* seventeen
ҳабдаҳум [habdahum] *adj.* seventeenth
ҳабс [habs] *n.* arrest
ҳабс кардан [habs kardan] *v.t.* imprison
ҳабсхона [habsxona] *n.* jail, prison
ҳаваскор [havaskor] *n.* amateur
ҳавасманд кардан [havasmand kardan] *v.t.* motivate, stimulate
ҳавз [havz] *n.* pool
ҳавза [havza] *n.* basin *(geo.)*
ҳавлии дарун [havlii darun] *n.* courtyard
ҳаво [havo] *n.* air, weather; **бо ҳавопаймо рафтан** [bo havopaymo raftan] go by air; **пойгоҳи ҳавопаймоӣ** [poygohi havopaymoi] air base
ҳаво тоза кардан [havo toza kardan] *v.t.* ventilate
ҳаво хунук кардан [havo xunuk kardan] *v.t.* air condition
ҳаводор [havodor] *n.* fan *(sports, etc.)*, enthusiast
ҳавоӣ [havoi] *adj.* aerial
ҳавокашӣ [havokashi] *n.* draft of air
ҳавола кардан [havola kardan] *v.t.* refer to
ҳавонавард [havonavard] *n.* pilot
ҳавопаймо [havopaymo] *n.* airplane
ҳавопаймоӣ [havopaymoi] *n.* aviation
ҳавосанҷ [havosanj] *n.* barometer
ҳавотозакунак [havotozakunak] *n.* ventilator
ҳавотозакунӣ [havotozakuni] *n.* ventilation
ҳавохоҳ [havoxoh] *n.* fan *(sports, etc.)*, enthusiast
ҳавохунуккунак [havoxunukkunak] *n.* air conditioner
ҳавохунуккунакдор [havoxunukkunakdor] *adj.* air-conditioned

ҳад [had] *n.* limit
ҳадаф [hadaf] *n.* target, objective, goal
ҳаёт [hayot] *n.* life
ҳаёҳуй [hayohuy] *n.* uproar, racket
ҳаждаҳ [hazhdah] *num.* eighteen
ҳаждаҳум [hazhdahum] *adj.* eighteenth
ҳазар кардан [hazar kardan] *v.t.* beware
ҳазм [hazm] *n.* digestion
ҳазм кардан [hazm kardan] *v.t.* digest
ҳазор [hazor] *num.* thousand
ҳазорпой [hazorpoy] *n.* centipede
ҳазорум [hazorum] *adj.* thousandth
ҳай кардан [hay kardan] *v.t.* drive, urge on
ҳайати коркунон [hayati korkunon] *n.* personnel
ҳайати ҳунармандон [hayati hunarmandon] *n.* cast *(of a movie, play, etc.)*
ҳайвон [hayvon] *n.* animal
ҳайз [hayz] *n.* menstruation, period
ҳайз дидан [hayz didan] *v.i.* menstruate, have one's period
ҳайкал [haykal] *n.* sculpture, statue
ҳайкал тарошидан [haykal taroshidan] *v.t.* sculpt
ҳайкалтарош [haykaltarosh] *n.* sculptor
ҳайкалтарошӣ [haykaltaroshi] *n.* sculpture *(artform)*
ҳайрат [hayrat] *n.* astonishment, surprise, amazement
ҳайратангез [hayratangez] *adj.* amazing, striking
ҳайрон кардан [hayron kardan] *v.t.* amaze, astonish
ҳақ [haq] *n.* fee; right
ҳақиқат [haqiqat] *n.* fact, reality, truth, validity
ҳақиқатан [haqiqatan] *adv.* indeed
ҳақиқӣ [haqiqi] *adj.* real, well-grounded, valid
ҳаққи хизмат [haqqi xizmat] *n.* sales commission
ҳал [hal] *n.* solution, settlement
ҳал кардан [hal kardan] *v.t.* solve
ҳалкунанда [halkunanda] *n.* solvent
ҳалкунӣ [halkuni] *n.* solution *(mixture of substances)*
ҳалқа [halqa] *n.* coil, link, loop
ҳалок шудан [halok shudan] *v.i.* perish
ҳалокат [halokat] *n.* ruin, perdition
ҳам [ham] *adv.* also, as well, too, even
ҳама [hama] *adj.* all, entire
ҳамааш [hamaash] *adj.* total
ҳамагӣ [hamagi] *adv.* in total
ҳамарзиш [hamarzish] *adj.* equivalent
ҳамвор [hamvor] *adj.* level, even, flat
ҳамвор кардан [hamvor kardan] *v.t.* make even
ҳамдард [hamdard] *adj.* sympathetic
ҳамдардӣ [hamdardi] *n.* sympathy
ҳамдардӣ кардан [hamdardi kardan] *v.i.* sympathize
ҳамеша [hamesha] *adv.* always, ever

ҳамешагӣ [hameshagi] *adv.* forever / *adj.* eternal, fixed, permanent
ҳамён [hamyon] *n.* purse, wallet
ҳамин хел [hamin xel] *adv.* in the manner shown, thus
ҳамкор [hamkor] *n.* associate, co-worker
ҳамкорӣ [hamkori] *n.* collaboration
ҳамкорӣ кардан [hamkori kardan] *v.i.* collaborate, cooperate
ҳамла [hamla] *n.* attack, assault; seizure *(med.)*
ҳамла кардан [hamla kardan] *v.t.* attack, assault
ҳамлу нақл [hamlu naql] *n.* transportation
ҳаммол [hammol] *n.* porter
ҳаммом [hammom] *n.* bath
ҳамнишин [hamnishin] *n.* associate
ҳамон [hamon] *adj.* same
ҳамон хеле ки [hamon xele ki] *adv.* just as
ҳамон ҳангоме ки [hamon hangome ki] as soon as
ҳампеша [hampesha] *n.* peer
ҳамроҳ [hamroh] *n.* companion, satellite / *adv.* along
ҳамроҳ рафтан [hamroh raftan] *v.t.* accompany
ҳамроҳӣ [hamrohi] *n.* companionship
ҳамсадо [hamsado] *n.* consonant
ҳамсар [hamsar] *n.* spouse, mate
ҳамсоя [hamsoya] *n.* neighbor
ҳамутоқ [hamutoq] *n.* roommate
ҳамфикрӣ [hamfikri] *n.* like-mindedness, harmony of opinion
ҳамхона [hamxona] *n.* housemate, roommate
ҳамчашмӣ [hamchashmi] *n.* rivalry, competition
ҳамчашмӣ кардан [hamchashmi kardan] *v.i.* contend
ҳамчун [hamchun] *adv.* like, as, just like
ҳамчунин [hamchunin] *adv.* likewise
ҳамҷинс кардан [hamjins kardan] *v.t.* assimilate
ҳамҷинсбоз [hamjinsboz] *n./adj.* homosexual, gay
ҳамшафат будан [hamshafat budan] *v.i.* adjoin
ҳамшираи тиббӣ [hamshirai tibbi] *n.* nurse
ҳангом [hangom] *n.* point in time, time
ҳангома [hangoma] *n.* sensation, sense of intense interest or excitement
ҳангоме ки [hangome ki] *conj.* when, while
ҳангуфт [hanguft] *adj.* enormous
ҳанӯз [hanüz] *adv.* still
ҳар [har] *adj.* each, every; **ҳар бор** [har bor] each time; **ҳар рӯз** [har rüz] every day
ҳар вақт [har vaqt] *pron.* anytime
ҳар кадом [har kadom] *adj./pron.* whichever
ҳар кӣ [har ki] *pron.* whoever
ҳар чӣ [har chi] *adj./pron.* whatever
ҳар ҷо ки [har jo ki] *adv./conj.* wherever

ҳаракат [harakat] *n.* motion, movement, traffic
ҳаракат кардан [harakat kardan] *v.i.* move
ҳаракатдиҳанда [harakatdihanda] *adj.* moving
ҳаргиз [hargiz] *adv.* never
ҳарза [harza] *n.* chatter, nonsense
ҳариф [harif] *n.* opponent, rival / *adj.* rival
ҳароммағз [harommaghz] *n.* spinal cord
ҳарорат [harorat] *n.* temperature
ҳарос [haros] *n.* fright
ҳаросонӣ [harosoni] *n.* panic
ҳаррӯза [harrüza] *adj.* usual, everyday
ҳартарафа [hartarafa] *adj.* versatile
ҳарф [harf] *n.* printing type; letter
ҳархела [harxela] *adj.* manifold
ҳарчанд [harchand] *conj.* although, though / *adv.* however
ҳасад [hasad] *n.* envy
ҳасад хӯрдан [hasad xürdan] *v.t.* envy
ҳасадхӯр [hasadxür] *adj.* envious
ҳасибча [hasibcha] *n.* sausage
ҳассос [hassos] *adj.* sensitive
ҳаста [hasta] *n.* nucleus; pit *(of a fruit)*
ҳастаӣ [hastai] *adj.* nuclear
ҳастӣ [hasti] *n.* existence
ҳасуд [hasud] *adj.* envious
ҳатто [hatto] *adv.* even
ҳафт [haft] *num.* seven
ҳафта [hafta] *n.* week
ҳафтод [haftod] *num.* seventy
ҳафтум [haftum] *adj.* seventh
ҳаҷ [haj] *n.* Hajj *(obligatory Islamic pilgrimage to Mecca)*
ҳаҷв [hajv] *n.* humor
ҳаҷм [hajm] *n.* mass, volume
ҳашарот [hasharot] *n.* insect
ҳашт [hasht] *num.* eight
ҳаштод [hashtod] *num.* eighty
ҳаштпо [hashtpo] *n.* octopus
ҳаштум [hashtum] *adj.* eighth
ҳезумхона [hezumxona] *n.* woodshed
ҳеҷ [hej] *adj.* no, none / *pron.* nothing
ҳеҷ кас [hej kas] *pron.* nobody, no one
ҳеҷ ҷо [hej jo] *pron.* nowhere
ҳизб [hizb] *n.* political party
ҳикоя [hikoya] *n.* story
ҳиққак [hiqqak] *n.* hiccup
ҳиққак задан [hiqqak zadan] *v.i.* hiccup
ҳилол [hilol] *n.* crescent
ҳимоя [himoya] *n.* protection, safeguard
ҳимоя кардан [himoya kardan] *v.t.* protect
ҳиндӣ [hindi] *n.* Hindi *(language)* / *adj.* Indian
ҳинду [hindu] *n.* Hindu; Indian
ҳис [his] *n.* feeling, sensation
ҳис кардан [his kardan] *v.t.* feel
ҳисоб [hisob] *n.* account, bill, calculation, score of a game or match
ҳисоби бонк [hisobi bonk] *n.* bank account
ҳисоб кардан [hisob kardan] *v.t.* calculate, reckon
ҳисобдор [hisobdor] *n.* accountant
ҳисобдорӣ [hisobdori] *n.* accounting
ҳисор [hisor] *n.* fortress

ҳисса [hissa] *n.* portion, segment, quota
ҳиҷо [hijo] *n.* syllable
ҳиштан [hishtan] *v.t.* abandon
ҳован [hovan] *n.* mortar *(used with a pestle for grinding spices, etc.)*
ҳодиса [hodisa] *n.* accident
ҳозир будан [hozir budan] *v.i.* be present, attend
ҳозира [hozira] *adj.* current, present, up-to-date
ҳозирҷавоб [hozirjavob] *adj.* witty
ҳоил [hoil] *n.* screen, partition
ҳоким [hokim] *n.* governor, mayor
ҳокимият [hokimiyat] *n.* authority
ҳола [hola] *n.* halo
ҳолазун [holazun] *n.* snail
ҳолат [holat] *n.* condition, situation, state, mood
ҳоло [holo] *adv.* now
ҳомӣ [homi] *n.* patron
ҳомуз [homuz] *n.* acid *(chemical compound)*
ҳомуздор [homuzdor] *adj.* acidic
ҳор [hor] *adj.* rabid
ҳорӣ [hori] *n.* rabies
ҳорра [horra] *adj.* tropical
ҳосил [hosil] *n.* crop, harvest
ҳосили ҷамъ [hosili jam'] *n.* sum *(in mathematics)*
ҳосилхез [hosilxez] *adj.* fertile
ҳоҷат [hojat] *n.* need
ҳоҷат доштан [hojat doshtan] *v.t.* need
ҳоҷатхона [hojatxona] *n.* latrine, lavatory
ҳоҷӣ [hoji] *n.* Hajj pilgrim
ҳубоб [hubob] *n.* bubble
ҳувайдо [huvaydo] *adj.* evident
ҳудуд [hudud] *n.* scope
ҳузур [huzur] *n.* attendance
ҳукм [hukm] *n.* judgment, verdict, sentence
ҳукм кардан [hukm kardan] *v.t.* sentence
ҳукмнома [hukmnoma] *n.* verdict
ҳукмрон [hukmron] *n.* ruler
ҳукмронӣ [hukmroni] *n.* domination
ҳукмронӣ кардан [hukmroni kardan] *v.t.* dominate, govern, rule
ҳукмфармо [hukmfarmo] *n.* dictator
ҳукмфармоӣ [hukmfarmoi] *n.* domination
ҳукумат [hukumat] *n.* government
ҳуқуқи муаллифӣ [huquqi muallifi] *n.* copyright
ҳуқуқвайронкунӣ [huquqvayronkuni] *n.* statutory offense
ҳунар [hunar] *n.* skill
ҳунарӣ [hunari] *adj.* artistic
ҳунарманд [hunarmand] *n.* actor, artisan / *adj.* skillful
ҳунарпеша [hunarpesha] *n.* actor
ҳурмат [hurmat] *n.* esteem, honor
ҳурмат кардан [hurmat kardan] *v.t.* honor, venerate
ҳусул [husul] *n.* acquisition
ҳуҷайра [hujayra] *n.* cell *(biological)*
ҳуҷайрагӣ [hujayragi] *adj.* cellular
ҳуҷра [hujra] *n.* jail cell
ҳуҷум [hujum] *n.* attack, assault, invasion

ҳуҷум кардан [hujum kardan] *v.t.* attack, assault
ҳуҷҷат [hujjat] *n.* record
ҳуш [hush] *n.* intelligence, consciousness, wit
ҳушёр [hushyor] *adj.* alert
ҳушёр кардан [hushyor kardan] *v.t.* alert
ҳуштак [hushtak] *n.* whistle
ҳуштак кашидан [hushtak kashidan] *v.i.* whistle
ҳӯппоқ задан [hüppoq zadan] *v.t.* snap one's fingers

Ч

чавгон [chavgon] *n.* club *(hockey, golf, etc.)*
чайқондан [chayqondan] *v.t.* rinse
чакана [chakana] *n.* retail
чакана фурӯхтан [chakana furüxtan] *v.t.* retail, sell at retail
чаканафурӯш [chakanafurüsh] *n.* retailer
чаканафурӯшӣ [chakanafurüshi] *n.* retail trade
чакидан [chakidan] *v.i.* trickle, leak
чакка [chakka] *n.* temple *(anat.)*; strained yogurt
чакра [chakra] *n.* drop
чақ-чақ [chaq-chaq] *n.* chat
чақ-чақ кардан [chaq-chaq kardan] *v.i.* chat
чаққон [chaqqon] *adj.* nimble
чалак [chalak] *n.* barrel, cask
чаласавод [chalasavod] *adj.* uneducated
чалачулпа [chalachulpa] *adj.* sloppy, poorly done
чалипо [chalipo] *n.* cross
чаман [chaman] *n.* lawn
чана [chana] *n.* sled
чана задан [chana zadan] *v.i.* bargain
чанбар [chanbar] *n.* circle, hoop
чанбари гул [chanbari gul] *n.* wreath
чанбарак [chanbarak] *n.* hoop
чанг [chang] *n.* claw; dust
чанг бардоштан [chang bardoshtan] *v.t.* dust
чангак [changak] *n.* hook
чангкашак [changkashak] *n.* vacuum cleaner
чангол [changol] *n.* claw
чанде [chande] *adj.* several
чандир [chandir] *adj.* elastic
чап [chap] *adj.* left
чападаст [chapadast] *adj.* left-handed
чаппа [chappa] *adj.* backward, reverse, upside-down
чаппа кардан [chappa kardan] *v.t.* tip over, turn upside-down, knock over
чаппа шудан [chappa shudan] *v.i.* get tipped over, get turned upside-down, get knocked over
чарбу [charbu] *n.* fat
чарм [charm] *n.* leather
чаро [charo] *adv./conj.* why
чароғ [charogh] *n.* headlight, lamp
чароғак [charoghak] *n.* lightning
чароғон [charoghon] *n.* illumination
чароғча [charoghcha] *n.* lightbulb
чарх [charx] *n.* tire, wheel
чарх задан [charx zadan] *v.i.* circulate, move through a circuit, spin, whirl
чарх занондан [charx zanondan] *v.t.* spin, turn

чарха [charxa] *n.* wheel
чархбол [charxbol] *n.* helicopter
чархзанӣ [charxzani] *n.* circulation
чархидан [charxidan] *v.i.* spin, turn
чархиш [charxish] *n.* turn
чархондан [charxondan] *v.t.* spin, turn
чархпӯш [charxpüsh] *n.* fender
часпак [chaspak] *adj.* adhesive, sticky
часпидан [chaspidan] *v.i.* adhere *(to an object, etc.)*, stick, cling
часпондан [chaspondan] *v.t.* attach, stick
чатоқ кардан [chatoq kardan] *v.t.* swindle
чатр [chatr] *n.* umbrella
чаҳор [chahor] *num.* four
чаҳорум [chahorum] *adj.* fourth
чашидан [chashidan] *v.t.* taste
чашой [chashoi] *n.* sense of taste
чашиш [chashish] *n.* taste
чашм [chashm] *n.* eye; compartment
чашм доштан [chashm doshtan] *v.i.* to expect
чашма [chashma] *n.* spring *(water)*
чашмак [chashmak] *n.* wink
чашмак задан [chashmak zadan] *v.i.* wink
чашмаки зону [chashmaki zonu] *n.* kneecap
чашмбар [chashmbar] *adj.* vivid
чашмдошт [chashmdosht] *n.* expectation
чемпион [chempion] *n.* champion
чен [chen] *n.* gauge, measure
чен кардан [chen kardan] *v.t.* gauge, measure
чентаноб [chentanob] *n.* tape measure
чердак [cherdak] *n.* attic, loft
чеҳра [chehra] *n.* face
чигил [chigil] *adj.* complicated, tangled
чигил кардан [chigil kardan] *v.t.* complicate, tangle
чигил шудан [chigil shudan] *v.i.* tangle
чидан [chidan] *v.t.* arrange, set *(the table, etc.)*; pluck, pick, harvest
чиз [chiz] *n.* thing, article, item, object
чизе [chize] *pron.* anything, something
чил [chil] *num.* forty
чиллик [chillik] *n.* clubs *(card suit)*
чиллик кардан [chillik kardan] *v.t.* cross *(arms, legs, etc.)*
чилликхол [chillikxol] *n.* clubs *(card suit)*
чилум [chilum] *adj.* fortieth
чимдӣ [chimdi] *n.* pinch
чимдӣ кардан [chimdi kardan] *v.t.* pinch
чин [chin] *n.* crease, wrinkle
чин кардан [chin kardan] *v.t.* wrinkle
чинӣ [chini] *n./adj.* Chinese
чипта [chipta] *n.* ticket
чирк [chirk] *n.* filth, dirt
чиркин [chirkin] *adj.* dirty, nasty
чирчирак [chirchirak] *n.* cricket *(insect)*
чистон [chiston] *n.* puzzle, riddle

чиҳил [chihil] *num.* forty
чиҳилум [chihilum] *adj.* fortieth
чӣ [chi] *adj./adv./pron.* what
чӣ гуна [chi guna] *adv.* how
чӣ тавр [chi tavr] *adv.* how
чӣ хел [chi xel] *adv.* how
чобук [chobuk] *adj.* agile, nimble
чодар [chodar] *n.* tent; veil *(in Islamic countries)*
чодарнишин [chodarnishin] *n.* nomad / *adj.* nomadic
чой [choy] *n.* tea
чойкаш [choykash] *n.* ladle
чойник [choynik] *n.* teapot
чойпулӣ [choypuli] *n.* gratuity, tip
чойпулӣ додан [choypuli dodan] *v.t.* give a gratuity, tip
чойхона [choyxona] *n.* teahouse
чойҷӯш [choyjüsh] *n.* kettle, teakettle
чок [chok] *n.* seam
чокар [chokar] *n.* servant
чоп [chop] *n.* edition, print, printing
чоп кардан [chop kardan] *v.t.* print
чопкунанда [chopkunanda] *n.* printer
чоплусӣ кардан [choplusi kardan] *v.t.* flatter
чор [chor] *num.* four
чора [chora] *n.* means, resources; redress, remedy
чорбоғ [chorbogh] *n.* park
чорум [chorum] *adj.* fourth
чордаҳ [chordah] *num.* fourteen
чордаҳум [chordahum] *adj.* fourteenth
чормағз [chormaghz] *n.* walnut
чорпаҳлӯ [chorpahlü] *adj.* stout
чорпой [chorpoy] *n.* beast
чорпояча [chorpoyacha] *n.* stool
чорраҳа [chorraha] *n.* crossroad
чорхез [chorxez] *n.* gallop
чорхез кардан [chorxez kardan] *v.i.* gallop
чорхонанусха [chorxonanusxa] *n.* check pattern, checkered pattern
чорчӯба [chorchüba] *n.* frame
чоршанбе [chorshanbe] *n.* Wednesday
чоряк [choryak] *n.* quarter
чоҳ [choh] *n.* well
чошнӣ [choshni] *n.* taste
чуқур [chuqur] *adj.* deep, profound
чуқурӣ [chuquri] *n.* depth, pit, deep hole
чунин [chunin] *adj.* such
чунки [chunki] *conj.* because
чурра [churra] *n.* hernia
чӯб [chüb] *n.* stick, wood
чӯббандӣ [chübbandi] *n.* scaffold
чӯббаст [chübbast] *n.* scaffold
чӯбдаст [chübdast] *n.* walking stick, cane, staff
чӯбдаста [chübdasta] *n.* bat *(stick)*
чӯбин [chübin] *adj.* wooden
чӯл [chül] *n.* steppe
чӯлоқ [chüloq] *adj.* crippled, lame
чӯлоқӣ [chüloqi] *n.* limp
чӯлпӣ [chülpi] *n.* strainer
чӯпон [chüpon] *n.* shepherd
чӯтка [chütka] *n.* brush
чӯҷа [chüja] *n.* chick

Ч

чаббидан [jabbidan] *v.t.* absorb
чав [jav] *n.* barley
чавдор [javdor] *n.* rye
чави русӣ [javi rusi] *n.* oat
чавоб [javob] *n.* answer, reply, response
чавоб додан [javob dodan] *v.t.* answer, respond, reply
чавобгар [javobgar] *adj.* liable, responsible
чавобгар донистан [javobgar donistan] *v.t.* blame
чавобгарӣ [javobgari] *n.* blame, liability
чавон [javon] *n.* adolescent, juvenile, youth / *adj.* young, adolescent, juvenile, youthful
чавона [javona] *n.* sprout
чавонӣ [javoni] *n.* youth
чавонмард [javonmard] *n.* guy
чавоҳирот [javohirot] *n.* jewelry
чавҳар [javhar] *n.* essence, extract
чадвал [jadval] *n.* schedule, timetable
чаз [jaz] *n.* jazz
чазо [jazo] *n.* penalty, punishment
чазо додан [jazo dodan] *v.t.* punish
чазр [jazr] *n.* low tide
чайб [jayb] *n.* pocket
чайра [jayra] *n.* porcupine
чалб кардан [jalb kardan] *v.i.* attract / *v.t.* involve
чалил [jalil] *adj.* majestic
чалолат [jalolat] *n.* majesty
чамъ [jam'] *n.* addition *(mathematics)*, total, plural / *adj.* plural / *prep.* plus
чамъ кардан [jam' kardan] *v.t.* add *(mathematics)*, total; assemble, convene; collect; focus
чамъ омадан [jam' omadan] *v.i.* assemble
чамъият [jam'iyat] *n.* society
чамъомад [jam'omad] *n.* assembly, convention
чамъулчамъ [jam'uljam'] *adj.* total
чанба [janba] *n.* aspect
чанг [jang] *n.* battle, fight, war
чанг кардан [jang kardan] *v.i.* battle, fight
чангал [jangal] *n.* forest, woods, jungle
чангидан [jangidan] *v.i.* fight
чангчӯй [jangjüy] *n./adj.* militant
чаннат [jannat] *n.* heaven
чаноб [janob] *n.* gentleman, mister *(Mr.)*, sir
чаноза [janoza] *n.* funeral
чануб [janub] *n.* south
чанубӣ [janubi] *adj.* southern, south
чараён [jarayon] *n.* course *(of a river or events)*, process, current, flow; **чараёни баркӣ** [jarayoni barqi] electric current
чарима [jarima] *n.* fine
чарӣ [jari] *n.* ravine
чарроҳ [jarroh] *n.* surgeon
чарроҳӣ [jarrohi] *n.* medical operation, surgery
часад [jasad] *n.* corpse
часадкушой [jasadkushoi] *n.* autopsy
частан [jastan] *v.i.* jump, bounce, leap
частухез кардан [jastuxez kardan] *v.i.* skip

чафо [jafo] *n.* oppression, unkindness
чафо кашидан [jafo kashidan] *v.i.* suffer, be oppressed
чаҳаннам [jahannam] *n.* hell
чаҳиш [jahish] *n.* jump, leap
чаҳон [jahon] *n.* world; **саросари чаҳон** [sarosari jahon] all around the world
чаҳонгард [jahongard] *n.* tourist
чаҳонӣ [jahoni] *adj.* worldwide
чаҳонгардӣ [jahongardi] *n.* tourism
чаҳондан [jahondan] *v.t.* bounce
чаҳонӣ [jahoni] *adj.* global
чашн [jashn] *n.* carnival, celebration, festival, holiday
чашн гирифтан [jashn giriftan] *v.i.* celebrate
чаъфарӣ [ja'fari] *n.* parsley
чевон [jevon] *n.* cabinet, cupboard
чевони деворӣ [jevoni devori] *n.* closet
чевони китоб [jevoni kitob] *n.* bookcase
чевони пӯшок [jevoni pūshok] *n.* chest of drawers
чеғ задан [jegh zadan] *v.t.* call out, call *(someone)*, scream
чигар [jigar] *n.* liver
чиддият [jiddiyat] *n.* seriousness, gravity
чиддӣ [jiddi] *adj.* earnest, grave, serious
чилав [jilav] *n.* rein
чилд [jild] *n.* volume *(book)*
чило [jilo] *n.* polish
чило додан [jilo dodan] *v.t.* polish, shine
чилчила [jiljila] *adj.* curly
чин [jin] *n.* gin
чингила [jingila] *adj.* curly
чингила кардан [jingila kardan] *v.t.* curl
чиноят [jinoyat] *n.* crime
чинояткор [jinoyatkor] *n.* criminal
чинояткорона [jinoyatkorona] *adj.* criminal
чинс [jins] *n.* gender, sex, species; jeans
чинсият [jinsiyat] *n.* sexuality
чинсӣ [jinsi] *adj.* sexual
чир [jir] *n.* suede
чисман [jisman] *adj.* physical
чиҳат [jihat] *n.* aspect
чиян [jiyan] *n.* nephew, niece
чо [jo] *n.* place
човид [jovid] *adj.* eternal, immortal
чоғ [jogh] *n.* jaw
чоғ задан [jogh zadan] *v.i.* chatter
чодугар [jodugar] *n.* magician
чодугарӣ [jodugari] *n.* magic
чодугарона [jodugarona] *adj.* magical
чое [joe] *adv.* someplace
чое ки [joe ki] *conj.* where
чозиб [jozib] *adj.* attractive, glamorous
чозиба [joziba] *n.* attraction; gravity *(force of attraction)*
чозибият [jozibiyat] *n.* glamor
чой [joy] *n.* place, space, accommodation, site, location
чой додан [joy dodan] *v.t.* accommodate
чойгир кардан [joygir kardan] *v.t.* settle
чойгир шудан [joygir shudan] *v.i.* settle
чойдод [joydod] *n.* real estate

чойпӯш [joypüsh] *n.* sheet *(bedding)*
чома [joma] *n.* robe
чомадон [jomadon] *n.* suitcase
чомашӯӣ [jomashüi] *n.* laundry
чомашӯйхона [jomashüyxona] *n.* laundry room
чон [jon] *n.* soul, spirit
чонвар [jonvar] *n.* animal, beast
чонвар обхокӣ [jonvari obxoki] *n.* amphibian
чонваршиносӣ [jonvarshinosi] *n.* zoology
чонишин [jonishin] *n.* pronoun; substitute / *adj.* substitute
чонишин кардан [jonishin kardan] *v.t.* substitute
чонканӣ [jonkani] *n.* agony
чонсахт [jonsaxt] *adj.* hardy
чорӣ [jori] *adj.* current
чорӣ шудан [jori shudan] *v.i.* flow
чосус [josus] *n.* spy, agent
чосусӣ кардан [josusi kardan] *v.i.* spy
чоҳил [johil] *adj.* ignorant
чоҳилӣ [johili] *n.* ignorance
чувол [juvol] *n.* sack
чуворӣ [juvori] *n.* corn
чуворимакка [juvorimakka] *n.* corn
чуғрофия [jughrofiya] *n.* geography
чудо [judo] *adj.* separate / *adv.* apart
чудо гузоштан [judo guzoshtan] *v.t.* insulate
чудо кардан [judo kardan] *v.t.* separate, detach, isolate
чудо шудан [judo shudan] *v.i.* separate
чудогона [judogona] *adj.* separate
чудогузорӣ [judoguzori] *n.* insulation
чудоӣ [judoi] *n.* separation
чудокунӣ [judokuni] *n.* partition
чуз [juz] *prep.* except
чуз он ки [juz on ki] *conj.* unless
чузвкаш [juzvkash] *n.* briefcase, portfolio
чузъ [juz'] *n.* ingredient
чузъӣ [juz'i] *adj.* topical
чумак [jumak] *n.* faucet, tap, nozzle
чумла [jumla] *n.* sentence, phrase
чумҳурият [jumhuriyat] *n.* republic
чумҳурихоҳ [jumhurixoh] *n.* republican
чумҳуриятӣ [jumhuriyati] *adj.* republican
чумҳурӣ [jumhuri] *n.* republic
чумъа [jum'a] *n.* Friday
чунбанда [junbanda] *adj.* moving
чунбидан [junbidan] *v.i.* move, shake, swing, wag
чунбиш [junbish] *n.* motion, movement
чунбондан [junbondan] *v.t.* move, rock, shake, swing, wag, wave
чуръат кардан [jur'at kardan] *v.i.* dare
чустан [justan] *v.t.* search, look for, hunt, seek
чустучӯ [justujü] *n.* search
чуфт [juft] *n.* couple, pair, equivalent, match / *adj.* even *(not odd)*; **шумораи чуфт** [shumorai juft] an even number

ҷӯй [jüy] *n.* canal *(above-ground)*, ditch, brook
ҷӯйбор [jüybor] *n.* brook
ҷӯр кардан [jür kardan] *v.t.* tune
ҷӯра [jüra] *n.* man or boy's male friend
ҷӯроб [jürob] *n.* sock
ҷӯршавӣ [jürshavi] *n.* combination
ҷӯш [jüsh] *n.* boil, boiling
ҷӯшидан [jüshidan] *v.i.* boil
ҷӯшондан [jüshondan] *v.t.* boil
ҷӯшухурӯш [jüshuxurüsh] *n.* enthusiasm

Ш

шаб [shab] *n.* night
шабака [shabaka] *n.* network
шабакия [shabakiya] *n.* retina
шабаҳ [shabah] *n.* ghost
шабнам [shabnam] *n.* dew
шабнишинӣ [shabnishini] *n.* dinner party
шабона [shabona] *adv.* overnight
шабпарак [shabparak] *n.* moth
шавқ [shavq] *n.* interest, zest
шавқ овардан [shavq ovardan] *v.t.* interest
шавқманд [shavqmand] *adj.* eager
шавқманд кардан [shavqmand kardan] *v.t.* encourage
шавқовар [shavqovar] *adj.* interesting
шавҳар [shavhar] *n.* husband
шавҳардор [shavhardor] *adj.* married *(woman)*
шавшув [shavshuv] *n.* noise
шағал [shaghal] *n.* pebble
шайтон [shayton] *n.* devil
шак [shak] *n.* doubt
шак доштан [shak doshtan] *v.t.* doubt
шакар [shakar] *n.* sugar
шакл [shakl] *n.* form, shape
шақаррос [shaqarros] *n.* crash
шақшақа [shaqshaqa] *n.* rattle
шақшақамор [shaqshaqamor] *n.* rattlesnake
шал кардан [shal kardan] *v.t.* paralyze
шалақ [shalaq] *adj.* rickety
шалӣ [shali] *n.* paralysis
шаллоқ [shalloq] *n.* slap
шаллоқ задан [shalloq zadan] *v.t.* slap
шалпас [shalpas] *n.* splash
шалпас задан [shalpas zadan] *v.i.* splash
шамол [shamol] *n.* wind
шамолрав [shamolrav] *adj.* windy
шампун [shampun] *n.* shampoo
шамшер [shamsher] *n.* sword
шамъ [sham'] *n.* candle
шамъдон [sham'don] *n.* candleholder
шанбе [shanbe] *n.* Saturday
шапарак [shaparak] *n.* butterfly
шар [shar] *n.* vice, evil
шараққос занондан [sharaqqos zanondan] *v.t.* slam
шараф [sharaf] *n.* glory, honor
шарбат [sharbat] *n.* juice, syrup
шарик [sharik] *n.* accomplice, partner

шарикдарс [sharikdars] *n.* schoolmate
шарикӣ [shariki] *adj.* shared
шарир [sharir] *adj.* wicked
шарқ [sharq] *n.* east
шарқӣ [sharqi] *adj.* eastern, east
шарм [sharm] *n.* shame
шарм дорондан [sharm dorondan] *v.t.* embarrass
шарманда [sharmanda] *adj.* embarrassed
шармандагӣ [sharmandagi] *n.* embarrassment
шармгин [sharmgin] *adj.* ashamed, shy
шармовар [sharmovar] *adj.* embarrassing, shameful, scandalous
шармондан [sharmondan] *v.t.* embarrass
шармсор кардан [sharmsor kardan] *v.t.* disgrace
шармсорӣ [sharmsori] *n.* disgrace
шароб [sharob] *n.* wine
шарора [sharora] *n.* spark
шарт [shart] *n.* bet
шарт кардан [shart kardan] *v.t.* bet
шартнома [shartnoma] *n.* contract
шарф [sharf] *n.* scarf
шарҳ [sharh] *n.* comment, commentary, explanation
шарҳ додан [sharh dodan] *v.i.* comment / *v.t.* explain
шарҳнопазир [sharhnopazir] *adj.* inexplicable, unaccountable
шаршара [sharshara] *n.* waterfall
шассӣ [shassi] *n.* chassis
шаст [shast] *n.* fishing rod / *num.* sixty
шатранҷ [shatranj] *n.* chess; **тахтаи шатранҷ** [taxtai shatranj] chessboard; **мӯҳраи шатранҷ** [mührai shatranj] chess piece
шаффоф [shaffof] *adj.* diaphanous, sheer
шах [shax] *n.* cliff / *adj.* erect, firm, stiff
шах кардан [shax kardan] *v.t.* stiffen
шах шудан [shax shudan] *v.i.* stiffen
шахс [shaxs] *n.* individual, person
шахсият [shaxsiyat] *n.* personality
шахсӣ [shaxsi] *adj.* individual, personal, subjective
шаҳр [shahr] *n.* city, town
шаҳрӣ [shahri] *adj.* urban
шаҳрванд [shahrvand] *n.* citizen, national
шаш [shash] *num.* six
шашка [shashka] *n.* checkers
шашум [shashum] *adj.* sixth
шаън [sha'n] *n.* dignity, glory
швед [shved] *n.* Swedish
шведӣ [shvedi] *n.* Swedish *(language)* / *adj.* Swedish
швейсариягӣ [shveysariyagi] *n./adj.* Swiss
шева [sheva] *n.* accent, dialect
шер [sher] *n.* lion
шероза [sheroza] *n.* adhesive tape
шеър [she'r] *n.* poem, poetry
шиддати беморӣ [shiddati bemori] *n.* fit *(med.)*
шиддатнок [shiddatnok] *adj.* strained, tense, vehement
шиддатнокӣ [shiddatnoki] *n.* tension, strain
шикам [shikam] *n.* abdomen, belly, stomach

шикамравӣ [shikamravi] *n.* diarrhea
шиканондан [shikanondan] *v.t.* break
шиканҷа [shikanja] *n.* torture
шиканҷа додан [shikanja dodan] *v.t.* torture
шикаст [shikast] *n.* defeat, wreck
шикаст додан [shikast dodan] *v.t.* defeat
шикастан [shikastan] *v.t./v.i.* break, wreck
шикор [shikor] *n.* hunt
шикор кардан [shikor kardan] *v.t.* hunt
шикорчӣ [shikorchi] *n.* hunter
шикоф [shikof] *n.* crack, leak
шикоят [shikoyat] *n.* complaint, grievance
шикоят кардан [shikoyat kardan] *v.i.* complain
шим [shim] *n.pl.* pants
шимол [shimol] *n.* north
шимолӣ [shimoli] *adj.* northern, north
шино [shino] *n.* swimming
шино кардан [shino kardan] *v.i.* swim
шиновар [shinovar] *n.* swimmer / *adj.* floating
шино шудан [shinovar shudan] *v.i.* float
шинондан [shinondan] *v.t.* place on the ground or other surface; settle
шинос [shinos] *n.* acquaintance *(person)* / *adj.* familiar
шинос кардан [shinos kardan] *v.t.* introduce
шинос шудан [shinos shudan] *v.i.* become acquainted, meet
шиноснома [shinosnoma] *n.* passport
шиносонидан [shinosonidan] *v.t.* acquaint, introduce
шиносоӣ [shinosoi] *n.* acquaintance *(with someone or something)*
шинохтан [shinoxtan] *v.t.* know *(someone)*, be acquainted, recognize
шиор [shior] *n.* slogan
шипанг [shipang] *n.* pavilion
шиппак [shippak] *n.* sandal, slipper
шир [shir] *n.* milk
шир додан [shir dodan] *v.t.* nurse *(a baby)*
шира [shira] *n.* extract, sap, syrup
ширavорӣ [shiravori] *n.* dessert
ширгарм [shirgarm] *adj.* tepid, lukewarm
ширеш [shiresh] *n.* glue
ширин [shirin] *adj.* sweet
ширинӣ [shirini] *n.* sweet
ширинтар кардан [shirintar kardan] *v.t.* sweeten
ширӣ [shiri] *adj.* dairy
ширкат [shirkat] *n.* company *(business enterprise)*, corporation, firm
ширхӯр [shirxür] *n.* mammal
шитоб [shitob] *n.* hurry, rush
шитобӣ [shitobi] *adj.* hasty
шитобкор [shitobkor] *adj.* hasty
шитобкорӣ [shitobkori] *n.* haste
шитобкорона [shitobkorona] *adj.* rash / *adv.* hastily, hurriedly
шитобон бурдан [shitobon burdan] *v.t.* rush
шитофтан [shitoftan] *v.i.* hurry, rush

шифер [shifer] *n.* roofing slate
шифо [shifo] *n.* cure
шифо додан [shifo dodan] *v.t.* cure, heal
шифо ёфтан [shifo yoftan] *v.i.* heal, recuperate
шифобахш [shifobaxsh] *adj.* therapeutic
шифт [shift] *n.* ceiling
шиша [shisha] *n.* bottle; glass
шишагин [shishagin] *adj.* glass
шишанах [shishanax] *n.* fiberglass
шишатозакунак [shishatozakunak] *n.* windshield wiper
шиштан [shishtan] *v.i.* sit
шогирд [shogird] *n.* pupil, student
шод [shod] *adj.* glad, merry, joyful
шодӣ [shodi] *n.* joy
шоир [shoir] *n.* poet
шоистаи писандидан [shoistai pisandidan] *adj.* admirable
шоколад [shokolad] *n.* chocolate
шоколадин [shokoladin] *adj.* chocolate; **тахтача шоколад** [taxtacha shokolad] chocolate bar
шол [shol] *n.* shawl
шом [shom] *n.* dusk, twilight, evening; Islamic prayer performed at dusk
шомиёна [shomiyona] *n.* tent
шомма [shomma] *n.* sense of smell
шона [shona] *n.* comb; shoulder
шона кардан [shona kardan] *v.t.* comb
шонздаҳ [shonzdah] *num.* sixteen
шонздаҳум [shonzdahum] *adj.* sixteenth
шоридан [shoridan] *v.i.* pour
шох [shox] *n.* horn, antler, branch
шохак [shoxak] *n.* antenna *(of insects and other living creatures)*; tentacle
шохча [shoxcha] *n.* twig
шоҳаншоҳ [shohanshoh] *n.* emperor
шоҳбулутранг [shohbulutrang] *adj.* maroon
шоҳгавазн [shohgavazn] *n.* elk
шоҳдухтар [shohduxtar] *n.* princess
шоҳзода [shohzoda] *n.* prince
шоҳид [shohid] *n.* witness
шоҳин [shohin] *n.* falcon
шоҳӣ [shohi] *adj.* royal
шоҳмот [shohmot] *n.* chess; **тахтаи шоҳмот** [taxtai shohmot] chessboard; **мӯҳраи шоҳмот** [mührai shohmot] chess piece
шоҳроҳ [shohroh] *n.* artery *(roadway)*, highway
шоҳтир [shohtir] *n.* beam, shaft
шояд [shoyad] *adv.* maybe, perhaps / *aux.* might
штепсел [shtepsel] *n.* electrical outlet
шубон [shubon] *n.* shepherd
шубҳа [shubha] *n.* doubt
шубҳа кардан [shubha kardan] *v.t.* doubt, mistrust
шубҳаомез [shubhaomez] *adj.* doubtful, questionable, suspicious
шудан [shudan] *v.i.* become
шуданӣ [shudani] *adj.* feasible
шудгор кардан [shudgor kardan] *v.t.* plow

шукуфа [shukufa] *n.* blossom
шукуфтан [shukuftan] *v.i.* bloom
шум [shum] *adj.* sinister
шумор [shumor] *n.* count, tally
шумора [shumora] *n.* number
шумурдан [shumurdan] *v.t.* count
шунаванда [shunavanda] *n.* listener
шунавой [shunavoi] *n.* sense of hearing
шунавондан [shunavondan] *v.t.* transmit sound
шунидан [shunidan] *v.i.* hear
шуоъ [shuo'] *n.* radius; ray
шурӯъ [shurü'] *n.* start
шурӯъ кардан [shurü' kardan] *v.t.* start
шурӯъ шудан [shurü' shudan] *v.i.* start
шустан [shustan] *v.t.* wash
шустанӣ [shustani] *adj.* washable
шутур [shutur] *n.* camel
шух [shux] *n.* thin layer, film; rock
шуш [shush] *n.* lung
шӯла [shüla] *n.* porridge
шӯр [shür] *adj.* salty
шӯрбо [shürbo] *n.* soup, stew
шӯриш [shürish] *n.* rebellion, revolt
шӯриш кардан [shürish kardan] *v.i.* rebel, revolt
шӯришгар [shürishgar] *n.* rebel
шӯрмоҳӣ [shürmohi] *n.* herring
шӯро [shüro] *n.* council
шӯрондан [shürondan] *v.t.* cause to move, agitate
шӯх [shüx] *n.* joker / *adj.* naughty
шӯхӣ [shüxi] *n.* joke, mischief
шӯхӣ кардан [shüxi kardan] *v.i.* joke
шӯҳрат [shührat] *n.* fame
шӯъба [shü'ba] *n.* department
шӯъла [shü'la] *n.* flame
шӯълавар шудан [shü'lavar shudan] *v.i.* flash

Э

элак [elak] *n.* small-holed sieve
элак кардан [elak kardan] *v.t.* sift
электрикӣ [elektriki] *adj.* electric
электронӣ [elektroni] *adj.* electronic
эмин [emin] *adj.* secure, safe
эронӣ [eroni] *n./adj.* Iranian
эҳсос [ehsos] *n.* emotion, feeling, sensation
эҳсос кардан [ehsos kardan] *v.t.* feel
эҳтиёт [ehtiyot] *n.* caution, care
эҳтиёткор [ehtiyotkor] *adj.* careful, cautious, wary, watchful; discreet, prudent
эҳтиёҷ [ehtiyoj] *n.* necessity, requirement
эҳтиёҷ доштан [ehtiyoj doshtan] *v.t.* require
эҳтимолӣ [ehtimoli] *adj.* likely, probable
эҳтиром [ehtirom] *n.* respect
эҳтиром кардан [ehtirom kardan] *v.t.* honor, respect
эҷодкор [ejodkor] *n.* maker
эшон [eshon] *n.* descendant of the Prophet Muhammad / *pron.* they, them
эълон [e'lon] *n.* advertisement, commercial, announcement, declaration

эълон карда шудан [e'lon karda shudan] *v.i.* advertise
эълон кардан [e'lon kardan] *v.t.* advertise, announce, declare
эътиборнок [e'tibornok] *adj.* reliable, having legal force, valid
эътимод доштан [e'timod doshtan] *v.t.* rely
эътироз [e'tiroz] *n.* objection, protest
эътироз кардан [e'tiroz kardan] *v.t.* object, protest
эътироф кардан [e'tirof kardan] *v.i.* admit, acknowledge, confess
эътироф [e'tirof] *n.* acknowledgement, confession

Ю

-ю [yu] *conj.* and *(after vowels)*
юз [yuz] *n.* cheetah
юзпаланг [yuzpalang] *n.* cheetah
юнонӣ [yunoni] *n./adj.* Greek

Я

ягон [yagon] *adj.* some
ягон кас [yagon kas] *pron.* anyone, somebody
ягон чиз [yagon chiz] *pron.* anything
ягон ҷо [yagon jo] *pron.* anywhere
ягона [yagona] *adj.* only, single, sole, unique
ягонагӣ [yagonagi] *n.* unity
ядак [yadak] *n.* trailer
ядро [yadro] *n.* nucleus
ядроӣ [yadroi] *adj.* nuclear
як [yak] *num.* one
як кардан [yak kardan] *v.t.* unite
як ҳангоме [yak hangome] *adv.* sometime
як шудан [yak shudan] *v.i.* unite with, join
якдилона [yakdilona] *adj.* unanimous
якка [yakka] *adj.* alone, lone, single, sole, lonely
яклухт [yakluxt] *adj.* entire
якоҳанг [yakohang] *adj.* monotonous
якрав [yakrav] *adj.* obstinate, stubborn
якранга [yakranga] *adj.* monotonous
яксон [yakson] *adj.* same
яксон набудан [yakson nabudan] *v.i.* differ
якум [yakum] *adj.* first
якумин [yakumin] *adj.* first, primary
якумӣ [yakumi] *n.* priority
якхел [yakxel] *adj.* alike, identical, same
якхел набудан [yakxel nabudan] *v.i.* differ
якхела [yakxela] *adj.* identical, standard, uniform
якҷониба [yakjoniba] *adj.* one-way
якҷоя [yakjoya] *adv.* together
якҷоя кардан [yakjoya kardan] *v.t.* combine, bring together
якҷоя шудан [yakjoya shudan] *v.i.* get together, come together
якҷояқунӣ [yakjoyakuni] *n.* combination
якчанд [yakchand] *adj.* several
якшанбе [yakshanbe] *n.* Sunday
яқин [yaqin] *adj.* definite, certain, sure

яқин кардан [yaqin kardan] *v.t.* make sure
яла кардан [yala kardan] *v.t.* undo, unfasten, unwrap
ялаққос [yalaqqos] *n.* flash
ялаққос задан [yalaqqos zadan] *v.i.* flash, sparkle
ялаққосӣ [yalaqqosi] *adj.* brilliant
январ [yanvar] *n.* January
янга [yanga] *n.* sister-in-law *(brother's wife)*
японӣ [yaponi] *n./adj.* Japanese
яра [yara] *n.* injury, wound
ярадор [yarador] *adj.* injured
ярадор кардан [yarador kardan] *v.t.* injure, wound
ярмарка [yarmarka] *n.* fair *(county, church, etc.)*
яроқ [yaroq] *n.* weapon
ярч [yarch] *n.* landslide
ятим [yatim] *n.* orphan
ятимхона [yatimxona] *n.* orphanage
ях [yax] *n.* ice
ях бандондан [yax bandondan] *v.t.* freeze
ях бастан [yax bastan] *v.i.* freeze
ях кардан [yax kardan] *v.i.* freeze
ях кунондан [yax kunondan] *v.t.* freeze, refrigerate
яхбаста [yaxbasta] *adj.* frozen
яхдон [yaxdon] *n.* refrigerator, ice box
яхин [yaxin] *adj.* icy
яхӣ [yaxi] *adj.* icy
яхкарда [yaxkarda] *adj.* frozen
яхмолакпарӣ кардан [yaxmolakpari kardan] *v.i.* ice-skate
яхмос [yaxmos] *n.* ice cream
яхпӯш [yaxpüsh] *adj.* ice-covered
яхчол [yaxchol] *n.* refrigerator
яҳудӣ [yahudi] *n.* Jew / *adj.* Jewish
яшми сабз [yashmi sabz] *n.* jade

English-Tajik Dictionary

A

a, an [э, эн] *art.* -е [-e]; **a boy** писаре [pisare]; **a book** китобе [kitobe]

abandon [абенден] *v.t.* падруд гуфтан [padrud guftan], тарк кардан [tark kardan], ҳиштан [hishtan]

abbreviate [абривиейт] *v.t.* мухтасар кардан [muxtasar kardan]

abbreviation [абривиейшан] *n.* ихтисор [ixtisor]

abdomen [эбдомен] *n.* шикам [shikam]

ability [абилити] *n.* тавоноӣ [tavonoi], қобилият [qobiliyat]

able [эибал] *adj.* тавоно [tavono], қобил [qobil]

abnormal [абнормал] *adj.* ғайриоддӣ [ghayrioddi]

aboard [аборд] *adv.* *(aboard a ship)* дар киштӣ [dar kishti]; *(aboard a plane)* дар ҳавопаймо [dar havopaymo]

abortion [аборшан] *n.* бачапартоӣ [bachapartoi], бачапартоёнӣ [bachapartoyoni]

about [абаут] *adv.* наздик [nazdik], тақрибан [taqriban] / *prep.* *(around, approximately)* тақрибан [taqriban], *(concerning)* дар бораи [dar borai]

above [эбав] *adv.* боло [bolo], ба боло [ba bolo] / *prep.* боло [bolo], дар боло [dar bolo]; **above all** [эбав ол] *adv.* болотар аз ҳама [bolotar az hama]

abroad [эброд] *adv./adj.* хориҷа [xorija]

absence [абсенс] *n.* ғайбат [ghaybat]

absent [абсент] *adj.* ғоиб [ghoib]

absolute [абсолют] *adj.* мутлақ [mutlaq]

absorb [эбзорб] *v.t.* ҷаббидан [jabbidan]

abstract [эбстрект] *adj.* муҷаррад [mujarrad]

absurd [абсурд] *adj.* бемаънӣ [bema'ni]

abundance [абанданс] *n.* фаровонӣ [farovoni]

abundant [абандант] *adj.* фаровон [farovon]

abuse [абюс] *n.* *(anguish)* озор [ozor], *(verbal abuse)* дашном [dashnom] / *v.t.* *(cause anguish)* озор додан [ozor dodan], *(abuse verbally)* дашном додан [dashnom dodan]

abusive [абюсив] *adj.* дашномдиҳанда [dashnomdihanda]

academic [экадемик] *adj.* академӣ [akademi]

academy [экадеми] *n.* академия [akademiya]

accelerate [экселерейт] *v.t.* тезондан [tezondan], суръат додан [sur'at dodan] / *v.i.* тезтар шудан [teztar shudan]

accelerator [экселерейтор] *n.* суръатфизо [sur'atfizo]

accent [эксент] *n.* лаҳҷа [lahja], шева [sheva]

accept [эксепт] *v.t.* қабул кардан [qabul kardan], пазируфтан [paziruftan]

acceptance [эксептанс] *n.* қабул [qabul], пазириш [pazirish]

access [эксес] *n.* дастрасӣ [dastrasi]
accessories [эксесориз] *n.* лавозимот [lavozimot]
accessory [эксесори] *n.* чизи фаръӣ [chizi far'i], чизи иловагӣ [chizi ilovagi] / *adj.* фаръӣ [far'i], иловагӣ [ilovagi]
accident [эксидент] *n.* ҳодиса [hodisa]
accidental [эксидентал] *adj.* тасодуфӣ [tasodufi]
accidentally [эксидентали] *adv.* тасодуфан [tasodufan]
accommodate [акомадейт] *v.t.* ҷой додан [joy dodan], гунҷондан [gunjondan]
accommodation [акомадейшан] *n.* ҷой [joy], манзил [manzil]
accompany [акапани] *v.t.* ҳамроҳ рафтан [hamroh raftan]
accomplice [акомплис] *n.* шарик [sharik]
accomplish [акомплиш] *v.t.* анҷом додан [anjom dodan]
accomplishment [акомплишмент] *n.* анҷом [anjom]
according to [акординг ту] *prep.* мувофиқи [muvofiqi]
account [экаунт] *n.* ҳисоб [hisob]; **bank account** ҳисоби бонк [hisobi bonk]
accountant [экаунтант] *n.* ҳисобдор [hisobdor]
accounting [экаунтинг] *n.* ҳисобдорӣ [hisobdori]
accumulate [экюмюлейт] *v.t.* андӯхтан [andüxtan], ғундоштан [ghundoshtan]
accurate [экюрет] *adj. (precise)* аниқ [aniq], дақиқ [daqiq], *(correct)* дуруст [durust]
accusation [акюзешан] *n.* тухмат [tühmat]
accuse [акюз] *v.t.* муттаҳам кардан [muttaham kardan]
accustom [акастам] *v.i.* одат кардан [odat kardan], омӯхта шудан [omüxta shudan]; **be accustomed to** … ба … омӯхта будан [ba … omüxta budan]
ace [эйс] *n.* зот [zot]; **ace of hearts** зоти таппон [zoti tappon]
ache [эйк] *n.* дард [dard] / *v.i.* дард кардан [dard kardan]
achieve [ачив] *v.t.* ноил шудан [noil shudan], анҷом додан [anjom dodan]
achievement [ачивмент] *n.* анҷом [anjom], ноилшавӣ [noilshavi]
acid [эсид] *n. (substance with a sour taste)* туршӣ [turshi], *(chemical)* ҳомуз [homuz] / *adj.* турш [tursh]
acidic [эсидик] *adj.* ҳомуздор [homuzdor]
acidity [эсидити] *n.* туршӣ [turshi]
acknowledge [экнолиҷ] *v.t.* *(admit)* эътироф кардан [e'tirof kardan], иқрор кардан [iqror kardan]; *(acknowledge sb)* ба эътибор гирифтан [ba e'tibor giriftan]
acknowledgment [экнолиҷмент] *n.* эътироф [e'tirof], иқрор [iqror]
acne [экни] *n.* гармича [garmicha], рихинак [rixinak]
acquaint [акуейнт] *v.t.* ошно кардан [oshno kardan], шиносонидан [shinosonidan]

acquaintance [акуейнтанс] *n. (knowledge of a person)* шиносоӣ [shinosoi], ошноӣ [oshnoi], *(person one knows)* шинос [shinos], ошно [oshno], *(knowledge of a subject)* шиносоӣ [shinosoi]

acquire [акуайр] *v.t. (gain possession)* ба даст овардан [ba dast ovardan]; *(learn)* ёд гирифтан [yod giriftan]

acquisition [экуизишан] *adj.* ҳусул [husul]

acre [эйкър] *n.* акр [akr]

across [экрос] *adv.* ба сӯйи дигар [ba süyi digar], сӯйи дигар [süyi digar] / *prep.* сар то сари [sar to sari]

act [экт] *n. (deed, action)* кор [kor], кирдор [kirdor]; *(of a play)* парда [parda], *(item on a program:, juggling act, magic act, etc.)* баромад [baromad] / *v.i. (perform in a play or movie, etc.)* бозӣ кардан [bozi kardan], бозидан [bozidan]; *(take action)* кор кардан [kor kardan]

action [экшан] *n.* кор [kor], амал [amal]

active [эктив] *adj.* фаъол [fa'ol]

activity [эктивити] *n.* фаъолият [fa'oliyat]

actor [эктор] *n.* ҳунарманд [hunarmand], ҳунарпеша [hunarpesha]

actual [экчуал] *adj.* воқеӣ [voqei]

acute [акют] *adj.* тез [tez]

A.D. [эй ди] *(abbrev. of* **Anno Domini***)* милодӣ [milodi]

adapt [адапт] *v.t.* созгор кардан [sozgor kardan] / *v.i.* созгор шудан [sozgor shudan]

adapter [адаптер] *n.* адаптер [adapter]

add [эд] *v.t. (include additional items)* афзудан [afzudan], илова кардан [ilova kardan], *(mathematics)* ҷамъ кардан [jam' kardan]

addition [адишон] *n. (sth additional)* илова [ilova], афзоиш [afzoish]; *(mathematics)* ҷамъ [jam']

additional [адишонал] *adj.* иловагӣ [ilovagi]

address [адрес] *n.* суроға [surogha], нишонӣ [nishoni] / *v.t.* нишонӣ навиштан [nishoni navishtan]

adequate [адекуат] *adj.* басанда [basanda], кофӣ [kofi]

adhere [адҳир] *v.i. (remain attached)* часпидан [chaspidan]; *(comply with)* риоя кардан [rioya kardan]

adhesive [адҳисив] *adj.* часпак [chaspak]

adjacent [адҷейсант] *adj.* наздик [nazdik]

adjective [адҷектив] *gram.* сифат [sifat]

adjoin [адҷойн] *v.i.* пайваста будан [payvasta budan], ҳамшафат будан [hamshafat budan]

adjust [адҷаст] *v.t.* таъдил кардан [ta'dil kardan]

administer [администър] *v.t.* идора кардан [idora kardan]

administration [администрейшан] *n.* идора [idora]

administrative [административ] *adj.* идорӣ [idori]

admirable [адмирабъл] *adj.* шоистаи писандидан [shoistai pisandidan]
admiral [адмирал] *n.* адмирал [admiral]
admire [адмайр] *v.t.* писандидан [pisandidan]
admission [адмишан] *n.* даромадан [daromadan], дохилшавӣ [doxilshavi]; **free admission** даромадани бепул [daromadani bepul]
admit [адмит] *v.t. (grant admission)* иҷозати даромадан додан [ijozati daromadan dodan]; *(acknowledge)* иқрор кардан [iqror kardan]
adolescent [адолесент] *n.* ҷавон [javon] / *adj.* ҷавон [javon]
adopt [адопт] *v.t. (accept)* пазируфтан [paziruftan], қабул кардан [qabul kardan]; *(adopt a child)* фарзанд хондан [farzand xondan]
adoption [адопшан] *n.* фарзандхонд [farzandxond]
adore [адор] *v.t. (worship)* парастидан [parastidan]; *(love greatly)* бисёр дӯст доштан [bisyor düst doshtan]
adult [адалт] *n.* болиғ [boligh] / *adj.* болиғ [boligh]
advance [адванс] *n. (progress)* пешрафт [peshraft]; *(pre-payment)* пешпардохт [peshpardoxt] / *v.t.* пеш кашидан [pesh kashidan] / *v.i.* пеш рафтан [pesh raftan]; **in advance** пешакӣ [peshaki]
advantage [адвантиҷ] *n. (superiority)* бартарӣ [bartari]; *(benefit)* фоида [foida]
adventure [адвенчур] *n.* саргузашт [sarguzasht]
adverb [адверб] *gram.* зарф [zarf]
adversary [адверсари] *n. (enemy)* душман [dushman]; *(rival)* рақиб [raqib]
advertise [адвертайз] *v.t.* эълон кардан [e'lon kardan] / *v.i.* эълон карда шудан [e'lon karda shudan]
advertisement [адвертайзмент] *n.* эълон [e'lon]
advice [адвайс] *n.* панд [pand], маслиҳат [maslihat]
advise [адвайз] *v.t.* панд додан [pand dodan], маслиҳат додан [maslihat dodan]
adviser [адвайзор] *n.* мушовир [mushovir]
aerial [эриял] *n.* антенна [antenna] / *adj.* ҳавоӣ [havoi]
affair [афейр] *n.* кор [kor]
affect [афект] *v.t.* таъсир кардан [ta'sir kardan]
affection [афекшан] *n.* меҳр [mehr]
affectionate [афеканит] *adj.* пурмеҳр [purmehr], меҳрубон [mehrubon]
affirm [афирм] *v.t.* исбот кардан [isbot kardan]
affirmation [афирмейшан] *n.* исбот [isbot]
afflict [афликт] *v.t.* ранҷондан [ranjondan], ғамгин кардан [ghamgin kardan]

affliction [афликшан] *n.* ғам [gham], бадбахтӣ [badbaxti]
afford [афорд] *v.t.* пули басанда доштан [puli basanda doshtan]
Afghan [эфген] *n./adj.* афғон [afghon]
afraid [афрейд] *adj.* тарсон [tarson]; **be afraid of** тарсидан аз [tarsidan az]
African [африкан] *n./adj.* африқоӣ [afriqoi]
after [афтер] *adv.* пас [pas], сипас [sipas], баъд [ba'd] / *prep.* пас аз [pas az], баъд аз [ba'd az]; **after us** пас аз мо [pas az mo]; **after all** охир [oxir]
afternoon [афтернун] *n.* пешин [peshin]
afterward [афтеруард] *adv.* сипас [sipas]
again [эгейн] *adv.* боз [boz]
against [эгейнст] *prep.* *(touching)* ба [ba]; *(in opposition)* бар зидди [bar ziddi]
age [эйҷ] *n.* *(duration of life)* син [sin], сол [sol]; *(era)* аср [asr]
agenda [аҷенда] *n.* рӯзномаи маҷлис [rüznomai majlis]
agent [эйҷент] *n.* *(one empowered to act)* гумошта [gumoshta]; *(spy)* ҷосус [josus]; *(substance: chemical, etc.)* омил [omil]
aggravate [эгривейт] *v.t.* бадтар кардан [badtar kardan]
aggressive [агресив] *adj.* таҷовузкор [tajovuzkor]
agile [эҷайл] *adj.* чобук [chobuk], зуд [zud]
agitate [эҷитейт] *v.t.* *(cause to move)* шӯрондан [shürondan]; *(make upset)* ба изтироб овардан [ba iztirob ovardan]
ago [эго] *adv.* пеш [pesh]; **long ago** кайҳо [kayho]
agony [эгони] *n.* ҷонканӣ [jonkani]
agree [эгри] *v.i.* *(be in accord)* мувофиқ будан [muvofiq budan], *(decide)* қарор доштан [qaror doshtan], забон як кардан [zabon yak kardan]
agreeable [эгриябъл] *adj.* дилписанд [dilpisand], форам [foram]
agreement [эгримент] *n.* *(contract)* иттифоқ [ittifoq], созиш [sozish]; *(harmony of opinion)* ҳамфикрӣ [hamfikri]; *(accord)* мувофиқат [muvofiqat]
agricultural [эгрикалчурал] *adj.* зироатӣ [ziroati]
agriculture [эгрикалчур] *n.* кишоварзӣ [kishovarzi], зироат [ziroat]
ahead [аҳед] *adj.* дар пеш [pesh] / *adv.* пешопеш [peshopesh], ба пеш [ba pesh]; **ahead of** пеш аз [pesh az]; **get ahead** дар пеш шудан [dar pesh shudan]; **go ahead** ба пеш рафтан [ba pesh raftan]
aid [эйд] *n.* ёрӣ [yori], кӯмак [kümak] / *v.t.* ёрӣ додан [yori dodan], кӯмак кардан [kümak kardan]
AIDS [эйдз] *n.* *(abbrev. of* **Acquired Immunodeficiency Syndrome***)* СПИД [SPID]

aim [эйм] *n.* *(target)* нишон [nishon], ҳадаф [hadaf]; *(intention)* ният [niyat] / *v.t.* *(have an intention)* ният доштан [niyat doshtan]; *(aim a gun, an arrow, etc.)* нишон гирифтан [nishon giriftan]

air [эр] *n.* ҳаво [havo]; **go by air** бо ҳавопаймо рафтан [bo havopaymo raftan]; **air base** пойгоҳи ҳавопаймоӣ [poygohi havopaymoi]

air condition [эр-кондишан] *v.t.* ҳаво хунук кардан [havo xunuk kardan]

air-conditioned [эр-кондишанд] *adj.* ҳавохунуккунакдор [havoxunukkunakdor]

air conditioner [эр-кондишнер] *n.* ҳавохунуккунак [havoxunukkunak]

air-conditioning [эр-кондишнинг] *n.* тасфияи ҳаво [tasfiyai havo]

air force [эрфорс] *n.* қувваҳои ҳарбии ҳавоӣ [quvvahoi harbii havoi]

airline [эрлайн] *n.* роҳи ҳавоӣ [rohi havoi]

airmail [эрмейл] *n.* почтаи ҳавоӣ [pochtai havoi]

airplane [эрплен] *n.* ҳавопаймо [havopaymo]

airport [эрпорт] *n.* фурудгоҳ [furudgoh]

aisle [айл] *n.* роҳрав [rohrav]

alarm [аларм] *n.* бонги хатар [bongi xatar] / *v.t.* ба изтироб андохтан [ba iztirob andoxtan]; **sound the alarm** бонги хатар задан [bongi xatar zadan]; **alarm clock** соати зангдор [soati zangdor]

alcohol [алкоҳол] *n.* спирт [spirt]; **alcoholic drink** нӯшокии спиртдор [nüshokii spirtdor]

alcoholic [алкоҳолик] *n.* майзада [mayzada] / *adj.* спиртдор [spirtdor]

alcove [алков] *n.* тахтмон [taxtmon], равоқ [ravoq]

ale [эйл] *n.* оби ҷави англисӣ [obi javi anglisi], пивои англисӣ [pivoi anglisi]

alert [алерт] *n.* бонги хатар [bongi xatar] / *adj.* ҳушёр [hushyor] / *v.t.* ҳушёр кардан [hushyor kardan]

alien [эйлиен] *adj.* *(foreign)* бегона [begona]; *(extra-terrestrial)* аз ситораи бегона [az sitorai begona]

align [алайн] *v.t.* дар саф овардан [dar saf ovardan]

alike [алайк] *adj.* монанд [monand], якхел [yakxel]

alive [алайв] *adj.* зинда [zinda]

all [ол] *adj.* ҳама [hama]

allergic [алерҷик] *adj.* аллергӣ [allergi]; *(be allergic)* аллергия доштан [allergiya doshtan]

allergy [алерҷи] *n.* аллергия [allergiya]

alley [али] *n.* тангкӯча [tangkücha], паскӯча [pasküchа]

alliance [алайанс] *n.* иттифоқ [ittifoq]

allow [алау] *v.t.* мондан [mondan]

ally [элай] *n.* иттифоқчӣ [ittifoqchi]

almond [алмонд] *n.* бодом [bodom]

almost [олмост] *adv.* тақрибан [taqriban]

aloft [алофт] *adj.* боло [bolo]
alone [алон] *adj.* танҳо [tanho]
along [алонг] *adv.* ҳамроҳ [hamroh]
aloud [алауд] *adv.* бо овози баланд [bo ovozi baland]
alphabet [алфабет] *n.* алифбо [alifbo]
already [олреди] *adv.* аллакай [allakay]
also [олсо] *adv.* ҳам [ham]
altar [олтар] *n. (of a church)* меҳроб [mehrob], *(sacrificial)* қурбонгоҳ [qurbongoh]
alter [олтер] *v.t.* дигаргун кардан [digargun kardan]
alteration [олтерейшан] *n.* дигаргунӣ [digarguni]
although [олдо] *conj.* агарчи [agarchi], ҳарчанд [harchand]
altitude [алтитюд] *n.* баландӣ [balandi]
altogether [олтугедер] *adv. (in total)* ҳамагӣ [hamagi], *(completely)* тамоман [tamoman]
aluminum [алуминам] *n.* алюминий [alyuminiy]
always [олуиз] *adv.* ҳамеша [hamesha]
a.m. [эй эм] *adj. (abbrev. of* **ante meridiem** *[before noon])* пагоҳӣ [pagohi]
amateur [амачър] *n.* ҳаваскор [havaskor]
amaze [амейз] *v.t.* ҳайрон кардан [hayron kardan]
amazing [амейзинг] *adj.* ҳайратангез [hayratangez]
ambassador [амбасадор] *n.* сафир [safir]
ambiguous [амбигюас] *adj.* духӯра [duxüra]
ambition [амбишан] *n.* мансабпарастӣ [mansabparasti]
ambitious [амбишас] *adj.* мансабпараст [mansabparast]
ambulance [амбюланс] *n.* мошини ёрии таъҷилӣ [moshini yorii ta'jili]
amendment [амендмент] *n.* ислоҳ [isloh]
American [американ] *n./adj.* амрикоӣ [amrikoi]
amid [амид] *prep.* миёни [miyoni]
ammonia [амония] *n.* аммиак [ammiak]
among [аманг] *prep.* миёни [miyoni]
amphibian [эмфибиян] *n.* ҷонвар обхокӣ [jonvari obxoki] / *adj.* обхокӣ [obxoki]
ample [эмпъл] *adj. (large amount)* фаровон [farovon]; *(sufficient)* басанда [basanda]
amplifier [эмплифайэр] *n.* қувватфизо [quvvatfizo]
amplify [эмплифай] *v.t.* баландтар кардан [balandtar kardan]
amputate [эмпютейт] *v.t.* бурида партофтан [burida partoftan]
amputation [эмпютейшан] *n.* буридапартоӣ [buridapartoi]
amuse [амюз] *v.t. (occupy)* андармон кардан [andarmon kardan], *(make laugh)* вақтчоқ кардан [vaqtchoq kardan], хандондан [xandondan]
amusement [амюзмент] *n.* кайф [kayf], лаззат [lazzat]

analogy [аналоҷи] *n. (similarity)* монандӣ [monandi], *(comparison based on similarity)* қиёс [qiyos]

analysis [анализис] *n.* таҳлил [tahlil]

analyze [аналайз] *v.t.* таҳлил кардан [tahlil kardan]

anarchy [энарки] *n.* бесарӣ [besari], беҳокимиятӣ [behokimiyati]

anatomy [анатоми] *n.* колбадшиносӣ [kolbadshinosi], анатомия [anatomiya]

ancestor [энсестар] *n.* ниё [niyo]

anchor [энкор] *n.* лангар [langar] / *v.i.* лангар андохтан [langar andoxtan]

ancient [эйншант] *adj.* бостон [boston], қадим [qadim]

and [энд] *conj.* -у [u], *(after vowels)* -ю [yu], ва [va]; **and so forth** *or* **and so on** ва ғайра [va ghayra]

anecdote [энекдот] *n.* латифа [latifa]

anemia [анимия] *n.* камхунӣ [kamxuni]

anesthesia [энестизия] *n.* анестизия [anesteziya]

angel [эйнҷал] *n.* фаришта [farishta]

anger [энгър] *n.* хашм [xashm] / *v.t.* хашмгин кардан [xashmgin kardan] / *v.i.* хашмгин шудан [xashmgin shudan]

angle [энгъл] *n.* кунҷ [kunj]; **right angle** кунҷи рост [kunji rost]

angry [ангри] *adj.* хашмгин [xashmgin]

anguish [энгуиш] *n.* азоб [azob], дард [dard]

animal [энимал] *n.* ҷонвар [jonvar], ҳайвон [hayvon]

ankle [энкъл] *n.* буҷулак [bujulak]

annex [энекс] *n.* бинои фаръӣ [binoi far'i] / *v.t.* ғасб кардан [ghasb kardan]

anniversary [аниварсари] *n.* солгард [solgard]

announce [анаунс] *v.t.* еълон кардан [e'lon kardan]

announcement [анаунсмант] *n.* еълон [e'lon]

annoy [аной] *v.t.* безор кардан [bezor kardan], озурдан [ozurdan]

annoyance [анойянс] *n.* безорӣ [bezori], озурдагӣ [ozurdagi]

annual [энюал] *adj.* солона [solona]

annul [анал] *v.t.* бекор кардан [bekor kardan], лағв кардан [laghv kardan]

anonymous [анонимас] *adj.* номаълум [noma'lum]

another [анадер] *adj.* дигар [digar]

answer [энсър] *n.* посух [posux], ҷавоб [javob] / *v.t.* посух додан [posux dodan], ҷавоб додан [javob dodan]

ant [энт] *n.* мӯрча [mürcha]

antenna [энтена] *n. (of an insect, etc.)* шохак [shoxak]; *(for transmission)* антенна [antenna]

anti- [энти] *pref.* зидди [ziddi]

antibiotic [энтибайотик] *n.* антибиотик [antibiotik] / *adj.* антибиотикӣ [antibiotiki]

anticipate [энтисипейт] *v.t. (realize beforehand)* пешбинӣ кардан [peshbini kardan] / *v.i. (expect)* чашм доштан [chashm doshtan]
anticipation [энтисипейшан] *n. (foresight)* пешбинӣ [peshbini]; *(expectation)* чашмдошт [chashmdosht]
antique [энтик] *n.* атиқа [atiqa] / *adj.* кӯҳна [kühna]; **antique shop** атиқафурӯшӣ [atiqafurüshi]
antiseptic [энтисептик] *adj.* зидди уфунӣ [ziddi ufuni], антисептикӣ [antiseptiki]
anxiety [энгзайити] *n.* ноороми [nooromi], нигаронӣ [nigaroni]
anxious [энкшас] *adj.* ноором [noorom], нигарон [nigaron]
any [эни] *adj. (some)* ягон [yagon]; *(all)* ҳама [hama]; *(each)* ҳар [har]
anybody [энибоди] *pron.* касе [kase]
anyone [эниуан] *pron.* ягон кас [yagon kas], касе [kase]
anything [энитинг] *pron.* ягон чиз [yagon chiz], чизе [chize]
anytime [энитайм] *adv.* ҳар вақт [har vaqt]
anywhere [эниуэр] *adv.* ягон ҷо [yagon jo], куҷое [kujoe]
apart [апарт] *adv.* ҷудо [judo]
apartment [апартмент] *n.* апортумон [aportumon]
apathetic [апатетик] *adj.* беҳавсала [behavsala], мурдадил [murdadil]
apologize [апологайз] *v.i.* узр хостан [uzr xostan], пӯзиш хостан [püzish xostan]
apology [апологи] *n.* узр [uzr], пӯзиш [püzish]
apparatus [апаратус] *n.* дастгоҳ [dastgoh], абзор [abzor]
apparel [аперел] *n.* пӯшок [püshok]
apparent [аперент] *adj.* падидор [padidor], дидашаванда [didashavanda]
appeal [апил] *v.i. (seek redress)* муроҷиат кардан [murojiat kardan]; *(attract)* ҷалб кардан [jalb kardan]
appear [апир] *v.i.* пайдо шудан [paydo shudan], намоён шудан [namoyon shudan]
appearance [апиранс] *n.* пайдоиш [paydoish]
appendicitis [апендисайтис] *n.* аппендисит [appendisit], омоси кӯррӯда [omosi kürrüda]
appendix [апендикс] *n. (addendum)* замима [zamima]; *(anatomical)* аппендикс [appendiks]
appetite [апетайт] *n.* иштиҳо [ishtiho]
appetizer [апетайзер] *n.* хӯриш [xürish], газак [gazak]
applaud [аплод] *v.t.* қарсак задан [qarsak zadan], каф задан [kaf zadan]
applause [аплоз] *n.* қарсакзанӣ [qarsakzani], кафкӯбӣ [kafkübi]
apple [эпъл] *n.* себ [seb]; **Adam's apple** хекиртак [xekirtak]
appliance [аплайанс] *n.* абзор [abzor], асбоб [asbob]

application [аппликейшан] *n.* *(usage)* корбурд [korburd]; *(request)* дархост [darxost]
apply [аплай] *v.t.* ба кор бурдан [ba kor burdan] / *v.i.* дархост кардан [darxost kardan]
appoint [апойнт] *v.t.* таъин кардан [ta'in kardan], гумоштан [gumoshtan]
appointment [апойнтмент] *n.* *(position)* вазифа [vazifa]; *(meeting)* мулоқот [muloqot]
appraisal [апрейзал] *n.* арзёбӣ [arzyobi]
appreciate [апришиейт] *v.t.* қадр донистан [qadr donistan]
appreciation [апришиейшан] *n.* қадрдонӣ [qadrdoni]
approach [апроч] *n.* наздикшавӣ [nazdikshavi] / *v.i.* наздик шудан [nazdik shudan]
appropriate [апроприят] *adj.* муносиб [munosib]
approval [апрувал] *n.* таҳсин [tahsin]
approve [апрув] *v.t.* писандидан [pisandidan], маъқул донистан [ma'qul donistan]
approximate [апроксимейт] *adj.* тақрибӣ [taqribi], тахминӣ [taxmini] / *v.t.* тахмин кардан [taxmin kardan]
approximately [апроксиметли] *adv.* тақрибан [taqriban], тахминан [taxminan]
apricot [эйприкот] *n.* зардолу [zardolu]
April [эйприл] *n.* апрел [aprel]
apron [эйпран] *n.* пешдоман [peshdoman]
apt [апт] *adj.* *(talented)* боистеъдод [boiste'dod]; *(suitable)* муносиб [munosib]
aptitude [аптитюд] *n.* *(talent)* истеъдод [iste'dod]; *(suitability)* муносибат [munosibat]
aquatic [акуэтик] *adj.* обӣ [obi]
Arab [араб] *n.* араб [arab] / *adj.* арабӣ [arabi]
Arabic [арабик] *n.* *(language)* арабӣ [arabi]
arbitrary [арбитрери] *adj.* ихтиёрӣ [ixtiyori], бедалел [bedalel]
arch [арч] *n.* тоқ [toq]
archaeologist [аркиёлоҷист] *n.* бостоншинос [bostonshinos]
archaeology [аркиёлоҷи] *n.* бостоншиносӣ [bostonshinosi]
architect [аркитект] *n.* меъмор [me'mor]
architectural [аркитекчурал] *adj.* меъморӣ [me'mori]
architecture [аркитекчур] *n.* меъморӣ [me'mori]
archive [аркайв] *n.* бойгонӣ [boygoni] / *v.t.* дар бойгонӣ гузоштан [dar boygoni guzoshtan]
arctic [арктик] *adj.* бисёр хунук [bisyor xunuk]; **Arctic** *n.* Қутби Шимолӣ [Qutbi Shimoli]; **Arctic Circle** Доираи Қутби Шимол [Doirai Qutbi Shimol]

area [эрия] *n. (mathematical)* масоҳат [masohat]; *(region)* ноҳия [nohiya]; *(subject)* соҳа [soha], доира [doira]

argue [аргю] *v.i.* баҳс кардан [bahs kardan]

argument [аргюмент] *n.* баҳс [bahs]

arise [арайз] *v.i. (get up)* хестан [xestan]; *(come into being)* пайдо шудан [paydo shudan]

arithmetic [аритметик] *n.* арифметика [arifmetika], илми ҳисоб [ilmi hisob]

arm [арм] *n.* бозу [bozu]

armchair [армчер] *n.* курсии паҳлӯдор [kursii pahlüdor]

Armenian [арминиян] *n. (person)* арман [arman]; *(language)* арманӣ [armani] / *adj.* арманӣ [armani]

armpit [армпит] *n.* зери бағал [zeri baghal]

army [арми] *n.* лашкар [lashkar], қӯшун [qüshun]

aroma [арома] *n.* хушбӯй [xushbüy], накҳат [nakhat]

around [араунд] *adv.* гирдогирд [girdogird] / *prep.* гирди [girdi]; **all around the world** саросари ҷаҳон [sarosari jahon]

arrange [аренҷ] *v.t.* чидан [chidan], ба тартиб овардан [ba tartib ovardan]

arrangement [арейнҷмент] *n.* тартиб [tartib]

arrest [арест] *n.* дастгирӣ [dastgiri], ҳабс [habs] / *v.t.* дастгир кардан [dastgir kardan]

arrival [арайвал] *n.* вуруд [vurud]

arrive [арайв] *v.i.* расидан [rasidan]

arrogance [эроганс] *n.* ғурур [ghurur], такаббур [takabbur]

arrogant [эрогант] *adj.* мағрур [maghrur], пуркибр [purkibr]

arrow [эро] *n.* тир [tir], ходанг [xadang]

art [арт] *n.* санъат [san'at]

artery [артери] *n. (roadway)* шоҳроҳ [shohroh], роҳи асосӣ [rohi asosi]; *(blood vessel)* сурхраг [surxrag]

article [артикъл] *n. (item)* чиз [chiz]; *(in a newspaper)* мақола [maqola]; *(gram.)* артикл [artikl]; *(legal)* модда [modda], банд [band]

artificial [артифишал] *adj.* сохтагӣ [soxtagi], сунъӣ [sun'i]

artisan [артизан] *n.* ҳунарманд [hunarmand], пешавар [peshavar]

artist [артист] *n.* санъаткор [san'atkor]

artistic [артистик] *adj.* санъатӣ [san'ati], ҳунарӣ [hunari]

as [эз] *adv.* ки [ki], ҳамон хеле ки [hamon xele ki]; **as well** ҳам [ham]; **as soon as** ҳамон ҳангоме ки [hamon hangome ki]; **just as** ҳамон хеле ки [hamon xele ki]

ash [эш] *n.* хокистар [xokistar]

ashamed [ашеймд] *adj.* шармгин [sharmgin]

ashtray [эштрей] *n.* хокистардон [xokistardon]

Asia [эйжа] *n.* Осиё [Osiyo]

Asian [эйжан] *n./adj.* осиёӣ [osiyoi]
aside [асайд] *adv.* ба як сӯ [ba yak sü]; **aside from** ғайр аз [ghayr az]
ask [эск] *v.t.* пурсидан [pursidan]
asleep [аслип] *adj./adv.* хобида [xobida]
aspect [эспект] *n.* ҷанба [janba], ҷиҳат [jihat]
asphalt [асфолт] *n.* асфалт [asfalt], қир [qir]
aspirin [эспирин] *n.* аспирин [aspirin]
assault [асолт] *n.* ҳуҷум [hujum], ҳамла [hamla] / *v.t.* ҳуҷум кардан [hujum kardan], ҳамла кардан [hamla kardan]
assemble [асембъл] *v.t.* ҷамъ кардан [jam' kardan] / *v.i.* ҷамъ омадан [jam' omadan]
assembly [асмбли] *n.* маҷлис [majlis]
assert [асерт] *v.t. (state positively)* исбот кардан [isbot kardan]; *(defend oneself)* (худро) мудофиа кардан [(xudro) mudofia kardan]
assertion [асершан] *n.* исбот [isbot]
assign [асайн] *v.t. (appoint or designate)* таъин кардан [ta'in kardan]; *(give homework, a job, etc.)* супурдан [supurdan]
assimilate [асимилейт] *v.t. (make similar)* ба худ монанд кардан [ba xud monand kardan], ҳамҷинс кардан [hamjins kardan]; *(physiological)* аз худ кардан [az xud kardan]
assist [асист] *v.t.* ёри додан [yori dodan], кӯмак кардан [kümak kardan]
assistance [асистанс] *n.* ёри [yori], кӯмак [kümak]
assistant [асистант] *n.* дастёр [dastyor], ёвар [yovar]
associate [асосиейт] *n.* ҳамкор [hamkor], ҳамнишин [hamnishin] / *v.t.* вобаста кардан [vobasta kardan], пайвастан [payvastan]
association [асосиейшан] *n.* анҷуман [anjuman]
assume [асюм] *v.t.* фарз кардан [farz kardan]
assurance [ашуранс] *n.* боваркунонӣ [bovarkunoni], дилпуркунӣ [dilpurkuni]
assure [ашур] *v.t.* бовар кунондан [bovar kunondan]
asthma [эстма] *n.* зиққи нафас [ziqqi nafas]
asthmatic [эстметик] *adj.* зиққи нафас [ziqqi nafas]
astonish [астониш] *v.t.* ҳайрон кардан [hayron kardan]
astray [астрей] *adj./adv.* гумроҳ [gumroh]
astringent [эстринҷент] *adj.* банданда [bandanda]
astrology [эстролоҷи] *n.* нуҷум [nujum]
astronomer [эстрономер] *n.* ситорашинос [sitorashinos]
astronomy [эстрономи] *n.* ситорашиносӣ [sitorashinosi]
astute [астют] *adj.* зирак [zirak], тез [tez]
asylum [асайлам] *n.* паноҳ [panoh]; **insane asylum** тиморхона [timorxona]

at [эт] *prep.* ба [ba]
atheism [эйтийизм] *n.* бединӣ [bedini], даҳригӣ [dahrigi]
atheist [эйтийист] *n.* бедин [bedin], даҳрӣ [dahri]
athlete [атлит] *n.* варзишгар [varzishgar]
athletics [атлетикс] *n.pl.* варзиш [varzish]
atmosphere [атмосфир] *n.* *(air)* ҳаво [havo]; *(ambiance or mood)* муҳит [muhit]
atom [атом] *n.* атом [atom]
attach [атеч] *v.t.* пайвастан [payvastan], часпондан [chaspondan]
attack [атек] *n.* ҳуҷум [hujum], ҳамла [hamla] / *v.t.* ҳуҷум кардан [hujum kardan], ҳамла кардан [hamla kardan]
attempt [атемпт] *n.* *(try)* кӯшиш [küshish]; *(assault)* суиқасд [suiqasd] / *v.i.* кӯшиш кардан [küshish kardan]
attend [атенд] *v.t.* *(be present)* ҳозир будан [hozir budan], мавҷуд будан [mavjud budan]; *(wait upon)* дастёрӣ кардан [dastyori kardan], хизмат кардан [xizmat kardan]
attendance [атендант] *n.* ҳузур [huzur], мавҷудият [mavjudiyat]
attendant [атендант] *n.* дастёр [dastyor], хизматгор [xizmatgor]
attention [атеншан] *n.* диққат [diqqat], таваҷҷӯҳ [tavajjüh]; **pay attention to** диққат кардан ба [diqqat kardan ba]
attentive [атентив] *adj.* бодиққат [bodiqqat]
attic [этик] *n.* утоқи зери тораки бом [utoqi zeri toraki bom], чердак [cherdak]
attitude [этитюд] *n.* назар [nazar], ақида [aqida]
attorney [атерни] *n.* вакил [vakil]; **attorney general** додситон [dodsiton]
attract [атрект] *v.t.* ҷалб кардан [jalb kardan], ба худ кашидан [ba xud kashidan]
attraction [атрекшан] *n.* дилкашӣ [dilkashi], ҷозиба [joziba]
attractive [атректив] *adj.* дилкаш [dilkash], ҷозиб [jozib]
attribute [атрибют] *n.* хусусият [xususiyat] / *v.t.* нисбат додан [nisbat dodan]
auction [окшан] *n.* музояда [muzoyada] / *v.t.* ба музояда гузоштан [ba muzoyada guzoshtan]
audience [одиенс] *n.* *(for sth visual)* тамошобинон [tamoshobinon]; *(for sth heard)* шунавандагон [shunavandagon]
auditory [одитори] *adj.* -и шунавоӣ [-i shunavoi]
augment [огмент] *v.t.* афзудан [afzudan], зиёд кардан [ziyod kardan]
August [огаст] *n.* август [avgust]
aunt [онт] *n.* *(paternal)* амма [amma]; *(maternal)* хола [xola]; *(paternal uncle's wife)* зани амак [zani amak]; *(maternal uncle's wife)* зани тағо [zani tagho]

Australian [остейлиян] *n./adj.* австралиягӣ [avstraliyagi]
authentic [отентик] *adj.* саҳеҳ [saheh], аслӣ [asli]
author [отор] *n.* муаллиф [muallif]
authority [оторити] *n.* ҳокимият [hokimiyat]
authorization [оторайзейшан] *n.* иҷозат [ijozat]
authorize [оторайз] *v.t.* иҷозат додан [ijozat dodan]
automatic [отометик] *adj.* худ ба худ [xud ba xud]
automation [отомейшан] *n.* автоматонӣ [avtomatoni]
automobile [отомобил] *n.* автомобил [avtomobil]
autonomous [отономас] *adj.* мухтор [muxtor]
autopsy [отопси] *n.* ҷасадкушоӣ [jasadkushoi]
autumn [отам] *n.* тирамоҳ [tiramoh], хазон [xazon]
availability [авейлабилити] *n. (accessibility)* дастрасӣ [dastrasi]; *(presence)* мавҷудӣ [mavjudi]
available [авейлабъл] *adj. (accessible)* дастрас [dastras]; *(present)* мавҷуда [mavjuda]
avenue [эвеню] *n. (means of access)* роҳ [roh]; *(broad street)* хиёбон [xiyobon]
average [эвриҷ] *n./adj.* миёна [miyona]; **on average** ба ҳисоби миёна [ba hisobi miyona]
aviation [эйвиейшан] *n.* ҳавопаймоӣ [havopaymoi]
avoid [авойд] *v.i.* дурӣ ҷустан [duri justan], канора гирифтан [kanora giriftan]
awake [ауэйк] *adj.* бедор [bedor] / *v.i.* бедор шудан [bedor shudan]
award [ауорд] *n.* мукофот [mukofot], подош [podosh] / *v.t.* мукофот додан [mukofot dodan], подош додан [podosh dodan]
aware [ауэр] *adj.* огоҳ [ogoh]
away [ауэй] *adj.* номавҷуда [nomavjuda] / *adv.* ба як сӯй [ba yak süy]
awful [офул] *adj.* даҳшатнок [dahshatnok]
awkward [окуард] *adj.* ноқулай [noqulay]
ax [экс] *n.* табар [tabar]
axis [эксис] *n.* меҳвар [mehvar]
axle [эксъл] *n.* тир [tir]
Azerbaijani [азербайҷани] *n./adj.* озарбойҷонӣ [ozarboyjoni]

B

baby [бейби] *n.* тифл [tifl], кӯдак [küdak]
back [бек] *n.* пушт [pusht] / *adj.* дар пушт [dar pusht] / *adv.* пуштнокӣ [pushtnoki]; **back up** *(an automobile, etc.)* пуштнокӣ рафтан [pushtnoki raftan]; **be back** пас омадан [pas omadan]; **back pain** дарди пушт [dardi pusht];
backbone [бекбон] *n.* аррапушт [arrapusht]
background [бекраунд] *n.* пасманзар [pasmanzar]
backward [бекуард] *adj.* чаппа [chappa] / *adv.* пуштнокӣ [pushtnoki]

bacon [бейкон] *n.* гӯшти хуки дуддодашуда [güshti xuki duddodashuda]
bacteria [бактирия] *n.* бактерия [bakteriya]
bacterial [бактириял] *adj.* бактериядор [bakteriyador]
bad [бед] *adj.* бад [bad], ганда [ganda]
badge [беч] *n.* нишон [nishon]
badly [бедли] *adv.* бад [bad], ганда [ganda]
bag [бег] *n.* халта [xalta]
baggage [бегич] *n.* бағоҷ [baghoj]
bail [бейл] *n.* замонат [zamonat]
bait [бейт] *n.* хӯр-хӯрак [xür-xürak], донаи дом [donai dom]
bake [бейк] *v.t.* пухтан [puxtan] / *v.i.* пухта шудан [puxta shudan]
baker [бейкер] *n.* нонвой [nonvoy], нонпаз [nonpaz]
balance [баланс] *n.* *(scale)* тарозу [tarozu]; *(equilibrium)* мувозина [muvozina]; *(equality)* баробарӣ [barobari]; *(symmetry)* таносуб [tanosub]
balcony [балкони] *n.* полкона [polkona], балкон [balkon]
bald [болд] *adj.* кал [kal]
ball [бол] *n.* тӯб [tüb]
balloon [балун] *n.* пуфак [pufak]
banana [банана] *n.* банан [banan]
band [банд] *n.* *(music group)* даста [dasta]; *(strip)* навор [navor]
bandage [бандач] *n.* бандина [bandina], бандиш [bandish]
banister [банистер] *n.* панҷара [panjara]
bank [банк] *n.* бонк [bonk]
banker [банкер] *n.* бонкир [bonkir]
bankrupt [бенкрапт] *adj.* варшикаст [varshikast]
banner [банер] *n.* байрақ [bayraq]
banquet [банкуэт] *n.* зиёфат [ziyofat]
baptism [баптизм] *n.* таъмид [ta'mid]
baptize [баптайз] *v.t.* таъмид кардан [ta'mid kardan]
bar [бар] *n.* *(for drinking)* майхона [mayxona], бар [bar]; *(bar-shaped object)* мила [mila]; **chocolate bar** тахтача шоколад [taxtacha shokolad]; **bar of soap** кулчаи собун [kulchai sobun]
barber [барбер] *n.* сартарош [sartarosh]
barbershop [барбершоп] *n.* сартарошхона [sartaroshxona]
bare [бер] *adj.* *(describing a person)* луч [luch], бараҳна [barahna]; *(describing a tree)* бебарг [bebarg]; *(describing a landscape)* бедору дарахт [bedoru daraxt]
bargain [баргин] *n.* харидуфурӯш [xaridufurüsh], муомила [muomila] / *v.i.* чана задан [chana zadan]
bark [барк] *n.* *(dog)* аккос [akkos]; *(tree)* пӯсти дарахт [püsti daraxt] / *v.i.* аккос задан [akkos zadan]
barley [барли] *n.* ҷав [jav]

barometer [барометер] *n.* ҳавосанҷ [havosanj]
barrack [барак] *n.* сарбозхона [sarbozxona], истиқоматгоҳи аскарон [istiqomatgohi askaron]
barrel [барел] *n.* чалак [chalak]
barren [барен] *adj.* *(not yielding crops)* бебор [bebor], беҳосил [behosil]; *(sterile)* нозо [nozo]
barrier [бариер] *n.* садд [sadd], девора [devora]; **break the sound barrier** аз садди садо гузаштан [az saddi sado guzashtan]
base [бейс] *n.* *(basis)* поя [poya], асос [asos]; *(headquarters of organization, mil., etc.)* пойгоҳ [poygoh]; *(chemical)* асос [asos]
baseball [бейсбол] *n.* бейсбол [beysbol]
basement [бейсмент] *n.* таҳхона [tahxona], зеризаминӣ [zerizamini]
basic [бейсик] *adj.* асосӣ [asosi]
basin [бейсин] *n.* *(for washing)* тағора [taghora], лаган [lagan]; *(geo.)* ҳавза [havza]
basis [бейсис] *n.* поя [poya], асос [asos]
basket [баскет] *n.* сабад [sabad]
basketball [баскетбол] *n.* баскетбол [basketbol]
bat [бат] *n.* *(stick)* чӯбдаста [chübdasta]; *(animal)* кӯршабпарак [kürshabparak]
batch [бач] *n.* даста [dasta]
bath [бат] *n.* ҳаммом [hammom]
bathe [бейд] *v.t.* оббозӣ кунондан [obbozi kunondan] / *v.i.* оббозӣ кардан [obbozi kardan]
bathroom [батрум] *n.* *(room for bathing)* гармоба [garmoba]; *(restroom)* ташноб [tashnob], хонаи дастшӯӣ [xonai dastshüi]
bathtub [баттаб] *n.* ванна [vanna]
batter [батер] *n.* хамири обгин [xamiri obgin] / *v.t.* кӯфтан [küftan], сахт задан [saxt zadan]
battery [батери] *n.* батарея [batareya]
battle [батл] *n.* ҷанг [jang], корзор [korzor] / *v.i.* ҷанг кардан [jang kardan]
bay [бей] *n.* халиҷ [xalij]
B.C. [би си] *(abbrev. of* **before Christ***)* қабл аз милод [qabl az milod]
be [би] *v.i.* будан [budan]
beach [бич] *n.* канори дарё [kanori daryo]
beak [бик] *n.* нӯл [nül]
beam (wood) [бим] *n.* болор [bolor], шоҳтир [shohtir]
bean [бин] *n.* лӯбиё [lübiyo]
bear [бер] *n.* хирс [xirs] / *v.t.* бурдан [burdan]
beard [бирд] *n.* риш [rish]
bearing [беринг] *n.* рафтор [raftor]
beast [бист] *n.* ҷонвар [jonvar], чорпой [chorpoy]
beat [бит] *n.* зарб [zarb] / *v.t.* задан [zadan]
beautiful [бютифул] *adj.* зебо [zebo]
beauty [бюти] *n.* зебоӣ [zeboi]

beaver [бивер] *n.* кундуз [qunduz]
because [биказ] *conj.* чунки [chunki], зеро [zero]
become [бикам] *v.i.* шудан [shudan]
bed [бед] *n.* кат [kat]
bedbug [бедбаг] *n.* тахтакана [taxtakana], ганг [gang]
bedroom [бедрум] *n.* хонаи хоб [xonai xob]
bee [би] *n.* занбӯри асал [zanbüri asal], оруи асал [orui asal]
beef [биф] *n.* гӯшти гов [güshti gov]
beer [бир] *n.* оби ҷав [obi jav], пиво [pivo]
beet [бит] *n.* лаблабу [lablabu]
beetle [битл] *n.* гамбуск [gambusk], қунғуз [qunghuz]
before [бифоре] *prep.* пеш аз [pesh az] / *adv.* пештар [peshtar]
beg [бег] *v.i. (request)* хоҳиш кардан [xohish kardan]; *(be a beggar)* гадоӣ кардан [gadoi kardan]
beggar [бегар] *n.* гадо [gado]
begin [бигин] *v.t.* сар кардан [sar kardan], оғоз кардан [oghoz kardan] / *v.i.* сар шудан [sar shudan], оғоз шудан [oghoz shudan]
beginner [бигинер] *n.* навкор [navkor], навомӯз [navomüz]
behalf [биҳаф] *n.* хотир [xotir]; **on behalf of** ба хотири [ba xotiri]
behave [биҳейв] *v.i.* рафтор кардан [raftor kardan]
behavior [биҳейвёр] *n.* рафтор [raftor], муомила [muomila]
behind [биҳайнд] *prep.* пушти [pushti], паси [pasi]
behold [биҳолд] *v.i.* дидан [didan]
being [бийинг] *n. (existence)* ҳастӣ [hasti]; *(creature)* офарида [ofarida]
belief [билиф] *n.* ақида [aqida]
believe [билив] *v.i.* бовар кардан [bovar kardan]
bell [бел] *n.* занг [zang]
belly [бели] *n.* шикам [shikam]
belong [билонг] *v.i.* аз он будан [az on budan]
belongings [билонгингз] *n.pl.* бору банд [boru band], дороӣ [doroi]
below [било] *prep.* дар зери [dar zeri]
belt [белт] *n.* камар [kamar], камарбанд [kamarband]
bench [бенч] *n.* харак [xarak]
bend [бенд] *v.t.* хамондан [xamondan], каҷ кардан [kaj kardan] / *v.i.* хамидан [xamidan], каҷ шудан [kaj shudan]
beneath [бинит] *prep.* зери [zeri], таги [tagi]
beneficial [бенефишал] *adj.* фоиданок [foidanok], манфиатбахш [manfiatbaxsh]
benefit [бенефит] *n.* фоида [foida], манфиат [manfiat] / *v.t.* фоида бахшидан [foida baxshidan] / *v.i.* манфиат гирифтан [manfiat giriftan]
benign [бинайн] *adj. (kind)* меҳрубон [mehrubon]; *(non-malignant)* безиён [beziyon]

bent [бент] *adj.* хамида [xamida], кач̣ [kaj]
berry [бери] *n.* буттамева [buttameva]
beside [бисайд] *prep.* пахлӯйи [pahlüyi]
best [бест] *adj./adv.* беҳтарин [behtarin]
bestow [бисто] *v.t.* бахшидан [baxshidan]
bet [бет] *n.* гарав [garav], шарт [shart] / *v.t.* гарав бастан [garav bastan], шарт кардан [shart kardan]
betray [битрей] *v.t.* хиёнат кардан [xiyonat kardan]
better [бетер] *adj./adv.* беҳтар [behtar]
between [битуин] *prep.* миёни [miyoni], байни [bayni]
beverage [беврич̣] *n.* нӯшоба [nüshoba], нӯшокӣ [nüshoki]
beware [биуэр] *v.t.* ҳазар кардан [hazar kardan]
beyond [биёнд] *prep.* онсӯйи [onsüyi]
bib [биб] *n.* ошхӯрак [oshxürak]
Bible [байбл] *n.* Инҷил [Injil]
bicycle [байсикал] *n.* дучарха [ducharxa]
big [биг] *adj.* калон [kalon]
bilingual [байлингюал] *adj.* дузабона [duzabona]
bill [бил] *n.* *(beak)* нӯл [nül]; *(legislative)* лоиҳаи қонун [loihai qonun]; *(bank note)* пули коғазӣ [puli koghazi]; *(list of costs)* ҳисоб [hisob]
billiards [билярдз] *n.* билярд [bilyard]
bin [бин] *n.* хамма [xamma]
bind [байнд] *v.t.* бастан [bastan]
biography [байографи] *n.* тарҷумаи ҳол [tarjumai hol], зиндагинома [zindaginoma]
biological [байолоҷикал] *adj.* -и зистшиносӣ [-i zistshinosi], биологӣ [biologi]
biologist [байолоҷист] *n.* зистшинос [zistshinos]
biology [байолоҷи] *n.* зистшиносӣ [zistshinosi], биология [biologiya];
bird [бирд] *n.* парранда [parranda]
birth [бирт] *n.* зоиш [zoish], таваллуд [tavallud]; **place of birth** зодгоҳ [zodgoh]
birth certificate [бирт сертификет] *n.* гувоҳиномаи зоиш [guvohinomai zoish]
birth control [бирт контрол] *n.* пешгирии обистанӣ [peshgirii obistani]
birthday [биртдей] *n.* зодрӯз [zodrüz], рӯзи таваллуд [rüzi tavallud]
biscuit [бискит] *n.* кулча [kulcha]
bit [бит] *n.* *(small piece)* порча [porcha], лӯнда [lünda]; *(short period of time)* муддати кӯтоҳ [muddati kütoh]; *(of a bridle)* сӯлуқ [süluq]
bite [байт] *v.t.* газидан [gazidan]
bitter [битер] *adj.* талх [talx]
black [блек] *adj.* сиёҳ [siyoh]
blackberry [блекбери] *n.* марминҷон [marminjon]
blackboard [блекборд] *n.* тахтаи синф [taxtai sinf]

bladder [бледер] *n.* пешобдон [peshobdon], масона [masona]
blade [блейм] *n.* теғ [tegh]
blame [блейм] *n.* ҷавобгарӣ [javobgari] / *v.t.* ҷавобгар донистан [javobgar donistan]
blanket [бланкет] *n.* кампал [kampal]
blast [бласт] *n. (strong wind)* тундбод [tundbod]; *(explosion)* тарқиш [tarqish]
blaze [блейз] *n.* аланга [alanga], оташ [otash]
bleak [блик] *adj. (without hope)* ноумед [noumed]; *(without shelter)* бепаноҳ [bepanoh]; *(cold)* хунук [xunuk]
bleed [блид] *v.i.* хун рафтан [xun raftan]
bless [блес] *v.t.* дуои хайр гуфтан [duoi xayr guftan]
blessed [блесд] *adj. (auspicious)* хуҷаста [xujasta]; *(fortunate)* некбахт [nekbaxt], некахтар [nekaxtar]
blessing [блесинг] *n. (prayer)* дуои хайр [duoi xayr]; *(boon)* баракат [barakat]
blind [блайнд] *adj.* кӯр [kür], нобино [nobino]
blindness [блайнднес] *n.* кӯрӣ [küri], нобиноӣ [nobinoi]
blink [блинк] *v.i.* мижа задан [mizha zadan]
block [блок] *n.* кунда [kunda]
blond [блонд] *adj.* малла [malla]; **blond-haired** малламӯй [mallamüy]
blood [блад] *n.* хун [xun]
bloom [блум] *v.i.* шукуфтан [shukuftan]
blossom [блосом] *n.* шукуфа [shukufa]
blouse [блаус] *n.* блузка [bluzka]
blow [бло] *v.t.* пуф кардан [puf kardan] / *v.i.* вазидан [vazidan]
blue [блу] *adj.* кабуд [kabud]
blueberry [блубери] *n.* меваи кабуд [mevai kabud]
blunt [блант] *adj.* кунд [kund]
blush [блаш] *v.i.* сурх шудан [surx shudan]
board [борд] *n.* тахта [taxta]; **board game** бозии рӯимизӣ [bozii rüimizi]
boarding school [бординг скул] *n.* мактаб-интернат [maktab-internat]
boat [бот] *n.* қаиқ [qaiq]
boating [ботинг] *n.* белкашӣ [belkashi], қаиқронӣ [qaiqroni]
body [боди] *n.* тан [tan], бадан [badan]
boil [бойл] *n. (med.)* даммал [dammal]; *(boiling)* ҷӯш [jüsh] / *v.t.* ҷӯшондан [jüshondan] / *v.i.* ҷӯшидан [jüshidan]
boiler [бойлер] *n.* обгармкунак [obgarmkunak]; **boiler room** дегхона [degxona]
bold [болд] *adj.* нотарс [notars]
bolt [болт] *n. (mechanical)* мехи печдор [mexi pechdor]; *(locking device)* ғалақа [ghalaqa]
bomb [бом] *n.* бомба [bomba] / *v.t. (bombard)* бомбаборон кардан [bombaboron kardan]; *(throw a bomb)* бомба андохтан [bomba andoxtan]

bone [бон] *n.* устухон [ustuxon]
bone marrow [бон меро] *n.* мағзи устухон [maghzi ustuxon]
book [бук] *n.* китоб [kitob]
bookcase [буккейс] *n.* ҷевони китоб [jevoni kitob]
bookmark [букмарк] *n.* хатчӯб [xatchüb]
bookstore [букстор] *n.* китбфурӯшӣ [kitobfurüshi]
boot [бут] *n.* патинка [patinka], мӯза [müza]
border [бордер] *n.* марз [marz], сарҳад [sarhad]
born [борн] *adj.* зода [zoda], зоида [zoida]
boss [бос] *n.* саркор [sarkor]
bottle [ботл] *n.* шиша [shisha]
bottom [ботом] *n.* таг [tag], таҳ [tah]
bounce [баунс] *v.t.* ҷаҳондан [jahondan] / *v.i.* ҷастан [jastan]
box [бокс] *n.* *(small box)* қуттӣ [qutti]; *(large box, trunk)* сандуқ [sanduq]
boxing [боксинг] *n.* бокс [boks], муштзанӣ [mushtzani]
boy [бой] *n.* писар [pisar], бача [bacha]
boyfriend [бойфренд] *n.* дӯстписар [düstpisar]
brain [брейн] *n.* мағз [maghz], майна [mayna]
brake [брейк] *n.* тормоз [tormoz] / *v.t.* тормоз додан [tormoz dodan]
branch [бренч] *n.* шох [shox]
brave [брейв] *adj.* далер [daler], диловар [dilovar]
Brazilian [бразилян] *n./adj.* бразилиягӣ [braziliyagi]
breach [брич] *n.* рахна [raxna] / *v.t.* рахна кардан [raxna kardan]
bread [бред] *n.* нон [non]
break [брейк] *n.* танаффус [tanaffus] / *v.t.* шиканондан [shikanondan], шикастан [shikastan] / *v.i.* шикастан [shikastan]; **coffee break** танаффуси қаҳванӯшӣ [tanaffusi qahvanüshi]; **school break** таътил [ta'til]
breakfast [брекфаст] *n.* ноништа [nonishta]
breathe [брид] *v.i.* нафас кашидан [nafas kashidan]
breeze [бриз] *n.* насим [nasim]
brick [брик] *n.* хишт [xisht] / *adj.* хиштин [xishtin]
bride [брайд] *n.* келин [kelin], арӯс [arüs]
brief [бриф] *adj.* кӯтоҳ [kütoh]
briefcase [брифкейс] *n.* ҷузвкаш [juzvkash]
bribe [брайб] *n.* ришва [rishva] / *v.t.* ришва додан [rishva dodan]
bright [брайт] *adj.* равшан [ravshan]
brilliant [бриляант] *adj.* дурахшон [duraxshon], ялаққосӣ [yalaqqosi]
bring [бринг] *v.t.* овардан [ovardan]
British [бритиш] *n./adj.* британиягӣ [britaniyagi]
broccoli [броколи] *n.* брокколи [brokkoli]
bronchitis [бронкайтис] *n.* бронхит [bronxit]
bronze [бронз] *n.* биринҷ [birinj] / *adj.* биринҷӣ [birinji]
broth [брот] *n.* пиёба [piyoba]

brother [брадер] *n.* бародар [barodar]
brush [браш] *n.* чӯтка [chütka]
brutal [брутал] *adj.* золим [zolim], бераҳм [berahm]
bubble [бабал] *n.* пуфак [pufak], ҳубоб [hubob]
bucket [бакит] *n.* сатил [satil]
budget [баҷит] *n.* буҷа [buja]
bulb [балб] *n. (lightbulb)* чароғча [charoghcha], лампочка [lampochka]; *(flower bulb)* бех [bex]
bullet [булет] *n.* тир [tir]
bundle [бандл] *n.* бӯғча [büghcha]
buoy [бой] *n.* пойобнамо [poyobnamo]
bureau [бюро] *n. (government agency)* бюро [byuro]; *(furniture)* комод [komod]
bureaucracy [бюрокраси] *n.* расмиятпарастӣ [rasmiyatparasti]
bureaucrat [бюрокрет] *n.* коғазбоз [koghazboz], расмиятпараст [rasmiyatparast]
bury [бери] *v.t.* дафн кардан [dafn kardan]
bus [бас] *n.* автобус [avtobus]
business [бизнес] *n.* кор [kor]
businessman [бизнесмен] *n.* корчаллон [korchallon]
busy [бизи] *adj.* серкор [serkor], машғул [mashghul]
but [бат] *conj.* аммо [ammo], лекин [lekin]
butter [батар] *n.* маска [maska]
butterfly [батарфлай] *n.* шапарак [shaparak]
buttocks [батокс] *n.pl.* сурин [surin]
button [батан] *n.* тугма [tugma]
buttonhole [батанҳол] *n.* сӯрохи тугма [süroxi tugma]
buy [бай] *v.t.* харидан [xaridan]
buyer [байер] *n.* харидор [xaridor]
by [бай] *prep. (close to, next to)* назди [nazdi], паҳлӯи [pahlüyi]; *(through)* ба василаи [ba vasilai]; *(at the edge of)* лаби [labi]; *(not later than, prior to)* пеш аз [pesh az]; *(in mathematics, e.g. divided by)* ба [ba]; *(to go by)* бо [bo]

C

cabbage [кебиҷ] *n.* карам [karam]
cabin [кебин] *n.* кулба [kulba]
cabinet [кебинет] *n.* ҷевон [jevon]
cable [кейбъл] *n.* кабел [kabel]
café [кафе] *n.* қаҳвахона [qahvaxona]
cafeteria [кафетирия] *n.* ошхона [oshxona]
caffeine [кафин] *n.* кофеин [kofein]
cage [кейк] *n.* қафас [qafas]
cake [кейк] *n.* торт [tort]
calcium [калсиям] *n.* калтсий [kaltsiy]
calculate [калкюлейт] *v.t.* ҳисоб кардан [hisob kardan]
calculation [калкюлейшан] *n.* ҳисоб [hisob]
calculator [калкюлейтор] *n.* калкулятор [kalkulyator]
calendar [календар] *n.* солнома [solnoma], тақвим [taqvim]

calf [каф] *n. (anat.)* соқ [soq]; *(animal)* гӯсола [güsola]
call [кол] *n.* бонг [bong], фарёд [faryod] / *v.t. (call out, call sb or sth)* ҷеғ задан [jegh zadan]; *(make a telephone call)* занг задан [zang zadan]
calm [ком] *n.* оромӣ [oromi] / *adj.* ором [orom] / *v.t.* ором кардан [orom kardan] / *v.i.* ором шудан [orom shudan]
camel [камел] *n.* шутур [shutur], уштур [ushtur]
camera [камера] *n.* аксгирак [aksgirak]
camp [камп] *n.* лагер [lager], урдугоҳ [urdugoh] / *v.i.* лагер сохтан [lager soxtan]
campsite [кампсайт] *n.* лагер [lager]
campus [кампас] *n. (college)* замини донишкада [zamini donishkada]; *(university)* замини донишгоҳ [zamini donishgoh]; *(school)* замини мактаб [zamini maktab]
can [кен] *n.* банка [banka], қуттӣ [qutti] / *aux.* тавонистан [tavonistan]; **I can go.** Ман рафта метавонам. [man rafta metavonam.]
Canadian [канейдиян] *n./adj.* канадагӣ [kanadagi]
canal [канал] *n. (above-ground)* ҷӯй [jüy]; *(subterranean)* корез [korez]; *(anatomical)* роҳ [roh]
cancel [кансел] *v.t.* лағв кардан [laghv kardan], бекор кардан [bekor kardan]
cancellation [кенселейшан] *n.* лағв [laghv]
cancer [кенсер] *n.* саратон [saraton]
candid [кендид] *adj.* рост [rost], ростгӯй [rostgüy]
candidate [кендидейт] *n.* номзад [nomzad]
candle [кендл] *n.* шамъ [sham']
candleholder [кендлхолдер] *n.* шамъдон [sham'don]
candy [кенди] *n.* конфет [konfet], қанд [qand]; **rock candy** набот [nabot]
cane [кейн] *n. (reed)* най [nay]; *(walking stick)* чӯбдаст [chübdast], асо [aso]
cannon [канон] *n.* тӯп [tüp]
canoe [кану] *n.* заврақи комагӣ [zavraqi komagi]
canteen [кантин] *n. (flask)* обдон [obdon], қумқума [qumquma]; *(cafeteria)* ошхонаи хурд [oshxonai xurd]
canvas [канвас] *n.* карбос [karbos]
cap [кеп] *n. (hat)* кулоҳ [kuloh]; *(lid or top)* сарпӯш [sarpüsh]
capable [кейпабъл] *adj.* қобил [qobil], тавоно [tavono]
capacity [капеситу] *n.* гунҷоиш [gunjoish]
cape [кейп] *n. (piece of clothing)* кифтпӯшак [kiftpüshak]; *(geo.)* димоға [dimogha]
capital [капитал] *n. (city)* пойтахт [poytaxt]; *(finance)* сармоя [sarmoya]; *(capital letter)* сарҳарф [sarharf]
capsule [капсул] *n.* ғилофак [ghilofak]

captain [каптин] *n. (of a ship)* сардори киштӣ [sardori kishti]; *(of a sports team)* роҳбар [rohbar], сардаста [sardasta]
car [кор] *n.* мошин [moshin]
carbohydrate [карбоҳайдрейт] *n.* карбогидрат [karbogidrat]
card [кард] *n.* қарта [qarta]
cardboard [кардборд] *n.* муқова [muqova]
care [кер] *n. (caution)* эҳтиёт [ehtiyot], диққат [diqqat]; *(concern)* парво [parvo]; *(nurture)* парвариш [parvarish], тимор [timor] / *v.i. (take care of)* парвардан [parvardan], тимор кардан [timor kardan]
careful [керфул] *adj.* эҳтиёткор [ehtiyotkor], бодиққат [bodiqqat]
careless [керлес] *adj.* беэҳтиёт [beehtiyot], бедиққат [bediqqat]
carnival [карнивал] *n.* ҷашн [jashn], ид [id]
carpenter [карпентер] *n.* дуредгар [duredgar]
carry [кари] *v.t.* бурдан [burdan]
carry-on [кари-он] *n. (luggage)* бағоҷи дастӣ [baghoji dasti]
cart [карт] *n.* ароба [aroba]
cartilage [карталич] *n.* тағояк [taghoyak]
carton [картон] *n.* қуттии муқовагӣ [quttii muqovagi]
cartoon [картун] *n.* карикатура [karikatura], расми хандаовар [rasmi xandaovar]
cartridge [картрич] *n.* патрон [patron]
carve [карв] *v.t.* кандакорӣ кардан [kandakori kardan]
carving [карвинг] *n.* кандакорӣ [kandakori]
case [кейс] *n. (legal)* парванда [parvanda]; *(med.)* қуттӣ [qutti]; *(situation)* ҳолат [holat]; *(grammatical)* падеж [padezh]; *(example)* мисол [misol]
cash [каш] *n.* пули нақд [puli naqd]
cashier [кашир] *n.* сандуқдор [sanduqdor], кассир [kassir]
cask [каск] *n.* чалак [chalak]
cast [каст] *n. (med.)* тахтачаи шикастабандӣ [taxtachai shikastabandi]; *(of a movie or play)* ҳайати ҳунармандон [hayati hunarmandon] / *v.t.* андохтан [andoxtan], партофтан [partoftan]
castle [касъл] *n.* қалъа [qal'a], кӯшк [küshk]
casual [кажуал] *adj.* беэътино [bee'tino], роҳат [rohat]
casualty [кажуалти] *n.* захмдор [zaxmdor]
cat [кат] *n.* пишак [pishak], гурба [gurba]
catalog [каталог] *n.* каталог [katalog]
catch [кач] *v.t. (take in hand)* қапидан [qapidan]; *(arrest)* дастгир кардан [dastgir kardan]
cathedral [катидрал] *n.* калисои ҷомеъ [kalisoi jome']
Catholic [католик] *n.* католик [katolik] / *adj.* католикӣ [katoliki]
Catholicism [католисизм] *n.* католитсизм [katolitsizm]
cattle [катъл] *n.* моли чорпой [moli chorpoy]

cauldron [колдран] *n.* деги калон [degi kalon]
cauliflower [колифлаур] *n.* гулкарам [gulkaram]
cause [коз] *n.* сабаб [sabab] / *v.t.* овардан [ovardan], сабаб шудан [sabab shudan]
caution [кошан] *n.* эҳтиёт [ehtiyot]
cautious [кошас] *adj.* эҳтиёткор [ehtiyotkor]
cave [кейв] *n.* ғор [ghor]
cease [сис] *v.i.* бас шудан [bas shudan]
cedar [сидар] *n.* дарахти ҷалғӯза [daraxti jalghüza]
ceiling [силинг] *n.* шифт [shift]
celebrate [селебрейт] *v.i.* ҷашн гирифтан [jashn giriftan]
celebration [селебрейшан] *n.* ҷашн [jashn]
cell [сел] *n.* *(biological)* ҳуҷайра [hujayra]; *(jail)* ҳуҷра [hujra]
cellar [селар] *n.* таҳхона [tahxona]
cello [чело] *n.* виолинчел [violinchel]
cellular [селюлар] *adj.* ҳуҷайрагӣ [hujayragi]
cellular phone [селюлар фон] *n.* телефони дастӣ [telefoni dasti]
cement [семент] *n.* симон [simon]
cemetery [семетери] *n.* гӯристон [güriston]
center [сентър] *n.* марказ [markaz]
centimeter [сентимитер] *n.* сантиметр [santimetr]
centipede [сентипид] *n.* ҳазорпой [hazorpoy]
central [сентрал] *adj.* марказӣ [markazi]
century [сенчури] *n.* садсола [sadsola], қарн [qarn]
ceramic [серамик] *n.* сафолӣ [safoli] / *adj.* сафолӣ [safoli]
cereal [сириял] *n.* ғалла [ghalla]
ceremony [серемони] *n.* маросим [marosim]
certain [сертан] *adj.* *(definite)* аниқ [aniq], яқин [yaqin]; *(some)* ягон [yagon]
certificate [сертификат] *n.* гувоҳинома [guvohinoma]; **birth certificate** гувоҳиномаи зоиш [guvohinomai zoish]
certify [сертифай] *v.t.* тасдиқ кардан [tasdiq kardan]
chain [чейн] *n.* занҷир [zanjir]
chair [чер] *n.* курсӣ [kursi]
chalk [чок] *n.* бӯр [bür]
challenge [чаленҷ] *n.* даъват [da'vat] / *v.t.* даъват кардан [da'vat kardan]
chamber [чеймбер] *n.* утоқ [utoq]; **bedchamber** хобгоҳ [xobgoh]
champion [чампян] *n.* чемпион [chempion], қаҳрамон [qahramon]
chance [чанс] *n.* тасодуф [tasoduf]
change [чейнҷ] *n.* *(alteration)* дигаргунӣ [digarguni], тағйир [taghyir]; *(coins)* пули майда [puli mayda]; *(balance of money)* бақияи пул [baqiyai pul] / *v.t.* дигаргун кардан [digargun kardan], иваз кардан [ivaz kardan] / *v.i.* дигаргун шудан [digargun shudan], тағйир ёфтан [taghyir yoftan]

changeable [чейнҷабъл] *adj.* ноустувор [noustuvor]
changing room [чейнчинг рум] *n.* хонаи пӯшоккашӣ [xonai püshokkashi]
channel [чанел] *n.* канал [kanal]
chaotic [кейотик] *adj.* харҷумарҷ [xarjumarj], бетартиб [betartib]
chapel [чапел] *n.* калисои хурд [kalisoi xurd]
chapter [чаптер] *n.* боб [bob]
character [каректер] *n.* *(temperament)* хӯй [xüy], табиат [tabiat]; *(role)* рол [rol], нақш [naqsh]
characteristic [каректеристик] *n.* хислати вижа [xislati vizha] / *adj.* вижа [vizha], хос [xos]
charge [чарҷ] *n.* *(responsibility or duty)* ӯҳда [ühda]; *(financial)* ҳисоб [hisob]; *(attack)* ҳамла [hamla] / *v.t.* *(responsibility or duty)* ба ӯҳда гузоштан [ba ühda guzoshtan]; *(financial)* ба ҳисоб гузоштан [ba hisob guzoshtan]; *(attack)* ҳамла кардан [hamla kardan]
charity [черити] *n.* хайрот [xayrot]
charm [чарм] *n.* *(pleasing manner)* дилрабоӣ [dilraboi]; *(amulet or talisman)* тӯмор [tümor], тилисм [tilism]; *(incantation)* афсун [afsun] / *v.t.* *(attract or delight)* дил рабудан [dil rabudan]; *(cast a spell)* афсун кардан [afsun kardan]
chart [чарт] *n.* нақша [naqsha], харита [xarita] / *v.t.* нақша кашидан [naqsha kashidan], харита кашидан [xarita kashidan]
charter [чартер] *n.* низомнома [nizomnoma] / *v.t.* киро кардан [kiro kardan]
chase [чейс] *n.* дунболагирӣ [dunbolagiri] / *v.t.* дунболагирӣ кардан [dunbolagiri kardan]
chassis [часис] *n.* шассӣ [shassi]
chat [чат] *n.* гуфтугӯ [guftugü], чақ-чақ [chaq-chaq] / *v.i.* чақ-чақ кардан [chaq-chaq kardan], гуфтугӯ кардан [guftugü kardan]
chatter [чатер] *n.* сафсата [safsata], ҳарза [harza] / *v.i.* ҷоғ задан [jogh zadan], лаққидан [laqqidan]
cheap [чип] *adj.* арзон [arzon]
check [чек] *n.* *(a halt)* таваққуф [tavaqquf], ист [ist]; *(verification)* назорат [nazorat], тафтиш [taftish]; *(form of payment)* чек [chek]; *(mark)* аломати қайд [alomati qayd] / *v.t.* *(halt or stop)* таваққуф кардан [tavaqquf kardan]; *(verify)* назорат кардан [nazorat kardan], тафтиш кардан [taftish kardan]; **check pattern** чорхонанусха [chorxonanusxa]
checkers [чекарз] *n.* шашка [shashka]
checkmate [чекмейт] *v.t.* мот кардан [mot kardan]
cheek [чик] *n.* рухсор [ruxsor]

cheese [чиз] *n.* панир [panir]
cheetah [чита] *n.* юз [yuz], юзпаланг [yuzpalang]
chemical [кемикал] *n.* моддаи химиявӣ [moddai ximiyavi] / *adj.* химиявӣ [ximiyavi]
chemistry [кемистри] *n.* химия [ximiya], кимиё [kimiyo]
cherish [чериш] *v.t.* парвардан [parvardan], навозиш кардан [navozish kardan]
cherry [чери] *n.* гелос [gelos]
chess [чес] *n.* шоҳмот [shohmot], шатранҷ [shatranj]; **chessboard** тахтаи шоҳмот [taxtai shohmot], тахтаи шатранҷ [taxtai shatranj]; **chess piece** мӯҳраи шоҳмот [mührai shohmot], мӯҳраи шатранҷ [mührai shatranj]
chest [чест] *n. (container)* сандуқ [sanduq]; *(anat.)* сина [sina]; **chest of drawers** ҷевони пӯшок [jevoni püshok], комод [komod]; **chest pains** дарди сари дил [dardi sari dil]
chew [чу] *v.t.* хойидан [xoyidan]
chick [чик] *n.* чӯҷа [chüja]
chicken [чикан] *n.* мурғ [murgh]
chief [чиф] *n.* сардор [sardor]
child [чайлд] *n.* кӯдак [küdak], бача [bacha]
childhood [чайлдхуд] *n.* кӯдакӣ [küdaki], бачагӣ [bachagi]
childish [чайлдиш] *adj.* бачагона [bachagona], кӯдакона [küdakona]
children [чилдрен]) *n.pl.* кӯдакон [küdakon], бачагон [bachagon]
chill [чил] *n.* сармо [sarmo], хунукӣ [xunuki] / *v.t.* хунук кардан [xunuk kardan]
chilly [чили] *adj.* хунук [xunuk], сард [sard]
chimney [чимни] *n.* дудкаш [dudkash]
chin [чин] *n.* манаҳ [manah], занах [zanax]
china [чайна] *n.* фахфур [faxfur] / *adj.* фахфурӣ [faxfuri]
Chinese [чайниз] *n./adj.* хитоӣ [xitoi], чинӣ [chini]
chip [чип] *n.* пешранда [peshranda], тароша [tarosha] / *v.t.* ранда кардан [randa kardan], тарошидан [taroshidan]
chisel [чизел] *n.* искана [iskana] / *v.t.* кандан [kandan]
chocolate [чоклат] *n.* шоколад [shokolad] / *adj.* шоколадин [shokoladin]
choice [чойс] *n.* писанд [pisand], интихоб [intixob]
choir [куайр] *n.* хор [xor], дастаи сарояндагон [dastai saroyandagon]
choke [чок] *v.t.* гулӯгир кардан [gulügir kardan], хафа кардан [xafa kardan]
cholesterol [колестерол] *n.* холестрин [xolestrin]
choose [чуз] *v.t.* баргузидан [barguzidan], интихоб кардан [intixob kardan] / *v.i.* баргузидан [barguzidan], писандидан [pisandidan]
chop [чоп] *v.t.* реза кардан [reza kardan]

chorus [корас] *n. (group of singers)* хор [xor], дастаи сарояндагон [dastai saroyandagon]; *(refrain)* гардон [gardon]

christen [крисан] *v.t.* номидан [nomidan]

Christian [крисчан] *n./adj.* насронӣ [nasroni]

Christianity [крисчиянити] *n.* дини насронӣ [dini nasroni]

Christmas [крисмас] *n.* мавлуди Исо [mavludi Iso]

chronic [кроник] *adj.* давомнок [davomnok]

church [чурч] *n.* калисо [kaliso]

cider [сайдер] *n. (alcoholic)* майи себ [mayi seb]; *(non-alcoholic)* шарбати себ [sharbati seb]

cigar [сигор] *n.* сигара [sigara]

cigarette [сигарет] *n.* сигарет [sigaret], сигор [sigor]

cinder [синдер] *n.* ангишти нимсӯз [angishti nimsüz]; **cinders** хокистар [xokistar]

cinema [синема] *n.* синамо [sinamo]

cinnamon [синамон] *n.* дорчин [dorchin]

circle [сиркъл] *n.* чанбар [chanbar], доира [doira]

circuit [сиркит] *n. (electronic)* контур [kontur]; *(circular course)* давра [davra]

circulate [сиркюлейт] *v.i. (move through a circuit)* гирд гаштан [gird gashtan], чарх задан [charx zadan]; *(disseminate)* паҳн шудан [pahn shudan]

circulation [сиркюлейшан] *n.* гардиш [gardish], чархзанӣ [charxzani]

circumcision [сиркамсижан] *n.* хатна [xatna]

circumference [сиркамференс] *n.* давра [davra]

circumstance [сиркамстанс] *n.* маврид [mavrid]

circus [сиркас] *n.* сирк [sirk]

cite [сайт] *v.t.* иқтибос овардан [iqtibos ovardan]

citizen [ситизен] *n.* шаҳрванд [shahrvand]

city [сити] *n.* шаҳр [shahr]

civilization [сивилайзейшан] *n.* тамаддун [tamaddun]

claim [клейм] *n.* даъво [da'vo] / *v.t.* даъво кардан [da'vo kardan]

clam [клам] *n.* клем [klem]

clap [клап] *v.t.* қарсак задан [qarsak zadan]

class [клас] *n.* синф [sinf]

classical [класикал] *adj.* классикӣ [klassiki]

classify [класифай] *v.t.* дастабандӣ кардан [dastabandi kardan], тасниф кардан [tasnif kardan]

classroom [класрум] *n.* синф [sinf], дарсхона [darsxona]

claw [кло] *n.* чангол [changol], чанг [chang]

clay [клей] *n.* гил [gil], лой [loy]

clean [клин] *adj.* пок [pok], тоза [toza] / *v.t.* пок кардан [pok kardan], тоза кардан [toza kardan]

cleaner [клинер] *n. (person)* фаррош [farrosh]

clear [клир] *adj.* соф [sof] / *v.t.* соф кардан [sof kardan]

clergy [клерҷи] *n.pl.* рӯҳониён [rühoniyon]

clerk [клерк] *n.* котиб [kotib]

clever [клевер] *adj.* зирак [zirak]
client [клайент] *n.* муштарӣ [mushtari]
cliff [клиф] *n.* шах [shax]
climate [клаймит] *n.* иқлим [iqlim], обу ҳаво [obu havo]
climax [клаймакс] *n.* авҷ [avj]
climb [клайм] *n.* болобарой [bolobaroi] / *v.t.* боло баромадан [bolo baromadan] / *v.i.* боло рафтан [bolo raftan]
cling [клинг] *v.i.* часпидан [chaspidan]
clinic [клиник] *n.* дармонгоҳ [darmongoh], клиника [klinika]
clip [клип] *n.* бандак [bandak] / *v.t.* исканҷа кардан [iskanja kardan]
clock [клок] *n.* соат [soat]
close [клос] *adj./adv.* наздик [nazdik]
close [клоз] *v.t.* бастан [bastan], пӯшонидан [püshonidan]
closed [клозд] *adj.* баста [basta]
closet [клозет] *n.* ҷевони деворӣ [jevoni devori]
cloth [клот] *n.* газвор [gazvor], порча [porcha]
clothe [клод] *v.t.* пӯшонидан [püshonidan]
clothes [клод] *n.pl.* пӯшок [püshok], либос [libos]
clothing [клодинг] *n.* пӯшок [püshok], либос [libos]
cloud [клауд] *n.* абр [abr]
cloudy [клауди] *adj.* абрнок [abrnok]
clown [клаун] *n.* масхарабоз [masxaraboz]
club [клаб] *n. (cudgel or stick)* калтак [kaltak], таёқ [tayoq]; *(organization)* клуб [klub], анҷуман [anjuman]; *(sports equipment)* чавгон [chavgon]; **clubs** *(card suit)* чилликхол [chillikxol], чиллик [chillik]
clue [клу] *n.* калид [kalid]
cluster [кластер] *n.* хӯша [xüsha], даста [dasta] / *v.i.* даста шудан [dasta shudan]
clutch [клач] *n. (mechanical part)* кӯпала [küpala], бастак [bastak] / *v.t.* сахт гирифтан [saxt giriftan]
coach [коч] *n. (sports)* омӯзгор [omüzgor]; *(economy class)* дараҷаи дуюм [darajai duyum]; *(carriage)* фойтун [foytun]
coal [кол] *n.* ангишт [angisht]
coarse [корс] *adj.* дурушт [durusht]
coast [кост] *n.* соҳил [sohil]
coat [кот] *n.* палто [palto]
cobra [кобра] *n.* мори айнакӣ [mori aynaki]
cobweb [кобуэб] *n.* тори тортанак [tori tortanak], тортанакхона [tortanakxona]
cock [кок] *n.* хурӯс [xurüs]
cocktail [коктейл] *n.* коктейл [kokteyl]
cocoa [коко] *n.* какав [kakav]
cod [код] *n.* равғанмоҳӣ [ravghanmohi]
code [код] *n.* рамз [ramz]; **code of conduct** қоидаи рафтор [qoidai raftor]; **moral code** қонуни ахлоқ [qonuni axloq]
coffee [кофи] *n.* қаҳва [qahva]

coffee pot [кофи пот] *n.* қаҳвачӯшонак [qahvajüshonak]
coffee shop [кофи шоп] *n.* қаҳвахона [qahvaxona]
coffin [кофин] *n.* тобут [tobut]
coil [койл] *n.* печ [pech], ҳалқа [halqa]
coin [койн] *n.* сикка [sikka], танга [tanga]
coincide [коинсайд] *v.i.* рост омадан [rost omadan]
coincidence [коинсиданс] *n.* тасодуф [tasoduf]
coincidental [коинсидентал] *adj.* тасодуфӣ [tasodufi]
cold [колд] *n.* хунукӣ [xunuki], сардӣ [sardi] / *adj.* хунук [xunuk], сард [sard]
collaborate [колаборейт] *v.i.* ҳамкорӣ кардан [hamkori kardan], иштирок кардан [ishtirok kardan]
collaboration [колаборейшан] *n.* ҳамкорӣ [hamkori], иштирок [ishtirok]
collar [колар] *n.* гиребон [girebon], ёқа [yoqa]
collect [колект] *v.t.* ғундоштан [ghundoshtan], ҷамъ кардан [jam' kardan]
collection [колекшан] *n.* маҷмӯа [majmüa]
college [колеҷ] *n.* донишкада [donishkada]
collide [колайд] *v.i.* бархӯрдан [barxürdan]
collision [колижан] *n.* бархӯрӣ [barxüri], садама [sadama]
colon [колон] *n.* *(anat.)* ғафсрӯда [ghafsrüda]; *(gram.)* аломати тақсим [alomati taqsim]
colonel [кернел] *n.* полковник [polkovnik], сарҳанг [sarhang]
colony [колони] *n.* мустамлика [mustamlika]
color [калар] *n.* ранг [rang]
column [колам] *n.* *(pillar)* сутун [sutun]; *(line)* саф [saf]
comb [ком] *n.* шона [shona] / *v.t.* шона кардан [shona kardan]
combination [комбинейшан] *n.* ҷӯршавӣ [jürshavi], якҷоякунӣ [yakjoyakuni]
combine [комбайн] *v.t.* якҷоя кардан [yakjoya kardan]
come [кам] *v.i.* омадан [omadan]
comedy [комеди] *n.* комедия [komediya]
comfort [комфорт] *n.* *(solace)* дилдорӣ [dildori], дилбардорӣ [dilbardori]; *(condition of ease)* оромӣ [oromi], роҳат [rohat] / *v.t.* дилдорӣ кардан [dildori kardan], дилбардорӣ кардан [dilbardori kardan]
comfortable [камфуртабал] *adj.* қулай [qulay]
comic [комик] *adj.* комедиявӣ [komediyavi]
comma [кома] *n.* вергул [vergul]
command [куманд] *n.* фармон [farmon] / *v.t.* фармон додан [farmon dodan]
commence [коменс] *v.i.* сар шудан [sar shudan], оғоз шудан [oghoz shudan]
comment [комент] *n.* шарҳ [sharh], тафсир [tafsir] / *v.i.* шарҳ додан [sharh dodan], тафсир кардан [tafsir kardan]

commentary [коментери] *n.* шарҳ [sharh], тафсир [tafsir]
commerce [комерс] *n.* савдо [savdo], тиҷорат [tijorat]
commercial [комершал] *n.* эълон [e'lon] / *adj.* тиҷоратӣ [tijorati]
commission [комишан] *n.* *(group of people)* комиссия [komissiya]; *(fee for services rendered)* ҳаққи хизмат [haqqi xizmat]
committee [комити] *n.* кумита [kumita]
common [комон] *adj.* *(ordinary)* оддӣ [oddi], омиёна [omiyona]; *(shared, e.g. money, resources, etc.)* муштарак [mushtarak], шарикӣ [shariki]; *(the same or identical, e.g. language, etc.)* якхела [yakxela]
communicate [комюникейт] *v.t.* хабар додан [xabar dodan]
communication [комюникейшан] *n.* хабардиҳӣ [xabardihi], хабаррасонӣ [xabarrasoni]
communism [комюнизм] *n.* коммунизм [kommunizm]
communist [комюнист] *n.* коммунист [kommunist] / *adj.* коммунистӣ [kommunisti]
compact [компакт] *n.* қуттии упо [quttii upo] / *adj.* зич [zich], ихчам [ixcham]
companion [компанян] *n.* ҳамроҳ [hamroh]
companionship [компанияншип] *n.* ҳамроҳӣ [hamrohi]
company [компани] *n.* *(companionship or fellowship)* ҳамроҳӣ [hamrohi]; *(business enterprise)* ширкат [shirkat]
compare [компер] *v.t.* муқоиса кардан [muqoisa kardan]
comparison [компарисон] *n.* муқоиса [muqoisa]
compartment [компартмент] *n.* хонача [xonacha], чашм [chashm]
compass [компас] *n.* қутбнамо [qutbnamo]
compatible [компатибъл] *adj.* ба ҳам мувофиқ [ba ham muvofiq]
competence [компетенс] *n.* ӯҳдабарой [ühdabaroi], кордонӣ [kordoni]
competent [компетент] *adj.* ӯҳдабаро [ühdabaro], кордон [kordon]
competition [компетишан] *n.* *(contest)* мусобиқа [musobiqa]; *(rivalry)* ҳамчашмӣ [hamchashmi], рақобат [raqobat]
complain [комплен] *v.i.* гила кардан [gila kardan], шикоят кардан [shikoyat kardan]
complaint [комплент] *n.* гила [gila], шикоят [shikoyat]
complete [комплит] *adj.* пурра [purra], мукаммал [mukammal] / *v.t.* пурра кардан [purra kardan], мукаммал кардан [mukammal kardan]
complicate [компликейт] *v.t.* чигил кардан [chigil kardan], печида кардан [pechida kardan], буғранҷ кардан [bughranj kardan]

complicated [компликейтед] *adj.* печида [pechida], буғранҷ [bughranj], чигил [chigil]
compliment [комплимент] *n.* таъриф [ta'rif] / *v.t.* таъриф кардан [ta'rif kardan]
comply [комплай] *v.i.* итоат кардан [itoat kardan]
compose [композ] *v.t.* таълиф кардан [ta'lif kardan]
composition [композишан] *n.* *(make-up)* таркиб [tarkib]; *(writing or music)* таълиф [ta'lif], тасниф [tasnif]; *(gram.)* пайвастшавӣ [payvastshavi]
compound [компаунд] *n.* *(chemical)* таркиб [tarkib] / *adj.* таркибӣ [tarkibi], мураккаб [murakkab]
comprehensive [компреҳенсив] *adj.* пурра [purra], мукаммал [mukammal]
comprise [компрайз] *v.t.* таркиб кардан [tarkib kardan]
compromise [компромайз] *n.* созиш [sozish]
computer [компютер] *n.* компютер [kompyuter]
conceal [консил] *v.t.* пинҳон кардан [pinhon kardan]
concede [консид] *v.t.* гузашт кардан [guzasht kardan]
conceit [консит] *n.* худписандӣ [xudpisandi], манманӣ [manmani]
concentrate [консентрейт] *v.i.* *(bring together)* якҷоя кардан [yakjoya kardan], ғун кардан [ghun kardan]; *(pay attention)* тамоми диққати худро додан [tamomi diqqati xudro dodan]
concept [консепт] *n.* ақида [aqida]
concern [консерн] *n.* ноороми [nooromi] / *v.t.* марбут будан [marbut budan]
concert [консерт] *n.* консерт [konsert]
concession [консешан] *n.* *(government grant to business, or the business itself)* имтиёз [imtiyoz]; *(sth conceded or given up)* гузашт [guzasht]
concise [консайс] *adj.* мухтасар [muxtasar]
conclusion [конклужан] *n.* анҷом [anjom]
concrete [конкрит] *n.* бетон [beton]
condemn [кондем] *v.t.* *(express disapproval)* мазаммат кардан [mazammat kardan], номаъқул шумурдан [noma'qul shumurdan]; *(pronounce judgment against)* маҳкум кардан [mahkum kardan]
condition [кондишан] *n.* ҳолат [holat]
condolence [кондоленс] *n.* таъзия [ta'ziya]
condom [кондом] *n.* презерватив [preservativ]
conduct [кондакт] *n.* рафтор [raftor], муомила [muomila] / *v.t.* идора кардан [idora kardan]
conductor [кондактор] *n.* *(on a train)* кондуктор [konduktor]; *(of electricity, etc.)* ноқил [noqil]
cone [кон] *n.* махрут [maxrut]
confess [конфес] *v.t.* иқрор кардан [iqror kardan], эътироф кардан [e'tirof kardan]

confession [конфешан] *n.* эътироф [e'tirof]
confidence [конфиденс] *n.* дилпурӣ [dilpuri]
confirm [конфирм] *v.t.* тасдиқ кардан [tasdiq kardan], таъкид кардан [ta'kid kardan]
confirmation [конфирмейшан] *n.* тасдиқ [tasdiq], таъкид [ta'kid]
conflict [конфликт] *n.* *(physical)* задухӯрд [zaduxürd]; *(of ideas)* ихтилоф [ixtilof]
confuse [конфюз] *v.t.* *(mistake for sth else)* монанд кардан [monand kardan]; *(throw off or cause a lack of clear thinking)* саросема кардан [sarosema kardan]
confusion [конфюжан] *n.* саросемагӣ [sarosemagi]
congratulate [конграчюлейт] *v.t.* табрик кардан [tabrik kardan], муборакбод гуфтан [muborakbod guftan]
congratulations [конграчюлейшан] *n.* табрик [tabrik], муборак [muborak]
congress [конгрес] *n.* конгресс [kongress]
conjunction [конҷанкшан] *gram.* пайвандак [payvandak]
connect [конект] *v.t.* *(join or bring together)* пайвастан [payvastan], пайванд кардан [payvand kardan]; *(via a communications circuit)* алоқаманд кардан [aloqamand kardan]
connection [конекшан] *n.* *(physical link)* пайваст [payvast]; *(association or relationship)* алоқа [aloqa], робита [robita]
conquer [конкер] *v.t.* фатҳ кардан [fath kardan], истило кардан [istilo kardan]
conquest [конкуест] *n.* фатҳ [fath], истило [istilo]
conscience [коншенс] *n.* виҷдон [vijdon]
conscientious [консиеншас] *adj.* бовиҷдон [bovijdon]
conscious [коншас] *adj.* *(awake or aware)* боҳуш [bohush]; *(deliberate)* барқасд [barqasd]
consent [консент] *n.* розигӣ [rozigi] / *v.t.* розигӣ додан [rozigi dodan]
consequence [консекуэнс] *n.* натиҷа [natija], оқибат [oqibat]
conservation [консервейшан] *n.* нигоҳдорӣ [nigohdori], муҳофизат [muhofizat]
conservative [консерватив] *adj.* кӯҳнапараст [kühnaparast]
conserve [консерв] *v.t.* нигоҳ доштан [nigoh doshtan], муҳофизат кардан [muhofizat kardan]
consider [консидер] *v.t.* *(think carefully)* дида баромадан [dida baromadan], мулоҳиза кардан [mulohiza kardan]; *(regard as)* ҳисоб кардан [hisob kardan], шумурдан [shumurdan]
consideration [консидерейшан] *n.* мулоҳиза [mulohiza]

consist [консист] *v.i.* иборат будан [iborat budan], таркиб ёфтан [tarkib yoftan]

consolation [консолейшан] *n.* дилбардорӣ [dilbardori], тасалло [tasallo]

console [консол] *n.* рафак [rafak] / *v.t.* дилдорӣ кардан [dildori kardan], дилбардорӣ кардан [dilbardori kardan]

consonant [консунант] *n.* ҳамсадо [hamsado]

constant [констант] *n.* константа [konstanta], бузургии пойдор [buzurgii poydor] / *adj. (without stopping)* беист [beist]; *(fixed or permanent)* пойдор [poydor]

constellation [констелейшан] *n.* бурҷ [burj], галаситора [galasitora]

constipation [констипейт] *n.* қабзият [qabziyat]

constitute [конститют] *v.t.* ташкил додан [tashkil dodan]

constitution [конститюшан] *n.* сарқонун [sarqonun]

consul [консул] *n.* консул [konsul]

consulate [консюлат] *n.* консулхона [konsulxona]

consult [консалт] *v.i.* машварат кардан [mashvarat kardan]

consultant [консалтант] *n.* мушовир [mushovir]

consume [консюм] *v.t.* сарф кардан [sarf kardan], истеъмол кардан [iste'mol kardan]

consumer [консюмер] *n.* сарфкунанда [sarfkunanda], истеъмолкунанда [iste'molkunanda]

consumption [консампшан] *n.* сарф [sarf], истеъмол [iste'mol]

contact [контект] *n.* алоқа [aloqa], тамос [tamos] / *v.t.* алоқа кардан [aloqa kardan], тамос гирифтан [tamos giriftan]

contact lens [контект ленз] *n.* линза [linza]

contagious [контейҷас] *adj.* сирояткунанда [siroyatkunanda]

contain [контейн] *v.t. (have capacity for)* гунҷондан [gunjondan], ҷой додан [joy dodan]; *(have or hold)* доштан [doshtan]

container [контейнер] *n.* зарф [zarf]

contaminate [контаминейт] *v.t.* олудан [oludan]

contend [контенд] *v.i.* ҳамчашмӣ кардан [hamchashmi kardan], рақобат кардан [raqobat kardan]

content [контент] *n.* окана [okana] / *adj.* розӣ [rozi], қонеъ [qone']

contest [контест] *n.* мусобиқа [musobiqa] / *v.t.* мубоҳиса кардан [mubohisa kardan]

continent [континент] *n.* қитъа [qit'a]

continue [кантиню] *v.i.* давом додан [davom dodan]

continuous [кантинюас] *adj.* давомдор [davomdor]

contraceptive [контрасептив] *n.* доруи пешгиркунандаи обистанӣ [dorui peshgirkunandai obistani] / *adj.* пешгиркунандаи обистанӣ [peshgirkunandai obistani]
contract [контрект] *n.* шартнома [shartnoma], аҳднома [ahdnoma]
contrary [контрери] *adj.* зид [zid], мухталиф [muxtalif]
contrast [контрест] *n.* зиддият [ziddiyat]
contribute [контрибют] *v.t.* *(assist)* ёрмандӣ расондан [yormandi rasondan]; *(contribute to a newspaper)* иштирок кардан [ishtirok kardan]
contribution [контрибюшан] *n.* ёрмандӣ [yormandi]
control [контрол] *n.* назорат [nazorat] / *v.t.* назорат кардан [nazorat kardan]
convene [конвин] *v.t.* ҷамъ кардан [jam' kardan]
convenience [конвиниенс] *n.* қулай будан [qulay budan], роҳат [rohat]
convent [конвент] *n.* дайр [dayr]
convention [конвеншан] *n.* *(meeting)* маҷлис [majlis], ҷамъомад [jam'omad]; *(custom)* оин [oin], расм [rasm]
conversation [конварсешан] *n.* гуфтугӯ [guftugü]
convert [конверт] *n.* навдин [navdin], навкеш [navkesh] / *v.t.* *(change)* дигаргун кардан [digargun kardan]; *(convert sb religiously)* ба кеши дигар даровардан [ba keshi digar darovardan]
convey [конвей] *v.t.* бурдан [burdan], кашондан [kashondan]
cook [кук] *n.* ошпаз [oshpaz] / *v.t.* пухтан [puxtan]
cookbook [кукбук] *n.* китоби ошпазӣ [kitobi oshpazi]
cookie [куки] *n.* кулчаи қандин [kulchai qandin]
cooking [кукинг] *n.* ошпазӣ [oshpazi]
cool [кул] *adj.* салқин [salqin] / *v.t.* хунук кардан [xunuk kardan], сард кардан [sard kardan]
cooperate [куоперейт] *v.i.* ҳамкорӣ кардан [hamkori kardan]
coordinate [куординейт] *v.t.* ба ҳамдигар мувофиқ кардан [ba hamdigar muvofiq kardan]
cop [коп] *n.* милиса [milisa]
copier [копиер] *n.* дастгоҳи нусхабардорӣ [dastgohi nusxabardori]
copper [копар] *n.* мис [mis]
copy [копи] *n.* нусха [nusxa] / *v.t.* *(make a copy)* нусха бардоштан [nusxa bardoshtan]; *(imitate)* тақлид кардан [taqlid kardan]
copyright [копирайт] *n.* ҳуқуқи муаллифӣ [huquqi muallifi]
coral [корал] *n.* марҷон [marjon]
cordially [кордяли] *adv.* самимона [samimona]
core [кор] *n.* ӯзак [üzak], дила [dila]

cork [корк] *n.* пӯка [püka], дахантиққӣ [dahantiqqi]
corn [корн] *n.* ҷуворӣ [juvori], ҷуворимакка [juvorimakka]
corner [корнар] *n.* гӯша [güsha], кунҷ [kunj]
corporation [корпорейшан] *n.* ширкат [shirkat]
corpse [корпс] *n.* ҷасад [jasad], лоша [losha]
correct [курект] *adj.* дуруст [durust] / *v.t.* дуруст кардан [durust kardan], ислоҳ кардан [isloh kardan]
correction [корекшан] *n.* ислоҳ [isloh]
correspond [кореспонд] *v.i.* мукотиба доштан [mukotiba doshtan]
correspondence [кореспонденс] *n.* мукотибот [mukotibot]
correspondent [кореспондент] *n.* хабарнигор [xabarnigor]
corridor [коридор] *n.* роҳрав [rohrav]
corrupt [корап] *adj.* ришватхӯр [rishvatxür]
corruption [корапшан] *n.* фасод [fasod]
cost [кост] *n.* нарх [narx], баҳо [baho] / *v.t.* истодан [istodan], нарх доштан [narx doshtan]
costume [костюм] *n.* *(clothing)* пӯшок [püshok]; *(theatrical garb)* пӯшоки театрӣ [püshoki teatri]
cot [кот] *n.* *(child's bed)* кати бачагона [kati bachagona]
cottage [котиҷ] *n.* кулба [kulba]
cotton [котон] *n.* пахта [paxta], пунба [punba] / *adj.* пахтагӣ [paxtagi], пахтагин [paxtagin]
couch [кауч] *n.* диван [divan]
cough [коф] *n.* сурфа [surfa] / *v.i.* сурфидан [surfidan]
could [куд] *aux.* *(past of* can*)* гузаштаи [guzashtai]
council [каунсил] *n.* шӯро [shüro]
count [каунт] *n.* *(tally)* шумор [shumor]; *(nobleman)* граф [graf] / *v.t.* шумурдан [shumurdan]
counter [каунтер] *n.* пештахта [peshtaxta]
counterfeit [каунтерфит] *adj.* сохта [soxta], қалбакӣ [qalbaki]
country [кантри] *n.* кишвар [kishvar], мамлакат [mamlakat]
couple [капал] *n.* ҷуфт [juft]
courage [куриҷ] *n.* далерӣ [daleri], диловарӣ [dilovari]
courageous *adj.* далер [daler], диловар [dilovar]
course [корс] *n.* *(academic)* курс [kurs]; *(process, course of events, course of a river)* ҷараён [jarayon]; **of course** албатта [albatta]
court [корт] *n.* *(legal)* додгоҳ [dodgoh], суд [sud]; *(royal)* дарбор [darbor]; *(sports facility)* корт [kort]
courtesy [куртеси] *n.* *(courteous behavior)* хушмуомилагӣ [xushmuomilagi]; *(favor)* некхоҳӣ [nekxohi]
courtyard [кортярд] *n.* ҳавлии дарун [havlii darun]

cousin [казин] *n. (son of paternal uncle)* амакбача [amakbacha]; *(son of paternal aunt)* аммабача [ammabacha]; *(son of maternal uncle)* тағобача [taghobacha]; *(son of maternal aunt)* холабача [xolabacha]; *(daughter of paternal uncle)* духтари амак [duxtari amak]; *(daughter of paternal aunt)* духтари амма [duxtari amma]; *(daughter of maternal uncle)* духтари тағо [duxtari tagho]; *(daughter of maternal aunt)* духтари хола [duxtari xola]

cover [кавер] *n.* пӯшиш [püshish] / *v.t.* пӯшондан [püshondan]

cow [коу] *n.* гов [gov]

coward [кауард] *n.* тарсончак [tarsonchak], буздил [buzdil]

crab [краб] *n.* харчанг [xarchang]

crack [крак] *n.* тарқ [tarq], шикоф [shikof] / *v.t.* тарқондан [tarqondan] / *v.i.* тарқидан [tarqidan]

cracker [кракер] *n.* кулчаи хушк [kulchai xushk]

cradle [креидал] *n.* гаҳвора [gahvora]

craft [крафт] *n.* пеша [pesha]

craftsman [крафтсман] *n.* пешавар [peshavar]

cramp [крамп] *n.* ихтилоҷ [ixtiloj]

crane [крейн] *n. (bird)* куланг [kulang]; *(mechanical)* крани борбардор [krani borbardor]

crash [краш] *n.* гулдуррос [guldurros], шақаррос [shaqarros] / *v.t.* гулдуррос зада афтондан [guldurros zada aftondan], таққи задан [taqqi zadan]

crate [крейт] *n.* сандуқ [sanduq]

crater [крейтер] *n.* танӯра [tanüra]

crawl [крол] *v.i.* хазидан [xazidan]

crazy [крейзи] *adj.* девона [devona]

cream [крим] *n. (dairy product)* саршир [sarshir], қаймоқ [qaymoq]; *(topical application)* крем [krem]

crease [крис] *n.* чин [chin]

create [криейт] *v.t.* офаридан [ofaridan]

creation [криейшан] *n.* офариниш [ofarinish]

creature [кричар] *n.* офарида [ofarida]

credit [кредит] *n.* вом [vom], қарз [qarz] / *v.t.* вом додан [vom dodan], қарз додан [qarz dodan]; **credit card** варақаи қарз [varaqai qarz]; **on credit** бақарз [baqarz]

creditor [кредитор] *n.* вомдиҳанда [vomdihanda], қарздиҳанда [qarzdihanda]

creep [крип] *v.i.* хазидан [xazidan]

crescent [кресант] *n.* ҳилол [hilol]

crest [крест] *n. (of a bird)* кокул [kokul]; *(of a wave)* теға [tegha]; *(coat-of-arms)* нишон [nishon]

crew [кру] *n.* бригада [brigada]

cricket [крикет] *n. (insect)* чирчирак [chirchirak]; *(sport)* крикет [kriket]

crime [крайм] *n.* ҷиноят [jinoyat]
criminal [криминал] *n.* ҷинояткор [jinoyatkor] / *adj.* ҷинояткорона [jinoyatkorona]
crippled [крипалд] *adj.* ланг [lang], чӯлоқ [chüloq]
crisis [крайсис] *n.* бӯҳрон [bühron]
criticism [критисизм] *n.* танқид [tanqid]
criticize [критисайз] *v.t.* танқид кардан [tanqid kardan]
crooked [крукид] *adj.* каҷ [kaj]
crop [кроп] *n.* ҳосил [hosil]
cross [крос] *n.* хоҷ [xoj], чалипо [chalipo], салиб [salib] / *v.t. (cross arms or legs, etc.)* чиллик кардан [chillik kardan]; *(cross a river, street, etc.)* гузаштан [guzashtan], убур кардан [ubur kardan]; **cross the street** аз кӯча гузаштан [az kücha guzashtan]
crossroad [кросрод] *n.* чорраҳа [chorraha]
crossword [кросвурд] *n.* кроссворд [krossvord]
crouch [крауч] *v.i.* зонуқат нишастан [zonuqat nishastan], сари ду пой нишастан [sari du poy nishastan]
crow [кро] *n.* калоғ [kalogh], зоғ [zogh]
crowd [крауд] *n.* тӯда [tüda], анбӯҳ [anbüh]
crowded [краудед] *adj.* пуропур [puropur]
crown [краун] *n.* тоҷ [toj]
crude [круд] *adj.* хом [xom], нопурра [nopurra]
cruel [крул] *adj.* сангдил [sangdil], золим [zolim]
cruise [круз] *n.* круиз [kruiz]; **go on a cruise** круиз рафтан [kruiz raftan]
crumb [крам] *n.* резгӣ [rezgi], пора [pora]
crumble [крамбъл] *v.i.* майда шудан [mayda shudan], пора-пора шудан [pora-pora shudan]
crunch [кранч] *v.t.* ғарчос кардан [gharchos kardan]
crush [краш] *v.t.* фушурдан [fushurdan]
crust [краст] *n.* қабат [qabat]
crutch [крач] *n.* асобағал [asobaghal]
cry [край] *n.* фарёд [faryod] / *v.t. (yell)* фарёд задан [faryod zadan]; *(weep)* гиристан [giristan], гиря кардан [girya kardan]
crystal [кристал] *n.* булӯр [bulür] / *adj.* булӯрин [bulürin]
cub [каб] *n.* бача [bacha] *(барои ҷонварҳо)*
cube [кюб] *n.* мукааб [mukaab]
cuff [каф] *n.* нӯгостин [nügostin], саростин [sarostin]
cultivate [калтивейт] *v.t.* коштан [koshtan]
cultivation [калтивейшан] *n.* кишт [kisht]
cultural [калчурал] *adj.* фарҳангӣ [farhangi]
culture [калчур] *n.* фарҳанг [farhang]
cup [кап] *n.* пиёла [piyola], косача [kosacha]

cupboard [кабурд] *n.* ҷевон [jevon]
curb [курб] *v.t.* боздоштан [bozdoshtan]
cure [кюр] *n.* дармон [darmon], шифо [shifo] / *v.t.* шифо додан [shifo dodan]
curious [кюрияс] *adj.* кунҷков [kunjkov]
curl [курл] *n.* зулф [zulf], каҷак [kajak] / *v.t.* ҷингила кардан [jingila kardan]; **curl up** *(one's body)* ба худ печидан [ba xud pechidan]
curly [курли] *adj.* ҷингила [jingila], ҷилҷила [jiljila]
currency [куренси] *n.* пул [pul]; **currency exchange** табдили пул [tabdili pul]
current [курент] *n.* ҷараён [jarayon] / *adj.* ҳозира [hozira], ҷорӣ [jori]; **electric current** ҷараёни барқӣ [jarayoni barqi]
curse [курс] *n.* нафрин [nafrin] / *v.t.* нафрин кардан [nafrin kardan]
curtain [куртан] *n.* парда [parda]
curve [курв] *n.* хам [xam] / *v.i.* хам шудан [xam shudan]
cushion [кушан] *n.* болишт [bolisht]
custard [кастард] *n.* фиринии тухмӣ [firinii tuxmi]
custom [кастом] *n.* оин [oin], расм [rasm]
customer [кастомер] *n.* фармоянда [farmoyanda], муштарӣ [mushtari]
customs [кастомз] *n.* гумрук [gumruk]; **customs official** гумрукчӣ [gumrukchi]
cut [кат] *n.* бuриш [burish] / *v.t.* буридан [buridan]
cute [кют] *adj.* ширин [shirin], дилкаш [dilkash]
cycle [сайкъл] *n.* гардиш [gardish], доира [doira]
cylinder [силиндер] *n.* устувона [ustuvona]
cynical [синикал] *adj.* бадбин [badbin]
cypress [сайпрес] *n.* сарв [sarv]

D

dad(dy) [дад*(и)*] *n.* додо [dodo], дада [dada]
daily [дейли] *adj.* рӯзона [rüzona]
dairy [дери] *adj.* ширӣ [shiri]; **dairy cow** гови дӯшой [govi düshoi]
dam [дам] *n.* банди об [bandi ob]
damage [дам] *n.* зиён [ziyon], осеб [oseb] / *v.t.* зиён расондан [ziyon rasondan], осеб овардан [oseb ovardan]
damn [дам] *v.t.* лаънат кардан [la'nat kardan]
damp [дамп] *adj.* намнок [namnok], заҳ [zah]
dampen [дампен] *v.t.* нам кардан [nam kardan]
dance [данс] *n.* рақс [raqs] / *v.i.* рақсидан [raqsidan]
danger [дейнҷар] *n.* хатар [xatar]
dangerous [дейнҷарас] *adj.* хатарнок [xatarnok]
dare [дер] *v.i.* ҷуръат кардан [jur'at kardan]
daring [деринг] *adj.* диловар [dilovar], нотарс [notars]
dark [дарк] *adj.* торик [torik]
darken [даркен] *v.t.* торик кардан [torik kardan]

darkness [даркнес] *n.* торикӣ [toriki]
dash [даш] *n. (hyphen)* тире [tire]; *(small amount)* камакак [kamakak]; *(run)* давиш [davish]
data [дейта] *n.pl.* маълумот [ma'lumot]
date [дейт] *n. (the day's date)* таърих [ta'rix]; *(a meeting with sb)* дидор [didor], вохӯрӣ [voxüri]; *(fruit)* хурмо [xurmo] / *v.t. (date a document)* таърих мондан [ta'rix mondan]
daughter [дотер] *n.* духтар [duxtar]
daughter-in-law [дотер-ин-ло] *n.* келин [kelin], арӯс [arüs]
dawn [дон] *n.* саседадам [sapedadam], саҳар [sahar]
day [дей] *n.* рӯз [rüz]
dead [дед] *adj.* мурда [murda]
deaf [деф] *adj.* кар [kar]
deal [дил] *n.* муомила [muomila], харидуфурӯш [xaridufurüsh] / *v.t.* бахш кардан [baxsh kardan] / *v.i.* муомила кардан [muomila kardan], харидуфурӯш кардан [xaridufurüsh kardan]; *(deal cards)* қарта кашидан [qarta kashidan]
dealer [дилер] *n.* фурӯшанда [furüshanda]
dear [дир] *adj. (esteemed or loved)* гиромӣ [giromi], азиз [aziz]; *(expensive)* гарон [garon], қимат [qimat]
death [дет] *n.* марг [marg]
debate [дебейт] *n.* мунозира [munozira], мубоҳиса [mubohisa] / *v.t.* мунозира кардан [munozira kardan], мубоҳиса кардан [mubohisa kardan]
debt [дет] *n.* қарз [qarz], вом [vom]; **in debt** қарздор [qarzdor]
decay [декей] *n.* пӯсиш [püsish] / *v.i.* пӯсидан [püsidan]
deceit [дисит] *n.* фиреб [fireb]
deceive [дисив] *v.t.* фирефтан [fireftan]
December [дисембар] *n.* декабр [dekabr]
decent [дисент] *adj.* муносиб [munosib], дуруст [durust]
deception [десепшан] *n.* фиреб [fireb]
decide [десайд] *v.t.* қарор додан [qaror dodan]
decimal [десимал] *adj.* даҳӣ [dahi]; **decimal point** нуқтаи даҳӣ [nuqtai dahi]
decision [десижан] *n.* қарор [qaror]
decisive [десайсив] *adj.* қатъӣ [qat'i]
deck [дек] *n. (of cards)* дастаи қарта [dastai qarta]; *(of a ship)* саҳни киштӣ [sahni kishti]
declaration [декларейшан] *n.* эълон [e'lon], изҳор [iz-hor]
declare [деклер] *v.t.* эълон кардан [e'lon kardan], изҳор кардан [iz-hor kardan]

decline [деклайн] *n.* пастшавӣ [pastshavi], таназзул [tanazzul] / *v.t. (decline a request or invitation, etc.)* рад кардан [rad kardan], қабул накардан [qabul nakardan] / *v.i. (decline in health)* бемадор шудан [bemador shudan]; *(decline in quantity, quality, etc.)* паст шудан [past shudan], таназзул кардан [tanazzul kardan]

decorate [декорейт] *v.t.* оростан [orostan], зеб додан [zeb dodan]

decoration [декорейшан] *n.* ороиш [oroish], зеб [zeb]

decrease [декрис] *n.* коҳиш [kohish] / *v.t.* камтар кардан [kamtar kardan] / *v.i.* камтар шудан [kamtar shudan]

dedicate [дедикейт] *v.t.* бахшидан [baxshidan]

dedication [дедикейшан] *n. (as in the beginning of a book)* номаи бахшиш [nomai baxshish]; *(devotion)* сарсупурдагӣ [sarsupurdagi]; *(loyalty)* вафодорӣ [vafodori]

deduction [дедакшан] *n. (from a total)* тарҳ [tarh]; *(logical)* қиёс [qiyos]

deed [дид] *n. (act)* кирдор [kirdor], карда [karda]; *(document)* санад [sanad]

deem [дим] *v.t.* донистан [donistan]

deep [дип] *adj.* чуқур [chuqur], жарф [zharf]

deer [дир] *n.* гавазн [gavazn]

defeat [дефит] *n.* шикаст [shikast] / *v.t.* шикаст додан [shikast dodan]

defect [дифект] *n.* нуқсон [nuqson] / *v.i.* ба тарафи душман гузаштан [ba tarafi dushman guzashtan]

defective [дифектив] *adj.* нуқсондор [nuqsondor]

defend [дифенд] *v.t.* дифоъ кардан [difo' kardan]

defendant [дефендант] *n.* айбдор [aybdor]

defense [дифенс] *n.* дифоъ [difo']

defer [дефер] *v.t.* мондан [monondan]

define [дефайн] *v.t.* таъриф кардан [ta'rif kardan]

definite [дефинит] *adj. (without doubt)* бешак [beshak]; *(certain)* аниқ [aniq], яқин [yaqin]; *(gram.)* муайян [muayyan]

definition [дефинишан] *n.* таъриф [ta'rif]

definitive [дефинитив] *adj. (conclusive)* қатъӣ [qat'i]; *(gram.)* муайянкунанда [muayyankunanda]

deflate [дифлейт] *v.t.* аз бод тиҳӣ кардан [az bod tihi kardan]

defy [дефай] *v.t.* фармонбардорӣ накардан [farmonbardori nakardan]

degree [дегри] *n.* дараҷа [daraja]; *(academic title)* унвон [unvon]

dehydrated [диҳайдрейт] *adj.* беоб [beob]

delay [делей] *n.* андармонӣ [andarmoni], таъхир [ta'xir] / *v.t.* андармон кардан [andarmon kardan], таъхир кардан [ta'xir kardan]

delete [делит] *v.t.* пок кардан [pok kardan]

deliberate [делиберат] *adj.* барқасд [barqasd]
delicacy [деликаси] *n.* *(quality of being)* назокат [nazokat]; *(choice food)* хӯроки хушхӯр [xüroki xushxür]
delicate [деликат] *adj.* нозук [nozuk]
delight [делайт] *n.* хурсандӣ [xursandi]
deliver [деливер] *v.t.* бурда расондан [burda rasondan]
delivery [деливери] *n.* бурдарасонӣ [burdarasoni]
demand [деманд] *n.* тақозо [taqozo] / *v.t.* тақозо кардан [taqozo kardan]
democracy [демокраси] *n.* демократия [demokratiya]
democratic [демократик] *adj.* демократӣ [demokrati]
demonstrate [демонстрейт] *v.t.* намоиш додан [namoish dodan] / *v.i.* намоиш дода шудан [namoish doda shudan]
demonstration [демонстрейшан] *n.* *(showing)* намоиш [namoish]; *(public rally)* тазоҳур [tazohur]
den [ден] *n.* лона [lona]
dense [денс] *adj.* зич [zich]
density [денсити] *n.* зичӣ [zichi]
dent [дент] *n.* ҷои фурӯрафта [joi furürafta] / *v.t.* зер кардан [zer kardan]
dental [дентал] *adj.* -и дандон [-i dandon]
dentist [дентист] *n.* духтури дандон [duxturi dandon], дандонпизишк [dandonpizishk]
deny [денай] *v.t.* инкор кардан [inkor kardan]
depart [департ] *v.i.* равона шудан [ravona shudan], рахсипор шудан [rahsipor shudan]
department [департмент] *n.* шӯъба [shü'ba]; **department store** фурӯшгоҳ [furüshgoh]
departure [депарчур] *n.* равонашавӣ [ravonashavi], раҳсипорӣ [rahsipori]
depend [депенд] *v.i.* вобаста будан [vobasta budan], тобеъ будан [tobe' budan]
dependent [депендент] *n.* нонхӯр [nonxür] / *adj.* вобаста [vobasta], тобеъ [tobe']
depict [депикт] *v.t.* тасвир кардан [tasvir kardan]
deport [депорт] *v.t.* аз кишвар берун кардан [az kishvar berun kardan]
depot [депо] *n.* ҷои исту таъмир [joi istu ta'mir]
depress [депрес] *v.t.* афсурда кардан [afsurda kardan]
depressed [депресд] *adj.* афсурда [afsurda]
depression [депрешан] *n.* *(emotional)* афсурдагӣ [afsurdagi]; *(economic)* таназзул [tanazzul]; *(geological)* пастхамӣ [pastxami]
deprive [депрайв] *v.t.* маҳрум кардан [mahrum kardan]
depth [депт] *n.* чуқурӣ [chuquri], жарфо [zharfo]
deputy [депюти] *n.* муовин [muovin], намоянда [namoyanda]

derive [дерайв] *v.t.* гирифтан [giriftan]
descend [десенд] *v.i.* фуровардан [furovardan]
descent [десент] *n. (coming down)* фурориш [furorish]; *(genetics)* нажод [nazhod]
describe [дескрайб] *v.t.* тавсиф кардан [tavsif kardan]
description [дескрипшан] *n.* тавсиф [tavsif]
desert [дезерт] *n.* биёбон [biyobon] / *v.t.* тарк кардан [tark kardan], ҳиштан [hishtan] / *v.i. (mil.)* аз хизмат гурехтан [az xizmat gurextan]
deserve [дезерв] *v.t.* сазовор будан [sazovor budan]
design [дезайн] *n.* тарҳ [tarh] / *v.t.* тарҳ кашидан [tarh kashidan]
designate [дезигнейт] *v.t.* таъин кардан [ta'in kardan]
designer [дезайнер] *n.* тарҳкаш [tarhkash]
desirable [дезайрабъл] *adj.* дилхоҳ [dilxoh], матлуб [matlub]
desire [дезайр] *n.* орзу [orzu], хоҳиш [xohish] / *v.t.* орзу кардан [orzu kardan], хоҳиш кардан [xohish kardan]
desk [деск] *n.* мизи хатнависӣ [mizi xatnavisi]
despair [деспер] *n.* ноумедӣ [noumedi] / *v.i.* ноумед шудан [noumed shudan]
dessert [дезерт] *n.* шираворӣ [shiravori], десерт [desert]
destiny [дестини] *n.* сарнавишт [sarnavisht]
destroy [дестрой] *v.t.* вайрон кардан [vayron kardan], хароб кардан [xarob kardan]
destruction [дестракшан] *n.* вайронӣ [vayroni], харобӣ [xarobi]
detach [детач] *v.t.* ҷудо кардан [judo kardan]
detain [детейн] *v.t.* андармон кардан [andarmon kardan], боздоштан [bozdoshtan]
detect [детект] *v.t.* ошкор кардан [oshkor kardan]
detection [детекшан] *n.* кашф [kashf]
detective [детектив] *n.* муфаттиши махфӣ [mufattishi maxfi]
detergent [детерҷент] *n.* хока [xoka]; **laundry detergent** хокаи пӯшокшӯӣ [xokai püshokshüi]; **dish detergent** хокаи зарфшӯӣ [xokai zarfshüi]
determination [детерминейшан] *n.* устуворӣ [ustuvori]
determine [детермин] *v.t.* барқарор кардан [barqaror kardan]
determined [детерминъд] *adj. (decisive or strong)* қатъӣ [qat'i]; *(steadfast)* устувор [ustuvor]
develop [девелоп] *v.t. (a plan)* таҳия кардан [tahiya kardan]; *(a country)* пешрафт додан [peshraft dodan]; *(an industry or resources)* ривоҷ додан [rivoj dodan]; *(film)* зоҳир кардан [zohir kardan] / *v.i.* пеш рафтан [pesh raftan]

development [девелопмент] *n.* пешрафт [peshraft]
deviation [дивиейшан] *n.* хамкунӣ [xamkuni]
device [девайс] *n.* абзор [abzor], асбоб [asbob]
devil [девил] *n.* шайтон [shayton]
devise [дивайз] *v.t.* андешида ёфтан [andeshida yoftan], ихтироъ кардан [ixtiro' kardan]
devout [диваут] *adj.* порсо [porso], диндор [dindor]
dew [дю] *n.* шабнам [shabnam]
diabetes [дайабитиз] *n.* бемории қанд [bemorii qand]
diabetic [дайабетик] *adj.* гирифтори бемории қанд [giriftori bemorii qand]
diagnosis [дайагносис] *n.* ташхис [tashxis]
diagonal [дайагонал] *adj.* уреб [ureb]
dial [дайал] *n.* лавҳаи соат [lavhai soat] / *v.t.* гирифтан [giriftan]; **dial a telephone number** рақами телефонро гирифтан [raqami telefonro giriftan]
dialect [дайялект] *n.* шева [sheva], лаҳҷа [lahja]
dialogue [дайалог] *n.* гуфтугӯ [guftugü], муколима [mukolima]
diameter [дайаметер] *n.* қутр [qutr]
diamond [дайманд] *n.* алмос [almos]; **diamond ring** ангуштарини алмосдор [angushtarini almosdor]; **diamonds** *(card suit)* хишт [xisht]
diamond-shaped [дайманд-шейпд] *adj.* алмосшакл [almosshakl]
diaper [дайпер] *n.* парпеч [parpech]
diarrhea [дайария] *n.* дарунравӣ [darunravi], шикамравӣ [shikamravi]
diary [дайри] *n.* дафтари хотира [daftari xotira]
dice [дайс] *n.pl.* мӯҳраҳо [mühraho]; *v.t.* ба шакли мукааб буридан [ba shakli mukaab buridan]
dictate [диктейт] *v.t.* дикта кардан [dikta kardan]
dictation [диктейшан] *n.* дикта [dikta]
dictator [диктейтор] *n.* ҳукмфармо [hukmfarmo]
dictionary [дикшанери] *n.* луғат [lughat], фарҳанг [farhang]
die [дай] *n. (pl.* **dice** [дайс]*)* мӯҳра [mühra]
die [дай] *v.i.* мурдан [murdan]
diesel [дизел] *n.* дизел [dizel]; **diesel fuel** сӯзишвории дизелӣ [süzishvorii dizeli]
diet [дайет] *n.* парҳез [parhez] / *v.i.* парҳез кардан [parhez kardan]
differ [дифер] *v.i.* фарқ доштан [farq doshtan], якхел набудан [yakxel nabudan], яксон набудан [yakson nabudan]
difference [диференс] *n.* фарқ [farq], тафовут [tafovut]
different [диферент] *adj.* мухталиф [muxtalif], дигарсон [digarson], дигархел [digarxel]

difficult [дификулт] *adj.* душвор [dushvor], мушкил [mushkil]
difficulty [дификулти] *n.* душворӣ [dushvori], мушкилӣ [mushkili]
dig [диг] *v.t.* кофтан [koftan], кандан [kandan]
digest [дайҷест] *v.t.* ҳазм кардан [hazm kardan], гуворидан [guvoridan]
digestion [дайҷесчан] *n.* ҳазм [hazm], гувориш [guvorish]
dignified [дигнифайд] *adj.* мӯҳтарам [mühtaram]
dignity [дигнити] *n.* иззат [izzat], шаън [sha'n]
diligent [диличент] *adj.* боғайрат [boghayrat], серкӯшиш [serküshish]
dim [дим] *adj.* хира [xira], норавшан [noravshan] / *v.t.* хира кардан [xira kardan]
dimension [дайменшан] *n.* андоза [andoza]
diminish [диминиш] *v.t.* паст кардан [past kardan], камтар кардан [kamtar kardan]
dine [дайн] *v.i.* хӯрдан [xürdan]
dining room [дайнинг рум] *n.* хонаи хӯрокхӯрӣ [xonai xürokxüri]
dinner [динер] *n.* хӯроки шом [xüroki shom]
dip [дип] *v.t.* ғӯтондан [ghütondan]; *(into water or sauce)* ба об/қайла андохтан [ba ob/qayla andoxtan]
diplomat [дипломат] *n.* дипломат [diplomat]
diplomatic [дипломатик] *adj.* дипломатӣ [diplomati]
direct [дайрект] *adj.* рост [rost], бевосита [bevosita], мустақим [mustaqim] / *adv.* рост [rost], мустақиман [mustaqiman] / *v.t.* идора кардан [idora kardan], роҳбарӣ кардан [rohbari kardan]
direction [дайрекшан] *n.* сӯй [süy], тараф [taraf]
director [дайректор] *n.* мудир [mudir]
directory [дайректори] *n.* рӯйхат [rüyxat]; **telephone directory** рақамномаи телефон [raqamnomai telefon]
dirt [дирт] *n. (earth or soil)* лой [loy], гил [gil]; *(filthy substance)* чирк [chirk]
dirty [дирти] *adj.* чиркин [chirkin], ифлос [iflos]
disagree [дисагри] *v.i.* мувофиқ набудан [muvofiq nabudan], носоз будан [nosoz budan]
disagreement [дисагримент] *n.* мухолифат [muxolifat], ноиттифоқӣ [noittifoqi], носозӣ [nosozi]
disappear [дисапир] *v.i.* нопадид шудан [nopadid shudan]
disappoint [дисапойнт] *v.t.* дилхунук кардан [dilxunuk kardan], маъюс кардан [ma'yus kardan]
disappointment [дисапойнтмент] *n.* дилхунукӣ [dilxunuki], маъюсӣ [ma'yusi]
disaster [дизастер] *n.* офат [ofat]; **natural disaster** офати табиӣ [ofati tabii]

discipline [дисиплин] *n. (state of order)* интизом [intizom]; *(branch of knowledge)* фан [fan]
discount [дискаунт] *n.* тахфиф [taxfif]
discover [дискавер] *v.t.* кашф кардан [kashf kardan]
discovery [дискавери] *n.* кашф [kashf]
discreet [дискрит] *adj.* эҳтиётkор [ehtiyotkor]
discriminate [дискриминейт] *v.i.* табъиз кардан [tab'iz kardan], ҳуқуқро поймол кардан [huquqro poymol kardan]
discuss [дискас] *v.t.* мубоҳиса кардан [mubohisa kardan]
discussion [дискашан] *n.* мубоҳиса [mubohisa]
disease [дизиз] *n.* беморӣ [bemori], касалӣ [kasali]
disgrace [дисгрейс] *n.* беобрӯӣ [beobrüi], шармсорӣ [sharmsori] / *v.t.* шармсор кардан [sharmsor kardan]
disguise [дисгайз] *n.* ниқоб [niqob] / *v.t. (wear a disguise)* ниқоб пӯшидан [niqob püshidan]; *(dissemble)* пардапӯш кардан [pardapüsh kardan]; **disguise one's intentions** ниятҳои худро пардапӯш кардан [niyathoi xudro pardapüsh kardan]
disgust [дисгаст] *n.* нафрат [nafrat]
disgusting [дисгастинг] *adj.* дилбеҷокунанда [dilbejokunanda], нафратангез [nafratangez]
dish [диш] *n.* зарф [zarf]
dishonest [дисонест] *adj.* беинсоф [beinsof]
dishonesty [дисонести] *n.* беинсофӣ [beinsofi]
disinfect [динфект] *v.t.* тамъиз кардан [tam'iz kardan]
disinfectant [дисинфектант] *n.* моддаи тамъиз [moddai tam'iz]
disk [диск] *n.* лаълича [la'licha]; **computer disk** диск [disk]
dislike [дислайк] *v.t.* дӯст надоштан [düst nadoshtan]
dismiss [дисмис] *v.t.* рухсат додан [ruxsat dodan]
disobey [дисобей] *v.t.* саркашӣ кардан [sarkashi kardan], гӯш накардан [güsh nakardan]
display [дисплей] *n.* намоиш [namoish] / *v.t.* намоиш додан [namoish dodan]
displease [дисплиз] *v.t.* хуш наомадан [xush naomadan], нафоридан [naforidan]
dispose [диспоз] *v.i. (get rid of)* дур кардан [dur kardan]; *(complete)* анҷом додан [anjom dodan]
dispute [диспют] *n. (disagreement)* муноқиша [munoqisha]; *(legal)* низоъ [nizo'] / *v.i.* муноқиша кардан [munoqisha kardan]
disregard [дисрегард] *n.* нописандӣ [nopisandi], беэътиноӣ [bee'tinoi] / *v.t.* писанд накардан [pisand nakardan], беэътиноӣ кардан [bee'tinoi kardan]
distance [дистанс] *n.* дурӣ [duri]

distant [дистант] *adj.* дур [dur]
distill [дистил] *v.t.* тақтир кардан [taqtir kardan]
distinct [дистинкт] *adj.* махсус [maxsus]
distinction [дистинкшан] *n.* фарқ [farq]
distinguish [дистингуиш] *v.t.* фарқ кардан [farq kardan]
distort [дисторт] *v.t.* таҳриф кардан [tahrif kardan], нодуруст нишон додан [nodurust nishon dodan]
distract [дистракт] *v.t.* ба ҷойи дигар ҷалб кардан [ba joyi digar jalb kardan]
distress [дистрес] *n.* пурайшонӣ [purayshoni]
distribute [дистрибют] *v.t.* тақсим кардан [taqsim kardan]
distribution [дистрибюшан] *n.* тақсимот [taqsimot]
district [дистрикт] *n.* ноҳия [nohiya]
distrust [дистраст] *n.* нобоварӣ [nobovari] / *v.t.* бовар накардан [bovar nakardan]
disturb [дистурб] *v.t.* ошуфтан [oshuftan], ташвиш додан [tashvish dodan]
ditch [дич] *n.* хандақ [xandaq], ҷӯй [jüy]
dive [дайв] *v.i.* ғӯта задан [ghüta zadan], ғаввосӣ кардан [ghavvosi kardan]
diver [дайвер] *n.* ғӯтазан [ghütazan], ғаввос [ghavvos]
diverse [дайверс] *adj.* гуногун [gunogun], рангоранг [rangorang]
divide [дивайд] *v.t.* тақсим кардан [taqsim kardan]; **to divide eight by four** ҳаштро ба чор тақсим кардан [hashtro ba chor taqsim kardan]
diving [дайвинг] *n.* ғӯтазанӣ [ghütazani], ғаввосӣ [ghavvosi]
division [дивижан] *n.* тақсимшавӣ [taqsimshavi]
divorce [диворс] *n.* талоқ [taloq] / *v.t.* талоқ додан [taloq dodan] / *v.i.* талоқ гирифтан [taloq giriftan]
dizziness [дизинес] *n.* сарчархзанӣ [sarcharxzani]
dizzy [дизи] *adj.* гиҷ [gij]; **I feel dizzy.** Сарам чарх мезанад. [Saram charx mezanad.]
do [ду] *v.t.* кардан [kardan] / *v.i.* басанда будан [basanda budan]
dock [док] *n.* таъмиргоҳи киштиҳо [ta'mirgohi kishtiho]
doctor [доктор] *n.* пизишк [pizishk], духтур [duxtur]
dog [дог] *n.* саг [sag]
doll [дол] *n.* лӯхтак [lüxtak]
dollar [долар] *n.* доллар [dollar]
dolphin [долфин] *n.* делфин [delfin]
domain [домейн] *n. (territory of rule or control)* қаламрав [qalamrav]; *(sphere)* соҳа [soha]
dome [дом] *n.* гунбаз [gunbaz], гунбад [gunbad]
domestic [доместик] *adj. (relating to the household)* хонагӣ [xonagi]; *(internal, e.g. politics/economics)* дохилӣ [doxili]

dominate [доминейт] *v.t.* ҳукмронӣ кардан [hukmroni kardan]
domination [доминейшан] *n.* ҳукмронӣ [hukmroni], ҳукмфармоӣ [hukmfarmoi]
donate [донейт] *v.t.* садақа додан [sadaqa dodan], бахшидан [baxshidan]
donation [донейшан] *n.* садақа [sadaqa], бахшиш [baxshish]
donkey [допки] *n.* хар [xar]
door [дор] *n.* дар [dar]
doorbell [дорбел] *n.* занги дар [zangi dar]
doorman [дорман] *n.* дарбон [darbon]
dose [дос] *n.* воя [voya]
dot [дот] *n.* нуқта [nuqta]
double [дабъл] *adj.* дучанд [duchand]
doubt [даут] *n.* шак [shak], шубҳа [shubha] / *v.t.* шак доштан [shak doshtan], шубҳа кардан [shubha kardan]
doubtful [даутфул] *adj.* шубҳаомез [shubhaomez]
dough [до] *n.* хамир [xamir]
dove [дав] *n.* кабӯтар [kabütar], кафтар [kaftar]
down [даун] *n.* пари нарм [pari narm] / *adv.* поин [poin]
dozen [дазен] *n.* дувоздаҳ дона [duvozdah dona]
draft [драфт] *n.* *(mil.)* даъват [da'vat]; *(preliminary version)* ангора [angora]; *(air)* ҳавокашӣ [havokashi]
drag [драг] *v.t.* кашола кардан [kashola kardan]
dragon [драгон] *n.* аждаҳо [azhdaho], аждар [azhdar]
drain [дрейн] *n.* тарнов [tarnov], новадон [novadon] / *v.t.* заҳбур кандан [zahbur kandan]
drama [драма] *n.* драма [drama]
draw [дро] *v.t.* расм кашидан [rasm kashidan]
drawing [дроинг] *n.* расм [rasm]
dread [дред] *n.* бим [bim] / *v.t.* бим доштан [bim doshtan]
dream [дрим] *n.* хоб [xob]
dreary [дрири] *adj.* дилгиркунанда [dilgirkunanda]
dress [дрес] *n.* *(clothing)* пӯшок [püshok]; *(woman's dress)* куртаи занона [kurtai zanona] / *v.t.* пӯшондан [püshondan] / *v.i.* пӯшидан [püshidan]
drift [дрифт] *n.* *(snow drift)* барфтӯда [barftüda] / *v.i.* *(drift with the wind)* аз рафти вазиши бод ронда шудан [az rafti vazishi bod ronda shudan]; *(drift in the water)* аз рафти ҷараёни об ронда шудан [az rafti jarayoni ob ronda shudan]
drill [дрил] *n.* парма [parma] / *v.t.* парма кардан [parma kardan]
drink [дринк] *n.* нӯшиданӣ [nüshidani]; *(soft drink)* нӯшоба [nüshoba]; *(alcoholic drink)* нӯшокии спиртдор [nüshokii spirtdor] / *v.t.* нӯшидан [nüshidan]
drive [драйв] *v.t.* рондан [rondan]
driver [драйвер] *n.* ронанда [ronanda]; **driver's license** гувоҳномаи ронандагӣ [guvohnomai ronandagi]

drizzle [дризъл] *v.i.* сим-сим боридан [sim-sim boridan]; **It's drizzling.** Сим-сим меборад. [Sim-sim meborad.]
drop [дроп] *n.* чакра [chakra], қатра [qatra] / *v.t.* афтондан [aftondan]
drown [драун] *v.t.* ғарқ кардан [gharq kardan] / *v.i.* ғарқ шудан [gharq shudan]
drug [драг] *n. (medicine)* дору [doru]; *(narcotic)* нашъа [nash'a]
drum [драм] *n.* таблак [tablak], дуҳул [duhul]
drunk [дранк] *adj.* маст [mast]
dry [драй] *v.t.* хушк [xushk]
dry cleaner [драй клинер] *n.* козургарии кимиёӣ [kozurgarii kimiyoi]
dryer [драйэр] *n.* хушккунак [xushkkunak]
duck [дак] *n.* мурғобӣ [murghobi]
due [дю] *adj.* муносиб [munosib], даркорӣ [darkori]
dull [дал] *adj. (blunt)* кунд [kund]; *(not bright)* хира [xira]
dumb [дам] *adj.* гунг [gung], лол [lol]
dung [данг] *n.* пору [poru], саргин [sargin]
during [дюринг] *prep.* зимни [zimni]
dusk [даск] *n.* шом [shom], нимторикӣ [nimtoriki]
dust [даст] *n.* чанг [chang], гард [gard] / *v.t.* чанг бардоштан [chang bardoshtan]
duster [дастер] *n.* латтаи чангбардорӣ [lattai changbardori]
dusty [дасти] *adj.* пурчанг [purchang], гардолуд [gardolud]
duty [дюти] *n.* вазифа [vazifa]; **on duty** навбатдор [navbatdor]; **off duty** аз навбатдорӣ озод [az navbatdori ozod]
dwell [дуэл] *v.i.* сокин будан [sokin budan], зиндагӣ кардан [zindagi kardan]
dwelling [дуэлинг] *n.* бошишгоҳ [boshishgoh], маскан [maskan]
dye [дай] *n.* ранг [rang] / *v.t.* ранг кардан [rang kardan]
dying [дайинг] *adj.* мурданӣ [murdani]
dynamic [дайнамик] *adj.* серамал [seramal]

E

each [ич] *adj.* ҳар [har] / *adv.* донаӣ [donai] / *pron.* ҳар як [har yak], ҳар кадом [har kadom]
eager [игер] *adj.* шавқманд [shavqmand]
eagle [игал] *n.* уқоб [uqob]
ear [ир] *n.* гӯш [güsh]
earache [ирейк] *n.* дарди гӯш [dardi güsh]
early [эрли] *adj./adv.* барвақт [barvaqt]; **early morning** пагоҳи барвақт [pagohi barvaqt]
earmuffs [ирмафс] *n.pl.* гӯшпӯшакҳо [güshpüshakho]
earn [эрн] *v.i. (earn money)* пул кор кардан [pul kor kardan]; *(earn a right)* ҳақ пайдо кардан [haq paydo kardan]
earnest [эрнест] *adj.* ҷиддӣ [jiddi]

earnings [эрнингз] *n.* *(salary)* моҳона [mohona], музд [muzd]; *(income)* даромад [daromad]
earphone [ирфон] *n.* гӯшмонак [güshmonak]
earplug [ирплаг] *n.* латтаи гӯш [lattai güsh]
earring [ирринг] *n.* гӯшвора [güshvora]
earth [эрт] *n.* замин [zamin]
earthquake [эрткуек] *n.* заминҷунбӣ [zaminjunbi]
east [ист] *adj.* ховарӣ [xovari], шарқӣ [sharqi] / *adv.* сӯйи ховар [süyi xovar] / *n.* ховар [xovar], офтоббаро [oftobbaro], шарқ [sharq]; **Middle East** Ховари Миёна [Xovari Miyona]
eastern [истерн] *adj.* ховарӣ [xovari], шарқӣ [sharqi]
easy [изи] *adj.* осон [oson];
easily [изили] *adv.* ба осонӣ [ba osoni]
eat [ит] *v.t.* хӯрдан [xürdan]
eccentric [эксентрик] *adj.* аҷиб [ajib]
echo [эко] *n.* акси садо [aksi sado], пажвок [pazhvok]
economical [экономикал] *adj.* иқтисодӣ [iqtisodi]
economics [экономикс] *n.* иқтисодиёт [iqtisodiyot]
economist [экономист] *n.* иқтисодчӣ [iqtisodchi]
economy [экономи] *n.* иқтисод [iqtisod]
edge [эҷ] *n.* лаб [lab], канор [kanor]
edible [эдибъл] *adj.* хӯрданӣ [xürdani]
edit [эдит] *v.t.* таҳрир кардан [tahrir kardan]
edition [эдишан] *n.* чоп [chop], нашр [nashr]
educate [эҷукейт] *v.t.* таълим додан [ta'lim dodan], омӯхтан [omüxtan]
education [эҷукейшан] *n.* таълиму тарбия [ta'limu tarbiya], омӯзиш [omüzish]
educational [эҷукейшунал] *adj.* таълимӣ [ta'limi]
eel [ил] *n.* мормоҳӣ [mormohi]
effect [эфект] *n.* асар [asar], таъсир [ta'sir]
effective [эфектив] *adj.* таъсирбахш [ta'sirbaxsh]
effort [эфорт] *n.* кӯшиш [küshish]
egg [эг] *n.* тухм [tuxm]
eggplant [эгплант] *n.* бодинҷон [bodinjon]
Egyptian [иҷипшан] *n./adj.* мисрӣ [misri]
eight [эйт] *num.* ҳашт [hasht]
eighteen [эйтин] *num.* ҳаждаҳ [hazhdah]
eighteenth [эйтинт] *adj.* ҳаждаҳум [hazhdahum]
eighth [эйт] *adj.* ҳаштум [hashtum]
eighty [эйти] *num.* ҳаштод [hashtod]
either ... or [айдер … ор] *conj.* ё … ё … [yo … yo …], хоҳ … хоҳ … [xoh … xoh …]
elastic [иластик] *n.* лас [las] / *adj.* чандир [chandir], ёзанда [yozanda]
elbow [элбо] *n.* оринҷ [orinj]
elderly [элдерли] *adj.* солхӯрда [solxürda] / *n.* солхӯрдагон [solxürdagon]
elect [элект] *v.t.* интихоб кардан [intixob kardan]
election [элекшан] *n.* интихобот [intixobot]

electric [электрик] *adj.* барқӣ [barqi], электрикӣ [elektriki]
electricity [электрисити] *n.* барқ [barq]
electronic [электроник] *adj.* электронӣ [elektroni]
elegant [элегант] *adj.* *(person)* босалиқа [bosaliqa]; *(object)* базеб [bazeb]
element [элемент] *n.* *(chemistry)* ансур [ansur]; *(component)* таркиб [tarkib]
elementary [элементари] *adj.* ибтидоӣ [ibtidoi]
elephant [элефант] *n.* фил [fil]
elevator [элеветур] *n.* лифт [lift]
eleven [элеван] *num.* ёздаҳ [yozdah]
eleventh [элевант] *adj.* ёздаҳум [yozdahum]
eliminate [элиминейт] *v.t.* бартараф кардан [bartaraf kardan], нест кардан [nest kardan]
elk [элк] *n.* шоҳгавазн [shohgavazn]
else [элс] *adj.* дигар [digar] / *adv.* боз [boz]
e-mail [и-мейл] *n.* алоқаи электронӣ [aloqai elektroni]
embargo [эмбарго] *n.* қадаған [qadaghan]
embark [эмбарк] *v.t.* сар кардан [sar kardan]
embarrass [эмберес] *v.t.* шарм дорондан [sharm dorondan], шармондан [sharmondan
embarrassed [эмбересд] *adj.* шарманда [sharmanda]
embarrassing [эмбересинг] *adj.* шармовар [sharmovar]
embarrassment [эмбересмент] *n.* шармандагӣ [sharmandagi]
embassy [эмбаси] *n.* сафоратхона [saforatxona]
emblem [эмблем] *n.* тамға [tamgha]
embrace [эмбрейс] *n.* оғӯш [oghüsh] / *v.t.* оғӯш кардан [oghüsh kardan], ба оғӯш кашидан [ba oghüsh kashidan]
embroider [эмбройдер] *v.t.* гулдӯзӣ кардан [guldüzi kardan]
embroidered [эмбройдерд] *adj.* гулдӯзӣ [guldüzi]
embroidery [эмбройдери] *n.* гулдӯзӣ [guldüzi]
emerald [эмралд] *n.* зумуррад [zumurrad]
emerge [эмерҷ] *v.i.* падид омадан [padid omadan]
emergency [эмерҷенси] *n.* вазъияти таъҷилӣ [vaz'iyati ta'jili]; **emergency assistance** ёрии таъҷилӣ [yorii ta'jili]; **emergency exit** баромадгоҳи эҳтиётӣ [baromadgohi ehtiyoti]
emigrant [эмигрант] *n.* муҳоҷир [muhojir]
emigrate [эмигрейт] *v.i.* муҳоҷират кардан [muhojirat kardan]
emigration [эмигрейшан] *n.* муҳоҷират [muhojirat]
emit [эмит] *v.t.* *(let out a scream, etc.)* баровардан [barovardan]; *(exude)* тарашшӯҳ кардан [tarashshüh kardan]
emotion [эмошан] *n.* эҳсос [ehsos]
emperor [эмперор] *n.* шоҳаншоҳ [shohanshoh], импаротӯр [imparotür]

emphasis [эмфасис] *n.* таъкид [ta'kid]
emphasize [эмфасайз] *v.t.* таъкид кардан [ta'kid kardan]
empire [эмпайр] *n.* импаротӯрӣ [imparotüri]
employ [эмплой] *v.t.* ба кор бурдан [ba kor burdan]
employee [эмплоӣ] *n.* корманд [kormand]
employer [эмплойер] *n.* корфармо [korfarmo]
employment [эмплоймент] *n.* кор [kor]
empty [эмпти] *adj.* тиҳӣ [tihi], холӣ [xoli] / *v.t.* тиҳӣ кардан [tihi kardan], холӣ кардан [xoli kardan]
enable [энейбъл] *v.t.* қобил кардан [qobil kardan], имконият додан [imkoniyat dodan]
enamel [инамел] *n. (protective or decorative coating)* мино [mino]; *(anat.)* сир [sir]; **tooth enamel** сири дандон [siri dandon]
enclose [энклоз] *v.t.* ба дарун гузоштан [ba darun guzoshtan]
enclosure [энкложур] *n.* замима [zamima]
encounter [энкаунтер] *n.* дучор [duchor], дучоршавӣ [duchorshavi] / *v.t.* дучор шудан [duchor shudan]
encourage [энкуриҷ] *v.t.* шавқманд кардан [shavqmand kardan]
encyclopedia [энсайклопидия] *n.* доиратулмаориф [doiratulmaorif]
end [энд] *n.* поён [poyon] / *v.i.* ба поён расидан [ba poyon rasidan]
ending [эндинг] *n.* поён [poyon], анҷом [anjom]
endorse [эндорс] *v.t.* писандидан [pisandidan], маъқул донистан [ma'qul donistan]
endurance [эндюранс] *n.* тоб [tob], тобоварӣ [tobovari]
endure [эндюр] *v.t.* тоб овардан [tob ovardan]
enemy [энеми] *n.* душман [dushman]
energetic [энерҷетик] *adj.* серҳаракат [serharakat]
energy [энерҷи] *n.* қувва [quvva], нерӯ [nerü]
engagement [энгейҷмент] *n.* номзадӣ [nomzadi]; **engagement ring** ангуштарини номзадӣ [angushtarini nomzadi]
engine [энҷин] *n.* муҳаррик [muharrik], мотор [motor]
engineer [энҷинир] *n.* муҳандис [muhandis]
English [инглиш] *n./adj.* англисӣ [anglisi]
engrave [энгрейв] *v.t.* кандакорӣ кардан [kandakori kardan]
engraving [энгрейвинг] *n.* кандакорӣ [kandakori]
enjoy [энҷой] *v.t.* кайф кардан [kayf kardan]
enjoyment [энҷоймент] *n.* кайф [kayf]
enlarge [энларҷ] *v.t.* калонтар кардан [kalontar kardan]
enormous *adj.* бузург [buzurg], ҳангуфт [hanguft]

enough [инаф] *adj.* басанда [basanda], кофӣ [kofi] / *adv.* ба қадри кифоя [ba qadri kifoya]
ensure [эншур] *v.t.* таъмин кардан [ta'min kardan]
enter [энтер] *v.i.* даромадан [daromadan]
enterprise [энтерпрайз] *n.* ташаббус [tashabbus]
entertain [энтертейн] *v.t.* *(amuse)* саргарм кардан [sargarm kardan]; *(receive guests)* меҳмон кардан [mehmon kardan]
entertaining [энтертейнинг] *adj.* саргармкунанда [sargarmkunanda]
entertainment [энтертейнмент] *n.* саргармкунӣ [sargarmkuni]
enthusiasm [энтузиазм] *n.* ҷӯшухурӯш [jüshuxurüsh]
entire [энтайр] *adj.* ҳама [hama], пурра [purra], яклухт [yakluxt]
entrance [энтранс] *n.* даромадгоҳ [daromadgoh]
entrust [энтраст] *v.t.* супурдан [supurdan]
entry [ентри] *n.* даромад [daromad]
envelop [энвелап] *v.t.* печондан [pechondan]
envelope [энвелоп] *n.* лифофа [lifofa]
envious [энвияс] *adj.* ҳасадхӯр [hasadxür], ҳасуд [hasud]
environment [энвайронмент] *n.* муҳит [muhit]
environs [энвайронз] *n.* атроф [atrof]
envy [энви] *n.* ҳасад [hasad] / *v.t.* ҳасад хӯрдан [hasad xürdan]
epidemic [эпидемик] *n.* паҳншавӣ [pahnshavi] / *adj.* *(widespread)* паҳншуда [pahnshuda]; *(infectious)* сирояткунанда [siroyatkunanda]
epilepsy [эпилепси] *n.* саръ [sar'], туткулоқ [tutquloq]
equal [икуал] *adj.* баробар [barobar] / *v.t.* баробар будан [barobar budan]
equality [икуалити] *n.* баробарӣ [barobari]
equator [икуэйтор] *n.* хати истиво [xati istivo]
equip [икуип] *v.t.* таҷҳиз кардан [tajhiz kardan]
equipment [икуипмент] *n.* асбобу анҷом [asbobu anjom], таҷҳизот [tajhizot]
equity [экуити] *n.* инсоф [insof]
equivalent [экуивалент] *adj.* ҳамарзиш [hamarzish], баробар [barobar]
era [эра] *n.* давра [davra]
erase [ирейс] *v.t.* пок кардан [pok kardan]
eraser [ирейсер] *n.* хаткӯркунак [xatkürkunak]
erect [ирект] *adj.* шах [shax], росткарда [rostkarda] / *v.t.* сохтан [soxtan]
error [эрор] *n.* хато [xato], иштибоҳ [ishtiboh]
escalator [эскалейтор] *n.* зинаи равон [zinai ravon]
escape [искейп] *n.* гурез [gurez] / *v.t.* гурехтан [gurextan]
escort [эскорт] *n.* дастаи посбонон [dastai posbonon] / *v.t.* посбонӣ карда гусел кардан [posboni karda gusel kardan], қаровулӣ карда бурдан [qarovuli karda burdan]

especially [эспешали] *adv.* ба вижа [ba vizha]
essay [эсей] *n.* иншо [insho]
essence [эсенс] *n.* ҷавҳар [javhar], асл [asl]
essential [эсеншал] *adj.* зарурӣ [zaruri]
establish [эстаблиш] *v.t.* барпо кардан [barpo kardan]
estate [эстейт] *n.* дороӣ [doroi], мулк [mulk]; **real estate** ҷойдод [joydod]
estimate [эстимейт] *n.* тахмин [taxmin], баровард [barovard] / *v.t.* тахмин кардан [taxmin kardan], баровард кардан [barovard kardan]
et cetera [этсетера] *n.* ва ғайра [va ghayra]
eternal [этрнал] *adj.* ҷовид [jovid], ҳамешагӣ [hameshagi]
ethical [этикал] *adj.* мувофиқи ахлоқу одоб [muvofiqi axloqu odob]
ethnic [этник] *adj.* нажодӣ [nazhodi]
ethnographer [этнографист] *n.* мардумшинос [mardumshinos]
ethnography [этнографи] *n.* мардумшиносӣ [mardumshinosi]
Europe [юроп] *n.* Аврупо [Avrupo]
European [юропиян] *n./adj.* аврупоӣ [avrupoi]
European Union [юропиян юинян] *n.* Иттиҳоди Аврупо [Ittihodi Avrupo]
evacuate [ивакюейт] *v.t.* тахлия кардан [taxliya kardan]
evacuation [ивакюейшан] *n.* тахлия [taxliya]
evaluation [ивалюейшан] *n.* арзёбӣ [arzyobi]
eve [ив] *n.* арафа [arafa]; **New Year's Eve** арафаи Соли нав [arafai Soli nav]
even [ивен] *adj. (of one level)* ҳамвор [hamvor]; *(not odd)* ҷуфт [juft] / *adv.* ҳатто [hatto], ҳам [ham] / *v.t.* ҳамвор кардан [hamvor kardan]
evening [ивнинг] *n.* шом [shom], бегоҳ [begoh]
event [эвент] *n.* рӯйдод [rüydod]
ever [эвер] *adv.* ҳамеша [hamesha]
every [эври] *adj.* ҳар [har]
everybody [эврибоди] *pron.* ҳар кас [har kas]
everyone [эвриуан] *pron.* ҳар кас [har kas]
everything [эвритинг] *pron.* ҳама [hama], ҳама чиз [hama chiz]
everywhere [эвриуэр] *adv.* ҳама ҷо [hama jo], ҳар ҷо [har jo]
evidence [эвиденс] *n.* исбот [isbot]
evident [эвдент] *adj.* ошкор [oshkor], намоён [namoyon], ҳувайдо [huvaydo]
evil [ивил] *n.* бадӣ [badi] / *adj.* бад [bad]
evolution [эволюшан] *n.* таҳаввул [tahavvul]
exact [эгзакт] *adj.* аниқ [aniq], дақиқ [daqiq]
exaggerate [эгзаҷерейт] *v.t.* муболиға кардан [muboligha kardan]
exaggeration [эгзаҷерейшан] *n.* муболиға [muboligha]

examination [эгзаминейшан] *n. (med.)* муоина [muoina]; *(test)* озмун [ozmun], имтиҳон [imtihon]

examine [эгзамин] *v.t.* муоина кардан [muoina kardan]

example [эгзампъл] *n.* мисол [misol]; **for example** масалан [masalan]

excavation [экскавейшан] *n.* ковиш [kovish]

exceed [эксид] *v.t.* зиёд шудан [ziyod shudan], зиёд баромадан [ziyod baromadan]

excellent [экселент] *adj.* бартарин [bartarin], олӣ [oli]

except [эксепт] *prep.* ҷуз [juz], ба ҷуз [ba juz]

exception [эксепшан] *n.* истисно [istisno]

excess [эксес] *n.* зиёдӣ [ziyodi]

exchange [эксчейнҷ] *n.* иваз [ivaz], алиш [alish], мубодила [mubodila] / *v.t.* иваз кардан [ivaz kardan], алиш кардан [alish kardan], мубодила кардан [mubodila kardan]

excite [эксайт] *v.t.* барангехтан [barangextan]

excitement [эксайтмент] *n.* барангезиш [barangezish]

exclaim [эксклейм] *v.t.* нидо кардан [nido kardan]

exclamation [эксcламейшан] *n.* нидо [nido]; **exclamation mark** аломати нидо [alomati nido]

exclude [эксклуд] *v.t.* роҳ надодан [roh nadodan], хориҷ кардан [xorij kardan]

excuse [екскюз] *n.* баҳона [bahona] / *v.t.* маъзур доштан [ma'zur doshtan], бахшидан [baxshidan]; **Excuse me!** Бубахшед! [Bubaxshed!]

execute [эгзекют] *v.t. (carry out)* иҷро кардан [ijro kardan]; *(kill)* куштан [kushtan]

executive [эгзекютив] *n.* иҷрогар [ijrogar]; **executive committee** кумитаи иҷроия [kumitai ijroiya]

exhale [эксҳейл] *v.i.* дам баровардан [dam barovardan], нафас баровардан [nafas barovardan]

exhaust [эгзост] *n. (engine fumes)* гуппос [guppos]]

exhausted [эгзостед] *adj. (physically)* ниҳоят монда [nihoyat monda], коркӯфта [korküfta]; *(finished, completed in terms of money, resources, etc.)* тамомшуда [tamomshuda]

exhibit [эгзибит] *n.* намоиш [namoish] / *v.t.* нишон додан [nishon dodan], намоиш додан [namoish dodan]

exile [эгзайл] *n.* бадарғагӣ [badarghagi] / *v.t.* бадарға кардан [badargha kardan]

exist [егзист] *v.i. (be)* будан [budan]; *(live)* зистан [zistan]

existence [егзистенс] *n.* ҳастӣ [hasti]

exit [эгзит] *n.* баромадгоҳ [baromadgoh] / *v.i.* баромадан [baromadan]

expand [экспанд] *v.t.* калонтар кардан [kalontar kardan], фарохтар кардан [faroxtar kardan]
expansion [экспаншан] *n.* фарохкунӣ [faroxkuni]
expect [экспект] *v.t.* чашм доштан [chashm doshtan]
expectation [экспектейшан] *n.* чашмдошт [chashmdosht]
expel [экспел] *v.t.* берун кардан [berun kardan]
expense [экспенс] *n.* харҷ [xarj], сарф [sarf]
expensive [экспенсив] *adj.* гарон [garon], қимат [qimat]
experience [экспириянс] *n.* таҷриба [tajriba] / *v.t.* таҷриба кардан [tajriba kardan]
expert [эксперт] *n.* кордон [kordon]
explain [эксплейн] *v.t.* шарҳ додан [sharh dodan]
explanation [эксπланейшан] *n.* шарҳ [sharh]
explode [эксплод] *v.i.* тарқидан [tarqidan] / *v.t.* тарқондан [tarqondan]
explore [эксплор] *v.t.* тадқиқ кардан [tadqiq kardan]
explosion [экспложан] *n.* тарқиш [tarqish]
export [экспорт] *n.* содирот [sodirot] / *v.t.* содирот кардан [sodirot kardan]
expose [экспоз] *v.t.* дучор кардан [duchor kardan], гирифтор кардан [giriftor kardan]
exposure [экспожур] *n.* *(photographic)* дараҷаи танвир [darajai tanvir]; *(to sth)* хӯрдан [xürdan]; *(to radiation)* шуоъ хӯрдан [shuo' xürdan]
express [экспрес] *adj./v.t.* изҳор кардан [iz-hor kardan], ифода кардан [ifoda kardan]
extend [экстенд] *v.t.* ёзондан [yozondan], кашида дароз кардан [kashida daroz kardan]
extension [экстеншан] *n.* ёзониш [yozonish]
external [экстернал] *adj.* берунӣ [beruni]
extinction [экстинкшан] *n.* нестшавӣ [nestshavi]; **in danger of extinction** дар зери тарси нестшавӣ [dar zeri tarsi nestshavi]
extinguish [экстингуиш] *v.t.* куштан [kushtan], хомӯш кардан [xomüsh kardan]
extra [экстра] *adj.* изофагӣ [izofagi], иловагӣ [ilovagi] / *adv.* ниҳоят [nihoyat]
extra-large [экстра-ларҷ] *adj.* ниҳоят калон [nihoyat kalon]
extract [экстрект] *n.* шира [shira], ҷавҳар [javhar] / *v.t.* баровардан [barovardan]
extradite [экстрадайт] *v.t.* (ҷинояткорро) ба кишвари худаш супурдан [(jinoyatkorro) ba kishvari xudash supurdan]
extraordinary [экстрординери] *adj.* фавқулодда [favqulodda]
extravagant [экстравагант] *adj.* газоф [gazof], ифроткор [ifrotkor]
extreme [экстрим] *adj.* *(dire)* қатъӣ [qat'i]; *(radical)* ифротӣ [ifroti]
extremely [экстримли] *adv.* ниҳоят [nihoyat]

exult [эгзалт] *v.i.* хурсандӣ кардан [xursandi kardan]
eye [ай] *n.* чашм [chashm]
eyeball [айбол] *n.* ғӯзаи чашм [ghüzai chashm]
eyebrow [айбрау] *n.* абрӯ [abrü], қош [qosh]
eyelash [айлаш] *n.* мижа [mizha]; **eyelashes** мижгон [mizhgon]
eyelid [айлид] *n.* пилки чашм [pilki chashm]
eyeliner [айлайнер] *n.* сурма [surma]

F

fabric [фабрик] *n.* газвор [gazvor]
façade [фасад] *n.* намо [namo]
face [фейс] *n.* рӯй [rüy], чеҳра [chehra]
facial [фейшал] *adj.* -и рӯй [-i rüy]; **facial muscles** мушакҳои рӯй [mushakhoi rüy]
facilitate [фасилитейт] *v.t.* осон кардан [oson kardan]
facility [фасилити] *n. (means)* васила [vasila]; *(amenity)* таҷҳизот [tajhizot], лавозимот [lavozimot]
fact [факт] *n.* ҳақиқат [haqiqat], амри воқеъ [amri voqe']; **in fact** дар ҳақиқат [dar haqiqat]
factory [фактори] *n.* завод [zavod], корхона [korxona], фабрика [fabrika]
faculty [факулти] *n. (ability)* қобилият [qobiliyat]; *(university department)* донишкада [donishkada], факулта [fakulta]; *(body of teachers)* ҳайати омӯзгорон [hayati omüzgoron]
fade [фейд] *v.i.* пажмурда шудан [pazhmurda shudan], пажмурдан [pazhmurdan]; **fade away** нест шудан [nest shudan]
faded [фейдед] *adj.* пажмурда [pazhmurda]
fail [фейл] *v.i.* ноком шудан [nokom shudan]
failure [фейлюр] *n.* нокомӣ [nokomi]
faint [фейнт] *adj. (weak)* суст [sust], нимҷон [nimjon]; *(light-colored)* хира [xira] / *v.i.* беҳуш шудан [behush shudan], аз ҳуш рафтан [az hush raftan]
fair [фер] *n.* ярмарка [yarmarka], бозор [bozor] / *adj. (just)* одил [odil], боинсоф [boinsof]; *(light-haired or -skinned)* равшан [ravshan]
fairy [фери] *n.* парӣ [pari]
fairy-tale [фери-тейл] *n.* афсона [afsona]
faith [фейт] *n.* имон [imon]
faithful [фейтфул] *adj.* вафодор [vafodor]
falcon [фолкан] *n.* шоҳин [shohin]
fall [фол] *n. (season)* тирамоҳ [tiramoh], хазон [xazon]; *(action of falling)* афтиш [aftish], ғалтиш [ghaltish] / *v.i.* афтидан [aftidan], афтодан [aftodan], ғалтидан [ghaltidan]
false [фолс] *adj.* бардурӯғ [bardurügh], сохта [soxta]; **false witness** гувоҳии бардурӯғ [guvohii bardurügh]; **false alarm** бонги хатари бардурӯғ [bongi xatari bardurügh]

falsify [фолсифай] *v.t.* сохтакорӣ кардан [soxtakori kardan], қалбакӣ кардан [qalbaki kardan]
fame [фейм] *n.* номдорӣ [nomdori], шӯҳрат [shührat]
familiar [фамиляр] *adj.* шинос [shinos], ошно [oshno]
family [фемили] *n.* оила [oila]
famous [феймас] *adj.* номдор [nomdor], машҳур [mashhur]
fan [фен] *n. (devotee)* ҳавохоҳ [havoxoh], ҳаводор [havodor]; *(mechanical device)* бодбезак [bodbezak]
fancy [фенсу] *adj.* пурнақшу нигор [purnaqshu nigor]
far [фар] *adj./adv.* дур [dur]
faraway [фарауэй] *adj.* дур [dur], дурдаст [durdast]
fare [фер] *n.* киропулӣ [kiropuli]
farm [фарм] *n.* киштзор [kishtzor], ферма [ferma]
farmer [фармер] *n.* деҳқон [dehqon], кишоварз [kishovarz]
farsighted [фарсайтед] *adj. (hyperopic)* дурбин [durbin]; *(prudent, having foresight)* дурандеш [durandesh]
fascinate [фесинейт] *v.t.* мафтун кардан [maftun kardan], дил рабудан [dil rabudan]
fascinating [фасинейтинг] *adj.* дилрабо [dilrabo]
fascination [фесинейшан] *n.* дилрабоӣ [dilraboi]
fashion [фешан] *n.* мод [mod]; **to come into fashion** мод шудан [mod shudan]
fashionable [фешнабъл] *adj.* модшуда [modshuda]
fast [фест] *adj.* тез [tez], зуд [zud]
fasten [фесен] *v.t.* бастан [bastan], маҳкам кардан [mahkam kardan]
fat [фет] *n.* чарбу [charbu] / *adj.* фарбеҳ [farbeh]
fatal [фейтал] *adj.* марговар [margovar], ногузир [noguzir]
father [фадер] *n.* падар [padar]
father-in-law [фадер-ин-ло] *n.* хусур [xusur]
fatty [фати] *adj.* равғанин [ravghanin], серравған [serravghan]
faucet [фосет] *n.* ҷумак [jumak]
fault [фолт] *n. (mistake, error)* тақсир [taqsir], айб [ayb], гуноҳ [gunoh]; *(defect)* нуқсон [nuqson]
faulty [фолти] *adj.* нуқсондор [nuqsondor]
favor [фейвур] *n.* хайрхоҳӣ [xayrxohi], некхоҳӣ [nekxohi]; **to do (sb) a favor** (ба касе) хайрхоҳӣ кардан [(ba kase) xayrxohi kardan]; **to look favorably** лутфомез нигаристан [lutfomez nigaristan]
favorite [фейвурит] *adj.* дӯстдошта [düstdoshta]
fax [факс] *n.* факс [faks] / *v.t.* факс фиристодан [faks firistodan]
fear [фир] *n.* тарс [tars] / *v.t.* тарсидан [tarsidan]
feasible [физибъл] *adj.* шуданӣ [shudani]

feast [фист] *n.* базм [bazm], зиёфат [ziyofat]
feather [федар] *n.* пар [par]
February [февруэри] *n.* феврал [fevral]
fee [фи] *n.* ҳақ [haq], пардохт [pardoxt]
feed [фид] *n.* хӯрок [xürok] / *v.t.* хӯрондан [xürondan], хӯрок додан [xürok dodan]
feel [фил] *v.t.* ҳис кардан [his kardan], эҳсос кардан [ehsos kardan] / *v.i.* ба назар расидан [ba nazar rasidan]
feeling [филинг] *n.* ҳис [his], эҳсос [ehsos]
fellow [фело] *n. (person)* одам [odam]; *(peer)* ҳампеша [hampesha]; *(comrade)* рафиқ [rafiq]
felt [фелт] *n.* намад [namad]
female [фимейл] *n.* зан [zan] / *adj.* занона [zanona]; *(animal)* мода [moda]
feminine [феминин] *adj.* занона [zanona]
fence [фенс] *n.* тавора [tavora], деворча [devorcha]
fender [фендер] *n.* чархпӯш [charxpüsh]
ferment [ферментл] *v.t.* турш кардан [tursh kardan]
fern [ферн] *n.* папоротник [paporotnik], фарн [farn]
ferry [фери] *n.* киштии гузора [kishtii guzora]
fertile [фертайл] *adj.* ҳосилхез [hosilxez], зархез [zarxez]
festival [фестивал] *n.* ҷашн [jashn], ид [id]
fever [фивер] *n.* таб [tab]
few [фю] *n.* кам [kam]
fiber [файбер] *n.* тор [tor], нах [nax]; **muscle fibers** торҳои мушак [torhoi mushak]
fiberglass [файберглес] *n.* шишанах [shishanax]
fiction [фикшан] *n.* афсона [afsona], гапи бофта [gapi bofta]
fiddle [фидъл] *n.* ғиҷҷак [ghijjak], камонча [kamoncha]
field [филд] *n. (cultivated area)* киштзор [kishtzor]; *(broad expanse of flat land)* майдон [maydon]; *(topic or subject)* соҳа [soha], доира [doira]
fierce [фирс] *adj.* дарранда [darranda], хунхор [xunxor]
fifteen [фифтин] *num.* понздаҳ [ponzdah]
fifteenth [фифтинт] *adj.* понздаҳум [ponzdahum]
fifth [фифт] *adj.* панҷум [panjum]
fiftieth [фифтият] *adj.* панҷоҳум [panjohum]
fifty [фифти] *num.* панҷоҳ [panjoh]
fig [фиг] *n.* анҷир [anjir]
fight [файт] *n.* ҷанг [jang] / *v.t.* мубориза бурдан [muboriza burdan] / *v.i.* ҷангидан [jangidan], ҷанг кардан [jang kardan]
figure [фигур] *n. (number)* рақам [raqam], адад [adad]; *(form)* андом [andom] / *v.t. (consider)* дар назар доштан [dar nazar doshtan]; *(calculate)* ҳисоб кардан [hisob kardan] / *v.i. (to appear in)* намоён шудан [namoyon shudan]

file [файл] *n. (collection of papers)* парванда [parvanda], папка [papka]; *(tool)* сӯҳон [sühon]; *(computer file)* файл [fayl] / *v.t. (smooth with a file)* сӯҳон кардан [sühon kardan]; *(keep on file)* бойгонӣ кардан [boygoni kardan]

fill [фил] *v.t.* анбоштан [anboshtan], пур кардан [pur kardan]

film [филм] *n. (photographic)* навор [navor]; *(movie)* филм [film]; *(thin layer)* шух [shux], пардача [pardacha], қаймоқак [qaymoqak]; *(film of ice)* қаймоқаки ях [qaymoqaki yax] / *v.t.* филм гирифтан [film giriftan]

filter [филтер] *n. (water filter)* обполо [obpolo]; *(light filter)* нурполо [nurpolo]; *(gas filter)* газполо [gazpolo]

filthy [филти] *adj.* мурдор [murdor]

final [файнал] *adj.* охирин [oxirin]

finally [файнали] *adv.* охир [oxir], дар охир [dar oxir]

finance [файнанс] *n. (finances)* молия [moliya], маблағ [mablagh] / *v.t.* маблағ додан [mablagh dodan]

financial [файнаншал] *adj.* молиявӣ [moliyavi], пулӣ [puli]

find [файнд] *n.* бозёфт [bozyoft] / *v.t.* ёфтан [yoftan], пайдо кардан [paydo kardan]

fine [файн] *n.* ҷарима [jarima] / *adj. (delicate)* борик [borik], маҳин [mahin]; *(well, good)* нағз [naghz]

finger [фингер] *n.* ангушт [angusht], панҷа [panja]

fingerprint [фингерпринт] *n.* нақши ангушт [naqshi angusht]

finish [финиш] *n. (end)* анҷом [anjom], поён [poyon]; *(on furniture, etc.)* дасткории такмилӣ [dastkorii takmili] / *v.t.* ба анҷом расондан [ba anjom rasondan] / *v.i.* анҷом ёфтан [anjom yoftan]

fire [файр] *n.* оташ [otash], алов [alov] / *v.t. (fire an employee)* бекор кардан [bekor kardan]; *(fire a missile)* сар додан [sar dodan], паррондан [parrondan]; *(shoot a weapon)* тир андохтан [tir andoxtan], паррондан [parrondan]

firm [фирм] *n.* ширкат [shirkat] / *adj. (hard)* сахт [saxt], шах [shax]; *(determined)* устувор [ustuvor]

first [фирст] *adj.* якум [yakum], нахуст [naxust], аввал [avval] / *adv. (at first, first of all)* аввалан [avvalan]

fish [фиш] *n.* моҳӣ [mohi] / *v.t.* моҳигирӣ кардан [mohigiri kardan], моҳӣ гирифтан [mohi giriftan] / *v.i.* ҷустан [justan]

fisherman [фишерман] *n.* моҳигир [mohigir]

fishing [фишинг] *n.* моҳигирӣ [mohigiri]; **to go fishing** ба моҳигирӣ рафтан [ba mohigiri raftan]

fist [фист] *n.* мушт [musht]

fit [фит] *n.* хурӯҷ [xurüj], шиддати бемори [shiddati bemori] / *adj.* короянда [koroyanda], муносиб [munosib] / *v.t.* соз кардан [soz kardan], муносиб кардан [munosib kardan] / *v.i.* андоза будан [andoza budan], короям будан [koroyam budan]; **to have a fit** шиддати беморӣ доштан [shiddati bemori doshtan], бисёр хашмгин шудан [bisyor xashmgin shudan]; **fit of coughing** хурӯҷи сурфа [xurüji surfa]

fitness [фитнес] *n. (physical)* тандурустӣ [tandurusti]; *(appropriateness)* муносибат [munosibat]; **fitness instructor** омӯзгори варзиш [omüzgori varzish]

five [файв] *num.* панҷ [panj]

fix [фикс] *v.t. (repair or correct)* дуруст кардан [durust kardan], дарбеҳ кардан [darbeh kardan]; *(appoint, set in place)* муқаррар кардан [muqarrar kardan]

flag [флаг] *n.* парчам [parcham], байрақ [bairaq]

flame [флейм] *n.* алов [alov], аланга [alanga], шӯъла [shü'la]

flannel [фланел] *n.* бумазӣ [bumazi]

flap [флап] *v.i.* афшондан [afshondan]

flash [флаш] *n.* ялаққос [yalaqqos], дурахш [duraxsh] / *v.i.* ялаққос задан [yalaqqos zadan], шӯълавар шудан [shü'lavar shudan]

flat [флат] *adj.* ҳамвор [hamvor]; **flat tire** сӯрохи чархи мошин [süroxi charxi moshin]

flatter [флатер] *v.t.* чоплусӣ кардан [choplusi kardan], хушомадгӯӣ кардан [xushomadgüi kardan]

flavor [флейвор] *n.* маза [maza] / *v.t.* хушмаза кардан [xushmaza kardan]

flaw [фло] *n.* норасоӣ [norasoi], камӣ [kami]

flea [фли] *n.* кайк [kayk]

flee [фли] *v.i.* гурехтан [gurextan]

fleet [флит] *n.* новгон [novgon], флот [flot] / *adj.* бодпо [bodpo], тезгард [tezgard]

flesh [флеш] *n.* гӯшт [güsht]

flight [флайт] *n.* парвоз [parvoz]

flirt [флирт] *n.* зани карашмадор [zani karashmador] / *v.i.* ноз кардан [noz kardan], карашма кардан [karashma kardan]

float [флот] *v.i.* шиновар шудан [shinovar shudan]

flock [флок] *n.* рама [rama], гала [gala]

flood [флад] *n.* сел [sel], селоб [selob]

floor [флор] *n. (of a room)* фарш [farsh]; *(level or storey)* ошёна [oshyona]

florist [флорист] *n.* гулфурӯш [gulfurüsh]
flour [флаур] *n.* орд [ord]
flow [фло] *n.* рафт [raft], ҷараён [jarayon] / *v.i.* равон шудан [ravon shudan], ҷорӣ шудан [jori shudan]
flower [флауер] *n.* гул [gul]
flu [флу] *n.* тимоб [timob], грипп [gripp]
fluent [флуэнт] *adj.* равон [ravon]
fluently [флуэнтли] *adv.* озодона [ozodona], равон [ravon]
fluff [флаф] *n.* пат [pat]
fluid [флуид] *n.* моеъ [moe'], чизи обакӣ [chizi obaki] / *adj.* обакӣ [obaki]
fly [флай] *n.* пашша [pashsha], магас [magas] / *v.i.* паридан [paridan], парвоз кардан [parvoz kardan]
foam [фом] *n.* кафк [kafk]
focus [фокас] *n.* марказ [markaz] / *v.t.* ҷамъ кардан [jam' kardan]
fog [фог] *n.* туман [tuman]
foggy [фоги] *adj.* *(meteorological)* тумангирифта [tumangirifta]; *(unclear)* норавшан [noravshan]
fold [фолд] *n.* қат [qat] / *v.t.* қат кардан [qat kardan], дуқат кардан [duqat kardan]
folder [фолдер] *n.* папка [papka]
follow [фоло] *v.i.* *(go/come behind)* аз паи рафтан [az pai raftan], аз паи омадан [az pai omadan]; *(follow sb/sth,e.g. a leader, established conventions, etc.)* пайравӣ кардан [payravi kardan]
follower [фолоэр] *n.* пайрав [payrav]
following [фолоинг] *adj.* дигар [digar], навбатӣ [navbati]
fond [фонд] *adj.* *(be fond of)* дӯст доштан [düst doshtan]
food [фуд] *n.* хӯрок [xürok]
fool [фул] *n.* нодон [nodon], аблаҳ [ablah]
foolish [фулиш] *adj.* нодон [nodon], аблаҳона [ablahona]
foot [фут] *n.* *(anat.)* пой [poy], по [po]; *(unit of measurement)* фут [fut]
football [футбол] *n.* футболи амрикоӣ [futboli amrikoi]
for [фор] *prep.* барои [baroi]
forbid [форбид] *v.t.* манъ кардан [man' kardan], қадаған кардан [qadaghan kardan]
forbidden [форбиден] *adj.* қадаған [qadaghan], манъшуда [man'shuda]
force [форс] *n.* зӯр [zür], қувва [quvva] / *v.t.* водор кардан [vodor kardan], водоштан [vodoshtan]; **by force** бо зӯрӣ [bo züri]
forearm [форарм] *n.* соид [soid]
forecast [форкаст] *n.* пешгӯӣ [peshgüi]
forehead [форҳед] *n.* пешона [peshona], пешонӣ [peshoni]
foreign [форен] *adj.* *(from a foreign land)* хориҷӣ [xoriji]; *(unfamiliar)* бегона [begona]
foreigner [форенер] *n.* хориҷӣ [xoriji]

foresight [форсайт] *n.* пешбинӣ [peshbini]
forest [форист] *n.* ҷангал [jangal]
forever [форевер] *adv.* ҳамешагӣ [hameshagi]
foreword [форвурд] *n.* пешгуфтор [peshguftor]
forget [форгет] *v.t.* фаромӯш кардан [faromüsh kardan] / *v.i.* аз ёд баромадан [az yod baromadan]
forget-me-not [форгет-ми-нот] *n.* марзангӯш [marzangüsh]
forgive [форгив] *v.t.* бахшидан [baxshidan]
forgotten [форготен] *adj.* фаромӯшшуда [faromüshshuda]
fork [форк] *n.* панҷа [panja]
form [форм] *n.* шакл [shakl] / *v.t.* ташкил додан [tashkil dodan], сохтан [soxtan] / *v.i.* падид омадан [padid omadan]
formal [формал] *adj.* расмӣ [rasmi]
formation [формейшан] *n.* ташкила [tashkila]
former [формер] *adj.* пештара [peshtara], пешин [peshin]
formula [формюла] *n.* формула [formula]
fort [форт] *n.* қалъача [qal'acha]
fortieth [фортият] *adj.* чиҳилум [chihilum], чилум [chilum]
fortnight [фортнайт] *n.* ду ҳафта [du hafta]
fortress [фортрес] *n.* қалъа [qal'a], ҳисор [hisor], диж [dizh]
fortunate [форчунат] *adj.* хушбахт [xushbaxt]
fortunately [форчунатли] *adv.* хушбахтона [xushbaxtona]
fortune [форчун] *n. (luck, fate)* бахт [baxt]; *(wealth)* боигарӣ [boigari], дороӣ [doroi]
forty [форти] *num.* чил [chil], чиҳил [chihil]
forward [форуард] *adv.* ба пеш [ba pesh]
fossil [фосил] *n. (animal)* ҷонвари сангшуда [jonvari sangshuda]; *(plant)* растании сангшуда [rastanii sangshuda]
foster [фостер] *v.t.* парвардан [parvardan]
foster brother [фостер брадер] *n.* бародари ширхӯра [barodari shirxüra]
foster sister [фостер систер] *n.* хоҳари ширхӯра [xohari shirxüra]
found [фаунд] *v.t.* барпо кардан [barpo kardan]
foundation [фаундешан] *n.* бунёд [bunyod]
founder [фаундер] *n.* бунёдкор [bunyodkor]
fountain [фаунтен] *n.* фаввора [favvora]
four [фор] *num.* чор [chor], чаҳор [chahor]
fourteen [фортин] *num.* чордаҳ [chordah]
fourteenth [фортинт] *adj.* чордаҳум [chordahum]
fourth [форт] *adj.* чорум [chorum], чаҳорум [chahorum]
fowl [фаул] *n.* мурғ [murgh]
fox [фокс] *n.* рӯбоҳ [rüboh]

fraction [фракшан] *n.* каср [kasr]
fragile [фраҷайл] *adj.* зудшикан [zudshikan]
frame [фрейм] *n.* чорчӯба [chorchüba] / *v.t.* ба чорчӯба гузоштан [ba chorchüba guzoshtan]
frantic [франтик] *adj.* бенӯхта [benüxta]
fraud [фрод] *n.* фиреб [fireb]
free [фри] *adj.* озод [ozod]
freedom [фридам] *n.* озодӣ [ozodi]
freeze [фриз] *v.t.* ях кунондан [yax kunondan], ях бандондан [yax bandondan] / *v.i.* ях кардан [yax kardan], ях бастан [yax bastan]
freight [фрейт] *n.* бор [bor]
French [френч] *n./adj.* фаронсавӣ [faronsavi]
frequency [фрикуэнси] *n.* суръат [sur'at]
frequent [фрикуэнт] *adj.* зуд-зуд [zud-zud]
frequently [фрикуэнтли] *adv.* зуд-зуд [zud-zud]
fresh [фреш] *adj.* тоза [toza], тару тоза [taru toza]
Friday [фрайдей] *n.* ҷумъа [jum'a], одина [odina]
fried [фрайд] *adj.* бирён [biryon]
friend [френд] *n.* дӯст [düst], рафиқ [rafiq]
friendly [френдли] *adj.* дӯстона [düstona]
friendship [френдшип] *n.* дӯстӣ [düsti]
fright [фрайт] *n.* тарс [tars], бим [bim], ҳарос [haros]
frighten [фрайтан] *v.t.* тарсондан [tarsondan]
frightening [фрайтнинг] *adj.* тарснок [tarsnok], бимнок [bimnok]
frog [фрог] *n.* қурбоққа [qurboqqa]
from [фром] *prep.* аз [az]
front [фронт] *adj.* пеш [pesh] / *n.* пеш [pesh]; **in front of** дар пеши [dar peshi]
frontier [фронтир] *n.* сарҳад [sarhad]
frost [фрост] *n.* хунукӣ [xunuki], сармо [sarmo]
frostbite [фростбайт] *n.* хунук занондагӣ [xunuk zanondagi]
frown [фраун] *v.i.* рӯй турш кардан [rüy tursh kardan]
frozen [фрозен] *adj.* яхкарда [yaxkarda], яхбаста [yaxbasta]
fruit [фрут] *n.* мева [meva]
frustrate [фрастрейт] *v.t.* барбод кардан [barbod kardan]
frustration [фрастрейшан] *n.* барбодравӣ [barbodravi]
fry [фрай] *v.t.* бирёндан [biryondan], бирён кардан [biryon kardan]
frying pan [фрайинг пан] *n.* тоба [toba]
fuel [фюл] *n.* сӯзишворӣ [süzishvori]
fugitive [фюҷитив] *n.* гуреза [gureza], гурезпо [gurezpo] / *adj.* гуреза [gureza]
full [фул] *adj.* пур [pur]
fun [фан] *n.* дилхушӣ [dilxushi], кайф [kayf]
function [фанкшан] *n.* вазифа [vazifa], кор [kor] / *v.i.* кор кардан [kor kardan]

fund [фанд] *n.* сармоя [sarmoya] / *v.t.* сармоя гузоштан [sarmoya guzoshtan]
fundamental [фандаментал] *adj.* асосӣ [asosi], бунёдӣ [bunyodi]
fundamentalist [фандаменталист] *n.* бунёдгаро [bunyodgaro]
funeral [фюнерал] *n.* ҷаноза [janoza]
fungus [фангас] *n.* пӯпанак [püpanak], мағор [maghor]
funnel [фанел] *n.* даҳана [dahana], қиф [qif]
funny [фани] *adj.* хандаовар [xandaovar]
fur [фур] *n.* мӯина [müina]
furious [фюрияс] *adj.* хашмгин [xashmgin], оташин [otashin]
furnace [фурнас] *n.* кӯра [küra], дош [dosh]
furnish [фурниш] *v.t.* *(add furniture)* мебелдор кардан [mebeldor kardan]; *(provide/ supply)* таъмин кардан [ta'min kardan]
furniture [фурничур] *n.* мебел [mebel]
further [фурдер] *adv.* илова бар ин [ilova bar in] / *adj.* дуртар [durtar]
fuselage [фюселаж] *n.* танаи ҳавопаймо [tanai havopaimo]
future [фючур] *n./adj.* ояанда [oyanda]

G

gag [гег] *n.* даҳонбанд [dahonband], тиққонҷ [tiqqonj]
gain [гейн] *n.* суд [sud], фоида [foida] / *v.t.* суд бурдан [sud burdan], фоида бурдан [foida burdan]
gall [гол] *n.* заҳра [zahra], зарда [zarda] / *v.t.* озурдан [ozurdan], озор додан [ozor dodan]
gall bladder [гол бледер] *n.* заҳрадон [zahradon]
gallery [гелери] *n.* *(art gallery)* нигористон [nigoriston]
gallon [гелон] *n.* галлон [gallon]
gallop [гелоп] *n.* чорхез [chorxez] / *v.i.* чорхез кардан [chorxez kardan]
gallstone [галстон] *n.* санги заҳрадон [sangi zahradon]
game [гейм] *n.* *(that one plays)* бозӣ [bozi]; *(wildlife)* ҷонварони шикоршаванда [jonvaroni shikorshavanda]
gang [генг] *n.* дастаи бадкорон [dastai badkoron]
gap [геп] *n.* фосила [fosila]
garage [гараж] *n.* гараж [garazh]
garbage [гарбиҷ] *n.* ахлот [axlot]
garden [гарден] *n.* боғ [bogh]
gardener [гарденер] *n.* боғбон [boghbon]
gargle [гаргъл] *v.i.* ғарғара кардан [gharghara kardan]
garlic [гарлик] *n.* сир [sir]
garment [гармент] *n.* пӯшок [püshok]
gas [гес] *n.* газ [gaz]
gasoline [гесолин] *n.* бензин [benzin]
gas station [гес стейшан] *n.* бензинфурӯшӣ [benzinfurüshi]

gassy [геси] *adj.* газгун [gazgun]
gate [гейт] *n.* дарвоза [darvoza]
gather [гедер] *v.t.* ғун кардан [ghun kardan], ғундоштан [ghundoshtan] / *v.i.* ғун шудан [ghun shudan]
gauge [гейҷ] *n.* чен [chen], андоза [andoza] / *v.t.* чен кардан [chen kardan], санҷидан [sanjidan]
gay [гей] *adj.* *(happy)* хуш [xush]; *(sexuality)* ҳамҷинсбоз [hamjinsboz]
gear [гир] *n.* механизм [mexanizm], данда [danda]
gem [ҷем] *n.* нақрасанг [naqrasang], санги қиматбаҳо [sangi qimatbaho]
gender [ҷендер] *n.* ҷинс [jins]
general [ҷенерал] *n.* генерал [general] / *adj.* умумӣ [umumi]; **in general** умуман [umuman]
generally [ҷенерали] *adv.* умуман [umuman], одатан [odatan]
generate [ҷенерейт] *v.t.* тавлид кардан [tavlid kardan], ба вуҷуд овардан [ba vujud ovardan]
generation [ҷенерейшан] *n.* насл [nasl]
generous [ҷенерас] *adj.* сахӣ [saxi], кушодадаст [kushodadast]
genetic [ҷенетик] *adj.* генетикӣ [genetiki]
genital [ҷенитал] *adj.* таносулӣ [tanosuli]
genitals [ҷениталз] *n.pl.* узвҳои таносул [uzvhoi tanosul]
genius [ҷинияс] *n.* *(the concept)* даҳо [daho], нубуғ [nubugh]; *(a person)* доҳӣ [dohi], нобиға [nobigha]
gentle [ҷентъл] *adj.* *(soft, not rough to the touch)* нарм [narm]; *(softly, not roughly)* оҳиста [ohista]; *(sweet, soft-hearted)* навозишкор [navozishkor], нармдил [narmdil]; *(well-mannered)* боадаб [boadab], илтифотнок [iltifotnok]
gentleman [ҷентълман] *n.* оқо [oqo], ҷаноб [janob]
geography [ҷиографи] *n.* ҷуғрофия [jughrofiya]
geology [ҷиолоҷи] *n.* заминшиносӣ [zaminshinosi]
Georgian [ҷорҷан] *n./adj.* гурҷӣ [gurji]
germ [ҷерм] *n.* микроб [mikrob]
German [ҷерман] *n.* олмонӣ [olmoni], немис [nemis] / *adj.* олмонӣ [olmoni], немисӣ [nemisi]
gesture [ҷесчур] *n.* имову ишорат [imovu ishorat] / *v.i.* имову ишорат кардан [imovu ishorat kardan]
get [гет] *v.t.* ба даст овардан [ba dast ovardan], гирифтан [giriftan]; **got to** бояд [boyad]; **get up** хестан [xestan]; **get on** *(bus, train, etc.)* савор шудан [savor shudan]; **get off** *(bus, train, etc.)* фаромадан [faromadan]; **get together** якҷоя шудан [yakjoya shudan]
ghost [гост] *n.* шабаҳ [shabah]
giant [ҷайант] *n.* одами азимҷусса [odami azimjussa] / *adj.* азим [azim]

gift [гифт] *n.* тӯҳфа [tühfa]
giggle [гигъл] *n.* қиқир-қиқир [qiqir-qiqir], қиқиррос [qiqirros] / *v.i.* қиқир-қиқир хандидан [qiqir-qiqir xandidan], қиқиррос задан [qiqirros zadan]
gild [гилд] *v.t.* зарандуд кардан [zarandud kardan]
gill [гил] *n.* ғалсама [ghalsama]
gilt [гилт] *n.* зарҳал [zarhal] / *adj.* зарандуд [zarandud]
gin [ҷин] *n.* ҷин [jin]
girl [гирл] *n.* духтар [duxtar]
girlfriend [гирлфренд] *n.* дӯстдухтар [düstduxtar]
give [гив] *v.t.* додан [dodan]
glad [глад] *adj.* шод [shod]
glamor [гламор] *n.* ҷозибият [jozibiyat]
glamorous [гламорус] *adj.* ҷозиб [jozib]
glance [гланс] *n.* нигоҳи сатҳӣ [nigohi sathi] / *v.i.* андак нигаристан [andak nigaristan]
gland [гланд] *n.* ғадуд [ghadud]
glare [глер] *n.* нигоҳи хашмгин [nigohi xashmgin] / *v.i.* хашмгинона нигаристан [xashmginona nigaristan]
glass [глас] *n.* шиша [shisha] / *adj.* шишагин [shishagin]
glasses [гласез] *n.pl.* айнак [aynak]
glimpse [глимпс] *n.* нигоҳи сатҳӣ [nigohi sathi]
global [глобал] *adj.* ҷаҳонӣ [jahoni]
globe [глоб] *n.* кура [kura]
gloom [глум] *n.* тирагӣ [tiragi]
gloomy [глуми] *adj.* тира [tira]
glory [глори] *n.* шаън [sha'n], шараф [sharaf]
glottis [глотис] *n.* роғи садопардаҳо [roghi sadopardaho]
glove [глав] *n.* дастпӯшак [dastpüshak], дасткаш [dastkash]
glow [гло] *n.* тобиш [tobish] / *v.i.* тобидан [tobidan]
glue [глу] *n.* ширеш [shiresh], елим [yelim] / *v.t.* бо ширеш часпондан [bo shiresh chaspondan], бо елим часпондан [bo yelim chaspondan]
go [го] *v.i.* рафтан [raftan]
goal [гол] *n. (objective)* ҳадаф [hadaf], нишон [nishon]; *(intention)* мақсад [maqsad]; *(sports)* дарвоза [darvoza]
goalkeeper [голкипер] *n.* дарвозабон [darvozabon]
goat [гот] *n.* буз [buz]
god [год] *n.* худо [xudo]
goddess [годес] *n.* олиҳа [oliha]
gold [голд] *n.* тилло [tillo], зар [zar] / *adj.* тиллоӣ [tilloi], зарин [zarin]
golden [голден] *adj. (made of gold)* тиллоӣ [tilloi], зарин [zarin]; *(gold-colored)* тиллоранг [tillorang], зарранг [zarrang]
golf [голф] *n.* голф [golf]
good [гуд] *n.* мол [mol], модда [modda] / *adj.* нағз [naghz], хуб [xub]
goodbye [гудбай] *n.* падруд [padrud]; **Goodbye!** Дар паноҳи Худо! [Dar panohi Xudo!]
goods [гудз] *n.pl.* мол [mol], молҳо [molho]

goose [гус] *n.* қоз [qoz]
gossip [госип] *n.* суханчин [suxanchin] / *v.i.* суханчинӣ кардан [suxanchini kardan]
govern [говерн] *v.t.* ҳукмронӣ кардан [hukmroni kardan]
government [говернмент] *n.* ҳукумат [hukumat]
governor [говернор] *n.* ҳоким [hokim]
grace [грейс] *n.* хушандомӣ [xushandomi]
graceful [грейсфул] *adj.* хушандом [xushandom]
gracefully [грейсфули] *adv.* хиромон [xiromon]
gracious [грейшас] *adj.* меҳрубон [mehrubon]
grade [грейд] *n. (degree)* дараҷа [daraja]; *(class)* синф [sinf]
gradual [греҷуал] *adj.* тадриҷӣ [tadriji], оҳиста-оҳиста [ohista-ohista]
graduate [греҷуейт] *v.t.* дараҷа бастан [daraja bastan] / *v.i.* тамом кардан [tamom kardan]
graft [грефт] *n.* пайванднавда [payvandnavda] / *v.t.* пайванд кардан [payvand kardan]
grain [грейн] *n.* ғалла [ghalla]
gram [грем] *n.* грамм [gramm]
grammar [гремар] *n.* грамматика [grammatika]
grand [гренд] *adj.* боазамат [boazamat]
grandchild [грендчайлд] *n.* набера [nabera]
grandfather [грендфадер] *n.* падаркалон [padarkalon], бобо [bobo]
grandmother [грендмадер] *n.* модаркалон [modarkalon], бибӣ [bibi]
granite [гренит] *n.* хоро [xoro]
grant [грент] *n.* пешкаш [peshkash], бахшиш [baxshish] / *v.t.* бахшидан [baxshidan]
grape [грейп] *n.* ангур [angur]; **grape juice** шарбати ангур [sharbati angur]
graph [греф] *n.* график [grafik]
graphic [грефик] *adj.* графикӣ [grafiki]
grasp [гресп] *v.t.* қапидан [qapidan]
grass [грес] *n.* сабза [sabza]
grasshopper [грасҳопер] *n.* малах [malax]
grateful [грейтфул] *adj.* сипосгузор [siposguzor]
gratitude [гретитюд] *n.* сипосгузорӣ [siposguzori]
grave [грейв] *n.* гӯр [gür], қабр [qabr] / *adj.* ҷиддӣ [jiddi]
gravel [гревел] *n.* сангреза [sangreza]
gravity [гравити] *n. (seriousness)* ҷиддият [jiddiyat]; *(force of attraction)* ҷозиба [joziba]
gray [грей] *adj.* хокистарӣ [xokistari]
grease [грис] *n.* равған [ravghan] / *v.t.* равған задан [ravghan zadan]
great [грет] *adj.* бузург [buzurg]
great-grandfather [грейт-грендфадер] *n.* бобокалон [bobokalon]

great-grandmother [грейт-грендмадер] *n.* бибикалон [bibikalon]
greatness [грейтнас] *n.* бузургӣ [buzurgi]
Greek [грик] *n./adj.* юнонӣ [yunoni]
green [грин] *adj.* сабз [sabz]
greenhouse [гринҳаус] *n.* гулхона [gulxona]
greet [грит] *v.t.* салом додан [salom dodan], дуруд гуфтан [durud guftan]
greeting [гритинг] *n.* салом [salom], дуруд [durud]
grief [гриф] *n.* андӯҳ [andüh]
grievance [гриванс] *n.* гила [gila], шикоят [shikoyat]
grieve [грив] *v.i.* ғусса хӯрдан [ghussa xürdan]
grill [грил] *n.* дастгоҳи кабобкунӣ [dastgohi kabobkuni] / *v.t.* кабоб кардан [kabob kardan]
grind [грайнд] *v.t.* орд кардан [ord kardan], кӯфтан [küftan], майда кардан [mayda kardan]
grip [грип] *n.* гир [gir] / *v.t.* шиддатнок гирифтан [shiddatnok giriftan]
groan [грон] *n.* нола [nola] / *v.i.* нолидан [nolidan]
grocer [гросер] *n.* баққол [baqqol]
grocery [гросери] *n.* баққолӣ [baqqoli]
groin [гройн] *n.* қадкашак [qadkashak]
groom [грум] *n.* домод [domod]
ground [граунд] *n.* замин [zamin] / *adj.* кӯфта [küfta]
groundwork [граундвурк] *n.* замина [zamina], бунёд [bunyod]
group [груп] *n.* гурӯҳ [gurüh]
grow [гро] *v.t. (cultivate)* коштан [koshtan], рӯёндан [rüyondan] / *v.i. (become bigger)* калон шудан [kalon shudan]; *(of plants)* рӯидан [rüidan], сабзидан [sabzidan]
growl [граул] *n.* ғуррос [ghurros] / *v.i.* ғуррос задан [ghurros zadan]
grown-up [грон-ап] *n.* қадрас [qadras], болиғ [boligh]
growth [грот] *n. (progress)* расиш [rasish]; *(increase)* афзоиш [afzoish]; *(of plants)* сабзиш [sabzish]; *(increase in size)* калоншавӣ [kalonshavi]
guarantee [гаранти] *n.* замонат [zamonat] / *v.t.* замонат кардан [zamonat kardan]
guard [гард] *n.* посбон [posbon], қаровул [qarovul] / *v.t.* посбонӣ кардан [posboni kardan], қаровулӣ кардан [qarovuli kardan]
guerilla [гурила] *n.* партизан [partizan] / *adj.* партизанӣ [partizani]
guess [гес] *n.* тахмин [taxmin] / *v.t.* тахмин карда ёфтан [taxmin karda yoftan] / *v.i.* тахмин кардан [taxmin kardan]
guest [гест] *n.* меҳмон [mehmon]
guesthouse [гестҳаус] *n.* меҳмонхона [mehmonxona]
guide [гайд] *n.* роҳнамо [rohnamo] / *v.t.* роҳ намудан [roh namudan], роҳнамоӣ кардан [rohnamoi kardan]

guidebook [гайдбук] *n.* роҳнамо [rohnamo], китобчаи роҳнамо [kitobchai rohnamo]
guilt [гилт] *n.* гуноҳгорӣ [gunohgori], айбдорӣ [aybdori]
guilty [гилти] *adj.* гуноҳгор [gunohgor], айбдор [aybdor]
guitar [гитар] *n.* гитара [gitara]
gulf [галф] *n.* халиҷ [xalij]
gum [гам] *n. (anat.)* вора [vora], милки дандон [milki dandon]; *(chewing gum)* сақич [saqich]
gun [ган] *n.* туфанг [tufang], милтиқ [miltiq]
gust [гаст] *n.* тундбод [tundbod]
gutter [гатер] *n.* нова [nova], новадон [novadon]
guy [гай] *n.* ҷавонмард [javonmard], мард [mard]
gymnasium [ҷимнейзиям] *n.* варзишгоҳ [varzishgoh]
gynecologist [гайнеколоҷист] *n.* духтури занҳо [duxturi zanho]
Gypsy [ҷипси] *n.* лӯлӣ [lüli]

H

habit [ҳебит] ***n.*** хӯй [xüy], одат [odat]
hail [ҳейл] *n.* жола [zhola], тагарг [tagarg]
hair [ҳер] *n.* мӯй [müy]
hairdresser [ҳердресер] *n.* сартарош [sartarosh]
hairy [ҳери] *adj.* сермӯй [sermüy], мӯйдор [müydor]
half [ҳеф] *n.* ним [nim] / *adj.* ним [nim], нисф [nisf]
hall [ҳол] *n.* толор [tolor]
hallway [ҳолуэй] *n.* роҳрав [rohrav]
halo [ҳейло] *n.* хиргоҳ [xirgoh], ҳола [hola]
hammer [ҳемер] *n.* болға [bolgha] / *v.t.* болға задан [bolgha zadan]
hand [ҳенд] *n. (anat.)* даст [dast]; *(of a watch/clock)* ақрабак [aqrabak]; **minute hand** ақрабаки дақиқашумор [aqrabaki daqiqashumor]; **hour hand** ақрабаки соатнамо [aqrabaki soatnamo] / *v.t.* **shake hands** вохӯрӣ кардан [voxüri kardan]; **hand over** супурдан [supurdan]
handbag [ҳендбаг] *n.* сумка [sumka]
handbook [ҳендбук] *n.* маълумотнома [ma'lumotnoma]
handicap [ҳендикап] *n.* монеа [monea]
handicapped [ҳендикапд] *adj.* ноқис [noqis]
handicraft [ҳендикрафт] *n.* сунъати дастӣ [sun'ati dasti]
handkerchief [ҳенкерчиф] *n.* дастрӯмолча [dastrümolcha]
handle [ҳендл] *n.* дастак [dastak]
handmade [ҳендмейд] *adj.* дастӣ [dasti]
handrail [ҳендрейл] *n.* панҷара [panjara]
handsome [ҳендсам] *adj.* хушрӯ [xushrü]
handy [ҳенди] *adj.* наздик [nazdik], бароҳат [barohat]

hang [ҳенг] *v.t.* овехтан [ovextan], овезон кардан [ovezon kardan] / *v.i.* овехта шудан [ovexta shudan], овезон карда шудан [ovezon karda shudan]; **hang one's self** худро овехта куштан [xudro ovexta kushtan]
hangar [ҳенгар] *n.* ангар [angar]
hanger [ҳенгер] *n.* пӯшоковезак [püshokovezak], либосовезак [libosovezak]
hangover [ҳенговер] *n.* хумор [xumor]
happen [ҳепен] *v.i.* рӯй додан [rüy dodan]
happiness [ҳепинес] *n.* шодӣ [shodi], хушӣ [xushi]
happy [ҳепи] *adj.* шод [shod], хушнуд [xushnud], хуш [xush]
harass [ҳарес] *v.t.* хавотир кардан [xavotir kardan], ба изтироб овардан [ba iztirob ovardan]
harbor [ҳарбор] *n.* лангаргоҳ [langargoh], бандар [bandar]
hard [ҳард] *adj.* сахт [saxt]
harden [ҳарден] *v.i.* сахт шудан [saxt shudan]
hardly [ҳардли] *adv.* тақрибан ҳеҷ [taqriban hej]
hardship [ҳардшип] *n.* сахтӣ [saxti], бечорагӣ [bechoragi]
hardy [ҳарди] *adj.* ҷонсахт [jonsaxt]
hare [ҳер] *n.* заргӯш [zargüsh]
harm [ҳарм] *n.* газанд [gazand], зиён [ziyon], зарар [zarar] / *v.t.* зиён расондан [ziyon rasondan], осеб овардан [oseb ovardan]
harmful [ҳармфул] *adj.* зиёнрасон [ziyonrason], осебнок [osebnok], зарарнок [zararnok]
harmless [ҳармлес] *adj.* безиён [beziyon], безарар [bezarar]
harness [ҳарнес] *n.* афзоли асп [afzoli asp] / *v.t.* бастан [bastan]; (a cart) ба ароба бастан [ba aroba bastan]
harp [ҳарп] *n.* уд [ud]
harsh [ҳарш] *adj.* *(severe)* сахт [saxt]; *(of lighting)* баланд [baland]
harvest [ҳарвест] *n.* ҳосил [hosil]
haste [ҳейст] *n.* шитобкорӣ [shitobkori]
hasty [ҳейсти] *adj.* шитобкор [shitobkor], шитобӣ [shitobi]
hat [ҳет] *n.* кулоҳ [kuloh]
hatch [ҳеч] *v.t.* тухм зер карда баровардан [tuxm zer karda barovardan] / *v.i.* аз тухм баровардан [az tuxm barovardan]
hate [ҳейт] *n.* нафрат [nafrat] / *v.t.* нафрат кардан [nafrat kardan]
haul [ҳол] *v.t.* кашидан [kashidan], кашола кардан [kashola kardan]
have [ҳав] *v.t.* доштан [doshtan]; **have to** бояд [boyad]
hawk [ҳок] *n.* пайғу [payghu], заған [zaghan], ғалевоҷ [ghalevoj]
hay [ҳей] *n.* беда [beda], хасбеда [xasbeda]
hazard [ҳезард] *n.* хатар [xatar]

haze [ҳейз] *n.* тумани тунук [tumani tunuk]

hazy [ҳейзи] *adj.* тумандор [tumandor]

he [ҳи] *pron.* ӯ [ü], вай [vay]

head [ҳед] *n.* сар [sar] / *v.t.* сардорӣ кардан [sardori kardan]

heading [ҳединг] *n.* сарлавҳа [sarlavha], унвон [unvon]

headlight [ҳедлайт] *n.* чароғ [charogh]

headline [ҳедлайн] *n.* сарлавҳа [sarlavha], унвон [unvon]

headquarters [ҳедкуортерз] *n.pl.* идораи марказӣ [idorai markazi]

heal [ҳил] *v.t.* даво кардан [davo kardan], шифо додан [shifo dodan] / *v.i.* сиҳат шудан [sihat shudan], шифо ёфтан [shifo yoftan]

health [ҳелт] *n.* тандурустӣ [tandurusti], сиҳатӣ [sihati]

healthy [ҳелти] *adj.* тандуруст [tandurust], сиҳат [sihat]

heap [ҳип] *n.* тӯда [tüda]

hear [ҳир] *v.t.* шунидан [shunidan]

hearing [ҳиринг] *n.* *(sense)* шунавоӣ [shunavoi]; *(legal)* додрасӣ [dodrasi]

heart [ҳарт] *n.* дил [dil]; *(card suit)* таппон [tappon]

heart attack [ҳарт атек] *n.* сактаи дил [saktai dil]

heartburn [ҳарт бурн] *n.* зардачӯш [zardajüsh]

hearth [ҳарт] *n.* оташдон [otashdon], дегдон [degdon]

hearty [ҳарти] *adj.* *(friendly, affectionate)* дӯстона [düstona], самимона [samimona]; *(healthy-looking)* сиҳат [sihat]

heat [ҳит] *n.* *(warmth)* гармӣ [garmi], тафт [taft]; *(of animals)* ӯгурхоҳӣ [ügurxohi], гушн [gushn]

heater [ҳитер] *n.* гармкунак [garmkunak]

heating [ҳитинг] *n.* гармкунӣ [garmkuni]; **central heating** гармкунии марказӣ [garmkunii markazi]

heaven [ҳеван] *n.* биҳишт [bihisht], ҷаннат [jannat]

heavy [ҳеви] *adj.* вазнин [vaznin], сангин [sangin], гарон [garon]

hedge [ҳеҷ] *n.* тавораи буттагӣ [tavorai buttagi]

hedgehog [ҳеҷҳог] *n.* хорпушт [xorpusht]

heel [ҳил] *n.* пошна [poshna]

height [ҳайт] *n.* *(size/stature)* қад [qad]; *(altitude)* баландӣ [balandi]

heir [эр] *n.* меросхӯр [merosxür]

helicopter [ҳеликоптер] *n.* вертолёт [vertolyot], чархбол [charxbol]

hell [ҳел] *n.* дӯзах [düzax], ҷаҳаннам [jahannam]

hello [ҳело] *n.* *(telephone greeting)* лаббай [labbay], бале [bale], ало [alo]; *(all-purpose greeting)* салом [salom], дуруд [durud]

helm [ҳелм] *n.* зимом [zimom]

helmet [ҳелмет] *n.* хӯд [xüd], кулаҳхӯд [kulahxüd]

help [ҳелп] *n.* ёрӣ [yori], кӯмак [kümak] / *v.t.* ёрӣ додан [yori dodan], кӯмак кардан [kümak kardan]

helper [ҳелпер] *n.* дастёр [dastyor], ёвар [yovar]

helpful [ҳелпфул] *adj.* судманд [sudmand], фоиданок [foidanok]
hemophilia [ҳимофилия] *n.* гемофилия [gemofiliya]
hen [ҳен] *n.* мокиён [mokiyon]
hepatitis [ҳепатайтис] *n.* қубод [qubod], зотулкабид [zotulkabid], зардпарвин [zardparvin]
her [ҳер] *adj.* аз они ӯ [az oni ü], аз они вай [az oni vay]; *pron.* ӯ [ü], вай [vay]
herd [ҳерд] *n.* пода [poda]
here [ҳир] *adv.* ин ҷо [in jo]; **right here** ҳамин ҷо [hamin jo]
hernia [ҳерния] *n.* чурра [churra], дабба [dabba]
hero [ҳиро] *n.* қаҳрамон [qahramon]
heroic [ҳероик] *adj. (of heroes)* қаҳрамонӣ [qahramoni]; *(like a hero)* қаҳрамонона [qahramonona]
heron [ҳерон] *n.* куланг [kulang]
herring [ҳеринг] *n.* шӯрмоҳӣ [shürmohi]
hers [ҳерз] *pron.* аз они ӯ [az oni ü], аз они вай [az oni vay]
herself [ҳерселф] *pron.* худаш [xudash]
hesitate [ҳезитейт] *v.i.* дудила шудан [dudila shudan]
hesitation [ҳезитейшан] *n.* дудилагӣ [dudilagi]
hiccup [ҳикап] *n.* ҳиққак [hiqqak] / *v.i.* ҳиққак задан [hiqqak zadan]
hidden [ҳиден] *adj.* пинҳонӣ [pinhoni]
hide [ҳайд] *v.t.* пинҳон кардан [pinhon kardan]/ *v.i.* пинҳон шудан [pinhon shudan]
high [ҳай] *adj.* баланд [baland]
highway [ҳайуей] *n.* шоҳроҳ [shohroh]
hike [ҳайк] *n.* гаштугузор [gashtuguzor] / *v.i.* гаштугузор кардан [gashtuguzor kardan]
hill [ҳил] *n.* теппа [teppa]
hilly [ҳили] *adj.* сертеппа [serteppa], гарева [gareva]
him [ҳим] *pron.* ӯ [ü], вай [vay]
himself [ҳимселф] *pron.* худаш [xudash]
hinder [ҳиндер] *v.t.* боздоштан [bozdoshtan], мамониат кардан [mamoniat kardan]
Hindu [ҳинду] *n.* ҳинду [hindu] / *adj.* -и ҳинду [-i hindu]
hinge [ҳинҷ] *n.* ошиқ-маъшуқ [oshiq-ma'shuq] / *v.i.* вобаста будан [vobasta budan]
hint [ҳинт] *n.* кинoя [kinoya] / *v.i.* бо киноя гуфтан [bo kinoya guftan]
hip [ҳип] *n.* сон [son]
hippopotamus [ҳипопотамус] *n.* баҳмут [bahmut], аспи обӣ [aspi obi]
hire [ҳайр] *v.t.* киро кардан [kiro kardan]
his [ҳиз] *pron.* аз они ӯ [az oni ü], аз они вай [az oni vay]
hiss [ҳис] *v.i.* фашшос задан [fashshos zadan]
historian [ҳисторияи] *n.* таърихшинос [ta'rixshinos]

historical [ҳисторикал] *adj.* таърихӣ [ta'rixi]
history [ҳистори] *n.* таърих [ta'rix]
hit [ҳит] *v.t.* задан [zadan]
hive [ҳайв] *n.* канду [kandu]
hoarse [ҳорс] *adj.* хиррӣ [xirri]
hobby [ҳоби] *n.* кори дӯстдошта [kori düstdoshta]
hockey [ҳоки] *n.* хоккей [xokkey]
hoe [ҳо] *n.* каланд [kaland]
hoist [ҳойст] *v.t.* бардоштан [bardoshtan], баланд кардан [baland kardan]
hold [ҳолд] *v.t.* доштан [doshtan], даст гирифтан [dast giriftan]
hole [ҳол] *n.* сӯрох [sürox]
holiday [ҳолидей] *n. (festive or holy day)* ҷашн [jashn], ид [id]; *(vacation)* рухсатӣ [ruxsati]
hollow [ҳоло] *adj.* ковок [kovok]
holy [ҳоли] *adj.* муқаддас [muqaddas]
home [ҳом] *n.* хона [xona]
homeland [ҳомланд] *n.* майҳан [mayhan], ватан [vatan]
homesick [ҳомсик] *adj.* ватанро пазмон [vatanro pazmon]
homesickness [ҳомсикнес] *n.* ҳасрати ватан [hasrati vatan]
hometown [ҳомтаун] *n.* шаҳри худ [shahri xud]
homework [ҳомвурк] *n.* вазифаи хонагӣ [vazifai xonagi]
homosexual [ҳомосекшуал] *n./adj.* ҳамҷинсбоз [hamjinsboz]
honest [онест] *adj.* софдил [sofdil], дурусткор [durustkor]
honesty [онести] *n.* дурусткорӣ [durustkori]
honey [ҳани] *n.* асал [asal], ангубин [angubin]
honeymoon [ҳанимун] *n.* моҳи асал [mohi asal]
honor [онор] *n.* шараф [sharaf], иззат [izzat] / *v.t.* эҳтиром кардан [ehtirom kardan], иззат кардан [izzat kardan]
hoof [ҳуф] *n.* сум [sum]
hook [ҳук] *n.* чангак [changak]
hoop [ҳуп] *n.* чанбар [chanbar], чанбарак [chanbarak]
hope [ҳоп] *n.* умед [umed] / *v.t.* умед доштан [umed doshtan], умедвор будан [umedvor budan]
hopeful [ҳопфул] *adj.* умедвор [umedvor]
hopeless [ҳоплес] *adj.* ноумед [noumed]
horizon [ҳорайзон] *n.* уфуқ [ufuq]
horizontal [ҳоризонтал] *adj.* уфуқӣ [ufuqi]
horn [ҳорн] *n. (of an animal)* шох [shox]; *(mus.)* буғ [bugh], карнай [karnay]; *(of a car)* буғ [bugh]
horrible [ҳорибъл] *adj.* даҳшатнок [dahshatnok]
horror [ҳорор] *n.* даҳшат [dahshat]
hors d'oeuvre [ордӯв] *n.* хӯриш [xürish], газак [gazak]
horse [ҳорс] *n.* асп [asp]; **on horseback** аспсавор [aspsavor]

horsepower [ҳорспауэр] *n.* қувваи асп [quvvai asp];
horseshoe [ҳорсшу] *n.* наъл [na'l]
hose [ҳоз] *n.* рӯда [rüda]
hospitable [ҳоспитабъл] *adj.* меҳмондӯст [mehmondüst], меҳмоннавоз [mehmonnavoz]
hospital [ҳоспитал] *n.* беморхона [bemorxona], касалхона [kasalxona]
host [ҳост] *n.* мизбон [mizbon] / *v.t.* меҳмон кардан [mehmon kardan]
hostage [ҳостиҷ] *n.* гаравгон [garavgon]
hostel [ҳостел] *n.* хобгоҳи умумӣ [xobgohi umumi]
hostess [ҳостес] *n.* мизбонзан [mizbonzan]
hostile [ҳостайл] *adj.* душманона [dushmanona]
hot [ҳот] *adj.* гарм [garm], тафсон [tafson]
hotel [ҳотел] *n.* меҳмонхона [mehmonxona]
hour [аур] *n.* соат [soat]
house [ҳаус] *n.* хона [xona]
household [ҳаусҳолд] *n.* хонадон [xonadon], хонавода [xonavoda]
housekeeper [ҳаускипер] *n.* кадбону [kadbonu]
housewife [ҳаусуайф] *n.* соҳибхоназан [sohibxonazan]
how [ҳау] *adv.* чӣ хел [chi xel], чӣ гуна [chi guna], чӣ тавр [chi tavr]
however [ҳауэвер] *adv.* ҳарчанд [harchand] / *conj.* аммо [ammo]
howl [ҳаул] *n.* уллос [ullos] / *v.i. (of an animal)* уллос кашидан [ullos kashidan]; *(cry loudly)* гиряву нола кардан [giryavu nola kardan]
hug [ҳаг] *n.* оғӯш [oghüsh] / *v.t.* оғӯш кардан [oghüsh kardan], ба оғӯш гирифтан [ba oghüsh giriftan]
huge [ҳюҷ] *adj.* бузург [buzurg]
human [ҳюман] *adj.* одамӣ [odami], инсонӣ [insoni], башарӣ [bashari]; **human being** одам [odam], инсон [inson]; **human rights** ҳуқуқи башар [huquqi bashar]
humane [ҳюмейн] *adj.* одамдӯст [odamdüst]
humanity [ҳюманити] *n.* башарият [bashariyat]
humble [ҳамбъл] *adj.* хоксор [xoksor], фурӯтан [furütan]
humid [ҳюмид] *adj.* намнок [namnok]
humidity [ҳюмидити] *n.* намнокӣ [namnoki]
humor [ҳюмор] *n.* зарофат [zarofat], ҳаҷв [hajv]
hump [ҳамп] *n.* кӯз [küz], кӯж [küzh]; *(of an animal)* кӯҳон [kühon]
hundred [ҳандред] *num.* сад [sad]
hundredth [ҳандредт] *adj.* садум [sadum]
hunger [ҳангер] *n.* гуруснагӣ [gurusnagi]
hungry [ҳангри] *adj.* гурусна [gurusna]
hunt [ҳант] *n.* шикор [shikor] / *v.t. (hunt game)* шикор кардан [shikor kardan]; *(search for)* ҷустан [justan]
hunter [ҳантер] *n.* шикорчӣ [shikorchi]
hurray [ҳурей] *interj.* ура [ura]
hurry [ҳари] *n.* шитоб [shitob] / *v.i.* шитофтан [shitoftan]

hurt [ҳурт] *n.* зиён [ziyon], осеб [oseb] / *v.t.* зиён расондан [ziyon rasondan], осеб овардан [oseb ovardan] / *v.i.* дард кардан [dard kardan]; **It hurts.** Дард мекунад. [Dard mekunad.]
husband [ҳазбанд] *n.* шавҳар [shavhar]
hut [ҳат] *n.* кулба [kulba]
hygiene [ҳайҷин] *n.* беҳдошт [behdosht]
hymn [ҳим] *n.* мадҳия [madhiya]
hyphen [ҳайфен] *n.* тире [tire]

I

I [ай] *pron.* ман [man]
ice [айс] *n.* ях [yax]
ice cream [айс крим] *n.* яхмос [yaxmos]
icon [айкон] *n.* икона [ikona], уқнус [uqnus]
icy [айси] *adj.* яхин [yaxin], яхӣ [yaxi]; *(ice-covered)* яхпӯш [yaxpüsh]
idea [айдия] *n.* ақида [aqida], андеша [andesha]
ideal [айдил] *n.* мақсади олӣ [maqsadi oli] / *adj.* *(best)* беҳтарин [behtarin]; *(imaginary, existing only in the mind)* хаёлӣ [xayoli]
identical [айдентикал] *adj.* якхел [yakxel]
identification [айдентификейшан] (*abbr.* **ID**) *n.* ташхис [tashxis]; **identification card** гувоҳномаи шахсӣ [guvohnomai shaxsi]
identify [айдентифай] *v.t.* ташхис кардан [tashxis kardan]
idiom [идиям] *n.* таъири рехта [ta'biri rexta], идиома [idioma]
idiot [идият] *n.* аблаҳ [ablah], аҳмақ [ahmaq]
idle [айдъл] *adj.* бекор [bekor]
if [иф] *conj.* агар [agar]
ignition [игнишан] *n.* афрӯзиш [afrüzish]; *(in a car or other device)* асбоби афрӯзиш [asbobi afrüzish]
ignorance [игнуранс] *n.* ҷоҳилӣ [johili], нодонӣ [nodoni]
ignorant [игнурант] *adj.* ҷоҳил [johil], нодон [nodon]
ignore [игнор] *v.t.* писанд накардан [pisand nakardan], ба эътибор нагирифтан [ba e'tibor nagiriftan]
ill [ил] *adj.* бемор [bemor], касал [kasal]
illegal [иллигал] *adj.* ғайриқонунӣ [ghayriqonuni]
illegible [иллеҷибъл] *adj.* нохоно [noxono]
illiterate [иллитерат] *adj.* бесавод [besavod]
illness [илнес] *n.* беморӣ [bemori], касалӣ [kasali]
illumination [илуминейшан] *n.* чароғон [charoghon]
illusion [илужан] *n.* фиреби ҳис [firebi his], ғалати тасаввур [ghalati tasavvur]
illustrate [иластрейт] *v.t.* *(provide illustrations)* суратдор кардан [suratdor kardan]; *(provide examples)* бо мисол фаҳмондан [bo misol fahmondan]
illustration [иластрейшан] *n.* расм [rasm], сурат [surat]

image [имеҷ] *n.* тимсол [timsol], тасвир [tasvir]
imagination [имаҷинейшан] *n.* пиндор [pindor], тасаввур [tasavvur]
imagine [имаҷин] *v.t.* пиндоштан [pindoshtan], тасаввур кардан [tasavvur kardan]
imitate [имитейт] *v.t.* тақлид кардан [taqlid kardan]
imitation [имитейшан] *n.* тақлид [taqlid]
immense [именс] *adj.* бузург [buzurg]
immoral [иммарал] *adj.* бадахлоқ [badaxloq]
immortal [иммортал] *adj. (of a person)* ҷовид [jovid]; *(of things/ideas)* намиранда [namiranda]
impasse [импас] *n.* роҳи сарбаста [rohi sarbasta]
impatient [импейшент] *adj.* бесабр [besabr]
imperfect [имперфект] *adj.* нопурра [nopurra], номукаммал [nomukammal]
implement [имплемент] *n.* асбоб [asbob], абзор [abzor] / *v.t.* иҷро кардан [ijro kardan]
imply [имплай] *v.t.* зимнан фаҳмондан [zimnan fahmondan]
impolite [импулайт] *adj.* беадаб [beadab]
import [импорт] *n.* воридот [voridot] / *v.t.* ворид кардан [vorid kardan]; **import duty** андози воридот [andozi voridot]
importance [импортанс] *n.* аҳамият [ahamiyat]
important [импортант] *adj.* аҳамиятнок [ahamiyatnok]
impose [импоз] *v.t. (impose an idea)* бо зӯрӣ талқин кардан [bo züri talqin kardan]; *(impose a tax)* андоз андохтан [andoz andoxtan]
impossible [импосибъл] *adj.* номумкин [nomumkin]
impotent [импотент] *adj.* бетаъсир [beta'sir], нотавон [notavon]
impress [импрес] *v.t. (impress sb)* таъсир кардан [ta'sir kardan]; *(impress with a seal)* мӯҳр задан [mührzadan]; *(instill or inculcate ideas)* талқин кардан [talqin kardan]; *(stamp a design)* сикка задан [sikka zadan]
impressive [импресив] *adj.* таъсирбахш [ta'sirbaxsh]
imprint [импринт] *v.t.* нақш бандондан [naqsh bandondan]
imprison [импризон] *v.t.* зиндонӣ кардан [zindoni kardan], ҳабс кардан [habs kardan]
improper [импропер] *adj.* номуносиб [nomunosib], беҷо [bejo]
improve [импрув] *v.t.* беҳтар кардан [behtar kardan] / *v.i.* беҳтар шудан [behtar shudan]
improvement *n.* беҳшавӣ [behshavi]
improvise [импрувайз] *v.t. (in speech)* бадеҳатан гуфтан [badehatan guftan]; *(in music)* бадеҳатан навохтан [badehatan navoxtan]

impulse [импалс] *n.* чунбиши беихтиёрона [junbishi beixtiyorona]
in [ин] *prep.* дар [dar]; **Come in!** Даро! [Daro!]
inability [инабилити] *n.* нотавонӣ [notavoni]
inaccessible [инаксесибъл] *adj.* дастнорас [dastnoras], каснорас [kasnoras]
inactive [инактив] *adj.* бефаъолият [befa'oliyat]
inaugurate [иногурейт] *v.t.* расман оғоз кардан [rasman oghoz kardan]
inauguration [иногурейшан] *n.* маросими кушод [marosimi kushod]
incentive [инсентив] *n.* ангеза [angeza]
inch [инч] *n.* дюйм [dyuym]
inclination [инклинейшан] *n.* майл [mayl]
incline [инклайн] *n.* нишеб [nisheb], майлон [maylon]
include [инклуд] *v.t.* даровардан [darovardan]
income [инкам] *n.* даромад [daromad]
incompetent [инкомпетент] *adj.* ноӯҳдабаро [noühdabaro], беҳунар [behunar]
incorrect [инкорект] *adj.* нодуруст [nodurust]
increase [инкрис] *n.* афзоиш [afzoish] / *v.i.* афзудан [afzudan]
indeed [индид] *adv.* ба ростӣ [ba rosti], ҳақиқатан [haqiqatan]
independence [индепенденс] *n.* истиқлол [istiqlol]
independent [индепендент] *adj.* мустақил [mustaqil]
index [индекс] *n.* феҳрист [fehrist], индекс [indeks]
index finger [индекс фингер] *n.* ангушти ишорат [angushti ishorat]
Indian [индиян] *n.* ҳинду [hindu] / *adj.* ҳиндӣ [hindi]
indicate [индикейт] *v.t.* нишон додан [nishon dodan], ишора кардан [ishora kardan]
indifferent [индиферент] *adj.* бепарво [beparvo]
indignation [индигнейшан] *n.* ранҷиш [ranjish]
indigo [индиго] *n.* нил [nil]
indirect [индайрект] *adj.* нороста [norosta], гирдогирд [girdogird]
individual [индивиҷюал] *n.* шахс [shaxs] / *adj.* шахсӣ [shaxsi]
Indonesian [индонижан] *n.* индонезиягӣ [indoneziyagi] / *adj.* индонезӣ [indonezi]
indoor [индор] *adj.* дарунӣ [daruni], хонагӣ [xonagi]
industrial [индастриял] *adj.* саноатӣ [sanoati]
industrious [индастрияс] *adj.* меҳнатдӯст [mehnatdüst]
industry [индастри] *n.* саноат [sanoat]
inefficient [инефишент] *adj.* ноӯҳдабаро [noühdabaro]
inexpensive [инекспенсив] *adj.* камарзиш [kamarzish]
infant [инфант] *n.* кӯдак [küdak]
infect [инфект] *v.t.* олуда кардан [oluda kardan], мубтало кардан [mubtalo kardan]
infection [инфекшан] *n.* мараз [maraz]

infectious [инфекшас] *adj.* сирояткунанда [siroyatkunanda], гузаранда [guzaranda]
inferior [инфериёр] *adj.* пастсифат [pastsifat], паст [past]
inflamed [инфлеймд] *adj.* варамкарда [varamkarda], газакгирифта [gazakgirifta]
inflammable [инфламабъл] *adj.* қобили даргирифтан [qobili dargiriftan]
inflammation [инфламейшан] *n.* газак [gazak], варам [varam]
inflatable [инфлейтабъл] *adj.* дам карда мешудагӣ [dam karda meshudagi]
inflation [инфлейшан] *n.* таваррум [tavarrum]
influence [инфлуэнс] *n.* таъсир [ta'sir] / *v.t.* таъсир гузоштан [ta'sir guzoshtan]
inform [информ] *v.t.* хабар кардан [xabar kardan]
information [информейшан] *n.* маълумот [ma'lumot], хабар [xabar]
infringe [инфринч] *v.t.* таҷовуз кардан [tajovuz kardan], халал додан [xalal dodan]
ingenious [инчинияс] *adj.* устокор [ustokor]
ingredient [ингридиент] *n.* ҷузъ [juz']; *(of a recipe)* маҳсулот [mahsulot]
inhabit [инҳабит] *v.t.* сокин будан [sokin budan]
inhabitant [инҳабитант] *n.* сокин [sokin]
inhale [инҳейл] *v.i.* нафас даровардан [nafas darovardan]
inherit [инҳерит] *v.t.* мерос гирифтан [meros giriftan]
inheritance [инҳеританс] *n.* мерос [meros]
initial [инишал] *n. (first letters of a name)* сарҳарфҳои ном [sarharfhoi nom] / *adj.* нахустин [naxustin]
initiative [инишатив] *n.* ташаббус [tashabbus]
inject [инчект] *v.t.* дору фиристодан [doru firistodan], тазриқ кардан [tazriq kardan]
injection [инчекшан] *n.* тазриқ [tazriq]
injure [инчур] *v.t.* осеб овардан [oseb ovardan], зарар кардан [zarar kardan], ярадор кардан [yarador kardan]
injured [инчурд] *adj.* ярадор [yarador]
injury [инчури] *n.* яра [yara], реш [resh], зарар [zarar]
ink [инк] *n.* сиёҳӣ [siyohi]
in-law [ин-ло] *n.* хеши ҳамсар [xeshi hamsar]
inn [ин] *n.* меҳмонхона [mehmonxona]
inner [инер] *adj.* дарунӣ [daruni]
innocent [иносент] *adj.* бегуноҳ [begunoh]
inoculate [инокюлейт] *v.t.* канондан [kanondan], пайванд кардан [payvand kardan]
inoculation [инокюлейшан] *n.* канондан(и) [kanondan(i)]
inquire [инкуайр] *v.i.* маълумот пурсидан [ma'lumot pursidan]

inquiry [инкуайри] *n.* пурсиш [pursish]
insane [инсейн] *adj.* девона [devona]
insect [инсект] *n.* ҳашарот [hasharot]
insert [инсерт] *v.t.* дарҷ кардан [darj kardan], даровардан [darovardan]
inside [инсайд] *n./adj.* дарун [darun]
insight [инсайт] *n.* басират [basirat]
insist [инсист] *v.i.* исрор кардан [isror kardan]
insistence [инсистенс] *n.* исрор [isror]
insomnia [инсомния] *n.* бехобӣ [bexobi], бедорхобӣ [bedorxobi]
inspect [инспект] *v.t.* тафтиш кардан [taftish kardan]
inspection [инспекшан] *n.* тафтиш [taftish]
inspector [инспектор] *n.* назоратчӣ [nazoratchi]
inspiration [инспирейшан] *n.* илҳом [ilhom]
inspire [инспайр] *v.t.* илҳом бахшидан [ilhom baxshidan]
install [инстол] *v.t.* барқарор кардан [barqaror kardan], гузоштан [guzoshtan]
installation [инстолейшан] *n.* барқарорӣ [barqarori], гузориш [guzorish]
instance [инстанс] *n.* *(example)* мисол [misol], назира [nazira]; *(event)* воқеа [voqea]
instant [инстант] *n.* дам [dam], лаҳза [lahza] / *adj.* фаврӣ [favri]
instantly [инстантли] *adv.* фавран [favran]
instead of [инстед] *prep.* ба ҷои [ba joi]
instep [инстеп] *n.* баландии рӯи пой [balandii rüi poy]
instinct [инстинкт] *n.* ғариза [ghariza], савқи табиӣ [savqi tabii]
institute [институт] *n.* институт [institut], бунгоҳ [bungoh] / *v.t.* барқарор кардан [barqaror kardan], барпо кардан [barpo kardan]
instruct [инстракт] *v.t.* омӯзондан [omüzondan], омӯхтан [omüxtan]
instruction [инстракшан] *n.* *(learning)* омӯзиш [omüzish]; *(how-to)* дастур [dastur]
instrument [инструмент] *n.* асбоб [asbob]
insufficient [инсуфишент] *adj.* нокифоя [nokifoya]
insulate [инсулейт] *v.t.* ҷудо гузоштан [judo guzoshtan]
insulation [инсулейшан] *n.* ҷудогузорӣ [judoguzori]
insult [инсалт] *n.* дашном [dashnom] / *v.t.* *(curse)* дашном додан [dashnom dodan]; *(cause insult)* таҳқир кардан [tahqir kardan]
insurance [иншуранс] *n.* бима [bima], суғурта [sughurta]
insure [иншур] *v.t.* суғурта кардан [sughurta kardan]
intelligence [интеличенс] *n.* ҳуш [hush], хирад [xirad], ақл [aql]
intelligent [интеличент] *adj.* хирадманд [xiradmand], зирак [zirak], боақл [boaql]

intend [интенд] *v.t.* қасд кардан [qasd kardan]
intense [интенс] *adj.* бошиддат [boshiddat]
intention [интеншан] *n.* ният [niyat], қасд [qasd]
interest [интерест] *n.* дилчаспӣ [dilchaspi], шавқ [shavq] / *v.t.* шавқ овардан [shavq ovardan]
interesting [интерестинг] *adj.* дилчасп [dilchasp], шавқовар [shavqovar]
interfere [интерфир] *v.t.* дахолат кардан [daxolat kardan], худро аралаш кардан [xudro aralash kardan]
interior [интириёр] *n.* дарун [darun], андарун [andarun] / *adj.* дарунӣ [daruni]
internal [интернал] *adj.* дарунӣ [daruni]
international [интернашунал] *adj.* байналмилалӣ [baynalmilali], байналхалқӣ [baynalxalqi]
Internet [интернет] *n.* интернет [internet]
interpreter [интерпретер] *n.* тарҷумон [tarjumon]
interrupt [интерапт] *v.t.* кандан [kandan], қатъ кардан [qat' kardan] / *v.i.* канда шудан [kanda shudan], қатъ шудан [qat' shudan]
interruption [интерапшан] *n.* кандашавӣ [kandashavi], қатъшавӣ [qat'shavi]
interval [интервал] *n.* фосила [fosila]
intervene [интервин] *v.i.* мудохила кардан [mudoxila kardan]
interview [интервю] *n.* мусоҳиба [musohiba] / *v.t.* мусоҳиба кардан [musohiba kardan]
intestine [интестин] *n.* рӯда [rüda]
intimate [интимат] *adj.* наздик [nazdik], маҳрам [mahram]
into [инту] *prep.* даруни [daruni], дар [dar]
intransitive [интрензитив] *gram.* монда [monda]
introduce [интродюс] *v.t.* шиносондан [shinosondan], шинос кардан [shinos kardan]
introduction [интродакшан] *n.* сарсухан [sarsuxan]
invade [инвейд] *v.t.* ҳуҷум карда даромадан [hujum karda daromadan]
invasion [инвейжан] *n.* тохтутоз [toxtutoz], ҳуҷум [hujum]
invent [инвент] *v.t.* ихтироъ кардан [ixtiro' kardan]
invention [инвеншан] *n.* ихтироъ [ixtiro']
inventory [инвентори] *n.* феҳрист [fehrist], инвентар [inventar]
invest [инвест] *v.t.* сармоя гузоштан [sarmoya guzoshtan]
investigate [инвестигейт] *v.t.* расидагӣ кардан [rasidagi kardan], таҳқиқ кардан [tahqiq kardan]
investigation [инвестигейшан] *n.* расидагӣ [rasidagi], таҳқиқ [tahqiq]
investment [инвестмент] *n.* сармоягузорӣ [sarmoyaguzori]

invisible [инвизибъл] *adj.* диданашаванда [didanashavanda], нонамоён [nonamoyon]
invitation [инвитейшан] *n.* даъват [da'vat], таклиф [taklif]; **invitation card** даъватнома [da'vatnoma], таклифнома [taklifnoma]
invite [инвайт] *v.t.* даъват кардан [da'vat kardan], таклиф кардан [taklif kardan]
invoice [инвойс] *n.* фактура [faktura]
involve [инволв] *v.t.* ҷалб кардан [jalb kardan]
Iranian [ираниан] *n./adj.* эронӣ [eroni]
iris [айрис] *n. (flower)* савсан [savsan]; *(anat.)* пардаи инабияи чашм [pardai inabiyai chashm]
Irish [айиш] *n./adj.* ирландӣ [irlandi]
iron [айърн] *n. (metal)* оҳан [ohan]; *(appliance)* дарзмол [darzmol], уттӣ [utti] / *adj.* оҳанин [ohanin] / *v.t.* дарзмол кардан [darzmol kardan], уттӣ кардан [utti kardan]
ironic [айроник] *adj.* истеҳзоомез [istehzoomez]
irony [айрони] *n.* истеҳзо [istehzo]
irreconcilable [ирреконсайлабъл] *adj.* оштинопазир [oshtinopazir]
irreversible [ирреверсибъл] *adj.* баргаштнопазир [bargashtnopazir]
irrigate [иригейт] *v.t.* обёрӣ кардан [obyori kardan]
irrigation [иригейшан] *n.* обёрӣ [obyori]
Islam [ислам] *n.* ислом [islom]
Islamic [исламик] *adj.* исломӣ [islomi]
island [айланд] *n.* ҷазира [jazira]
Ismaili [исмайли] *n.*/исмоилӣ [ismoili]
isolate [айсулейт] *v.t.* ҷудо кардан [judo kardan]
Israeli [изрейли] *n./adj.* исроилӣ [isroili]
issue [ишу] *n. (of stamps, coinage, etc.)* барориш [barorish]; *(publication)* нашр / *v.t. (issue stamps, coins, etc.)* баровардан [barovardan]; *(give)* додан [dodan]
it [ит] *pron.* ӯ [ü], вай [vay]
Italian [италиян] *n./adj.* итолиёӣ [itoliyoi]
italics [айталикс] *n.* курсив [kursiv]
itch [ич] *n.* хоришак [xorishak] / *v.i.* хоридан [xoridan]
item [айтем] *n.* модда [modda]
its [итс] *adj.* аз они ӯ [az oni ü], аз они вай [az oni vay]
itself [итселф] *pron.* худаш [xudash]
ivory [айвори] *n.* оҷ [oj]
ivy [айви] *n.* ошиқпечон [oshiqpechon]

J

jacket [ҷекит] *n.* пиҷак [pijak], куртка [kurtka]
jade [ҷейд] *n.* яшми сабз [yashmi sabz]

jail [чейл] *n.* зиндон [zindon], ҳабсхона [habsxona]
jam [чем] *n.* мураббо [murabbo]
janitor [ченитор] *n.* фаррош [farrosh]
January [ченюери] *n.* январ [yanvar]
Japanese [чепаниз] *n./adj.* японӣ [yaponi]
jar [чор] *n.* банка [banka]
jaw [чо] *n.* чоғ [jogh]
jazz [чез] *n.* чаз [jaz]
jealous [челас] *adj.* бадрашк [badrashk]
jealousy [челаси] *n.* бадрашкӣ [badrashki]
jeans [чинз] *n.pl.* чинс [jins], шими чинс [shimi jins]
jelly [чели] *n.* полуда [poluda], желе [zhele]
jellyfish [челифиш] *n.* медуза [meduza]
jerk [черк] *n.* *(movement)* такон [takon]; *(person)* бадзот [badzot] *v.t.* тakoндан [takondan]
jersey [черзи] *n.* фуфайка [fufayka]
jet [чет] *n.* *(of water)* фавра [favra]
Jew [чу] *n.* яҳудӣ [yahudi]
jewel [чул] *n.* санги гаронбаҳо [sangi garonbaho]
jewelry [чулри] *n.* зевар [zevar], чавоҳирот [javohirot]
Jewish [чуиш] *adj.* яҳудӣ [yahudi]
job [чоб] *n.* кор [kor], вазифа [vazifa]
jog [чог] *n.* тела [tela], такон [takon] / *v.i.* оҳиста давидан [ohista davidan]
join [чойн] *v.t.* *(connect)* пайвастан [payvastan]; *(unite with or become part of)* як шудан [yak shudan], муттаҳид гардидан [muttahid gardidan]
joint [чойнт] *n.* банд [band], буғум [bughum]
joke [чок] *n.* шӯхӣ [shüxi] / *v.i.* шӯхӣ кардан [shüxi kardan]
joker [чокер] *n.* шӯх [shüx]
journal [чурнал] *n.* *(diary)* дафтари хотира [daftari xotira]; *(publication)* журнал [zhurnal], маҷалла [majalla]
journalist [чурналист] *n.* журналист [zhurnalist], рӯзноманигор [rüznomanigor]
journey [чурни] *n.* сафар [safar] / *v.i.* сафар кардан [safar kardan]
joy [чой] *n.* шодӣ [shodi]
judge [чач] *n.* довар [dovar] / *v.t.* суд кардан [sud kardan]
judgment [чачмант] *n.* ҳукм [hukm]
jug [чаг] *n.* кӯза [küza]
juggle [чагл] *v.t.* жонглёрӣ кардан [zhonglyori kardan]
juice [чус] *n.* шарбат [sharbat], сок [sok]
July [чулай] *n.* июл [iyul]
jump [чамп] *n.* чаҳиш [jahish] / *v.i.* частан [jastan]
junction [чанкшан] *n.* чои пайванд [joi payvand]; *(railroad)* узели роҳи оҳан [uzeli rohi ohan]
June [чун] *n.* июн [iyun]
jungle [чангл] *n.* чангал [jangal]
junior [чуняр] *adj.* хурдсол [xurdsol]

junk [ҷанк] *n.* кӯҳнакола [kühnakola], латта-путта [latta-putta]
jury [ҷури] *n.* жюри [zhyuri], ҳайати доварон [hayati dovaron]
just [ҷаст] *adj.* одил [odil], боинсоф [boinsof] / *adv.* нав [nav], навакак [navakak]
justice [ҷастис] *n.* адлия [adliya], дод [dod]
justification [ҷастификейшан] *n.* сафедкунӣ [safedkuni]
justify [ҷастифай] *v.t.* сафед кардан [safed kardan]
juvenile [ҷувенайл] *n.* ҷавон [javon] / *adj.* ҷавон [javon], хурдсол [xurdsol]; **juvenile delinquent** ҷинояткори хурдсол [jinoyatkori xurdsol]

K

kangaroo [кангару] *n.* кенгуру [kenguru]
Kazakh [казак] *n. (person)* қазоқ [qazoq]; *(language)* қазоқӣ [qazoqi] / *adj.* қазоқ [qazoq]
keel [кил] *n.* синчи киштӣ [sinji kishti]
keen [кин] *adj.* тез [tez]
keep [кип] *v.t.* нигоҳ доштан [nigoh doshtan]
keeper [кипър] *n.* нигоҳдоранда [nigohdoranda], посбон [posbon]
kennel [кенъл] *n.* сагхона [sagxona], хоначаи саг [xonachai sag]
kernel [кернъл] *n.* дона [dona]
kerosene [керосин] *n.* карасин [karasin]
kettle [кетъл] *n.* чойҷӯш [choyjüsh]
key [ки] *n.* калид [kalid]
keyboard [киборд] *n.* сафҳаи калид [safhai kalid], тугмахона [tugmaxona]
keyhole [киҳол] *n.* сӯрохи қуфл [süroxi qufl]
khaki [каки] *adj.* хокӣ [xoki], хокиранг [xokirang]
kick [кик] *n.* лагад [lagad]; *(penalty kick)* тӯби ҷаримавӣ [tübi jarimavi] / *v.t.* лагад задан [lagad zadan]; *(kick out)* касе ба кӯча бароварда партофтан [kase ba kücha barovarda partoftan]
kid [кид] *n. (child)* кӯдак [küdak]; *(young goat)* бузича [buzicha] / *v.i.* шӯхӣ кардан [shüxi kardan]
kidnap [киднап] *v.t.* рабудан [rabudan]
kidney [кидни] *n.* гурда [gurda]
kill [кил] *v.t.* куштан [kushtan]
kilo(gram) [кило(грам)] *n.* кило(грамм) [kilo(gramm)]
kilometer [киломитар] *n.* километр [kilometr]
kind [кайнд] *n.* гуна [guna] / *adj.* меҳрубон [mehrubon]; **kind of** каме [kame]
kindergarten [киндергартън] *n.* боғча [boghcha]
kindle [киндъл] *v.t.* даргирондан [dargirondan], афрӯхтан [afrüxtan]
kindness [кайнднас] *n.* меҳрубонӣ [mehruboni]

king [кинг] *n.* подшоҳ [podshoh]
kingdom [кингдам] *n.* подшоҳӣ [podshohi]
kiosk [киоск] *n.* дӯкончa [dükoncha]
Kirghiz [киргиз] *n. (person)* қирғиз [qirghiz]; *(language)* қирғизӣ [qirghizi] / *adj.* қирғиз [qirghiz];
kiss [кис] *n.* бӯса [büsa] / *v.t.* бӯсидан [büsidan]
kitchen [кичън] *n.* ошхона [oshxona], ошпазхона [oshpazxona]
kite [кайт] *n.* бодбарак [bodbarak]
kitten [китън] *n.* гурбача [gurbacha], пишакбача [pishakbacha]
knapsack [напсак] *n.* борхалта [borxalta]
knead [нид] *v.t.* сириштан [sirishtan]
knee [ни] *n.* зону [zonu]
kneecap [никеп] *n.* чашмаки зону [chashmaki zonu]
kneel [нил] *v.i.* дузону шудан [duzonu shudan]
knife [найф] *n.* корд [kord]
knit [нит] *v.t./v.i.* бофтан [boftan]
knock [нок] *n.* тақ-тақ [taq-taq] / *v.i.* тақ-тақ кардан [taq-taq kardan]
knot [нот] *n.* гиреҳ [gireh] / *v.t.* гиреҳ бастан [gireh bastan]
know [но] *v.t.* донистан [donistan]; *(be acquainted)* шинохтан [shinoxtan] / *v.i.* донистан [donistan], огоҳ будан [ogoh budan]
knowledge [нолич] *n.* дониш [donish]
knuckle [накъл] *n.* банди ангушт [bandi angusht]
Koran [коран] *n.* Қуръон [Qur'on]
Korean [куриян] *n./adj.* кореягӣ [koreyagi]
kosher [кошер] *adj.* кошер [kosher], ҳалол барои яҳудиён [halol baroi yahudiyon]

L

label [лейбъл] *n.* ёрлиқ [yorliq] / *v.t.* ёрлиқ часпондан [yorliq chaspondan]
labor [лейбър] *n. (work)* меҳнат [mehnat]; *(childbirth)* дарди ҳамл [dardi haml]; **go into labor** дардаш гирифтан [dardash giriftan]
laboratory [леборатри] *n.* лаборатория [laboratoriya], озмоишгоҳ [ozmoishgoh]
laborer [лейборер] *n.* меҳнаткаш [mehnatkash]
labyrinth [лебиринт] *n.* лабиринт [labirint], (ҷои) пурпечухамӣ [(joi) purpechuxami]
lack [лек] *n.* камӣ [kami] / *v.t.* камбуд доштан [kam doshtan]
ladder [ледър] *n.* нардбон [nardbon]
ladle [лейдъл] *n.* обгардон [obgardon], чойкаш [choykash]
lady [лейди] *n.* хонум [xonum]
lake [лейк] *n.* кӯл [kül]
lamb [лем] *n.* барра [barra]
lame [лейм] *adj.* ланг [lang], чӯлоқ [chüloq]

lamp [лемп] *n.* чароғ [charogh]
lamppost [лемппост] *n.* фонуси кӯчагӣ [fonusi küchagi]
land [ленд] *n.* замин [zamin]; *(dry land)* хушкӣ [xushki], замин [zamin]; *(country)* кишвар [kishvar] / *v.t.* ба хушкӣ овардан [ba xushki ovardan] / *v.i.* фуроварда шудан [furovarda shudan]
landlord [лендлоорд] *n.* заминдор [zamindor], соҳиби замин [sohibi zamin]
landmark [лендмарк] *n.* фарсангсор [farsangsor]; **historical landmark** ҷои таърихӣ [joi ta'rixi]
landscape [лендскейп] *n.* манзара [manzara]
landslide [лендслайд] *n.* ярч [yarch]
lane [лейн] *n.* тангкӯча [tangkücha]
language [ленгвич] *n.* забон [zabon]; **native language** забони модарӣ [zaboni modari]
lantern [лентърн] *n.* фонус [fonus]
lap [леп] *n.* доман [doman]
lapel [лапел] *n.* зеҳкалон [zehkalon]
lapse [лепс] *n.* *(failure, error)* хато [xato]; *(pause)* даранг [darang]
lard [лард] *n.* равғани хук [ravghani xuk]
large [ларҷ] *adj.* калон [kalon]
laryngitis [леринҷайтас] *n.* ларингит [laringit]
laser [лейзър] *n.* лазер [lazer]
last [лест] *adj.* охирин [oxirin] / *v.i.* кашол ёфтан [kashol yoftan]; **at last** билохира [biloxira]
latch [леч] *n.* ғалақаи дар [ghalaqai dar] / *v.i.* ғалақаи дарро гузарондан [ghalaqai darro guzarondan]
late [лейт] *adj.* дер [der] / *adv.* дер [der], бевақт [bevaqt]
lately [лейтли] *adv.* дар қарибӣ [dar qaribi], ба наздикӣ [ba nazdiki]
lathe [лейд] *n.* дастгоҳи дуредгарӣ [dastgohi duredgari]
lather [ледър] *n.* кафки собун [kafki sobun]
Latin [летин] *n./adj.* лотинӣ [lotini]
Latin American *adj.* Амрикои Лотинӣ [Amrikoi Lotini]
latitude [летитюд] *n.* арз [arz]
latrine [латрин] *n.* халоҷо [xalojo], ҳоҷатхона [hojatxona]
latter [летър] *adj.* *(last, second)* охирин [oxirin], дуюм [duyum]; *(recent)* чанде пеш рӯйдода [chande pesh rüydoda]; *pron.* дуюм [duyum]
laugh [лаф] *n.* ханда [xanda] / *v.i.* хандидан [xandidan], ханда кардан [xanda kardan]
laughter [лефтър] *n.* ханда [xanda]
launch [лонч] *n.* баркас [barkas] / *v.t.* паррондан [parrondan], сар додан [sar dodan], ба кор андохтан [ba kor andoxtan]
laundry [лондри] *n.* ҷомашӯӣ [jomashüi]; **laundry room** ҷомашӯйхона [jomashüyxona]

lavatory [леватори] *n.* ҳоҷатхона [hojatxona]
lavish [левиш] *adj.* кушодадаст [kushodadast], сахӣ [saxi]
law [ло] *n.* қонун [qonun]; **against the law** ғайриқонунӣ [ghayriqonuni]
lawful [лофул] *adj.* қонунӣ [qonuni]
lawn [лон] *n.* чаман [chaman]
lawsuit [лосут] *n.* мурофиа [murofia]
lawyer [лойер] *n.* адвокат [advokat]
laxative [лексатив] *n.* исҳоловар [is-holovar], доруи дарунронӣ [dorui darunroni]
lay [лей] *v.t.* гузоштан [guzoshtan], ниҳодан [nihodan]
layer [лайар] *n.* қабат [qabat]
lazy [лейзи] *adj.* танбал [tanbal]
lead [лед] *n.* сурб [surb] / *v.t. (provide leadership)* роҳбарӣ кардан [rohbari kardan]; *(show the way)* роҳнамоӣ кардан [rohnamoi kardan] / *v.i.* ба пеш будан [ba pesh budan]
leader [лидър] *n.* роҳбар [rohbar]
leadership [лидършип] *n.* роҳбарӣ [rohbari]
leaf [лиф] (*pl.* **leaves** [ливз] барг [barg]) *n.* барг [barg]
leak [лик] *n.* сӯрох [sürox], шикоф [shikof] / *v.t.* рехтан [rextan] / *v.i.* таровида гузаштан [tarovida guzashtan]
lean [лин] *adj.* лоғар [loghar] / *v.t.* такя кунондан [takya kunondan] / *v.i.* такя кардан [takya kardan]
leap [лип] *n.* ҷаҳиш [jahish] / *v.i.* ҷастан [jastan]
leap year [лип йер] *n.* соли кабиса [soli kabisa]
learn [лърн] *v.t.* омӯхтан [omüxtan], ёд гирифтан [yod giriftan] / *v.i.* хабар шудан [xabar shudan], хабардор шудан [xabardor shudan]
learner [лърнър] *n.* омӯзанда [omüzanda]
lease [лис] *n.* иҷора [ijora], киро [kiro] / *v.t.* иҷора кардан [ijora kardan], киро кардан [kiro kardan] / *v.i.* ба иҷора додан [ba ijora dodan]
least [лист] *adj.* камтарин [kamtarin] / *adv.* ҳеҷ [hej], асло [aslo]; **at least** камаш [kamash]
leather [ледър] *n.* чарм [charm]
leave [лив] *v.t. (place, put, allow to remain)* мондан [mondan], гузоштан [guzoshtan]; *(abandon, forsake)* тарк кардан [tark kardan] / *v.i.* равона шудан [ravona shudan], рафтан [raftan]
leaves. *See* **leaf**
lecture [лекчър] *n.* лексия [leksiya]
left [лефт] *adj.* чап [chap] / *adv.* аз чап [az chap]
left-handed [лефт-ҳандид] *adj.* чападаст [chapadast]
leg [лег] *n.* пой [poy], линг [ling]

legal [лигъл] *adj.* қонунӣ [qonuni]
legality [лигалити] *n.* қонунӣ будан [qonuni budan]
legend [леҷанд] *n.* афсона [afsona]
legible [леҷибъл] *adj.* хоно [xono]
legislation [леҷислейшан] *n.* қонунбарорӣ [qonunbarori], қонунгузорӣ [qonunguzori]
legitimate [леҷитамит] *adj.* қонунӣ [qonuni]
leisure [лежър] *n.* фароғат [faroghat], вақти дамгирӣ [vaqti damgiri]
lemon [леман] *n.* лимӯ [limü]
lend [ленд] *v.t.* қарз додан [qarz dodan]
length [ленгт] *n.* дарозӣ [darozi]
lengthen [ленгтън] *v.t.* дарозтар кардан [daroztar kardan]
lens [ленз] *n.* линза [linza]
lentil [лентал] *n.* наск [nask]
leopard [лепард] *n.* паланг [palang]
less [лес] *adj./adv.* камтар [kamtar]
lesson [лесан] *n.* дарс [dars]
let [лет] *v.t.* мондан [mondan], гузоштан [guzoshtan]
letter [летър] *n.* нома [noma], хат [xat]
lettuce [летас] *n.* коҳу [kohu]
level [левъл] *n.* сатҳ [sath], дараҷа [daraja] / *adj.* баробар [barobar]
lever [левар] *n.* фашанг [fashang]
liability [лаябилити] *n.* масъулият [mas'uliyat], ҷавобгарӣ [javobgari]
liable [лаяабъл] *adj.* масъул [mas'ul], ҷавобгар [javobgar]
liar [лаяр] *n.* дуруғгӯй [durughgüy]
libel [лайбъл] *n.* тӯҳмат [tühmat], бӯҳтон [bühton] / *v.t.* тӯҳмат кардан [tühmat kardan], бӯҳтон кардан [bühton kardan]
liberal [либрал] *adj.* бисёр [bisyor], кушодадаст [kushodadast]; *(political)* либералӣ [liberali]
liberty [либърти] *n.* озодӣ [ozodi]
librarian [лайбрериян] *n.* китобдор [kitobdor], корманди китобхона [kormandi kitobxona]
library [лайбрери] *n.* китобхона [kitobxona]
license [лайсанс] *n.* иҷозат [ijozat], рухсат [ruxsat]; **driver's license** иҷозатномаи ронандагӣ [ijozatnomai ronandagi]; **export license** иҷозатномаи содирот [ijozatnomai sodirot]
lick [лик] *v.t.* лесидан [lesidan]
lid [лид] *n.* сарпӯш [sarpüsh]
lie [лай] *n.* дуруғ [durugh] / *v.i.* *(tell a lie)* дуруғ гуфтан [durugh guftan]; *(be at rest)* дароз кашидан [daroz kashidan]
lieutenant [лутенант] *n.* лейтенант [leytenant]
life [лайф] *n.* зиндагӣ [zindagi], ҳаёт [hayot], зиндагонӣ [zindagoni]
lifeless [лайфлес] *adj.* беҷон [bejon], бедам [bedam]

lifetime [лайфтайм] *n.* умр [umr]

lift [лифт] *n. (elevator)* лифт [lift] / *v.t.* баланд кардан [baland kardan], бардоштан [bardoshtan]

light [лайт] *n.* равшанӣ [ravshani], нур [nur] / *adj. (color)* равшан [ravshan]; *(weight)* сабук [sabuk] / *v.t.* даргиронидан [dargirondan], афрӯхтан [afrüxtan]

lighten [лайтън] *v.t. (make brighter)* равшан кардан [ravshan kardan]; *(reduce weight)* сабуктар кардан [sabuktar kardan]

lighthouse [лайтҳаус] *n.* минои баҳрӣ [minoi bahri]

lightning [лайтнинг] *n.* барқ [barq], чароғак [charoghak]

like [лайк] *adj.* монанд [monand] / *adv.* ҳамчун [hamchun], мисли [misli] / *v.t.* дӯст доштан [düst doshtan], нағз дидан [naghz didan]

likely [лайкли] *adv.* эҳтимолӣ [ehtimoli], мумкин [mumkin]

likewise [лайквайз] *adv.* ҳамчунин [hamchunin]

limb [лим] *n.* дасту по [dastu po], узв [uzv], аъзо [a'zo]

lime [лайм] *n. (fruit)* лимӯ [limü]; *(calcium oxide)* оҳак [ohak]

limit [лимит] *n.* ҳад [had]

limp [лимп] *n.* лангӣ [langi], чӯлоқӣ [chüloqi] / *v.i.* лангидан [langidan], лангон-лангон гаштан [langon-langon gashtan]

line [лайн] *n.* хат [xat], рах [rax] / *v.t.* хат кашидан [xat kashidan]

linen [линан] *n.* катон [katon]

lining [лайнинг] *n.* астар [astar], остар [ostar]

link [линк] *n.* банд [band], ҳалқа [halqa] / *v.t.* қисматбандӣ кардан [qismatbandi kardan], пайвастан [payvastan]

lion [лайян] *n.* шер [sher]

lip [лип] *n.* лаб [lab]

liqueur [ликюр] *n.* ликёр [likyor]

liquid [ликуид] *n.* моеъ [moe'], чизи обакӣ [chizi obaki] / *adj.* обакӣ [obaki]

liquor [ликър] *n.* нӯшокии спиртӣ [nüshokii spirti], арақ [araq]

list [лист] *n.* рӯйхат [rüyxat], феҳрист [fehrist] / *v.t.* ба рӯйхат даровардан [ba rüyxat darovardan]

listen [лисен] *v.t.* гӯш кардан [güsh kardan]

listener [лиснар] *n.* шунаванда [shunavanda]

literary [литерери] *adj.* адабӣ [adabi]

literature [литерачус] *n.* адабиёт [adabiyot]

litter *n. (palanquin)* тахти равон [taxti ravon]

little [литал] *n.* кам [kam]; **little by little** кам-кам [kam-kam] / *adj.* майда [mayda]; **a little bit** каме [kame] / *adv.* каме [kame]

live [лайв] *adj.* зинда [zinda]

live [лив] *v.i.* зиндагӣ кардан [zindagi kardan], зистан [zistan]

lively [лайвли] *adj.* зиндадил [zindadil], пурҷӯшухурӯш [purjüshuxurüsh]

liver [ливар] *n.* ҷигар [jigar]
living room [ливинг рум] *n.* меҳмонхона [mehmonxona]
lizard [лизард] *n.* калтакалос [kaltakalos], калпеса [kalpesa]
load [лод] *n.* бор [bor] / *v.t.* бор кардан [bor kardan]
loaf [лоф] *n.* буханка [buxanka]; **loaf of bread** буханкаи нон [buxankai non]
loan [лон] *n.* вом [vom], қарз [qarz] / *v.t.* қарз додан [qarz dodan]
lobby [лоби] *n.* даҳлез [dahlez], хонаи даромад [xonai daromad]
lobster [лобстар] *n.* харчанг [xarchang]
lock [лок] *n.* қуфл [qufl] / *v.t.* қуфл кардан [qufl kardan]
locomotive [локомотив] *n.* локомотив [lokomotiv]
locust [локуст] *n.* малах [malax]
lodge [лоҷ] *n.* қаравулхона [qaravulxona] / *v.i.* иҷора нишастан [ijora nishastan], истиқомат кардан [istiqomat kardan]
lodging [лоҷинг] *n.* истиқоматгоҳ [istiqomatgoh]
loft [лофт] *n.* чердак [cherdak]
log *n.* ғӯлачӯб [ghülachüb]
logic [лоҷик] *n.* мантиқ [mantiq]
logical [лоҷикал] *adj.* мантиқӣ [mantiqi], бомантиқ [bomantiq]
lone [лон] *adj.* якка [yakka], танҳо [tanho], тоқа [toqa]
lonely [лонли] *adj.* якка [yakka], танҳо [tanho], тоқа [toqa]
long [лонг] *adj.* дароз [daroz]; **a long time** бисёр вақт [bisyor vaqt] / *adv.* бисёр вақт [bisyor vaqt], муддати дароз [muddati daroz] / *v.i.* пазмон шудан [pazmon shudan], зор шудан [zor shudan]
longitude [лонҷитюд] *n.* тӯл [tül]
look [лук] *n.* нигоҳ [nigoh] / *v.i. (look at)* нигоҳ кардан [nigoh kardan], нигаристан [nigaristan]; *(look for)* ҷустан [justan]
loom [лум] *n.* дастгоҳи бофандагӣ [dastgohi bofandagi]
loop [луп] *n.* ҳалқа [halqa], гиреҳ [gireh]
loose [лус] *adj.* фаҳул [fahul], кушод [kushod]
loosen [лусан] *v.t.* суст кардан [sust kardan], сусттар кардан [susttar kardan]
lord [лорд] *n.* хоҷа [xoja]
lose [луз] *v.t. (a possession)* гум кардан [gum kardan]; *(metaphorically)* аз даст додан [az dast dodan] / *v.i.* бохтан [boxtan], бой додан [boy dodan]
loss [лос] *n.* гум кардан [gum kardan], аздастдиҳӣ [azdastdihi]; *(business)* зиён [ziyon]
lost [лост] *adj.* гумшуда [gumshuda], гумкарда [gumkarda]
lot [лот] *n. (a lot)* бисёр [bisyor]; *(draw lots)* қуръа *(*партофтан*)* [qur'a *(*partoftan*)*]; *(fortune)* сарнавишт [sarnavisht]
loud [лауд] *adj.* баланд [baland]

loudspeaker [лаудспикър] *n.* карнайи радио [karnayi radio]
love [лав] *n.* ишқ [ishq], муҳаббат [muhabbat] / *v.t./v.i.* дӯст доштан [düst doshtan]
lovely [лавли] *adj.* диловез [dilovez]
lover [лавър] *n.* ошиқ [oshiq]
low [ло] *adj.* паст [past]
loyal [лоял] *adj.* вафодор [vafodor]
luck [лак] *n.* бахт [baxt]; **good luck** хушбахтӣ [xushbaxti]; **bad luck** бадбахтӣ [badbaxti]
luckily [лакили] *adv.* хушбахтона [xushbaxtona]
lucky [лаки] *adj.* хушбахт [xushbaxt]
luggage [лагиҷ] *n.* бағоҷ [baghoj]
lump [ламп] *n.* кулӯхпора [kulüxpora]
lunar [лунар] *adj.* қамарӣ [qamari]
lunatic [лунатик] *n.* девона [devona]
lunch [ланч] *n.* ноништаи дуюм [nonishtai duyum], хӯроки пешин [xüroki peshin]; **to have lunch** *v.* ноништаи дуюм кардан [nonishtai duyum kardan], хӯроки пешин кардан [xüroki peshin kardan]
lung [ланг] *n.* шуш [shush]
luxurious [лагжурияс] *adj.* бошукӯҳ [boshuküh], бокарруфар [bokarrufar]
luxury [лагжъри] *n.* люкс [lyuks]
lye [лай] *n.* ишқороб [ishqorob]

M

machine [машин] *n.* мошин [moshin]
mad [мед] *adj. (insane)* девона [devona]; *(furious)* хашмгин [xashmgin]
madam [медам] *n.* хонум [xonum]
magazine [мегазин] *n.* маҷалла [majalla], журнал [zhurnal]
magic [меҷик] *n.* ҷодугарӣ [jodugari]
magical [меҷикал] *adj.* ҷодугарона [jodugarona]
magician [меҷишан] *n.* ҷодугар [jodugar]
magnet [мегнит] *n.* оҳанрабо [ohanrabo], магнит [magnit]
magnetic [мегнетик] *adj.* магнитнок [magnitnok]
magnificent [мегнифисант] *adj.* бошукӯҳ [boshuküh]
magnify [мегнифай] *v.t.* калон кардан [kalon kardan]
maid [мейд] *n.* хизматгорзан [xizmatgorzan]
mail [мейл] *n.* почта [pochta]
main [мейн] *adj.* асосӣ [asosi]
mainland [мейнланд] *n.* материк [materik]
maintain [мейнтейн] *v.t.* нигоҳ доштан [nigoh doshtan]
maintenance [мейнтенанс] *n.* нигоҳ доштан(и) [nigoh doshtan(i)], тармимӣ [tarmimi]
majestic [маҷестик] *adj.* ҷалил [jalil], боазамат [boazamat]
majesty [меҷести] *n.* ҷалолат [jalolat], азамат [azamat]

major [мейҷър] *n.* майор [mayor] / *adj.* асосӣ [asosi], муҳим [muhim]
majority [маҷорити] *n.* аксарият [aksariyat]
make [мейк] *n.* сохт [soxt] / *v.t.* сохтан [soxtan], тайёр кардан [tayyor kardan]
maker [мейкър] *n.* офаринанда [ofarinanda], эҷодкор [ejodkor]
makeup [мейк-ап] *n.* косметика [kosmetika]
male [мейл] *n. (animal)* нар [nar]; *(human)* мард [mard]
malignant [малигнант] *adj.* бадният [badniyat], бадқасд [badqasd]; *(med.)* зиёнрасон [ziyonrason]
mammal [мемал] *n.* ширхӯр [shirxür]
man [мен] *n.* мард [mard], одам [odam]
manage [менич] *v.t.* идора кардан [idora kardan]
management [меничмант] *n.* идора [idora]
manager [менеҷер] *n.* мудир [mudir]
maneuver [манувър] *v.i.* манёвр кардан [manyovr kardan]
manhood [менҳуд] *n. (being a man)* мардонагӣ [mardonagi]; *(maturity)* балоғат [baloghat]
manifold [менифолд] *n.* гуногун [gunogun], ҳархела [harxela]
manipulate [манипюлейт] *v.t.* кор кардан [kor kardan]; *(tamper with or falsify)* фиребгарӣ кардан [firebgari kardan]
mankind [менкайнд] *n.* башарият [bashariyat]
mannequin [манекин] *n.* манекен [maneken], одамак [odamak]
manner [менер] *n.* тарз [tarz]
mansion [меншан] *n.* кох [kox]
manufacture [менюфекчур] *n.* сохт [soxt] / *v.t.* сохтан [soxtan]
manure [манюр] *n.* пору [poru]
manuscript [менюскрипт] *n.* дастнавис [dastnavis]
many [мени] *adj.* бисёр [bisyor]
map [меп] *n.* харита [xarita]
marathon [мератон] *n.* марафон [marafon]
marble [марбл] *n.* мармар [marmar]
March [марч] *n.* март [mart]
mare [мер] *n.* модиён [modiyon], байтал [baytal]
margarine [марҷарин] *n.* маргарин [margarin]
margin [марҷин] *n.* канор [kanor]
marine [марин] *adj.* баҳрӣ [bahri], дарёӣ [daryoi]
mark [марк] *n.* нишона [nishona], тамға [tamgha]
market [маркет] *n.* бозор [bozor]
marketing [маркетинг] *n.* бозорёбӣ [bozoryobi]
marmalade [мармалейд] *n.* мармалод [marmalod]
maroon [марун] *adj.* дорчинӣ [dorchini], шоҳбулутранг [shohbulutrang]
marriage [мариҷ] *n.* никоҳ [nikoh], издивоҷ [izdivoj]

married [марид] *adj.* хонадор [xonador]; *(married man)* зандор [zandor]; *(married woman)* шавҳардор [shavhardor]
marrow [маро] *n.* *(bone marrow)* мағз [maghz]
marry [мари] *v.t.* издивоҷ кардан [izdivoj kardan]
marsh [марш] *n.* ботлоқ [botloq]
marshal [маршал] *n.* маршал [marshal]
marvelous [марвелас] *adj.* тааҷҷубовар [taajjubovar], аҷоиб [ajoib]
masculine [маскюлин] *adj.* мардона [mardona]; *(gram.)* ҷинси мардона [jinsi mardona]
mash [маш] *v.t.* молида мулоим кардан [molida muloim kardan], фишурда мулоим кардан [fishurda muloim kardan]
mask [маск] *n.* ниқоб [niqob]
mass [мас] *adj.* бисёр [bisyor] / *n.* миқдори бисёр [miqdori bisyor]; *(figurative)* анбӯҳ [anbüh], тӯда [tüda]; *(majority)* аксарият [aksariyat]
massage [масаж] *n.* масҳ [mas-h]
massive [масив] *adj.* бузург [buzurg], калон [kalon]
mast [маст] *n.* сутуни киштӣ [sutuni kishti]
master [мастер] *n.* усто [usto], устод [ustod]; *(owner)* соҳиб [sohib]
mastery [мастери] *n.* устогӣ [ustogi], маҳорат [mahorat]
mat [мат] *n.* бӯрё [büryo]
match [мач] *n.* *(equal, counterpart)* ҷуфт [juft]; *(used to light fire)* гӯгирд [gügird]; *(sports)* бозӣ [bozi]; **soccer match** бозии футбол [bozii futbol]
mate [мейт] *n.* *(spouse)* ҳамсар [hamsar]; *(buddy)* рафиқ [rafiq]
material [матириял] *n.* *(cloth)* матоъ [mato'], газвор [gazvor]; **raw material** моли хом [moli xom]
mathematics [математикс] *n.* математика [matematika]
matter *n.* *(substance)* модда [modda]; *(subject)* мавзӯъ [mavzü']; **What's the matter?** Чӣ шудааст? [Chi shudaast?]
mattress [матрес] *n.* бистар [bistar]
mature [мачур] *adj.* болиғ [boligh]
maturity [мачурити] *n.* балоғат [baloghat]
maximum [максимам] *n.* миқдори зиёдтарин [miqdori ziyodtarin] / *adj.* *(biggest)* калонтарин [kalontarin]; *(most)* бештарин [beshtarin]
may [мей] *verbal aux.* мумкин аст [mumkin ast]
May [мей] *n.* май [may]
maybe [мейби] *adv.* шояд [shoyad]
mayonnaise [мейонейз] *n.* майонез [mayonez]
mayor [мейяр] *n.* мир [mir], ҳоким [hokim]
maze [мейз] *n.* (ҷои) пурпечухамӣ [(joi) purpechuxami]

me [ми] *pron.* ман [man], маро [maro]
meadow [медо] *n.* марғзор [marghzor]
meager [мигъp] *adj.* кам [kam], нокифоя [nokifoya]
meal [мил] *n.* хӯрок [xürok], тановул [tanovul]
mean [мин] *n.* миёна [miyona] / *adj.* паст [past]
meaning [мининг] *n.* маъно [ma'no], маънӣ [ma'ni]
means [минз] *n.* восита [vosita], василa [vasila], чора [chora]
meantime [минтайм] *n.* фосила [fosila] / *adv. (in the meantime, meanwhile)* дар зимни он [dar zimni on]
measure [межур] *n.* чен [chen]; *v.t.* чен кардан [chen kardan]
meat [мит] *n.* гӯшт [güsht]
mechanic [механик] *n.* механик [mexanik]
medal [медал] *n.* медал [medal]
medical [медикал] *adj.* тиббӣ [tibbi]
medicine [медисин *n.* *(medication)* дору [doru]; *(the science of medicine)* пизишкӣ [pizishki], тиб [tib]
medium [мидиям] *n.* миёна [miyona]; *(means)* восита [vosita] / *adj.* миён [miyon], мобайн [mobayn]
meet [мит] *v.t.* вохӯрдан [voxürdan], мулоқот кардан [muloqot kardan] / *v.i. (come together)* ҷамъ шудан [jam' shudan], якҷоя шудан [yakjoya shudan]; *(be introduced)* шинос шудан [shinos shudan]
meeting [митинг] *n.* вохӯрӣ [voxüri], мулоқот [muloqot]
melon [мелан] *n.* харбуза [xarbuza]
melt [мелт] *v.t.* гудохтан [gudoxtan], об кардан [ob kardan] / *v.i.* об шудан [ob shudan]
member [мембър] *n.* узв [uzv]
membrane [мембрейн] *n.* мембрана [membrana]
memoir [мемуар] *n.* ёддоштҳо [yoddoshtho], хотираҳо [xotiraho]
memorize [меморайз] *v.t.* аз ёд кардан [az yod kardan], аз бар кардан [az bar kardan]
memory [мемури] *n.* ёд [yod]; *(reminiscence)* хотира [xotira], ёддошт [yoddosht]
menace [менис] *n.* дӯғ [dügh], пӯписа [püpisa], таҳдид [tahdid]
mend [менд] *v.t.* ислоҳ кардан [isloh kardan], дуруст кардан [durust kardan]
men's room [менз рум] *n.* ҳоҷатхонаи мардона [hojatxonai mardona]
mental [ментал] *adj.* фикрӣ [fikri]
mention [меншан] *n.* номбар [nombar], зикр [zikr] / *v.t.* ном бурдан [nom burdan], зикр кардан [zikr kardan]
menu [меню] *n.* меню [menyu], номгӯи хӯрокҳо [nomgüi xürokho]
merchandise [мерчандайз] *n.* мол [mol]
merchant [мерчант] *n.* савдогар [savdogar], тоҷир [tojir]
merciful [мерсифул] *adj.* раҳмдил [rahmdil], меҳрубон [mehrubon]

merciless [мерсилес] *adj.* берахм [berahm], сангдил [sangdil]
mercy [мерси] *n.* меҳрубонӣ [mehruboni], раҳм [rahm], раҳмдилӣ [rahmdili]
merely [мирли] *adv.* танҳо [tanho], фақат [faqat]
merit [мерит] *n.* бартарӣ [bartari], сифат [sifat]
merry [мери] *adj.* шод [shod], фархунда [farxunda]
mesh [меш] *n.* тӯр [tür]
mess [мес] *n.* бетартибӣ [betartibi]
message [месич] *n.* пайғом [payghom], паём [payom]
messenger [месинчар] *n.* хабаррасон [xabarrason], қосид [qosid], пайк [payk]
metal [метал] *n.* фулуз [fuluz], металл [metall]
meter [митар] *n.* метр [metr]
method [метад] *n.* равиш [ravish], тарз [tarz]
methodical [методикал] *adj.* мунтазам [muntazam], мураттаб [murattab]
Mexican [мексикан] *n./adj.* мексикоӣ [meksikoi]
microphone [майкрофон] *n.* микрофон [mikrofon]
microscope [майкроскоп] *n.* заррабин [zarrabin], микроскоп [mikroskop]
mid [мид] *adj.* ним [nim], миёна [miyona]
midday [мид-дей] *n.* нимрӯз [nimrüz], нисфирӯз [nisfirüz]
middle *adj.* миёнҷой [miyonjoy], миёна [miyona], васат [vasat]
Middle Ages асрҳои миёна [asrhoi miyona]
middle-aged [мидал ейҷиз] *adj.* миёнсол [miyonsol]
midnight [миднайт] *n.* нимишаб [nimishab], нисфишаб [nisfishab]
midwife [мидуайф] *n.* момодоя [momodoya], доя [doya]
might [майт] *verbal aux.* шояд [shoyad]
migrate [майгрейт] *v.i.* кӯчидан [küchidan]
mild [майлд] *adj.* муътадил [mu'tadil]
mile [майл] *n.* мил [mil]
militant [милитант] *adj.* ҷангҷӯй [jangjüy]
military [милитери] *n.* лашкар [lashkar], қӯшун [qüshun], артиш [artish]
milk [милк] *n.* шир [shir]
mill [мил] *n.* осиёб [osiyob], осиё [osiyo]; *(factory)* фабрика [fabrika], завод [zavod]
miller [милар] *n.* осиёбон [osiyobon]
millimeter [милимитар] *n.* миллиметр [millimetr]
million [милян] *n.* миллион [million]
mind [майнд] *n.* фикр [fikr], зеҳн [zehn], хирад [xirad] / *v.t. (remember, keep in mind)* дар ёд доштан [dar yod doshtan]; *(dislike)* ҳисси ногувор кардан [hissi noguvor kardan]
mindful [майндфул] *adj.* бодиққат [bodiqqat]
mindless [майндлес] *adj.* бемаънӣ [bema'ni]
mine [майн] *n.* кон [kon] / *pron.* аз они ман [az oni man], -и ман [-i man]

mingle [мингъл] *v.i.* омехта шудан [omexta shudan], аралашкарда шудан [aralashkarda shudan]
minimum [минимам] *n.* миқдори камтарин [miqdori kamtarin]
mining [майнинг] *n.* конканӣ [konkani]
minister [министер] *n.* вазир [vazir]
ministry [министри] *n.* вазорат [vazorat]
minor [майнар] *n.* хурдсол [xurdsol] / *adj.* хурд [xurd], ночиз [nochiz]
minority [майнорити] *n.* ақаллият [aqalliyat]
mint [минт] *n.* пудина [pudina]
minus [майнас] *prep.* тарҳ [tarh], минус [minus]
minute [минит] *n.* дақиқа [daqiqa]
minute [мийнют] *adj.* майда [mayda], реза [reza]
miracle [ммиракл] *n.* мӯъҷиза [mü'jiza]
miraculous [миракюлас] *adj.* мӯъҷизакорона [mü'jizakorona]
mirage [мираж] *n.* сароб [sarob]
mire [майр] *n.* лой [loy]
mirror [мирор] *n.* оина [oina]
misadventure [мисадвенчур] *n.* бадбахтӣ [badbaxti]
mischief [мисчиф] *n.* шӯхӣ [shüxi]
misdeed [мисдид] *n.* бадкирдорӣ [badkirdori]
miser [майзър] *n.* хасис [xasis]
misery [мизари] *n.* азоб [azob], бенавоӣ [benavoi], бечорагӣ [bechoragi]
misfortune [мисфорчун] *n.* бадбахтӣ [badbaxti]
mislay [мислей] *v.t.* дар ҷои фаромӯшшуданӣ гзоштан [dar joi faromüshshudani guzoshtan]
misplace [мисплейс] *v.t.* дар ҷои фаромӯшшуданӣ гузоштан [dar joi faromüshshudani guzoshtan]
Miss [мис] *n.* хонумдухтар [xonumduxtar]
miss [мис] *n.* хато [xato] / *v.t.* хато кардан [xato kardan]; *(miss sb)* (касеро) пазмон шудан (kasero) pazmon shudan
missile [мисайл] *n.* мушак [mushak], ракета [raketa]
mission [мишан] *n.* супориш [suporish]; *(diplomatic)* сафорат [saforat]
mist [мист] *n.* туман [tuman]
mistake [мистейк] *n.* хато [xato], иштибоҳ [ishtiboh] / *v.t.* хато кардан [xato kardan], иштибоҳ кардан [ishtiboh kardan]
mistaken [мистейкан] *adj.* бархато [barxato], ғалат [ghalat]
mister (Mr.) [мистар] *n.* ҷаноб [janob], оқо [oqo]
mistress [мистрас] *n. (head of household)* кадбону [kadbonu]
mistrust [мистраст] *v.t.* бовар накардан [bovar nakardan], шубҳа кардан [shubha kardan]
misunderstanding [мисандарстандинг] *n.* ғалатфаҳмӣ [ghalatfahmi], каҷфаҳмӣ [kajfahmi]

mix [микс] *n.* хелҳо [xelho], хелҳои мол [xelhoi mol], ассортимент [assortiment] / *v.t.* омехтан [omextan], аралаш кардан [aralash kardan]
mixture [миксчар] *n.* омезиш [omezish], аралаш [aralash]
moan [мон] *n.* нола [nola], фиғон [fighon]
mode [мод] *n.* тариқа [tariqa], тарз [tarz]
model [модел] *n.* намуна [namuna], тамсила [tamsila]
modem [модем] *n.* модем [modem]
modification [модификейшан] *n.* тағйирёбӣ [taghyiryobi], дигаргуншавӣ [digargunshavi]
modify [модифай] *v.t.* тағйир додан [taghyir dodan], дигаргун кардан [digargun kardan]
modular [модюлар] *adj.* модулӣ [moduli]
module [модюл] *n.* модул [modul]
moist [мойст] *adj.* нам [nam], тар [tar]
moisten [мойсан] *v.t.* нам кардан [nam kardan], тар кардан [tar kardan]
moisture [мойсчар] *n.* намӣ [nami], тарӣ [tari]
mold [молд] *n.* қолиб [qolib], нусха [nusxa]; *(fungus)* пӯпанак [püpanak] / *v.t.* аз рӯи қолиб сохтан [az rüi qolib soxtan], аз рӯи нусха кор кардан [az rüi nusxa kor kardan]
mom(my) [мом*(и)*] *n.* нана [nana], она [ona], оча [ocha]
moment [момент] *n.* лаҳза [lahza], дам [dam]
monarch [монарк] *n.* подшоҳ [podshoh]
monarchy [монарки] *n.* ҳукумати подшоҳӣ [hukumati podshohi]
monastery [монастери] *n.* дайр [dayr]
Monday [мандей] *n.* душанбе [dushanbe]
money [мани] *n.* пул [pul]
monitor [монитор] *n.* *(computer)* сафҳаи намоиш [safhai namoish]
monk [манки] *n.* роҳиб [rohib]
monkey [манки] *n.* маймун [maymun], бӯзина [büzina]
monopoly [монополи] *n.* монополия [monopoliya], инҳисор [inhisor]
monotonous [монотанас] *adj.* якоҳанг [yakohang], якранга [yakranga]
monster [монстар] *n.* дев [dev], аждар [azhdar]
monstrous [монстрас] *adj.* *(terrifying)* даҳшатангез [dahshatangez]; *(huge)* бузург [buzurg]
month [мант] *n.* моҳ [moh]
mood [муд] *n.* ҳолат [holat], димоғ [dimogh]
moon [мун] *n.* моҳ [moh]; **full moon** моҳи пурра [mohi purra]
moonlight [мунлайт] *n.* моҳтоб [mohtob]
mop [моп] *n.* пайкора [paykora] / *v.t.* бо пайкора шустан [bo paykora shustan]
moral [морал] *n.* ахлоқ [axloq]

more [мор] *adj./adv.* беш [besh], бештар [beshtar] / *adv.* боз [boz]
moreover [моровар] *adv.* илова бар [ilova bar]
morning [морнинг] *n.* пагоҳӣ [pagohi], бомдод [bomdod], субҳ [subh]
mortar [мортар] *n. (building material)* оҳак [ohak]; *(mil.)* мортира [mortira]; *(kitchen vessel)* ҳован [hovan]
mortgage [моргич] *n.* гарав [garav]
mosque [моск] *n.* масҷид [masjid]
mosquito [мускито] *n.* хомӯшак [xomüshak]
most [мост] *adj.* бештарин [beshtarin], аксарият [aksariyat] / *adv.* бештарин [beshtarin]
moth [мот] *n.* шабпарак [shabparak], парвона [parvona]; *(clothes moth)* куя [kuya]
mother [мадер] *n.* модар [modar]
mother-in-law [мадер-ин-ло] *n.* хушдоман [xushdoman]
motion [мошан] *n.* ҳаракат [harakat], ҷунбиш [junbish]
motivate [мотивейт] *v.t.* далел овардан [dalel ovardan], ҳавасманд кардан [havasmand kardan]
motivation [мотивейшан] *n.* далел [dalel], сабаб [sabab]
motive [мотив] *n.* далел [dalel]
motor [мотор] *n.* мотор [motor], муҳаррик [muharrik]
motorcycle [моторсайкл] *n.* мотосикл [motosikl]
mount *v.t. (get on)* савор кардан [savor kardan]; *(put up)* баланд кардан [baland kardan] / *v.i.* боло рафтан [bolo raftan], савор шудан [savor shudan]
mountain [маунтан] *n.* кӯҳ [küh]; **mountain climbing** кӯҳнавардӣ [kühnavardi]; **mountain climber** кӯҳнавард [kühnavard]
mourn [морн] *v.t.* сӯгворӣ кардан [sügvori kardan], азодорӣ кардан [azodori kardan]
mourning [морнинг] *n.* сӯгворӣ [sügvori], азодорӣ [azodori]
mouse [маус] *n.* муш [mush]
mouth [маут] *n.* даҳон [dahon], даҳан [dahan]
mouthpiece [маутпис] *n. (mus.)* лабгир [labgir]
move [мув] *v.t.* ҷунбондан [junbondan], ғеҷондан [ghejondan]; *(to a new house, country)* кӯчондан [küchondan] / *v.i.* ҷунбидан [junbidan], ҳаракат кардан [harakat kardan]; *(to a new house, country)* кӯчидан [küchidan]
movement [мувмант] *n.* ҷунбиш [junbish], ҳаракат [harakat]
movie [муви] *n.* синамо [sinamo]
moving [мувинг] *adj.* ҷунбанда [junbanda], ҳаракатдиҳанда [harakatdihanda]
Mrs. [мисиз] *n.* хонум [xonum]
much [мач] *adj./adv.* бисёр [bisyor], хеле [xele]

mud [мад] *n.* лой [loy], гил [gil]
muffle [мафъл] *v.t.* пахш кардан [paxsh kardan], хомӯш кардан [xomüsh kardan]
muffler [мафлър] *n.* *(scarf)* рӯймоли гарданпеч [rüymoli gardanpech]; *(mechanical part)* садонишонак [sadonishonak]
mug [маг] *n.* қадаҳи дастадор [qadahi dastador], кружка [kruzhka]
multiplication [малтипликейшан] *n.* зарбзанӣ [zarbzani]
multiply [малтиплай] *v.t.* афзоёндан [afzoyondan], зиёд кардан [ziyod kardan]; *(mathematics)* зарб задан [zarb zadan]
municipality [мюнисипалити] *n.* мунисипалитет [munisipalitet]
murder [мурдер] *n.* қатл [qatl], куштор [kushtor] / *v.t.* куштан [kushtan], қатл кардан [qatl kardan]
murderer [мърдеръп] *n.* қотил [qotil], одамкуш [odamkush]
muscle [масъл] *n.* мушак [mushak]
muscular [маскюлър] *adj.* сермушак [sermushak]
museum [мюзиям] *n.* музей [muzey], осорхона [osorxona]
mushroom [машрум] *n.* занбӯруғ [zanbürugh], қорч [qorch]
music [мюзик] *n.* мусиқӣ [musiqi]
musician [мюзишан] *n.* навозанда [navozanda]
Muslim [муслим] *n.* мусалмон [musalmon] / *adj.* мусалмонӣ [musalmoni]
mussel [масъл] *n.* мидия [midiya]
must [маст] *verbal aux.* бояд [boyad]
mustache [масташ] *n.* мӯйлаб [müylab], бурут [burut]
mustard [мастард] *n.* хардал [xardal]
mute [мют] *adj.* гунг [gung], лол [lol]
mutiny [мютини] *n.* исён [isyon]
mutton [матън] *n.* гӯшти гӯсфанд [güshti güsfand]
mutual [мючуал] *adj.* дутарафа [dutarafa]
muzzle [мазъл] *n.* *(snout)* фук [fuk], пӯз [püz]; *(device)* пӯзбанд [püzband]
my [май] *adj.* аз они ман [az oni man], -и ман [-i man], -ам [-am]
myself [майселф] *pron.* худам [xudam]
mystery [мистри] *n.* роз [roz], сир [sir]
myth [мит] *n.* афсона [afsona]
mythology [митолоҷи] *n.* афсонашиносӣ [afsonashinosi]

N

nail [нейл] *n.* *(fastener)* мех [mex]; *(anat.)* нохун [noxun] / *v.t.* мех задан [mex zadan]
naive [найив] *adj.* содда [sodda], соддадил [soddadil]

naked [нейкид] *adj.* луч [luch], бараҳна [barahna]
name [нейм] *n.* ном [nom]; **first name** ном [nom]; **last name** насаб [nasab], фамилия [familiya] / *v.t.* номидан [nomidan]
namely [неймли] *adv.* махсусан [maxsusan]
nanny [нени] *n.* доя [doya], бачабардор [bachabardor], парастор [parastor]
nap [неп] *n.* пинак [pinak], ғанаб [ghanab] / *v.i.* пинак кардан [pinak kardan], ғанаб кардан [ghanab kardan]
napkin [непкин] *n.* сачоқ [sachoq]
narcotic [наркотик] *n.* нашъа [nash'a] / *adj.* нашъадор [nash'ador]
narrate [нерейт] *v.t.* нақл кардан [naql kardan]
narrator [нерейтор] *n.* ноқил [noqil]
narrow [неро] *adj.* танг [tang]
narrow-minded [неро-майндед] *adj.* тангназар [tangnazar]
nasty [нести] *adj.* чиркин [chirkin], ганда [ganda]
nation [нейшан] *n.* миллат [millat], кишвар [kishvar]
national [нешънал] *n.* шаҳрванд [shahrvand] / *adj.* миллӣ [milli], давлатӣ [davlati]
nationality [нешъналити] *n.* миллат [millat], миллият [milliyat]
nationwide [нейшануайд] *adj.* дар тамоми кишвар [dar tamomi kishvar]
native [нейтив] *n. (man)* одами маҳаллӣ [odami mahalli]; *(woman)* зани маҳаллӣ [zani mahalli] / *adj.* бумӣ [bumi], маҳаллӣ [mahalli]; *(land)* ватан [vatan], майҳан [mayhan]; *(language)* забони модарӣ [zaboni modari]
natural [нечърал] *adj.* табиӣ [tabii]
naturally [нечърали] *adv.* табиатан [tabiatan]
naughty [ноти] *adj.* шӯх [shüx]
nausea [нозия] *n.* дилбеҷошавӣ [dilbejoshavi]
nauseated [нозиейтед] *adj.* дилбеҷо [dilbejo]
nauseating [нозиейтинг] *adj.* қайовар [qayovar], дилбеҷокунанда [dilbejokunanda]
nauseous [ношас] *adj.* қайовар [qayovar], дилбеҷокунанда [dilbejokunanda]
naval [нейвал] *adj.* баҳрӣ [bahri], дарёӣ [daryoi]
navel [нейвал] *n.* ноф [nof]
navigate [невигейт] *v.t.* киштиронӣ кардан [kishtironi kardan]
navigation [невигейшан] *n.* киштиронӣ [kishtironi]
navy [нейви] *n.* флоти ҳарбӣ [floti harbi]
near [нир] *adj./adv.* наздик [nazdik]
nearby [нирбай] *adj.* наздик [nazdik] / *adv.* аз паҳлӯи [az pahlüi]
nearly [нирли] *adv.* наздики [nazdiki], тақрибан [taqriban]

nearsighted [нирсайтид] *adj.* наздикбин [nazdikbin]
neat [нит] *adj.* покиза [pokiza], мунтазам [muntazam]
necessary [несесери] *adj.* даркорӣ [darkori], лозим [lozim], зарурӣ [zaruri]
necessity [несесити] *n.* зарурат [zarurat], эҳтиёҷ [ehtiyoj]
neck [нек] *n.* гардан [gardan]
necklace [неклас] *n.* гарданбанд [gardanband]
necktie [нектай] *n.* галстук [galstuk]
need [нид] *n.* ниёз [niyoz], ҳоҷат [hojat] / *v.t.* ниёз доштан [niyoz doshtan], ҳоҷат доштан [hojat doshtan]
needle [нидал] *n.* сӯзан [süzan]
needless [нидлас] *adj.* нодаркор [nodarkor], беҳуда [behuda]
negation [нигейшан] *n.* инкор кардан(и) [inkor kardan(i)], рад кардан(и) [rad kardan(i)]
negative [негатив] *n.* *(photographic)* негатив [negativ] / *adj.* манфӣ [manfi]
neglect [неглект] *v.t.* бенигоҳубин мондан [benigohubin mondan]
negotiate [нигошиейт] *v.i.* музикирот кардан [muzokirot kardan], гуфтушунид кардан [guftushunid kardan]
negotiation [нигошиейшан] *n.* гуфтушунид [guftushunid], музокира [muzokira]
neighbor [нейбър] *n.* ҳамсоя [hamsoya]
neighborhood [нейбърҳуд] *n.* маҳалла [mahalla]
neither [найдар] *adj.* ҳеҷ як [hej yak], ҳеҷ кадом [hej kadom] / *pron.* ҳеҷ кадом [hej kadom] / *conj.* на [na]; **neither ... nor ...** на ... на ... [na ... na ...]; **neither this nor that** на ину на он [na inu na on]
nephew [нефю] *n.* ҷиян [jiyan]; *(brother's son)* бародарзода [barodarzoda]; *(sister's son)* хоҳарзода [xoharzoda]
nerve [нерв] *n.* асаб [asab]
nervous [нервас] *adj.* асабӣ [asabi], асабонӣ [asaboni]
nest [нест] *n.* лона [lona], ошёна [oshyona] / *v.i.* лона сохтан [lona soxtan], ошёна сохтан [oshyona soxtan]
net [нет] *n.* тӯр [tür] / *adj.* холис [xolis]; **net weight** вазни холис [vazni xolis] / *v.t.* бо тӯр гирифтан [bo tür giriftan]
network [нетвурк] *n.* шабака [shabaka]
neural [нюрал] *adj.* асабӣ [asabi]
neuralgia [нюралҷия] *n.* асабдард [asabdard], невралгия [nevralgiya]
neurologist [нюролоҷист] *n.* невропатолог [nevropatolog]
neurotic [нюротик] *adj.* неврозӣ [nevrozi]
neuter [нютар] *adj.* беҷинс [bejins]
neutral [нютрал] *adj.* бетараф [betaraf]

neutrality [нютралити] *n.* бетарафӣ [betarafi]
never [невар] *adv.* ҳаргиз [hargiz], ҳеҷ гоҳ [hej goh]
new [ню] *adj.* нав [nav]
newborn [нюборн] *n./adj.* навзод [navzod]
news [нюз] *n.* навигарӣ [navigari], хабар [xabar]; **good news** мужда [muzhda]
newspaper [нюзпепар] *n.* рӯзнома [rüznoma]
newsstand [нюзстанд] *n.* дӯконча [dükoncha], дӯкончаи рӯзнома [dükonchai rüznoma]
New Year [ню йир] *n.* Соли нав [soli nav]; **New Year's Eve** арафаи Соли нав [arafai Soli nav]
next [некст] *adj.* оянда [oyanda], дигар [digar] / *adv.* сипас [sipas], пас [pas], баъд [ba'd]; **next to** паҳлӯи [pahlüi]
nice [найс] *adj.* нағз [naghz]
niche [ниш] *n.* тоқча [toqcha]
nickel [никъл] *n. (metal)* никел [nikel]
nickname [никнейм] *n.* лақаб [laqab]
niece [нис] *n.* ҷиян [jiyan]; *(brother's daughter)* духтари бародар [duxtari barodar]; *(sister's daughter)* духтари хоҳар [duxtari xohar]
night [найт] *n.* шаб [shab]
nightclub [найтклаб] *n.* дискотека [diskoteka]
nightmare [найтмер] *n.* сиёҳӣ [siyohi], хоби даҳшатовар [xobi dahshatovar]
nimble [нимбъл] *adj.* чобук [chobuk], чаққон [chaqqon]
nine [найн] *num.* нӯҳ [nüh]
nineteen [найнтин] *num.* нӯздаҳ [nüzdah]
nineteenth [найнтинт] *adj.* нӯздаҳум [nüzdahum]
ninety [найнти] *num.* навад [navad]
ninth [найнт] *adj.* нӯҳум [nühum]
nitrogen [найтроҷин] *n.* азот [azot], нитроген [nitrogen]
no [но] *adj.* ҳеҷ [hej] / *adv.* не [ne]; *(opp. of yes)* не [ne]
noble [ноъл] *n.* ашроф [ashrof], асилзода [asilzoda] / *adj.* бошараф [bosharaf]
nobody [нободи] *pron.* ҳеҷ кас [hej kas]
noise [нойз] *n.* ғавғо [ghavgho], шавшув [shavshuv]
noisy [нойзи] *adj.* серғавғо [serghavgho], сершавшув [sershavshuv]
nomad [номад] *n.* чодарнишин [chodarnishin]
nominate [номинейт] *v.t.* таъйин кардан [ta'yin kardan]
nomination [номинейшан] *n.* таъйин кардан(и) [ta'yin kardan(i)]
none [нан] *pron.* ҳеҷ кадом [hej kadom], ҳеҷ [hej]
nonsense [нонсенс] *n.* ҳарза [harza], ёва [yova]
noodle [нудал] *n.* угро [ugro]
noon [нун] *n.* нимрӯз [nimrüz], пешин [peshin]
no one [но ван] *pron.* ҳеҷ кас [hej kas]
nor [нор] *conj.* на [na]
normal [нормал] *adj.* оддӣ [oddi]
normality [нормалити] *n.* ҳолати оддӣ [holati oddi]

normally [нормали] *adv.* одатан [odatan], маъмулан [ma'mulan]
north [норт] *n.* шимол [shimol] / *adj.* шимолӣ [shimoli]
northeast [нортист] *n.* шимолу шарқ [shimolu sharq] / *adj.* шимолу шарқӣ [shimoly sharqi]
northern [нордерн] *adj.* шимолӣ [shimoli]
northwest [нортуест] *n.* шимолу ғарб [shimolu gharb] / *adj.* шимолу ғарбӣ [shimolu gharbi]
nose [ноз] *n.* бинӣ [bini]
nostril [нострал] *n.* сӯрохи бинӣ [süroxi bini]
not [нот] *adv.* не [ne]
notarize [нотарайз] *v.t.* тасдиқ кардан [tasdiq kardan]
note [нот] *n.* аломат [alomat], нишона [nishona]; *(short letter)* хатча [xatcha]; *(mus.)* нота [nota] / *v.t.* дар ёд доштан [dar yod doshtan], дида мондан [dida mondan]
notebook [нотбук] *n.* дафтар [daftar]
nothing [натинг] *pron.* ҳеҷ [hej]
notice [нотис] *n.* *(sign)* аломат [alomat]; *(attention)* таваҷҷӯҳ [tavajjüh] / *v.t.* дар ёд доштан [dar yod doshtan], дида мондан [dida mondan]
noticeable [нотисабъл] *adj.* намоён [namoyon], ошкор [oshkor]
notification [нотификейшан] *n.* огоҳинома [ogohinoma], хабарнома [xabarnoma]
notify [нотифай] *v.t.* огоҳонидан [ogohonidan], хабар додан [xabar dodan]
notion [ношан] *n.* ақида [aqida]
noun [наун] *gram.* исм [ism]
nourish [нуриш] *v.t.* *(feed)* хӯрондан [xürondan]; *(keep alive/take care of)* парвардан [parvardan]
nourishing [нуришинг] *adj.* хӯрокдиҳанда [xürokdihanda]
nourishment [нуришмант] *n.* хӯрокдиҳӣ [xürokdihi], хӯрок [xürok]
novel [новал] *n.* роман [roman], китоби бадеӣ [kitobi badei] / *adj.* нав [nav], навбаромад [navbaromad]
novelty [новалти] *n.* *(newness)* навӣ [navi], *(something new)* чизи нав [chizi nav]
November [новембар] *n.* ноябр [noyabr]
now [нау] *adv.* акнун [aknun], ҳоло [holo]; **up to now** то ҳоло [to holo]
nowhere [новер] *adv.* ҳеҷ ҷо [hej jo]
noxious [нокшас] *adj.* осебнок [osebnok], зарарнок [zararnok]
nozzle [нозъл] *n.* ҷумак [jumak]
nuance [нуанс] *n.* оҳанг [ohang]
nuclear [нуклияр] *adj.* ядроӣ [yadroi], ҳастаӣ [hastai]
nucleus [нуклияс] *n.* ядро [yadro], ҳаста [hasta]
nude [нюд] *adj.* луч [luch], бараҳна [barahna]
nudity [нюдити] *n.* бараҳнагӣ [barahnagi]

nuisance [нюсанс] *n.* заҳмат [zahmat]
null [нал] *adj.* лағв [laghv], бекор [bekor]
nullify [налифай] *v.t.* лағв кардан [laghv kardan], бекор кардан [bekor kardan]
numb [нам] *adj.* карахт [karaxt], беҳис [behis]
number [намбър] *n.* шумора [shumora], рақам [raqam]
numerous [нюмерас] *adj.* сершумор [sershumor], бисёр [bisyor]
nun [нан] *n.* роҳиба [rohiba]
nurse [нурс] *n. (med.)* ҳамшираи тиббӣ [hamshirai tibbi]; *(nanny/ wet nurse)* доя [doya] / *v.t. (give milk)* маккондан [makkondan], шир додан [shir dodan]; *(take care of)* парвардан [parvardan]
nursery [нурсери] *n.* хонаи кӯдакон [xonai küdakon]; *(agricultural/ horticultural)* парвардахона [parvardaxona], ниҳолхона [niholxona]
nut [нат] *n.* мағз [maghz]
nutrition [нутришан] *n.* хӯрокдиҳӣ [xürokdihi]
nutritious [нутришас] *adj.* хӯрокдиҳанда [xürokdihanda]

O

oak [ок] *n.* булут [bulut]
oar [ор] *n.* бели қаиқ [beli qaiq]
oat [от] *n.* ҷави русӣ [javi rusi]
oath [от] *n.* савганд [savgand], қасам [qasam]
oatmeal [отмил] *n.* шӯлаи ҷави русӣ [shülai javi rusi]
obedience [обидиянс] *n.* фармонбардорӣ [farmonbardori]
obedient [обидиянт] *adj.* фармонбардор [farmonbardor]
obey [обей] *v.t.* фармонбардорӣ кардан [farmonbardori kardan]
object [обҷект] *n. (thing)* чиз [chiz]; *(goal)* нишон [nishon], ҳадаф [hadaf]; *(gram.)* пуркунанда [purkunanda] / *v.t.* эътироз кардан [e'tiroz kardan]
objection [обҷекшан] *n.* еътироз [e'tiroz]
objective [обҷектив] *adj.* беғараз [begharaz], бетараф [betaraf]; *(goal)* нишон [nishon], ҳадаф [hadaf]
obligation [облигейшан] *n.* вазифа [vazifa]
oblige [облайҷ] *v.t.* водор намудан [vodor kardan], маҷбур кардан [majbur kardan]
oblong [облонг] *n.* чизи дарозрӯя [chizi darozrüya] / *adj.* дарозрӯя [darozrüya]
obscene [обсин] *adj.* бешарм [besharm], беодоб [beodob]
obscure [обскюр] *adj.* тира [tira], мубҳам [mubham] / *v.t.* тира кардан [tira kardan], мубҳам кардан [mubham kardan]
observation [обзервейшан] *n.* назорат [nazorat], дидбонӣ [didboni]
observatory [обзерватори] *n.* расадхона [rasadxona]

observe [обзерв] *v.t.* тамошо кардан [tamosho kardan]
obstacle [обстикал] *n.* монеа [monea]
obstetrician [обстетришан] *n.* акушер [akusher], духтури занҳо [duxturi zanho]
obstinate [обстинат] *adj.* якрав [yakrav]
obstruct [обстракт] *v.t.* душвор кардан [dushvor kardan], банд кардан [band kardan]
obstruction [обстракшан] *n.* сад [sad], душворӣ [dushvori]
obtain [обтейн] *v.t.* пайдо кардан [paydo kardan], ба даст даровардан [ba dast darovardan]
obtainable [обтейнабал] *adj.* пайдокунӣ [paydokuni], бадастдарорӣ [badastdarori]
obvious [обвияс] *adj.* ошкор [oshkor]
occasion [окейжан] *n.* мавқеъ [mavqe'], маврид [mavrid]
occasional [окейжанал] *adj.* гоҳ-гоҳ [goh-goh]
occasionally [окейжанали] *adv.* гоҳ-гоҳӣ [goh-gohi]
occult [окалт] *adj.* пинҳонӣ [pinhoni]
occupation [окюпейшан] *n. (mil.)* ишғол [ishghol]; *(profession)* касб [kasb]
occupied [окюпайд] *adj. (busy)* машғул [mashghul]; *(under mil. occupation)* ишғол кардашуда [ishghol kardashuda]
occupy [окюпай] *v.t.* машғул кардан [mashghul kardan]; *(mil.)* ишғол кардан [ishghol kardan]
occur [окур] *v.i.* рӯй додан [rüy dodan], воқеъ шудан [voqe' shudan]
occurrence [окуранс] *n.* рӯйдод [rüydod], воқеа [voqea]
ocean [ошан] *n.* уқёнус [uqyonus]
o'clock [оъклок] *adv.* соати [soati]; **nine o'clock** соати нӯҳ [soati nüh]
October [остобар] *n.* октябр [oktyabr]
octopus [октопус] *n.* ҳаштпо [hashtpo]
odd [од] *adj. (strange)* аҷиб [ajib], ғариб [gharib]; *(not even)* тоқ [toq]
oddity [одити] *n.* чизи аҷиб [chizi ajib], чизи ғариб [chizi gharib]
odor [одор] *n.* бӯй [büy]
odorless [одорлес] *adj.* бебӯй [bebüy]
of [ов] *prep.* аз [az]
off [оф] *adv.* ба як сӯ [ba yak sü], дур [dur] / *adj.* бекор [bekor], хомӯш [xomüsh] / *prep.* аз [az], аз рӯйи [az rüyi]
offend [офенд] *v.t.* хафа кардан [xafa kardan]
offense [офенс] *n.* хафагӣ [xafagi]
offensive [офенсив] *adj.* хафагиангез [xafagiangez]
offer [офар] *n.* пешниҳод [peshnihod], таклиф [taklif] / *v.t.* пешниҳод кардан [peshnihod kardan], таклиф кардан [taklif kardan]
office [офис] *n.* идора [idora], корхона [korxona]; *(position of duty)* вазифа [vazifa]

officer [офисар] *n.* афсар [afsar]
official [офишал] *n.* мансабдор [mansabdor] / *adj.* расмӣ [rasmi]
often [офан] *adv.* тез-тез [tez-tez], зуд-зуд [zud-zud]
oil [ойл] *n. (cooking, motor, etc.)* равған [ravghan]; **crude oil** нафт [naft]; **oil well** чоҳи нафт [chohi naft] / *v.t.* равған молидан [ravghan molidan]
oily [ойли] *adj.* равғанӣ [ravghani], равғандор [ravghandor]
ointment [ойнтмант] *n.* марҳам [marham]
OK [оке] *adv.* майлаш [maylash]
old [олд] *adj. (for inanimate objects)* кӯҳна [kühna]; *(elderly)* пир [pir]
old-fashioned [олд-фашанд] *adj.* қадима [qadima], аздаҳонмонда [azdahonmonda]
olive [олив] *n.* зайтун [zaytun]; **olive green** зайтунранг [zaytunrang]; **olive oil** равғани зайтун [ravghani zaytun]
olympic [олимпик] *adj.* олимпӣ [olimpi]; **Olympic Games** Бозиҳои олимпӣ [Bozihoi olimpi]
omelet(te) [омлет] *n.* омлет [omlet]
omission [омишан] *n.* ғафлат [ghaflat]
omit [омит] *v.t.* ғафлат кардан [ghaflat kardan]
on [он] *prep.* рӯйи [rüyi], ба [ba], сари [sari]; **on schedule** сари вақт [sari vaqt]
once [ванс] *adv.* як бор [yak bor], як мартаба [yak martaba]; **at once** зуд [zud], фавран [favran]; **once in a while** гоҳ-гоҳ [goh-goh]
one [ван] *num.* як [yak]
onion [анян] *n.* пиёз [piyoz]
only [онли] *adj.* ягона [yagona] / *adv.* танҳо [tanho]
ooze [уз] *v.i.* таровидан [tarovidan]
open [опан] *adj.* кушода [kushoda], боз [boz] / *v.t.* кушодан [kushodan], боз кардан [boz kardan] / *v.i.* кушода шудан [kushoda shudan]
opening [опанинг] *n.* кушоиш [kushoish]
opera [опера] *n.* опера [opera]
operate [опарейт] *v.t.* идора кардан [idora kardan], ба кор андохтан [ba kor andoxtan]
operation [опарейшан] *n.* амал [amal]; *(med.)* ҷарроҳӣ [jarrohi]; *(mil.)* амалиёти ҳарбӣ [amaliyoti harbi]
operator [опарейтор] *n.* оператор [operator]
opinion [опинян] *n.* гумон [gumon]
opponent [опонант] *n.* ҳариф [harif], мухолиф [muxolif]
opportunity [опортюнити] *n.* фурсат [fursat]
oppose [опоз] *v.t.* мухолифат кардан [muxolifat kardan]
opposite [опозит] *n.* акс [aks], зид [zid] / *adj.* рӯ ба рӯ [rü ba rü], муқобил [muqobil]
opposition [опозишан] *n.* мухолифат [muxolifat], *(political opposition [pl.])* мухолифин [muxolifin]

oppress [опрес] *v.t.* ситам кардан [sitam kardan]
oppression [опрешан] *n.* ситам [sitam], ҷафо [jafo]
oppressive [опресив] *adj.* ситамкунанда [sitamkunanda]
optical [оптикал] *adj.* оптикӣ [optiki]
optician [оптишан] *n.* оптик [optik]
optimist [оптимист] *n.* некбин [nekbin]
optimistic [оптимистик] *adj.* некбин [nekbin]
option [опшан] *n.* хостагирӣ [xostagiri], интихоб [intixob]
optional [опшанал] *adj.* ғайриҳатмӣ [ghayrihatmi]
or [ор] *conj.* ё [yo]
oral [орал] *adj.* даҳанакӣ [dahanaki]
orange [оринҷ] *n. (fruit)* афлесун [aflesun], пӯртахол [pürtaxol]; *(color)* норинҷӣ [norinji] / *adj.* норинҷӣ [norinji]; **orange juice** оби афлесун [obi aflesun]
orchard [орчард] *n.* боғи мевадор [boghi mevador]
orchestra [оркестра] *n.* оркестр [orkestr]
order [ордар] *n. (command)* фармон [farmon]; *(in a restaurant, etc.)* фармоиш [farmoish] / *v.t. (command)* фармон додан [farmon dodan]; *(purchase)* фармоиш додан [farmoish dodan]
ordinary [ординери] *adj.* оддӣ [oddi], рӯзмарра [rüzmarra]
ore [ор] *n.* маъдан [ma'dan]
organ [орган] *n. (anat.)* олат [olat], узв [uzv]; *(mus.)* арғунун [arghunun]
organic [органик] *adj.* табиӣ [tabii]
organization [органайзейшан] *n.* ташкилот [tashkilot]
organize [органайз] *v.t.* ташкил кардан [tashkil kardan]
origin [ориҷин] *n.* асл [asl]
original [ориҷинал] *adj.* аслӣ [asli]
originally [ориҷинали] *adv.* аслан [aslan]
ornament [орнамент] *n.* ороиш [oroish]
orphan [орфан] *n.* ятим [yatim], сағир [saghir];
orphanage [орфаниҷ] *n* ятимхона [yatimxona]
oscillate [осилейт] *v.i.* ларзидан [larzidan]
ostracism [острасизм] *n.* бадарғакунӣ [badarghakuni], табъид [tab'id]
ostrich [острич] *n.* шутурмурғ [shuturmurgh]
other [адар] *adj.* дигар [digar]
otherwise [адаруайз] *adv.* вагарна [vagarna]
ounce [аунс] *n.* унтсия [untsiya]
our [аур] *adj.* аз они мо [az oni mo], -амон [-amon]
ours [аурз] *pron.* аз они мо [az oni mo]
ourselves [аурселвз] *pron.* худамон [xudamon]
out [аут] *adv.* берун [berun], ба берун [ba berun]
outcast [ауткаст] *n.* бадарғашуда [badarghashuda]

outcome [ауткам] *n.* натиҷа [natija]
outdoor [аутдор] *adj.* берун аз хона [berun az xona]
outer [аутар] *adj.* берунӣ [beruni]
outline [аутлайн] *n.* тарҳ [tarh], ангора [angora] / *v.t.* тарҳ кашидан [tarh kashidan]
outside [аутсайд] *n./adv.* берун [berun] / *adj.* берунӣ [beruni] / *prep.* берун аз [berun az]
outskirts [аутскиртс] *n.* канор [kanor]; *(of a city)* маҳалли дурдаст [mahalli durdast]
outstanding [аутстандинг] *adj.* барҷаста [barjasta]
oval [овал] *adj.* байзавӣ [bayzavi]
oven [аван] *n.* танӯр [tanür], оташдон [otashdon]
over [овар] *adv.* болои [boloi]
overalls [оваролз] *n.* либоси кор [libosi kor]
overcast [оваркаст] *adj.* абрнок [abrnok]
overdue [овардю] *adj.* таъхир кардашуда [ta'xir kardashuda], аз вақт гузаронда [az vaqt guzaronda]
overlook [оварлук] *v.t.* надида мондан [nadida mondan] / *v.i.* маҳалро аз баландие дидан [mahalro az balandie didan]
overnight [оварнайт] *adv.* шабона [shabona]
overseas [оварсиз] *adj.* хориҷӣ [xoriji] / *adv.* дар кишварҳои бегона [dar kishvarhoi begona]
overtime [овартайм] *adj.* зиёда аз вақти муқаррарӣ [ziyoda az vaqti muqarrari]
overweight [оваруейт] *adj.* вазни барзиёд [vazni barziyod]
owe [о] *v.t.* қарздор будан [qarzdor budan]
owl [аул] *n.* чуғз [jughz], бум [bum]
own [он] *adj.* худ [xud] / *v.t.* соҳиб будан [sohib budan]
owner [онар] *n.* соҳиб [sohib]
ox [окс] *n.* (*pl.* **oxen**) [оксан] барзагов [barzagov]
oxygen [оксиҷан] *n.* оксиген [oksigen]
oyster [ойстар] *n.* садафак [sadafak]
ozone [озон] *n.* озон [ozon]

P

pace [пейс] *n.* *(step)* қадам [qadam], гом [gom]; *(speed)* суръат [sur'at] / *v.t.* бо қадам чен кардан [bo qadam chen kardan]
pack [пек] *v.t.* печонда бастан [pechonda bastan]; *(fill up)* пур кардан [pur kardan] / *v.i.* печонда баста шудан [pechonda basta shudan]
package [пекиҷ] *n.* той [toy], бандча [bandcha], даста [dasta]
packing [пекинг] *n.* борбандӣ [borbandi]
pagan [пейган] *n.* бутпараст [butparast] / *adj.* -и бутпарастӣ [-i butparasti]
page [пейҷ] *n.* саҳифа [sahifa]
pail [пейл] *n.* сатил [satil]
pain [пейн] *n.* дард [dard] / *v.t.* дард кардан [dard kardan]

painful [пейнфул] *adj.* дарднок [dardnok]
painless [пейнлас] *adj.* бедард [bedard]
paint [пейнт] *n.* ранг [rang] / *v.t. (paint a picture)* расм кашидан [rasm kashidan]; *(paint a wall, door, etc.)* ранг кардан [rang kardan] / *v.i.* рассомӣ кардан [rassomi kardan]
painter [пейнтер] *n.* наққош [naqqosh], рассом [rassom]
painting [пейнтинг] *n.* расм [rasm]; *(the art of painting)* рассомӣ [rassomi], наққошӣ [naqqoshi]
pair [пер] *n.* ҷуфт [juft]
pajamas [паҷамаз] *n.pl.* пойҷома [poyjoma]
Pakistani [пекистени] *n./adj.* покистонӣ [pokistoni]
pal [пел] *n. (man/boy's male friend)* ҷӯра [jüra]; *(woman/girl's female friend)* дугона [dugona]; *(friend)* дӯст [düst]
palace [палас] *n.* кох [kox], қаср [qasr]
pale [пейл] *adj.* рангпарида [rangparida], нимранг [nimrang]
palette [пелет] *n.* лавҳачаӣ рассомӣ [lavhachai rassomi]
palm [пом] *n.* кафи даст [kafi dast]
palm tree [пом три] *n.* нахл [naxl]
palpitation [палпитейшан] *n.* тапиш [tapish]; **heart palpitations** тапиши дил [tapishi dil]
pamphlet [пемфлет] *n.* китобча [kitobcha]
pan [пен] *n.* тоба [toba]
panic [пеник] *n.* воҳима [vohima], ҳаросонӣ [harosoni]; *v.i.* ба воҳима афтодан [ba vohima aftodan]
pant [пент] *v.i.* ба зӯр нафас кашидан [ba zür nafas kashidan]
panties [пантиз] *n.pl.* пӯшоки таги занона [püshoki tagi zanona]
pantry [пентри] *n.* анбор [anbor]
pants [пентс] *n.pl.* шим [shim]
paper [пейпър] *n.* коғаз [koghaz] / *adj.* коғазин [koghazin]
parachute [перашут] *n.* парашют [parashyut] / *v.t.* бо парашют партофтан [bo parashyut partoftan] / *v.i.* бо парашют паридан [bo parashyut paridan]
parade [парейд] *n.* парад [parad], роҳпаймоӣ [rohpaymoi]
paradise [перадайс] *n.* биҳишт [bihisht]
paragraph [перагреф] *n.* абзатс [abzats]
parallel [перaлел] *adj.* мувозӣ [muvozi]
paralysis [перaлисис] *n.* шалӣ [shali]
paralyze [пералайз] *v.t.* шал кардан [shal kardan]
parasite [перасайт] *n.* паразит [parazit]
parasitic [пераситик] *adj.* паразитӣ [paraziti]
parcel [парсал] *n.* коғазпеч [koghazpech], пакет [paket]
parchment [парчмант] *n.* пергамент [pergament]

pardon [пардан] *n.* бахшиш [baxshish] / *v.t.* бахшидан [baxshidan]
parent [перант] *n. (father)* падар [padar]; *(mother)* модар [modar]; *(parents)* падару модар [padaru modar], волидайн [volidayn]
parish [периш] *n. (administrative division)* маҳалли истиқомати қавми ягон калисо [mahalli istoqomati qavmi yagon kaliso]; *(church members)* қавми ягон калисо [qavmi yagon kaliso]
park [парк] *n.* боғ [bogh], чорбоғ [chorbogh] / *v.t.* мошин мондан [moshin mondan]
parking lot [паркинг лот] *n.* ҷои мошинмонӣ [joi moshinmoni]
parliament [парлимент] *n.* порлумон [porlumon]
parliamentary [парлиментари] *n.* порлумонӣ [porlumoni]
parrot [перат] *n.* тӯтӣ [tüti]
parsley [парсли] *n.* ҷаъфарӣ [ja'fari]
part [парт] *n.* қисм [qism]; **car part** қисми мошин [qismi moshin] / *v.i.* аз ҳамдигар ҷудо шудан [az hamdigar judo shudan]
partial [паршъл] *adj.* нопурра [nopurra], як андоза [yak andoza]
participate [партисипейт] *v.i.* иштирок кардан [ishtirok kardan]
particle [партикъл] *n.* зарра [zarra]
particular [партикюлар] *adj.* махсус [maxsus]
partition [партишан] *n.* ҷудокунӣ [judokuni], тақсимкунӣ [taqsimkuni]
partner [партнър] *n.* шарик [sharik]
party [парти] *n.* базм [bazm]; *(dinner party)* шабнишинӣ [shabnishini]; *(political party)* ҳизб [hizb], партия [partiya]; *(group of people)* даста [dasta]
pass [пес] *n. (permit)* роҳхат [rohxat]; *(geo.)* ағба [aghba], кӯтал [kütal] / *v.t.* гузаштан [guzashtan]
passage [песаҷ] *n.* гузаргоҳ [guzargoh]
passenger [песенҷер] *n.* мусофир [musofir]; **passenger train** поезди мусофиркашӣ [poezdi musofirkashi]
passerby [песербай] *n. (pl.* **passersby***)* роҳгузар [rohguzar]
passion [пешан] *n. (love, romance)* ишқ [ishq]; *(interest)* шавқ [shavq]
passionate [пешанит] *adj.* пурҷӯшухурӯш [purjüshuxurüsh]; *(romantic)* пуршаҳват [purshahvat]
passive [песив] *adj.* суст [sust], беҳаракат [beharakat]
passport [песпорт] *n.* шиносномa [shinosnoma], паспорт [pasport]
password [песвурд] *n.* номи шаб [nomi shab]
past [пест] *n.* гузашта [guzashta] / *adj.* гузашта [guzashta]

paste [пейст] *n. (thick mixture)* хамир [xamir]; *(glue)* елим [yelim] / *v.t.* елим кардан [yelim kardan], часпондан [chaspondan]
pasteurized [песчурайзд] *adj.* пастеризатсия кардашуда [pasterizatsiya kardashuda]
pastime [пестайм] *n.* вақтгузаронӣ [vaqtguzaroni], саргармӣ [sargarmi]
pastry [пейстри] *n.* пирог [pirog], пирожнӣ [pirozhni]
patch [печ] *n.* пина [pina], дарбеҳ [darbeh]; *(vegetable patch)* пал [pal] / *v.t.* пина кардан [pina kardan], дарбеҳ кардан [darbeh kardan]
patent [петент] *n.* патент [patent]
path [пет] *n.* пайроҳа [payroha]
pathetic [патетик] *adj.* риққатовар [riqqatovar]
patience [пейшенс] *n.* сабр [sabr]
patient [пейшент] *n.* бемор [bemor] / *adj.* босабр [bosabr]
patriot [пейтрият] *n.* ватандӯст [vatandüst]
patriotic [пейтриётик] *adj.* ватандӯст [vatandüst]
patrol [патрол] *n.* дастаи посбонон [dastai posbonon] / *v.i.* посбонӣ кардан [posboni kardan]
patron [пейтран] *n.* ҳомӣ [homi]
pattern [патерн] *n.* намуна [namuna]
paunch [пончʼ] *n.* ишкамба [ishkamba]
pause [поз] *n.* таваққуф [tavaqquf] / *v.t.* таваққуф кардан [tavaqquf kardan] / *v.i.* таваққуф шудан [tavaqquf shudan]
pave [пейв] *v.t.* фарш кардан [farsh kardan]
pavement [пейвмент] *n.* пиёдагард [piyodagard]
pavilion [павилян] *n.* шипанг [shipang]
paw [по] *n.* панҷа [panja], пой [poy]
pawn [пон] *n. (chess piece)* пиёда [piyoda] / *v.t.* гарав гузоштан [garav guzoshtan]
pay [пей] *n.* музд [muzd] / *v.t.* пардохтан [pardoxtan], пул додан [pul dodan]; *(pay attention)* таваҷҷӯҳ кардан [tavajjüh kardan]
payment [пеймент] *n.* пардохт [pardoxt]
pea [пи] *n.* нахӯд [naxüd]
peace [пис] *n. (lack of fighting/ war)* оштӣ [oshti], сулҳ [sulh]; *(tranquility)* оромиш [oromish], осоиш [osoish]
peaceful [писфул] *adj. (tranquil)* ором [orom], осоишта [osoishta]; *(peace-loving)* сулҳдӯст [sulhdüst]
peach [пич] *n.* шафтолу [shaftolu]
peacock [пикок] *n.* товус [tovus]
peak [пик] *n. (highest level)* авҷ [avj]; *(geo.)* қулла [qulla], ситеғ [sitegh]
peanut [пинат] *n.* финдиқи заминӣ [findiqi zamini]
pear [пер] *n.* нок [nok], мурӯд [murüd]
pearl [перл] *n.* марворид [marvorid]

peasant [пезант] *n.* деҳқон [dehqon]
pebble [пебъл] *n.* шағал [shaghal]
pedal [педал] *n.* педал [pedal]
pedestrian [педестриян] *n.* пиёдагард [piyodagard]; **pedestrian crossing** гузаргоҳи пиёдагардон [guzargohi piyodagardon]
pediatrician [пидиятришан] *n.* духтури кӯдакон [duxturi küdakon]
peel [пил] *n.* пӯст [püst] / *v.t.* пӯст кандан [püst kandan]
peg [пег] *n.* мехи чӯбин [mexi chübin]
pen [пен] *n.* ручка [ruchka]
penalty [пеналти] *n.* ҷазо [jazo], сазо [sazo]
pencil [пенсил] *n.* қалам [qalam]
penetrate [пенетрейт] *v.t.* нуфуз кардан [nufuz kardan]
penicillin [пенисилин] *n.* пенитсиллин [penitsillin]
penknife [пеннайф] *n.* кордча [kordcha]
pension [пеншан] *n.* нафақа [nafaqa]
pensioner [пеншанер] *n.* нафақахӯр [nafaqaxür]
people [пипал] *n.* мардум [mardum], халқ [xalq]
pepper [пепер] *n. (black pepper)* мурч [murch]; **red pepper** мурчи сурх [murchi surx]; **chili pepper** қаламфур [qalamfur]; **bell pepper** қаламфури булғорӣ [qalamfuri bulghori]
peppermint [пеперминт] *n.* пудина [pudina]
perceive [персив] *v.t.* дарк кардан [dark kardan], дарёфтан [daryoftan]
percent [персент] *n.* дарсад [darsad]
percentage [персентиҷ] *n.* дарсад [darsad]
perception [персепшан] *n.* дарк [dark], дарёфт [daryoft]
perch [перч] *n.* ходачаи катаки мурғ [xodachai kataki murgh]; *(fish)* аломоҳӣ [alomohi]
perfect [перфект] *adj.* комил [komil]
perform [перформ] *v.i.* иҷро кардан [ijro kardan]
performance [перформанс] *n.* иҷро [ijro]
perfume [перфюм] *n.* атр [atr]
perhaps [перҳапс] *adv.* шояд [shoyad]
peril [перил] *n.* хатар [xatar]
period [пирияд] *n. (gram.)* нуқта [nuqta]; *(segment of time)* муддат [muddat], давра [davra]; *(a woman's menstruation)* ҳайз [hayz]; **to have one's period** ҳайз дидан [hayz didan]
periodic [пириёдик] *adj.* даврӣ [davri]
periodical [пириёдикал] *n.* нашрияи даврӣ [nashriyai davri]
peripheral [периферал] *adj.* ғайримарказӣ [ghayrimarkazi]; **peripheral nervous system** *(anat.)* системаи ғайримарказии асабҳо [sistemai ghairimarkazii asabho]
perish [периш] *v.i.* ҳалок шудан [halok shudan]

perishable [перишабал] *adj.* тезвайроншаванда [tezvayronshavanda]
permanence [перманенс] *n.* пойдорӣ [poydori]
permanent [перманент] *adj.* пойдор [poydor]
permission [пермишан] *n.* иҷозат [ijozat]
permit [пермит] *n.* иҷозатнома [ijozatnoma] / *v.t.* иҷозат додан [ijozat dodan]
perpendicular [перпендикюлар] *adj.* амудӣ [amudi]
Persian [пержан] *n.* *(language)* порсӣ [porsi], форсӣ [forsi]
persist [персист] *v.i.* истодагарӣ кардан [istodagari kardan]
person [персон] *n.* кас [kas], шахс [shaxs]
personal [персонал] *adj.* шахсӣ [shaxsi]
personality [персоналити] *n.* шахсият [shaxsiyat]
personnel [персонел] *n.* ҳайати кормандон [hayati kormandon]
perspective [перспектив] *n.* перспектива [perspektiva]
perspire [перспайр] *v.i.* арақ кардан [araq kardan]
perspiration [перспирейшан] *n.* арақ [araq]
persuade [персуейд] *v.t.* бовар кунондан [bovar kunondan]
pessimist [песимист] *n.* бадбин [badbin]
pessimistic [песимистик] *adj.* бадбин [badbin]
pester [пестер] *v.t.* безор кардан [bezor kardan]
pet [пет] *n.* ҷонвари хонагӣ [jonvari xonagi] / *v.t.* навозиш кардан [navozish kardan]
petal [петал] *n.* гулбарг [gulbarg]
petition [петишан] *n.* ариза [ariza], илтимоснома [iltimosnoma]
petrol [петрол] *n., Br. see* **gas** *and* **gasoline**
petroleum [петролиям] *n.* нафт [naft]
petty [пети] *adj. (insignificant)* майда [mayda]; *(petty person)* майдагап [maydagap]
phantom [фантом] *n.* хаёл [xayol]
pharmaceutical [фармасутикал] *adj.* -и дорусозӣ [-i dorusozi]
pharmacist [фармасист] *n.* дорусоз [dorusoz]
pharmacology [фармаколоҷи] *n.* дорушиносӣ [dorushinosi], фармакология [farmakologiya]
pharmacy [фармаси] *n.* дорухона [doruxona]
phase [фейз] *n.* марҳала [marhala], муддат [muddat]
pheasant [фезант] *n.* тазарв [tazarv]
phenomenon [феноменон] *n. (pl.* **phenomena***)* падида [padida]
philosophy [философи] *n.* фалсафа [falsafa]
phlegm [флем] *n.* балғам [balgham]
phone [фон] *see* **telephone**
phonetic [фонетик] *adj.* фонетикӣ [fonetiki]

phonetics [фонетикс] *n.pl.* фонетика [fonetika]
photocopy [фотокопи] *n.* фотонусха [fotonusxa] / *v.t.* фотонусха гирифтан [fotonusxa giriftan]
photo(graph) [фото(граф)] *n.* сурат [surat], акс [aks]
photograph [фотограф] *v.t.* сурат гирифтан [surat giriftan], акс гирифтан [aks giriftan]
photographer [фотографер] *n.* суратгир [suratgir], аксгир [aksgir]
photography [фотографи] *n.* суратгирӣ [suratgiri], аксгирӣ [aksgiri]
phrase [фрейз] *n.* ҷумла [jumla], ифода [ifoda] / *v.t.* ифода кардан [ifoda kardan]
phrasebook [фрейзбук] *n.* китоби гуфтугӯ [kitobi guftugü]
physical [физикал] *adj.* ҷисман [jisman]
physician [физишан] *n.* духтур [duxtur], пизишк [pizishk]
physicist [физисист] *n.* физик [fizik]
physics [физикс] *n.* физика [fizika]
piano [пиано] *n.* фортепяно [fortepyano]
pick [пик] *n.* зоғнӯл [zoghnül] / *v.t. (choose)* хоста гирифтан [xosta giriftan], интихоб кардан [intixob kardan]; *(pluck/harvest)* чидан [chidan]
pickle [пикъл] *n.* намакоб [namakob] / *v.t.* дар намак хобондан [dar namak xobondan]
pickpocket [пикпокет] *n.* кисабур [kisabur]
picnic [пикник] *n.* сайри чорбоғ [sayri chorbogh]
picture [пикчур] *n.* сурат [surat], тасвир [tasvir] / *v.t.* сурати чизеро ба худ гирифтан [surati chizero ba xud giriftan]
picturesque [пикчуреск] *adj.* хушманзара [xushmanzara]
pie [пай] *n.* пирог [pirog], санбӯса [sanbüsa]
piece [пис] *n.* порча [porcha], тикка [tikka]
pierce [пирс] *v.t.* халондан [xalondan], сӯрох кардан [sürox kardan]
pig [пиг] *n.* хук [xuk]
pigeon [пиҷан] *n.* кафтар [kaftar], кабӯтар [kabütar]
pile [пайл] *n.* тӯда [tüda] / *v.t.* ҷамъ кардан [jam' kardan] / *v.i.* ҷамъ шудан [jam' shudan]
piles [пайлз] *n. (med.)* бавосир [bavosir]
pilgrim [пилгрим] *n.* зиёраткунанда [ziyoratkunanda]; *(Hajj pilgrim)* ҳоҷӣ [hoji]
pilgrimage [пилграмиҷ] *n.* зиёрат [ziyorat]; *(Hajj)* ҳаҷ [haj]
pill [пил] *n.* ҳаб [hab]
pillar [пилар] *n.* сутун [sutun]
pillow [пило] *n.* болишт [bolisht]
pillowcase [пилокейс] *n.* ҷилди болишт [jildi bolisht]
pilot [пайлат] *n.* ҳавонавард [havonavard], халабон [xalabon]

pimple [пимпъл] *n.* гармича [garmicha], рихинак [rixinak]
pin [пин] *n.* сӯзанак [süzanak]
pincers [пинсерз] *n.pl.* анбӯр [anbür]
pinch [пинч] *n.* чимдӣ [chimdi] / *v.t.* чимдӣ кардан [chimdi kardan]
pine [пайн] *n.* санавбар [sanavbar]
pineapple [пайнапъл] *n.* ананас [ananas]
pink [пинк] *adj.* гулобӣ [gulobi]
pint [пайнт] *n.* пинта [pinta]
pioneer [пайёнир] *n.* пионер [pioner], навкор [navkor]
pious [пайас] *adj.* порсо [porso], диндор [dindor]
pipe [пайп] *n.* қубур [qubur]; *(mus.)* карнай [karnay]
piper [пайпър] *n.* карнайчӣ [karnaychi]
pirate [пайрат] *n.* роҳзани дарёӣ [rohzani daryoi]
pistol [пистол] *n.* таппонча [tapponcha]
piston [пистон] *n.* поршен [porshen]
pit [пит] *n.* *(hole)* мағок [maghok], чуқурӣ [chuquri]; *(in fruit)* ҳаста [hasta]
pitcher *n.* *(container)* кӯза [küza]
pity [пити] *n.* дилсӯзӣ [dilsüzi] / *v.i.* дилсӯз будан [dilsüz budan]
place [плейс] *n.* ҷой [joy], ҷо [jo]; **place of birth** зодгоҳ [zodgoh]; **to take place** рӯй додан [rüy dodan] / *v.t.* ниҳодан [nihodan], гузоштан [guzoshtan]
plague [плейг] *n.* офат [ofat] / *v.t.* озор додан [ozor dodan]
plain [плейн] *n.* дашт [dasht] / *adj.* *(simple)* содда [sodda]; *(obvious)* ошкор [oshkor]
plan [план] *n.* нақша [naqsha], план [plan] / *v.t.* план гузоштан [plan guzoshtan], тартиб додан [tartib dodan]; *(architectural)* нақша кашидан [naqsha kashidan]
plane [плейн] *see* **airplane**
planet [планет] *n.* сайёра [sayyora]
plank [планк] *n.* тахта [taxta]
plant [плант] *n.* растанӣ [rastani]; *(factory)* фабрика [fabrika] / *v.t.* *(sow seeds)* коштан [koshtan]; *(place on the ground)* шинондан [shinondan]
plasma [плазма] *n.* плазма [plazma]
plaster [пластер] *n.* гач [gach] / *v.t.* андовидан [andovidan], андова кардан [andova kardan]
plastic [пластик] *n.* пластик [plastik] / *adj.* пластмасӣ [plastmasi], пластикӣ [plastiki]
plate [плейт] *n.* *(small plate)* табақча [tabaqcha]; *(serving plate)* табақ [tabaq]
plateau [плато] *n.* пуштакӯҳ [pushtaküh]
platform [платформ] *n.* платформа [platforma]
platinum [платинум] *n.* тиллои сафед [tilloi safed], платина [platina]
play [плей] *n.* песа [pesa] / *v.t.* *(play a game/role)* бозӣ кардан [bozi kardan]; *(play an instrument)* навохтан [navoxtan] / *v.i.* бозидан [bozidan], бозӣ кардан [bozi kardan]

player [плейър] *n. (one who plays a game, etc.)* бозингар [bozingar]; *(musician)* навозанда [navozanda]
playground [плейграунд] *n.* майдончаи бачагон [maydonchai bachagon]
playing field [плейинг филд] *n.* майдони бозӣ [maydoni bozi]
plea [пли] *n.* мудофиа [mudofia]
plead [плид] *v.i.* мудофиа кардан [mudofia kardan]
pleasant [плезант] *adj.* форам [foram]
please [плиз] *v.t.* хушнуд кардан [xushnud kardan], форидан [foridan] / *adv.* илтимос [iltimos]
pleasure [плежър] *n.* хурсандӣ [xursandi]
plenty [пленти] *n.* фаровонӣ [farovoni]
pliers [плайърз] *n.pl.* анбӯр [anbür]
plot [плот] *n. (of a novel)* сужет [suzhet]; *(political)* суиқасд [suiqasd]; *(of land)* қитъаи замин [qit'ai zamin] / *v.t.* нақша кашидан [naqsha kashidan]
plow [плау] *n.* сипор [sipor] / *v.t.* шудгор кардан [shudgor kardan]
plug [плаг] *n.* тиққонҷ [tiqqonj], пӯка [püka]; *(electrical outlet)* штепсел [shtepsel] / *v.t.* тиққондан [tiqqondan]
plum [плам] *n.* олу [olu]
plumber [пламър] *n.* водопроводчӣ [vodoprovodchi], налдавон [naldavon]
plume [плум] *n.* пар [par]
plump [пламп] *adj.* ғафс [ghafs]
plunge [планҷ] *v.i.* ғӯта задан [ghüta zadan]
plural [плурал] *n./adj./gram.* ҷамъ [jam']
plus [плас] *n.* аломати ҷамъ [alomati jam'] / *prep.* ҷамъ [jam']
p.m. [пи эм] *adj. (abbrev. of* **post meridiem** *[after noon])* бегоҳӣ [begohi]
pneumonia [нимония] *n.* варами шуш [varami shush]
pocket [покит] *n.* ҷайб [jayb], киса [kisa]
pod [под] *n.* ғилофак [ghilofak]
poem [поем] *n.* шеър [she'r]
poet [поет] *n.* шоир [shoir]
poetry [поетри] *n.* шеър [she'r]
point [пойнт] *n.* нуқта [nuqta]; *(sharp end)* нӯг [nüg] / *v.i. (point out)* нишон додан [nishon dodan]
poison [пойзон] *n.* заҳр [zahr]
poisonous [пойзонус] *adj.* заҳрдор [zahrdor]
pole [пол] *n.* хода [xoda]; *(telephone/telegraph)* симчӯб [simchüb]; *(geo.)* қутб [qutb]
Pole [пол] *n.* полшагӣ [polshagi], леҳистонӣ [lehistoni]
police [полис] *n.* милиса [milisa]
policy [полиси] *n.* санади суғурта [sanadi sughurta]; **insurance policy** ҳуҷҷати васиқаи бима [hujjati vasiqai bima]

polish [полиш] *n.* пардоз [pardoz], ҷило [jilo] / *v.t.* пардоз додан [pardoz dodan], ҷило додан [jilo dodan]
Polish [полиш] *n./adj.* полшагӣ [polshagi], лаҳистонӣ [lahistoni]
polite [полайт] *adj.* боадаб [boadab]
political [политикал] *adj.* сиёсӣ [siyosi]
politician [политишан] *n.* сиёсатмадор [siyosatmador]
politics [политикс] *n.pl.* сиёсат [siyosat]
poll [пол] *n.* овоздиҳӣ [ovozdihi]
pollute [полют] *v.t.* олудан [oludan]
polluted [полютид] *adj.* олуда [oluda]
pollution [полюшан] *n.* олудагӣ [oludagi]
pond [понд] *n.* толоб [tolob]
pony [пони] *n.* тоту [totu]
pool [пул] *n.* ҳавз [havz]
poor [пур] *adj. (in wealth)* камбағал [kambaghal]; *(unfortunate)* бечора [bechora]
pope [поп] *n.* папа [papa], поп [pop]
pop music [поп мюзик] *n.* мусиқии поп [musiqii pop]
poppy [попи] *n.* хашхош [xashxosh], кӯкнор [küknor]
population [попюлейшан] *n.* аҳолӣ [aholi]
porcelain [порсалин] *n.* фахфур [faxfur]
porch [порч] *n.* айвон [ayvon]
porcupine [поркюпайн] *n.* ҷайра [jayra]
pore [пор] *n.* масома [masoma]
pork [порк] *n.* гӯшти хук [güshti xuk]
porridge [порич] *n.* шӯла [shüla]
port [порт] *n.* бандар [bandar]
portable [портабъл] *adj.* ихчамсохт [ixchamsoxt]
porter [портър] *n.* ҳаммол [hammol], боркаш [borkash]
portfolio [портфолио] *n.* ҷузвкаш [juzvkash]
portion [поршан] *n.* ҳисса [hissa], қисм [qism], бархаш [barx]
portrait [портрет] *n.* сурат [surat]
Portuguese [порчугиз] *n./adj.* португалӣ [portugali]
position [позишан] *n.* мавқеъ [mavqe']; *(government post)* вазифа [vazifa]
positive [позитив] *adj.* мусбӣ [musbi]
possess [позес] *v.t.* соҳиб будан [sohib budan]
possession [позешан] *n.* тасарруф [tasarruf], дошта [doshta]
possessive [позесив] *adj.* соҳибӣ [sohibi]
possible [посибъл] *adj.* мумкин [mumkin]
post [пост] *n. (pole or stake)* хода [xoda], чӯб [chüb]; *(mail)* почта [pochta]; *(position to which one is appointed)* вазифа [vazifa] / *v.t. (send)* фиристодан [firistodan]; *(send by mail)* бо почта фиристодан [bo pochta firistodan]; *(put up)* часпондан [chaspondan]

postcard [посткард] *n.* хати кушода [xati kushoda], корти пустӣ [korti pusti]
posterity [постерити] *n.* авлод [avlod], зуррият [zurriyat]
postmark [постмарк] *n.* маркаи почта [markai pochta], тамбр [tambr]
post office [пост офис] *n.* идораи почта [idorai pochta]
postpone [постпон] *v.t.* ба таъхир андохтан [ba ta'xir andoxtan]
pot [пот] *n.* дег [deg]
potato [потейто] *n.* картошка [kartoshka]
pottery [потери] *n.* кулолӣ [kuloli]
pouch [пауч] *n.* халтача [xaltacha]
poultry [полтри] *n.* паррандаҳои хонагӣ [parrandahoi xonagi]
pound [паунд] *n.* фунт [funt] / *v.t.* кӯфтан [küftan]
pour [пор] *v.t.* рехтан [rextan] / *v.i.* рехтан [rextan], шоридан [shoridan]
powder [паудэр] *n.* хока [xoka], гард [gard]
power [пауэр] *n.* нерӯ [nerü], қувва [quvva], тавоноӣ [tavonoi]
powerful [пауэрфул] *adj.* тавоно [tavono], нерӯманд [nerümand], қавӣ [qavi]
practical [практикъл] *adj.* амалӣ [amali]
practically [практикли] *adv.* тақрибан [taqriban]
practice [практис] *n.* *(experience)* таҷриба [tajriba]; *(practical application)* амал [amal]; *(skilled work)* маҳорат [mahorat] / *v.t./v.i.* машқ кардан [mashq kardan]
praise [прейз] *n.* ситоиш [sitoish] / *v.t.* ситоиш кардан [sitoish kardan]
praiseworthy [прейзворди] *adj.* шоистаи ситоиш [shoistai sitoish]
pram [прам] *n.* аробачаи бачагона [arobachai bachagona]
prawn [прон] *n.* креветка [krevetka]
pray [прей] *v.i.* намоз хондан [namoz xondan], дуо кардан [duo kardan]
prayer [прейэр] *n.* дуо [duo]
preach [прич] *v.t.* хатибӣ кардан [xatibi kardan]
precarious [прикерияс] *adj.* ноустувор [noustuvor]
precede [пресид] *v.t.* пешопеш рафтан [peshopesh raftan], пеш гузаштан [pesh guzashtan]
precious [прешас] *adj.* гаронбаҳо [garonbaho], қиматбаҳо [qimatbaho]
precise [пресайс] *adj.* аниқ [aniq], дақиқ [daqiq]
predict [предикт] *v.t.* пешгӯӣ кардан [peshgüi kardan]
prefer [префер] *v.t.* беҳтар донистан [behtar donistan]
preference [преференс] *n.* бартарӣ [bartari]
prefix [префикс] *gram.* префикс [prefiks]
pregnant [прегнант] *adj.* обистан [obistan], бордор [bordor]

prejudice [пречидис] *n.* бадгумонӣ [badgumoni]
preparation [препарейшан] *n.* тайёрӣ [tayyori]
prepare [препейр] *v.t.* тайёр кардан [tayyor kardan], омода кардан [omoda kardan] / *v.i.* тайёр шудан [tayyor shudan], омода шудан [omoda shudan]
preposition [препозишан] *gram.* пешоянд [peshoyand]
prescribe [прескрайб] *v.t.* дору фармудан [doru farmudan]
prescription [прескрипшан] *n.* коғаздору [koghazdoru]
present [презент] *n.* тӯҳфа [tühfa] / *adj.* ҳозира [hozira] / *v.t.* тақдим кардан [taqdim kardan], пешкаш кардан [peshkash kardan]
presently [презентли] *adv.* ҳозир [hozir], ба зудӣ [ba zudi]
preserve [презерв] *n. (fruit preserves)* мураббо [murabbo] / *v.t.* нигоҳ доштан [nigoh doshtan], муҳофизат кардан [muhofizat kardan]
president [президент] *n.* президент [prezident]
press [прес] *n.* матбуот [matbuot] / *v.t.* фушурдан [fushurdan]
pressure [прешур] *n.* фишор [fishor] / *v.t.* фишор додан [fishor dodan]
prestige [престиж] *n.* обрӯ [obrü]
pretty [прити] *adj.* зебо [zebo], дилкаш [dilkash] / *adv.* анча [ancha], хуб [xub]
prevent [превент] *v.t.* пешгирӣ кардан [peshgiri kardan]
prevention [превеншан] *n.* пешгирӣ [peshgiri]
preventive [превентив] *adj.* пешгирикунанда [peshgirikunanda]
previous [привияс] *adj.* пешина [peshina]
price [прайс] *n.* баҳо [baho], нарх [narx] / *v.t.* нарх мондан [narx mondan]
priceless [прайслес] *adj.* бебаҳо [bebaho]
pride [прайд] *n.* ифтихор [iftixor]
priest [прист] *n.* кашиш [kashish]
primary [праймери] *adj. (first)* якумин [yakumin], нахустин [naxustin]; *(beginning)* ибтидоӣ [ibtidoi]
prime [прайм] *adj. (basic)* асосӣ [asosi]; *(top-quality)* умда [umda]
prince [принс] *n.* шоҳзода [shohzoda]
princess [принсес] *n.* шоҳдухтар [shohduxtar]
principal [принсипал] *n.* хӯҷаин [xüjain], соҳибкор [sohibkor] / *adj.* асосӣ [asosi]
principle [принсипал] *n.* усул [usul], асос [asos]
print [принт] *n.* чоп [chop] / *v.t.* чоп кардан [chop kardan]
printer [принтер] *n.* чопкунанда [chopkunanda]
printing [принтинг] *n.* чоп [chop]

priority [прайорити] *n.* якумӣ [yakumi], приоритет [prioritet]

prison [призан] *n.* зиндон [zindon], ҳабсхона [habsxona]

prisoner [признер] *n.* зиндонӣ [zindoni]

privacy [прайваси] *n.* танҳоӣ [tanhoi]

private [прайвит] *adj.* хусусӣ [xususi]

privilege [привлич] *n.* имтиёз [imtiyoz]

prize [прайз] *n.* мукофот [mukofot], подош [podosh]

probable [пробабъл] *adj.* эҳтимолӣ [ehtimoli]

probably [пробабли] *adv.* эҳтимол ки [ehtimol ki]

problem [проблем] *n.* масъала [mas'ala], проблема [problema]

procedure [просичур] *n.* расму қоида [rasmu qoida]; *(med.)* муоличa [muolija]

proceed [просид] *v.i.* давом додан [davom dodan]

process [просес] *n.* равиш [ravish], рафт [raft]

produce [продюс] *v.t.* истеҳсол кардан [istehsol kardan], тавлид кардан [tavlid kardan]

product [продакт] *n.* маҳсул [mahsul]

profession [профешон] *n.* пеша [pesha], касб [kasb]

professional [профешонал] *adj.* касбӣ [kasbi]

professor [професор] *n.* профессор [professor]

profile [профайл] *n.* нимрух [nimrux]

profit [профит] *n.* суд [sud] / *v.i.* суд бурдан [sud burdan]

profound [профаунд] *adj.* чуқур [chuqur]

program [програм] *n.* программа [programma]; *(plan)* нақша [naqsha]; *(radio/television/concert)* барнома [barnoma] / *v.t.* программа сохтан [programma soxtan]

programmer [програмер] *n.* программасоз [programmasoz]

progress [прогрес] *n.* пешрафт [peshraft], тараққӣ [taraqqi] / *v.i.* пешрафт кардан [peshraft kardan], тараққӣ кардан [taraqqi kardan]

progressive [прогресив] *adj.* пешравона [peshravona], мутараққӣ [mutaraqqi]

prohibit [проҳибит] *v.t.* манъ кардан [man' kardan]

prohibition [проҳибишан] *n.* манъ [man'], қадаған [qadaghan]

project [проҷект] *n.* лоиҳа [loiha], нақша [naqsha]

projector [проҷектор] *n.* нурафкан [nurafkan]

promenade [променейд] *n.* *(stroll)* сайру гашт [sayru gasht]; *(place to stroll)* ҷои сайру гашт [joi sayru gasht]

promise [промис] *n.* ваъда [va'da] / *v.t.* ваъда додан [va'da dodan]

pronoun [пронаун] *n.* ҷонишин [jonishin]

pronounce [пронаунс] *v.t.* талаффуз кардан [talaffuz kardan]

pronunciation [пронансиейшан] *n.* талаффуз [talaffuz]
proof [пруф] *n.* исбот [isbot]
propaganda [пропаганда] *n.* таблиғот [tablighot]
propel [пропел] *v.t.* рондан [rondan], ба пеш рондан [ba pesh rondan]
propeller [пропелер] *n.* парра [parra]; *(airplane)* парраи ҳавопаймо [parrai havopaymo]
proper [пропер] *adj.* муносиб [munosib]
property [проперти] *n.* мол [mol]
prophecy [професи] *n.* пешгӯӣ [peshgüi]
prophet [профет] *n.* пайғамбар [payghambar]
proposal [пропозал] *n.* пешниҳод [peshnihod]
propose [пропоз] *v.t.* пешниҳод кардан [peshnihod kardan]
proprietor [пропрайетор] *n.* доранда [doranda], соҳиб [sohib]
prose [проз] *n.* наср [nasr]
prosecutor [просекютор] *n.* *(public prosecutor)* додситон [dodsiton]
prospective [проспектив] *adj.* интизордошта [intizordoshta], мунтазира [muntazira]
prosper [проспер] *v.i.* равнақ ёфтан [ravnaq yoftan], гул-гул шукуфтан [gul-gul shukuftan]
prosperity [просперити] *n.* равнақ [ravnaq], давлатмандӣ [davlatmandi]
prosperous [просперас] *adj.* давлатманд [davlatmand]
prostate [простейт] *n.* простата [prostata]; **prostate cancer** саратони простата [saratoni prostata]
prostitute [проститют] *n.* танфурӯш [tanfurüsh]
protect [протект] *v.t.* мудофиа кардан [mudofia kardan], ҳимоя кардан [himoya kardan]
protection [протекшан] *n.* мудофиа [mudofia], ҳимоя [himoya]
protein [протин] *n.* сафеда [safeda]
protest [протест] *n.* эътироз [e'tiroz] / *v.t.* эътироз кардан [e'tiroz kardan]
Protestant [протестант] *n.* протестант [protestant] / *adj.* протестантӣ [protestanti]
Protestantism [протестантизм] *n.* протестантизм [protestantizm]
proud [прауд] *adj.* сарбаланд [sarbaland], ифтихорманд [iftixormand]
prove [прув] *v.t.* исбот кардан [isbot kardan]
proverb [проверб] *n.* зарбулмасал [zarbulmasal]
provide [провайд] *v.t.* омода кардан [omoda kardan]; **provided that** ба шарте ки [ba sharte ki]
province [провинс] *n.* вилоят [viloyat]
prudent [прудент] *adj.* фарзона [farzona], эҳтиёткор [ehtiyotkor]

prune [прун] *n.* олуқоқ [oluqoq]
psychiatrist [сайкайатрист] *n.* духтури касалиҳои рӯҳӣ [duxturi kasalihoi rühi]
psychological [сайколоҷикал] *adj.* равонӣ [ravoni], рӯҳӣ [rühi]
psychologist [сайколоҷист] *n.* равоншинос [ravonshinos], рӯҳшинос [rühshinos]
psychology [сайколоҷи] *n.* равоншиносӣ [ravonshinosi], рӯҳшиносӣ [rühshinosi]
pub [паб] *n.* майхона [mayxona], майкада [maykada]
public [паблик] *adj.* умумӣ [umumi]
publication [пабликейшан] *n.* нашр [nashr]
publicity [паблисити] *n.* реклама [reklama]
publish [паблиш] *v.t.* нашр кардан [nashr kardan]
publisher [паблишър] *n.* нашркунанда [nashrkunanda]
pudding [пудинг] *n.* фиринӣ [firini]
puff [паф] *n.* вазиш [vazish]
pull [пул] *v.t.* кашидан [kashidan]
pulley [пули] *n.* ғарғара [gharghara]
pulse [палс] *n.* набз [nabz]
pump [памп] *n.* насос [nasos] / *v.t.* бо насос кашида баровардан [bo nasos kashida barovardan]
pumpkin [пампкин] *n.* каду [kadu]
punch [панч] *n.* мушт [musht] / *v.t.* мушт задан [musht zadan]
punctuate [панкчуейт] *v.t.* аломатҳои китобатӣ гузоштан [alomathoi kitobati guzoshtan]
punctuation [панкчуейшан] *n.* аломатҳои китобатӣ [alomathoi kitobati]
puncture [панкчър] *n.* сӯрох [sürox] / *v.t.* халонда сӯрох кардан [xalonda sürox kardan]
punish [паниш] *v.t.* сазо додан [sazo dodan], ҷазо додан [jazo dodan]
punishment [панишмент] *n.* сазо [sazo], ҷазо [jazo]
pupil [пюпил] *n. (student)* шогирд [shogird], талаба [talaba]; *(anat.)* мардумак [mardumak], гавҳарак [gavharak]
puppet [папет] *n.* зоча [zocha], лӯхтак [lüxtak]
puppy [папи] *n.* сагбача [sagbacha]
purchase [пурчис] *n.* харид [xarid] / *v.t.* харидан [xaridan]
pure [пюр] *adj.* покиза [pokiza], беғубор [beghubor], холис [xolis]
purification [пюрификейшан] *n.* полоиш [poloish]
purify [пюрифай] *v.t.* полудан [poludan]
purple [пурпъл] *adj.* арғувонӣ [arghuvoni]
purpose [пурпас] *n.* қасд [qasd]; **on purpose** барқасд [barqasd]

purse [пурс] *n.* ҳамён [hamyon], қапчуқ [qapchuq]
pursue [пурсю] *v.t.* дунболагирӣ кардан [dunbolagiri kardan], таъқиб кардан [ta'qib kardan]
pus [пас] *n.* рим [rim]
push [пуш] *n.* тела [tela] / *v.t.* тела додан [tela dodan] / *v.i.* фишор овардан [fishor ovardan]
puzzle [пазъл] *n.* чистон [chiston]
pyramid [пирамид] *n.* аҳром [ahrom]

Q

quail [куейл] *n.* бедона [bedona], вартиш [vartish]
quaint [куейнт] *adj.* дерина [derina], кӯҳна [kühna]
qualified [куалифайд] *adj.* корозмуда [korozmuda], боихтисос [boixtisos]
qualify [куалифай] *v.i.* дараҷаи ихтисосро муайян кардан [darajai ixtisosro muayyan kardan]
quality [куалити] *n.* сифат [sifat]
qualm [куам] *n.* дилбеҷошавӣ [dilbejoshavi], дилбеҳузурӣ [dilbehuzuri]
quantity [куантити] *n.* миқдор [miqdor], андоза [andoza]
quarantine [куарантин] *n.* карантин [karantin]
quarrel [куарел] *n.* низоъ [nizo'] / *v.i.* низоъ андохтан [nizo' andoxtan]
quarry [куари] *n.* кони санг [koni sang]
quart [куарт] *n.* кварта [kvarta]
quarter [куартер] *n.* чоряк [choryak]
quarterly [куартерли] *adj.* кварталӣ [kvartali] / *adv.* семоҳа [semoha]
quartz [куартз] *n.* квартс [kvarts]
queasy [куизи] *adj.* нимҷон [nimjon]
queen [куин] *n.* малика [malika], зани шоҳ [zani shoh]
queer [куир] *adj.* аҷиб [ajib]
query [куери] *n.* пурсиш [pursish], савол [savol] / *v.t.* пурсидан [pursidan]
question [куесчан] *n.* пурсиш [pursish], савол [savol] / *v.t.* пурсидан [pursidan]
quick [куик] *adj.* зуд [zud], тез [tez]
quiet [куайет] *n.* беовозӣ [beovozi] / *adj.* ором [orom], беовоз [beovoz]
quilt [куилт] *n.* кӯрпа [kürpa]
quit [куит] *v.i.* тарк кардан [tark kardan]
quite [куайт] *adv.* комилан [komilan]
quota [куота] *n.* ҳисса [hissa], саҳм [sahm]
quotation [куотейшан] *n.* иқтибос [iqtibos]
quote [куот] *n.* иқтибос [iqtibos]; *(stock market)* қурб [qurb] / *v.t.* иқтибос овардан [iqtibos ovardan]

R

rabbit [ребит] *n.* харгӯш [xargüsh]
rabid [ребид] *adj.* ҳор [hor]

rabies [рейбиз] *n.* ҳорӣ [hori]
race [рейс] *n. (competition)* пойга [poyga]; *(horse race)* аспдавонӣ [aspdavoni]; *(ethnicity)* нажод [nazhod]
racial [решал] *adj.* нажодӣ [nazhodi]
rack [рек] *n.* тиргак [tirgak], поя [poya]
racket [рекет] *n. (noise, uproar)* ҳаёҳуй [hayohuy]; *(tennis racket)* ракеткаи теннис [raketkai tennis]
radiator [рейдиетор] *n.* гармкунак [garmkunak]
radical [редикал] *adj.* тарафдори чорабиниҳои қатъӣ [tarafdori chorabinihoi qat'i], радикал [radikal]
radio [рейдио] *n.* радио [radio]
radioactive [рейдиоактив] *adj.* радиоактив [radioaktiv]
radius [рейдияс] *n.* шуоъ [shuo']
raffle [рефъл] *n.* лотерея [lotereya]
raft [рефт] *n.* амад [amad], сал [sal]
rafting [рефтинг] *n.* амадронӣ [amadroni], салронӣ [salroni]
rag [рег] *n.* латта [latta]
rage [рейҷ] *n.* хашм [xashm]
ragged [регед] *adj.* дарида [darida], порашуда [porashuda]
raid [рейд] *n.* тохтутоз [toxtutoz] / *v.t.* тохтутоз кардан [toxtutoz kardan]
railing [рейлинг] *n.* панҷара [panjara]
railroad [рейлрод] *n.* роҳи оҳан [rohi ohan]
railway [рейлуей] *n.* роҳи оҳан [rohi ohan]
rain [рейн] *n.* борон [boron] / *v.i.* борон боридан [boron boridan]
rainbow [рейнбо] *n.* рангинкамон [ranginkamon], тирукамон [tirukamon]
raincoat [рейнкот] *n.* боронӣ [boroni]
rainy [рейни] *adj.* серборон [serboron]
raise [рейз] *v.t. (standards, salaries, etc.)* баланд кардан [baland kardan]; *(rear children)* парвардан [parvardan], калон кардан [kalon kardan]
raisin [рейзин] *n.* мавиз [maviz]
rake [рейк] *n.* хаскашак [xaskashak] / *v.t.* бо хаскашак тӯда кардан [bo xaskashak tüda kardan]
rally [рели] *n.* ҷамъи оммавӣ [jam'i ommavi] / *v.t.* боз ҷамъ кардан [boz jam' kardan] / *v.i.* боз ҷамъ шудан [boz jam' shudan], боз қавӣ шудан [boz qavi shudan]
ramble [рембъл] *v.i.* бесарунӯг гап задан [besarunüg gap zadan]
ramification [ремификейшан] *n. (branch/subordinate part)* шоха [shoxa]; *(consequence)* оқибат [oqibat]
ramp [ремп] *n.* пастхамӣ [pastxami], нишеб [nisheb]
rancid [ренсид] *adj.* талхшуда [talxshuda]

random [рендом] *adj.* тасодуфӣ [tasodufi]
range [рейнч] *n. (distance)* якчанд [yakchand]; *(mountain range)* қаторкӯҳ [qatorküh]
rank [ренк] *n. (row/line)* саф [saf], қатор [qator]; *(position/post)* рутба [rutba], мансаб [mansab] / *v.t.* *(put in a line or row)* саф кашондан [saf kashondan]; *(classify)* тасниф кардан [tasnif kardan]
ransack [ренсек] *v.t.* ғорат кардан [ghorat kardan]
ransom [ренсом] *n.* фидия [fidiya] / *v.t.* пул дода озод кардан [pul doda ozod kardan], фидия дода халос кардан [fidiya doda xalos kardan]
rape [рейп] *n.* ба номус таҷовуз кардан(и) [ba nomus tajovuz kardan(i)] / *v.t.* ба номус таҷовуз кардан [ba nomus tajovuz kardan]
rapid [репид] *adj.* тез [tez]
rare [рер] *adj.* камёб [kamyob]
rash [реш] *n.* доначаҳо [donachaho] / *adj.* беандеша [beandesha], шитобкорона [shitobkorona]
raspberry [резбери] *n.* тамашк [tamashk]
rat [рет] *n.* калламуш [kallamush]
rate [рейт] *n.* нарх [narx]; *(speed)* тезӣ [tezi], суръат [sur'at]; **foreign exchange rate** қурби валюта [qurbi valyuta]
rather [радер] *adv.* беҳтар [behtar], бартар [bartar]; **I'd rather** беҳтар медонам [behtar medonam]
ratification [ретификейшан] *n.* тасдик [tasdiq]
ratify [ретифай] *v.t.* тасдиқ кардан [tasdiq kardan]
ration [решан] *n.* озуқа [ozuqa], воя [voya] / *v.t.* воясозӣ кардан [voyasozi kardan], ба вояҳо тақсим кардан [ba voyaho taqsim kardan]
rational [решонал] *adj.* оқил [oqil]
rattle [ретъл] *n.* шақшақа [shaqshaqa]
rattlesnake [ретълснейк] *n.* шақшақамор [shaqshaqamor]
ravine [равин] *n.* сой [soy], ҷарӣ [jari]
raw [ро] *adj.* хом [xom]
ray [рей] *n.* шуоъ [shuo']
razor [рейзор] *n.* риштарошак [rishtaroshak], ришгирак [rishgirak]; **razor blade** теғ [tegh], поку [poku]
reach [рич] *n.* дастрас [dastras] / *v.t.* расидан [rasidan]; **within reach** дар дастрас (будан) dar dastras (budan)
react [риакт] *v.i.* вокуниш доштан [vokunish doshtan]
reaction [риакшан] *n.* вокуниш [vokunish], аксуламал [aksulamal]
read [рид] *v.t.* хондан [xondan]
reader [ридър] *n.* хонанда [xonanda]
reading [ридинг] *n.* хониш [xonish]

ready [реди] *adj.* тайёр [tayyor], омода [omoda]
real [рил] *adj.* ҳақиқӣ [haqiqi], воқеӣ [voqei]
reality [риялити] *n.* ҳақиқат [haqiqat], воқеият [voqeiyat]
realize [риялайз] *v.t.* фаҳмидан [fahmidan], пай бурдан [pay burdan]
reap [рип] *v.t.* даравидан [daravidan]
reappear [риапир] *v.i.* боз намудор шудан [boz namudor shudan]
rear [рир] *n.* пушт [pusht], ақиб [aqib]; **in the rear** дар пушт(и) [dar pusht(i)]
reason [ризон] *n. (ability to reason)* хирад [xirad], ақл [aql]; *(reason for sth)* далел [dalel], сабаб [sabab] / *v.i.* андешидан [andeshidan]
reasonable [ризонабъл] *adj.* боандеша [boandesha], хирадманд [xiradmand]
reassure [риашур] *v.t.* боз итминон додан [boz itminon dodan]
rebate [рибейт] *n.* тахфиф [taxfif], кам кардани нарх [kam kardani narx]
rebel [ребел] *n.* шӯришгар [shürishgar] / *v.i.* шӯриш кардан [shürish kardan], қиём кардан [qiyom kardan]
rebellion [ребелян] *n.* шӯриш [shürish], қиём [qiyom]
rebuff [рибаф] *v.t.* рад кардан [rad kardan]
recall [рикол] *v.t. (repeal)* бекор кардан [bekor kardan]; *(recollect)* ба ёд овардан [ba yod ovardan]
receipt [ресит] *n.* забонхат [zabonxat]
receive [ресив] *v.t.* дарёфт кардан [daryoft kardan]; *(receive sb)* пазироӣ кардан [pHaziroi kardan]
receiver [ресивър] *n.* гиранда [giranda]; **telephone receiver** гӯшаки телефон [güshaki telefon]
recent [рисент] *adj.* нав [nav]
recently [рисентли] *adv.* ба наздикӣ [ba nazdiki]
reception [ресепшан] *n.* пазироӣ [piziroi]; **official reception** маҷлиси қабул [majlisi qabul]
recipe [ресипи] *n.* ретсепт [retsept]
reciprocity [ресипросити] *n.* дутарафа будан(и) [dutarafa budan(i)]
recite [ресайт] *v.t.* сухангарӣ кардан [suxangari kardan], нақл кардан [naql kardan]
reckon [рекан] *v.t.* ҳисоб кардан [hisob kardan]
recognition [рекагнишан] *n.* шинохтан(и) [shinoxtan(i)]
recognize [рекагнайз] *v.t.* шинохтан [shinoxtan]; **to officially recognize** ба расмият шинохтан [ba rasmiyat shinoxtan]
recommend [рекаменд] *v.t.* тавсия кардан [tavsiya kardan]
recommendation [рекамендейшан] *n.* тавсия [tavsiya]
recompense [рекомпенс] *n.* подош [podosh], талофӣ [talofi] / *v.t.* подош додан [podosh dodan], талофӣ додан [talofi dodan], товон додан [tovon dodan]

reconcile [рекансайл] *v.t.* оштӣ додан [oshti dodan]
reconciliation [рекансилиейшан] *n.* оштӣ [oshti]
record [рекорд] *n.* ёддошт [yoddosht], ҳуҷҷат [hujjat], гувоҳинома [guvohinoma]; *(world record/sports record)* рекорд [rekord]
record [рикорд] *v.t.* навишта гирифтан [navishta giriftan], ёддошт кардан [yoddosht kardan]
recover [рекавер] *v.i. (recover from sickness)* сиҳат шудан [sihat shudan]; *(find again)* боз ёфтан [boz yoftan]; *(collect [from a disaster zone, etc.])* боз ҷамъ кардан [boz jam' kardan]
recreation [рекриейшан] *n.* вақтхушӣ [vaqtxushi]
recruit [рекрут] *n.* сарбози нав [sarbozi nav] / *v.t.* одам чида гирифтан [odam chida giriftan];
recruitment [рекрутмент] *n.* *(mil.)* сарбозгирӣ кардан [sarbozgiri kardan]
rectangle [ректангл] *n.* росткунҷа [rostkunja]
rectangular [ректангюлар] *adj.* росткунҷа [rostkunja]
recuperate [рекуперейт] *v.i.* сиҳат шудан [sihat shudan], шифо ёфтан [shifo yoftan]
recurrence [рекуренс] *n.* такрор [takror]
recurring [рекуринг] *adj.* навбатӣ [navbati]
recycle [рисайкъл] *v.t.* партовҳоро истифода бурдани [partovhoro istifoda burdan]
recycling [рисайклинг] *n.* истифодаи партов [istifodai partov], партовтозакунӣ [partovtozakuni]
red [ред] *adj.* сурх [surx]
reddish [редиш] *adj.* сурхак [surxak], сурхтоб [surxtob]
redness [реднас] *n.* сурхӣ [surxi]
reduce [редюс] *v.t.* камтар кардан [kamtar kardan], пасттар кардан [pasttar kardan]
reduction [редакшан] *n.* камшавӣ [kamshavi], пастшавӣ [pastshavi]
reed [рид] *n.* най [nay]
reef [риф] *n.* харсанги зериобӣ [xarsangi zeriobi]; **coral reef** обсанги марҷонӣ [obsangi marjoni]
reel [рил] *n.* ғалтак [ghaltak]
refer [рефер] *v.t.* нисбат додан [nisbat dodan]; **to refer to** ҳавола кардан [havola kardan]
reference [референс] *n. (reference book)* маълумотнома [ma'lumotnoma]; *(letter of reference)* тавсиянома [tavsiyanoma]
refill [рифил] *v.t.* боз пур кардан [boz pur kardan]
refine [рифайн] *v.t.* тоза кардан [toza kardan], полудан [poludan]
refinery [рифайнери] *n.* полоишгоҳ [poloishgoh]
refit [рифит] *v.t.* таъмир кардан [ta'mir kardan]

reflect [рефлект] *v.i.* мунъакис шудан [mun'akis shudan]; *(think)* андеша кардан [andesha kardan] / *v.t.* мунъакис кардан [mun'akis kardan]

reflection [рефлекшан] *n.* инъикос [in'ikos]

reform [реформ] *v.i.* ислоҳот даровардан [islohot darovardan]

refresh [рефреш] *v.t.* тароват бахшидан [tarovat baxshidan], серун кардан [serun kardan]

refreshment [рефрешмент] *n. (food)* хӯриш [xürish]; *(drink)* нӯшокӣ [nüshoki], нӯшоба [nüshoba]

refrigerate [рефриҷерейт] *v.t.* ях кунондан [yax kunondan]

refrigerator [рефриҷерейтор] *n.* яхдон [yaxdon], яхчол [yaxchol]

refuge [рефюҷ] *n.* паноҳ [panoh], паноҳгоҳ [panohgoh]

refugee [рефюҷи] *n.* паноҳанда [panohanda], гуреза [gureza]

refund [рифанд] *n.* баргардондани пул [bargardondani pul] / *v.t.* пул баргардондан [pul bargardondan]

refusal [рефюзал] *n.* раддия [raddiya]

refuse [рефюз] *n.* ахлот [axlot] / *v.t.* рад кардан [rad kardan], даст кашидан [dast kashidan]

regard [регард] *n.* *(consideration)* мулоҳиза [mulohiza]; *(esteem)* ҳурмат [hurmat], эҳтиром [ehtirom] / *v.t.* *(look)* нигоҳ кардан [nigoh kardan], нигаристан [nigaristan]; *(pay consideration)* мулоҳиза кардан [mulohiza kardan]

regarding [регардиг] *prep.* дар бораи [dar borai]

regime [режим] *n.* тартибот [tartibot]; *(government)* сохти давлатӣ [soxti davlati], давлат [davlat]

region [риҷон] *n.* минтақа [mintaqa], ноҳия [nohiya]

regional [риҷонал] *adj.* маҳаллӣ [mahalli]

register [реҷистер] *n.* рӯйхат [rüyxat], дафтари қайд [daftari qayd] / *v.t.* қайд кардан [qayd kardan], рӯйхат кардан [rüyxat kardan]

registered letter [реҷистерд летер] *n.* номаи супоришӣ [nomai suporishi]

regret [регрет] *n.* пушаймонӣ [pushaymoni], афсӯс [afsüs] / *v.t.* пушаймон шудан [pushaymon shudan], афсӯс хӯрдан [afsüs xürdan]

regular [регюлар] *adj.* мунтазам [muntazam], ботартиб [botartib]

regulation [регюлейшан] *n.* танзим [tanzim]

rehabilitation [риҳабилитейшан] *n.* таҷдид [tajdid]; *(med.)* офият [ofiyat]

rehearsal [реҳерсал] *n.* машқ [mashq]

rehearse [реҳерс] *v.t.* машқ кардан [mashq kardan]
reimburse [риимбурс] *v.t.* товон додан [tovon dodan], талофӣ додан [talofi dodan]
rein [рейн] *n.* ҷилав [jilav], лаҷом [lajom]
reinforce [риинфорс] *v.t.* маҳкам кардан [mahkam kardan]
reject [реҷект] *v.t.* рад кардан [rad kardan]
rejection [реҷекшан] *n.* рад [rad]
relapse [рилапс] *n.* такрор [takror], такроршавӣ [takrorshavi]
relate [релейт] *v.t.* нақл кардан [naql kardan]
relationship [релейшаншип] *n.* нисбат [nisbat]; муносибат [munosibat]; *(connection)* алоқа [aloqa], робита [robita]; *(familial)* хешӣ [xeshi]
relative [релатив] *n.* хеш [xesh] / *adj.* нисбӣ [nisbi]
relax [релакс] *v.i.* *(untense)* суст шудан [sust shudan]; *(rest)* дам гирифтан [dam giriftan] / *v.t.* суст кардан [sust kardan]
relaxation [релаксейшан] *n.* дамгирӣ [damgiri]
release [релис] *n.* раҳоӣ [rahoi] / *v.t.* раҳонидан [rahonidan], озод кардан [ozod kardan]
reliable [релайабъл] *adj.* эътиборнок [e'tibornok], боэътимод [boe'timod]
relief [релиф] *n.* таскин [taskin], сабукӣ [sabuki]
relieve [релив] *v.t.* сабук кардан [sabuk kardan], таскин додан [taskin dodan]
religion [религҷан] *n.* дин [din]
religious [релиҷас] *adj.* *(pertaining to religion)* динӣ [dini]; *(religiously observant)* диндор [dindor]
rely [релай] *v.i.* эътимод доштан [e'timod doshtan]
remain [ремейн] *v.i.* мондан [mondan]
remaining [ремейнинг] *adj.* боқимонда [boqimonda], мондагӣ [mondagi]
remark [ремарк] *n.* қайд [qayd] / *v.i.* қайд карда мондан [qayd karda mondan], ба назар гирифтан [ba nazar giriftan]
remedy [ремеди] *n.* дору [doru], чора [chora] / *v.t.* *(remedy a situation/problem)* дуруст кардан [durust kardan]; *(remedy a disease/disorder)* сиҳат кардан [sihat kardan]
remember [ремембер] *v.t.* ёд кардан [yod kardan] / *v.i.* ба ёд омадан [ba yod omadan]
remind [ремайнд] *v.t.* ба ёд овардан [ba yod ovardan]
reminder [ремайндер] *n.* ёдоварӣ [yodovari], огоҳӣ [ogohi]
remit [римит] *v.t.* *(send)* фиристодан [firistodan]; *(slacken)* суст кардан [sust kardan]
remittance [римитанс] *n.* пули фиристодашуда [puli firistodashuda], пулфиристонӣ [pulfiristoni]
remorse [риморс] *n.* пушаймонӣ [pushaymoni]
remote [ремот] *adj.* дурдаст [durdast]

remove [ремув] *v.t.* кашидан [kashidan], бардоштан [bardoshtan]
renew [реню] *v.t.* аз нав барпо кардан [az nav barpo kardan], аз нав сар кардан [az nav sar kardan]
renewal [ренюал] *n.* азнавсозӣ [aznavsozi]
renounce [ренаунс] *v.t.* инкор кардан [inkor kardan], гардан тофтан [gardan toftan]
renovate [реновейт] *v.t.* аз нав кардан [az nav kardan], тоза кардан [toza kardan]
renovation [реновейшан] *n.* навкунӣ [navkuni]
rent [рент] *n.* иҷора [ijora] / *v.t. (rent from)* иҷора гирифтан [ijora giriftan]; *(rent to)* ба иҷора додан [ba ijora dodan]
reorganize [риорганайз] *v.t.* аз нав ташкил кардан [az nav tashkil kardan]
repair [рипер] *n.* таъмир [ta'mir], тармим [tarmim] / *v.t.* таъмир кардан [ta'mir kardan], тармим кардан [tarmim kardan]
repeat [рипит] *n.* такрор [takror] / *v.i. (repeat an action or occurrence)* такрор кардан [takror kardan], дубора кардан [dubora kardan]; *(repeat a word or sentence)* дубора гуфтан [dubora guftan]
repel [репел] *v.t.* аз худ дур кардан [az xud dur kardan]; *(repel with force)* зада гардондан [zada gardondan]
repent [репент] *v.i.* тавба кардан [tavba kardan]
repetition [репетишан] *n.* такрор [takror]
replace [риплейс] *v.t. (replace sth)* иваз кардан [ivaz kardan], алиш кардан [alish kardan]; *(replace sb)* ба ҷои (касе) таъин кардан [ba joi (kase) ta'in kardan]
reply [риплай] *n.* посух [posux] / *v.i.* посух додан [posux dodan]
report [репорт] *n.* гузориш [guzorish] / *v.t.* гузориш додан [guzorish dodan] / *v.i.* рӯзноманигорӣ кардан [rüznomanigori kardan], хабарнигорӣ кардан [xabarnigori kardan]
reporter [репортер] *n.* рӯзноманигор [rüznomanigor], хабарнигор [xabarnigor]
represent [репрезент] *v.t.* намоён кардан [namoyon kardan]
representative [репрезентатив] *n.* намоянда [namoyanda]
repression [репрешан] *n.* фурӯнишонӣ [furünishoni]
reprimand [репримaнд] *n.* сарзаниш [sarzanish] / *v.t.* сарзаниш кардан [sarzanish kardan]
reproduce [рипродюс] *v.t.* аз нав ба вуҷуд овардан [az nav ba vujud ovardan]
reproduction [рипродакшан] *n.* азнавбавуҷудоварӣ [aznavbavujudovari]
reptile [рептайл] *n.* хазанда [xazanda]
republic [репаблик] *n.* ҷумҳурӣ [jumhuri], ҷумҳурият [jumhuriyat]
republican [репабликан] *n.* ҷумҳурихоҳ [jumhurixoh] / *adj.* ҷумҳуриятӣ [jumhuriyati]

reputation [репютейшан] *n.* ном [nom], обрӯ [obrü]
request [рекуест] *n.* хоҳиш [xohish], дархост [darxost] / *v.t.* хоҳиш кардан [xohish kardan], дархост кардан [darxost kardan]
require [рикуайр] *v.t.* ниёзманд будан [niyozmand budan], эҳтиёҷ доштан [ehtiyoj doshtan]
requirement [рикуайрмент] *n.* ниёз [niyoz], ҳоҷат [hojat]
rescue [рескю] *n.* раҳоӣ [rahoi], наҷот [najot] / *v.t.* раҳонидан [rahonidan], наҷот додан [najot dodan]
research [рисерч] *n.* пажӯҳиш [pazhühish], таҳқиқ [tahqiq] / *v.t.* пажӯҳиш кардан [pazhühish kardan], таҳқиқ кардан [tahqiq kardan]
resemblance [ризембланс] *n.* монандӣ [monandi]
resemble [ризембъл] *v.t.* монанд будан [monand budan]
resent [ризент] *v.t.* ранҷидан [ranjidan]
reservation [резервейшан] *n. (at a hotel/restaurant)* брон [bron], пешакӣ гирифтан(и) [peshaki giriftan(i)]; *(doubt/misgiving)* шубҳа [shubha]
reserve [резерв] *n.* захира [zaxira]; *(mil.)* запас [zapas] / *v.t.* нигоҳ доштан [nigoh doshtan], захира кардан [zaxira kardan]; *(reserve in advance)* пешакӣ гирифтан [peshaki giriftan], брон кардан [bron kardan]
reserved [резервъд] *adj.* *(kept aside)* нигоҳдошта [nigohdoshta], захиракарда [zaxirakarda]; *(obtained in advance)* пешакӣ гирифта [peshaki girifta]
reservoir [резервуар] *n.* обанбор [obanbor]
reside [ризайд] *v.i.* зиндагӣ кардан [zindagi kardan], истиқомат кардан [istiqomat kardan]
residence [резиденс] *n.* истиқоматгоҳ [istiqomatgoh]
resident [резидент] *n.* сокин [sokin]
residue [резидю] *n.* пасмонда [pasmonda]
resign [ризайн] *v.i.* истеъфо додан [iste'fo dodan]
resignation [резигнейшан] *n.* истеъфо [iste'fo]
resin [резин] *n.* қатрон [qatron]
resist [резист] *v.t.* муқовимат кардан [muqovimat kardan]
resistance [резистанс] *n.* муқовимат [muqovimat]
resistant [резистант] *adj.* муқовиматкунанда [muqovimatkunanda]
resort [резорт] *n. (last resort)* чора [chora]; *(health resort)* осоишгоҳ [osoishgoh]
respect [респект] *n.* эҳтиром [ehtirom] / *v.t.* эҳтиром кардан [ehtirom kardan]
respirator [респирейтор] *n.* респиратор [respirator]
respond [респонд] *v.i.* посух додан [posux dodan], ҷавоб додан [javob dodan]
response [респонс] *n.* посух [posux], ҷавоб [javob]

responsible [респонсибъл] *adj.* масъул [mas'ul], ҷавобгар [javobgar]
rest [рест] *n.* дамгирӣ [damgiri] / *v.i.* дам гирифтан [dam giriftan]
restaurant [рестронт] *n.* ресторан [restoran]
restless [рестлес] *adj.* беқарор [beqaror], ноором [noorom]
restore [рестор] *v.t.* баргардондан [bargardondan], пас додан [pas dodan]
restrain [рестрейн] *v.t.* боздоштан [bozdoshtan], фурӯ нишондан [furü nishondan]; **to restrain oneself** худдорӣ кардан [xuddori kardan]
restrict [рестрикт] *v.t.* маҳдуд кардан [mahdud kardan]
restriction [рестрикшан] *n.* маҳдудият [mahdudiyat]
result [резалт] *n.* натиҷа [natija] / *v.i.* **to result in** баромадан [baromadan]
résumé [резаме] *n.* хулоса [xulosa]
resume [резюм] *v.t.* аз нав сар кардан [az nav sar kardan]
retail [ритейл] *n.* чакана [chakana] / *v.t.* **to sell at retail** чакана фурӯхтан [chakana furüxtan] / *adj.* **retail trade** савдои чакана [savdoi chakana], чаканафурӯшӣ [chakanafurüshi]
retailer [ритейлър] *n.* чаканафурӯш [chakanafurüsh]
retain [ритейн] *v.t.* нигоҳ доштан [nigoh doshtan]
retina [ретина] *n.* шабакия [shabakiya]
retire [ретайр] *v.i. (to leave)* худро дур кашидан [xudro dur kashidan]; *(to end one's career)* хонанишин шудан [xonanishin shudan]
retired [ретайрд] *adj.* хонанишин [xonanishin]
return [ретурн] *n.* бозгашт [bozgasht], баргашт [bargasht] / *v.t.* баргардондан [bargardondan], пас додан [pas dodan] / *v.i.* баргаштан [bargashtan], бозгаштан [bozgashtan]
reunite [риюнайт] *v.t.* аз нав як кардан [az nav yak kardan]
reveal [ревил] *v.t.* намоён кардан [namoyon kardan], падидор кардан [padidor kardan]
revelation [ревелейшан] *n.* ваҳӣ [vahy], илҳом [ilhom]
revenge [ревенҷ] *n.* интиқом [intiqom]
revenue [ревеню] *n.* даромад [daromad]
reverse [реверс] *n.* пушт [pusht] / *adj.* чаппа [chappa], баръакс [bar'aks] / *v.t.* пуштнокӣ рафтан [pushtnoki raftan]
review [ревю] *n.* тафтиши дубора [taftishi dubora] / *v.t.* аз нав дида баромадан [az nav dida baromadan], аз назар гузарондан [az nazar guzarondan]
revise [ревайз] *v.t.* тасҳеҳ кардан [tas-heh kardan], ислоҳ кардан [isloh kardan]
revive [ревайв] *v.t.* зинда кардан [zinda kardan] / *v.i.* зинда шудан [zinda shudan]
revocation [ревокейшан] *n.* лағв [laghv]

revoke [ревок] *v.t.* бекор кардан [bekor kardan], лағв кардан [laghv kardan]
revolt [револт] *n.* шӯриш [shürish] / *v.i.* шӯриш кардан [shürish kardan]
revolution [революшан] *n. (political)* инқилоб [inqilob]; *(rotation)* гардиш [gardish]
revolve [револв] *v.t.* гардондан [gardondan] / *v.i.* гардидан [gardidan]
reward [реуард] *n.* подош [podosh], инъом [in'om] / *v.t.* подош додан [podosh dodan], инъом додан [in'om dodan]
rhyme [райм] *n.* қофия [qofiya]
rhythm [ридъм] *n.* вазн [vazn]
rib [риб] *n.* қабурға [qaburgha]
ribbon [рибан] *n.* навор [navor], лента [lenta]
rice [райс] *n.* биринҷ [birinj]
rich [рич] *adj.* доро [doro], бой [boy], давлатманд [davlatmand]
rickety [рикети] *adj.* лиққонак [liqqonak], шалақ [shalaq]
riddle [ридал] *n.* чистон [chiston]
ride [райд] *n.* саворӣ [savori] / *v.t.* савор шудан [savor shudan]
rider [райдър] *n.* савор [savor]
ridge [риҷ] *n.* теға [tegha]; *(geo.)* қаторкӯҳ [qatorküh]
ridiculous [ридикюлас] *adj.* масхараомез [masxaraomez]
rifle [райфъл] *n.* милтиқ [miltiq], туфанг [tufang]
right [райт] *n.* ҳақ [haq] / *adj. (correct)* дуруст [durust]; *(opp. of left)* рост [rost]
right-handed [райт-ҳандед] *adj.* ростадаст [rostadast]
rigid [риҷид] *adj.* сахт [saxt]
rim [рим] *n.* лаб [lab], канор [kanor]
rind [райнд] *n.* пӯст [püst], пӯчоқ [püchoq]
ring [ринг] *n.* ангуштарин [angushtarin] / *v.t./v.i.* занг задан [zang zadan]
rinse [ринс] *v.t.* чайқондан [chayqondan]
riot [райат] *n.* исъён [is'yon] / *v.i.* исъён кардан [is'yon kardan]
rip [рип] *n.* даридагӣ [daridagi], порагӣ [poragi] / *v.t.* даррондан [darrondan], пора кардан [pora kardan] / *v.i.* даридан [daridan], пора шудан [pora shudan]
ripe [райп] *adj.* пухта [puxta], расида [rasida]
rise [райз] *n.* баландшавӣ [balandshavi], афзоиш [afzoish] / *v.i.* баланд шудан [baland shudan]; *(go up)* ба боло рафтан [ba bolo raftan]; *(get up, stand up)* хестан [xestan]; *(rise up)* бархостан [barxostan]
risk [риск] *n.* хатар [xatar] / *v.t.* ба хатар андохтан [ba xatar andoxtan]
rival [райвал] *n./adj.* рақиб [raqib], ҳариф [harif]
rivalry [райвалри] *n.* рақобат [raqobat], ҳамчашмӣ [hamchashmi]
river [ривър] *n.* дарё [daryo], рӯд [rüd]
road [род] *n.* роҳ [roh]

roar [рор] *n.* ғурриш [ghurrish], ғуррос [ghurros] / *v.i.* ғурридан [ghurridan], ғуррос задан [ghurros zadan]

roast [рост] *n.* кабоб [kabob] / *adj.* кабоб кардашуда [kabob kardashuda] / *v.t.* кабоб кардан [kabob kardan]

rob [роб] *v.t.* ғорат кардан [ghorat kardan], дуздидан [duzdidan]; *(to rob travelers/ commit highway robbery)* роҳзанӣ кардан [rohzani kardan]

robber [робер] *n.* ғоратгар [ghoratgar], дузд [duzd]; *(highway robber)* роҳзан [rohzan]

robbery [робери] *n.* ғорат [ghorat], дуздӣ [duzdi]; *(highway robbery)* роҳзанӣ [rohzani]

robe [роб] *n.* халат [xalat], ҷома [joma]

robin [робин] *n.* саъба [ca'ba], нору [noru]

robot [робот] *n.* робот [robot]

rock [рок] *n.* харсанг [xarsang], шух [shux] / *v.t.* ҷунбондан [junbondan], алвонҷ додан [alvonj dodan]

rocket [рокет] *n.* ракета [raketa]

rock music [рок мюзик] *n.* мусиқии рок [musiqii rok]

rocky [роки] *adj.* серхарсанг [serxarsang], сершух [sershux]

rod [род] *n.* мила [mila]; *(fishing)* шаст [shast]

role [рол] *n.* рол [rol], нақш [naqsh]

roll [рол] *n. (bread)* булка [bulka] / *v.t.* ғелондан [ghelondan] / *v.i.* ғелида рафтан [ghelida raftan], ғел задан [ghel zadan]

rolling pin [ролинг пин] *n.* тирак [tirak]

romance [руманс] *n.* ошиқӣ [oshiqi]

romantic [румантик] *adj.* ошиқона [oshiqona]

roof [руф] *n.* бом [bom]

room [рум] *n.* утоқ [utoq]

roommate [руммейт] *n.* ҳамутоқ [hamutoq], ҳамхона [hamxona]

rooster [рустар] *n.* хурӯс [xurüs]

root [руд] *n.* реша [resha]

rope [роп] *n.* арғамчин [arghamchin], расан [rasan]

rosary [розари] *n.* тасбеҳ [tasbeh]

rose [роз] *n.* садбарг [sadbarg], гул [gul] / *adj.* гулобӣ [gulobi]

rosebush [розбуш] *n.* гулбутта [gulbutta], буттаи гули садбарг [buttai guli sadbarg]

rot [рот] *v.i.* пӯсидан [püsidan], тосидан [tosidan]

rotten [ротен] *adj.* пӯсида [püsida], тосида [tosida]

rouge [руж] *n.* сурхӣ [surxi]

rough [раф] *adj.* дурушт [durusht]

round [раунд] *adj.* гирд [gird], лӯнда [lünda]

routine [рутин] *n.* тартиб [tartib], низом [nizom] / *adj.* оддӣ [oddi]

row [ро] *n.* қатор [qator] / *v.t.* бел кашидан [bel kashidan], бел задан [bel zadan]

rowboat [робот] *n.* қаиқ [qaiq]
royal [роял] *adj.* шоҳӣ [shohi], подшоҳӣ [podshohi]
rub [раб] *v.t.* молидан [molidan]
rubber [рабер] *n.* резина [rezina], каучук [kauchuk]
ruby [руби] *n.* лаъл [la'l], ёқути сурх [yoquti surx]
rucksack [раксек] *n.* борхалта [borxalta]
rudder [радер] *n.* суккон [sukkon]
rude [руд] *adj.* дағал [daghal], қӯрс [qürs]
rug [раг] *n.* қолин [qolin], гилем [gilem]
ruin [руин] *n.* ҳалокат [halokat], нобудшавӣ [nobudshavi]; *(ruins)* хароба [xaroba], вайрона [vayrona] / *v.t.* вайрон кардан [vayron kardan], хароб кардан [xarob kardan]
rule [рул] *n.* *(regulation/law)* дастур [dastur], қоида [qoida], қонун [qonun]; *(governing authority)* ҳукмронӣ [hukmroni], идора [idora] / *v.t.* *(exercise authority over, govern)* ҳукмронӣ кардан [hukmroni kardan], идора кардан [idora kardan]; *(draw a line)* хат кашидан [xat kashidan]
ruler [рулер] *n.* *(measuring tool)* хаткашак [xatkashak]; *(political)* ҳукмрон [hukmron]
rum [рам] *n.* ром [rom]
rumble [рамбъл] *n.* гулдуррос [guldurros] / *v.i.* гулдуррос задан [guldurros zadan]
rumor [румор] *n.* овоза [ovoza]
run [ран] *n.* дав [dav], тохт [toxt] / *v.i.* давидан [davidan], тохтан [toxtan]
runner [ранер] *n.* *(person who runs)* даванда [davanda]; *(device on which sth moves)* давак [davak]
running [ранинг] *n.* даводавӣ [davodavi]
rush [раш] *n.* *(hurry/haste)* шитоб [shitob]; *(reed)* най [nay], қамиш [qamish] / *v.t.* шитобон бурдан [shitobon burdan] / *v.i.* шитофтан [shitoftan]
Russian [рашан] *n.* рус [rus]; *(language)* русӣ [rusi] / *adj.* русӣ [rusi]
rust [раст] *n.* занг [zang] / *v.t.* занг занондан [zang zanondan] / *v.i.* занг задан [zang zadan]
rustic [растик] *adj.* рустоӣ [rustoi]
rusty [расти] *adj.* зангзада [zangzada]
rye [рай] *n.* ҷавдор [javdor]

S

saccharin [сакарин] *n.* сахарин [saxarin]
sack [сек] *n.* ҷувол [juvol], халта [xalta]
sacred [секрид] *adj.* муқаддас [muqaddas]
sacrifice [секрифайс] *n.* қурбон [qurbon] / *v.t.* қурбон кардан [qurbon kardan] / *v.i.* қурбон шудан [qurbon shudan]
sad [сед] *adj.* андӯҳгин [andühgin], ғамгин [ghamgin]

sadden [седен] *v.t.* андӯҳгин кардан [andühgin kardan], ғамгин кардан [ghamgin kardan] / *v.i.* андӯҳгин шудан [andühgin shudan], ғамгин шудан [ghamgin shudan]

saddle [седъл] *n.* зин [zin] / *v.t.* зин кардан [zin kardan]

sadness [саднес] *n.* андӯҳ [andüh], ғам [gham]

safe [сейф] *n.* сейф [seyf] / *adj. (without danger)* бехатар [bexatar]; *(secure)* эмин [emin]

safeguard [сейфгард] *n.* замонат [zamonat], ҳимоя [himoya]

safety [сейфти] *n. (lack of danger)* бехатарӣ [bexatari]; *(security)* амният [amniyat]

sail [сейл] *n.* бодбон [bodbon] / *v.t.* киштӣ рондан [kishti rondan] / *v.i.* бо киштӣ сафар кардан [bo kishti safar kardan]

sailboat [сейлбот] *n.* киштии бодбондор [kishtii bodbondor]

sailor [сейлор] *n.* баҳрнавард [bahrnavard], дарёнавард [daryonavard]

saint [сейнт] *n.* валӣ [vali]

sake [сейк] *n.* хотир [xotir]; **for the sake of** аз барои [az baroi], ба хотири [ba xotiri]; **for God's sake** аз барои Худо [az baroi Xudo]

salable [сейлабъл] *adj.* бозоргир [bozorgir]

salad [селад] *n.* салат [salat]

salary [селари] *n.* моҳона [mohona], музд [muzd]

sale [сейл] *n.* фурӯш [furüsh]; **for sale** фурӯшӣ [furüshi]

salesman [сейлзман] *n.* фурӯшанда [furüshanda], фурӯшгор [furüshgor]

sales tax [сейлз текс] *n.* андози гардиш [andozi gardish]

salmon [самон] *n.* озодмоҳӣ [ozodmohi]

salt [салт] *n.* намак [namak] / *v.t. (add salt)* намак андохтан [namak andoxtan]; *(preserve with salt)* намак задан [namak zadan]

salty [салти] *adj.* шӯр [shür], намакин [namakin]

salute [салут] *n.* салют [salyut] / *v.t.* салют додан [salyut dodan]

salvation [селвейшан] *n.* наҷот [najot], растагорӣ [rastagori]

salve [салв] *n.* марҳами шифобахш [marhami shifobaxsh]

same [сейм] *adj.* ҳамон [hamon], якхел [yakxel], яксон [yakson]

sample [сампъл] *n.* намуна [namuna] / *v.t.* санҷидан [sanjidan], озмудан [ozmudan]; *(sample food/drink)* чашида дидан [chashida didan]

sanctuary [сенкчуери] *n. (holy place)* ибодатгоҳ [ibodatgoh]; *(refuge)* паноҳгоҳ [panohgoh]

sand [сенд] *n.* рег [reg]

sandal [сандал] *n.* шиппак [shippak]

sandpaper [сендпейпър] *n.* коғази сунбода [koghazi sunboda]

sandwich [сендуич] *n.* сандвич [sandvich]

sane [сейн] *adj.* оқил [oqil]
sanitary [сенитери] *adj.* беҳдоштӣ [behdoshti], санитарӣ [sanitari]
sanity [санити] *n.* саломати ақл [salomati aql]
sap [сеп] *n.* шира [shira]
sapphire [сефайр] *n.* ёқути кабуд [yoquti kabud]
sardine [сардин] *n.* сардина [sardina]
satellite [сетелайт] *n.* ҳамроҳ [hamroh], моҳвора [mohvora]; **planetary satellite** ҳамроҳи сайёра [hamrohi sayyora]
satisfaction [сетисфакшан] *n.* қаноат [qanoat]
satisfactory [сетисфактори] *adj.* қаноатбахш [qanoatbaxsh]
satisfied [сетисфайд] *adj.* қонеъ [qone'], қаноатманд [qanoatmand]
satisfy [сетисфай] *v.t.* қонеъ гардондан [qone' gardondan]
Saturday [сетурдей] *n.* шанбе [shanbe]
sauce [сос] *n.* қайла [qayla], сарҷӯш [sarjüsh]
saucepan [соспан] *n.* дегча [degcha]
saucer [сосер] *n.* тақсимича [taqsimicha]
sausage [сосич] *n.* ҳасибча [hasibcha], колбаса [kolbasa]
savage [севиҷ] *n.* одами ваҳшӣ [odami vahshi] / *adj.* ваҳшӣ [vahshi], ваҳшиёна [vahshiyona]
save [сейв] *v.t.* наҷот додан [najot dodan], раҳо кардан [raho kardan]; *(save money, etc.)* пасандоз кардан [pasandoz kardan]
savings [сейвингс] *n.* пули пасандоз кардашуда [puli pasandoz kardashuda]
savior [сейвёр] *n.* раҳокунанда [rahokunanda], наҷотдиҳанда [najotdihanda]
savor [сейвор] *n.* маза [maza] / *v.t.* маза карда хӯрдан [maza karda xürdan]
savory [сейвори] *adj.* бомаза [bomaza]
saw [со] *n.* арра [arra] / *v.t.* арра кардан [arra kardan]
sawdust [содаст] *n.* аррамайда [arramayda]
say [сей] *v.t./v.i.* гуфтан [guftan]
saying [сейинг] *n.* мақол [maqol], масал [masal]
scab [скеб] *n.* карахш [karaxsh]
scaffold [скефолд] *n.* чӯббандӣ [chübbandi], чӯббаст [chübbast]
scald [скалд] *n.* ҷои сӯхтагӣ [joi süxtagi] / *v.t.* оби ҷӯш рехта сӯзондан [obi jüsh rexta süzondan]
scale [скейл] *n.* *(for measurement)* миқёс [miqyos]; *(mus.)* қаторовоз [qatorovoz]; *(of fish)* пулакча [pulakcha]; *(scales [for weighing])* тарозу [tarozu]
scan [скен] *v.t.* аз назар гузарондан [az nazar guzarondan]; *(mechanically scan)* тафсил дидан бо шуоъи локатор [tafsil didan bo shuo'i lokator]
scandal [скендал] *n.* расвоӣ [rasvoi]
scandalous [скендалас] *adj.* шармовар [sharmovar]

Scandinavian [скендинейвиян] *n.* скандинав [skandinav] / *adj.* скандинавӣ [skandinavi]
scar [скар] *n.* доғ [dogh], из [iz]
scarce [скерс] *adj.* кам [kam], нокифоя [nokifoya]; *(rare)* камёб [kamyob]
scare [скер] *v.t.* тарсондан [tarsondan]
scarecrow [скеркро] *n.* хӯса [xüsa], матарс [matars]
scarf [скарф] *n.* гарданпеч [gardanpech], шарф [sharf]
scarlet [скарлет] *adj.* суп-сурх [sup-surx], гулгун [gulgun]
scatter [скетер] *v.t.* пароканда кардан [parokanda kardan], пошидан [poshidan] / *v.i.* пароканда шудан [parokanda shudan], пошида шудан [poshida shudan]
scene [син] *n.* манзара [manzara]; *(theatrical)* намоиш [namoish]
scenery [синери] *n.* манзара [manzara]; *(theatrical)* ороиши саҳна [oroishi sahna]
scent [сент] *n.* хушбӯӣ [xushbüy], накҳат [nakhat]
schedule [скеҷуал] *n.* ҷадвал [jadval] / *v.t.* муайян кардан [muayyan kardan]
scheme [ским] *n.* *(plan)* нақша [naqsha], тарҳ [tarh]; *(plot/intrigue)* найранг [nayrang], дасиса [dasisa]
scholar [сколар] *n.* донишманд [donishmand], олим [olim]
scholarship [сколаршип] *n.* донишмандӣ [donishmandi]; *(financial aid for school)* стипендия [stipendiya]
school [скул] *n.* мактаб [maktab]
schoolchild [скулчайлс] *n.* мактаббача [maktabbacha], мактабхон [maktabxon]
schoolmate [скулмейт] *n.* шарикдарс [sharikdars]
schoolteacher [скултичър] *n.* муаллим [muallim], омӯзгор [omüzgor]
science [сайанс] *n.* илм [ilm], фан [fan]
scientific [сайантифик] *adj.* илмӣ [ilmi]
scientist [сайантист] *n.* донишманд [donishmand], олим [olim]
scissors [сизърз] *n.* қайчӣ [qaychi]
scold [сколд] *v.t.* сарзаниш кардан [sarzanish kardan]
scope [скоп] *n.* доира [doira], ҳудуд [hudud]
score [скор] *n.* *(notch)* нишона [nishona]; *(of a game)* ҳисоб [hisob] / *v.t.* *(mark with a notch)* нишона кардан [nishona kardan]; *(score a goal)* гол задан [gol zadan]
scorn [скорн] *n.* таҳқир [tahqir] / *v.t.* таҳқир кардан [tahqir kardan]
scorpion [скорпян] *n.* каждум [kazhdum]
scour [скаур] *v.t.* *(clean)* тоза кардан [toza kardan], шустан [shustan]; *(search thoroughly)* кофтуков кардан [koftukov kardan], шадалинг зада гаштан [shadaling zada gashtan]
scrap [скрап] *n.* порча [porcha]

scrape [скрейп] *v.t.* харошидан [xaroshidan], тарошидан [taroshidan]
scratch [скрач] *n.* изи ханҷол [izi xanjol] / *v.t.* ханҷол кардан [xanjol kardan]
scream [скрим] *v.i.* дод задан [dod zadan], ҷеғ задан [jegh zadan]
screen [скрин] *n.* *(partition)* ҳоил [hoil], парда [parda]; *(movie screen)* экрани кино [ekrani kino]; *(television screen)* оинаи нилгун [oinai nilgun] / *v.t.* *(cover or shield)* панаҳ кардан [panah kardan], пеш гирифтан [pesh giriftan]; *(test)* озмудан [ozmudan]
screw [скру] *n.* мехи печдор [mexi pechdor], печ [pech] / *v.t.* тоб дода сахт кардан [tob doda saxt kardan]
screwdriver [скрудрайвер] *n.* печтобак [pechtobak], мурваттобак [murvattobak]
scribble [скрибъл] *v.t.* харошидан [xaroshidan]
scrub [скраб] *v.t.* бо чӯтка тоза кардан [bo chütka toza kardan]
scruple [скрупъл] *n.* дудилагӣ [dudilagi]
scrupulous [скрупюлас] *adj.* бовиҷдон [bovijdon]
sculpt [скалпт] *v.i.* ҳайкал тарошидан [haykal taroshidan]
sculptor [скалптор] *n.* ҳайкалтарош [haykaltarosh]
sculpture [скалпчур] *n.* ҳайкал [haykal]; *(the art of sculpture)* ҳайкалтарошӣ [haykaltaroshi]
scum [скам] *n.* кафк [kafk]
scythe [сайд] *n.* пойдос [poydos], доси дастадароз [dosi dastadaroz]
sea [си] *n.* баҳр [bahr], дарё [daryo]
seacoast [сикост] *n.* соҳили баҳр [sohili bahr]
seagull [сигал] *n.* моҳихӯрак [mohixürak]
seahorse [сиҳорс] *n.* аспаки баҳрӣ [aspaki bahri]
seal [сил] *n.* *(animal)* тюлен [tyulen]; *(sth that secures or closes)* мӯҳр [mühr], тамға [tamgha] / *v.t.* *(affix a seal)* мӯҳр задан [mühr zadan]; *(seal up)* хамира молидан [xamira molidan]
sealant [силант] *n.* хамира [xamira]
seam [сим] *n.* дарз [darz], чок [chok]
seamstress [симстрес] *n.* дӯзанда [düzanda]
seaport [сипорт] *n.* бандаргоҳи баҳрӣ [bandargohi bahri]
search [серч] *n.* кофтуков [koftukov], ҷустуҷӯ [justujü] / *v.t.* ҷустан [justan], кофтан [koftan]
seasick [сисик] *adj.* касали баҳрӣ [kasali bahri]
seasickness [сисикнес] *n.* касалии баҳрӣ [kasalii bahri]
season [сизан] *n.* фасл [fasl]
seasonal [сизанал] *adj.* фаслӣ [fasli]
seat [сит] *n.* *(place to sit)* нишастгоҳ [nishastgoh]; *(chair)* курсӣ [kursi]
seawater [сиуатер] *n.* оби баҳрӣ [obi bahri]

seaweed [сиуид] *n.* растании баҳрӣ [rastanii bahri]
seclusion [секлужан] *n.* гӯшанишинӣ [güshanishini]
second [секанд] *n.* сония [soniya] / *adj.* дуюм [duyum]
secret [сикрет] *n.* роз [roz], сир [sir] / *adj.* пинҳонӣ [pinhoni], ниҳонӣ [nihoni]
secretary [секретери] *n.* котиб [kotib]
section [секшан] *n.* қисм [qism]
secular [секюлар] *adj.* ғайридинӣ [ghayridini]
secure [секюр] *adj.* эмин [emin] / *v.t.* таъмин кардан [ta'min kardan]
security [секюрити] *n.* амният [amniyat]
sedate [седейт] *adj.* ором [orom] / *v.t.* ором кардан [orom kardan]
seduce [седюс] *v.t.* фирефтан [fireftan]
seduction [седакшан] *n.* фиреб [fireb]
see [си] *v.t.* дидан [didan] / *v.i.* фаҳмидан [fahmidan]
seed [сид] *n.* тухм [tuxm]
seek [сик] *v.t.* ҷустан [justan]
seem [сим] *v.i.* намудан [namudan], ба назар намудан [ba nazar namudan]; **It seems to me that …** Ба назарам менамояд ки … [Ba nazaram menamoyad ki …]
segment [сегмент] *n.* қисмат [qismat], ҳисса [hissa]
seize [сиз] *v.t.* қапидан [qapidan], рабудан [rabudan]
seizure [сижур] *n.* *(confiscation)* мусодира [musodira]; *(med.)* ҳамла [hamla]
seldom [селдом] *adv.* кам [kam]
select [селект] *v.t.* хоста гирифтан [xosta giriftan], ҷудо карда гирифтан [judo karda giriftan]
selection [селекшан] *n.* интихоб [intixob]
self [селф] *adj.* худ [xud]
sell [сел] *v.t.* фурӯхтан [furüxtan]
seller [селар] *n.* фурӯшанда [furüshanda]
semicolon [семайколон] *n.* нуқтавергул [nuqtavergul]
senate [сенат] *n.* сенат [senat]
senator [сенатор] *n.* сенатор [senator]
send [сенд] *v.t.* фиристодан [firistodan], равона кардан [ravona kardan]
sender [сендер] *n.* фиристанда [firistanda]
senior [синёр] *n./adj.* калон [kalon]
sensation [сенсейшан] *n.* *(feeling)* ҳис [his], эҳсос [ehsos]; *(state of intense interest/excitement)* ҳангома [hangoma]
sense [сенс] *n.* *(feeling)* ҳис [his], эҳсос [ehsos]; *(consciousness)* ҳуш [hush]; *(meaning)* маъно [ma'no]
senseless [сенслес] *adj.* *(without feeling)* беҳис [behis], карахт [karaxt]; *(without meaning)* бемаънӣ [bema'ni]; *(without consciousness)* беҳуш [behush]
sensitive [сенситив] *adj.* ҳассос [hassos]
sentence [сентенс] *n.* *(gram.)* ҷумла [jumla]; *(legal)* ҳукми суд [hukmi sud] / *v.t.* ҳукм кардан [hukm kardan]

separate [сепарейт] *adj.* ҷудо [judo], ҷудогона [judogona]
separate [сепарет] *v.t.* ҷудо кардан [judo kardan] / *v.i.* ҷудо шудан [judo shudan]
separation [сепарейшан] *n.* ҷудоӣ [judoi]
September [септембер] *n.* сентябр [sentyabr]
septic [септик] *adj.* пӯсида [püsida], септикӣ [septiki]; **to become septic** септикӣ шудан [septiki shudan]
sequel [сикуал] *n.* давом [davom]
sergeant [сарҷент] *n.* сержант [serzhant]
series [сириз] *n.* силсила [silsila]
serious [сирияс] *adj.* ҷиддӣ [jiddi]
sermon [сермон] *n.* вазъ [vaz'], хутба [xutba]
serum [серум] *n.* хуноба [xunoba]
servant [сервант] *n.* нӯкар [nükar], чокар [chokar], хизматгор [xizmatgor]
serve [серв] *v.t.* хизмат кардан [xizmat kardan]
service [сервис] *n.* хизмат [xizmat]
session [сешан] *n.* маҷлис [majlis]
set [сет] *n.* даста [dasta], маҷмӯа [majmüa] / *v.t.* *(put sth down, place sth)* гузоштан [guzoshtan]; *(set the table)* чидан [chidan]; *(set a price)* таъин кардан [ta'in kardan] / *v.i.* фурӯ рафтан [furü raftan], ғуруб кардан [ghurub kardan]
settle [сетъл] *v.t.* ҷойгир кардан [joygir kardan], шинондан [shinondan] / *v.i.* ҷойгир шудан [joygir shudan], кӯчида омадан [küchida omadan]
settlement [сетълмент] *n.* *(habitation)* деҳа [deha]; *(solution to a problem)* ҳал [hal], оқибат [oqibat]
seven [севен] *num.* ҳафт [haft]
seventeen [севентин] *num.* ҳабдаҳ [habdah]
seventeenth [севентинт] *adj.* ҳабдаҳум [habdahum]
seventh [севент] *adj.* ҳафтум [haftum]
seventy [севенти] *num.* ҳафтод [haftod]
several [северал] *adj.* якчанд [yakchand], чанде [chande]
severe [севир] *adj.* сахт [saxt]
sew [со] *v.t.* дӯхтан [düxtan]
sewer [суер] *n.* канализатсия [kanalizatsiya]
sewing [соинг] *n.* дӯхт [düxt]
sex [секс] *n.* ҷинс [jins]
sexual [секшуал] *adj.* ҷинсӣ [jinsi]
sexuality [секшуалити] *n.* ҷинсият [jinsiyat]
shabby [шаби] *adj.* фарсуда [farsuda], фарсудашуда [farsudashuda]
shade [шейд] *n.* *(place of shadow)* соягоҳ [soyagoh]; *(shadow)* соя [soya]; *(variation of a color, meaning, etc.)* тобиш [tobish]; *(lamp shade)* сарпӯши чароғ [sarpüshi charogh]
shadow [шадо] *n.* соя [soya]

shady [шейди] *adj. (having shade)* серсоя [sersoya], соядор [soyador]; *(questionable, of dubious character)* шубҳаомез [shubhaomez]

shaft [шафт] *n.* ходa [xoda], шохтир [shohtir], даста [dasta]

shaggy [шаги] *adj.* пахмоқ [paxmoq], сермӯй [sermüy], серпашм [serpashm]

shake [шейк] *v.t.* такондан [takondan], ҷунбондан [junbondan] / *v.i.* ларзидан [larzidan], ҷунбидан [junbidan]

shallow [шало] *adj.* рӯякӣ [rüyaki]; *(of water)* пастоб [pastob]

sham [шам] *n.* бардурӯғӣ [bardurüghi]

shame [шейм] *n.* шарм [sharm], хиҷолат [xijolat]; **What a shame.** Ҳайф аст. [Hayf ast.]

shameless [шеймлес] *adj.* бешарм [besharm]

shampoo [шампу] *n.* шампун [shampun]

shape [шейп] *n.* шакл [shakl] / *v.t.* сохтан [soxtan], офаридан [ofaridan]

share [шер] *n. (portion)* ҳисса [hissa]; *(of a company)* саҳм [sahm] / *v.t.* тақсим кардан [taqsim kardan] / *v.i.* иштирок кардан [ishtirok kardan]

shareholder [шерҳолдер] *n.* саҳмдор [sahmdor]

shark [шарк] *n.* кӯсамоҳӣ [küsamohi], акула [akula]

sharp [шарп] *adj.* тез [tez], бурро [burro]

sharpen [шарпен] *v.t.* тез кардан [tez kardan]

shave [шейв] *v.t.* тарошидан [taroshidan]

shaving cream [шейвинг крим] *n.* креми риштарошӣ [kremi rishtaroshi]

shawl [шол] *n.* шол [shol]

she [ши] *pron.* вай [vay], ӯ [ü] *(*барои занону духтарон*)*

shear [шир] *v.t.* қайчӣ кардан [qaychi kardan]

shears [ширс] *n. (for wool)* қайчии пашмчинӣ [qaychii pashmchini]; *(for gardening)* қайчии токбурӣ [qaychii tokburi]

shed [шед] *n.* анбор [anbor]; *(woodshed)* ҳезумхона [hezumxona] / *v.t. (shed tears, blood, etc.)* рехтан [rextan]; *(shed light)* равшан кардан [ravshan kardan]; *(shed skin)* пӯст партофтан [püst partoftan]

sheep [шип] *n.* гӯсфанд [güsfand]

sheer [шир] *adj. (transparent)* шаффоф [shaffof]; *(steep)* ростфуромада [rostfuromada]

sheet [шит] *n. (bedding)* ҷойпӯш [joypüsh], малофа [malofa]; *(of paper)* варақа [varaqa]

shelf [шелф] *n. (pl.* **shelves***)* раф [raf]

shell [шел] *n. (of nuts, seeds, etc.)* пӯчоқ [püchoq]; *(of animals)* зиреҳ [zireh]; *(of sea creatures)* гӯшмоҳӣ [güshmohi]; *(mil.)* тири тӯп [tiri tüp]

shellfish [шелфиш] *n.* моллюскҳо [mollyuskho]
shelter [шелтер] *n.* паноҳ [panoh], сарпаноҳ [sarpanoh] / *v.t.* паноҳ додан [panoh dodan]
shepherd [шеперд] *n.* чӯпон [chüpon], шубон [shubon]
shield [шилд] *n.* сипар [sipar]
shift [шифт] *n.* ивазкунӣ [ivazkuni], дигаркунӣ [digarkuni] / *v.t.* иваз кардан [ivaz kardan] / *v.i.* ҷой иваз кардан [joy ivaz kardan]
shine [шайн] *v.t.* ҷило додан [jilo dodan] / *v.i.* дурахшидан [duraxshidan], тобидан [tobidan]
ship [шип] *n.* киштӣ [kishti] / *v.t.* бо киштӣ бор кардан [bo kishti bor kardan]
shirt [ширт] *n.* курта [kurta], пероҳан [perohan]
shiver [шивер] *v.i.* ларзидан [larzidan]
shock [шок] *n.* такон [takon]; *(med.)* садама [sadama] / *v.t.* такондан [takondan]
shoe [шу] *n.* пойафзол [poyafzol], кафш [kafsh]
shoehorn [шуҳорн] *n.* кафчаи кафшпӯшӣ [kafchai kafshpüshi]
shoelace [шулейс] *n.* бандаки пойафзол [bandaki poyafzol]
shoe polish [шу полиш] *n.* локи пойафзол [loki poyafzol]
shoot [шут] *v.t.* тир андохтан [tir andoxtan], паррондан [parrondan]
shop [шоп] *n.* дӯкон [dükon], мағоза [maghoza] / *v.i.* харид кардан [xarid kardan]
shopkeeper [шопкипер] *n.* дӯкондор [dükondor]
shopping [шопинг] *n.* харид [xarid]
shore [шор] *n.* соҳил [sohil], канор [kanor]
short [шорт] *adj.* кӯтоҳ [kütoh]; *(of short stature)* қадпаст [qadpast]
shortage [шортиҷ] *n.* камӣ [kami], норасоӣ [norasoi]
shorten [шортен] *v.t.* кӯтоҳ кардан [kütoh kardan]
shortly [шортли] *adv.* ба зудӣ [ba zudi]
shorts [шортс] *n.* шими кӯтоҳ [shimi kütoh]
should [шуд] *v.i.* боистан [boistan]
shoulder [шолдер] *n.* шона [shona], китф [kitf], дӯш [düsh]
shove [шав] *n.*тела [tela] / *v.t.* тела додан [tela dodan]
shovel [шавал] *n.* бел [bel]
show [шо] *n.* намоиш [namoish], тамошо [tamosho] / *v.t.* нишон додан [nishon dodan]
shower [шауер] *n.* душ [dush] / *v.i.* душ кардан [dush kardan]
shrewd [шруд] *adj.* зирак [zirak], борикбин [borikbin]
shrimp [шримп] *n.* креветка [krevetka]
shrine [шрайн] *n.* мазор [mazor], сағона [saghona]
shrink [шринк] *v.t.* коҳондан [kohondan], хурд кардан [xurd kardan] / *v.i.* костан [kostan], хурд шудан [xurd shudan]

shuffle [шафъл] *v.t.* тагу рӯ кардан [tagu rü kardan]; **shuffle cards** қартаҳоро тагу рӯ кардан [qartahoro tagu rü kardan]

shut [шат] *v.t.* пӯшондан [püshondan], бастан [bastan]

shy [шай] *adj.* шармгин [sharmgin]

sick [сик] *adj.* касал [kasal], бемор [bemor]

sickness [сикнас] *n.* касалӣ [kasali], беморӣ [bemori]

side [сайд] *n. (of a person/ object)* паҳлӯ [pahlü]; *(direction)* сӯй [süy], сӯ [sü]

sidewalk [сайдвок] *n.* пиёдагард [piyodagard]

sideways [сайдвейз] *adv.* аз паҳлӯ [az pahlü]

sieve [сив] *n. (small-holed)* элак [elak]; *(large-holed)* ғалбер [ghalber]

sift [сифт] *v.t.* бехтан [bextan], элак кардан [elak kardan]

sigh [сай] *n.* оҳ [oh] / *v.i.* оҳ кашидан [oh kashidan]

sight [сайт] *n. (sense)* биниш [binish], биноӣ [binoi]; *(a sight/scene)* манзара [manzara]

sign [сайн] *n.* аломат [alomat], ишора [ishora] / *v.t.* имзо кардан [imzo kardan] / *v.i.* ишора кардан [ishora kardan]

signal [сигнал] *n.* ишора [ishora]

signature [сигначур] *n.* имзо [imzo]

significance [сигнификанс] *n. (meaning)* маъно [ma'no]; *(importance)* аҳамият [ahamiyat]

signify [сигнифай] *v.t.* маъно доштан [ma'no doshtan]

silence [сайланс] *n.* хомӯшӣ [xomüshi] / *v.t.* хомӯш кардан [xomüsh kardan]

silent [сайлант] *adj.* хомӯш [xomüsh]

silk [силк] *n.* абрешим [abreshim] / *adj.* абрешимӣ [abreshimi]

silly [сили] *adj.* аблаҳ [ablah]

silver [силвар] *n.* нуқра [nuqra], сим [sim]

similar [симилар] *adj.* монанд [monand]

similarity [симиларити] *n.* монандӣ [monandi]

simmer [симер] *v.i.* оҳиста ҷӯшидан [ohista jüshidan]

simple [симпъл] *adj.* содда [sodda]

simplify [симплифай] *v.t.* осонтар кардан [osontar kardan]

simply [симпли] *adv. (only, merely)* танҳо [tanho], фақат [faqat]; *(plainly)* бенозунузона [benozunuzona]

simulate [симюлейт] *v.t.* вонамуд кардан [vonamud kardan], сохтакорӣ кардан [soxtakori kardan]

simulation [симюлейшан] *n.* вонамуд [vonamud], амсиласозӣ [amsilasozi]

sin [син] *n.* гуноҳ [gunoh] / *v.i.* гуноҳ кардан [gunoh kardan]

since [синс] *adv. (before)* пеш [pesh], пештар [peshtar]; *(from before until now)* аз пештар то ҳоло [az peshtar to holo] / *prep.* аз вақте ки [az vaqte ki]

sincere [синсир] *adj.* самимӣ [samimi]
sincerity [синсерити] *n.* ихлос [ixlos], самимият [samimiyat]
sinew [синю] *n.* пай [pay]
sing [синг] *v.t./v.i.* сурудан [surudan]
singer [сингер] *n.* сароянда [saroyanda]
singing [сингинг] *n.* сурудхонӣ [surudxoni]
single [сингъл] *adj.* якка [yakka], ягона [yagona]
single room [сингъл рум] *n.* утоқи яккаса [utoqi yakkasa]
sinister [синистер] *adj.* шум [shum], тарсангез [tarsangez]
sink [синк] *n.* дастшӯяк [dastshüyak]
sip [сип] *n.* қулт [qult] / *v.t.* як қулт нӯшидан [yak qult nüshidan]
sir [сир] *n.* ҷаноб [janob]
sister [систер] *n.* хоҳар [xohar]
sister-in-law [систер-ин-ло] *n. (brother's wife)* янга [yanga]; *(wife's sister)* хоҳарарӯс [xohararüs]; *(husband's sister)* хоҳаршӯй [xoharshüy]
sit [сит] *v.i.* нишастан [nishastan], шиштан [shishtan]
site [сайт] *n.* ҷой [joy], маҳал [mahal]
situation [сичюейшан] *n.* ҳолат [holat], вазъият [vaz'iyat]
six [сикс] *num.* шаш [shash]
sixteen [сикстин] *num.* шонздаҳ [shonzdah]
sixteenth [сикстинт] *adj.* шонздаҳум [shonzdahum]
sixth [сикст] *adj.* шашум [shashum]
sixty [сиксти] *num.* шаст [shast]
size [сайз] *n.* қад [qad], андоза [andoza]
skate [скейт] *n. (footwear)* асбоби яхмолакпарӣ; *(type of fish)* суфрамоҳӣ / *v.i.* яхмолакпарӣ кардан [yaxmolakpari kardan]
skeleton [скелетон] *n.* устухонбандӣ [ustuxonbandi]
sketch [скеч] *n.* ангора [angora]
ski [ски] *n.* лижа [lizha] / *v.i.* лижаронӣ кардан [lizharoni kardan]
skid [скид] *v.i.* андармон шудан [andarmon shudan]
skill [скил] *n.* ҳунар [hunar]
skillful [скилфул] *adj.* ҳунарманд [hunarmand]
skim [ским] *v.t.* қаймоқ гирифтан [qaymoq giriftan]
skim milk [ским милк] *n.* шири қаймоқаш гирифтагӣ [shiri qaymoqash giriftagi]
skin [скин] *n.* пӯст [püst]
skinny [скини] *adj.* лоғар [loghar]
skip [скип] *v.i.* ҷастухез кардан [jastuxez kardan]
skirt [скирт] *n.* доман [doman]
skull [скал] *n.* косаи сар [kosai sar]
sky [скай] *n.* осмон [osmon]
slack [слек] *adj.* суст [sust]
slam [слем] *v.t.* шароққос занондан [sharaqqos zanondan]

slang [сленг] *n.* забони гуфтугӯӣ [zaboni guftugüi]
slant [слент] *n.* нишеб [nisheb] / *v.i.* кaҷ шудан [kaj shudan]
slap [слеп] *n.* шаллоқ [shalloq] / *v.t.* шаллоқ задан [shalloq zadan]
slash [слеш] *v.t.* зада буридан [zada buridan], кафондан [kafondan]
slate [слейт] *n. (stone)* варақасанг [varaqasang]; *(roofing slate)* шифер [shifer]
slave [слейв] *n.* банда [banda], ғулом [ghulom]
slavery [слейвари] *n.* бандагӣ [bandagi]
sled [след] *n.* чана [chana]
sleek [слик] *adj.* силиқ [siliq]
sleep [слип] *v.i.* хобидан [xobidan]
sleepy [слипи] *adj.* хоболуд [xobolud]
sleeve [слив] *n.* остин [ostin]
slender [слендар] *adj.* борик [borik]
slice [слайс] *n.* порча [porcha] / *v.t.* буридан [buridan]
slight [слайт] *adj. (a little bit)* кам [kam]; *(slight of build)* тунук [tunuk] / *n.* беҳурматӣ [behurmati]
slim [слим] *adj.* борик [borik]
sling [слинг] *n.* фалахмон [falaxmon]
slip [слип] *n.* лағжиш [laghzhish] / *v.i.* лағжидан [laghzhidan]
slipper [слипер] *n.* кафши хонапӯшӣ [kafshi xonapüshi], шиппак [shippak]
slippery [слипери] *adj.* лағжонак [laghzhonak]
slogan [слоган] *n.* шиор [shior]
slope [слоп] *n.* нишеб [nisheb], нишебӣ [nishebi]
sloppy [слопи] *adj. (messy)* бетартиб [betartib]; *(of work)* нимкола [nimkola], чалачулпа [chalachulpa]
slot [слот] *n.* сӯрох [sürox]
sloth [слот] *n. (animal)* коҳилак [kohilak]; *(laziness)* танбалӣ [tanbali], коҳилӣ [kohili]
slow [сло] *adj.* оҳиста [ohista] / *v.t.* суст кардан [sust kardan] / *v.i.* суст шудан [sust shudan]
sluggish [слагиш] *adj.* суст [sust]
sluice [слуис] *n.* дарвозаи обпарто [darvozai obparto]
slum [сламз] *n.* маҳалҳои ноободи камбағалон [mahalhoi noobodi kambaghalon]
small [смол] *adj.* хурд [xurd], майда [mayda]
smart [смарт] *adj. (intelligent)* зирак [zirak]; *(well-dressed)* хушсарулибос [xushsarulibos]
smash [смаш] *v.t.* хароб кардан [xarob kardan]
smell [смел] *n.* бӯй [büy]; *(sense of smell)* бӯйоӣ [büyoi], шомма [shomma] / *v.t.* бӯидан [büidan], бӯй кардан [büy kardan] / *v.i.* бӯй додан [büy dodan]
smile [смайл] *n.* лабханд [labxand], табассум [tabassum] / *v.i.* лабханд кардан [labxand kardan], табассум кардан [tabassum kardan]

smith [смит] *n.* оҳангар [ohangar]
smog [смог] *n.* смог [smog]
smoke [смок] *n.* дуд [dud] / *v.i.* сигор кашидан [sigor kashidan]
smoky [смоки] *adj.* пурдуд [purdud], дуднок [dudnok]
smooth [смуд] *adj.* суфта [sufta]
smuggle [смагъл] *v.t.* қочоқ бурдан [qochoq burdan]
smuggler [смаглер] *n.* қочоқчӣ [qochoqchi]
smuggling [смаглинг] *n.* қочоқчигӣ [qochoqchigi]
snack [снак] *n.* газак [gazak], хӯриш [xürish]; **snack bar** ошхонача [oshxonacha]
snail [снейл] *n.* тӯқумшуллуқ [tüqumshulluq], ҳолазун [holazun]
snake [снейк] *n.* мор [mor]
snap [снап] *v.t.* *(bite)* газидан [gazidan]; *(snap one's fingers)* ҳӯппоқ задан [hüppoq zadan]; *(break)* шикастан [shikastan] / *v.i.* *(emit a snapping sound)* қарс-қурс кардан [qars-qurs kardan]; *(answer rudely)* посухи нешдор гуфтан [posuxi neshdor guftan]
snarl [снарл] *v.i.* дандон нишон додан [dandon nishon dodan]
snatch [снач] *v.t.* кашида гирифтан [kashida giriftan]
sneakers [сникерз] *n.* кафши теннис [kafshi tennis]
sneeze [сниз] *n.* атса [atsa] / *v.i.* атса задан [atsa zadan]
snob [сноб] *n.* нозпарвард [nozparvard]
snobbish [снобиш] *adj.* нозпарвард [nozparvard], нозпарвардона [nozparvardona]
snore [снор] *v.i.* хуррок кашидан [xurrok kashidan]
snort [снорт] *n.* фирқ-фирқ [firq-firq] / *v.i.* фирқ-фирқ кардан [firq-firq kardan]; **to snort with laughter** қиқиррос зада хандидан [qiqirros zada xandidan]
snout [снаут] *n.* пӯз [püz], фук [fuk]
snow [сно] *n.* барф [barf] / *v.i.* барф боридан [barf boridan]
snowflake [снофлейк] *n.* зарраи барф [zarrai barf]
snowstorm [сносторм] *n.* бӯрон [büron]
so [со] *adv.* *(in the manner shown, thus)* ин хел [in xel], ҳамин хел [hamin xel]; *(to such an extent)* ин қадар [in qadar]
soak [сок] *v.t.* тар кардан [tar kardan] / *v.i.* тар шудан [tar shudan]
soaking [сокинг] *n.* таршавӣ [tarshavi]
soap [соп] *n.* собун [sobun] / *v.t.* собун задан [sobun zadan]
soar [софт] *v.i.* бол наҷунбона парвоз кардан [bol najunbonda parvoz kardan], баланд парвоз кардан [baland parvoz kardan]
sob [соб] *v.i.* зор-зор гиристан [zor-zor giristan]
soccer [сокер] *n.* футбол [futbol]
social [сошал] *adj.* иҷтимоӣ [ijtimoi]

socialism [сошализм] *n.* сотсиализм [sotsializm]
socialist [сошалист] *n.* сотсиалист [sotsialist] / *adj.* сотсиалистӣ [sotsialisti]
society [сосайэти] *n.* ҷамъият [jam'iyat]
sock [сок] *n.* ҷӯроб [jürob]
socket [сокет] *n. (electric)* штепсел [shtepsel]; *(eye)* косаи чашм [kosai chashm]
soda [сода] *n.* сода [soda]
sodium [содям] *n.* натрий [natriy]
sofa [софа] *n.* диван [divan]
sofa-bed [софа-бед] *n.* диванкат [divankat]
soft [софт] *adj.* нарм [narm], мулоим [muloim]
soft drink [софт дринк] *n.* нӯшоба [nüshoba]
soil [сойл] *n.* хок [xok], замин [zamin]
solar [солар] *adj.* офтобӣ [oftobi]
soldier [солҷер] *n.* сарбоз [sarboz], аскар [askar]
sole [сол] *n. (of a shoe)* таг [tag]; *(of a foot)* кафи пой [kafi poy]; *(fish)* камбала [kambala] / *adj.* ягона [yagona], якка [yakka]
solid [солид] *n.* ҷисми сахт [jismi saxt] / *adj. (firm)* сахт [saxt], устувор [ustuvor]; *(sound, as in an argument or reasoning)* асоснок [asosnok]
solution [солюшан] *n. (resolution to a problem)* ҳал [hal]; *(mixture of substances)* ҳалкунӣ [halkuni], обкунӣ [obkuni]
solve [солв] *v.t.* ҳал кардан [hal kardan]
solvent [солвент] *n.* ҳалкунанда [halkunanda], обкунанда [obkunanda]
somber [сомбер] *adj.* тира [tira]
some [сам] *adj.* ягон [yagon]
somebody [самбоди] *pron.* касе [kase], ягон кас [yagon kas]
somehow [самҳау] *adv.* ким-чӣ хел [kim-chi xel]
someone [самуан] *pron.* ким-кӣ [kim-ki]
someplace [самплейс] *adv.* ҷое [joe], ким-куҷо [kim-kujo]
something [самтинг] *pron.* чизе [chize], ким-чӣ [kim-chi]
sometime [самтайм] *adv.* як ҳангоме [yak hangome]; **sometimes** гоҳо [goho], гоҳ-гоҳ [goh-goh]
somewhat [самуат] *adv.* каме [kame], андак [andak]
somewhere [самуер] *adv.* дар ҷое [dar joe], дар куҷое [dar kujoe]
son [сан] *n.* писар [pisar], бача [bacha]
song [сонг] *n.* суруд [surud]
son-in-law [сан-ин-ло] *n.* домод [domod]
soon [сун] *adv.* ба зудӣ [ba zudi], ба наздикӣ [ba nazdiki]; **as soon as** ҳамин ки [hamin ki]
sore [сор] *n.* реш [resh] / *adj.* дарднок [dardnok]
sore throat [сор трот] *n.* дарди гулӯ [dardi gulü]
sorrow [соро] *n.* андӯҳ [andüh], ғам [gham]
sorry [сори] *adj.* пушаймон [pushaymon], мутаассиф [mutaassif]; **I'm sorry.** Бубахшед. [Bubaxshed.]

sort [сорт] *n.* хел [xel], гуна [guna] / *v.t.* хел-хел кардан [xel-xel kardan], ба хелҳо ҷудо кардан [ba xelho judo kardan]

soul [сол] *n.* ҷон [jon], рӯҳ [rüh]

sound [саунд] *n.* садо [sado], овоз [ovoz] / *adj. (healthy)* тандуруст [tandurust]; *(sound thinking)* дуруст [durust], асоснок [asosnok]; *(firm, solid)* устувор [ustuvor] / *v.i.* садо додан [sado dodan]

soup [суп] *n.* шӯрбо [shürbo]

sour [саур] *adj.* турш [tursh]

source [сорс] *n.* сарчашма [sarchashma]

south [саут] *n.* ҷануб [janub] / *adj.* ҷанубӣ [janubi] / *adv.* ба ҷануб [ba janub], сӯи ҷануб [süi janub]

southeast [саутист] *n.* ҷануби шарқ [janubi sharq] / *adj.* ҷануби шарқӣ [janubi sharqi]

southeastern [саутистерн] *adj.* ҷануби шарқӣ [janubi sharqi]

southern [садерн] *adj.* ҷанубӣ [janubi]

southwest [саутуест] *n.* ҷануби ғарб [janubi gharb] / *adj.* ҷануби ғарбӣ [janubi gharbi]

southwestern [саутустерн] *adj.* ҷануби ғарбӣ [janubi gharbi]

souvenir [сувенир] *n.* *(memento)* ёдгорӣ [yodgori]; *(gift brought from travel)* савғотӣ [savghoti], армуғон [armughon]

sovereign [соверин] *adj.* соҳибистиқлол [sohibistiqlol]

sow [сау] *n.* модахук [modaxuk]

sow [со] *v.t.* коштан [koshtan], коридан [koridan]

soy [сой] *n.* соя [soya]; **soy sauce** қайлаи соя [qaylai soya]

space [спейс] *n. (cosmic)* фазо [fazo]; *(place, a portion of space)* ҷой [joy]

spade [спейд] *n. (tool)* бел [bel]; **spades** *(suite in cards)* қарамашшоқ [qaramashshoq], холи зоғи сиёҳ [xoli zoghi siyoh]

Spanish [спаниш] *n./adj.* испанӣ [ispani]

spare part [спер парт] *n.* қисми эҳтиётӣ [qismi ehtiyoti]

spark [спарк] *n.* шарора [sharora] / *v.t.* афрӯхтан [afrüxtan]

sparkle [спаркъл] *v.i.* ялаққос задан [yalaqqos zadan]

spark plug [спарк плаг] *n.* шамъи афрӯзиш [sham'i afrüzish]

sparrow [спаро] *n.* гунҷишк [gunjishk]

spatial [спейшал] *adj.* фазоӣ [fazoi], маконӣ [makoni]

speak [спик] *v.t.* гуфтан [guftan] / *v.i.* гап задан [gap zadan]

speaker [спикер] *n. (person)* суханвар [suxanvar], нотиқ [notiq]; *(loudspeaker)* карнай [karnay]

special [спешал] *adj.* вижа [vizha], махсус [maxsus], хос [xos]

specialist [спешалист] *n.* мутахассис [mutaxassis]
species [спишиз] *n.* ҷинс [jins]
specify [спесифай] *v.t.* тасниф кардан [tasnif kardan]
specimen [спесимен] *n.* намуна [namuna]
spectator [спектейтор] *n.* тамошобин [tamoshobin], бинанда [binanda]
speech [спич] *n.* *(oration)* суханронӣ [suxanroni]; *(faculty of speech)* сухан [suxan], нутқ [nutq]
speed [спид] *n.* суръат [sur'at], тезӣ [tezi] / *v.i.* босуръат рафтан [bosur'at raftan]
speedometer [спидометер] *n.* суръатсанҷ [sur'atsanj]
spell [спел] *v.t.* навишта шудан [navishta shudan]
spend [спенд] *v.t.* сарф кардан [sarf kardan]
sphere [сфир] *n.* кура [kura]
spice [спайс] *n.* дорувор [doruvor], адвия [adviya]
spicy [спайси] *adj.* тунд [tund], тундмаза [tundmaza]
spider [спайдер] *n.* тортанак [tortanak]
spiderweb [спайдер веб] *n.* тори тортанак [tori tortanak], тортанакхона [tortanakxona]
spill [спил] *n.* резиш [rezish] / *v.t.* резондан [rezondan], рехтан [rextan] / *v.i.* рехтан [rextan], рехта шудан [rexta shudan]
spin [спин] *v.t.* *(spin thread, etc.)* ресидан [residan], риштан [rishtan]; *(make sth turn)* чарх занондан [charx zanondan], гардондан [gardondan] / *v.i.* *(turn)* чарх задан [charx zadan]
spinach [спинач] *n.* испаноқ [ispanoq], исфаноҷ [isfanoj]
spinal column [спайнал колам] *see* **backbone**, **spine**
spinal cord [спайнал корд] *n.* ҳароммағз [harommaghz]
spine [спайн] *n.* аррапушт [arrapusht], сутунмӯҳра [sutunmühra]
spiral [спайрал] *adj.* морпеч [morpech]
spire [спайр] *n.* нӯк [nük]
spirit [спирит] *n.* ҷон [jon], рӯҳ [rüh], равон [ravon]
spiritual [спиритуал] *adj.* рӯҳонӣ [rühoni], маънавӣ [ma'navi]
spit [спит] *n.* оби даҳан [obi dahan] / *v.t.* туф кардан [tuf kardan]
spite [спайт] *n.* кина [kina]; **in spite of** бо вуҷуди [bo vujudi], қатъи назар аз [qat'i nazar az]
splash [сплаш] *n.* шалпас [shalpas], лаппиш [lappish] / *v.t.* пошидан [poshidan] / *v.i.* шалпас задан [shalpas zadan], лаппас задан [lappas zadan]
splint [сплинт] *n.* тахтача [taxtacha], тахтачабанд [taxtachaband]
splinter [сплинтер] *n.* реза [reza], пора [pora] / *v.i.* кафидан [kafidan]
spoil [спойл] *v.t.* *(ruin/destroy)* вайрон кардан [vayron kardan]; *(spoil a child)* эркаю вайрон кардан [erkayu vairon kardan] / *v.i.* *(go bad)* гандидан [gandidan]; *(become ruined/destroyed)* вайрон шудан [vayron shudan]

spoke [спок] *n.* парраи чарх [parrai charx]
sponge [спанч] *n.* исфанҷ [isfanj]
sponsor [спонсор] *n.* зомин [zomin] / *v.t.* зомин будан [zomin budan]
spontaneous [спонтейнияс] *adj.* худ аз худ пайдошуда [xud az xud paydoshuda], беихтиёрона [beixtiyorona]
spool [спул] *n.* найча [naycha]
spoon [спун] *n.* қошуқ [qoshuq]
sport [спорт] *n.* варзиш [varzish], спорт [sport]
sportsman [спортсман] *n.* варзишгар [varzishgar]
spot [спот] *n. (mark/stain)* доғ [dogh], лакка [lakka], хол [xol]; *(location)* ҷой [joy], маҳал [mahal] / *v.t. (mark with spots)* доғдор кардан [doghdor kardan], лаккадор кардан [lakkador kardan]; *(see)* дидан [didan]; *(find)* ёфтан [yoftan]
spout [спаут] *n.* фавра [favra]
sprain [спрейн] *n.* рагканӣ [ragkani] / *v.* раг кандан [rag kandan]
spray [спрей] *n.* туман [tuman], ғубор [ghubor] / *v.t.* пошидан [poshidan]
spread [спред] *v.t.* паҳн кардан [pahn kardan] / *v.i.* паҳн шудан [pahn shudan]
spring [спринг] *n. (season)* баҳор [bahor]; *(mechanical)* фанар [fanar]; *(jump)* ҷаҳиш [jahish]; *(water welling up from the earth)* чашма [chashma]; *(source or origin)* сарчашма [sarchashma] / *v.i.* ҷастан [jastan], хез задан [xez zadan]
sprinkle [спринкъл] *v.t.* пошидан [poshidan]
sprint [спринт] *v.i.* ба масофаи наздик тохтан [ba masofai nazdik toxtan]
sprout [спраут] *n.* навда [navda], ҷавона [javona] / *v.i.* сабзидан [sabzidan], неш задан [nesh zadan], навда баровардан [navda barovardan]
spur [спур] *n.* маҳмез [mahmez] / *v.t.* маҳмез задан [mahmez zadan]
spy [спай] *n.* ҷосус [josus] / *v.i.* ҷосусӣ кардан [josusi kardan]
square [скуер] *n. (shape)* квадрат [kvadrat], мураббаъ [murabba']; *(town square)* майдон [maydon] / *adj.* квадратӣ [kvadrati], мураббаъ [murabba']
squash [скуаш] *n. (vegetable)* каду [kadu]; *(sport)* сквош [skvosh] / *v.t.* пачақ кардан [pachaq kardan]
squint [скуинт] *v.i.* каҷ нигаристан [kaj nigaristan]
squirrel [скуирел] *n.* санҷоб [sanjob]
stable [стейбъл] *n.* оғил [oghil], аспхона [aspxona] / *adj.* устувор [ustuvor]
stadium [стейдям] *n.* стадион [stadion], майдони варзиш [maydoni varzish]
staff [стаф] *n. (stick or pole)* асо [aso], чӯбдаст [chübdast]; *(personnel)* ҳайати коркунон [hayati korkunon]
stage [стейҷ] *n. (period of time in a process)* марҳала [marhala]; *(theatrical)* саҳна [sahna]

stain [стейн] *n.* доғ [dogh], лакка [lakka] / *v.t.* доғдор кардан [doghdor kardan], лаккадор кардан [lakkador kardan] / *v.i.* доғдор шудан [doghdor shudan], лаккадор шудан [lakkador shudan]

stained glass [стейнд глес] *n.* шишаи ранга [shishai ranga]

stainless [стейнлес] *adj.* доғдорнашуда [doghdornashuda], лаккадорнашуда [lakkadornashuda]

stainless steel [стейнлес стил] *n.* пӯлоди зангногир [pülodi zangnogir]

stair [стер] *n.* зина [zina], зинапоя [zinapoya]

staircase [стеркейс] *n.* зина [zina], зинапоя [zinapoya], пиллагон [pillagon]

stake [стейк] *n.* мехи чӯбин [mexi chübin]

stale [стейл] *adj.* кӯҳна [kühna], қоқ [qoq]

stalk [сток] *n.* поя [poya] / *v.t.* пинҳонӣ наздик шудан [pinhoni nazdik shudan]

stall [стол] *n.* охур [oxur]

stammer [стамер] *n.* забон гирифтагӣ [zabon giriftagi], лакнати забон [laknati zabon] / *v.i.* забон гирифта гап задан [zabon girifta gap zadan], лакнати забон доштан [laknati zabon doshtan]

stamp [стамп] *n. (postage)* тамбри пустӣ [tambri pusti], маркаи почта [markai pochta]; *(seal)* мӯҳр [mühr] / *v.t.* мӯҳр задан [mühr zadan]

stand [станд] *n.* дӯконча [dükoncha]; **newspaper stand** дӯкончаи рӯзнома [dükonchai rüznoma] / *v.t.* рост мондан [rost mondan] / *v.i.* истодан [istodan]

standard [стандард] *n.* стандарт [standart]; *(criterion)* меъёр [me'yor]; *(flag)* парчам [parcham]; *(standard of living)* сатҳи зиндагӣ [sathi zindagi] / *adj.* якхела [yakxela], стандартӣ [standarti]

standing [стандинг] *adj. (in a standing position)* истода [istoda]; *(permanent, fixed)* пайваста [payvasta], ҳамешагӣ [hameshagi]; **standing order** низомнома [nizomnoma]

star [стар] *n.* ситора [sitora]

starch [старч] *n.* оҳор [ohor], нишоста [nishosta] / *v.t.* оҳор додан [ohor dodan]

stare [стер] *v.i.* чашм наканда нигоҳ кардан [chashm nakanda nigoh kardan]

starfish [старфиш] *n.* ситораи баҳрӣ [sitorai bahri]

start [старт] *n.* оғоз [oghoz], шурӯъ [shurü'] / *v.t.* сар кардан [sar kardan], шурӯъ кардан [shurü' kardan] / *v.i.* *(begun)* сар шудан [sar shudan], шурӯъ шудан [shurü' shudan]; *(move suddenly)* якбора ларзидан [yakbora larzidan], як қад паридан [yak qad paridan]

starter [стартер] *n. (auto)* корандози муҳаррик [korandozi muharrik]

starvation [старвейшан] *n.* гуруснамонӣ [gurusnamoni], қаҳтӣ [qahti]

state [стейт] *n. (state of being)* ҳолат [holat]; *(country)* кишвар [kishvar]; *(administrative unit of a country)* иёлат [iyolat] / *v.i.* баён кардан [bayon kardan], изҳор кардан [iz-hor kardan]

statement [стейтмент] *n.* баён [bayon], изҳор [iz-hor]

statesman [стейтсман] *n.* арбоби сиёсат [arbobi siyosat]

station [стейшан] *n.* истгоҳ [istgoh]

stationary [стейшанери] *adj.* ғайрисайёр [ghayrisayyor], доимӣ [doimi]

stationery [стейшонери] *n.* асбоби хатнависӣ [asbobi xatnavisi]

statistic [статистик] *n.* статистика [statistika], омор [omor]

statistical [статистикал] *adj.* статистикӣ [statistiki], оморӣ [omori]

statue [стачу] *n.* ҳайкал [haykal], пайкара [paykara], муҷассама [mujassama]

status [статус] *n.* вазъият [vaz'iyat]

status quo [статус куо] *n.* вазъияти даврাи муайян [vaz'iyati davrai muayyan]

statutory [стачутори] *adj.* қонунӣ [qonuni]; **statutory offence** ҳуқуқвайронкунӣ [huquqvayronkuni]

stay [стей] *v.i.* мондан [mondan]

steady [стеди] *adj.* устувор [ustuvor]

steak [стейк] *n.* бифштекс [bifshteks]

steal [стил] *v.t.* дуздидан [duzdidan] / *v.i. (be stolen)* дуздида шудан [duzdida shudan]; *(move silently)* пинҳонӣ гаштан [pinhoni gashtan]

steam [стим] *n.* буғ [bugh] / *v.t. (cook)* дар буғ пухтан [dar bugh puxtan]; *(expose to steam)* буғ додан [bugh dodan] / *v.i. (be cooked)* дар буғ пухта шудан [dar bugh puxta shudan]; *(be exposed to steam)* буғ дода шудан [bugh doda shudan]

steamed [стимд] *adj.* дампухт [dampuxt]

steamship [стимшип] *n.* киштии буғ [kishtii bugh]

steel [стил] *n.* пӯлод [pülod] / *adj.* пӯлодин [pülodin]

steer [стир] *v.t.* рондан [rondan], идора кардан [idora kardan] / *v.i.* ронда шудан [ronda shudan]

stem [стем] *n.* тана [tana]

step [степ] *n.* қадам [qadam], гом [gom] / *v.i.* қадам задан [qadam zadan]

stepbrother [степбрадер] *n.* randoмandar

stepdaughter [степдотер] *n.* духтарандар [duxtarandar]

stepfather [степфадер] *n.* падарандар [padarandar]

stepmother [степмадер] *n.* модарандар [modarandar]

steppe [степ] *n.* дашт [dasht], чӯл [chül]

stepsister [степсистер] *n.* хоҳарандар [xoharandar]

stepson [степсан] *n.* писарандар [pisarandar]

stereotype [стириётайп] *n. (printing)* қолаби чоп [qolabi chop]
sterile [стерайл] *adj. (infertile woman)* нозо [nozo]; *(free of bacteria)* тамъизшуда [tam'izshuda]
sterilize [стерилайз] *v.t. (clean of bacteria)* тамъиз кардан [tam'iz kardan]; *(render male incapable of reproducing)* ахта кардан [axta kardan]; *(render female incapable of reproducing)* нозо кардан [nozo kardan]
stern [стерн] *adj.* сахтгир [saxtgir]
stethoscope [стетоскоп] *n.* стетоскоп [stetoskop]
stew [сту] *n.* шӯрбо [shürbo]
steward [стуард] *n.* стюард [styuard]
stewardess [стуардес] *n.* стюардесса [styuardessa]
stick [стик] *n.* чӯб [chüb], калтак [kaltak] / *v.t.* часпондан [chaspondan] / *v.i.* часпидан [chaspidan]
sticky [стики] *adj.* часпак [chaspak]
stiff [стиф] *adj.* хамнашаванда [xamnashavanda], сахт [saxt], шах [shax]
stiffen [стифен] *v.t.* шах кардан [shax kardan] / *v.i.* шах шудан [shax shudan]
still [стил] *adj. (without movement)* беҳаракат [beharakat]; *(quiet)* ором [orom] / *adv.* ҳанӯз [hanüz]
stimulant [стимюлант] *n.* доруи ҳавасмандкунанда [dorui havasmandkunanda]
stimulate [стимюлейт] *v.t.* ҳавасманд кардан [havasmand kardan], барангехтан [barangextan]
sting [стинг] *n.* неш [nesh] / *v.t.* неш задан [nesh zadan], газидан [gazidan]
stir [стир] *v.t.* тагу рӯ кардан [tagu rü kardan]
stirrup [стирап] *n.* узангу [uzangu], рикоб [rikob]
stitch [стич] *n.* кӯк [kük]
stock [сток] *n. (reserve)* захира [zaxira]; *(goods in a store)* хелҳои мол [xelhoi mol]; *(share in a company)* саҳм [sahm] / *v.t.* захира кардан [zaxira kardan]
stockholder [стокҳолдер] *n.* саҳмдор [sahmdor]
stocking [стокинг] *n.* ҷӯроб [jürob], ҷӯроби дароз [jürobi daroz]
stock market [сток маркет] *n.* бозори саҳом [bozori sahom]
stomach [стамак] *n.* меъда [me'da], шикам [shikam]
stomachache [стамакейк] *n.* дарди шикам [dardi shikam]
stone [стон] *n.* санг [sang] / *adj.* сангин [sangin], сангӣ [sangi]
stool [стул] *n.* чорпояча [chorpoyacha]
stop [стоп] *n. (ceasing of activity)* ист [ist]; *(bus/trainstop)* истгоҳ [istgoh] / *v.t. (seal or close)* бастан [bastan], маҳкам кардан [mahkam kardan]; *(stop from moving or doing)* боздоштан [bozdoshtan] / *v.i.* истодан [istodan]; **Stop!** *(imperative)* исто! [Isto!]

storage [сторич] *n.* нигоҳдорӣ [nigohdori]; **storage room** хонаи нигоҳдорӣ [xonai nigohdori]
store [стор] *n. (shop)* дӯкон [dükon], мағоза [maghoza]; *(stock or reserve)* захира [zaxira] / *v.t.* захира кардан [zaxira kardan]
storeroom [сторрум] *n.* хонаи нигоҳдорӣ [xonai nigohdori], анбор [anbor]
stork [сторк] *n.* лаклак [laklak]
storm [сторм] *n.* тӯфон [tüfon]
stormy [сторми] *adj.* пуртӯфон [purtüfon]; *(full of waves)* пурмавҷ [purmavj]
story [стори] *n. (level of a building)* ошёна [oshyona]; *(account, tale)* қисса [qissa], ҳикоя [hikoya]; **tell a story** қисса гуфтан [qissa guftan], ҳикоя нақл кардан [hikoya naql kardan]
stout [стаут] *adj.* тануманд [tanumand], чорпаҳлӯ [chorpahlü]
stove [стов] *n.* ӯҷоқ [üjoq]
straight [стрейт] *adj.* рост [rost]
strain [стрейн] *v.t. (stretch or pull tight)* таранг кардан [tarang kardan]; *(remove impurities)* полондан [polondan], софӣ кардан [sofi kardan]
strainer [стрейнер] *n.* чӯлпӣ [chülpi], баракгирак [barakgirak]
strait [стрейт] *n.* гулӯгоҳ [gulügoh]
strange [стрейнч] *adj.* аҷиб [ajib], ғариб [gharib]
stranger [стрейнҷер] *n.* бегона [begona], одами бегона [odami begona]
strangle [странгъл] *v.t.* буғӣ кардан [bughi kardan]
strap [страп] *n.* тасма [tasma]
straw [стро] *n.* коҳ [koh]
strawberry [строберн] *n.* қулфинай [qulfinay]
streak [стрик] *n.* хат [xat], рах [rax]
stream [стрим] *n.* ҷӯй [jüy], ҷӯйбор [jüybor]
street [стрит] *n.* кӯча [kücha]
strength [стренгт] *n.* тоб [tob], зӯр [zür], қудрат [qudrat]
strengthen [стренгтен] *v.t.* тақвият додан [taqviyat dodan]
stress [стрес] *n. (gram.)* зада [zada]; *(emphasis)* таъкид [ta'kid]; *(pressure)* фишор [fishor] / *v.t.* таъкид кардан [ta'kid kardan]; *(be stressed)* зиқ будан [ziq budan]
stressed out [стресд аут] *adj.* зиқшуда [ziqshuda]
stretch [стреч] *v.t.* таранг кардан [tarang kardan]
stretcher [стречер] *n.* занбар [zanbar]
strict [стрикт] *adj.* сахтгир [saxtgir]
strike [страйк] *n.* корпартоӣ [korpartoi] / *v.t. (hit)* задан [zadan] / *v.i. (go on strike)* корпартоӣ кардан [korpartoi kardan]
striking [страйкинг] *adj.* ҳайратангез [hayratangez]
string [стринг] *n.* тор [tor]
strip [стрип] *n.* навор [navor] / *v.t.* луч кардан [luch kardan] / *v.i.* луч шудан [luch shudan]

stripe [страйп] *n.* рах [rax]
striped [страйпд] *adj.* рахдор [raxdor], рах-рах [rax-rax]
stroke [строк] *n. (blow, impact)* зарба [zarba]; *(of a pen)* хат [xat]; *(heat stroke)* офтобзанӣ [oftobzani]; *(med.)* сакта [sakta] / *v.t.* сила кардан [sila kardan]
strong [стронг] *adj.* пурзӯр [purzür], нерӯманд [nerümand], қавӣ [qavi]
structure [стракчур] *n. (arrangement)* сохт [soxt]; *(construction)* сохтмон [soxtmon], бино [bino]
struggle [страгъл] *n.* талош [talosh] / *v.i.* талош кардан [talosh kardan]
stub [стаб] *v.t.* пешпо хӯрдан [peshpo xürdan]
stubborn [стабурн] *adj.* якрав [yakrav]
student [стюдент] *n.* шогирд [shogird], донишҷӯ [donishjü]
study [стади] *n. (work of art)* ангора [angora]; *(learning)* омӯзиш [omüzish] / *v.t.* омӯхтан [omüxtan], ёд гирифтан [yod giriftan] / *v.i.* дарс хондан [dars xondan]
stuff [стаф] *n.* модда [modda], чиз [chiz] / *v.t.* пур кардан [pur kardan]
stumble [стамбъл] *v.i.* дакка хӯрдан [dakka xürdan]
stun [стан] *v.t.* гиҷ кардан [gij kardan]
stupid [ступид] *adj.* аҳмақ [ahmaq], нодон [nodon]
style [стайл] *n. (architectural, literary, etc.)* сабк [sabk], услуб [uslub]; *(fashion)* мод [mod]
stylish [стайлиш] *adj.* модшуда [modshuda]
subdue [сабдю] *v.t.* зердаст кардан [zerdast kardan], мутеъ кардан [mute' kardan]
subject [сабҷект] *n. (topic of discussion)* мавзӯъ [mavzü']; *(area of study)* фан [fan]
subjective [сабҷестив] *adj.* шахсӣ [shaxsi]
submarine [сабмарин] *n.* киштии зериобӣ [kishtii zeriobi] / *adj.* зериобӣ [zeriobi]
submit [сабмит] *v.t.* пешниҳод кардан [peshnihod kardan] / *v.i.* тан додан [tan dodan], таслим шудан [taslim shudan]
subscribe [сабскрайб] *v.i.* обуна кардан [obuna kardan]
subscription [сабскрипшан] *n.* обуна [obuna]
subsidy [сабсиди] *n.* ёрии пулӣ [yorii puli]
substance [сабстанс] *n. (essence)* ҷавҳар [javhar], асл [asl]; *(matter)* модда [modda]
substantial [сабстаншал] *adj.* асосӣ [asosi], аслӣ [asli]
substitute [сабститют] *n.* ҷонишин [jonishin] / *adj.* ҷонишин [jonishin] / *v.t.* ҷонишин кардан [jonishin kardan]
subtitle [сабтайтъл] *n.* сарлавҳаи зер [sarlavhai zer]
subtle [сатъл] *adj.* нозук [nozuk]
subtract [сабтракт] *v.t.* тарҳ кардан [tarh kardan]

suburb [сабурб] *n.* атрофи шаҳр [atrofi shahr], музофоти шаҳр [muzofoti shahr]
subway [сабуэй] *n.* метро [metro]
succeed [саксес] *v.i.* комёб шудан [komyob shudan]
success [саксес] *n.* комёбӣ [komyobi]
such [сач] *adj.* чунин [chunin]; **such as** ҳамчун [hamchun]
suck [сак] *v.t.* макидан [makidan]
sudden [саден] *adj.* ногаҳонӣ [nogahoni]
suddenly [саденли] *adv.* ногаҳон [nogahon]
suede [суэйд] *n.* ҷир [jir]
suffer [сафер] *v.i.* ранҷ бурдан [ranj burdan], азоб дидан [azob didan], ҷафо кашидан [jafo kashidan]
suffice [суфайс] *v.i.* басанда будан [basanda budan], кифоя будан [kifoya budan]
sufficient [суфишант] *adj.* басанда [basanda], кифоя [kifoya]
suffix [сафикс] *n.* бандак [bandak]
sugar [шугар] *n. (granulated)* шакар [shakar]; *(lump)* қанд [qand]; **sugar bowl** қанддон [qanddon]
suggest [саҷест] *v.t.* илқо кардан [ilqo kardan], пешниҳод кардан [peshnihod kardan]
suggestion [саҷесчан] *n.* илқо [ilqo], пешниҳод [peshnihod]
suicide [суисайд] *n.* худкушӣ [xudkushi]; **to commit suicide** худкушӣ кардан [xudkushi kardan]
suit [сут] *n. (set of similar things)* даста [dasta]; *(set of clothes)* кастум [kastum]; *(legal)* даъво [da'vo] / *v.t. (be appropriate)* муносиб будан [munosib budan]; *(look attractive)* зебидан [zebidan]
suitable [сутабъл] *adj.* муносиб [munosib]
suitcase [суткейс] *n.* ҷомадон [jomadon]
suitor [сутър] *n. (man courting a woman)* хостгор [xostgor]; *(one making a request)* хоҳишкунанда [xohishkunanda]
sullen [сален] *adj.* туршрӯй [turshrüy]
sum [сам] *n. (amount)* маблағ [mablagh]; *(mathematical)* ҳосили ҷамъ [hosili jam'] / *v.t. (sum up)* ҷамъ кардан [jam' kardan]
summary [самари] *n.* хулоса [xulosa]
summer [самер] *n.* тобистон [tobiston] / *adj.* тобистона [tobistona]
summit [самит] *n.* қулла [qulla], ситеғ [sitegh]
sun [сан] *n.* хуршед [xurshed], офтоб [oftob]
sunbathe [санбейд] *v.i.* худро офтоб додан [xudro oftob dodan]
sunburn [санбурн] *n.* сӯхтагӣ аз офтоб [süxtagi az oftob]
Sunday [сандей] *n.* якшанбе [yakshanbe]
sunflower [санфлауэр] *n.* офтобпараст [oftobparast]; **sunflower seed** донаи офтобпараст [donai oftobparast]

sunglasses [санглaсез] *n.* айнак офтобпанаҳ [aynaki oftobpanah]
sunny [сани] *adj.* офтобӣ [oftobi]
sunrise [санрайз] *n.* тулӯи офтоб [tulüi oftob]
sunscreen [санскрин] *n.* равғани офтобпанаҳ [ravghani oftobpanah]
sunset [сансет] *n.* ғуруби офтоб [ghurubi oftob]
sunshine [саншайн] *n.* офтоб [oftob]
sunstroke [санстрок] *n.* офтобзанӣ [oftobzani]
suntan [сантен] *n.* сиёҳӣ аз офтоб [siyohi as oftob]; **suntan lotion** равғани офтобпанаҳ [ravghani oftobpanah]
superficial [суперфишал] *adj.* рӯякӣ [rüyaki]
superior [супириёр] *adj.* бартар [bartar], бартарин [bartarin]
supermarket [супермаркет] *n.* супермаркет [supermarket]
superstitious [суперстишас] *adj.* хурофотпараст [xurofotparast]
supervise [супервайз] *v.t.* назорат кардан [nazorat kardan]
supervisor [супервайзор] *n.* назоратчӣ [nazoratchi]
supper [сапер] *n.* хӯроки шом [xüroki shom]
supplement [саплемент] *n.* илова [ilova], такмил [takmil] / *v.t.* пурра кардан [purra kardan], мукаммал кардан [mukammal kardan]
supply [саплай] *n.* таъминот [ta'minot] / *v.t.* таъмин кардан [ta'min kardan]
support [сапорт] *n.* *(backing, assistance)* ёрӣ [yori]; *(alliance, political support)* тарафдорӣ [tarafdori]; *(prop, physical support)* такя [takya]; *(corroboration)* тақвият [taqviyat] / *v.t. (financially, etc.)* ёрӣ додан [yori dodan]; *(the roof, a structure, etc.)* дошта истодан [doshta istodan]; *(corroborate)* тақвият додан [taqviyat dodan]
supporter [сапортер] *n.* тарафдор [tarafdor]
suppose [сапоз] *v.i.* фарз кардан [farz kardan], гумон доштан [gumon doshtan], пиндоштан [pindoshtan]
suppress [сапрес] *v.t.* хомӯш кардан [xomüsh kardan], фурӯ нишондан [furü nishondan]
surcharge [сурчарҷ] *n.* пардохти барилова [parodoxti barilova]
sure [шур] *adj.* дилпур [dilpur], яқин [yaqin], мутмаин [mutmain] / *v.i.* **to make sure of sth** яқин кардан [yaqin kardan], боварӣ ҳосил кардан [bovari hosil kardan]
surety [шурети] *n.* *(self-assurance)* дилпурӣ [dilpuri]; *(security)* замонат [zamonat]
surf [сурф] *n.* мавҷҳои ба соҳил бархӯранда [mavjhoi ba sohil barxüranda]
surface [сурфис] *n.* сатҳ [sath]
surgeon [сурҷан] *n.* ҷарроҳ [jarroh]
surgery [сурҷари] *n.* ҷарроҳӣ [jarrohi]

surly [сурли] *adj.* туршрӯй [turshrüy]
surname [сурнейм] *n.* насаб [nasab]
surpass [сурпас] *v.t.* пеш гузаштан [pesh guzashtan], пешдастӣ кардан [peshdasti kardan]
surplus [сурплас] *n.* моли барзиёд [moli barziyod] / *adj.* барзиёд [barziyod]
surprise [сурпрайз] *n.* *(feeling)* ҳайрат [hayrat], таачуб [taajub]; *(unexpected event)* ҳодисаи ногаҳонӣ [hodisai nogahoni]; *(gift)* тӯҳфа [tühfa] / *v.t.* ба ҳайрат андохтан [ba hayrat andoxtan], ба таачуб овардан [ba taajub ovardan]
surrender [сурендер] *v.t.* супурдан [supurdan], таслим кардан [taslim kardan] / *v.i.* таслим шудан [taslim shudan], тан додан [tan dodan]
surround [сураунд] *v.t.* миёнагир кардан [miyonagir kardan], иҳота кардан [ihota kardan]
surrounding [сураундинг] *adj.* фарогиранда [farogiranda], иҳотакунанда [ihotakunanda]
surroundings [сураундингз] *n.pl.* муҳит [muhit]
survive [сурвайв] *v.i.* зинда мондан [zinda mondan]
survivor [сурвайвор] *n.* бозмонда [bozmonda]
suspect [саспенд] *n.* гумонбар [gumonbar] / *v.i.* гумон кардан [gumon kardan]
suspend [саспенд] *v.t.* *(hang)* овехтан [ovextan]; *(halt temporarily)* муваққатан таваққуф кардан [muvaqqatan tavaqquf kardan]
suspenders [саспендерз] *n.* шалворбанди китфӣ [shalvorbandi kitfi]
suspense [саспенс] *n.* нигаронӣ [nigaroni], ноороми [nooromi]; *adj.* пурмоҷаро [purmojaro]
suspicion [саспишан] *n.* гумони бад [gumoni bad]
suspicious [саспишас] *adj.* *(having suspicions)* бадгумон [badgumon]; *(arousing suspicion)* шубҳаомез [shubhaomez]
sustain [састейн] *v.t.* *(keep)* нигоҳ доштан [nigoh doshtan]; *(endure)* тоб овардан [tob ovardan]
swallow [суало] *n.* *(of food or water)* қулт [qult]; *(bird)* парасту [parastu], фароштурук [faroshturuk] / *v.t.* фурӯ бурдан [furü burdan]
swamp [суамп] *n.* ботлоқ [botloq], мурдоб [murdob]
swan [свон] *n.* турна [turna], қу [qu]
swarm [суарм] *n.* оила [oila], тӯда [tüda] / *v.i.* тӯда-тӯда парвоз кардан [tüda-tüda parvoz kardan]
swear [суэр] *v.i.* *(make an oath)* савганд хӯрдан [savgand xürdan], қасам хӯрдан [qasam xürdan]; *(curse)* дашном додан [dashnom dodan]

sweat [суэт] *n.* арақ [araq] / *v.i.* арақ кардан [araq kardan]
sweater [суэтер] *n.* свитер [sviter]
Swede [суид] *n.* швед [shved]
Swedish [суидиш] *adj.* шведӣ [shvedi]
sweep [суип] *v.t.* рӯфтан [rüftan]
sweet [сuит] *n.* ширинӣ [shirini] / *adj.* ширин [shirin]
sweeten [суитен] *v.t.* ширинтар кардан [shirintar kardan]
swell [суэл] *v.i.* омосидан [omosidan], варам кардан [varam kardan]
swelling [суэлинг] *n.* омос [omos], варам [varam]
swift [суифт] *adj.* тезгард [tezgard], бодпо [bodpo]
swim [суим] *v.i.* шино кардан [shino kardan], оббозӣ кардан [obbozi kardan]
swimmer [суимер] *n.* шиновар [shinovar], оббоз [obboz]
swimming [суиминг] *n.* шино [shino], шиноварӣ [shinovari], оббозӣ [obbozi]
swimming pool [суиминг пул] *n.* истахри шино [istaxri shino], ҳавзи шиноварӣ [havzi shinovari]
swindle [суиндъл] *v.t.* чатоқ кардан [chatoq kardan]
swindler [суиндлер] *n.* фиребгар [firebgar]
swing [суинг] *n.* арғунчак [arghunchak] / *v.t.* алвонҷ додан [alvonj dodan], ҷунбондан [junbondan] / *v.i.* алвонҷ хӯрдан [alvonj xürdan], ҷунбидан [junbidan]
Swiss [суис] *n./adj.* швейсариягӣ [shveysariyagi]
switch [суич] *n. (electric)* калидак [kalidak] / *v.t.* иваз кардан [ivaz kardan]; **to switch on** даргиронидан [dargirondan]; **to switch off** куштан [kushtan], хомӯш кардан [xomüsh kardan]
sword [сорд] *n.* шамшер [shamsher]
syllable [силабъл] *n.* ҳиҷо [hijo]
symbol [симбол] *n.* рамз [ramz], нишона [nishona], аломат [alomat]
symbolic [символик] *adj.* рамзӣ [ramzi]
sympathetic [симпатетик] *adj.* ҳамдард [hamdard]
sympathize [симпатайз] *v.i.* ҳамдардӣ кардан [hamdardi kardan]
sympathy [симпати] *n.* ҳамдардӣ [hamdardi]
symphony [симфони] *n.* симфония [simfoniya]
symptom [симптом] *n.* аломат [alomat], нишона [nishona]
synagogue [синагог] *n.* каниса [kanisa], куништ [kunisht]
synonym [синоним] *n.* муродиф [murodif]
syntax [синтакс] *n.* наҳв [nahv]
synthetic [синтетик] *adj.* синтетикӣ [sintetiki]
syringe [сиринҷ] *n.* сӯзандору [süzandoru]
syrup [сирап] *n.* шира [shira], шарбат [sharbat]

system [систем] *n.* тартиб [tartib], система [sistema]; **metric system** системаи метрӣ [sistemai metri]
systematic [систематик] *adj.* мураттаб [murattab]

T

table [тейбъл] *n.* миз [miz]
tablecloth [тейбълклот] *n.* дастархон [dastarxon]
tablespoon [тейбълспун] *n.* қошуқи хӯрокхӯрӣ [qoshuqi xürokxüri]
tablet [теблет] *n.* *(notepad)* дафтар [daftar]; *(pill)* ҳаб [hab]
table tennis [тейбъл теннис] *n.* тенниси рӯйи миз [tennisi rüyi miz]
tack [тек] *n.* *(thumbtack)* мехи сарпаҳни хурд [mexi sarpahni xurd]
tact [тект] *n.* боодобӣ [boodobi]
tactful [тектфул] *adj.* боодоб [boodob], боодобона [boodobona]
tactic [тектик] *n.* тактик [taktik]; **tactics** тактика [taktika]
tag [тег] *n.* ёрлиқ [yorliq], тамғакоғаз [tamghakoghaz]
tail [тейл] *n.* дум [dum]
taillight [тейллайт] *n.* чароғи ақиб [charoghi aqib]
tailor [тейлор] *n.* дарзӣ [darzi] / *v.t.* дарзигӣ кардан [darzigi kardan]
Tajik [таҷик] *n.* *(person)* тоҷик [tojik]; *(language)* тоҷикӣ [tojiki] / *adj.* тоҷик [tojik]
take [тейк] *v.t.* гирифтан [giriftan]
talc/talcum powder [талк] *n.* талқ [talq]
talent [телент] *n.* истеъдод [iste'dod]
talented [телентед] *adj.* боистеъдод [boiste'dod]
talk [ток] *n.* гуфтугӯ [guftugü], суҳбат [suhbat] / *v.i.* гап задан [gap zadan]
talkative [токатив] *adj.* лаққӣ [laqqi], сергап [sergap], пургӯ [purgü]
tall [тол] *adj.* қадбаланд [qadbaland]
tame [тейм] *adj.* ром [rom], дастомӯз [dastomüz] / *v.t.* ром кардан [rom kardan], дастомӯз кардан [dastomüz kardan]
tamper [темпер] *v.t.* дахолат кардан [daxolat kardan], мутаассир кардан [mutaassir kardan]
tampon [темпон] *n.* латта [latta]
tan [тен] *adj.* *(color)* қаҳвагӣ [qahvagi]; *(suntanned)* аз офтоб сиёҳшуда [az oftob siyohshuda] / *v.t.* ош додан [osh dodan], даббоғӣ кардан [dabboghi kardan] / *v.i.* аз офтоб сиёҳ шудан [az oftob siyoh shudan]
tangerine [тенҷерин] *n.* норанг [norang]
tangle [тенгъл] *v.t.* чигил кардан [chigil kardan] / *v.i.* чигил шудан [chigil shudan]
tank [тенк] *n.* *(mil.)* танк [tank]; *(gas tank)* баки бензин [baki benzin]
tanker [тенк] *n.* *(oil tanker)* киштии нафткашон [kishtii naftkashon]; *(gasoline tanker)* бензинкаш [benzinkash]

tap [теп] *n. (light hit)* зарбаи оҳиста [zarbai ohista]; *(knock)* тақ-тақ [taq-taq]; *(faucet)* ҷумак [jumak] / *v.t. (knock)* тақ-тақ кардан [taq-taq kardan]; *(hit lightly)* оҳиста задан [ohista zadan]; *(listen secretly)* пинҳонӣ гӯш кардан [pinhoni güsh kardan]
tape [тейп] *n. (narrow strip, cassette tape)* навор [navor]; *(adhesive tape)* шероза [sheroza] / *v.t. (stick with tape)* бо шероза часпондан [bo sheroza chaspondan]; *(put on tape)* сабт кардан [sabt kardan], ба навор сабт кардан [ba navor sabt kardan]
tape measure [тейп межур] *n.* чентаноб [chentanob]
tape recorder [тейп рекордер] *n.* магнитофон [magnitofon]
tapestry [тапестри] *n.* гобелен [gobelen]
tar [тар] *n.* қатрон [qatron]
target [таргет] *n.* нишон [nishon] / *v.t.* нишон гирифтан [nishon giriftan]
tariff [тариф] *n.* тариф [tarif]
tart [тарт] *adj.* данд [dand], турш [tursh]
task [теск] *n.* вазифа [vazifa], кор [kor]
taste [тейст] *n. (flavor)* маза [maza]; *(sense of taste)* чашоӣ [chashoi]; *(a taste of sth)* чашиш [chashish], чошнӣ [choshni]; *(personal preference)* майл [mayl]; *(sense of style)* салиқа [saliqa] / *v.t.* чашидан [chashidan] / *v.i.* маза додан [maza dodan]
tasty [тейсти] *adj.* бомаза [bomaza]
tavern [теверн] *n.* майхона [mayxona]
tax [текс] *n.* андоз [andoz]
tax-free [текс-фри] *adj.* аз андоз озод [az andoz ozod]
taxi [текси] *n.* таксӣ [taksi]
tea [ти] *n.* чой [choy]; **black tea** чои сиёҳ [choy siyoh]; **green tea** чои кабуд [choy kabud], чои сабз [choy sabz] / *v.* **to make tea** чой дам кардан [choy dam kardan]
teach [тич] *v.t.* омӯхтан [omüxtan], ёд додан [yod dodan]
teacher [тичер] *n.* омӯзгор [omüzgor], муаллим [muallim]
teacup [тикап] *n.* пиёла [piyola]
teahouse [тиҳаус] *n.* чойхона [choyxona]
teakettle [тикетъл] *n.* чойҷӯш [choyjüsh]
team [тим] *n.* даста [dasta], команда [komanda]
teapot [типот] *n.* чойник [choynik]
tear [тир] *n.* ашк [ashk]
tear [тер] *n.* даридагӣ [daridagi], порагӣ [poragi] / *v.t.* даррондан [darrondan], пора кардан [pora kardan] / *v.i.* даридан [daridan], пора шудан [pora shudan]
tease [тиз] *v.t.* безор кардан [bezor kardan], озор додан [ozor dodan]
teaspoon [тиспун] *n.* қошуқча [qoshuqcha]
technical [техникал] *adj.* техникӣ [texniki]

technician [текнишан] *n.* техник [texnik]
teenager [тинейҷер] *n.* наврас [navras], навбора [navbora]
telegram [телеграм] *n.* телеграмма [telegramma]
telephone [телефон] *n.* телефон telefon] / *v.t.* телефон кардан [telefon kardan], занг задан [zang zadan]
telephone directory [телефон дайректори] *n.* китоби телефон [kitobi telefon], рақамномаи телефон [raqamnomai telefon]
telescope [телескоп] *n.* телескоп [teleskop]
television [телевижан] *n.* телевизор [televizor], телевизион [televizion]
tell [тел] *v.t.* гуфтан [guftan], нақл кардан [naql kardan]
temper [темпер] *n.* хӯй [xüy], табиат [tabiat]
temperate *adj.* муътадил [mu'tadil], миёна [miyona]
temperature [темперачур] *n.* ҳарорат [harorat]
temple [темпъл] *n. (place of worship)* маъбад [ma'bad]; *(anat.)* чакка [chakka]
temporary [темпорери] *adj.* муваққатӣ [muvaqqati], даргузар [darguzar]
tempt [темпт] *v.t.* иғво кардан [ighvo kardan], васваса кардан [vasvasa kardan]
temptation [темптейшан] *n.* иғво [ighvo], васваса [vasvasa]
ten [тен] *num.* даҳ [dah]
tenacious [тенейшас] *adj.* суботкор [subotkor], мустаҳкам [mustahkam]
tenant [тенант] *n.* иҷорагир [ijoragir]
tend [тенд] *v.t. (look after)* нигоҳубин кардан [nigohubin kardan]; *(nurse)* парасторӣ кардан [parastori kardan] / *v.i. (tend to)* моил будан [moil budan]
tendency [тенденси] *n.* майл [mayl]
tender [тендер] *adj. (affectionate)* навозишкор [navozishkor], меҳрубон [mehrubon]; *(soft)* нарм [narm], мулоим [muloim]
tendon [тендан] *n.* пай [pay]
tennis [тенис] *n.* теннис [tennis]
tenor [тенар] *n.* тенор [tenor]
tense [тенс] *n. (gram.)* замон [zamon] / *adj. (pulled tight, taut)* таранг [tarang]; *(strained, politically tense)* шиддатнок [shiddatnok]
tension [теншан] *n. (tautness)* тарангшавӣ [tarangshavi]; *(political tension)* шиддатнокӣ [shiddatnoki]
tent [тент] *n.* чодар [chodar], хиргоҳ [xirgoh], шомиёна [shomiyona]
tentacle [тентакъл] *n.* шохак [shoxak]
tentative [тентатив] *adj.* озмоишӣ [ozmoishi]
tenth [тент] *adj.* даҳум [dahum]
tenuous [тенюас] *adj.* борик [borik], маҳин [mahin]
tepid [тепид] *adj.* ширгарм [shirgarm]
term [терм] *n. (period of time)* муддат [muddat]; *(semester)* семестр [semestr]

terminate [терминейт] *v.t.* хатм кардан [xatm kardan], ба поён расондан [ba poyon rasondan]
termite [термайт] *n.* мирук [miruk], арзамӯрак [arzamürak]
terrace [терас] *n.* айвон [ayvon], пешайвон [peshayvon]
terrestrial [терестриял] *adj.* *(relating to land)* заминӣ [zamini]; *(non-aquatic)* хушкигард [xushkigard]
terrible [терибъл] *adj.* фоҷианок [fojianok], даҳшатнок [dahshatnok]
terribly [терибли] *adv.* ниҳоят [nihoyat], аз ҳад берун [az had berun]
terrific [терифик] *adj.* бисёр хуб [bisyor xub]
territory [територи] *n.* хок [xok], сарзамин [sarzamin]
terror [терор] *n.* даҳшат [dahshat]
terrorism [тероризм] *n.* терроризм [terrorizm]
terrorist [терорист] *n.* террорист [terrorist]
test [тест] *n.* озмоиш [ozmoish], санҷиш [sanjish], имтиҳон [imtihon] / *v.t.* озмудан [ozmudan], санҷидан [sanjidan], имтиҳон кардан [imtihon kardan]
testify [тестифай] *v.i.* гувоҳӣ додан [guvohi dodan]
testimony [тестимони] *n.* гувоҳӣ [guvohi]
text [текст] *n.* матн [matn]
textbook [текстбук] *n.* китоби дарсӣ [kitobi darsi]
textile [текстайл] *n.* газвор [gazvor]
than [дан] *conj.* аз [az]
thank [танк] *v.t.* сипосгузорӣ кардан [siposguzori kardan], ташаккур гуфтан [tashakkur kardan], раҳмат гуфтан [rahmat guftan]; **thank you** ташаккур [tashakkur], раҳмат [rahmat]
thankful [танкфул] *adj.* сипосгузор [siposguzor]
thankfulness [танкфулнес] *n.* сипосгузорӣ [siposguzori]
thanks [танкс] *n.pl.* сипосгузорӣ [siposguzori]
that [дат] *adj./pron.* он [on] / *conj.* ки [ki]
thaw [то] *v.t.* об кардан [ob kardan] / *v.i.* об шудан [ob shudan]
the [да] *art. no equivalent in Tajik*
theater [театер] *n.* театр [teatr]
their [дейр] *pron.* аз они онҳо [az oni onho], -и онҳо [-i onho]
them [дем] *pron.* онҳо [onho], эшон [eshon]
theme [тим] *n.* мавзӯъ [mavzü']
themselves [демселвз] *pron.* худашон [xudashon]
then [ден] *adv.* сипас [sipas], пас [pas]
theology [тиёлоҷи] *n.* илоҳиёт [ilohiyot]
theoretical [теоретикал] *adj.* назариявӣ [nazariyavi]
theory [тири] *n.* назария [nazariya]
therapeutic [терапютик] *adj.* шифобахш [shifobaxsh]

therapy [терапи] *n.* терапия [terapiya], муоличаи бе усулҳои ҷарроҳӣ [muolijai be usulhoi jarrohi]
there [дер] *adv.* он ҷо [on jo]
therefore [дерфор] *adv.* бинобар ин [binobar in], пас [pas]
thermometer [термометер] *n.* ҳароратсанҷ [haroratsanj]
thermos [термос] *n.* термос [termos]
thermostat [термостат] *n.* термостат [termostat]
these [диз] *pron.* инҳо [inho]
thesis [тисис] *n.* рисола [risola]
they [дей] *pron.* онҳо [onho], эшон [eshon]
thick [тик] *adj.* ғафс [ghafs]
thicken [тикен] *v.t.* ғафс кардан [ghafs kardan] / *v.i.* ғафс шудан [ghafs shudan]
thickness [тикнес] *n.* ғафсӣ [ghafsi]
thief [тиф] *n.* *(pl.* **thieves***)* дузд [duzd]
thigh [тай] *n.* рон [ron]
thimble [тимбл] *n.* ангуштпона [angushtpona]
thin [тин] *adj.* тунук [tunuk]
thing [тинг] *n.* чиз [chiz]
think [тинк] *v.i.* андешидан [andeshidan], фикр кардан [fikr kardan]
third [тирд] *adj.* сеюм [seyum]
thirst [тирст] *n.* ташнагӣ [tashnagi]
thirsty [тирсти] *adj.* ташна [tashna]
thirteen [тиртин] *num.* сездаҳ [sezdah]
thirteenth [тиртинт] *adj.* сездаҳум [sezdahum]
thirty [тирти] *num.* сӣ [si]
this [дис] *adj./pron.* ин [in]
thorn [торн] *n.* хор [xor]
thorough [торо] *adj.* пухтакор [puxtakor], дақиқ [daqiq]
thoroughfare [торофер] *n.* *(main road)* роҳи асосӣ [rohi asosi]; *(crossing)* гузаргоҳ [guzargoh]
those [доз] *pron.* онҳо [onho]
though [до] *conj.* агарчи [agarchi], ҳарчанд [harchand]
thought [тот] *n.* андеша [andesha], фикр [fikr]
thoughtful [тотфул] *adj.* андешаманд [andeshamand]
thousand [таузанд] *num.* ҳазор [hazor]
thousandth [таузандт] *adj.* ҳазорум [hazorum]
thread [тред] *n.* нах [nax], ресмон [resmon]
threat [трет] *n.* таҳдид [tahdid]
threaten [третен] *v.t.* таҳдид кардан [tahdid kardan]
three [три] *num.* се [se]
threshold [трешҳолд] *n.* остона [ostona]
thrift [трифт] *n.* сарфаҷӯӣ [sarfajüi]
thrifty [трифти] *adj.* сарфаҷӯй [sarfajüy]
thrive [трайв] *v.i.* гул-гул шукуфтан [gul-gul shukuftan], равнақ ёфтан [ravnaq yoftan]
throat [трот] *n.* гулӯ [gulü]
throb [троб] *v.i.* задан [zadan], тапидан [tapidan]
throne [трон] *n.* тахт [taxt], авранг [avrang]
throttle [тротл] *n.* дроссел [drossel] / *v.t.* хафа кардан [xafa kardan]
through [тру] *prep.* аз [az], аз миёни [az miyoni]

throughout [труаут] *adv.* саросар [sarosar], сар то сар [sar to sar]
throw [тро] *n.* партоиш [partoish] / *v.t.* партофтан [partoftan], андохтан [andoxtan]; **throw up** партфтан [partoftan], қай кардан [qay kardan]; **throw away** бароварда партофтан [barovarda partoftan]
thumb [там] *n.* нарангушт [narangusht], сарангушт [sarangusht]
thunder [тандер] *n.* тундар [tundar], раъд [ra'd]
Thursday [турздей] *n.* панҷшанбе [panjshanbe]
thyme [тайм] *n.* сесанбар [sesanbar]
tick [тик] *n. (insect)* кана [kana]
ticket [тикет] *n.* чипта [chipta], билет [bilet]
tickle [тикъл] *v.t.* қитиқ кардан [qitiq kardan] / *v.i.* хоридан [xoridan]
tide [тайд] *n.* мадду ҷазр [maddu jazr]; **high tide** мад [mad]; **low tide** ҷазр [jazr]
tidy [тайди] *adj.* ботартиб [botartib]
tie [тай] *n. (bond)* ришта [rishta]; *(necktie)* галстук [galstuk]; *(even score)* дуранг [durang] / *v.t. (a knot, a necktie, etc.)* бастан [bastan]; *(a score)* бозиро дуранг кардан [boziro durang kardan]
tiger [тайгер] *n.* бабр [babr]
tight [тайт] *adj.* танг [tang]
tights [тайтс] *n. (art. of clothing)* колготки [kolgotki]
tighten [тайтен] *v.t.* танг кардан [tang kardan] / *v.i.* танг шудан [tang shudan]
tile [тайл] *n.* кошин [koshin], сафол [safol]
tilt [тилт] *v.i.* хам шудан [xam shudan]
timber [тимбер] *n.* чӯбу тахта [chübu taxta]
time [тайм] *n.* вақт [vaqt]; *(point in time)* ҳангом [hangom]; *(occasion)* бор [bor]
timetable [таймтейбъл] *n.* ҷадвал [jadval]
tin [тин] *n.* арзиз [arziz], қалъагӣ [qal'agi]; **tin can** банка [banka], қуттича [qutticha]
tingle [тингъл] *v.i.* каме сӯзиш кунондан [kame süzish kunondan], андаке сих задан [andake six zadan]
tint [тинт] *n.* тобиш [tobish], тобиши ранг [tobishi rang] / *v.t.* тобиши нав додан [tobishi nav dodan], ранг кардан [rang kardan]
tiny [тайни] *adj.* майдаяк [maydayak]
tip [тип] *n. (end of an object)* нӯг [nüg], сар [sar]; *(of a spear, arrow, etc.)* пайкон [paykon]; *(gratuity)* чойпулӣ [choypuli]; *(piece of advice)* маслиҳат [maslihat] / *v.t. (give a gratuity)* чойпулӣ додан [choypuli dodan]; *(push over)* чаппа кардан [chappa kardan], ғалтондан [ghaltondan]; *(give advice)* маслиҳат додан [maslihat dodan] / *v.i. (be tipped over, fall over)* чаппа шудан [chappa shudan], ғалтидан [ghaltidan]

tiptoe [типто] *n.* нӯги по [nügi po] / *v.i.* бо нӯги по гаштан [bo nügi po gashtan]
tire [тайр] *n.* чарх [charx], чархи мошин [charxi moshin] / *v.t.* хаста кардан [xasta kardan], монда кардан [monda kardan] / *v.i.* хаста шудан [xasta shudan], монда шудан [monda shudan]
tired [тайрд] *adj.* хаста [xasta], монда [monda]
tiredness [тайрднес] *n.* хастагӣ [xastagi], мондагӣ [mondagi]
tireless [тайрлес] *adj.* хастанашаванда [xastanashavanda], монданашаванда [mondanashavanda]
tiresome [тайрсам] *adj.* *(boring)* дилгиркунанда [dilgirkunanda]; *(causing fatigue)* хастакунанда [xastakunanda]
tissue [тишу] *n.* *(tissue paper)* коғази папирос [koghazi papiros]; *(anat.)* бофта [bofta]; **connective tissue** бофтаи пайвасткунанда [boftai payvastkunanda]
title [тайтъл] *n.* *(of a book, play, movie, etc.)* сарлавҳа [sarlavha], унвон [unvon]; *(of a person)* лақаб [laqab], унвон [unvon]
to [ту] *prep.* ба [ba]
toad [тод] *n.* ғук [ghuk]
tobacco [тобако] *n.* тамоку [tamoku]
today [тудей] *adv.* имрӯз [imrüz]
toe [то] *n.* ангушти пой [angushti poy]
together [тугедер] *adv.* якҷоя [yakjoya]
toil [тойл] *n.* меҳнат [mehnat] / *v.i.* меҳнат кашидан [mehnat kashidan]
toilet [тойлет] *n.* хало [xalo]
token [токен] *n.* нишона [nishona]
tolerance [толеранс] *n.* бардошт [bardosht], таҳаммул [tahammul]
tolerate [толерейт] *v.t.* бардошт кардан [bardosht kardan], тоқат кардан [toqat kardan]
toll [тол] *n.* боҷ [boj]
tomato [томейто] *n.* помидор [pomidor]
tomb [тум] *n.* гӯр [gür], қабр [qabr]
tomorrow [туморо] *adv.* пагоҳ [pagoh], фардо [fardo]
ton [тан] *n.* тонна [tonna]
tone [тон] *n.* *(of voice, a book, etc.)* оҳанг [ohang]; *(mus.)* парда [parda], оҳанг [ohang]; *(shade of color)* тобиш [tobish]
tongs [тонгз] *n.* анбӯр [anbür], оташгирак [otashgirak]; **fire tongs** оташгирак [otashgirak]; **sugar tongs** қандшиканак [qandshikanak]
tongue [танг] *n.* забон [zabon]
tonnage [таниҷ] *n.* тоннаж [tonnazh]
tonsils [тонсилз] *n.pl.* ғадуди бодомшакл [ghadudi bodomshakl]
too [ту] *adv.* *(also)* ҳам [ham], низ [niz]; *(excessively)* зиёд [ziyod]
tool [тул] *n.* асбоб [asbob], абзор [abzor]

tooth [тут] *n.* дандон [dandon]
toothache [тутейк] *n.* дарди дандон [dardi dandon]
toothbrush [тутбраш] *n.* чӯткаи дандон [chütkai dandon]
toothpaste [тутпейст] *n.* хамири дандон [xamiri dandon]
top [топ] *n. (uppermost point)* сар [sar], нӯг [nüg]; *(mountain peak)* қулла [qulla]; *(lid)* сарпӯш [sarpüsh]; *(toy)* ғирғирак [ghirghirak] / *adj.* баландтарин [balandtarin]
topic [топик] *n.* мавзӯъ [mavzü']
topical [топикал] *adj. (med.)* ҷузъӣ [juz'i]
torch [торч] *n.* машъал [mash'al]
torment [тормент] *n.* азоб [azob] / *v.t.* азоб додан [azob dodan]
tornado [торнейдо] *n.* гирдбоди сахт [girdbodi saxt]
torrent [торент] *n.* селоба [seloba]
torture [торчур] *n.* шиканҷа [shikanja] / *v.t.* шиканҷа додан [shikanja dodan]
toss [тос] *v.t.* партофтан [partoftan]
total [тотал] *n.* ҷамъ [jam'] / *adj.* ҷамъулҷамъ [jam'uljam'], ҳамааш [hamaash] / *v.t.* ҷамъ кардан [jam' kardan]
totalitarian [тоталитериян] *adj.* тоталитарӣ [totalitari]
totally [тотали] *adv.* тамоман [tamoman]
touch [тач] *n.* ламс [lams] / *v.t.* даст расондан [dast rasondan]
touching [тачинг] *adj.* пуртаъсир [purta'sir], риққатовар [riqqatovar]
touchy [тачи] *adj.* зудранҷ [zudranj]
tough [таф] *adj. (not soft)* сахт [saxt], дурушт [durusht]; *(difficult)* душвор [dushvor]
toughen [тафен] *v.t.* сахт кардан [saxt kardan]
toughness [тафнес] *n.* сахтӣ [saxti], дурруштӣ [durushti]
tour [тур] *n.* сафар [safar], давр [davr] / *v.t.* сафар кардан [safar kardan], давр задан [davr zadan]
tourism [туризм] *n.* ҷаҳонгардӣ [jahongardi], саёҳат [sayohat]
tourist [турист] *n.* ҷаҳонгард [jahongard], сайёҳ [sayyoh]
tournament [турнамент] *n.* мусобиқа [musobiqa]
tow [то] *v.t.* кашида бурдан [kashida burdan]
toward [тоард] *prep.* сӯи [süi], ба сӯи [ba süi]
tower [тауер] *n.* бурҷ [burj], манора [manora]
town [таун] *n.* шаҳр [shahr], шаҳри хурд [shahri xurd]
toy [той] *n.* бозича [bozicha]
trace [трейс] *n.* пай [pay], из [iz] / *v.t. (draw)* нақша кашидан [naqsha kashidan]; *(track or shadow)* аз пай афтода ёфтан [az pay aftoda yoftan]
trachea [трейкия] *n.* нои нафас [noi nafas]

track [трак] *n.* пай [pay], из [iz]; *(railroad)* роҳи оҳан [rohi ohan] / *v.t.* *(hunt)* аз пай афтода ёфтан [az pay aftoda yoftan]; *(make tracks)* нақши пой мондан [naqshi poy mondan]; *(to track in dirt)* чиркин кардан [chirkin kardan]

traction [тракшан] *n.* кашиш [kashish]

tractor [трактор] *n.* трактор [traktor]

trade [трейд] *n.* *(vocation)* пеша [pesha], касб [kasb]; *(commerce)* савдо [savdo] / *v.t.* алиш кардан [alish kardan] / *v.i.* савдо кардан [savdo kardan]

trader [трейдър] *n.* савдогар [savdogar]

tradition [традишан] *n.* анъана [an'ana]

traditional [традишанал] *adj.* анъанавӣ [an'anavi]

traffic [трафик] *n.* рафтуомад [raftuomad], ҳаракат [harakat] / *v.i.* савдо кардан [savdo kardan]

tragedy [трачеди] *n.* фоҷиа [fojia]

tragic [трачик] *adj.* фоҷианок [fojianok]

trail [трейл] *n.* пайроҳа [payroha] / *v.t.* кашондан [kashondan] / *v.i.* кашонда шудан [kashonda shudan]

trailer [трейлер] *n.* ядак [yadak]

train [трейн] *n.* поезд [poezd], қатор [qator] / *v.t.* тарбия кардан [tarbiya kardan]

trainer [трейнер] *n.* омӯзгор [omüzgor]; **physical trainer** омӯзгори варзиш [omüzgori varzish]

training [трейнинг] *n.* тарбия [tarbiya], омӯзиш [omüzish]

trait [трейт] *n.* хусусият [xususiyat]

traitor [трейтор] *n.* хоин [xoin], хиёнаткор [xiyonatkor]

trance [тренс] *n.* *(med.)* изтирор [iztiror]; *(state of ecstacy)* ваҷд [vajd]

transaction [трензекшан] *n.* додугирифт [dodugirift], муомила [muomila]

transfer [тренсфер] *n.* вогузорӣ [voguzori] / *v.t.* *(cause to pass from one side or place to another)* гузарондан [guzarondan]; *(move sth or sb to a different location)* кӯчондан [küchondan]; *(give sth over)* вогузоштан [voguzoshtan]

transit [трензит] *n.* транзит [tranzit]

transitive [трензитив] *adj.* *(gram.)* гузаранда [guzaranda]

translate [трензлейт] *v.t.* тарҷума кардан [tarjuma kardan]

translation [трензлейшан] *n.* тарҷума [tarjuma]

translator [трензлейтор] *n.* тарҷумон [tarjumon]

transmission [трензмишан] *n.* ирсол [irsol]; *(of knowledge)* ошнокунӣ [oshnokuni]; *(radio)* радиошунавонӣ [radioshunavoni]

transmit [трензмит] *v.t.* *(cause to go from one place to another)* расондан [rasondan], гузарондан [guzarondan]; *(of sound)* шунавондан [shunavondan]; *(of knowledge)* ошно кардан [oshno kardan], омӯхтан [omüxtan]

transport [транспорт] *n.* боркашонӣ [borkashoni], ҳамлу нақл [hamlu naql] / *v.t.* кашондан [kashondan], кӯчондан [küchondan]
trap [треп] *n.* дом [dom], қапқон [qapqon] / *v.t.* ба дом андохтан [ba dom andoxtan]
trap-door [треп-дор] *n.* палкона [palkona]
trash [треш] *n.* кӯҳнакола [kühnakola]
travel [тревел] *n.* сафар [safar] / *v.i.* сафар кардан [safar kardan]
traveler [тревелер] *n.* мусофир [musofir]
tray [трей] *n.* лаълӣ [la'li]
treason [тризан] *n.* хиёнат [xiyonat]
treasure [трежур] *n.* ганҷ [ganj]
treasurer [трежурер] *n.* ганҷур [ganjur], ганҷдор [ganjdor]
treasury [трежури] *n.* ганҷина [ganjina]
treat [трит] *n.* лаззат [lazzat] / *v.t. (treat to a meal)* меҳмон кардан [mehmon kardan]; *(treat a sickness)* муолиҷа кардан [muolija kardan] / *v.i.* муомила доштан [muomila doshtan]
treatment [тритмент] *n.* *(med.)* муолиҷа [muolija]; *(manner of behavior)* муомила [muomila], рафтор [raftor]
treaty [трити] *n.* аҳднома [ahdnoma], паймон [paymon]
tree [три] *n.* дарахт [daraxt]
tremble [трембъл] *v.i.* ларзидан [larzidan]
trench [тренч] *n.* хандақ [xandaq]
trend [тренд] *n.* равия [raviya], майлон [maylon]
trespass [треспас] *v.i.* аз хатти сарҳад пинҳонӣ гузаштан [az xatti sarhad pinhoni guzashtan]
trial [трайал] *n. (experiment, test)* озмоиш [ozmoish], санҷиш [sanjish]; *(legal)* муҳокима [muhokima], суд [sud]
triangle [трайангъл] *n.* секунҷа [sekunja]
triangular [трайангюлар] *adj.* секунҷа [sekunja]
tribe [трайб] *n.* қабила [qabila]
tribute [трибют] *n.* боҷ [boj]
trick [трик] *n. (card/magic trick)* найрангбозӣ [nayrangbozi]; *(deceit)* фиреб [fireb] / *v.t.* фирефтан [fireftan]
trickle [трикъл] *n.* фаврак [favrak] / *v.i.* чакидан [chakidan], таровидан [tarovidan]
tricycle [трайсикъл] *n.* сечарха [secharxa]
trifle [трайфъл] *n.* якпула чиз [yakpula chiz], ночиз [nochiz]
trigger [тригер] *n. (of a lock, apparatus)* забонак [zabonak], дандонак [dandonak]; *(of a gun)* камонаки милтиқ [kamonaki miltiq] / *v.t.* сабаб шудан [sabab shudan]

trimester [трайместер] *n.* *(period of three months)* муддати семоҳа [muddati semoha]; *(academic)* триместр [trimestr]

triumph [трайамф] *n.* пирӯзӣ [pirüzi] / *v.i.* пирӯз шудан [pirüz shudan]

trivial [тривиял] *adj.* ночиз [nochiz]

troops [трупс] *n.* лашкар [lashkar]

tropic [тропик] *n.* мадор [mador]; **Tropic of Cancer** мадори Саратон [madori Saraton]

tropical [тропикал] *adj.* ҳорра [horra], тропикӣ [tropiki]

tropics [тропикс] *n.pl.* баҳористон [bahoriston], минтақаҳои ҳорра [mintaqahoi horra]

trouble [трабъл] *n.* ташвиш [tashvish] / *v.t.* ташвиш додан [tashvish dodan]

troublesome [трабълсам] *adj.* пурзаҳмат [purzahmat]

trout [траут] *n.* гулмоҳӣ [gulmohi]

trowel [трауел] *n.* белча [belcha]

truant [труант] *n.* бачаи мактабгурез [bachai maktabgurez] / *adj.* мактабгурез [maktabgurez]

truck [трак] *n.* мошини боркаш [moshini borkash]

true [тру] *adj.* рост [rost]

truffle [трафъл] *n.* занбӯруғи тагихокӣ [zanbürughi tagixoki]

truly [трули] *adv.* ба ростӣ [ba rosti]

trump [трамп] *n.* кузур [kuzur] / *v.t.* бо кузур задан [bo kuzur zadan]

trunk [транк] *n.* *(of tree)* тана [tana]; *(torso)* колбад [kolbad], тан [tan]; *(of an animal)* хартум [xartum]; *(box)* сандуқ [sanduq]; *(suitcase)* ҷомадон [jomadon]

trust *n.* бовар [bovar], дилпурӣ [dilpuri] / *v.t.* бовар доштан [bovar doshtan], дилпур будан [dilpur budan]

trusting [трастинг] *adj.* зудбовар [zudbovar]

trustworthy [траствурди] *adj.* сазовори эътимод [sazovori e'timod]

truth [трут] *n.* ростӣ [rosti], ҳақиқат [haqiqat]

truthful [трутфул] *adj.* ростгӯй [rostgüy]

try [трай] *v.t.* *(test)* озмудан [ozmudan], санҷидан [sanjidan]; *(legal)* муҳокима кардан [muhokima kardan], суд кардан [sud kardan]; *(taste)* чашидан [chashidan] / *v.i.* кӯшидан [küshidan], кӯшиш кардан [küshish kardan]

tube [тюб] *n.* қубур [qubur], найча [naycha]

Tuesday [тюздей] *n.* сешанбе [seshanbe]

tug [таг] *v.i.* кашола кардан [kashola kardan], кашидан [kashidan]

tulip [тюлип] *n.* лола [lola]

tumor [тюмор] *n.* омос [omos], варам [varam]

tune [тюн] *n.* наво [navo], оҳанг [ohang] / *v.t.* ҷӯр кардан [jür kardan], соз кардан [soz kardan]

tunnel [танал] *n.* туннел [tunnel]

turbine [турбин] *n.* турбина [turbina]
turkey [турки] *n.* мурғи марҷон [murghi marjon]
Turkish [туркиш] *n.* турк [turk] / *adj.* туркӣ [turki]
Turkmen [туркмен] *n.* *(person)* туркман [turkman]; *(language)* туркманӣ [turkmani] / *adj.* туркман [turkman]
turmoil [турмойл] *n.* мағал [maghal], тӯпаланг [tüpalang]
turn [турн] *n.* чархиш [charxish] / *v.t.* чархонидан [charxonidan] / *v.i.* чархидан [charxidan]
turtle [туртал] *n.* сангпушт [sangpusht]
tweezers [туизарз] *n.* мӯйчинак [müychinak]
twelfth [туелфт] *adj.* дувоздаҳум [duvozdahum]
twelve [туелв] *num.* дувоздаҳ [duvozdah]
twentieth [туентият] *adj.* бистум [bistum]
twenty [туенти] *num.* бист [bist]
twice [туайс] *adv.* ду бор [du bor]
twig [туиг] *n.* шохча [shoxcha]
twilight [туайлайт] *n.* нимторикӣ [nimtoriki], шом [shom]
twin [туин] *n.* дугоник [dugonik]
twinge [туинҷ] *n.* дарди сахт [dardi saxt]
twinkle [туинкъл] *v.i.* йилт-йилт кардан [yilt-yilt kardan]
twist [туист] *n.* тоб [tob] / *v.t./v.i.* тофтан [toftan]
two [ту] *num.* ду [du]
type [тайп] *n.* *(kind)* хел [xel]; *(printing type)* ҳарф [harf]
typewriter [тайпрайтер] *n.* мошинка [moshinka], мошини хатнависӣ [moshini xatnavisi]
typical [типикал] *adj.* намунавӣ [namunavi]
typist [тайпист] *n.* рӯнавискунанда [rünaviskunanda]

U

ugly [агли] *adj.* безеб [bezeb]
ulcer [алсер] *n.* захм [zaxm]; **stomach ulcer** захми меъда [zaxmi me'da]
ultraviolet [алтравайлет] *adj.* ултрабунафш [ultrabunafsh]; **ultraviolet rays** шуоъҳои ултрабунафш [shuo'hoi ultrabunafsh]
umbrella [амбрела] *n.* чатр [chatr]; *(parasol)* соябон [soyabon]
unable [анейбл] *adj.* нотавон [notavon], беқобилият [beqobiliyat]; **I am unable to come.** Ман омада наметавонам. [Man omada nametavonam.]
unacceptable [анексептабл] *adj.* номақбул [nomaqbul]
unaccountable [анакаунтабл] *adj.* *(inexplicable)* шарҳнопазир [sharhnopazir]; *(without responsibility)* бемасъулият [bemas'uliyat]
unanimous [юненимас] *adj.* якдилона [yakdilona]
unarmed [анармд] *adj.* беяроқ [beyaroq]

unauthorized [аноторайзд] *adj. (without permission)* беиҷозат [beijozat]; *(without authority)* беваколат [bevakolat]
unavoidable [анавойдабл] *adj.* ногузир [noguzir]
unaware [анауэр] *adj.* бехабар [bexabar]
unbearable [анберабл] *adj.* тоқатфарсо [toqatfarso], тахаммулнопазир [tahammulnopazir]
uncertain [ансертан] *adj. (doubtful)* шубҳаомез [shubhaomez]; *(hesitant)* дудила [dudila]
uncle [анкъл] *n. (paternal)* амак [amak]; *(maternal)* тағо [tagho]
uncomfortable [анкамфтурбл] *adj.* ноқулай [noqulay]
unconscious [анконшас] *adj.* беҳуш [behush]
uncover [анкавер] *v.t. (find out)* фош кардан [fosh kardan]; *(remove covering)* луч кардан [luch kardan]
undamaged [андемиҷд] *adj.* безиён [beziyon]
undecided [андесайдед] *adj.* дудила [dudila]
under [андер] *adv.* зер [zer], таг [tag] / *prep. (beneath)* зери [zeri], таги [tagi]; *(less than)* камтар аз [kamtar az]
undergo [андерго] *v.i.* гирифтор шудан [giriftor shudan], дучор шудан [duchor shudan]
underground [андерграунд] *adj.* зеризаминӣ [zerizamini]; *(secret)* пинҳонӣ [pinhoni]
underline [андерлайн] *v.t.* ба зер хат кашидан [ba zer xat kashidan]
underneath [андернит] *prep.* дар зери [dar zeri]
undershirt [андерширт] *n.* куртаи таг [kurtai tag]
undersign [андерсайн] *v.t.* дар зери нома имзо кардан [dar zeri noma imzo kardan]
understand [андерстенд] *v.t.* фаҳмидан [fahmidan]
understanding [андерстендинг] *n. (comprehension)* фаҳмиш [fahmish]; *(mutual agreement)* тафоҳум [tafohum]
undertake [андертейк] *v.t.* ба ӯҳда гирифтан [ba ühda giriftan]
underwater [андеруотер] *adj.* зериобӣ [zeriobi]
underwear [андеруэр] *n.* пӯшоки таг [püshoki tag]
undo [анду] *v.t.* кушодан [kushodan], яла кардан [yala kardan]
uneasiness [анизинес] *n.* ноороми [nooromi]
uneasy [анизи] *adj.* ноором [noorom]
uneducated [анедюкейтед] *adj.* чаласавод [chalasavod], бесавод [besavod]
unemployed [анемплойд] *adj.* бекор [bekor]
unemployment [анемплоймент] *n.* бекорӣ [bekori]
unending [анендинг] *adj.* бепоён [bepoyon]
unequal [аникуал] *adj.* нобаробар [nobarobar]

unfair [анфер] *adj.* беинсоф [beinsof], беадолат [beadolat]
unfamiliar [анфамиляр] *adj.* ноошно [nooshno], ношинос [noshinos]
unfasten [анфесен] *v.t.* яла кардан [yala kardan]
unfortunate [анфорчунат] *adj.* бадбахт [badbaxt]
unfortunately [анфорчунатли] *adv.* мутаассифона [mutaassifona]
unfriendly [анфрендли] *adj.* бадхоҳона [badxohona], душманона [dushmanona]
unhappy [анҳепи] *adj.* нохуш [noxush]
unhealthy [анҳелти] *adj.* нохуш [noxush], бемор [bemor]
uniform [юниформ] *n.* пӯшоки расмӣ [püshoki rasmi], форма [forma] / *adj.* якхела [yakxela]
unimportant [анимпортант] *adj.* беаҳамият [beahamiyat]
unintentional [анинтеншонал] *adj.* беқасд [beqasd]
union [юнян] *n.* иттиҳод [ittihod], иттифоқ [ittifoq]
unique [юник] *adj.* ягона [yagona], беҳамто [behamto]
unisex [юнисекс] *adj.* бечинс [bejins]
unit [юнит] *n.* воҳид [vohid]
unite [юнайт] *v.t.* як кардан [yak kardan], муттаҳид кардан [muttahid kardan]
United Nations [юнайтед нейшанз] *n.* Созмони милали муттаҳид [Sozmoni milali muttahid]
unity [юнити] *n.* ягонагӣ [yagonagi]
universal [юниверсал] *adj.* умумӣ [umumi]
universe [юниверс] *n.* кайҳон [kayhon]
university [юниверсити] *n.* донишгоҳ [donishgoh]
unjust [анҷаст] *adj.* беадолат [beadolat]
unknown [аннон] *adj.* номаълум [noma'lum], ношинос [noshinos]
unless [анлес] *conj.* ҷуз он ки [juz on ki]
unlike [анлайк] *adj.* монанднабуда [monandnabuda], ноҳамгун [nohamgun]
unlikely [анлайкли] *adj.* аз эҳтимол дур [az ehtimol dur]
unload [анлод] *v.t.* фуровардан [furovardan]
unlucky [анлаки] *adj.* бадбахт [badbaxt]
unnecessary [аннесесери] *adj.* *(not needed)* нодаркор [nodarkor]; *(excessive)* барзиёд [barziyod]
unofficial [анофишал] *adj.* ғайрирасмӣ [ghayrirasmi]
unpack [анпек] *v.t* кушодан [kushodan]
unpleasant [анплезант] *adj.* нофорам [noforam], дилнокаш [dilnokash]
unpopular [анпопюлар] *adj.* омманофаҳм [ommanofahm]
unrest [анрест] *n.* ошӯб [oshüb]
unsafe [ансейф] *adj.* хатарнок [xatarnok]

unsatisfactory [ансетисфектори] *adj.* ғайриқаноатбахш [ghayriqanoatbaxsh]
unskilled [анскилд] *adj.* беихтисос [beixtisos]
unstable [анстейбл] *adj.* ноустувор [noustuvor]
unsuccessful [ансаксесфул] *adj.* ноком [nokom], бемуваффақият [bemuvaffaqiyat]
untie [антай] *v.t.* яла кардан [yala kardan], кушодан [kushodan]
until [антил] *prep.* то [to]
untrue [антру] *adj.* нодуруст [nodurust]
unwell [ануэл] *adj.* бемадор [bemador], бемор [bemor]
unwrap [анреп] *v.t.* яла кардан [yala kardan], кушодан [kushodan]
up [ап] *adj. (above)* боло [bolo]; *(out of bed)* хеста [xesta]; *(higher)* баландтар [balandtar]; *(better)* беҳтар [behtar]; **The sun is up.** Офтоб баромад. [Oftob baromad]; **The children are up.** Бачаҳо хестанд. [Bachaho xestand] / *adv.* боло [bolo]; **up until now** то акнун [to aknun] / *prep.* боло [bolo], ба боло [ba bolo]
upkeep [апкип] *n.* нигоҳдорию таъмир [nigohdoriyu ta'mir]
upon [апон] *prep.* рӯйи [rüyi], бар [bar]
upper [апер] *adj.* болоӣ [boloi], боло [bolo]
uproar [апрор] *n.* ғавғо [ghavgho]
upset [апсет] *adj. (knocked over)* чаппа [chappa]; *(unhappy)* хафа [xafa] / *v.t. (knock over)* чаппа кардан [chappa kardan]; *(offend)* хафа кардан [xafa kardan]
upsetting [апсетинг] *adj.* хафасозанда [xafasozanda]
upside down [апсайд даун] *adv.* чаппа [chappa]
upstairs [апстерз] *adj.* боло [bolo] / *adv.* ба боло [ba bolo]
upstream [апстрим] *adv.* ба муқобили ҷараён [ba muqobili jarayon]
up-to-date [ап-ту-дейт] *adj.* ҳозира [hozira]
upward [апуард] *adv.* сӯйи боло [süyi bolo]
urban [урбан] *adj.* шаҳрӣ [shahri]
urge [урҷ] *n. (impulse)* ангеза [angeza]; *(desire)* орзу [orzu] / *v.t. (to drive)* ҳай кардан [hay kardan], рондан [rondan]; *(to excite)* барангехтан [barangextan]; *(to persuade)* бовар кунондан [bovar kunondan]
urgency [урҷенси] *n.* таъҷилӣ [ta'jili], зарурат [zarurat]
urgent [урҷент] *adj.* таъҷилӣ [ta'jili]
urinary [юринери] *adj.* пешобӣ [peshobi]
urinate [юринейт] *v.i.* пешоб кардан [peshob kardan]
urine [юрин] *n.* пешоб [peshob]
urn [урн] *n.* устадон [ustadon]
us [ас] *pron.* мо [mo]

usage [юсич] *n.* корбурд [korburd], истеъмол [iste'mol]
use [юс] *n. (usage)* корбурд [korburd], истеъмол [iste'mol]; *(benefit)* фоида [foida]; **It's of use.** Фоида дорад. [Foida dorad]
use [юз] *v.t.* ба кор бурдан [ba kor burdan], истифода кардан [istifoda kardan]; *(utilize)* **I use** ба кор мебарам. [ba kor mebaram]; **use up** тамом кардан [tamom kardan]
used [юзд] *adj.* нимдошт [nimdosht]
useful [юсфул] *adj.* фоиданок [foidanok]
useless [юслес] *adj.* бефоида [befoida]
user [юзер] *n.* истеъмолкунанда [iste'molkunanda]
usher [ашер] *n.* тафтишкунандаи чипта [taftishkunandai chipta]
usual [южуал] *adj.* ҳаррӯза [harrüza], одатӣ [odati]
usually [южуали] *adv.* одатан [odatan]
utensil [ютенсил] *n.* абзор [abzor]; **utensils** лавозимот [lavozimot]; **kitchen utensils** зарфҳои ошпазхона [zarfhoi oshpazxona]
uterus [ютерас] *n.* бачадон [bachadon]
utility [ютилити] *n.* фоида [foida]; **public utilities** хизматҳои умумӣ [xizmathoi umumi]
utilize [ютилайз] *v.t.* ба кор бурдан [ba kor burdan], истифода кардан [istifoda kardan]
utmost [атмост] *adj.* бештарин [beshtarin]
utter [атер] *adj.* пурра [purra], тамом [tamom] / *v.t.* гуфтан [guftan]
Uzbek [узбек] *n. (person)* узбак [uzbak]; *(language)* узбакӣ [uzbaki] / *adj.* узбак [uzbak]

V

vacancy [вейканси] *n.* ҷойи тиҳӣ [joyi tihi]
vacant [вейкант] *adj.* тиҳӣ [tihi], холӣ [xoli]
vacation [вейкейшан] *n.* *(from work)* рухсатӣ [ruxsati]; *(from school)* таътил [ta'til]
vaccinate [вексинейт] *v.t.* ваксина гузарондан [vaksina guzarondan]
vaccination [вексинейшан] *n.* ваксинагузаронӣ [vaksinaguzaroni]
vaccine [вексин] *n.* ваксина [vaksina]
vacuum [векюм] *n.* чангкашак [changkashak] / *v.t.* бо чангкашак пок кардан [bo changkashak pok kardan]
vague [вейг] *adj.* норавшан [noravshan], номуайян [nomuayyan]
vain [вейн] *adj. (without result)* беҳуда [behuda]; *(egotistical)* худбин [xudbin]; **in vain** беҳуда [behuda]
valet [велей] *n.* хизматгор [xizmatgor]
valiant [велянт] *adj.* далер [daler], диловар [dilovar]

valid [велид] *adj. (just, well-grounded)* ҳақиқӣ [haqiqi]; *(having legal force)* эътиборнок [e'tibornok]
validity [велидити] *n.* ҳақиқат [haqiqat]
valley [вели] *n.* дара [dara], водӣ [vodi]
valuable [велюбал] *n.* чизи гаронбаҳо [chizi garonbaho] / *adj.* баҳодор [bahodor], арзишдор [arzishdor], гаронбаҳо [garonbaho]
value [велю] *n.* арзиш [arzish] / *v.t.* нарх мондан [narx mondan]
valve [велв] *n. (mechanical)* сарпӯшак [sarpüshak]; *(anat.)* қапқоқ [qapqoq]; **heart valve** қапқоқи дил [qapqoqi dil]
van [вен] *n.* автомобили каппадори боркаш [avtomobili kappadori borkash]
vanilla [ванила] *n.* ванил [vanil]
vanish [вениш] *v.i.* нопадид шудан [nopadid shudan], нонамоён шудан [nonamoyon shudan]
vapor [вейпор] *n.* буғ [bugh]
variable [вериябл] *n.* андозаи тағйирёбанда [andozai taghyiryobanda] / *adj.* тағйирёбанда [taghyiryobanda]
variation [вериейшан] *n.* тағйир [taghyir], дигаргунӣ [digarguni]
variety [варайети] *n.* рангорангӣ [rangorangi]
various [верияс] *adj.* гуногун [gunogun]
varnish [варниш] *n.* лок [lok] / *v.t.* лок задан [lok zadan]
vary [вери] *v.t.* дигаргун кардан [digargun kardan], тағйир додан [taghyir dodan] / *v.i.* дигаргун шудан [digargun shudan], тағйир ёфтан [taghyir yoftan]
vase [вейс] *n.* гулдон [guldon]
vault [волт] *n. (bank)* зеризаминӣ [zerizamini]; *(funeral)* дахма [daxma]
VCR [ви си ар] *n. (abbrev. of* **videocassette recorder***)* видеомагнитофон [videomagnitofon]
veal [вил] *n.* гӯшти гӯсола [güshti güsola]
vegetable [веҷетабл] *n.* сабзавот [sabzavot]
vegetarian [веҷетериян] *n.* гӯштнахӯранда [güshtnaxüranda] / *adj.* бегӯшт [begüsht]
vegetation [веҷетейшан] *n.* растаниҳо [rastaniho]
vehement [веемент] *adj.* шиддатнок [shiddatnok]
vehicle [вийикл] *n.* воситаи ҳамлу нақл [vositai hamlu naql]
veil [вейл] *n. (as worn in Islamic countries)* чодар [chodar]; *(as worn by a bride)* ниқоби тур [niqobi tur]
vein [вейн] *n.* сиёҳраг [siyohrag], раги варид [ragi varid]
velvet [велвет] *n.* бахмал [baxmal] / *adj.* бахмалин [baxmalin]
venerate [венерейт] *v.t.* ҳурмат кардан [hurmat kardan], парастидан [parastidan]

venereal [венириял] *adj.* *(disease)* бемории олоти таносул [bemorii oloti tanosul]
vengeance [венҷанс] *n.* интиқом [intiqom]
venom [венам] *n.* заҳр [zahr]
vent [вент] *n.* сӯрохи ҳавотозакунӣ [süroxi havotozakuni]
ventilate [вентилейт] *v.t.* ҳаво тоза кардан [havo toza kardan]
ventilation [вентилейшан] *n.* ҳавотозакунӣ [havotozakuni]
ventilator [вентилейтор] *n.* ҳавотозакунак [havotozakunak]
ventricle [вентрикл] *n.* меъдача [me'dacha]
venture [венчур] *n.* ташаббуси бохатар [tashabbusi boxatar]
verb [верб] *n.* феъл [fe'l]
verbal [вербал] *adj.* феълӣ [fe'li]
verdict [вердикт] *n.* ҳукм [hukm], ҳукмнома [hukmnoma]
verge [верҷ] *n.* лаб [lab], канор [kanor]; **on the verge of** дар дами [dar dami]
verification [верификейшан] *n.* тасдиқ [tasdiq]
verify [верифай] *v.t.* тасдиқ кардан [tasdiq kardan]
vermouth [вермут] *n.* вермут [vermut]
versatile [версатайл] *adj.* ҳартарафа [hartarafa]
verse [верс] *n.* назм [nazm]
version [вержан] *n.* *(explanation)* тафсир [tafsir], шарҳ [sharh]; *(translation)* тарҷума [tarjuma]
versus [версас] *prep.* дар муқобили [dar muqobili]
vertebra [вертебра] *n.*, мӯҳра [mühra], мӯҳраи аррапушт [mührai arrapusht]; *(anat.)* аррапушт [arrapusht], сутунмӯҳра [sutunmühra]
vertical [вертикал] *adj.* амудӣ [amudi]
very [вери] *adv.* бисёр [bisyor], хеле [xele]
vessel [весал] *n.* *(ship)* киштӣ [kishti]; *(blood vessel)* раг [rag]; *(container)* зарф [zarf]
vest [вест] *n.* камзӯлча [kamzülcha]
veteran [ветеран] *n.* сарбози пуртаҷриба [sarbozi purtajriba] / *adj.* пуртаҷриба [purtajriba]
veterinarian [ветеринериян] *n.* байтор [baytor], духтури ҷонварҳо [duxturi jonvarho]
veterinary [ветеринери] *adj.* байторӣ [baytori]
via [виа] *prep.* ба воситаи [ba vositai]
vial [вайал] *n.* шишаи хурд [shishai xurd]
vibrate [вайбрейт] *v.i.* ларзидан [larzidan]
vibration [вайбрейшан] *n.* ларзиш [larzish]
vice [вайс] *n.* *(evil)* бадӣ [badi], шар [shar]; *(mechanical)* гира [gira]
vice president [вайс президент] *n.* ноиб-президент [noib prezident]

vicinity [висинити] *n.* гирду атроф [girdu atrof]
vicious [вишас] *adj.* бисёр бад [bisyor bad]
victim [виктим] *n.* қурбонӣ [qurboni]
victory [виктори] *n.* пирӯзӣ [pirüzi], зафар [zafar]
video [видио] *n.* видео [video]
videotape [видиотейп] *n.* видеокассета [videokasseta]; **videotape recorder** видеомагнитофон [videomagnitofon]
view [вю] *n.* манзара [manzara] / *v.t.* нигаристан [nigaristan], нигоҳ кардан [nigoh kardan]; **point of view** нуқтаи назар [nuqtai nazar]
vigor [вигор] *n.* зӯр [zür]
villa [вила] *n.* кӯшк [küshk], вилла [villa]
village [виличҷ] *n.* деҳа [deha], қишлоқ [qishloq]
vine [вайн] *n.* ток [tok]
vinegar [винегар] *n.* сирко [sirko]
vineyard [винярд] *n.* токзор [tokzor]
violate [вайолейт] *v.t.* вайрон кардан [vayron kardan]
violation [вайолейшан] *n.* вайроншавӣ [vayronshavi]; **traffic violation** вайрон кардани қоидаҳои ҳаракати роҳ [vayron kardani qoidahoi harakati roh]
violence [вайленс] *n.* сахтӣ [saxti]
violent [вайлент] *adj.* сахт [saxt]
violet [вайлет] *n.* бунафша [bunafsha] / *adj.* бунафш [bunafsh]
violin [вайолин] *n.* скрипка [skripka], ғиҷҷак [ghijjak]
violoncello [вайолончело] *n.* виолончел [violonchel]
viral [вайрал] *adj.* вирусӣ [virusi]
virgin [вирҷин] *n.* дӯшиза [düshiza], бокира [bokira]
virtual [вирчуал] *adj.* амалӣ [amali]
virtually [вирчуали] *adv.* амалан [amalan]
virtue [вирчуал] *n.* некӯӣ [nekũi], неккирдорӣ [nekkirdori]
virus [вайрас] *n.* вирус [virus]
visa [виза] *n.* раводид [ravodid]
visibility [визибилити] *n.* намоёнӣ [namoyoni]
visible [визибл] *adj.* намоён [namoyon], дидашаванда [didashavanda]
vision [вижан] *n.* *(sense of sight)* биниш [binish], биноӣ [binoi]; *(intelligent foresight)* басират [basirat]; *(apparition)* рӯъё [rü'yo]
visit [визит] *n.* мулоқот [muloqot], боздид [bozdid] / *v.t.* боздид кардан [bozdid kardan], барои дидан рафтан [baroi didan raftan]
visitor [визитор] *n.* меҳмон [mehmon]
visor [вайзор] *n.* *(sun visor)* офтобпанаҳ [oftobpanah]
visual [вижуал] *adj.* басарӣ [basari]
vital [вайтал] *adj.* зарур [zarur], даркор [darkor]

vitality [вайтелити] *n.* қобилияти зист [qobiliyati zist]
vitamin [вайтамин] *n.* витамин [vitamin]
vivid [вивид] *adj.* чашмбар [chashmbar], дурахшон [duraxshon]
vocabulary [вокебюлери] *n.* луғат [lughat]
vocal [вокал] *adj.* овозӣ [ovozi]
voice [войс] *n.* овоз [ovoz], садо [sado] / *v.t.* ифода кардан [ifoda kardan]
void [войд] *adj.* *(empty)* тиҳӣ [tihi], холӣ [xoli]; *(ineffective, null)* ботил [botil]
volcano [волкейно] *n.* оташфишон [otashfishon]
volt [волт] *n.* волт [volt]
voltage [волтич] *n.* волтаж [voltazh]
volume [волюм] *n.* *(book)* ҷилд [jild]; *(mass)* ҳаҷм [hajm]; *(capacity)* гунҷоиш [gunjoish]; *(sound)* овоз [ovoz]
voluntary [волантери] *adj.* ихтиёрӣ [ixtiyori]
volunteer [волантир] *n.* довталаб [dovtalab]
vomit [вомит] *v.i.* қай кардан [qay kardan]
vote [вот] *n.* *(individual vote)* овоз [ovoz]; *(ballot, the process of voting)* овоздиҳӣ [ovozdihi]; *(eligibility to vote)* ҳаққи райъ [haqqi ray'] / *v.i.* овоз додан [ovoz dodan]
voter [вотер] *n.* овоздиҳанда [ovozdihanda]
voucher [ваучер] *n.* *(guaranty)* кафолатнома [kafolatnoma]; *(receipt)* забонхат [zabonxat]
vow [вау] *n.* савганд [savgand], қасам [qasam] / *v.t.* савганд хӯрдан [savgand xürdan], қасам хӯрдан [qasam xürdan]
vowel [вауэл] *n.* садонок [sadonok]
voyage [вояч] *n.* сафари киштӣ [safari kishti] / *v.i.* бо киштӣ сафар кардан [bo kishti safar kardan]
vulgar [валгур] *adj.* дағал [daghal], дурушт [durusht]

W

wad [вод] *n.* кулӯла [kulüla], кулӯх [kulüx]
wade [вейд] *v.i.* дар об роҳ рафтан [dar ob roh raftan]
wag [вег] *v.t.* ҷунбондан [junbondan] / *v.i.* ҷунбидан [junbidan]; **to wag the tail** дум ҷунбондан [dum junbondan]
wage [вейч] *n.* *(wages)* моҳона [mohona], музд [muzd]
wagon [вегон] *n.* ароба [aroba]
waist [вейст] *n.* миён [miyon], камар [kamar]
wait [вейт] *n.* интизорӣ [intizori] / *v.i.* мунтазир шудан [muntazir shudan]; *(wait on sb)* (ба касе) хизмат расондан [(ba kase) xizmat rasondan]
waiter [вейтер] *n.* пешхизмат [peshxizmat]

waiting room [вейтинг рум] *n.* қабулгоҳ [qabulgoh]
waitress [вейтрес] *n.* пешхизмат [peshxizmat]
wake [вейк] *v.t.* бедор кардан [bedor kardan] / *v.i.* бедор шудан [bedor shudan]
walk [вок] *n.* гардиш [gardish] / *v.t.* гардондан [gardondan] / *v.i.* роҳ рафтан [roh raftan], гаштан [gashtan]; **to take a walk** гардиш кардан [gardish kardan]
wall [вол] *n.* девор [devor]
wallet [волит] *n.* қапчуқ [qapchuq], ҳамён [hamyon]
walnut [волнат] *n.* чормағз [chormaghz]
wand [вонд] *n.* чӯбчаи ҷодугарӣ [chübchai jodugari]
wander [вондер] *v.i.* гаштугузор кардан [gashtuguzor kardan]; **to wander aimlessly** саргардон будан [sargardon budan]
want [вонт] *n.* хоҳиш [xohish] / *v.t.* хостан [xostan]
war [вор] *n.* ҷанг [jang]
wardrobe [вордроб] *n.* гардероб [garderob]
ware [вер] *n.* мол [mol]
warehouse [верҳаус] *n.* анбор [anbor]
warm [ворм] *adj.* гарм [garm]
warmth [вормт] *n.* гармӣ [garmi]
warn [ворн] *v.t.* пешакӣ огоҳонидан [peshaki ogohonidan]
warning [ворнинг] *n.* огоҳӣ [ogohi]
warrant [ворант] *n.* фармон [farmon], амри хаттӣ [amri xatti]
warranty [воранти] *n.* кафолатнома [kafolatnoma]
wart [ворт] *n.* озах [ozax]
wary [вери] *adj.* эҳтиёткор [ehtiyotkor]
wash [вош] *v.t.* шустан [shustan]
washable [вошабл] *adj.* шустанӣ [shustani]
washing machine [вошинг машин] *n.* мошини ҷомашӯӣ [moshini jomashüi]
wasp [восп] *n.* занбӯр [zanbür], ору [oru]
waste [вейст] *n.* *(refuse)* ахлот [axlot]; *(careless expense)* исроф [isrof] / *v.t.* исроф кардан [isrof kardan], талаф кардан [talaf kardan]
wasteful [вейстфул] *adj.* талафкор [talafkor]
wastepaper basket [вейстпейпер бескет] *n.* ахлотқуттӣ [axlotqutti]
watch [воч] *n.* соат [soat] / *v.t.* *(look at steadily)* тамошо кардан [tamosho kardan]; *(guard)* қаровулӣ кардан [qarovuli kardan] / *v.i.* дида баромадан [dida baromadan], нигоҳ кардан [nigoh kardan]
watchful [вочфул] *adj.* эҳтиёткор [ehtiyotkor]
watchman [вочмен] *n.* посбон [posbon]
water [вотер] *v.t.* об додан [ob dodan]; *n.* об [ob]; **fresh water** оби ширин [obi shirin]; **salt water** оби шӯр [obi shür]; **drinking water** оби нӯшиданӣ [obi nüshidani]

watercolor [вотеркалар] *n.* акварел [akvarel], ранги обӣ [rangi obi]
waterfall [вотерфол] *n.* шаршара [sharshara], обшор [obshor]
watermelon [вотермелон] *n.* тарбуз [tarbuz]
waterproof [вотерпруф] *adj.* обногузар [obnoguzar]
water-ski [вотер-ски] *v.i.* лижаронии обӣ кардан [lizharonii obi kardan]
watery [вотери] *adj.* обакӣ [obaki]
watt [вот] *n.* ватт [vatt]
wave [вейв] *n.* мавҷ [mavj] / *v.t.* ҷунбондан [junbondan]; **to wave the hand** даст ҷунбондан [dast junbondan]
wavelength [вейвленгт] *n.* дарозии мавҷ [darozii mavj]
waver [вейвер] *v.i.* дудила шудан [dudila shudan]
wax [векс] *n.* мум [mum] / *v.t.* мум задан [mum zadan]
way [вей] *n.* роҳ [roh]; **to lose one's way** роҳи худро гум кардан [rohi xudro gum kardan]; **one-way** якҷониба [yakjoniba]
wayward [вейвард] *adj.* худсар [xudsar]
we [ви] *pron.* мо [mo]
weak [вик] *adj.* суст [sust], заиф [zaif]
weaken [викен] *v.t.* суст кардан [sust kardan], заиф кардан [zaif kardan]
weakness [викнес] *n.* сустӣ [susti], заифӣ [zaifi]
wealth [велт] *n.* бойгарӣ [boygari], дороӣ [doroi]
wealthy [велти] *adj.* бой [boy], доро [doro]
weapon [вепон] *n.* ярок [yaroq], аслиҳа [asliha]
wear [вер] *v.t.* пӯшидан [püshidan]; **to wear away** соидан [soidan]
weary [вири] *adj.* коҳида [kohida], хаста [xasta]
weather [ведер] *n.* ҳаво [havo]; **weather forecast** пешгӯии ҳаво [peshgüii havo]
weave [вив] *v.t.* бофтан [boftan]
weaver [вивер] *n.* бофанда [bofanda]
web [веб] *n.* бофта [bofta]; **spiderweb** тортанакхона [tortanakxona]
website [вебсайт] *n.* сомонаи интернетӣ [somonai interneti]
wedding [вединг] *n.* тӯй [tüy], арӯсӣ [arüsi]; **wedding ring** ангуштарини никоҳ [angushtarini nikoh]
wedge [веҷ] *n.* фона [fona]; **to drive a wedge** фона задан [fona zadan]
Wednesday [венздей] *n.* чоршанбе [chorshanbe]
weed [вид] *n.* алафи бегона [alafi begona] / *v.t.* хишова кардан [xishova kardan]
week [вик] *n.* ҳафта [hafta]; **per week** ҳафтаӣ [haftai]
weekday [викдей] *n.* рӯзи кор [rüzi kor]
weekend [викенд] *n.* рӯзҳои дамгирӣ [rüzhoi damgiri]
weep [вип] *v.i.* гиря кардан [girya kardan], зор-зор гиристан [zor-zor giristan]

weigh [вей] *v.t. (determine weight)* баркашидан [barkashidan]; *(ponder)* санҷидан [sanjidan]
weight [вейт] *n.* вазн [vazn]; *(for exercise)* вазна [vazna]; *(for weighing)* санги тарозу [sangi tarozu]; **to gain weight** фарбеҳ шудан [farbeh shudan], гӯшт гирифтан [güsht giriftan]; **to lose weight** лоғар шудан [loghar shudan], камгӯшт шудан [kamgüsht shudan]
weird [вирд] *adj.* аҷиб [ajib]
welcome [велкам] *n.* пазирой [paziroi] / *v.t.* хуш омадед гуфтан [xush omaded guftan]; **Welcome to …** Ба … хуш омадед [Ba … xush omaded]
weld [велд] *v.t.* кафшер кардан [kafsher kardan]
welding [велдинг] *n.* кафшер [kafsher]
welfare [велфер] *n.* некӯаҳволӣ [nekühahvoli]
well [вел] *n.* чоҳ [choh] / *adj.* тандуруст [tandurust], нағз [naghz], хуб [xub] / *adv.* нағз [naghz], хуб [xub]; **as well** ҳам [ham]; **I am well.** Нағзам. [Naghzam.]
west [вест] *n.* бохтар [boxtar], ғарб [gharb] / *adj.* бохтарӣ [boxtari], ғарбӣ [gharbi] / *adv.* ба сӯи бохтар [ba süi boxtar], ба сӯи ғарб [ba süi gharb]
western [вестерн] *adj.* бохтарӣ [boxtari], ғарбӣ [gharbi]
wet [вет] *adj.* тар [tar] / *v.t.* тар кардан [tar kardan]
whale [вейл] *n.* кит [kit]
wharf [ворф] *n.* ҷои киштибандӣ [joi kishtibandi]
what [ват] *adj./adj.* чӣ [chi] / *pron.* чӣ [chi]; **What is this?** Ин чист? [In chist?]
whatever [ватевер] *adv./pron.* ҳар чӣ [har chi]
wheat [вит] *n.* гандум [gandum]
wheel [вил] *n.* чарха [charxa], чарх [charx]
wheelbarrow [вилберо] *n.* занбар [zanbar]
wheeze [виз] *n.* хиррос [xirros] / *v.i.* хиррос задан [xirros zadan]
when [вен] *adv.* кай [kay] / *conj.* ҳангоме ки [hangome ki], вақте ки [vaqte ki]
where [вер] *adv.* куҷо [kujo] / *conj.* ҷое ки [joe ki]
wherever [веревер] *adv./conj.* ҳар ҷо ки [har jo ki], куҷо ки [kujo ki]
which [вич] *adj.* кадом [kadom] / *pron.* ки [ki]
whichever [вичевер] *adj./pron.* ҳар кадом [har kadom]
while [вайл] *n.* муддат [muddat] / *conj.* ҳангоме ки [hangome ki], вақте ки [vaqte ki]; **for a while** муддате [muddate]
whip [вип] *n.* тозиёна [toziyona], қамчин [qamchin] / *v.t.* тозиёна задан [toziyona zadan]
whirl [вирл] *v.i.* чарх задан [charx zadan]
whirlpool [вирлпул] *n.* гирдоб [girdob]
whisk [виск] *n.* гардгир [gardgir]

whisker [вискер] *n.* мӯйлаб [müylab], бурут [burut]

whiskey, whisky [виски] *n.* виски [viski]

whisper [виспер] *n.* пичиррос [pichirros] / *v.i.* пичирос задан [pichirros zadan]

whistle [висл] *n.* ҳуштак [hushtak] / *v.i.* ҳуштак кашидан [hushtak kashidan]

white [вайт] *adj.* сафед [safed]

whiten [вайтен] *v.t.* сафед кардан [safed kardan]

who [ҳу] *pron.* кӣ [ki]

whoever [ҳуевер] *pron.* ҳар кӣ [har ki]

whole [ҳол] *adj.* пурра [purra], тамом [tamom]

wholesale [ҳолсейл] *adj.* кӯтара [kütara]

wholesome [ҳолсам] *adj.* гуворо [guvoro]

whom [ҳум] *pron.* киро [kiro]

whose [ҳуз] *adj.* аз они кӣ [az oni ki]

why [вай] *adv.* чаро [charo], барои чӣ [baroi chi] / *conj.* чаро [charo]

wick [вик] *n.* пилта [pilta], фатила [fatila]

wicked [викед] *adj.* бад [bad], шарир [sharir]

wicker [викер] *adj.* бофта [bofta]; **wicker basket** сабади бофта [sabadi bofta]

wide [вайд] *adj.* фарох [farox], васеъ [vase']

widen [вайден] *v.t.* фарохтар кардан [faroxtar kardan]

widespread [вайдспред] *adj.* паҳн кардашуда [pahn kardashuda]

widow [видо] *n.* бева [beva], бевазан [bevazan]

widower [видоэр] *n.* бева [beva], бевамард [bevamard]

width [видт] *n.* бар [bar], фарохӣ [faroxi]

wield [вилд] *v.t.* идора кардан [idora kardan]

wife [вайф] *n.* зан [zan], хонум [xonum]

wig [виг] *n.* мӯйи сохта [müyi soxta]

wild [вайлд] *adj.* ёбоӣ [yoboi], ваҳшӣ [vahshi]

wilderness [вилдернес] *n.* ҷои нообод [joi noobod]

wildlife [вайлдлайф] *n.* мавҷудот [mavjudot], олами зинда [olami zinda]

will [вил] *n. (choice, wish)* ирода [iroda]; *(self-discipline)* худдорӣ [xuddori]; *(legal)* васият [vasiyat] / *v.i.* хостан [xostan], ирода кардан [iroda kardan] / *verbal aux.* хостан [xostan]

willing [вилинг] *adj.* розӣ [rozi]

willingly [вилингли] *adv.* ихтиёрӣ [ixtiyori]

willow [вило] *n.* бед [bed]; **weeping willow** маҷнунбед [majnunbed]

win [вин] *n.* бурд [burd] / *v.t.* бурдан [burdan] / *v.i.* пирӯз шудан [piruz shudan]

wind [винд] *n.* бод [bod], шамол [shamol]

wind [вайнд] *v.t./v.i.* тофтан [toftan]

windmill [виндмил] *n.* осиёби бодӣ [osiyobi bodi]

window [виндо] *n.* тиреза [tireza]

windowsill [виндосил] *n.* зертахтаи тиреза [zertaxtai tireza]
windshield [виндшилд] *n.* оинаи шамолгардон [oinai shamolgardon]; **windshield wiper** шишатозакунак [shishatozakunak]
windy [винди] *adj.* сершамол [sershamol], шамолрав [shamolrav]
wine [вайн] *n.* май [may], шароб [sharob]
wing [винг] *n.* бол [bol]
wink [винк] *n.* чашмак [chashmak] / *v.i.* чашмак задан [chashmak zadan]
winner [винер] *n.* баранда [baranda]
winter [винтер] *n.* зимистон [zimiston]
wipe [вайп] *v.t.* пок кардан [pok kardan]
wire [вайр] *n.* сим [sim] / *v.t.* симро пайваст кардан [simro payvast kardan]
wisdom [виздам] *n.* хирад [xirad], ақл [aql]
wise [вайз] *adj.* хирадманд [xiradmand], оқил [oqil]
wish [виш] *n.* хоҳиш [xohish], орзу [orzu] / *v.t.* хостан [xostan], орзу кардан [orzu kardan]
wit [вит] *n.* ҳуш [hush], хирад [xirad]
witch [вич] *n.* соҳира [sohira]
with [вит] *prep.* бо [bo]
withdraw [витдро] *v.t.* *(pull back)* якбора ақиб кашидан [yakbora aqib kashidan]; *(take out money)* пулро пас гирифтан [pulro pas giriftan] / *v.i.* якбора ақиб гаштан [yakbora aqib gashtan]
withdrawal [витдроуал] *n.* пас гирифтани пул [pas giriftani pul]
wither [видер] *v.i.* пажмурда шудан [pazhmurda shudan]
withhold [витҳолд] *v.t.* нигоҳ доштан [nigoh doshtan]
within [видин] *adv.* дар [dar] / *prep.* дар [dar], даруни [daruni]
without [видаут] *prep.* бе [be]
withstand [витстенд] *v.t.* бардоштан [bardoshtan]
witness [витнес] *n.* гувоҳ [guvoh], шоҳид [shohid] / *v.t.* дидан [didan]
witty [вити] *adj.* аскиягӯй [askiyagüy], ҳозирҷавоб [hozirjavob]
wolf [вулф] *n.* гург [gurg]
woman [вуман] *n.* зан [zan]
womb [вум] *n.* бачадон [bachadon]
wonder [вандер] *v.i.* тааҷҷуб кардан [taajjub kardan]
wonderful [вандерфул] *adj.* тааҷҷубовар [taajjubovar]
wood [вуд] *n.* чӯб [chüb]
wooden [вуден] *adj.* чӯбин [chübin]
woods [вудс] *n.* ҷангал [jangal]
wool [вул] *n.* пашм [pashm]
woolen [вулен] *adj.* пашмин [pashmin]
word [вурд] *n.* вожа [vozha], сухан [suxan], калима [kalima]; **word-for-word** вожа ба вожа [vozha ba vozha]
work [вурк] *n.* кор [kor] / *v.i.* кор кардан [kor kardan]
workday [вуркдей] *n.* рӯзи кор [rüzi kor]

worker [воркер] *n.* коргар [korgar]
workplace [воркплейс] *n.* ҷои кор [joi kor]
workshop [воркшоп] *n.* коргоҳ [korgoh], корхона [korxona]
world [ворлд] *n.* ҷаҳон [jahon], дунё [dunyo], гетӣ [geti], олам [olam]
worldwide [ворлдвайд] *adj.* ҷаҳонӣ [jahoni]
worm [ворм] *n.* кирм [kirm]
worn out [ворн аут] *adj.* фарсуда [farsuda]
worried [ворид] *adj.* ноором [noorom]
worry [вори] *n.* ноороми [nooromi], фикр [fikr] / *v.i.* хавотир шудан [xavotir shudan]
worse [ворс] *adj./adv.* бадтар [badtar]
worship [воршип] *n.* парастиш [parastish] / *v.t.* парастидан [parastidan]
worshipper [воршипер] *n.* парастанда [parastanda]
worst [ворст] *adj.* бадтарин [badtarin] / *adv.* бадтар аз ҳама [badtar az hama]
worth [ворт] *n.* арзиш [arzish] / *adj.* арзанда [arzanda]; **It's not worth it.** Намеарзад. [Namearzad.], Ба дард намехӯрад. [Ba dard namexürad.]; **It's worth two dollars.** Ду доллар меарзад. [Du dollar mearzad.]
worthless [вортлес] *adj.* *(useless)* бефоида [befoida]; *(inconsequential)* ночиз [nochiz]; *(valueless)* беарзиш [bearzish]
worthwhile [вортвайл] *adj.* арзишдор [arzishdor], фоиданок [foidanok]
wound [вунд] *n.* захм [zaxm], яра [yara] / *v.t.* захмдор кардан [zaxmdor kardan], ярадор кардан [yarador kardan]
wrap [реп] *v.t.* печондан [pechondan]
wrapping paper [репинг пейпер] *n.* коғази чизпечонӣ [koghazi chizpechoni]
wrath [рет] *n.* хашм [xashm]
wreath [рит] *n.* чанбари гул [chanbari gul], занҷирча [zanjircha]
wreck [рек] *n.* шикаст [shikast] / *v.t.* шикастан [shikastan]
wrench [ренч] *n.* калид [kalid]; **monkey wrench** мурваткушои бозшаванда [murvatkushoi bozshavanda]
wrestle [ресл] *v.t.* гӯштӣ гирифтан [güshti giriftan]
wrestler [реслер] *n.* гӯштингир [güshtingir]
wrestling [реслинг] *n.* гӯштӣ [güshti]
wrinkle [ринкл] *n.* чин [chin], ожанг [ozhang] / *v.t.* чин кардан [chin kardan]
wrist [рист] *n.* банди даст [bandi dast]
wristwatch [риствоч] *n.* соати дастӣ [soati dasti]
write [райт] *v.t.* навиштан [navishtan]
writer [райтар] *n.* нависанда [navisanda]
writing [райтинг] *n.* хат [xat]; **in writing** хаттӣ [xatti]

wrong [ронг] *adj.* нодуруст [nodurust], ғалат [ghalat]

X

xenophobia [зенофобия] *n.* душмании бегона [dushmanii begona]
xenophobic [зенофобик] *adj.* душмани бегона [dushmani begona]
Xmas *n. (abbrev. of* **Christmas***)* ихтисори Christmas [ixtisori Christmas]
X-ray [экс рей] *n.* рентген [rentgen] / *v.t.* бо рентген дидан [bo rentgen didan]
xylophone [зайлофон] *n.* ксилофон [ksilofon]

Y

yacht [ят] *n.* яхта [yaxta]
yank [йенк] *v.t.* кандан [kandan], канда гирифтан [kanda giriftan]
yard [ярд] *n. (backyard)* ҳавлӣ [havli]; *(unit of measurement)* ярд [yard]
yarn [ярд] *n.* нахи бофандагӣ [naxi bofandagi]
yawn [ён] *n.* хамёза [xamyoza] / *v.i.* хамёза кашидан [xamyoza kashidan]
year [йир] *n.* сол [sol]
yearly [йирли] *adj.* солона [solona], ҳарсола [harsola]
yearn [йерн] *v.i.* орзу кардан [orzu kardan]
yeast [йист] *n.* хамиртурш [xamirtursh]
yell [йел] *n.* дод [dod], фарёд [faryod] / *v.i.* дод задан [dod zadan], фарёд задан [faryod zadan]
yellow [яло] *adj.* зард [zard]
yes [йес] *adv.* ҳа [ha], ҳо [ho], бале [bale]
yesterday [йестердей] *n.* дина [dina], дирӯз [dirüz]
yet [йет] *adv./conj.* ҳанӯз [hanüz]
yield [йилд] *n.* ҳосил [hosil] / *v.t.* супурдан [supurdan]
yoga [йога] *n.* йога [yoga]
yogurt [йогурт] *n.* мост [most], ҷурғот [jurghot]
yoke [йок] *n.* юғ [yugh]
yolk [йок] *n.* зардии тухм [zardii tuxm]
yonder [йондер] *adv.* он ҷо [on jo]
you [ю] *pron. (singular/ informal)* ту [tu]; *(plural/ polite)* шумо [shumo]
young [янг] *adj.* ҷавон [javon]
your [юр] *pron. (singular/ informal)* аз они ту [az oni tu]; *(plural/polite)* аз они шумо [az oni shumo]
yourself [юрселф] *pron. (informal)* худат [xudat]; *(formal/polite)* худатон [xudaton]
youth [ют] *n. (condition of being young)* ҷавонӣ [javoni]; *(young person)* ҷавон [javon]
youthful [ютфул] *adj.* ҷавон [javon], хурдсол [xurdsol]

Z

zeal [зил] *n.* ғайрат [ghayrat]
zealous [зелас] *adj.* ғаюр [ghayur]

zebra [зибра] *n.* гӯрхар [gürxar]
zenith [зенит] *n.* авҷ [avj]
zero [зиро] *num.* сифр [sifr], нол [nol]
zest [зест] *n.* шавқ [shavq]
zigzag [зигзег] *n.* хати каҷу килеб [xati kaju kileb] / *v.i.* каҷу килеб гаштан [kaju kileb raftan]
zinc [зинк] *n.* руҳ [ruh]
zip [зип] *v.t.* бо занҷирак гузарондан [bo zanjirak guzarondan]
zip code [зип код] *n.* индекси почта [indeksi pochta]
zipper [зипер] *n.* занҷирак [zanjirak]
zodiac [зодийэк] *n.* бурҷи дувоздаҳгона [burji duvozdahgona]; **signs of the zodiac** аломатҳои бурҷи дувоздаҳгона [alomathoi burji duvozdahgona]
zone [зон] *n.* минтақа [mintaqa]
zoo [зу] *n.* боғи ҳайвонот [boghi hayvonot]
zoological [зуолоҷикал] *adj.* -и ҷонваршиносӣ [-i jonvarshinosi]
zoology [зуолоҷи] *n.* ҷонваршиносӣ [jonvarshinosi]
Zoroastrian [зороэстриян] *n./adj.* зардуштӣ [zardushti]

www.ingramcontent.com/pod-product-compliance
Lightning Source LLC
Jackson TN
JSHW060705190426
101040JS00035B/445

* 9 7 8 0 7 8 1 8 1 2 3 3 7 *